Intimate Relationships

The McGraw-Hill Social Psychology Series

This popular series of paperback titles is written by authors about their particular field of expertise and is meant to complement any social psychology course. The series includes:

Berkowitz, Leonard: *Aggression: Its Causes, Consequences, and Control*

Brown, Jonathon: *The Self*

Burn, Shawn, M.: *The Social Psychology of Gender*

Brannigan, Gary G., and Matthew Merrens: *The Social Psychologists: Research Adventures*

Ellyson, Steve L. and Amy G. Halberstadt: *Explorations in Social Psychology: Readings and Research*

Fiske, Susan T. and Shelley E. Taylor: *Social Cognition, 2/e*

Schroeder, David, Louis Penner, John Dovidio, and Jane Piliavan: *The Psychology of Helping and Altruism: Problems and Puzzles*

Keough, Kelli A., and Julio Garcia: *Social Psychology of Gender, Race, and Ethnicity: Readings and Projects*

Milgram, Stanley: *The Individual in a Social World, 2/e*

Myers, David G.: *Exploring Social Psychology, 2/e*

Pines, Ayala M. and Christina Maslach: *Experiencing Social Psychology: Readings and Projects, 4/e*

Plous, Scott: *The Psychology of Judgment and Decision Making*

Ross, Lee and Richard E. Nisbett: *The Person and the Situation: Perspectives of Social Psychology*

Rubin, Jeffrey Z., Dean G. Pruitt, and Sung Hee Kim: *Social Conflict: Escalation, Stalemate, and Settlement, 2/e*

Triandis, Harry C.: *Culture and Social Behavior*

Zimbardo, Philip G. and Michael R. Leippe: *The Psychology of Attitude Change and Social Influence*

Intimate Relationships

FOURTH EDITION

Rowland S. Miller
Sam Houston State University

Daniel Perlman
University of British Columbia

Sharon S. Brehm
Indiana University Bloomington

Boston   Burr Ridge, IL   Dubuque, IA   Madison, WI   New York
San Francisco   St. Louis   Bangkok   Bogotá   Caracas   Kuala Lumpur
Lisbon   London   Madrid   Mexico City   Milan   Montreal   New Delhi
Santiago   Seoul   Singapore   Sydney   Taipei   Toronto

 **Higher Education**

INTIMATE RELATIONSHIPS
Published by McGraw-Hill, a business unit of The McGraw-Hill Companies, Inc., 1221 Avenue of the Americas, New York, NY, 10020. Copyright © 2007, 2002, 1992, 1985 by The McGraw-Hill Companies, Inc. All rights reserved. No part of this publication may be reproduced or distributed in any form or by any means, or stored in a database or retrieval system, without the prior written consent of The McGraw-Hill Companies, Inc., including, but not limited to, in any network or other electronic storage or transmission, or broadcast for distance learning.

Some ancillaries, including electronic and print components, may not be available to customers outside the United States.

This book is printed on acid-free paper.

4 5 6 7 8 9 0 FGR/FGR 0 9 8 7

ISBN-13: 978-0-07-293801-2
ISBN-10: 0-07-293801-3

Vice President and Editor-in-Chief:
    Emily Barrosse
Publisher: *Beth Mejia*
Executive Editor: *Michael J. Sugarman*
Senior Developmental Editor: *Judith Kromm*
Editorial Coordinator: *Katherine C. Russillo*
Marketing Manager: *Melissa S. Caughlin*
Managing Editor: *Jean Dal Porto*
Project Manager: *Meghan Durko*
Art Director: *Jeanne Schreiber*
Art Editor: *Katherine McNab*
Designer: *Marianna Kinigakis*

Cover Credit: *Lilith by Anahit Vart, 2003;*
    Art for After Hours/SuperStock, Inc.
Photo Research Coordinator: *Nora Agbayani*
Photo Researcher: *Emily Tietz*
Production Supervisor: *Janean A. Utley*
Senior Media Producer: *Stephanie George*
Media Project Manager: *Kathleen Boylan*
Composition: *10/12 Palatino,*
    by Interactive Composition Corporation
Printing: *45 # New Era Matte Plus,*
    by Quebecor World

Credits: The credits section for this book begins on page C1 and is considered an extension of the copyright page.

Library of Congress Cataloging-in-Publication Data

Intimate relationships / Rowland S. Miller . . . [et al.].—4th ed.
        p. cm.—(The McGraw-Hill series in social psychology)
    Includes bibliographical references and index.
    ISBN-13: 978-0-07-293801-2 (softcover : alk. paper)
    ISBN-10: 0-07-293801-3 (softcover : alk. paper)
    1. Family life education. 2. Interpersonal relations.   I. Miller, Rowland S.   II. Series.
HQ10.I58 2007
306.707—dc21

                                                                        2005054309

The Internet addresses listed in the text were accurate at the time of publication. The inclusion of a Web site does not indicate an endorsement by the authors or McGraw-Hill, and McGraw-Hill does not guarantee the accuracy of the information presented at these sites.

www.mhhe.com

Contents

Part Two
BASIC PROCESSES IN INTIMATE RELATIONSHIPS

Part Five
LOSING AND ENHANCING RELATIONSHIPS

Foreword

Intimate relationships are at the core of the human experience, forming the basic plot line in life's drama across all its stages. We are attracted to some people, come to like and love some, have romantic and sexual relationships with some, marry and give support and comfort to partners, and suffer when those relationships end badly instead of with their promised happy endings. Intimate relationships fulfill basic human needs for belonging and caring, and they involve strong emotional attachments to others. It is now well known that the single best protection anyone can have against the risks of many mental or physical illnesses is to have a viable social support network. Intimate relationships provide those networks. They are connections with other people we can call upon when we are distressed, and in turn, we can give our aid and care to our partners when they are in need. When middle-aged, successful business people are asked how their lives might be different if they had to do it all over again, they never say that they would work more; rather, most report that they would make more time for family and friends and loving relationships.

Given the obvious centrality of intimate relationships in our lives, it is curious that the topic is relatively new in the history of social psychology. It has emerged as an exciting field of research and practice only in the past few decades. Previously, scholarly interest had focused on dyads and small groups, often public ones, as people competed or cooperated, negotiated and bargained, conformed, complied, or resisted. But a hardy band of researchers, including the three co-authors of this book, began to demonstrate that it was possible to systematically investigate the subtle features of interpersonal dynamics in order to understand some of the ingredients that go into liking, loving, and sexual relationships. As research unfolded, the net of interested investigators extended from social psychology to personality, to cognitive psychology, to developmental psychology, to evolutionary psychology, to sociology, to family studies, to communication studies, and to human ecology. These perspectives combined to offer us new insights about the nature of intimate relationships.

Sharon Brehm's first two editions of *Intimate Relationships* in this **McGraw-Hill Social Psychology Series** were major contributors to the growth of the field of close relationships. Her books were the most successful of any of our other fine monographs in terms of sales and critical acclaim. Sharon's books were authoritative without being tedious, accessible to both faculty and students without being simplistic or going for "pop appeal." What she accomplished in her landmark books was to create scholarly texts that could be respected by her colleagues *and* enjoyed by students.

How has this fourth edition built upon that firm foundation to give ***Intimate Relationships*** a fresh new look—transforming it into something much better, yet much the same? How can you revise such a successful book without sacrificing either the breadth of scientific coverage or the depth of its appealingly friendly "authorial voice"? Simple. You create a team of co-authors who love the book and have them engage in a major makeover of its earlier versions, refashioning the best of the old into something wiser and even more reader friendly. Rowland (Rody) Miller, the new lead author of the book, accepted the challenge to take the tiller in hand and set sail for familiar destinations, but with new ports of call all along the way. He directed the team in a thorough update of the highly success-ful third edition. Which means that you will find in this new edition: five chapters totally rewritten from scratch; over 875 new references; 20 new topics that were not in the previous index (from flirting and mate poaching to fMRI studies of love, and more); and extended coverage of a dozen core topics (from attachment styles, to cohabitation, to forgiveness, and much more).

As in introductory psychology texts, which I have lived with and by for the past three decades, some authors are focused on "getting it right," even at the sake of being boring, while others are focused on "making it interesting," even at the sake of sacrificing scientific credibility. *Intimate Relationships* gets it right but is also a great read. What remains constant—and is a comfort for the con-tented users of previous editions—is the familiar sequence of chapters and the similar organization of information within chapters.

For teachers, this fourth edition will be a blessing because of the new peda-gogical supports for users. Instructors will delight in the IM with many readily usable class materials; in having a solid test bank; and in a course web site that offers PowerPoint slides that outline each chapter. There are few relatively in-expensive paperbacks in any field that can boast of such comprehensive sup-plementary support for instructors. As the research, theory, and applications of close relationships expand and deepen, this field is becoming "hot" for scholars and now for a new generation of teachers and students. *Intimate Relationships* will help to move the development of this field into more energetic research and more inspired teaching.

So, I say "Ciao" to the new senior co-author, Rody Miller, along with dear-est greetings to my long-time friend, Sharon Brehm. And I welcome you, dear reader, to join the group of similarly situated students who will enjoy and ben-efit from the scholarship, wonderfully engaging writing style, and the obvious dedication of this team of authors to the science of close relationships as trans-lated into this exciting literary form.

Philip G. Zimbardo
Series Consulting Editor
San Francisco, California

Preface

Welcome to *Intimate Relationships!* We're delighted that you are holding this book in your hands. There are few fields of behavioral science that are as dynamic, vibrant, and busy as the study of our intimate connections to others, and wonderful new insights are constantly emerging. We have had much to do in preparing this new edition! Nevertheless, our overarching goals have remained the same: Although the book can be of genuine interest to the general public, we have sought to provide college audiences with broad, reader-friendly coverage of relationship science that observes rigorous standards of scholarship but that preserves the personal appeal of its subject matter. Our hope is that you'll not be able to find a more complete or more accessible overview of the modern science of close relationships.

What's New to This Edition

This edition contains more than 875 new references, most of them from the last three years. As a result, there is new discussion of various topics that were not mentioned in prior editions. Here's some of what's new to this edition.

Online dating	Flirting
Narcissism	Sex differences in sexual desire
Ostracism	Immersive virtual environments
Mate poaching	The Speaker-Listener Technique
Hurt feelings	Short-term and long-term mating
Compassionate love	Appetitive and aversive motivations
Growth and Destiny beliefs	The rules of relationships
Tradeoffs in mate selection	fMRI studies of love
The Early Years of Marriage Project	

Several recently-developed research instruments are also newly included, providing readers opportunities to inspect the tools used in relationship research (and, if they wish, to test themselves). These additions include the following:

Hendrick, Dicke, & Hendrick's (1998) *Relationship Assessment Scale*
Arriaga & Agnew's (2001) *Commitment Scale*
Loving & Agnew's (2001) *Inventory of Desirable Responding in Relationships*
Mills, Clark, Ford, & Johnson's (2004) *Measure of Communal Strength*

There is also expanded coverage of a variety of topics. Among them are the following:

Cohabitation	Self-esteem and its relational effects
Forgiveness	Sociocultural correlates of divorce

Premarital breakups	Relationship maintenance mechanisms
The PAIR project	Adjustment to divorce
Sociometer theory	Lying in close relationships
Attachment styles	Reconstructive memory

Finally, each chapter now ends with a thought-provoking vignette that encourages the reader to consider how that chapter's material applies to various relational dilemmas. There are also more illustrations, tables, and figures throughout the work. Add it all up, and the 4th edition is definitely a fresher, thoroughly updated, new-and-improved work.

What Hasn't Changed

Nevertheless, we did not attempt to reinvent the wheel. The 3rd edition of this book was very well received, so we have retained its organization. Those familiar with the 3rd edition will find the same chapters in the same places. In order to accommodate new material, two topics, *self-verification* and *shyness*, have moved to new locations, but they are still covered in the same detail.

Vital influences on close relationships are again introduced in chapter 1. Thereafter, they are mentioned throughout the book, providing a welcome coherence to the text's broad coverage. As various concepts are applied to new topics, footnotes also remind readers where to find definitions that will refresh their memories.

Most importantly, the book retains the accessible, appealing style that won such praise in prior editions. We are honored to have the opportunity to describe relationship science to you; we are excited by the field and proud to participate in it, and we hope it shows.

For Instructors

An Instructor's Manual and Test Bank is available, and Dan Perlman maintains a course website that contains item analyses of exam questions; he is happy to share them with you at d.Perlman@ubc.ca. PowerPoint slides that outline each chapter are also available from McGraw-Hill.

A Partnership

This book is all about relationships, and we feel that the partnership you share with us as a reader is especially important. We invite you to tell us what you think. What did you like about our work? How can we improve it? Feel free to write your lead author, Rowland Miller, at miller@shsu.edu. As Ralph Waldo Emerson said, "Tis the good reader that makes the good book."

We wish you a good read. And feel free to share your experience with a friend or loved one. We hope the book will benefit you and your relationships, and to both you and your intimate partners, we wish a "bon voyage" in reading and, most importantly, in relating.

PART ONE

An Introduction to the Study of Intimate Relationships

CHAPTER 1

The Building Blocks of Relationships

THE NATURE AND IMPORTANCE OF INTIMACY ◆ The Nature of Intimacy ◆ The Need to Belong ◆ THE INFLUENCE OF CULTURE ◆ Sources of Change ◆ THE INFLUENCE OF EXPERIENCE ◆ THE INFLUENCE OF INDIVIDUAL DIFFERENCES ◆ Sex Differences ◆ Gender Differences ◆ Personality ◆ Self-Esteem ◆ THE INFLUENCE OF HUMAN NATURE ◆ THE INFLUENCE OF INTERACTION ◆ THE DARK SIDE OF RELATIONSHIPS ◆ FOR YOUR CONSIDERATION ◆ CHAPTER SUMMARY

How's this for a vacation? Imagine yourself in a nicely appointed suite with a pastoral view. You've got cable, video games, and wireless Web access, plenty of books and magazines, and all the supplies for your favorite hobby. Delightful food and drink are provided, and you have your favorite entertainments at hand. But there's a catch: No one else is around. You're completely alone. You have almost everything you want except for other people. You have no phone or e-mail, and you can't visit any chat rooms. Instant messaging is unavailable. No one else is even in sight, and you cannot interact with anyone else in any way.

How's that for a vacation? A few of us would enjoy the solitude for a while, but most of us would quickly find it surprisingly stressful to be completely detached from other people (Schachter, 1959). Most of us need others even more than we realize, and there's a reason prisons sometimes use *solitary confinement* as a form of punishment: Human beings are a very social species. People suffer when they are deprived of close contact with others, and at the core of our social nature is our need for intimate relationships.

Our relationships with others are a central aspect of our lives: a source of great joy when things go well, but a cause of great sorrow when they go poorly. Our relationships are indispensable and vital, and for that reason it can be important to understand how our relationships get started, how they grow and operate, and how, sometimes, they end in a haze of anger and pain.

This book will promote your own understanding of close relationships. Drawing on psychology, sociology, communication studies, and family studies, it describes what social scientists have learned about relationships through careful research. This is a different, more scientific view of relationships than you'll find in magazines or the movies; it's more reasoned, more cautious, and often less romantic. You'll also find that this book is not a how-to manual.

Intimacy takes many forms, and each of us must bring his or her beliefs, values, and personal experiences to bear on the information presented here. The purposes of this book are to guide you through the diverse foci of relationship science and to help you arrive at your own conclusions about relationships.

To set the stage for the discoveries to come, we'll first define our subject matter. What are intimate relationships? Why do they matter so much? Then, we'll consider the fundamental building blocks of close relationships: the cultures we inhabit, the experiences we encounter, the personalities we possess, the human origins we all share, and the interactions we conduct. In order to understand relationships, we must first comprehend who we are, *where* we are, and how we got there.

THE NATURE AND IMPORTANCE OF INTIMACY

Relationships come in all shapes and sizes. People have parents and may have children; they have colleagues at work or classmates at school; they encounter grocery clerks, physicians, and office staff; they have friends; and they have lovers. This book concentrates on just the last two types of partnerships, which exemplify *intimate* relationships. Our primary focus is on intimate relationships between adults (although we do discuss childhood friendships in chapter 7).

The Nature of Intimacy

What, then, is intimacy? The answer can depend on whom you ask, because intimacy is a multifaceted concept with several different components (Lippert & Prager, 2001; Prager & Roberts, 2004). However, both researchers (Laurenceau et al., 2004; Reis & Patrick, 1996) and laypeople (Marston et al., 1998; Monsour, 1992; Parks & Floyd, 1996) agree that intimate relationships differ from more casual associations in at least six specific ways: **knowledge, caring, interdependence, mutuality, trust,** and **commitment.**

First, intimate partners have extensive personal, often confidential, *knowledge* about each other. They share information about their histories, preferences, feelings, and desires that they do not reveal to most of the other people they know. Intimate partners also *care* about each other, feeling more affection for one another than they do for most others. Intimacy increases when people believe that their partners know and understand them and appreciate them (Reis & Gable, 2003).

The lives of intimate partners are also intertwined: What each partner does affects what the other partner wants to do and can do. *Interdependence* between intimates—the extent to which they need and influence each other—is frequent (they often affect each other), strong (they have a meaningful impact on each other), diverse (they influence each other in many different ways), and enduring (they influence each other over long periods of time). When relationships are interdependent, one's behavior affects one's partner as well as oneself (Berscheid, Snyder, & Omoto, 2004).

Please circle the picture below that best describes your **current** relationship with your partner.

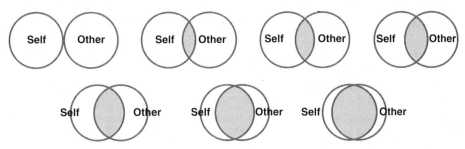

FIGURE 1.1. The inclusion of other in the self scale.
How intimate is a relationship? Asking people to pick the picture that portrays a
particular partnership does a remarkably good job of assessing the closeness they feel.
Source: Aron et al., 2004.

As a result of these close ties, people who are intimate also consider themselves to be a couple instead of two entirely separate individuals. They exhibit
a high degree of *mutuality*, which means that they recognize the overlap between their lives and think themselves as "us" instead of "me" and "her" (or
"him") (Fitzsimons & Kay, 2004; Levinger & Snoek, 1972). In fact, that change in
outlook—from "I" to "us"—often signals the subtle but significant moment in a
developing relationship when new partners first acknowledge their attachment
to each other (Agnew et al., 1998). Indeed, researchers sometimes assess the
amount of intimacy in a close relationship by simply asking partners to rate the
extent to which they "overlap" (Aron, Mashek, & Aron, 2004). The Inclusion of
Other in the Self Scale (see Figure 1.1) is a straightforward measure of mutuality that does a remarkably good job of distinguishing between intimate and
more causal relationships (Agnew et al., 2004).

A quality that makes these close ties tolerable is *trust*, the expectation that
an intimate partner will treat one fairly and honorably (Holmes, 1991). People
expect that no undue harm will result from their intimate relationships, and
they expect their partners to be responsive to their needs and concerned for
their welfare (Reis, Clark, & Holmes, 2004). When such trust is lost, people often
become wary and reduce the openness and interdependence that characterize
closeness (Jones, Crouch, & Scott, 1997).

Finally, intimate partners are ordinarily *committed* to their relationships.
That is, they expect their partnerships to continue indefinitely, and they invest
the time, effort, and resources that are needed to realize that goal. Without such
commitment, people who were once very close may find themselves less and
less interdependent and knowledgeable about each other as time goes by and
they slowly drift apart.

None of these components is absolutely required for intimacy to occur,
and each may exist when the others are absent. For instance, spouses in a stale,
unhappy marriage may be very interdependent, closely coordinating the practical details of their daily lives but still live in a psychological vacuum devoid

of much affection, openness, or trust. Such partners would certainly be more intimate than mere acquaintances are, but they would undoubtedly feel less close to one another than they used to (for instance, when they decided to marry), when more of the components were present. In general, our most satisfying and meaningful intimate relationships include all six of these defining characteristics (Fletcher, Simpson, & Thomas, 2000a; Simpson, Fletcher, & Campbell, 2001). Still, intimacy can exist to a lesser degree when only some of them are in place. And as unhappy marriages demonstrate, intimacy can also vary enormously over the entire course of a relationship.

Thus, there is no one kind of intimate relationship (Goodwin & Cramer, 2002; Haslam & Fiske, 1999). Indeed, perhaps the most fundamental lesson about relationships is a very simple one: They do come in all shapes and sizes. This variety is a source of great complexity, but it can also be a source of endless fascination. (And that's why we wrote this book!)

The Need to Belong

Our focus on intimate relationships means that we will not consider a wide variety of the interactions that you have with others each day. For instance, we will not examine the relationships you have with most of your classmates. Should we be so particular? Is such a focus justified? The answers, of course, are yes. Although our casual interactions with strangers, acquaintances, and others can be very influential (Miller, 2001), there's something special about intimate relationships. In fact, a powerful and pervasive drive to establish intimacy with others may be a basic part of our human nature. According to theorists Roy Baumeister and Mark Leary (1995), we *need* frequent, pleasant interactions with intimate partners in lasting, caring relationships if we're to function normally. There is a human **need to belong** in close relationships, and if the need is not met, a variety of problems follow.

Our need to belong is presumed to necessitate "regular social contact with those to whom one feels connected" (Baumeister & Leary, 1995, p. 501). In order to fulfill the need, we are driven to establish and maintain close relationships with other people; we require interaction and communion with those who know and care for us. We don't need a lot of close relationships, just a few; when the need to belong is satiated, our drive to form additional relationships is reduced. (Thus, when it comes to relationships, quality is more important than quantity.) It also doesn't matter much *who* our partners are; as long as they provide us stable affection and acceptance, our need can be satisfied. Thus, if their spouses die after a long marriage, people are often able to find replacement partners who—though they may be quite different from their previous partners—are nonetheless able to satisfy the widow's or widower's need to belong.

Some of the support for this theory comes from the ease with which we form relationships with others and from the tenacity with which we then resist the dissolution of our existing social ties. Indeed, when a valued relationship is in peril, we may find it hard to think about anything else—and the resulting preoccupation and strong emotion show how much our partnerships mean to us. The potency of the need to belong may also be why being entirely alone for a long period of time is so stressful (Schachter, 1959); anything that threatens our sense of connection to other people can be hard to take (Dean & Gardner, 2003).

In fact, some of the strongest evidence supporting a need to belong comes from studies of people who have lost their close ties to others (Ryff & Singer, 2000). Such losses impair one's health (Levin, 2000). Spouses whose marriages have turned angry and antagonistic (Kiecolt-Glaser et al., 1993) or who have actually been divorced (Kiecolt-Glaser & Newton, 2001) have higher blood pressure and weaker immune systems than those whose relationships are happier. And if such people continue to leave their social needs unfulfilled, they're likely to die younger than those who are happily attached to others. Across the life span, people who have few friends or lovers have much higher mortality rates than do those who are closely connected to caring partners (Berkman & Glass, 2000); in one extensive study, people who lacked close ties to others were two to three times more likely to die over a nine-year span (Berkman & Syme, 1979).

The quality of our relationships also affects our mental health (Kim & McKenry, 2002). Day by day, people who have pleasant interactions with others who care for them are more satisfied with their lives than are those who lack such social contact (Nezlek et al., 2002). And around the world, people who get and stay married are generally happier than are those who are less committed to an intimate partnership (Fleeson, 2004). In addition, a variety of problems such as depression, alcoholism, eating disorders, and schizophrenia are more likely to afflict those whose social needs are unfulfilled than those who have adequate ties to others (Segrin, 1998). On the surface (as we explain in detail in chapter 2), such patterns do not necessarily mean that bad relationships *cause* such problems; after all, people who are prone to schizophrenia may find it difficult to form loving relationships in the first place. Nevertheless, it does appear that a lack of intimacy can both cause such problems and/or make them worse (Assh & Byers, 1996; Segrin, 1998). In general, our well-being seems to depend on how well we satisfy the need to belong.

Why should we need intimacy so much? Why are we such a social species? One possibility is that the need to belong *evolved* over eons, gradually becoming a natural tendency in all human beings (Baumeister & Leary, 1995). That argument goes this way: Because early humans lived in small tribal groups surrounded by a difficult environment full of saber-toothed tigers, people who were loners were less likely than gregarious humans to have children who would grow to maturity and reproduce. In such a setting, a tendency to form stable, affectionate connections to others would have been evolutionarily *adaptive*, making it more likely that one's children would survive and thrive. As a result, our species slowly came to be characterized by people who cared deeply about what others thought of them and who sought acceptance and closeness from others. Admittedly, this view—which represents a provocative way of thinking about our modern behavior (and about which we'll have more to say later in this chapter)—is speculative. Nevertheless, whether or not this evolutionary account is entirely correct, there is little doubt that now, in the twenty-first century, almost all of us care deeply about the quality of our attachments to others. We are also at a loss, prone to illness and maladjustment, when we have insufficient intimacy in our lives. We know that food, water, and shelter are essential for life, but the need to belong suggests that intimacy with others is essential for a good, long life as well (Brewer, 2004).

Now, let's examine the major influences that will determine what sort of relationships we construct when we seek to satisfy the need to belong. We'll start with a counterpoint to our innate need for intimacy: the changing cultures that provide the norms that govern our intimate relationships.

THE INFLUENCE OF CULTURE

We know it seems like ancient history—cell phones and DVDs and the Internet and AIDS didn't exist—but let's look back at 1960, which may have been around the time that your grandparents were deciding to marry. If they were a typical couple, they would have married in their early twenties, before she was 21 and before he was 23.[1] They probably would not have lived together, or "cohabited," without being married because almost no one did at that time. And it's also unlikely that they would have had a baby without being married; 95 percent of the children born in the United States in 1960 had parents who were married to each other. Once they settled in, your grandmother probably did not work outside the home—most women didn't—and when her kids were preschoolers, it's quite likely that she stayed home with them all day; most women did. It's also likely that their children—in particular, your mom or dad—grew up in a household in which both of their parents were present at the end of the day.

Now, however, things are different. The last several decades have seen dramatic changes in the cultural context in which we conduct our close relationships. Indeed, you shouldn't be surprised if your grandparents are astonished and consternated by the cultural landscape that *you* face today. In the United States

- Fewer people are marrying than ever before. Almost everyone (94 percent) married at some point in their lives in 1960, but more people remain unmarried today. Demographers now predict that only 85 percent of young adults will ever marry (Popenoe & Whitehead, 2004).
- People are waiting longer to marry. On average, a woman is now 25 years old when she marries for the first time, and a man is 27; these are the oldest such ages in American history (Popenoe & Whitehead, 2004). That's much

[1]These and the following statistics were obtained from the U.S. Census Bureau at www.census.gov and the U.S. National Center for Health Statistics at www.cdc.gov/nchs, and from various other reports, including Kreider & Fields, 2002; Popenoe & Whitehead, 2004; and Sallee, 2003.

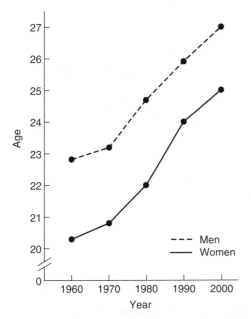

FIGURE 1.2. Average age of first marriage in the U.S.
American men and women are waiting longer to
get married than ever before.

older than your grandparents probably were when they got married (see
Figure 1.2). More than a third of all Americans now remain unmarried into
their middle thirties, and *most* African-Americans (53 percent) have never
married when they reach age 34 (Krieder & Simmons, 2003).

- People routinely live together even when they're not married. Cohabitation
  was very rare in 1960—only 5 percent of all adults ever did it—but it is now
  ordinary. Half of your classmates will at some time live with a lover without being married. In fact, almost one-third of American households
  (32 percent) are made up of an unmarried man and woman living together
  (Bramlett & Mosher, 2002).

- People often have babies even when they're not married. This was an uncommon event in 1960; only 5 percent of the babies born in the United States that
  year had unmarried mothers. Some children were *conceived* out of wedlock,
  but their parents usually got married before they were born. Not so now. In
  2002, *one-third* (33 percent) of the babies born in the U.S. had mothers who
  were not married (Sallee, 2003), and this was the highest rate ever recorded
  (Popenoe & Whitehead, 2004).

- About half of all marriages end in divorce. The likelihood that a married
  couple would someday divorce skyrocketed from 1960 to 1980 (see
  Figure 1.3). After peaking in the early 1980s, the divorce rate has dropped
  slightly, but divorces are still more than twice as common as they were

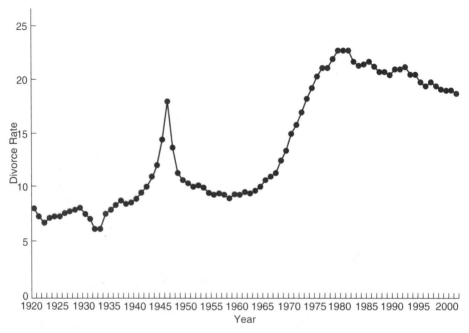

FIGURE 1.3. Divorce rates in the U.S.
After an extraordinary increase from the mid-1960s to 1980, the American divorce rate
has leveled off and even declined slightly in recent years. But half the marriages that
begin this year are still expected to ultimately end in divorce.
Note: The figure illustrates the divorce rate per 1,000 married women age 15 and older in the United States.
Source: National Center for Health Statistics, 2005.

when your grandparents married (National Center for Health Statistics, 2004). And the best guess is that an American couple getting married this year is more likely to divorce sometime down the road than to live happily ever after (Carter & Snow, 2004).

- Most children (about 60 percent) live in a single-parent home sometime during their childhoods. As a result of the higher divorce and unmarried-birth rates, it's now *un*likely that an American child will live with both parents throughout his or her entire youth. Indeed, at any one time, more than a third (34 percent) of the children in the U.S. are living with only one of their parents (Popenoe & Whitehead, 2004).

- Most preschool children have mothers who work outside the home. In 1960, more than three-quarters of American mothers stayed home all day when their children were too young to go to school, but fewer than half of them do so now. Fifty-five percent of the women who gave birth in 2000 returned to work before their babies were one year old (Sallee, 2003). Even if a child lives with both parents, neither of them is likely to be a full-time caregiver at home all day.

Compared with marriages that took place a generation ago, today's newlyweds are older, more likely to have children from a previous marriage, and more likely to be committed to their careers as well as to their families.

These remarkable changes suggest that some of our shared assumptions about the role that marriage and parenthood will play in our lives have changed substantially in recent years. Once upon a time, everybody got married, usually soon after they left college, and happy or sad, they were likely to stay with those partners. Pregnant people felt they *had* to get married, and cohabitation was known as "living in sin." But not so anymore. Marriage is now a *choice*, even if a baby is on the way, and increasing numbers of us are putting it off or not getting married at all. If we do marry, we're less likely to consider it a solemn, life-long commitment (Myers, 2000). In general, recent years have seen enormous change in the cultural norms that used to encourage people to get, and stay, married (Putnam, 2000; Stanfield & Stanfield, 1997).

Do these changes matter? Almost certainly they do. Cultural standards provide a foundation for our relationships (Huston, 2000; Thornton & Young-DeMarco, 2001); they shape our expectations and define what patterns are thought to be normal. Let's consider, in particular, the huge rise in the rates of cohabitation that have occurred in recent years. Most high school seniors now believe that it is a "good idea" for a couple to live together before they get married so that they can find out if they "really get along" (Bachman, Johnston, & O'Malley, 2001). Such attitudes make cohabitation a reasonable choice and, as we have seen, most people now cohabit before they ever marry. However, cohabitation does not make it more likely that a subsequent marriage will be successful; if anything, cohabitation *increases* a couple's risk that they will later divorce (Booth & Crouter, 2002; Smock, 2000), and there are probably several reasons why. Couples who choose to cohabit are typically less committed to each other than are those who marry (Waite & Gallagher, 2000), and they typically encounter less satisfaction and more infidelity than married people do (Cohan & Kleinbaum, 2002; Treas & Giesen, 2000). As a result, the longer that people cohabit, the less enthusiastic about marriage—and the more accepting of divorce—they become (Axinn & Barber, 1997). Cohabitation seems to undermine the positive attitudes toward marriage, and the determination to make a marriage work, that support marital success (Popenoe & Whitehead, 2002). So, widespread acceptance of cohabitation as a "trial marriage" may actually make divorce more, not less, likely in the long run.

Complicating things is the possibility that Western cultures such as the United States have become "increasingly individualistic and hedonistic" since you were born (Glenn & Weaver, 1988, p. 323). Arguably, we have come to expect more from our intimate partnerships—more pleasure and delight, and fewer hassles and sacrifices—even as cultural changes have made it easier to end a marriage or even avoid one altogether (Attridge & Berscheid, 1994). Consequently, fewer people get married and fewer marriages last.

Sources of Change

Thus, the patterns of your intimate relationships in the twenty-first century may differ from those experienced by prior generations, and there are undoubtedly several reasons why. One likely influence is our culture's increasing level of *socioeconomic development*. There is a general trend for a society to harbor more single people, tolerate more divorces, and support a later age of marriage the more industrialized and affluent it becomes (South, Trent, & Shen, 2001). Education and financial resources allow people to travel more widely and be more independent. With more options, fewer of us may be motivated to tie ourselves to just one partner for our entire lives. In addition, when both partners in a close relationship work long hours outside their home, they may have less time to devote to maintaining and enjoying their partnership (Amato et al., 2003).

Western cultures also emphasize individual liberty, encouraging people to pursue personal fulfillment, and if anything, this *individualism* has become more pronounced in recent years (Myers, 2000). Eastern cultures promote a more collective sense of self in which people feel more closely tied to their families and social groups, and the divorce rates in such cultures (such as Japan) are much lower than they are in the United States (Triandis, McCusker, & Hui, 1990).

New *technology* matters, too. Modern reproductive technologies allow single women to bear children fathered by men picked from a catalog at a sperm bank whom the women have never met! Women can also control their fertility, having children only when they choose, and American women are having fewer children than they used to (Sallee, 2003); consequently, fewer marriages are maintained for the "sake of the children." Technology may also play a role in reducing our ties to others: More and more of our leisure time is absorbed by private, often solitary entertainments such as playing video games or surfing the Web instead of socializing with friends or neighbors (Putnam, 2000). People who would have hosted parties in 1960 are now often sitting home alone watching video and computer screens.

However, an even more important—but more subtle—influence on the norms that govern relationships may be the relative numbers of young men and women in a given culture. Societies in which men are more numerous than women tend to have very different standards than those in which women outnumber men. We're describing a culture's **sex ratio,** a simple count of the number of men for every 100 women in a specific population. When the sex ratio is high, there are more men than women, and when the sex ratio is low, there are fewer men than women. A sex ratio of 100 means that there are equal numbers of women and men. In the United States, women are usually in their twenties, marrying a man two years older (on average), when they marry for the first time; thus, relationship researchers usually compute sex ratios that compare the number of women to the number of men who are slightly older.

The baby boom that followed World War II caused the American sex ratio, which was very high in 1960, to plummet to low levels at the end of that decade. For a time after the war, more babies were born each year than in the preceding year; this meant that when the "boomers" entered adulthood, there were fewer older men than younger women, and the sex ratio dropped. However, when birthrates began to slow and fewer children entered the demographic pipeline, each new flock of women was smaller than the preceding flock of men, and the American sex ratio crept higher in the 1990s (see Figure 1.4). Since then, reasonably stable birthrates among "boomer" parents have resulted in fairly equal numbers of marriageable men and women today. The most recent U.S. Census revealed that there were 86 unmarried men for every 100 unmarried women in the United States when the twenty-first century began (Kreider & Simmons, 2003).

These changes may have been more important than most people realize. Cultures with high sex ratios (in which there aren't enough women) tend to support traditional, old-fashioned roles for men and women (Pedersen, 1991; Secord, 1983). The women stay home raising children while the men work outside the home. Such cultures also tend to be sexually conservative. The ideal newlywed is a virgin bride, unwed pregnancy is shameful, and open cohabitation is rare. Divorce is discouraged. In contrast, cultures with low sex ratios (in which there are too few men) tend to be less traditional and more permissive. Women are encouraged to work and support themselves, and they are allowed (if not encouraged) to have sexual relationships outside of marriage. If a pregnancy occurs, unmarried motherhood is an option (Barber, 2001). Women even wear shorter skirts (Barber, 1999). The specifics vary with each historical period, but this general pattern has occurred throughout history (Guttentag & Secord, 1983). Ancient Rome, which was renowned for its sybaritic behavior? A low sex ratio. Victorian England,

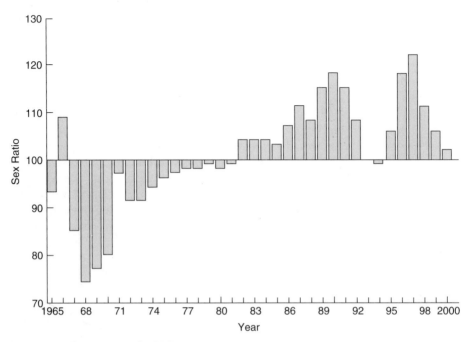

FIGURE 1.4. Sex ratios in the U.S.
American sex ratios were very low during the "sexual revolution" of the late 1960s, but there are more similar numbers of young men and women in the population now.

famous for its prim and proper ways? A high sex ratio. The Roaring Twenties, a footloose and playful decade? A low sex ratio. And in more recent memory, the "sexual revolution" and the advent of "women's liberation" in the late 1960s? Take another look at Figure 1.4.

Theorists Marcia Guttentag and Paul Secord (1983) argued that such cultural changes are not accidental. In their view, a society's norms evolve to promote the interests of its most powerful members, those who hold economic, political, and legal power. In the cultures we just mentioned, those people have been men. As a result, the norms governing relationships usually change to favor the interests of men as the numbers of available men and women change.

This is a daring assertion. After all, recent decades have seen enormous improvement in the status of American women, and few of us would want to change that. But let's think it through. When sex ratios are high, there aren't enough women to go around. If a man is lucky enough to attract a woman, he'll want to keep her. And (a) encouraging women to be housewives who are financially dependent on their husbands, and (b) discouraging divorce, are ways to do just that (and that's the way things were in 1960). On the other hand, when sex ratios are low, there are plenty of women, and men may be less interested in being tied down to just one of them. Thus, women work and delay marriage, and couples divorce more readily if dissatisfaction sets in.

Thus, the remarkable changes in the norms for American relationships since 1960 may be due, in part, to dramatic fluctuations in American sex ratios. Indeed, we may already be seeing the effects of the higher sex ratios of the late 1990s. The U.S. divorce rate, which *doubled* from 1967 to 1980, has leveled off and has even dropped slightly. Politicians now care about "family values." Teenagers are being more sexually responsible; the U.S. birthrate for unmarried teen mothers (although still higher than in other industrialized countries) is now lower than it's been for thirty years (Curtin & Martin, 2000). With roughly equal numbers of men and women now approaching marriageable age, it's likely that the cultural pendulum will swing back to sexual norms that are less permissive than those of the 1980s but not as restrained as those of 1960.

We should note that Guttentag and Secord's (1983) explanation of the operation of sex ratios—that things work to the advantage of men—is speculative. However, there is a rough but real link between a culture's proportions of men and women and its relational norms, and it serves as a compelling example of the manner in which culture can affect our relationships. To a substantial degree, what we expect and what we accept in our dealings with others can spring from the standards of the time and place in which we live.

THE INFLUENCE OF EXPERIENCE

Our relationships are also affected by the histories and experiences we bring to them, and there may be no better example of this than the global orientations toward relationships known as **attachment styles.** Years ago, developmental researchers (e.g., Bowlby, 1969) realized that infants displayed various patterns of attachment to their major caregivers (usually their mothers). The prevailing assumption was that whenever they were hungry, wet, or scared, some children found responsive care and protection to be reliably available. A loving and nurturing caregiver always came when they called, and youngsters who enjoyed such protection came to rely on others comfortably. They learned that other people were trustworthy sources of security and kindness. As a result, such children developed a **secure** style of attachment: They happily bonded with others, and they readily developed relationships characterized by relaxed trust.

Other children encountered different situations. For some, attentive care was unpredictable and inconsistent. Their caregivers were warm and interested on some occasions but distracted, anxious, or unavailable on others. These children thus developed fretful, mixed feelings about others known as **anxious-ambivalent** attachments. Being uncertain of when (or if) a departing caregiver would return, such children became nervous and clingy, displaying excessive neediness in their relationships with others.

Finally, for a third group of children, care was provided reluctantly by rejecting or hostile adults. Such children learned that little good came from depending on others, and they withdrew from others with an **avoidant** style of attachment. Avoidant children were often suspicious of and angry at others, and they did not easily form trusting, close relationships.

TABLE 1.1. Attachment Styles

Which of the following best describes your feelings? (Make your choice before reading the labels given at the end of this table.)

A. I find it relatively easy to get close to others and am comfortable depending on them and having them depend on me. I don't often worry about being abandoned or about someone getting too close to me.

B. I am somewhat uncomfortable being close to others; I find it difficult to trust them completely, difficult to allow myself to depend on them. I am nervous when anyone gets too close, and often, love partners want me to be more intimate than I feel comfortable being.

C. I find that others are reluctant to get as close as I would like. I often worry that my partner doesn't really love me or won't want to stay with me. I want to merge completely with another person, and this desire sometimes scares people away.

The first type of attachment style is described as "secure," the second as "avoidant," and the third as "anxious/ambivalent."

Source: From Shaver, Hazan, & Bradshaw, 1988.

The important point, then, is that researchers believed that early interpersonal experiences shaped the course of one's subsequent relationships. Indeed, attachment processes became a popular topic of research because the different styles were so obvious in many children. When they were faced with a strange, intimidating environment, for instance, secure children ran to their mothers, calmed down, and then set out to bravely explore the unfamiliar new setting (Ainsworth, Blehar, Waters, & Wall, 1978). Anxious-ambivalent children cried and clung to their mothers, ignoring the parents' reassurances that all was well. And avoidant children actually shunned their mothers, keeping their distance and evading close contact even when they were scared. As these examples suggest, the different styles of attachment could generally be linked to quite different patterns of friendship and play among young children as well (Koski & Shaver, 1997).

Still, attachment styles took on new relevance for relationship researchers when Cindy Hazan and Phillip Shaver (1987) demonstrated that similar orientations toward close relationships could also be observed among *adults*. In one of their studies, Hazan and Shaver invited readers of the *Rocky Mountain News* to participate in a "love quiz" by selecting the paragraph in Table 1.1 that fit them best; as you can see, each paragraph describes one of the attachment styles. Most people reported a secure style, but a substantial minority (about 40 percent) said they were *in*secure by picking either the avoidant or anxious-ambivalent self-description. In addition, the three groups of people reported childhood memories and current attitudes toward love and romance that fit their styles. Secure people generally held positive images of themselves and others and remembered their parents as loving and supportive. In contrast, insecure people viewed others with uncertainty or distrust and remembered their parents as inconsistent or cold.

With provocative results like these, attachment research quickly became one of the hottest fields in relationship science (see Cassidy & Shaver, 1999). Wide-ranging surveys have since shown that about 60 percent of us are secure, 25 percent avoidant, and 10 percent anxious-ambivalent (Mickelson, Kessler, & Shaver, 1997). And importantly, attachment tendencies seem to broadly influence our thoughts, feelings, and behavior in our adult relationships. People with secure styles tend to be more satisfied with their intimate partnerships than avoidant or anxious-ambivalent people are (Feeney, 1999). Avoidant people have a lack of faith in others that leads them to warily avoid interdependent intimacy, whereas anxious-ambivalent people seek such closeness but nervously fret that it won't last (Feeney, 1998). Both groups are less comfortable and relaxed in intimate relationships than secure people are.

Over time, there have been several theoretical and methodological advances in studies of attachment; researchers now recognize *four* different styles instead of three and assess them with more sophisticated measures than the simple paragraphs in Table 1.1. We'll bring you up to date on the latest thinking about attachment in chapter 8. For now, the important point is that attachment styles appear to be orientations toward relationships that are largely *learned* from our experiences with others. They are a prime example of the manner in which the proclivities and perspectives we bring to a new relationship emerge in part from our experiences in prior partnerships.

Let's examine this idea more closely. Any relationship is shaped by many different influences—that's the point of this chapter—and both babies and adults affect through their own behavior the treatment they receive from others. As any parent knows, for instance, babies are born with various temperaments and arousal levels. Some newborns have an easy, pleasant temperament, whereas others are fussy and excitable. Inborn differences in personality and emotionality make some children easier to parent than others, and caregivers may be especially attentive to bubbly, happy infants who are usually in good moods. Thus, the quality of parenting a baby receives can depend, in part, on the child's own personality and behavior; in this way, people's attachment style may be influenced by the traits with which they were born (Carver, 1997).

On the other hand, a child's temperament has only a moderate effect on the kind of parenting he or she receives (Vaughn & Bost, 1999), and people do not seem to be genetically predisposed to develop certain kinds of attachment styles (Waller & Shaver, 1994). Instead, just as developmental theorists originally assumed, our experiences seem to play a key role in shaping the styles we bring to subsequent relationships. Mothers' behavior toward their infants when the babies are newborns predicts what styles of attachment the children will have when they are older (Isabella, 1998): Moms who are content with closeness and who enjoy intimacy tend to have children who share that style, whereas insecure mothers tend to have insecure children. In fact, it's possible to predict with 75 percent accuracy what attachment style a child will have by assessing the mother's style before her baby is even born (Fonagy,

Steele, & Steele, 1991)! Moreover, when mothers with difficult, irritable babies are trained to be sensitive and responsive parents, their toddlers are much more likely to end up securely attached to them than they would have been in the absence of such training (van den Boom, 1994, 1995). Thereafter, the parenting adolescents receive as seventh graders predicts how they will behave in their own romances and friendships when they are young adults; teenagers who have nurturing and supportive relationships with their parents behave more warmly toward their lovers (Conger et al., 2000) and friends (Cui et al., 2002) years later. Youngsters apparently import the lessons they learn at home into their subsequent relationships with others (Feeney, 1999).

We're not prisoners of our experiences as children, however, because our attachment styles continue to be shaped by the experiences we encounter as adults (Davila & Cobb, 2003; Davila & Sargent, 2003). Being learned, attachment styles can be *un*learned, and over time, attachment styles can and do change (Baldwin & Fehr, 1995). A bad breakup can make a formerly secure person insecure, and a good relationship can gradually make an avoidant person less wary of intimacy (Kirkpatrick & Hazan, 1994; Ruvolo, Fabin, & Ruvolo, 2001). As many as a third of us may encounter real change in our attachment styles over a two-year period (Fuller & Fincham, 1995), and the good news is that the avoidant and anxious-ambivalent styles are more likely to change than a secure style is (Davila, Burge, & Hammen, 1997).

Nevertheless, once they have been established, attachment styles can also be stable and long-lasting, as they lead people to create new relationships that reinforce their existing tendencies (Scharfe & Bartholomew, 1994). By remaining aloof and avoiding interdependency, for instance, avoidant people may never learn that some people can be trusted and closeness can be comforting—and that perpetuates their avoidant style. In the absence of dramatic new experiences, people's styles of attachment can persist for decades (Fraley, 2002; Klohnen & Bera, 1998).

Thus, our global beliefs about the nature and worth of close relationships appear to be shaped by our experiences within them. By good luck or bad, our earliest notions about our own interpersonal worth and the trustworthiness of others emerge from our interactions with our major caregivers, and thus they start us down a path of trust or fear. But that journey never stops, and later obstacles or aid from fellow travelers may divert us and change our routes. Our learned styles of attachment to others may either change with time or persist indefinitely, all depending on our interpersonal experiences.

THE INFLUENCE OF INDIVIDUAL DIFFERENCES

Once they are formed, attachment styles also exemplify the idiosyncratic personal characteristics that people bring to their partnerships with others. We're all individuals with singular combinations of experiences and traits that shape our abilities and preferences, and the differences among us can influence our relationships. In romantic relationships, for instance, some pairings of attachment styles in the two partners are better—that is, more satisfying and stable—than others (Jones & Cunningham, 1996). Consider the mismatch that results when an anxious-ambivalent person falls in love with an avoidant partner; one of them may be unnerved by the other's emotional distance, while the other may be annoyed by the first's clingy intrusiveness. Both partners are likely to be less at ease than they would be with lovers who had more secure attachment styles.

Of course, the possibility that we can get along better with some people than with others is no surprise; we all know that. In this section of the chapter, we'll move beyond that simple truth in two ways. First, we'll explore the nature of individual differences, which are often gradual and subtle instead of abrupt. Then, we'll show that individual differences influence our behavior in close relationships. We'll consider four different types of individual variation: sex differences, gender differences, personalities, and self-esteem.

Sex Differences

At this moment, you're doing something rare. You're reading an academic textbook about relationship science, and that's something most people will never do. This is probably the *first* serious text you've ever read about relationships, too, and that means that we need to confront—and hopefully correct—some of the stereotypes you may hold about the differences between men and women in intimate relationships.

This may not be easy. Many of us are used to thinking that men and women have very different approaches to intimacy—that, for instance, "men are from Mars, women are from Venus." In a well-known book with that title, the author asserted that:

> men and women differ in all areas of their lives. Not only do men and women communicate differently but they think, feel, perceive, react, respond, love, need, and appreciate differently. They almost seem to be from different planets, speaking different languages and needing different nourishment. (Gray, 1992, p. 5)

Wow. Men and women sound like they're members of different species. No wonder heterosexual relationships are sometimes problematic!

But the truth is more subtle. Human traits obviously vary across a wide range, and (in most cases) if we graph the number of people who possess a certain talent or ability, we'll get a distinctive chart known as a *normal curve*. Such curves describe the frequencies with which particular levels of some trait can be found in people, and they demonstrate that (a) most people have talents or abilities that are only slightly better or worse than average, and (b) extreme levels of most traits, high or low, are very rare. Consider height, for example: A few people are very short or very tall, but the vast majority of us are only an inch or two shorter or taller than the average for our sex.

Why should we care about this? Because many lay stereotypes about men and women portray the sexes as having very different ranges of interests, styles, and abilities. As one example, men are often portrayed as being more interested in sex than women are (see Box 1.1), and the images of the sexes that people hold

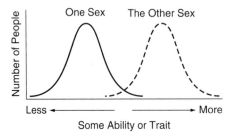

FIGURE 1.5. An imaginary sex difference. Popular stereotypes portray the sexes as being very different, with almost no overlap between the styles and preferences of the two sexes. This is *not* the way things really are.

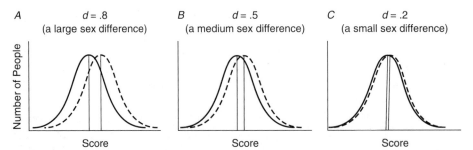

FIGURE 1.6. Actual sex differences take the form of overlapping normal curves. The three graphs depict large, medium, and small sex differences, respectively. (To keep them simple, they portray the ranges of attitudes or behavior as being the same for both sexes. This isn't always the case in real life.)

often seem to resemble the situation pictured in Figure 1.5: The difference between the average man and the average woman is presumed to be large, and there is almost no overlap between the sexes at all. But, despite the "Mars" and "Venus" stereotypes, this is *not* the way things really are. As we'll see in chapter 9, men do tend to have higher sex drives, on average, than women do. Nevertheless, *actual* sex differences take the form of the graphs shown in Figure 1.6, which depict ranges of interests and talents that *overlap* to a substantial extent (Schwartz & Rutter, 1998).

The three graphs in Figure 1.6 illustrate sex differences that are considered by researchers to be large, medium, and small, respectively. Formally, they differ with respect to a *d* statistic that specifies the size of a difference between groups.[2]

[2]To get a *d* score in these cases, you compute the difference between the average man and the average woman, and divide it by the average difference of the scores *within* each sex (which is the standard deviation of those scores). The resulting *d* value tells you how large the sex difference is compared to the usual amount by which men and women differ among themselves.

In the realm of sexual attitudes and behavior, graph A depicts the general size of the difference between men and women in incidence of masturbation (men masturbate more frequently), graph B illustrates the sex difference in sexual permissiveness (men approve of a wider range of behavior and are more accepting of casual sex), and graph C depicts the difference in number of sexual partners (men have more) (Oliver & Hyde, 1993). Obviously, these real-life examples look nothing like the stereotype pictured in Figure 1.5. More specifically, these examples make three vital points about psychological sex differences:

- Some differences are real, but quite small. (Don't be confused by researchers' terminology; when they talk about a "significant" sex difference, they're usually referring to a *"statistically* significant"—that is, numerically reliable—difference, and it may not be large at all.) Almost all of the differences between men and women that you will encounter in this book fall in the small to medium range.
- The range of behavior and opinions among members of a given sex is always *huge* compared to the average difference between the sexes. Some men may be very permissive, but other men are not permissive at all, and the two groups of men resemble each other much less than the average man and the average woman do. Another way to put this is that despite the sex difference in sexual permissiveness, a highly permissive man has more in common with the average *woman* on this trait than he does with a low-scoring *man.*
- The overlap in behavior and opinions is so large that many members of one sex will always score higher than the average member of the other sex. With a sex difference of medium size (with men higher and a *d* value of .5), one-third of all women will still score higher than the average man. What this means is that if you're looking for folks with permissive attitudes, you shouldn't just look for *men* because you heard that "men are more permissive than women"; you should look for permissive *people,* many of whom will be women despite the difference between the sexes.

The bottom line is that men and women usually overlap so thoroughly that they are much more similar than different on most of the dimensions and topics of interest to relationship science (Burn, 1996; Schwartz & Rutter, 1998). Indeed, the label "sex *differences"* is actually misleading because it emphasizes dissimilarities more than likenesses and gives the wrong impression. And it's really misguided to suggest that men and women come from different planets, because it simply isn't true. "Research does *not* support the view that men and women come from different cultures, let alone separate worlds" (Canary & Emmers-Sommer, 1997, p. vi). According to the careful science of relationships you'll study in this book, it's more accurate to say that "men are from North Dakota, women are from South Dakota" (Wood & Dindia, 1998, p. 32). (Or, as a bumper sticker we saw one day suggests: "Men are from Earth. Women are from Earth. Deal with it.")

Thus, sex differences in intimate relationships tend to be much less noteworthy and influential than laypeople often think. Common sense tends to

---

BOX 1.1

Combating Simplistic Stereotypes

Here's a joke that showed up in our e-mail one day:

How to Impress a Woman:
Compliment her. Cuddle her. Kiss her. Caress her. Love her. Comfort her. Protect her. Hug her. Hold her. Spend money on her. Wine and dine her. Listen to her. Care for her. Stand by her. Support her. Go to the ends of the earth for her.
How to Impress a Man:
Show up naked. Bring beer.

It's a cute joke. But it may not be harmless. It reinforces the stereotypes that women seek warmth and tenderness in their relationships, whereas men simply seek unemotional sex. In truth, men and women differ little in their desires in close relationships; they're not "opposite" sexes at all (Schwartz & Rutter, 1998). Although individuals of both sexes may differ substantially from each other, the differences between the average man and the average woman are rather small. Both women *and* men generally want their intimate partners to provide them lots of affection and warmth (Canary & Emmers-Sommer, 1997).

But so what? What are the consequences of wrongly believing that men are all alike, having little in common with women? Pessimism and hopelessness, for two (Metts & Cupach, 1990). People who really believe that the sexes are very different are less likely to try to repair their heterosexual relationships when conflicts occur (as they inevitably do). Thinking of the other sex as a bunch of aliens from another world is not only inaccurate, it can be damaging, forestalling efforts to understand a partner's point of view and preventing collaborative problem-solving. For that reason, we'll try to do our part to avoid perpetuating wrongful impressions by comparing men and women to the *other* sex, not the *opposite* sex, for the remainder of this book.

---

glorify and exaggerate sex differences, perhaps because it's easy to classify individuals as either men or women and convenient to apply simple stereotypes to them. But now that you're reading a serious text on intimate relationships, you need to think more carefully about sex differences and interpret them more reasonably. There are interesting and occasionally important sex differences that are meaningful parts of the fabric of relationships, and we'll encounter several of them in the chapters that follow. But they occur in the context of even broader similarities between the sexes, and the differences are always modest when they are compared to the full range of human variation. It's more work, but also more sophisticated and accurate, to think of individual differences, not sex differences, as the more important influences on interpersonal interaction. People differ among themselves whether they are male or female (as in the case of attachment styles), and these variations are usually much more consequential than sex differences are.

Gender Differences

We need to complicate things further by distinguishing between sex differences and *gender* differences in close relationships. When people use the terms carefully, sex differences refer to biological distinctions between men and women that spring naturally from their physical natures. In contrast, gender differences refer to social and psychological distinctions that are created by our cultures and up-bringing (Burn, 1996; Canary & Emmers-Sommer, 1997). For instance, when they are parents, women are mothers and men are fathers—that's a sex difference—but the common belief that women are more loving, more nurturant parents than men reflects a gender difference. Many men are capable of just as much tenderness and compassion toward the young as any woman is, but if we expect and encourage women to be the primary caregivers of our children, we can create cultural gender differences in parenting styles that are not natural or inborn at all.

Distinguishing sex and gender differences is often tricky, because the social expectations and training we apply to men and women are often confounded with their biological sex (Eagly & Wood, 1999). For instance, because women lactate and men do not, people often assume that predawn feedings of a newborn baby are the mother's job and that women are better than men at such things—even when the baby is being fed formula from a bottle that was warmed in a microwave! It's not always easy to disentangle the effects of biology and culture in shaping our interests and abilities. Nevertheless, the distinction between sex and gender differences is important, because some influential differences between men and women in relationships—gender differences—are largely *taught* to us as we grow up.

The best examples of this are our **gender roles,** the patterns of behavior that are culturally expected of "normal" men and women. Men, of course, are sup-posed to be "masculine," which means that they are expected to be assertive, self-reliant, decisive, competent, and competitive. Women are expected to be "feminine," or warm, sensitive, emotionally expressive, and kind. They're the "opposite" sexes to most people, and to varying degrees men and women are ex-pected to specialize in different kinds of social behavior all over the world (Williams & Best, 1990). However, people inherit only about a quarter to a third of their tendencies to be assertive or kind; most of these behaviors are learned (Cleveland, Udry, & Chantala, 2001; Lippa & Hershberger, 1999). In thorough-going and pervasive ways, cultural processes of socialization and modeling (rather than biological sex differences) lead us to expect that all men should be tough and all women should be tender (Burn, 1996).

Nevertheless, those stereotypes don't describe real people as well as you might think (Carothers & Reis, 2004); only *half* of us have attributes that fit these gender role expectations cleanly (Bem, 1993). Instead of being just "masculine" or "feminine," a sizable minority of people—about 35 percent—are both assertive *and* warm, sensitive *and* self-reliant. Such people possess both sets of the compe-tencies that are stereotypically associated with being male and with being female, and are said to be **androgynous.** If androgyny seems odd to you, you're probably just using a stereotyped vocabulary: On the surface, being "masculine" sounds

TABLE 1.2. Gender Roles

Instrumental Traits	Expressive Traits
Assertiveness	Warmth
Self-Reliance	Tenderness
Ambition	Compassion
Leadership	Kindness
Decisiveness	Sensitivity to Others

Our culture encourages men to be highly instrumental and women to be highly expressive, but which of these talents do you *not* want in an intimate companion?

incompatible with also being "feminine." In fact, because those terms are confusing, relationship researchers often use alternatives, referring to the "masculine" task-oriented talents as **instrumental** traits and to the "feminine" social and emotional skills as **expressive** traits (Spence & Helmreich, 1981). And it's not all that remarkable to find both sets of traits in the same individual. An androgynous person would be one who could effectively, emphatically stand up for himself or herself in a heated salary negotiation but who could then go home and sensitively, compassionately comfort a preschool child whose pet parakeet had died. A lot of people, those who specialize in either instrumental *or* expressive skills, would feel at home in one of those situations but not both. Androgynous people would be comfortable and capable in both domains.

In fact, the best way to think of instrumentality and expressiveness is as two separate sets of skills that may range from low to high in either men or women. Men who fulfill our traditional expectations are high in instrumentality but low in expressiveness, and are stoic, "macho" men. Traditional women are high in expressiveness but low in instrumentality; they're warm and friendly but not assertive or dominant. Androgynous people are both instrumental and expressive. The rest of us—about 15 percent—are either high in the skills typically associated with the other sex (and are said to be "cross-typed") or low in both sets of skills (and are said to be "undifferentiated"). Equal proportions of men and women fall into the androgynous, cross-typed, and undifferentiated categories, so, as with sex differences, it's simplistic and inaccurate to think of men and women as wholly distinct groups of people with separate, different traits (Bem, 1993; Carothers & Reis, 2004).

In any case, gender differences are of particular interest to relationship researchers because, instead of making men and women more compatible, they "may actually be responsible for much of the *incompatibility*" that causes relationships to fail (Ickes, 1985, p. 188). From the moment they meet, for instance, traditional men and women enjoy and like each other less than androgynous people do. In a classic experiment, Ickes and Barnes (1978) paired men and women in couples in which (a) both partners fit the traditional gender roles or (b) one or both partners were androgynous. The two people were introduced to each other and then simply left alone for five minutes in a waiting room while the researchers covertly videotaped their interaction. The results were striking. The traditional couples talked less, looked at each other less, laughed and smiled less, and afterward reported that they liked each other less than did the other couples. (Think about it: Stylistically, what do a masculine man and a feminine woman have in common?) When an androgynous man met a traditional woman, an androgynous woman met a traditional man, or two androgynous people got together, they got along much better than traditional men and women did.

More importantly, the disadvantage faced by traditional couples does not disappear as time goes by. Surveys of marital satisfaction demonstrate that such couples—who have marriages in which both spouses adhere to stereotyped gender roles—are generally *less* happy with their marriages than nontraditional couples are (Helms-Erickson, McHale, & Proulx, 2002; Zammichieli, Gilroy, & Sherman, 1988). With their different styles and different domains of expertise, masculine men and feminine women simply do not find as much pleasure in each other as less traditional, less stereotyped people do.

Perhaps this should be no surprise. When human beings devote themselves to intimate partnerships, they want affection, warmth, and understanding (Reis et al., 2000). People who are low in expressiveness—who are not very warm, tender, sensitive people—do not readily provide such warmth and tenderness (Basow & Rubenfeld, 2003). As a result, men or women who are married to spouses with low expressiveness are chronically less satisfied than are those whose partners are more sensitive, understanding, and kind (Miller, Huston, & Caughlin, 2003; Steiner-Pappalardo & Gurung, 2002). For this reason, traditional gender roles do men a disservice, depriving them of skills that would make them more rewarding husbands.

On the other hand, people who are low in instrumentality—who are low in assertiveness and personal strength—tend to have low self-esteem and to be less well-adjusted than those who have better task-oriented skills (Aubé et al., 1995). People feel better about themselves when they are competent and effective at "taking care of business" (Reis et al., 2000), so traditional gender roles

Instrumental, masculine people often feel ill at ease when they are asked to provide warm, sensitive support to others.

© *Reprinted with permission of King Features Syndicate.*

also do women a disservice, depriving them of skills that would facilitate more accomplishments and achievements.

The upshot of all this is that both instrumentality and expressiveness are valuable traits, and the happiest, best-adjusted, most effective people possess both sets of skills (Helgeson & Fritz, 1999; Saragovi et al., 2002). In particular, the most desirable spouses, those who are most likely to have contented, satisfied partners, are people who are both instrumental and expressive (Bradbury, Campbell, & Fincham, 1995). And in fact, when they're given a choice, most people say that they'd prefer androgynous dating partners or spouses to those who are merely masculine or feminine (Green & Kenrick, 1994).

So, it's ironic that we still tend to put pressure on those who do not rigidly adhere to their "proper" gender roles. Women who display as much competitiveness and assertiveness as men risk being perceived as pushy, impolite, and "unladylike" (Morrow & Cikasa, 2004) and as actually unsuited for some jobs (Rudman & Glick, 1999). If anything, however, gender expectations are stricter for men than for women; girls can be tomboys and nobody frets too much, but if a boy is too feminine, people really worry (Sandnabba & Ahlberg, 1999). American gender roles may be changing slowly but surely; in particular, American women are becoming more instrumental with each new generation (Twenge, 1997), and young adults of both sexes are gradually becoming more egalitarian and less traditional in their views of men and women (Bryant, 2003). Nonetheless, even if they limit our individual potentials and are right only half the time, gender stereotypes persist. Today we still expect and encourage men to be instrumental and women to be expressive (Prentice & Carranza, 2002), and such expectations are important complications for many of our close relationships.

Personality

Some consequential differences among people (such as attachment styles and gender differences) are affected by experience and may change over a few years' time, but other individual differences are more stable and lasting. Personality traits may influence people's behavior in their relationships across their entire lifetimes (Soldz & Vaillant, 1999), with only gradual change over long periods of time (Caspi et al., 2003; Shiner, Masten, & Roberts, 2003).

Personality researchers have identified a handful of central traits that characterize people all over the world (McCrae & Costa, 1997), and most of them seem to affect the quality of the relationships people have (see Box 1.2). On the positive side, extraverted, agreeable, and conscientious people have more, and more pleasant, relationships than do those who score lower on those traits (Bouchard, Lussier, & Sabourin, 1999; Watson, Hubbard, & Wiese, 2000a). Cheerful and enthusiastic moods are experienced often by extraverted and agreeable people (DeNeve & Cooper, 1998), and people in such happy moods tend to have fun and rewarding interactions with others (Vittengl & Holt, 1998). Conscientious people are reliable and dependable and can be trusted to keep

---

BOX 1.2

The Big Five Personality Traits

A small cluster of fundamental traits does a good job of describing the broad themes in behavior, thoughts, and emotions that distinguish one person from another (Wiggins, 1996). These key characteristics are called the Big Five traits by personality researchers, and most—but not all—of them appear to be very influential in intimate relationships. Which one of these would you assume does not matter much?

Extraversion—the extent to which people are outgoing, gregarious, talkative, and sociable versus cautious, reclusive, and shy.

Agreeableness—the degree to which people are good-natured, cooperative, and trusting versus irritable, cranky, and hostile.

Conscientiousness—the extent to which people are responsible, dutiful, and dependable versus unreliable and careless.

Neuroticism—the degree to which people are impulsive and prone to worry, anxiety, and anger.

Openness to experience—the degree to which people are imaginative, unconventional, and artistic versus conforming, uncreative, and stodgy.

The five traits are not listed in order of importance, but it is the last one, openness, that seems to have little to do with success and satisfaction in close relationships. The other four all make a difference.

---

their promises. Over time, these traits make one a desirable spouse (Watson et al., 2000a).

The most important of the Big Five traits, however, may be the one that has a negative impact: neuroticism (Asendorpf, 2002). The more neurotic people are, the less satisfied with their partnerships they tend to be (Karney & Bradbury, 1997). Neurotic people are prone to anger and anxiety, and those unhappy tendencies tend to result in unpleasant, pessimistic, and argumentative interactions with others (Caughlin, Huston, & Houts, 2000; Furr & Funder, 1998). In fact, a remarkable study that tracked 300 couples over a span of forty-five years found that a full 10 percent of the satisfaction and contentment spouses would experience in their marriages could be predicted from measures of their neuroticism when they were still engaged (Kelly & Conley, 1987). The less neurotic the partners were, the happier their marriages turned out to be. Everyone has good days and bad days, but some of us have *more* bad days (and fewer good ones) than other people—and those unlucky folks are especially likely to have unhappy, disappointing relationships.

Working alongside the global influences of the Big Five traits are other more specific personality variables that regulate our relationships, and we'll mention several in later chapters. For now, let's note that people's personalities affect their relationships more than their relationships affect their personalities (Asendorpf & Wilpers, 1998). Whether or not people ever marry, for instance, seems at least in part to be in their genes (Johnson et al., 2004). Some people are born with personalities that make them more likely than others to marry later in life, and these tendencies are not much affected by the experiences that they encounter. However, even our enduring personality traits can be shaped to a degree by our relationships (Robins, Caspi, & Moffitt, 2002). Dissatisfying and abusive relationships can gradually make us more anxious and neurotic, and warm, rewarding partnerships may make us more agreeable over time. But these effects are subtle, and our relationships probably have much bigger effects on the last individual difference we will consider: the self-evaluations we bring to our transactions with others.

Self-Esteem

Most of us like ourselves, but some of us do not. Our evaluations of ourselves constitute our **self-esteem**, and when we hold positive and favorable judgments of our skills and traits, our self-esteem is high; when we doubt ourselves, self-esteem is low. Because people with high self-esteem are generally healthier and happier than are those with low self-regard (Crocker & Luhtanen, 2003), it's widely assumed that it's good to feel good about yourself (Baumeister, 1998).

But how do people come to like themselves? A provocative, leading theory argues that self-esteem is a subjective gauge, a **"sociometer,"** that measures the quality of our relationships with others (Leary, 2003; Leary & Baumeister, 2000). When others like us, we like ourselves; when other people regard us positively and value their relationships with us, self-esteem is high. However, if we don't interest others—if others seem not to care whether or not we are part of their lives—self-esteem is low. Self-esteem operates in this manner, according to sociometer theory, because it is an evolved mechanism that serves our need to belong. This argument suggests that, because their reproductive success depended on staying in the tribe and being accepted by others, early humans became sensitive to any signs of exclusion that might precede rejection by others. Self-esteem became a psychological gauge that alerted people to declining acceptance by others, and dislike or disinterest from others gradually caused people to dislike themselves.

This perspective nicely fits most of what we know about the origins and operation of self-esteem (Leary, 2004; Leary & Baumeister, 2000). There's no question, for instance, that people feel better about themselves when they think they're attractive to the other sex (Brase & Guy, 2004). And the receptions we receive from others clearly affect our subsequent self-evaluations (Nezlek, 2001). In particular, events that involve interpersonal rejection damage our self-esteem in a way that other disappointments do not. Leary and his colleagues demonstrated this point in a clever study in which research participants were led to believe that they would be excluded from an attractive group either through bad luck—they had been randomly selected to be sent home—or because they had been voted out by the other members of the group (Leary et al., 1995). Even though the same desirable opportunity was lost in both situations, the people who had been personally rejected felt much worse about themselves than did those whose loss was impersonal. It's also interesting to note that public events that are witnessed by others affect people's self-esteem more than do private events that are otherwise identical but are known only to the individuals themselves. In this and several other respects (Leary & Baumeister, 2000), whether we realize it or not (Leary et al., 2003), our self-evaluations seem to be much affected by what we think others think of us.

Here is further evidence, then, that we humans are a very social species: It's very hard to like ourselves (and, indeed, it would be unrealistic to do so) if others don't like us, too. In most cases, people with chronically low self-esteem have developed their negative self-evaluations through an unhappy history of failing to receive sufficient acceptance and appreciation from other people.

And sometimes, this is very unfair. Some people are victimized by abusive relationships through no fault of their own, and, despite being likable people with fine social skills, they develop low self-esteem as a result of mistreatment from others. What happens when those people enter new relationships with kinder, more appreciative partners? Does the new feedback they receive slowly improve their self-esteem?

Not necessarily. A compelling series of studies by Sandra Murray and her colleagues has demonstrated that people with low self-esteem sometimes sabotage their relationships by underestimating their partners' love for them (Murray et al., 2001) and perceiving disregard where none exists (Murray et al., 2002). People with low self-regard find it hard to believe that they are well and truly loved by their partners (Murray et al., 1998) and, as a result, they are less optimistic that their loves will last than are people with higher self-esteem. This leads them to overreact to their partners' occasional bad moods (Bellavia & Murray, 2003); they feel more rejected, experience more hurt, and get more angry than do those with higher self-esteem. And these painful feelings make it harder for them to behave constructively in response to their imagined peril. Whereas people with high self-regard draw closer to their partners and seek to repair the relationship when frustrations arise, people with low self-esteem defensively distance themselves, stay surly, and behave badly (Murray, Bellavia et al., 2003). They also feel even worse about themselves (Murray, Griffin et al., 2003).

Altogether, Murray's studies revealed that the self-doubts and thin skins of people with low self-esteem lead them to make mountains out of molehills. They wrongly perceive small bumps in the road as worrisome signs of declining affection and commitment in their partners. Then, they respond with obnoxious, self-defeating hurt and anger that cut them off from the reassurance they crave. By comparison, people with higher self-esteem correctly shrug off the same small bumps and remain confident of their partners' acceptance and positive regard. The unfortunate net result is that once it is formed,

TABLE 1.3. How My Partner Sees Me

Sandra Murray and her colleagues use this scale in their studies of self-esteem in close relationships. People with high self-esteem believe that their partners hold them in high regard, but people with low self-esteem worry that their partners do not like or respect them as much. What do you think your partner thinks of you? — — — — — — — —

   In many ways, your partner may see you in roughly the same way you see yourself. Yet in other ways, your partner may see you differently than you see yourself. For example, you may feel quite shy at parties, but your partner might tell you that you really seem quite relaxed and outgoing on these occasions. On the other hand, you and your partner may both agree that you are quite intelligent and patient.

   For each trait or attribute that follows, please indicate *how you think that your partner sees you*. For example, if you think that your partner sees the attribute "self-assured" as moderately characteristic of you, you would choose "5".

   Respond using the scale below. Please enter your response in the blank to the left of each trait or attribute listed.

1	2	3	4	5	6	7	8	9
not at all characteristic		somewhat characteristic		moderately characteristic		very characteristic		completely characteristic

My partner sees me as . . .

___	Kind and Affectionate	___	Tolerant and Accepting
___	Critical and Judgmental	___	Thoughtless
___	Self-Assured	___	Patient
___	Sociable/Extraverted	___	Rational
___	Intelligent	___	Understanding
___	Lazy	___	Distant
___	Open and Disclosing	___	Complaining
___	Controlling and Dominant	___	Responsive
___	Witty and Humorous	___	Immature
___	Moody	___	Warm

low self-esteem may be hard to overcome; even after ten years of marriage, people with low self-esteem still tend to believe that their spouses love and accept them less than those faithful spouses really do (Murray, Holmes, & Griffin, 2000).

   Thus, our self-esteem appears to both result from, and then subsequently influence, our interpersonal relationships. What we think of ourselves seems to be dependent, at least in part, on the quality of our connections to others. And those self-evaluations affect our ensuing interactions with new partners, who provide us further evidence of our interpersonal worth. In fundamental ways, what we know of ourselves emerges from our partnerships with others, and matters thereafter.

BOX 1.3

An Individual Difference that's Not Much of a Difference: Homosexuality

We haven't said anything about gays or lesbians until now, and that's because there hasn't been much to say. There are few differences of any note between heterosexuals and homosexuals on any of the topics we've covered so far. For instance, gay men and lesbians exhibit the same attachment styles in the same proportions as heterosexual men and women do (Ridge & Feeney, 1998), and they, too, are happier with partners of high (rather than low) expressivity (Kurdek & Schmitt, 1986a).

There are some potentially important differences, on average, between homosexuals and heterosexuals. Gay men tend to be more expressive than heterosexual men are (Cohen, 2002), and lesbians tend to be better educated and to have higher self-esteem than their heterosexual sisters do (Rothblum & Factor, 2001). But the big difference between homosexual and heterosexual relationships is that a gay couple is comprised of two men and a lesbian couple of two women. To the extent that there are meaningful sex and gender differences in the way people conduct their relationships, they will show up in homosexual couples—not because of their

sexual orientation but because of the sex of the people involved (Mackey, Diemer, & O'Brien, 2000). Otherwise, there are scant differences between homosexual and heterosexual relationships. They operate in very similar manners (Peplau & Spalding, 2000). Homosexuals fall in love the same way, for instance, and they feel the same passions, experience the same doubts, and feel the same commitments as heterosexuals do (Kurdek, 1994b, 1998a; Kurdek & Schmitt, 1986b). Except for the sex of the partner, homosexual romances and partnerships are very much like heterosexual relationships (Baeccman, Folkesson, & Norlander, 1999).

So, we don't have to write two different books on intimate relationships; the same patterns exist in both heterosexual and homosexual partnerships. We'll certainly mention homosexuality where it's appropriate, but it won't be a major theme in this book because we'd typically just be reiterating what we've said in this box: The processes of close relationships are very similar in heterosexual and homosexual couples (Peplau & Spalding, 2000)—and there's often not much else to say.

THE INFLUENCE OF HUMAN NATURE

Now that we have surveyed several individual characteristics that distinguish people from one another, we can address the possibility that our relationships display some underlying themes that reflect the animal nature shared by all humankind. Our concern here is with evolutionary influences that have shaped close relationships over thousands of generations, instilling in us certain tendencies that are found in everyone (Kenrick & Trost, 2000; Winston, 2002).

Evolutionary psychology starts with three fundamental assumptions. First, *natural selection* has helped make us the species we are today. Motives such as the need to belong have presumably come to characterize human beings because they were *adaptive,* conferring some sort of reproductive advantage to those who possessed them (Barber, 2002b; Barrett, Dunbar, & Lycett, 2002). Thus, as we suggested earlier, the early humans who sought cooperative close-ness with others were probably more likely than asocial loners to have children who grew up to have children of their own. Over time, then, to the extent that the desire to affiliate with others is heritable (and it is, Tellegen et al., 1988), nat-ural selection would have made the need to belong more prevalent, with fewer and fewer people being born without it. In keeping with this example, evolu-tionary principles assert that any universal psychological mechanism exists in its present form because it consistently solved some problem of survival or reproduction in the past (Buss, 2004).

Second, evolutionary psychology suggests that men and women should differ from one another only to the extent that they have historically faced dif-ferent reproductive dilemmas (Buss & Kenrick, 1998; Geary, 1998). Thus, men and women should behave similarly in close relationships except in those instances in which different, specialized styles of behavior would allow better access to mates or promote superior survival of one's offspring. Are there such situations? Let's answer that question by posing two hypothetical queries:

> If, during one year, a man has sex with 100 different women, how many chil-dren can he father? (The answer, of course, is "lots, perhaps as many as 100.")

> If, during one year, a woman has sex with 100 different men, how many children can she have? (Probably just one.)

Obviously, there's a big difference in the minimum time and effort that men and women have to invest in each child they produce. For a man, the minimum requirement is a single ejaculation; given access to receptive mates, a man might father hundreds of children during his lifetime. But a woman can have children only until her menopause, and each child she has requires an enormous invest-ment of time and energy. These biological differences in men's and women's **parental investment** in their children may have supported the evolution of different strategies for selecting mates (Geary, 2000). Conceivably, given their more limited reproductive potential, women in our ancestral past who chose their mates carefully reproduced more successfully (with their children surviv-ing to have children of their own) than did women who were less thoughtful and deliberate in their choices of partners. In contrast, men who promiscuously pursued every available sexual opportunity probably reproduced more successfully. If they flitted from partner to partner, their children may have been less likely to survive, but what they didn't offer in quality (of parenting) they could make up for in quantity (of children). Thus, today—as this evolutionary account predicts—women do choose their sexual partners more carefully than men do. They insist on smarter, friendlier, more prestigious, and more emo-tionally stable partners than men will tolerate (Barrett et al., 2002; Kenrick et al., 1990), and are less accepting of casual, uncommitted sex than men are (Gangestad & Simpson, 1993). Perhaps this sex difference evolved over time.

Another reproductive difference between the sexes is that a woman always knows for sure whether or not a particular child is hers. By comparison, a man suffers **paternity uncertainty;** unless he is completely confident that his mate has been faithful to him, he cannot be absolutely certain that her child is his (Buss & Schmitt, 1993). Perhaps for that reason, men are especially vigilant toward the threat of marital infidelity, and they generally feel less certain that their mates have been faithful to them than women do (Paul, Foss, & Galloway, 1993). This difference, too, may have evolved over time.

An evolutionary perspective also makes use of a distinction between *short-term* and *long-term* mating strategies (Buss & Schmitt, 1993). Both men and women seem to pursue different sorts of attributes in the other sex when they're having a brief fling than when they're entering a longer, more committed relationship. In particular, men have a greater desire than women do for sexual liaisons of short duration (Schmitt, Shackelford, Duntley et al., 2001), they are more interested in brief affairs with a variety of partners, and when they enter new relationships, they're ready to have sex sooner than women are (Schmitt, Shackelford, & Buss, 2001). As a result, men are particularly attracted to women who seem to be sexually available and "easy"—at least in the short-term (Schmitt, Couden, & Baker, 2001). However, if they think about settling down, the same men who consider promiscuous women to be desirable partners in casual relationships often prefer chaste women as prospective spouses (Buss, 2000, 2004). Men also tend to seek wives who are young and pretty. When they're thinking long-term, men value physical attractiveness more than women do, and as men age, they marry women increasingly younger than themselves (Buss, 2004, Kenrick & Keefe, 1992).

Women exhibit different patterns. When women select short-term mates—particularly when they have extramarital affairs (Greiling & Buss, 2000)—they seek sexy, charming, dominant men with lots of masculine appeal. But when they evaluate potential husbands, they look for good financial prospects, men with incomes and resources who presumably can provide a safe environment for their children (Kenrick et al., 2001), even when those men aren't the sexiest guys in the pack (Gangestad & Simpson, 2000). In general, women care more than men do about the financial prospects and status of their long-term partners (Buss, 2004).

The effort to delineate human nature by identifying patterns of behavior that are found in all of humanity is one of the compelling aspects of the evolutionary perspective. In fact, the different preferences we just mentioned—with men valuing good looks and women valuing good incomes—have been found in dozens of cultures, everywhere they have been studied around the world (Buss, 2004).[3] However, an evolutionary perspective does not imply that culture is unimportant.

---

[3]Here's a chance for you to rehearse what you learned earlier in this chapter about sex differences. Men and women differ in the importance they attach to physical attractiveness and income, but that does not mean that women don't care about looks and men don't care about money. And as we'll see in chapter 3, men and women mostly want the *same* things, such as warmth, emotional stability, and generous affection, from their romantic partners. The sex differences we just described are real, but looks and money are less important than other valuable characteristics that men and women both want (Baker & Miller, 2004). Finally, before we finish this footnote, do you see how differential parental investment may help create the sex differences we've mentioned here? Think about it, and we'll return to this point in chapter 3.

Indeed, a third basic assumption of evolutionary psychology is that cultural influences determine whether evolved patterns of behavior are adaptive—and cultural change occurs faster than evolution does (Crawford, 1998). Thus, our species displays patterns of behavior that *were* adaptive eons ago, but not all of those inherited tendencies may fit the modern environments we inhabit now (Gaulin & McBurney, 2001). For instance, cavemen may have reproduced successfully if they mated with every possible partner, but modern men may not: In just the last two generations, we have seen (1) the creation of reproductive technologies—such as birth control pills—that allow women complete control of their fertility and (2) the spread of a lethal virus that is transmitted through sexual contact (the human immunodeficiency virus that causes AIDS). These days, an interest in sexual variety and an openness to multiple partners are probably less adaptive for men than they were millions of years ago. Conceivably, modern men may reproduce more successfully if they display a capacity for commitment and monogamy that encourages their partners to allow a pregnancy to occur. But the human race is still evolving. Natural selection will ultimately favor styles of behavior that fit this new environment, but it will take several thousand generations for such adaptations to occur. (And how will our cultures have changed by then?)

Thus, an evolutionary perspective provides a fascinating explanation for common patterns in modern relationships (Simpson & Gangestad, 2001). Certain themes and some sex differences exist because they spring from evolved psychological mechanisms that were useful long ago. We are not robots who are mindlessly enacting genetic directives, but we do have inherited habits that are triggered by the situations we encounter (Buss & Kenrick, 1998). Moreover, our habits may fit our modern situations to varying degrees. Behavior results from the interplay of both personal and situational influences, but some common reactions in people result from evolved human nature itself:

> The pressures to which we have been exposed over millenia have left a mental and emotional legacy. Some of these emotions and reactions, derived from the species who were our ancestors, are unnecessary in a modern age, but these vestiges of a former existence are indelibly printed in our make-up. (Winston, 2002, p. 3)

This is a provocative point of view that has attracted both acclaim and criticism. On the one hand, the evolutionary perspective has prompted intriguing new discoveries, most of which are consistent with the ideas it asserts (Buss, 2004; Gaulin & McBurney, 2001). On the other hand, assumptions about the primeval social environments from which human nature emerged are necessarily speculative (Eagly, 1997). In addition, an evolutionary model is not the only reasonable explanation for many of the patterns at issue. For instance, women may have to pick their mates more carefully than men do because cultures routinely allow women to control fewer financial resources (Eagly & Wood, 1999); arguably, women have to be concerned about their spouses' incomes because it's hard for them to earn as much money themselves (Wood & Eagly, 2002). If women filled similar roles and had social status as high as men's, some of the sex differences we described above might be much reduced (Eagly & Diekman, 2003; Johannesen-Schmidt & Eagly, 2002).

In any case, there *are* notable patterns in human relationships that appear everywhere, regardless of culture, and we'll describe several of them in later chapters. Whether it evolved or was a social creation (or both), there is a human nature, and it affects our intimate relationships.

THE INFLUENCE OF INTERACTION

The final building block of relationships is the interaction that the two partners share. So far, we have had much to say about the idiosyncratic experiences and personalities that individuals bring to a relationship, but it's time to acknowledge that relationships are often much more than the sum of their parts. Relationships emerge from the *combination* of their participants' histories and talents (Robins, Caspi, & Moffitt, 2000), and those amalgamations may be quite different from the simple sum of the individuals who create them (Reis, Capobianco, & Tsai, 2002). Chemists are used to thinking this way; when they mix two elements (such as hydrogen and oxygen) they often get a compound (such as water) that doesn't resemble either of its constituent parts. In a similar fashion, the relationship two people create results from contributions from each of them but may only faintly resemble the relationships they share with other people.

Moreover, a relationship emanates from the dynamic give-and-take of its participants day by day; it's a fluid *process* rather than a static, changeless thing (Berscheid, 1999). Individually, two partners inevitably encounter fluctuating moods and variable health and energy; then, when they interact, their mutual influence on one another may produce a constantly changing variety of outcomes. Over time, of course, unmistakable patterns of interaction may distinguish one relationship from another (Zayas, Shoda, & Ayduk, 2002). Still, at any given moment, a relationship may be an inconstant entity, the product of shifting transactions of complex people.

Overall, then, relationships are constructed of diverse influences that may range from the fads and fashions of current culture to the basic nature of the human race. Working alongside those generic influences are a variety of idiosyncratic factors such as personality and experience, some of them learned and some of them inherited. And ultimately, two people who hail from the same planet but who may otherwise be different—to a degree—in every other respect, begin to interact. The result may be frustrating or fulfilling, but the possibilities are always fascinating—and that's what relationships are made of.

THE DARK SIDE OF RELATIONSHIPS

We began this chapter by asserting the value of intimacy to human beings, so, to be fair, we should finish it by admitting that intimacy has potential costs as well. We need intimacy—we suffer without it—but distress and displeasure sometimes result from our dealings with others. Indeed, relationships can be disappointing in so many ways that whole books can, and have been, written about their pitfalls (Kowalski, 1997, 2001; Spitzberg & Cupach, 1998)! When they're close to others, people may fear that their sensitive secrets will be revealed or turned against them. They may dread the loss of autonomy and personal control that comes with interdependency (Baxter, 2004), and they may worry about being abandoned by those on whom they rely (Hatfield, 1984). They recognize that there is dishonesty in relationships and that people sometimes confuse sex with love (Firestone & Catlett, 1999). And in fact, most of us (56 percent) have had a very troublesome relationship in the last five years (Levitt, Silver, & Franco, 1996), so these are not empty fears.

As you might expect after our discussion of attachment styles, some people fear intimacy more than others (Greenfield & Thelen, 1997). Indeed, some of us anxiously expect that others will reject us, and we live on edge waiting for the relational axe to fall (Downey, Feldman, & Ayduk, 2000). But whether our fears are overstated or merely realistic, we're all likely to experience unexpected, frustrating costs in our relationships on occasion (Miller, 1997b). And the deleterious consequences of chronic aggravation and annoyance on our physical health can be substantial (Kiecolt-Glaser et al., 2002; Krause & Shaw, 2002).

So why take the risk? Because we are a social species. We need each other. We prematurely wither and die without intimate connections to other people. Relationships can be complex, but they are essential parts of our lives, so they are worth understanding as thoroughly as possible. We're glad you're reading this book, and we'll try to facilitate your understanding in the chapters that follow.

FOR YOUR CONSIDERATION

Marc and Wendy met during their junior years in college, and they instantly found a lot to like in each other. Wendy was pretty and very feminine and rather meek, and Marc liked the fact that he was able to entice her to have sex with him on their second date. Wendy was susceptible to his charms because she unjustly doubted her desirability, and she was excited that a dominant, charismatic man found her attractive. They started cohabitating during their senior years and married six months after graduation. They developed a traditional partnership, with Wendy staying home when their children were young and Marc applying himself to his career. He succeeded in his profession, winning several lucrative promotions, but Wendy began to feel that he was married more to his work than to her. She wanted him to talk to her more, and he began to wish that she was eating less and taking better care of herself.

In your opinion, what does the future hold for Marc and Wendy? How happy will they be with each other in another ten years? Why?

CHAPTER SUMMARY

The Nature and Importance of Intimacy

This book focuses on adult friendships and romantic relationships, topics that most of us find endlessly fascinating.

The Nature of Intimacy. Intimate relationships differ from more casual associations in at least six specific ways: *knowledge, caring, interdependence, mutuality, trust,* and *commitment.* None of these components is required for intimacy to occur, and relationships come in all shapes and sizes, but our most meaningful relationships include all six components.

The Need to Belong. Humans display a need to belong, a drive to maintain regular interaction with affectionate, intimate partners. When the need is not met for short periods, people become distressed and distracted. More severe consequences, such as poor physical and mental health, may follow if the need remains unfulfilled over time. The need to belong probably evolved over eons, favoring those early humans who sought stable, affectionate connections to others. We are a very social species.

The Influence of Culture

Cultural norms regarding relationships in the United States have changed dramatically over the last forty years. Fewer people are marrying than ever before, and those who do wait longer to marry. Then, half of all new marriages end in divorce. People routinely live together and often have babies even when they're not married, and such cohabitation appears to make a future divorce more, not less, likely. As a result of these trends, most American youths will live in a single-parent home before they're eighteen.

Sources of Change. High levels of socioeconomic development, increasing individualism, and new technology contribute to cultural change. So does the *sex ratio,* the number of men who are available for every 100 women in a population. Cultures with high sex ratios are characterized by sexually conservative behavior and traditional roles for men and women. In contrast, low sex ratios are correlated with permissive, less traditional behavior. This pattern may promote the interests of a society's most powerful members—men.

The Influence of Experience

Children's interactions with their major caregivers produce three different styles of attachment. *Secure* children bond happily with others and trust them; *anxious-ambivalent* children are nervous and clingy; and *avoidant* children are suspicious of others and do not trust them readily. Remarkably, similar orientations toward close relationships can also be observed among adults. Most of us (60 percent) are secure, but a quarter of us are avoidant, and 10 percent are anxious-ambivalent.

These orientations appear to be learned. Attachment styles can change, and a third of us—mostly those with avoidant or anxious-ambivalent styles—may encounter meaningful change in our styles over a two-year period. Thus, our global beliefs about the nature and worth of close relationships appear to be shaped by our experiences within them.

The Influence of Individual Differences

There's wide variation in people's abilities and preferences, but individual differences are more often gradual and subtle instead of abrupt. Nevertheless, such differences influence our behavior in close relationships in important ways.

Sex Differences. Despite lay beliefs that men and women are quite different, the distributions of their behavior and interests in intimate relationships take the form of substantially *overlapping normal curves.* Careful analysis indicates that some sex differences, although real, are quite small. The range of variation among members of a given sex is always large compared to the average difference between the sexes, and the overlap of the sexes is so substantial that many members of one sex will always score higher than the average member of the other sex. Thus, the sexes are much more similar than different on most of the topics and dimensions of interest to relationship science. Men and women are not from Mars and Venus, they're from North Dakota and South Dakota.

Gender Differences. *Sex* differences refer to biological distinctions between men and women that spring naturally from their physical natures, whereas *gender* differences refer to social and psychological distinctions that are taught to people by their cultures. Classifying a distinction between men and women as a sex or gender difference isn't always easy, but gender roles—the patterns of behavior that are culturally expected of normal men and women—are unquestionably gender differences. Men are expected to be dominant and assertive, women to be warm and emotionally expressive. These expectations only fit half of us, however. A third of us are *androgynous* and possess both *instrumental,* task-oriented skills and *expressive,* social and emotional talents. In fact, people can be high or low in either instrumentality or expressiveness, but traditional gender roles encourage us to specialize in one and not the other.

Such specialization is disadvantageous in close relationships. Men and women who adhere to traditional gender roles do not like each other, either at first meeting or later during a marriage, as much as less stereotyped, androgynous people do. This may be because expressiveness makes one a rewarding partner in intimate relationships, and instrumentality fosters personal adjustment, and only androgynous people enjoy both assets.

Personality. Personality traits are stable tendencies that characterize people's thoughts, feelings, and behavior across their whole lives. Extraversion, agreeableness, and conscientiousness help produce pleasant relationships, but neurotic people are less satisfied with their partnerships than are those with less neuroticism. These traits may be influential because they affect the chronic moods with which people approach others. Extraverted and agreeable people tend to be cheerful and enthusiastic, whereas neurotic people tend to feel anxious and fearful.

Self-Esteem. What we think of ourselves stems, in part, from our interactions with others. The *sociometer* theory argues that self-esteem is a subjective gauge of the quality of our relationships; if others regard us positively, self-esteem is high, but if others don't want to associate with us, self-esteem is low.

People who have low self-esteem undermine and sabotage their close relationships by underestimating their partners' love for them and overreacting to imagined threats. People with high self-esteem draw closer to their partners when frustrations arise, but people with low self-esteem distance themselves, behave badly, and feel even worse about themselves.

The Influence of Human Nature

An evolutionary perspective on modern relationships starts with three assumptions. First, natural selection shapes humankind, and any universal psychological mechanism exists because it was adaptive in the past. Second, men and women should differ only to the extent that they routinely faced historically different reproductive dilemmas. Such differences probably occurred; men and women make different *parental investments* in their offspring, and men suffer *paternity uncertainty* that does not plague women. Perhaps as a result, women choose their mates more carefully than men do, but men are especially vigilant toward the threat of marital infidelity. The sexes also pursue different mates when they're interested in a long, committed relationship than they do when they're interested in a short-term affair. Finally, the evolutionary perspective assumes that cultural influences determine whether inherited habits are still adaptive—and some of them may not be. Altogether, this point of view has attracted both adherents and critics. Still, whatever its source, there is a human nature, and it directs our intimate relationships.

The Influence of Interaction

Relationships result from the combinations of their participants' histories and talents, and thus are often more than the sum of their parts. The shifting, changeable interactions that two partners share are the result of their fluctuating moods and variable energy, and they demonstrate that relationships are fluid processes rather than static entities.

The Dark Side of Relationships

There are potential costs, as well as rewards, to intimacy. People may fear exposure, a loss of control, or abandonment. Such fears afflict some people more than others, but we all experience unexpected costs on occasion. So why take the risk? Because we are a social species, and we need each other.

CHAPTER 2

Research Methods

A Brief History of Relationship Science ✦ Developing a Question ✦ Obtaining Participants ✦ Choosing a Design ✦ Correlational Designs ✦ Experimental Designs ✦ Developmental Designs ✦ Selecting a Setting ✦ The Nature of Our Data ✦ Self-Reports ✦ Observations ✦ Physiological Measures ✦ Archival Materials ✦ Couples' Reports ✦ The Ethics of Such Endeavors ✦ Interpreting and Integrating Results ✦ A Final Note ✦ For Your Consideration ✦ Chapter Summary

Students often dread chapters on research methods, regarding them as distractions to be endured before getting to "the good stuff." You're probably interested in topics like love, sex, and jealousy, for instance, but do not have a burning desire to understand research designs and procedures. Chapters like this one often seem tangential to what students really want to know.

However, for several reasons, some basic knowledge of the methods of inquiry is especially valuable for consumers of relationship science. For one thing, there are more charlatans and imposters competing for your attention in this field than in most others (Stanovich, 2004). Bookstores and websites are full of ideas offered by people who don't really study relationships at all but who (a) base suggestions and advice on their own idiosyncratic experiences, or (b) simply make them up (Honeycutt, 1996). Appreciating the difference between trustworthy, reliable information and simple gossip can save you money and disappointment. Furthermore, misinformation about relationships is more likely to cause people real inconvenience than are misunderstandings in other sciences. People who misunderstand the nature of astronomical black holes, for instance, are much less likely to take action that will be disadvantageous to them than are people who are misinformed about the effects of divorce on children. Studies of relationships often have real human impact in everyday life (Bradbury, 2002).

Indeed, this book speaks more directly to topics that affect you personally than most other texts you'll ever read. Because of this, you have a special responsibility to be an informed consumer who can distinguish flimsy whimsy from solid truths.

This isn't always easy. As we'll see in this chapter, there may be various ways to address a specific research question, and each may have its own particular advantages and disadvantages. Reputable scientists gather and evaluate information systematically and carefully, but no single technique may provide the indisputable answers they seek. A thoughtful understanding of relationships often requires us to combine information from many studies, evaluating diverse facts with judicious discernment. This chapter provides the overview of research methods and the history of the field that you need to make such judgments.

Only basic principles are described here, but they should help you decide what evidence to accept and what to question. Hopefully, when we're done, you'll be better equipped to distinguish useful research evidence from useless anecdotes or mere speculation. For even more information, don't hesitate to consult other sources such as Duck (1997) and Sansone, Morf, and Panter (2004).

A BRIEF HISTORY OF RELATIONSHIP SCIENCE

Isaac Newton identified some of the basic laws of physics more than 400 years ago (back in 1687). Biology and chemistry have been around for just as long. The systematic study of human relationships, on the other hand, is a recent invention that is so new and so recent that most of the scientists who have ever studied human intimacy are still alive! This is no small matter. Because relationship science has a short history, it is less well-known than most other sciences, and for that reason it is less well understood. Very few people outside of colleges and universities appreciate the extraordinary strides this new discipline has made in the last forty years.

It's remarkable that it took scientists so long to begin studying relationships, because philosophers have always been keenly interested in the nature of friendship and intimacy. As an example, Table 2.1 provides a sampling of observations about relationships made by ancient philosophers; they pondered faithfulness, shyness, beauty, marital satisfaction, jealousy, and bereavement, among other issues. (But be forewarned: They were not always correct!)

Of all these ancient authors, Aristotle, who lived more than 2,300 years ago (circa 384–322 B.C.), may have analyzed close relationships most insightfully

TABLE 2.1. A Sample of Interpersonal Comments in the Writings of Early Philosophers

Friendship makes prosperity more brilliant, and lightens adversity by dividing and sharing it. (Cicero)

It goes far toward making a man faithful to let him understand that you think him so, and he that does but suspect I will deceive him, gives me a sort of right to do it. (Seneca)

Shyness is in fact an excess of modesty. (Plutarch)

What is beautiful is good. (Sappho)

Love must be fostered with soft words. (Ovid)

He that is not jealous, is not in love. (St. Augustine)

By all means marry; if you get a good wife, you'll be happy. If you get a bad one, you'll become a philosopher. (Socrates)

If you marry wisely, marry your equal. (Ovid)

There is no grief that time does not lessen and soften. (Cicero)

(see Books VIII and IX of his *Nicomachean Ethics*). He believed that "Man is by nature a social animal," and thought that there were three different kinds of friendships. In relationships based on utility, Aristotle argued, we are attracted to others because of the help they provide. In relationships based on pleasure, we are attracted to others because we find them pleasant and engaging. And in relationships based on virtue, we are attracted to others because of their virtuous character. Relationships of virtue were the highest form, Aristotle believed, because they were the only type in which partners were liked for themselves rather than as merely means to an end. They were also the longest lasting; Aristotle felt that a relationship of utility or pleasure would evaporate if the benefits provided by one's partner dwindled, but a friendship based on virtue would endure as long as the partner remained pure.

Aristotle gave relational matters considerable attention, as you can see. He was also right some of the time; remember Aristotle when you read about the modern reward theory of attraction in chapter 3. However, Aristotle only contemplated relationships; he did not engage in systematic efforts to determine whether his musings were correct. Neither did the many poets and philosophers such as Aquinas, Montaigne, Kant, and Emerson, who wrote on love and friendship between Aristotle's era and the end of the nineteenth century (see Pakaluk, 1991).

When modern psychology and sociology began to emerge in the late 1800s, theorists often incorporated relationships into their seminal formulations. Freud felt that parent-child relationships were crucial in human development. Durkheim believed that *anomie* (or being socially disconnected) was associated with suicide. Simmel wrote about dyads, or partnerships that involve just two people. These intellectuals sought support for their beliefs—for instance, Freud had his patients and Durkheim examined social statistics—but their primary contributions were conceptual.

Relationship science may have finally begun when Will S. Monroe (1898) asked 2,336 children in western Massachusetts to identify the traits and habits they considered to be important in selecting friends. (They mentioned such attributes as kindness, cheerfulness, and honesty.) This simple procedure marked a significant shift in the study of relationships—a change from analyses that were primarily philosophical to those that were grounded in data and empirical evidence.

In the years immediately after Monroe's pioneering project, very few similar studies were done. A trickle of historically important studies of children's friendships (e.g., Moreno, 1934), courtship (e.g., Waller, 1937), and marriages and families (see Broderick, 1988) began in the 1930s, but relatively few relationship studies were done before World War II. After the war, several important field studies, such as Whyte's (1955) *Street Corner Society* and Festinger, Schachter, and Back's (1950) study of student friendships in campus housing, attracted attention and respect. Still, relationships did not become a broad focus of research until an explosion of studies put the field on the scientific map in the 1960s and 1970s.

One of the most influential developments during that period was the new emphasis on laboratory experiments in social psychology. In a quest for precision that yielded unambiguous results, researchers began studying specific influences on relationships that they were able to control and manipulate. For instance, in a prominent line of research on the role of attitude similarity in liking, Donn Byrne and his colleagues (e.g., Byrne & Nelson, 1965a) asked people to inspect an attitude survey that had supposedly been completed by a stranger in another room, and then asked them how much they liked the stranger. What the participants didn't know was that the researchers had prepared the survey either to agree or disagree with the participants' own attitudes (which had been assessed earlier). This manipulation of attitude similarity had clear effects: Apparent agreement caused people to like the stranger more than disagreement did.

Procedures like these demonstrated that some of the sources of liking could be understood through lab experiments, and their methodological rigor satisfied researchers' desires for clarity and concision. They legitimized and popularized the study of interpersonal attraction, making it an indispensable part of social psychology textbooks for the first time. In retrospect, however, these investigations often did a poor job of representing the natural complexity of real relationships. The participants in many of Byrne's experiments never actually met that other person or interacted with him or her in any way. Indeed, in the procedure we have been discussing, a meeting couldn't occur because the stranger didn't actually exist! In this "phantom stranger" technique, people were merely reacting to check marks on a piece of paper and were the only real participants in the study. The researchers were measuring attraction to someone who wasn't even there. Byrne and his colleagues chose this method, limiting their investigation to one carefully controlled aspect of relationship development, in order to study it conclusively. However, they also created a rather sterile situation that lacked the immediacy and drama of chatting with someone face-to-face on a blind date.

But don't underestimate the importance of studies like these: They demonstrated that relationships could be studied scientifically, and they suggested that such investigations had enormous promise. They really brought relationship science to the attention of fellow scholars for the first time. And in the decades since, through the combined efforts of family scholars, psychologists, sociologists, and communication researchers, relationship science has grown and evolved to encompass new methods of considerable complexity and sophistication. Today, relationship science (Felmlee & Sprecher, 2000; Gottman & Notarius, 2002):

- often uses diverse samples of people drawn from all walks of life,
- examines varied types of family, friendship, and romantic relationships,
- frequently studies those relationships over long periods of time,
- studies both the pleasant and unpleasant aspects of relationships, and
- often follows relationships in their natural settings.

TABLE 2.2. A Typical Rochester Interaction Record

Date: ____   Time: ____   A.M./P.M. Length: ____ hours ____ minutes
List the initials, and sex of up to 3 main participants: _____
If there were more than 3 people, how many: Males _____ Females _____
Now rate the interaction on the following dimensions:

How **intimate** was it	superficial	1 2 3 4 5 6 7	meaningful
Did **you disclose:**	very little	1 2 3 4 5 6 7	a great deal
Did **others disclose:**	very little	1 2 3 4 5 6 7	a great deal
The **quality** was?	unpleasant	1 2 3 4 5 6 7	very pleasant
How **satisfied** were you?	less than expected	1 2 3 4 5 6 7	more than expected

Here are some examples of how the field currently operates:

- At the University of Rochester, Ladd Wheeler, John Nezlek, and Harry Reis developed the Rochester Interaction Record (or RIR), a short form with which research participants record important details about their ordinary dealings with others soon after they occur each day. (See Table 2.2.) The RIR captures information about authentic, natural interactions; studies typically compile these reports over a week or more, allowing the patterns in people's interactions to stand out.
- At the University of Texas at Arlington, William Ickes and his colleagues study spontaneous, unscripted interactions between people (who have sometimes just met) by leaving them alone on a comfortable couch for a few minutes while their conversation is covertly videotaped (Ickes, 2003). The camera is actually hidden in another room across the hall and can't be seen even if you're looking directly at it, so there's no clue that anyone is watching. (See Figure 2.1.) Afterwards, participants can review the tapes of their interaction in private cubicles where they are invited to report what they were thinking—and what they thought their partners were thinking—at each point in the interaction. The method thus provides an objective video-taped record of the interaction, and participants' thoughts and feelings and perceptions of one another can be obtained, too. (Visit this lab at http://www.uta.edu/psychology/faculty/ickes/social_lab/.)
- At the University of Washington (http://www.gottman.com/research/family/), John Gottman and his colleagues invite married couples to a pleasant setting where they may take several hours revisiting the disagreement that caused their last argument. They know that they are being videotaped, but after a while they typically become so absorbed in the interaction that the cameras are forgotten. The researchers may even take physiological measurements such as heart rate and electrodermal responses from the participants. Painstaking second-by-second analysis of the biological, emotional, and behavioral reactions he observes allows Gottman to predict

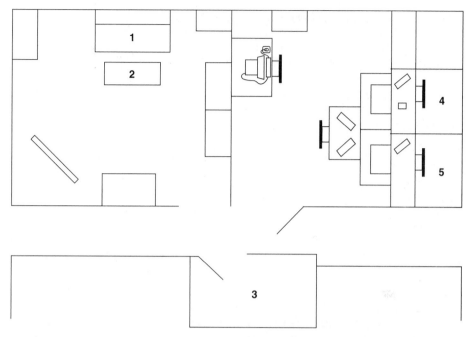

FIGURE 2.1. Schematic diagram of William Ickes's lab at the University of Texas at Arlington.

Participants in a typical study will be left alone on a couch (1)—the only place to sit—in a spacious room. A microphone hidden under a coffee table (2) and a video camera completely out of sight in another room (3) record their conversation. Afterwards, the participants may offer insights into what they were thinking during their interaction when they watch their videotape in individual viewing rooms (4 and 5).

with 93 percent accuracy which of the couples will, and which will not, divorce years later (Gottman & Levenson, 2000).

- At the University of Texas at Austin (http://www.utexas.edu/research/pair/), Ted Huston and his colleagues (e.g., Huston & Houts, 1998) continue to monitor the outcomes experienced by 168 couples who joined a marital research project, the Processes of Adaptation in Intimate Relationships (or PAIR) project, years ago. In 1981, newlywed couples in Pennsylvania were invited to participate in the PAIR investigation by providing extensive reports about the nature and status of their relationships. Since then, although many of them are now divorced and others have moved elsewhere, researchers have conducted brief follow-up interviews with these people every few years. Entire marriages are being carefully tracked from start to finish as time goes by.
- In a similar and even larger Early Years of Marriage Project run by Terri Orbuch and Joseph Veroff (2002), 199 white couples and 174 black couples from the area surrounding Detroit, Michigan, have been interviewed intermittently since they were married in 1986. The project is taking specific note of the influences of social and economic conditions on marital satisfaction,

and it allows comparisons of the outcomes encountered by white and black Americans. In 2000, 14 years after the project began, 29 percent of the white couples and 50 percent of the black couples had already divorced (Orbuch et al., 2002).

We hope that you're impressed by the creativity and resourcefulness embodied in these methods of research. (We are!) But as notable as they are, they barely scratch the surface in illustrating the current state of relationship science. Although still young, the field is now supported by hundreds of scholars around the world who hail from diverse scientific disciplines and whose work appears in several different professional journals devoted entirely to personal relationships. Look in your campus library for issues of the *Journal of Marriage and the Family*, the *Journal of Social and Personal Relationships*, and the journal simply entitled *Personal Relationships*.

You can also check out the International Association for Relationship Research, the world's largest organization of relationship scientists, at http://www.iarr.org.

DEVELOPING A QUESTION

How do these scholars study relationships? The first step in any scientific endeavor is to ask a question, and in a field like this one, some questions emerge from *personal experience*. Relationship researchers have an advantage over many other scientists in being unusually close to their subject matter; their own experiences in close relationships can alert them to important processes, and they are sometimes hip deep in the very swamps they are trying to drain (Miller, 2003)! Broader *social problems* also suggest questions for careful study. For instance, the huge increase in the American divorce rate from 1960 to 1980 resulted in a considerable amount of research on divorce as social scientists took note of the culture's changes.

Questions also come from *previous research*: Studies that answer one question may raise new ones. And still other questions are suggested by *theories* that strive to offer explanations for relational events. If a theory says that certain things should happen under given conditions, scientists will be curious to see if those predictions are correct. Research on intimate relationships involves questions that spring from all of these sources; scientists will put together their personal observations, their recognition of social problems, their knowledge of previous research, and their theoretical perspectives to create the questions they ask (Fiske, 2004).

The questions themselves are usually of two broad types. First, researchers may seek to *describe* some event or series of events as it naturally occurs. In this case, their goal is to delineate the nature of events as fully and accurately as they can. Alternatively, researchers can seek to establish the *causal connections* between events to determine which events have meaningful effects on subsequent outcomes and which do not. This distinction has many ramifications, both for the scientists who conduct research and for those who consume it.

For the researchers, the specific question often determines the design of the investigation. For instance, John Gottman's marital research at the University of Washington generally began with the descriptive goal of identifying the behaviors that differentiated happy spouses from those who were discontented. As that goal was met, Gottman began to determine whether such behavior could predict the fate of a marriage as time went by, and if so, why. The initial studies, which had descriptive goals, gradually provided the foundation for subsequent—and even more complex—investigations of the causal connections between certain types of behavior and marital distress. But it took time, and a variety of different procedures and research designs, before the tasks of description and causal connections were both complete (Gottman & Notarius, 2000).

There are two points here for consumers of relationship research. First, different studies have different goals, and discerning consumers judge investigations with respect to their intended purposes. If an exploratory study seeks mainly to describe a newly-noticed phenomenon, we shouldn't criticize it for leaving us uncertain about the causes and the effects of that phenomenon; those are different questions to be addressed later, after we specify what we're talking about. Second, and more importantly, thoughtful consumers resist the temptation to draw causal connections from studies with descriptive goals. Only certain research designs allow any insight into the causal connections between events, and clever consumers do not jump to unwarranted conclusions that the research results do not support. We'll return to this point later in this chapter.

OBTAINING PARTICIPANTS

So, whose relationships get studied? Relationship researchers usually recruit participants in one of two ways. The first approach is to use anyone who is readily available and who consents to participate; this is a **convenience sample** because it is (comparatively) convenient for the researcher to obtain. University professors who study intimate relationships often work with college students who are required to be research participants as part of their course work. Clinical psychologists may study distressed couples who come to their clinics seeking help. Researchers may also advertise for volunteers through the mass media or local community organizations. Although some specific characteristics must sometimes be met (so that a study may involve only dating partners who have known each other for less than two months), researchers who use convenience samples are usually glad to get the help of everyone they can.

In contrast, projects that use a **representative sample** strive to ensure that their participants resemble the entire population of people who are relevant to the research question. A study of marriage, for example, would need, in theory, a sample that is representative of all married people—all ages, all nationalities, and all socioeconomic levels. No such study has ever been conducted, and it probably never will be. If nothing else, the people who voluntarily consent to participate in a research study may be somewhat different from those who

The people in a representative sample reflect the demographic characteristics (sex, age, race, etc.) of the entire population of people that the researchers wish to study.

BOX 2.1

The Challenge of Volunteer Bias in Relationship Research

Regardless of whether investigators use convenience or representative sampling, they still face the problem of **volunteer bias:** Of the people invited to participate, those who do may differ from those who don't. In one illustration of this problem, Karney et al. (1995) simply asked 3,606 couples who had applied for marriage licenses in Los Angeles County whether they would participate in a longitudinal study of their relationships. Only 18 percent of the couples said that they would, and that's a typical rate in procedures of this sort. But their marriage licenses, which were open to the public, provided several bits of information about them (e.g., their addresses, their ages, and their jobs). The volunteers differed from those who refused to participate in sev-

eral ways; they were better educated, employed in higher-status jobs, and more likely to have cohabited. If the researchers had carried out a complete study with these people, would these characteristics have affected their results?

The answer may depend on what questions are asked, but volunteer bias can color the images that emerge from relationship research. People who volunteer for studies dealing with sexual behavior, for instance, tend to be more sexually experienced and active than nonvolunteers (Wiederman, 1999). This is a subtle form of sampling bias that can limit the applicability of research results among those who did not participate in a particular study.

choose not to participate (see Box 2.1). Still, some studies have tried to obtain samples that are representative of the adult population of individual countries or other delimited groups. And studies that are straightforward enough to be conducted over the Internet can attract very large samples that are much more diverse than those found on any one campus or even in any one country (Birnbaum, 2004; Gosling et al., 2004).

On the one hand, there is no question that if we seek general principles that apply to most people, representative samples are better than convenience samples (Miller, 2004). With convenience samples, there is always the danger that the results we obtain apply only to people who are just like our participants—students at a certain university, clients in a certain clinic, or volunteers from a certain area of the country. Attitudes, in particular, can vary considerably from one group to the next. On the other hand, many processes studied by relationship researchers are basic enough that they don't differ substantially across demographic groups; people all over the world, for instance, share similar standards about the nature of physical beauty (see chapter 3). To the extent that research examines fundamental aspects of the ways humans react to each other, there's little disadvantage to convenience samples because basic processes operate similarly from group to group.

Let's consider a specific example. Back in 1978, Russell Clark sent men and women out across the campus of Florida State University to proposition members of the other sex. Individually, they approached unsuspecting targets and randomly assigned them to one of three invitations (see Table 2.3); some people were simply asked out on a date, whereas other people were asked to have sex! The notable results were that no woman accepted the offer of sex from a stranger, but 75% of the men did—and that was more men than accepted the date!

This was a striking result, but so what? The study involved a small convenience sample on just one campus. Perhaps the results told us more about the odd desperation of men at FSU than they did about men and women in general. In fact, Clark had trouble getting the study published because of reviewers' concerns about the generality of the results. So, in 1982, he and Elaine Hatfield

TABLE 2.3. "Would You Go To Bed With Me Tonight?"

In Clark and Hatfield's (1989) studies, college students walking across campus encountered a stranger of the other sex who said, "Hi, I've noticed you around campus, and I find you very attractive," and then offered one of the three invitations below. What percentage of the students accepted the various offers?

	Percentages Saying "Yes"	
Invitations	Men	Women
"Would you go out with me tonight?"	50%	56%
"Would you come over to my apartment tonight?"	69%	6%
"Would you go to bed with me tonight?"	75%	0%

tried again; they repeated the study at FSU and got the same results (Clark & Hatfield, 1989).

Well, still so what? It was four years later, but the procedure had still only been tried in Tallahassee. If you give this example some thought, you'll be able to generate several reasons why the results could be limited to one particular time and one particular place.

We'd like to suggest a different perspective. Let's not fuss too much about the exact percentage of college men in Florida or elsewhere who would consent to sex with a stranger. That's exactly the kind of specific attitude that may vary some from one demographic group to another. Instead of endlessly criticizing or, even worse, dismissing the results of the Clark and Hatfield (1989) studies, let's recognize their limitations but not miss their point: Men were generally more accepting of casual sex than women were. When somebody actually asked, men were more likely to say "yes" to casual sex than women were. Stated generally, that's exactly the conclusion that has now been drawn from more recent investigations involving over 20,000 participants from every major region of the world (Schmitt & the International Sexuality Description Project, 2003; Schmitt et al., 2001), and Clark and Hatfield were among the very first to document this sex difference. Their method was simple, and their sample was limited, but they were onto something, and their procedure detected a basic pattern that really does seem to exist.

So, it's absolutely true that the Clark and Hatfield (1989) studies were not perfect. That's a judgment with which Clark and Hatfield (2003) themselves agree! But as long as their results are considered thoughtfully and judiciously, even small studies using convenience samples like these can be important contributions to relationship science. (In fact, about half of all relationship research is conducted with convenience samples comprised of college students [de Jong Giervald, 1995]. Do *your* relationships operate differently from those of other people?) Representative samples provide desirable reassurance that scientific results can be widely applied, but representative samples are difficult—and expensive—to obtain (Acitelli, 1997).

Many researchers have neither the money nor the personnel to contact people dispersed across a large geographic area. And even if they can contact a representative group of people, they may not be able to afford the payment and other expenses required to ask more than just a few questions of their participants.

Relationship science often presents dilemmas like these: Choices must be made, but no flawless option is available. In such cases, our confidence in our collective understanding of relationships rests on a gradual accumulation of knowledge with varied methods (Reis, 2002). Here, diversity is an asset. Different investigators study a given topic in different ways (Houts, Cook, & Shadish, 1986). Any single study may have some imperfections, but those weaknesses may be answered by another study's strengths. With a series of investigations, each approaching a problem from a different angle, we gradually delineate the truth. As a thoughtful consumer of relationship science, you should try to think the way the scientists do: No one study is perfect. Be cautious. Diverse methods are valuable. Wisdom takes time. But the truth is out there, and we're getting closer all the time.

CHOOSING A DESIGN

Once we have formulated a research question and obtained some participants, we need to arrange our observations in a way that will answer our question. This section describes several different research designs that often appear in relationship science.

Correlational Designs

A **correlation** allows us to answer the questions, "Do two events, x and y, change together? That is, are variations in x and y related in some way?" Correlations are numbers that can range from -1.00 to $+1.00$. The larger (the absolute value of) a correlation is, the more highly related two events are. If x and y are perfectly *positively* correlated (which means they go up and down together—as x goes up, so does y; as y goes down, so does x), we will obtain a correlation of $+1.00$. If x and y are perfectly *negatively* correlated (so that they change in opposite directions—as x goes up, y goes down; as x goes down, y goes up), we will obtain a correlation of -1.00. When x and y have no relationship at all, their correlation is 0. Some examples of these patterns are shown in Figure 2.2.

The question of whether two events change together is enormously important, and very common. Consider a question we'll answer in chapter 6: Do people who feel fairly treated by their partners also tend to feel satisfied with those relationships? Are perceptions of unfair treatment linked to dissatisfaction with a romantic partner? A correlational study designed to answer that question would typically assess naturally occurring patterns of satisfaction and fairness in a large number of couples without trying to influence or manipulate the couples' behavior in any way. The participants' feelings would be carefully measured, and a reliable connection between satisfaction and fairness would help us understand the nature of contentment in close relationships.

On the other hand, even if there was a correlation between fairness and satisfaction there'd be a lot we wouldn't know. Indeed, unsophisticated consumers often misinterpret the results of correlational designs. A correlation tells us that an association exists between two things, but it does *not* tell us *how* or *why* those things are related. Correlations do not tell us about the causal connections between events. Be careful not to assume too much when you encounter a correlation; many different plausible causal connections may all be possible when a correlation exists. Here are three straightforward possibilities:

- x may cause y—in the example of fairness and satisfaction, it could be that being fairly treated causes people to feel satisfied. *Or,*
- y may cause x—it could be that being satisfied causes people to feel fairly treated. *Or,*

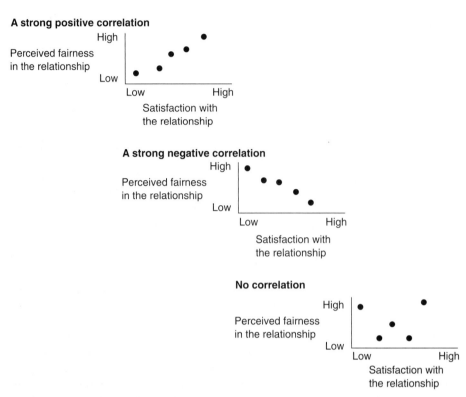

FIGURE 2.2. Correlational patterns.

- some other influence, a third variable, may cause both x and y, and the only reason x and y are related is because of their common cause. The two events x and y may not affect each other at all, and some other influence, such as being in a good mood, may cause people to feel both satisfied and fairly treated.

Any of these three, along with many other more complex chains of events, may be possible when x and y are correlated. If all we have is a correlation, all we know is that two events are related. We don't know what causal connections are involved.

Sometimes, however, we have lots of correlations. If our design includes measures of several different variables, or if we have taken our measurements on several different occasions over time, a number of sophisticated statistical analyses (e.g., partial correlations, path analysis, structural equation modeling) can rule out some of the possible causal connections that make correlational findings ambiguous. If you're interested, advanced statistics texts (e.g., Grimm & Yarnold, 1995) offer more details. For now, the important point is that these procedures enable us to get close to making defensible causal statements based on correlational data. Although we should be very careful not to turn a simple correlation into a causal connection, we should also realize that advanced statistical techniques make it possible to draw some reasonable conclusions about cause and effect within a correlational design.

Experimental Designs

When it's possible, a simpler way to investigate causal connections is to use an experimental design. **Experiments** provide more straightforward information about causes and their effects than correlational designs do because experimenters create and control the conditions they study. In a true experiment, researchers will intentionally manipulate one or more variables and randomly assign participants to the different conditions they have created to see how those changes affect people. Thus, instead of just asking "Do *x* and *y* change together?" experimenters ask "If we change *x*, what happens to *y*?"

Let's illustrate the difference between an experiment and a correlational study by reconsidering Donn Byrne's classic work on attitude similarity and attraction (e.g., Byrne & Nelson, 1965a, 1965b). Had Byrne wished to test his belief that similarity and liking were related, he could have simply measured partners' attitudes and their liking for each other. He would have obtained a positive correlation between similarity and liking, but he wouldn't have been sure what it meant. Similarity could lead to liking. On the other hand, liking someone could lead people to share that person's attitudes and gradually cause similarity. And so on. Simple correlations are informative, but they're also ambiguous.

What Byrne did instead was an experiment. Once his participants arrived at his lab, Byrne flipped a coin to determine randomly who would encounter a similar stranger and who would encounter one who didn't agree with them at all. He *controlled* that apparent agreement or disagreement, and it was the only difference between the two situations in which participants found themselves. With this procedure, when Byrne observed higher liking for the similar stranger, he could reasonably conclude that the greater agreement had *caused* the higher liking. How? Because the participants were randomly assigned to the two situations, the different degrees of liking could not be due to differences in the people who encountered each situation; on average, the two groups of participants were identical. Moreover, they all had identical experiences in the experiment except for the apparent similarity of the stranger. The only reasonable explanation for the different behavior Byrne observed was that similarity leads to liking. His experiment clearly showed that the manipulated cause, attitude similarity, had a noticeable effect, higher liking.

Experiments provide clearer, more definitive tests of causal connections than other designs do. Done well, they clearly delineate cause and effect (Haslam & McGarty, 2004). Why, then, do researchers ever do anything else? The answer lies in the fact that experimenters must be able to control and manipulate the events they wish to study. Byrne could control the information that his participants received about someone they had never met, but he couldn't manipulate other important factors in intimate relationships. We still can't. (How do you create full-fledged experiences of romantic love in a laboratory?) You can't do experiments on events you cannot control.

So, correlational and experimental designs each have their own advantages (Mark & Reichardt, 2004). With a correlational design, we can study compelling events in the real world—commitment to a relationship, passionate love, unsafe sex—and examine the links among them. But correlational designs are limited in what they can tell us about the causal relationships among events. With an experimental design, we can examine causal connections, but we are limited in the events we can study. Once again, there is no perfect solution—and that is another reason to study the same topic in different ways, from different perspectives.

Developmental Designs

Developmental designs study the manner in which behavior or events change over time. There are three major types of such designs.

Cross-Sectional Designs

The most common type of developmental design, a **cross-sectional design,** compares different people at different stages or ages in a developmental process. If we wished to examine risk factors for divorce at different stages of marriage, for instance, we could ask divorced couples who had been married for various lengths of time about the chief complaints that caused their divorces. We might find an association between the duration of marriages and the reasons they fail.

As this example suggests, cross-sectional designs are correlational designs, so we should be careful about the conclusions we draw from them. What if we found that marital infidelity was the leading cause of divorce after thirty years of marriage but that arguments over money were the primary complaints after only five years? Should we assume that infidelity is more common after years and years of the same old thing? Do spouses become more threatened by infidelity as they age? Not necessarily. We need to remember that our cross-sectional design is comparing people who married around 1976 to others who married in 2001. We're not only comparing people who were married for different lengths of time, but we're also comparing people who grew up in

In a cross-sectional design, researchers obtain responses from people from different age groups. To see if musical preferences differ with age, for example, we could ask 20-year-olds and 60-year-olds to evaluate various entertainers.

different circumstances. For all we know, their complaints about marriage haven't changed with the years, and their concerns just reflect the different eras in which the marriages started.

As you can see, the correlations that result from cross-sectional designs are always open to a specific kind of ambiguity: the different social, cultural, and political events our participants have experienced. Whenever we find a correlation between age and any other variable, we must carefully question whether it is really age that is involved or a difference in the backgrounds of our different age groups.

Longitudinal Designs

Cross-sectional designs confuse age with history. However, if we recruit participants who are all the same age and follow them over time as they get older, we have a study in which people's history is the same but their age changes. This is a **longitudinal design,** in which the same people are followed with repeated measurements over a period of time. If we repeatedly monitor the complaints of married couples who joined our study as newlyweds and who continue to participate as they grow older—as Ted Huston and his colleagues (e.g., Huston, Caughlin et al., 2001) are doing with the PAIR project— we will be using a longitudinal design. If the same people fought over money in their twenties but became increasingly concerned about marital infidelity in their fifties, we might assume that their worries had changed and that age and marital maturity were the causes of it.

But are the participants' ages the only things that might have changed over those thirty years? Probably not. Longitudinal designs do a better job of disentangling history and age than cross-sectional designs do, but they're still not perfect. Dramatic changes in the surrounding culture can still be mistaken for the effects of age and experience. What if some epidemic that affected women more than men changed the sex ratio so that 50-year-old men became much more numerous than 50-year-old women? Our discussion of sex ratios in chapter 1, suggests that people faced with an increasingly high sex ratio would adopt more conservative sexual attitudes and be more concerned about marital infidelity. In such a case, what appears in our study to be a normal developmental change in marital concerns could really be a temporary cultural shift that doesn't affect most marriages at all! Even though we tried to control for historical effects by ensuring that all our participants had the same general histories, we may still end up studying history rather than age.

If we are very persistent and clever, we could generally rule out historical influences by combining longitudinal and cross-sectional designs. We could start out with two groups, people who are 20 and another group of people who are 40, and follow both groups until they reach their middle fifties. If, at age 55, members of both groups developed a distinct concern about marital infidelity, then we might really begin to believe that, regardless of their idiosyncratic historical experiences, older people fear infidelity.

Of course, a study like this wouldn't be easy (Pomerantz, Ruble, & Bolger, 2004). In fact, there would be enormous logistical difficulties involved in conducting a single investigation that takes thirty years! One of the bigger problems facing longitudinal designs is **participant attrition,** the loss of participants over time (West, Biesanz, & Kwok, 2004). People move away and cannot be located, or they get busy or bored and just don't want to continue participating in the study. And the longer the study goes on, the greater these problems become. Long-term longitudinal studies sometimes end up with a small and select group of people who have stayed with the study from start to finish. Indeed, even if the study started with a representative sample, it may not have one when it's done.

Retrospective Designs

Given the difficulties of staying in touch with our participants over the course of a longitudinal study, maybe we should go backward rather than forward in time. Why don't we just ask people about their past experiences rather than trying to follow them through the future? We can, of course, and many studies of intimate relationships use such a **retrospective design.** Sometimes, long periods of time are involved ("What major arguments did you have before you got married?"); sometimes very short periods are studied ("How pleasant were your interactions with your spouse over the last twenty-four hours?").

Retrospective designs are very flexible. If we are worried about historical influences, we can ask people of different ages to think back to the same younger age, and see if they recall similar experiences. Indeed, if people had perfect memories, retrospective designs would be extremely useful. Unfortunately, of course, no one has perfect recall (e.g., Karney & Frye, 2002). As we will see later in this chapter (and again in chapter 4), there are difficulties with asking people about their lives; and these problems increase dramatically if we ask people about events that took place long ago (Frye & Karney, 2004). Whenever we rely on retrospective reports, we cannot know whether we are getting a clear picture of the past or one that has been contaminated by more recent events.

Overall, then, this review of developmental designs supports the same point we made earlier: No one type of research design is perfect, but each type has its uses. The focus on change over time provided by developmental designs is particularly valuable in research on intimate relationships. Our significant relationships with others are often long-term events, and we need to understand how they may change as time goes by.

SELECTING A SETTING

Now that we've developed our research question, recruited our participants, and chosen our design, we still have to select a setting in which to conduct our investigation. The usual choices include (a) a laboratory or (b) a natural, everyday environment, such as a couple's home. Either choice has advantages and disadvantages. (But you're getting used to that now, aren't you?) The lab offers the advantage of greater control over extraneous, unwanted influences.

Researchers can regulate the exact experiences their participants will have and arrange the physical environment itself to fit the purposes of the study. Natural settings offer the advantage of obtaining more typical behavior, as people will usually feel more comfortable and relaxed in their ordinary surroundings.

The disadvantages of these two settings are mirror images of their benefits. A laboratory may elicit artificial behavior that tells us little about what people usually do. On the other hand, natural settings may be full of distractions that are quite irrelevant to the research question but that heavily influence participants' behavior. People do behave differently in different environments, so we need to be sensitive to the possible impact of our setting on the results we obtain (Shoda, 2004).

In addition to its physical location, another aspect of the setting is the assignment that participants are given. Our procedure may entail specific directions and a limited choice of activities—this would be a *structured* situation—or it may allow people to do whatever they want, an *unstructured* assignment. Laboratory investigations often involve more structure than studies in naturalistic settings, but this isn't always the case. William Ickes's studies at the University of Texas at Arlington are sometimes very unstructured (e.g., couples are just left alone for a few minutes to do whatever they please), whereas an interview that takes place in a couple's home may be quite structured (telling the couple exactly what we want them to do).

The pros and cons of these two approaches resemble those of the physical settings we've already mentioned. Structured assignments give researchers more command over the behaviors they observe but can evoke reactions that are more contrived. Unstructured tasks elicit more realistic, more ordinary behavior but run the risk that the desired behaviors will not occur. The exact amount of structure varies widely in studies of intimate relationships, but most investigations require at least some structure. If, like John Gottman at the University of Washington, we were interested in studying disagreements between spouses, just watching and waiting for a fight would be a very frustrating way to proceed. It might never happen! Thus, Gottman straightforwardly asks his participants to revisit the topic of their last argument but then leaves them alone and lets them proceed without further interference.

A final consideration is relevant only for studies that take a fairly structured approach. Some behaviors are difficult to study because they are rare, or unpleasant, or very intimate (or all three). One way to overcome these difficulties is to have subjects **role-play** the behavior we're trying to understand—to act "as if" they were jealous, for instance, or were having an argument, or were trying to entice someone into bed. Role-play studies vary a great deal in how realistic they are. At one extreme, participants may be asked to read a story involving the relevant behavior and to imagine those events happening to them. Such *scenarios* are always less vivid than the real events would be, and they allow people to respond in a cool, collected fashion that may be quite different from the impulsive and emotional reactions they display when such events really take place. At the other extreme, studies known as *simulations* ask people to act

---

BOX 2.2

High-Tech Role-Playing

An intriguing new tool in relationship science is the use of *immersive virtual environments* (or IVEs) to study human interaction (Blascovich et al., 2002). In an IVE study, participants interact with three-dimensional computer representations of other people; they wear headsets that control what they see, and as they move through space in an empty room, the visual feedback they receive responds to their actual movements. It's like really being inside an elaborate video game.

Of course, participants know that the things they see aren't really happening. Nevertheless, an IVE can be an absorbing experience that generates behavior that resembles people's actions in real life (Bailenson et al., 2003). And the technique allows researchers precise control over the appearance, actions, and reactions of the virtual partners with whom the participants interact. Researchers can create exactly the same situation over and over, or they can vary the situation in subtle ways that would be hard to regulate with real-life actors and assistants. Verisimilitude versus control: Here's another research tool with important advantages and disadvantages, and we'll probably be hearing more about it in the years to come.

---

out a particular role in a hypothetical situation. For example, an investigator might ask a couple to pretend that they are angry with each other and then observe how they behave. This strategy is more engrossing, but participants still know that they are only pretending. Role-play studies are an ethically defensible way of studying emotionally charged topics, but people may do what they think they *should* do in these situations rather than what they really *would* do if the events actually occurred. Once again, there are both advantages and disadvantages to consider.

THE NATURE OF OUR DATA

We now need to consider just what data we're actually collecting. Are we recording others' judgments and perceptions of a relationship, or are we inspecting specific interactions ourselves? Two major types of research measures are described here: (a) people's own reports about their thoughts, feelings, and behaviors and (b) observations of people's behavior. We'll also examine three other kinds of data that are variations on these themes: couples' reports in which self-report and observation are combined, physiological measures, and archival evidence. No matter what data we use, our measures of behavior should have psychometric **validity** and **reliability.** That is, we should really be measuring the events we're trying to measure (that's validity), and, if those events aren't changing, we should get the same scores time after time (that's reliability).

Self-Reports

The most common means of studying intimate relationships is to ask people about their experiences. Such responses are **self-reports,** and they can be obtained in a variety of formats: through written questionnaires, verbal interviews, or even unstructured diaries in which participants write about whatever comes to mind (Harvey, Hendrick, & Tucker, 1988). The common theme linking such techniques is that people are telling us about their experiences—we're not watching them ourselves. Otherwise, the exact nature of participants' self-reports may vary in several ways. Self-reports may be

- *Retrospective versus concurrent.* Are people telling us about past events or are they keeping track of something happening now?
- *Global versus specific.* Do the self-reports summarize feelings or behaviors in broad, general terms (e.g., "How active is your sex life?"), or do they describe specific, concrete events (e.g., "How many times did you have sexual intercourse in the past week?")?
- *Subjective versus objective.* Does the self-report call for a subjective, feeling-based judgment (e.g., "How satisfying is your relationship?") or an objective, fact-based response (e.g., "Did your partner give you a present for your birthday?")?

Self-report data have important benefits. For one thing, they can tell us about the meaning that relational events have for those who experience them, and those meanings may be much richer and more important than an outside observer may know (Bruess & Pearson, 1993). For instance, an observer who sees Margaret bring ice cream home for Kathy may regard Margaret's behavior as kind and thoughtful, but nothing more. However, if Kathy knows that Margaret went to lots of trouble to find the special kind of ice cream that Kathy really loves, Margaret's gift may mean much more to Kathy than anyone else can readily appreciate. To the extent that self-reports allow us to "get inside people's heads" and understand their personal points of view, we obtain invaluable information that can help us understand the workings of relationships.

Self-report data are also inexpensive and easy to obtain. Investigators do not need elaborate equipment, research assistants, or an expansive laboratory. All they need is paper, some pencils, and willing participants. Consider, for instance, the short self-report measure provided in Table 2.4: Those seven questions do a remarkably good job of assessing people's satisfaction with their close relationships. For most purposes, there's no reason to ask more elaborate questions or use other means to distinguish happy, satisfied lovers from those who are less content because those seven straightforward questions work just fine (Hendrick, Dicke, & Hendrick, 1998). Self-report measures can be very efficient and very informative (Wegener & Fabrigar, 2004). Still (and this probably isn't a surprise!), self-reports may also present potential problems. Following are three major concerns.

TABLE 2.4. The Relationship Assessment Scale

Circle the answer below each question that best describes your current romantic relationship.

1. How well does your partner meet your needs?

1	2	3	4	5
not at all	somewhat	moderately well	very well	extremely well

2. In general, how satisfied are you with your relationship?

1	2	3	4	5
not at all	somewhat	moderately	very	extremely

3. How good is your relationship compared to most?

1	2	3	4	5
not at all	somewhat	moderately	very	extremely

4. How often do you wish you hadn't gotten into this relationship?

1	2	3	4	5
never	rarely	occasionally	often	very often

5. To what extent has your relationship met your original expectations?

1	2	3	4	5
not at all	somewhat	moderately well	very well	extremely well

6. How much do you love your partner?

1	2	3	4	5
not at all	somewhat	moderately	very much	extremely

7. How many problems are there in your relationship?

1	2	3	4	5
none	a few	some	many	very many

To determine your score, reverse the ratings you provided on items 4 and 7. If you circled a 1, change it to a 5; if you answered 2, make it a 4; 4 becomes 2, and 5 becomes 1. Then add up your answers. The higher your score, the more content you are with your relationship.

Source: Hendrick, Dicke, & Hendrick, 1998.

Participants' Interpretations of the Questions

Self-reports always occur in response to a researcher's instructions or questions. If the participants misinterpret what the researcher means or intends, their subsequent self-reports can be misleading. For instance, what do you think virginity means? Berger and Wenger (1973) found that 41 percent of their participants (who were both men and women) accepted "she brings herself to climax" as a possible way for a woman to lose her virginity! Thus, even an apparently simple question such as "Are you a virgin?" could be misunderstood, generating false conclusions. In fact, undetected problems with people's comprehension of terms describing sexual behavior may be a major problem in sexuality research (Wiederman, 2004).

Difficulties in Recall or Awareness

There is considerable controversy about just how accurately people can remember and report on things that have happened to them (Davis, 1999; Kruglanski, 1996), but there is general agreement that people are most accurate when they describe specific, objective events that have occurred recently. People are more likely to be inaccurate, and to fill in their memory gaps with their present beliefs and opinions, when we ask them to make global, subjective reports about things that happened long ago (Feeney & Cassidy, 2003). In particular, if a passionate romance ends in pain and discontent, the disappointed lovers are likely to have a very hard time remembering how happy and enthusiastic they felt months earlier when they had just fallen in love (Grote & Frieze, 1998).

Bias in Participants' Reports

A final major worry about self-report data involves the possibility of systematic bias or distortion in people's reports. Even when they want to be helpful, people may not necessarily tell the truth. This may occur for two reasons. First, they may not know what the truth is. That is, the participants' own perceptions may be distorted so that, although they are being honest, their reports aren't accurate. One example of this (which we'll mention again in chapter 4) is the **self-serving bias** that leads people to overestimate their responsibility for positive events in their relationships and to underestimate their blame for the bad times. People like to think of themselves in a positive light, so they tend to take the credit for their successes but duck the fault for their failures. If nothing else, domestic partners think they do a larger share of the housework than they really do (Ross & Sicoly, 1979)! Mistakes like this are interesting in their own right, and they are not dishonest attempts to mislead anyone, because they reflect people's genuine, if erroneous, views. Nevertheless, researchers need to be aware that they are sometimes obtaining participants' *perceptions* of the truth, which may differ somewhat from the whole, unvarnished truth.

A more serious problem occurs when people are reluctant to tell the truth as they see it. The best known example of this is the **social desirability bias,** which refers to distortion that results from people's wishes to make good impressions on others. Participants will be reluctant to admit anything that makes them look bad or that portrays them in an undesirable light. For instance, concerns about social acceptance may make some people hesitate to honestly report their same-sex attractions and behavior to researchers; as a result, there is continuing argument about the real prevalence of homosexuality (Cameron & Cameron, 1998; Michaels, 1996). Procedures that guarantee participants' anonymity help reduce social desirability problems, but bias can still creep into various self-reports.

This bias is so important that Timothy Loving and Christopher Agnew (2001) have developed a scale to measure people's tendencies to misrepresent their relationships to others (see Table 2.5). How concerned are you with what others learn about your relationships?

TABLE 2.5. The Motive to Make Your Relationship Look Good to Others

These five items come from the Inventory of Desirable Responding in Relationships. Answer them by thinking about your current relationship and rating your agreement with each item using this scale:

1	2	3	4	5	6	7
not true			somewhat true			very true

1. It is important to me that others are not aware of any negative thoughts I may have about my partner.

2. I make it a point never to disagree with my partner in the presence of others.

3. It is very important to me that others do not see my partner and I argue.

4. I never tell others about disagreements or quarrels my partner and I have.

5. It is important to me that others only see the good side of my relationship with my partner.

The average rating for college-aged women ranges from 4.5 to 6.7, and the average range is 3.6 to 5.8 for men. Below those ranges, you are less likely than most people to try to make your relationship look good to others, and above those ranges, you work harder than most to portray your partnership in a desirable light.

Source: Loving & Agnew (2001).

Observations

Another way to collect information about intimate relationships is to observe behavior directly. Scientific observations are rarely casual undertakings. Researchers often develop written manuals to teach their observers what to watch; they also conduct extensive practice sessions and usually go to great lengths to ensure that there is high *interrater reliability* (or good agreement among the observers). And the observations themselves are often hard work, involving painstaking attention to detail.

Some studies involve direct observations of ongoing behavior, whereas others use audio or video recordings from which observations are made at a later time. The amount of time that is analyzed also varies widely. One method of observation, called **experience-sampling,** uses intermittent, short periods of observation to capture samples of behavior that actually occur over longer periods of time. In experience-sampling, investigators may randomly sample short spans of time when a target behavior is likely to occur, perhaps scattering several periods of observation through different times on different days. For instance, in one clever technique, research participants carry small tape recorders that automatically switch on for 30 seconds every 12 minutes (Mehl & Pennebaker, 2003); if a conversation is occurring, a portion is recorded, and researchers can later determine what people were talking about and with whom. Experience-sampling can also be used with self-reports; participants can be given beepers that signal them to record who they're talking to or what they're doing at random intervals during the day. Experience-sampling can be very efficient, but it, like any technique of observation, faces a fundamental problem if we are interested in relatively rare events (such as arguments, episodes of jealousy, or consoling a partner after a misfortune): The event may not occur while the observations are being made.

When researchers do encounter the behaviors they seek to understand, their observations usually involve one or more of the following techniques:

- *Notes.* Here, observers record in writing everything they notice. Notes tend to be rich in interesting detail, but they also tend to have low interrater reliability.
- *Ratings.* When observers make ratings, they try to characterize what they have seen in relatively global (and usually subjective) terms. For example, if they're watching a couple arguing, they might rate the extent to which the interaction is "constructive and problem-solving" or "argumentative and hostile." With carefully developed rating scales and extensive training of observers, it's usually possible to obtain ratings that are reasonably reliable.
- *Coding.* Coding procedures focus on very specific behaviors such as the amount of time people speak during an interaction, the number of smiles they display, or the number of times they touch each other. Because coding is typically more objective than either narratives or ratings, it is usually quite reliable; nevertheless, complex schemes that require the coding of several different behaviors will require extensive training of observers.
- *Sequential observations.* More complex observations may focus on the *sequence* of interaction between two or more individuals (e.g., Bakeman & Gottman, 1997). Here, investigators examine the effects one person's behavior has on the subsequent behavior of others. When Susan smiles during a conversation, for example, is John more likely to smile back at her later on? Sequential observations are complicated and are usually limited to relatively short periods of time. Nevertheless, they can represent the back-and-forth flow of interaction with a high level of sophistication.

Observations like these generally avoid the disadvantages of self-reports. Trained observers are usually immune to misinterpretations of the researchers' intent, faulty memories, or self-serving biases. On the other hand, we need self-reports if we're to understand people's personal perceptions of their experiences. Observational studies may also be expensive; they often consume hours and hours of observers' time and sometimes require expensive equipment.

Observational research can also suffer from the problem of **reactivity:** People may change their behavior when they know they are being observed (Webb et al., 1981). Participants may be just as concerned with creating a good impression when they know others are watching as they are when they fill out a questionnaire or answer an interviewer's questions. Cromwell and Olson (1975) described an incident in which an experimenter working with couples had to leave the room for a moment; she did not intend to record what happened in her absence, but she forgot to turn off the recorder, and the couple was unaware that their conversation was still being taped. The experimenter later found (probably to her dismay) that the couple had engaged in an animated conversation that ended with one partner saying, "She's coming back; we'll have to be more careful."

But even when people don't try to act in socially desirable ways, the presence of an observer may subtly influence their behavior. In order to avoid such problems of reactivity, some investigators have devised elaborate, creative methods of observation. For example, Christensen (1979) got families to allow hidden microphones into a room where family conversations often occurred. The microphones were hooked to a timer that selected a random fifteen-minute period for recording when the family was home each day. Thus, the families knew that their interactions were being recorded, but they never knew when. Presumably, it was such a nuisance trying to create good impressions for hours each day—when most of the time it didn't matter—that the participants soon began to act naturally in spite of being observed.

Physiological Measures

Of course, we can avoid the potential problem of reactivity if we observe behavior that people cannot consciously control, and physiological measures of people's autonomic and biochemical reactions often do just that. Physiological measures assess such responses as heart rate, blood pressure, genital arousal, and hormone production to determine how interactions with others affect people physically. For instance, studies of loneliness (Cacioppo et al., 2000; Hawkley et al., 2003) have examined brain waves during sleep and levels of cortisol (a stress hormone) in saliva to determine that lonely people sleep restlessly and are rather anxious. Other investigations have found that people who have unhappy marriages exhibit poor immune system responses, making them more prone to various infections (Kiecolt-Glaser, 1999). Physiological measures are obviously impartial and objective, and they allow relationship researchers to explore the important ties between our interactions and our health. With the right instruments, it is even possible for researchers to take continuous measures of physiological responses while participants are engaged in various activities.

Archival Materials

Historical **archives** also avoid the problem of reactivity. Personal documents such as photographs and diaries, public media such as newspapers and magazines, and governmental records such as marriage licenses and census information can all be valuable sources of data about relationships (see Webb et al., 1981), and when these get dated, they become "archival" information. The use of marriage licenses in the study of volunteer bias we discussed in Box 2.1 is one example of the use of archival materials. In another study that examined the correlation between past physical attractiveness and current income, researchers rated people's attractiveness in old university yearbook photos (Frieze, Olson, & Russell, 1991). (What did they find? See chapter 3!)

Archival materials allow researchers to study past eras, and they are typically inexpensive to use. Obviously, they are also "nonreactive," because inspection of archival data does not change the behaviors being studied. Archival data can be limited, however. In particular, the material that has been saved from some previous era may not contain all the information a researcher would really like to have.

Couples' Reports

A final type of data involves self-reports in which each member of a couple provides reports of his or her own behavior but also acts as an observer of his or her partner's behavior. Thus, when the partners' perspectives are compared, couples' reports provide both a self-report and an observation of the same event. This is often fascinating, in part because there is sometimes little agreement between the partners' reports (Christensen, Sullaway, & King, 1983; Elwood & Jacobson, 1982). A husband may report showing affection to his wife, for example, when she doesn't perceive his actions to be affectionate at all. Couples' reports agree more when they get a chance to practice making their ratings and when they are asked to describe objective, specific events instead of making global, subjective judgments. However, the couple's disagreement about the general nature of their interactions is not necessarily a bad thing; it can be interesting in its own right. What does it mean when Betty and Barney do not agree on what Betty did? It may be useful to find out.

THE ETHICS OF SUCH ENDEAVORS

Obviously, research on relationships occasionally requires investigators to ask questions about sensitive topics or to observe private behavior. Should we pry into people's personal affairs?

This really isn't an issue we pose lightly. Although it's enormously valuable and sorely needed, relationship science presents important ethical dilemmas. Just asking people to fill out questionnaires describing their relationships may have subtle but lasting effects on those partnerships (McGregor & Holmes, 1999). When we ask people to specify what they get out of a relationship or to rate their love for their partners, for instance, we focus their attention on delicate matters they may not have thought much about. We encourage them to evaluate their relationships, and stimulate their thinking. Moreover, we arouse their natural curiosity about what their partners may be saying in response to the same questions. In general, a researcher's innocent inquiries run the risk of alerting people to relationship problems or frustrations they didn't know they had (Rubin & Mitchell, 1976).

Simulations and other observational studies may have even more impact. Consider John Gottman's (1994a) method of asking spouses to revisit the issue that caused their last argument: He doesn't encourage people to quarrel and bicker, but some of them do. Spouses that disagree sourly and bitterly are at much greater risk for divorce than are spouses who disagree with grace and humor, and Gottman's work has illuminated the specific styles of behavior that forecast trouble ahead. This work is extremely important. But does it do damage? Should we actually invite couples to return to a disagreement that may erode their satisfaction even further?

The answer to that question isn't simple. Relationship scientists ordinarily are very careful to safeguard the welfare of their participants (Kimmel, 2004). Detailed information is provided to potential participants before a study begins so that they can make an informed decision about whether or not to participate. Their consent to participate is voluntary and can be withdrawn at any time. After the data are collected, the researchers provide prompt feedback that explains any experimental manipulations and describes the larger purposes of the investigation. Final reports regarding the outcomes of the study are often made available when the study is complete. In addition, when ticklish matters are being investigated, researchers may provide information about where participants can obtain couples' counseling should they wish to do so; psychological services may even be offered for free.

As you can see, relationship science is based on compassionate concern for the well-being of its participants. People are treated with respect, thanked warmly for their efforts, and may even be paid for their time. They may also enjoy their experiences and benefit from them. For instance, newlyweds who were asked about their reactions to one laboratory study (Bradbury, 1994) were much more likely to have positive feelings about their experience than mixed or negative feelings (72 percent versus 3 percent). In a longitudinal study of marriages, participants who made frequent self-reports felt more competent as spouses than did those in a control condition who provided only minimal data (Veroff, Hatchett, & Douvan, 1992). At least some of the time, participation in relationship studies can be interesting and enlightening (Hughes & Surra, 2000). Still, should we be trying to study such private and intimate matters as close relationships?

The answer from here is absolutely yes. There's another side to the issue of ethics we haven't yet mentioned: science's ethical imperative to gain knowledge that can benefit humanity. In a culture in which more marriages are failures than successes (Carter & Snow, 2004), it would be unethical *not* to try to understand how relationships work. Intimate relationships can be a source of the grandest, most glorious pleasure human beings experience, but they can also be a source of terrible suffering and appalling destructiveness. It is inherently ethical, we believe, to try to learn how the joy might be increased and the misery reduced.

INTERPRETING AND INTEGRATING RESULTS

This isn't a statistics text (and we know you're pleased by that), but there are some aspects of the way relationship scientists do business that the thoughtful consumer of the field should understand. Most relationship studies subject the data they obtain to statistical analysis in order to determine whether their results are statistically "significant." This is a calculation of how likely it is that the results (e.g., the observed correlations or the effects of the manipulated variables in an experiment) could have occurred by chance. If it's rather unlikely that the results could be due to chance—the standard convention is that the risk must be 5 percent or less—we have a "significant" result. All of the research results reported in this book are significant results. You can also be confident that the studies that have obtained these results have passed critical inspection by other scientists. This does not mean, however, that every single specific result we may mention is unequivocally, positively true: Some of them might have occurred by chance, reflecting the influence of odd samples of people or unwanted mistakes of various sorts. When scientific results in psychology, sociology, or communication studies are significant, it means that chance occurrence is unlikely, not that chance occurrence is impossible.

The data obtained in relationship studies can also present unique challenges and complexities. Here are three examples:

Paired, interdependent data. Most statistical procedures assume that the scores of different participants are independent and do not influence each other, and when there's no apparent connection between one participant and the next, this is typically true. If researchers study the correlation between marital satisfaction and personal health in 100 different wives, for example, one woman's responses have no effect on the data obtained from other women, and the individual observations are independent. However, if the women's husbands are included, there probably *will* be a connection between the spouses' responses. A wife's contentment with her marriage may be influenced by both her husband's satisfaction and his health—indeed, the researchers may be studying these very patterns—and her answers are *not* independent of his.

The point here is that data obtained from relationship partners are often interdependent and can't be analyzed with the same techniques that are used in simpler investigations. Relationship researchers recognize that special statistical procedures are advisable for analyzing data collected from couples (e.g., Gonzalez & Griffin, 2004).

Different levels of analysis. Relationship researchers must also choose between two entirely different levels of analysis, one focusing on the individuals who make up couples and the other focusing on the couples themselves (Kenny, Bolger, & Kashy, 2002). For instance, researchers may examine how an individual's attachment style affects the interactive outcomes he or she obtains, or they may examine how the styles of two different partners combine to affect the quality of their relationship. The first of these questions analyzes individuals, but the second analyzes dyads, and relationship scholars must be careful to ensure that their procedures fit the level of analysis of interest to them.

Three sources of influence. Furthermore, even if we ignore situational and cultural influences, relationships are routinely shaped by influences from three different sources (of both individual and dyadic types). Specifically, relationships emerge from the individual contributions of the separate partners *and* from the unique effects of how they combine as a pair. For example, imagine that Fred and Wilma have a happy marriage. One reason for this may be the fact that Fred is an especially pleasant fellow who gets along well with everyone, including Wilma. Alternatively (or, perhaps, in addition), Wilma may be the one who's easy to live with. However, Fred and Wilma may also have a better relationship with each other than they could have with anyone else because of the unique way their individual traits combine; the whole may be more than the sum of its parts. Relationship researchers often encounter phenomena that result from the combination of all three of these influences, the two individual partners and the idiosyncratic partnership they share. Sophisticated statistical analyses are required to study all of these components at once (see Campbell & Kashy, 2002), another indication of the complexity of relationship science.

So what's our point here? We've noted that studies of close relationships tackle intricate matters and that statistical significance testing involves probabilities, not certainties. Should you take everything we say with a grain of salt, doubting us at every turn? Well, yes and no. We want you to be more thoughtful and less gullible, and we want you to appreciate the complexities underlying the things you're about to learn. Remember to think like a scientist: No study is perfect, but the truth is out there. We put more faith in patterns of results that are obtained by different investigators working with different samples of participants. We are also more confident when results are replicated with diverse methods.

For these reasons, scientists now do frequent **meta-analyses,** which are studies that statistically combine the results from several prior studies (Wood & Christensen, 2004). In a meta-analysis, an investigator compiles all existing studies of a particular phenomenon and combines their results to identify the themes they contain. If the prior studies all produce basically the same result, the meta-analysis makes that plain; if there are discrepancies, the meta-analysis may reveal why.

With tools like this at its disposal, relationship science has made enormous strides despite its short history and the complexity of its subject matter. And despite our earlier cautions, most of the things we have to tell you in this text are dependable facts, reliable results you can see for yourself if you do what the researchers did. Even more impressively, most of them are facts that had not been discovered when your parents were born.

A FINAL NOTE

In our desire to help you be more discerning, we've spent most of this chapter noting various pros and cons of diverse procedures, usually concluding that no single option is the best one in all cases. We hoped to encourage you to be more thoughtful about the complexities of good research. But in closing, let us reassure you that relationship science is in better shape than all of these uncertainties may make it seem. The variety of methods with which researchers study relationships is a *strength*, not a weakness (Ickes, 2000). And the field's judicious ability to differentiate what it does and does not yet know is a mark of its honesty and its developing maturity and wisdom.

People like easy answers. They like their information cut-and-dried. Many people actually prefer simple nonsense—like the idea that men come from Mars and women come from Venus—to the scientific truth, if the truth is harder to grasp. However, as a new consumer of the science of relationships, you have an obligation to prefer facts to gossip, even if you have to work a little harder to make sense of their complexities. Don't mistake scientific caution for a lack of quality. To the contrary, we want to leave you with the thought that it demonstrates scientific respectability to be forthright about the strengths and weaknesses of one's discipline. It's more often the frauds and imposters who claim they are always correct than the cautious scientists, who are really trying to get it right.

FOR YOUR CONSIDERATION

Chris and Jill had to participate in research studies if they wanted to pass the Introductory Psychology course they were taking together, so they signed up for a study of "Relationship Processes." They had been dating for two months, and the study was seeking "premarital romantic couples," and they liked the fact that they would be paid five dollars if they both participated. So, they attended a session with a dozen other couples in which they were separated and seated on opposite sides of a large room. They read and signed a permission form that noted they could quit anytime they wanted and then started to work on a long questionnaire.

Some of the questions were provocative. They were asked how many different people they had had sex with in the last year and how many people they wanted to have sex with in the next five years. Then, they were asked to answer the same questions again, this time as they believed the other would. Chris had never pondered such questions before, and he realized, once he thought about it, that he actually knew very little about Jill's sexual history and future intentions. That night, he was a little anxious, wondering and worrying about Jill's answers to those questions.

In your opinion, was this research procedure ethical? Would you like to complete a similar questionnaire? Why?

CHAPTER SUMMARY

A Brief History of Relationship Science

Philosophers such as Aristotle have been concerned with the analysis of close relationships for over 2,000 years. However, the scientific study of relationships is a recent endeavor that has come of age in the last thirty years. Since its blossoming in contrived lab experiments during the 1960s, the field has grown to include the longitudinal study of all types of relationships in their natural settings around the world.

Developing a Question

Research questions come from a number of sources, including personal experience, recognition of social problems, the results of prior research, and theoretical predictions. The questions themselves are usually of two types: They seek either to describe events or to delineate causal connections among variables. A given research program will often involve both approaches.

Obtaining Participants

Convenience samples are composed of participants who are easily available to the researcher. Findings based on such samples may not apply readily to other people, although this is rarely a problem when basic processes of behavior are involved. *Representative samples* are selected to reflect the demographic characteristics of the population of interest. They are expensive to select and maintain, so the time available with each participant is often limited. Both types of samples can suffer from volunteer bias.

Choosing a Design

Correlational Designs. A correlation describes the strength and direction of an association between two variables. Correlations are inherently ambiguous because events can be related for a variety of reasons. By themselves, correlations do not necessarily indicate the presence of any causal connection between events.

Experimental Designs. In experiments, researchers control and manipulate the conditions they study, allowing them to examine cause-and-effect relationships among events. Experiments are very informative, but many events cannot be studied experimentally for practical or ethical reasons.

Developmental Designs. Developmental designs study changes in behavior or events over time. There are three kinds of developmental designs. *Cross-sectional designs* compare participants from different age groups or time periods; however, because these people have different histories, the source of any differences obtained in cross-sectional research is often ambiguous. *Longitudinal* research follows the same group of participants across time. Such studies often suffer from *participant attrition,* the loss of participants as time goes by. *Retrospective designs* rely on participants' recall of past events, but people's memories can be inaccurate.

Selecting a Setting

Research can be conducted in laboratories or in real-world settings such as a couple's home. Laboratory research emphasizes control but may pay the price of artificiality. Real-world settings can promote more natural behavior, but control over extraneous variables is reduced. The participants' duties may be highly structured, entailing specific directions, or relatively unstructured, allowing them to do whatever they want. *Role-play* studies allow researchers to examine highly emotional events in an ethical manner but may fail to indicate what people really do in such situations.

The Nature of Our Data

Self-Reports. Relationship research often asks participants directly about their thoughts, feelings, and behavior. Self-reports are convenient and provide information about participants' personal perceptions. However, participants may misunderstand the researchers' questions, have faulty memories, and be subject to *self-serving* and *social desirability biases*. Overall, self-reports are more accurate when they focus on recent, specific, and objective events instead of global, subjective impressions of events long past.

Observations. When we observe people's behavior, reliability is a crucial concern. When interrater reliability is high, different observers agree on their observations. *Experience-sampling* is often used in observational research: A set of different, usually brief, observations are made at times randomly selected from a longer period of interest. Observations may take the form of detailed narratives, global ratings, the coding of specific behaviors, and sequential observations. They avoid the problems of self-reports, but pose their own problems: Observations are expensive to conduct, and participants' behavior may change when they know they are being observed.

Physiological Measures. Measurements of people's autonomic and hormonal changes indicate how social interaction affects people's physical well-being.

Archival Material. Historical records are nonreactive and allow researchers to compare the present with the past.

Couples' Reports. Couples' reports combine self-reports and observations— each partner is asked to report his or her own thoughts, feelings, and behavior, and each also acts as an observer of the other partner's behavior. Couples' reports often disagree, a fact that intrigues, rather than distresses, researchers.

The Ethics of Such Endeavors

Participation in relationship research may change people's relationships by encouraging them to think carefully about the situations they face. As a result, researchers take pains to protect the welfare of their participants. Information about the study is provided in advance, and participation is voluntary. Counseling is sometimes offered. Properly conducted, research on relationships can contribute to more enduring and satisfying relationships. Participants may even benefit from participating in couples' studies.

Interpreting and Integrating Results

Statistical analysis determines the likelihood that results could have occurred by chance. When this likelihood is very low, the results are said to be significant. Some such results may still be due to chance, however, so the thoughtful consumer does not put undue faith in any one study. Results that occur repeatedly with different samples of participants and with a variety of methods inspire greater confidence. *Meta-analysis* can lend confidence to conclusions by statistically combining results from several studies. Nevertheless, relationship researchers face several unique statistical and interpretative problems such as (a) paired, interdependent data, (b) different levels of analysis, and (c) influences from both the individual partners and their mutual interactions.

A Final Note

Scientific caution is appropriate, but it should not be mistaken for weakness or imprecision. Relationship science is in great shape.

PART TWO

Basic Processes in Intimate Relationships

Attraction

How do intimate relationships get started? What sets the processes of friendship or romance in motion? Obviously, the specifics vary widely. Relationships can begin under all kinds of circumstances, in all sorts of places—in the classroom, on a blind date, at work, in a grocery store, or on the Web. But psychologically, the first big step toward a relationship is always the same: interpersonal attraction, the desire to approach someone. Feelings of attraction don't guarantee that a relationship will develop, but they do open the door to the possibility.

Because attraction plays such a crucial role in so many different kinds of relationships, it has been the focus of an enormous amount of research (Berscheid & Reis, 1998). We will draw on that work in this chapter and discuss several major factors that appear to be particularly important in the beginning of an intimate relationship. But first, let's consider a basic principle about how attraction works.

THE FUNDAMENTAL BASIS OF ATTRACTION: A MATTER OF REWARDS

The most fundamental assumption about interpersonal attraction is that we are attracted to others whose presence is rewarding to us (Clore & Byrne, 1974; Lott & Lott, 1974). Two different types of rewards influence attraction: direct rewards we receive from our interaction with others and indirect rewards that are merely associated with another's presence. Direct rewards refer to all the positive consequences we obtain from being with someone. When people shower us with interest and approval, we enjoy the rewarding attention and acceptance. When people are witty and beautiful, we take pleasure in their rewarding characteristics. And when people give us access to desired goods such as money or status, we are glad to receive those benefits. Most of the time, the more of these rewards that people provide us, the more attracted we are to them.

But what about just being in someone's company under pleasant circumstances? What happens when your team scores the winning touchdown in a close game, and Pat is right beside you? Will you be attracted to Pat even though Pat did not cause the happy event? Such things do happen (Byrne & Murnen, 1988; Pelham, Mirenberg, & Jones, 2002). In attraction by association, our feelings about another person result from the emotional tone of the surrounding situation. If Pat is present during a pleasant event, we may experience a positive emotional response the next time we interact with Pat.

These two kinds of rewards—direct and indirect-by-association—highlight the interactive nature of attraction (Gifford & Gallagher, 1985; Wright, Ingraham, & Blackmer, 1985). Most people simply think that they are attracted to someone if he or she is an appealing person, but it's really more complex than that. Attraction does involve the perceived characteristics of the person who seems attractive, but it also depends on the needs, preferences, and desires of the person who becomes attracted and on the situation in which the two people find themselves. Our own needs and personalities can affect how we perceive others and react to the situation, and the situation itself can modify our preferences and our perceptions. Attraction is based on rewarding experiences with another person, but those rewarding experiences can come about in a variety of ways that depend on the time, place, and people involved. We consider a number of possible routes to attraction in this chapter, starting with a basic prerequisite—being there.

PROXIMITY: LIKING THOSE NEAR US

We might get to know someone in a chat room online, but isn't conversation more rewarding when we can hear others' voices, see their smiles, and actually hold their hands? Most of the time, relationships are more rewarding when they involve people who are near one another (who are physically, as well as psychologically, close). Indeed, our physical **proximity** to others often determines whether or not we ever meet them in the first place. More often than not, our friendships and romances grow out of interactions with those who are nearby. To meet people is not necessarily to love them, but to love them we must first meet them!

In fact, there is a clear connection between physical proximity and interpersonal attraction, and a few feet can make a big difference. Think about your Relationships classroom: Who have you gotten to know since the semester started? Who is a new friend? It's likely that the people you know and like best sit near you in class. In one study in which strangers were assigned seats in a

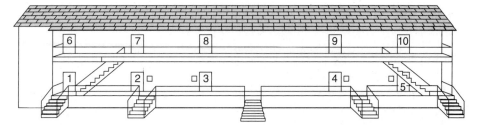

FIGURE 3.1. Schematic diagram of a student apartment building at MIT.

TABLE 3.1. Friendship Choices in Campus Housing at MIT

Two hundred seventy people living in buildings like that pictured in Figure 3.1 were asked to list their three closest companions. Among those living on the same floor of a given building, here's how often the residents named someone living:

1 door away	41% of the time
2 doors away	22%
3 doors away	16%
4 doors away	10%

Only 88 feet separated residents living four doors apart, at opposite ends of the same floor, but they were only one-quarter as likely to become friends as were people living in adjacent apartments. Evidently, small distances played a large part in determining who would and who would not be friends.

---

classroom, students were much more likely to become friends with those sitting near them than with those sitting across the room, even though the room was reasonably small (Segal, 1974).

A similar phenomenon occurs in student apartment complexes. In a classic study, Festinger, Schachter, and Back (1950) examined the friendships among students living in campus housing at the Massachusetts Institute of Technology. Residents were randomly assigned to apartments in seventeen different buildings that were all like the one pictured in Figure 3.1. People who lived close to each other were much more likely to become friends than were those whose apartments were further apart. Indeed, the chances that residents would become friends were closely related to the distances between their apartments, as Table 3.1 shows. Remarkably, the same result was also obtained from one building to the next: People were more likely to know and like residents of other buildings that were close to their own. Obviously, even small distances have a much larger influence on our relationships than most people realize. Whenever we choose the exact place where we will live or work or go to school, we also take a major step toward determining who the significant others in our lives will be. We know we are choosing a location; we may not fully realize we are also choosing the people we will meet.

Convenience: Proximity Is Rewarding, Distance Is Costly

Why does proximity have such influence? One answer is that when others are nearby, it's easy to enjoy whatever rewards they offer. Everything else being equal, a partner who is nearby has a big advantage over one who is far away (Gilbertson, Dindia, & Allen, 1998): The expense and effort of interacting with a distant partner—such as long-distance phone bills and hours on the road—make a distant relationship more costly overall than one that is closer to home. Distant relationships are less rewarding, too; an expression of love in an e-mail message is less pleasant than an actual kiss on the cheek. Thus, long-distance romantic relationships are generally less satisfying than are romances with partners who are nearby (Van Horn et al., 1997).

The only notable thing about this result is that anyone should find it surprising. However, lovers who have to endure a period of separation may blithely believe, because their relationship has been so rewarding up to that point, that some time apart will not affect their romance. If so, they may be surprised by the difference distance makes. When a relationship that enjoys the convenience of proximity becomes inconvenient due to distance, it may suffer more than anyone suspected. Even those who are already married are more likely to get divorced when they live apart than when they live together (Rindfuss & Stephen, 1990). Absence does *not* seem to make the heart grow fonder.

Familiarity: Repeated Contact

Proximity also makes it more likely that two people will cross paths often and become more familiar with each other. Folk wisdom suggests that "familiarity breeds contempt," but research evidence disagrees. Instead of being irritating, repeated contact with—or **mere exposure** to—someone usually increases our liking for him or her (Bornstein, 1989). Even if we have never talked to them, we tend to like people whose faces we recognize more than those whose faces are unfamiliar to us.

Moreland and Beach (1992) provided an interesting example of the mere exposure effect when they had college women attend certain classes either fifteen times, ten times, or five times during a semester. The women never talked to anyone and simply sat there, but they were present in the room frequently, sometimes, or rarely. Then, at the end of the semester, the real students were given pictures of the women and asked for their reactions. The results were very clear: The more familiar the women were, the more attracted to them the students were. And they were all liked better than women the students had never seen at all.

Thus, because proximity often leads to familiarity, and familiarity leads to liking, frequent contact with someone not only makes interaction more convenient, it may make that person seem more attractive. As another example, it may not be surprising, then, that heterosexual people who actually know gay men or lesbians have more positive attitudes toward homosexuals than do those who have no contact with gays or lesbians (Herek & Capitanio, 1996).

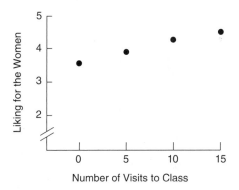

FIGURE 3.2. The Mere Exposure Effect in College Classrooms.
Even though they never interacted with anyone, women were liked more by other students the more often they visited a class.
Source: Moreland & Beach, 1992.

BOX 3.1

Virtual Proximity

Back in chapter 1, we suggested that technological changes can affect relationships, and a superb example of that lies in the access to others that we now take for granted on the Internet. In some respects, e-mail, instant messaging, and VOIP (Voice Over Internet Protocol) capabilities have simply provided us new ways to keep in touch with the friends that we already have (Tyler, 2002). But the Web has brought changes, too. It's now cheaper and easier than it used to be to maintain a relationship over long distances (Gunn, Guillory, & Gunn, 2002), and, perhaps more importantly, it's much easier to meet for the first time far-flung others with similar interests (Bargh & McKenna, 2004).

Not only are there chat rooms and bulletin boards for every taste, but there is also an online industry in singles websites such as Yahoo Personals and Matchmaker.com that allow people to announce themselves to potential partners who may be dozens of miles (or states!) away. The most popular of these websites, Match.com, is visited by about six million different people each month ("Romance," 2003). The singles websites typically allow people to browse their pages for free, but you must subscribe to the service to be able to contact any of the people you find there. Some of them also ask subscribers about their tastes and use various schemes to pair people with other subscribers who will be a good match for them. One site, eHarmony.com, has even received a patent for the "marital satisfaction formula" with which it searches for compatible partners among its flock (Konrad, 2004).

Most relationships still develop between two people who are in reasonably close physical proximity to one another. Nevertheless, it is now possible for people who are separated by great distances to find each other and fall in love.

The Power of Proximity

Of course, there are limits to the power of proximity to increase attraction. Constant exposure to anything—a favorite food or song, or perhaps even a lover—can be boring when saturation sets in (Bornstein, 1989). Familiarity enhances attraction, but overexposure does not. And close proximity to obnoxious, disagreeable people does not necessarily get us to like them better (Ebbesen, Kjos, & Konecni, 1976). The best conclusion to make about proximity is that it accentuates our feelings about others. If we're able to get along with people, we like them better when they're nearby. However, if they annoy us, proximity may only make things worse.

Indeed, a study in a condominium complex in California (Ebbesen et al., 1976) found that although most of the residents' friends lived nearby, most of their enemies did, too! Only rarely did people report that they really disliked someone who lived several buildings away from them. Instead, they despised fellow residents who were close enough to annoy them often—by playing music too loudly, letting pets run wild, and so on. Evidently, proximity makes interaction more likely, but it cannot guarantee that what follows will be desirable. We tend to be attracted to those who are near us, but if our contact with them becomes unpleasant, we may like them even less, not more.

PHYSICAL ATTRACTIVENESS: LIKING THOSE WHO ARE LOVELY

After proximity brings people together, what's the first thing we're likely to notice about those we meet? Their looks, of course. And, although we all know that there is much more to people than their external appearance, looks count. Physical attractiveness has a substantial influence on the first impressions that people form of one another. In general, right or wrong, we tend to assume that good-looking people are more likable, better people than those who are unattractive (Etcoff, 1999).

The Bias for Beauty: "What Is Beautiful Is Good"

Imagine that you are given a photograph of a stranger's face and, using only that information, you're asked to guess at the personality and prospects the person possesses. Studies of judgments like these routinely find that physically attractive people are presumed to be interesting, sociable people who are likely to encounter personal and professional success in life and love (see Table 3.2). In general, we seem to use the crude stereotype that what is beautiful is good; we assume that attractive people have desirable traits that complement their desirable appearances (Langlois et al., 2000). And we seem to make these judgments automatically, without any conscious thought; a beautiful face triggers a positive evaluation the moment we see it (Cheng, Ferguson, & Chartrand, 2003).

We don't expect good-looking strangers to be wonderful in every respect. The attractiveness stereotype leads us to assume that beautiful people are vivacious and socially skilled, and reasonably intelligent and well-adjusted, but

TABLE 3.2. What Is Beautiful Is Good

Both male and female research participants judged that physically attractive people were more likely than physically unattractive people to have the following characteristics:

Kind	Interesting
Strong	Poised
Outgoing	Sociable
Nurturant	Exciting dates
Sensitive	Better character
Sexually warm and responsive	

These same judges also believed that, compared to those who were unattractive, physically attractive people would have futures that involved:

More prestige	Happier marriages
More social and professional success	More fulfilling lives

Source: Findings from Dion, Berscheid, & Walster, 1972.

it does not affect our judgments of their integrity, responsibility, or compassion (Collins, 2004; Eagly et al., 1991). There is even a downside to beauty; gorgeous people are assumed to be more likely to be vain and promiscuous (Dermer & Theil, 1975). Still, there's no question that attractive people make better overall impressions on strangers than less attractive people do.

The bias for beauty exists in Eastern as well as Western cultures, but the specific advantages attributed to attractive people vary somewhat from place to place. In Korea, for instance, pretty people are presumed to be sociable, intelligent, and socially skilled, just as they are in the United States. However, in keeping with Korea's collectivist culture (which emphasizes group harmony), attractive people are also presumed to be concerned with the well-being of others, a result that is not obtained in the West (Wheeler & Kim, 1997). The physical attractiveness stereotype may be pervasive, but its specific content seems to depend on the specific values of a culture.

The bias for beauty may also lead people to confuse beauty with talent. In the workplace, physically attractive people are more likely to be hired after a job interview and to receive higher rates of pay (Hamermesh & Biddle, 1994). If you rate the looks of people with MBA degrees from the University of Pittsburgh on a 1 to 5 scale, each one-point increase in physical attractiveness is worth $2,600 in average annual salary for men and $2,150 for women (Frieze, Olson, & Russell, 1991). Good-looking attorneys earn higher incomes and are more likely to become partners in their firms than are lawyers of lesser looks (Biddle & Hamermesh, 1998), and attractive professors get better teaching evaluations from their students than unattractive instructors do (Hamermesh & Parker, 2005). Attractive people even make better impressions in court; good-looking culprits convicted of misdemeanors in Texas get lower fines than they would have received had they been less attractive (Downs & Lyons, 1991).

But are the interactions and relationships of beautiful people really any different from those of people who are less pretty? We'll address that question shortly. First, though, we need to assess whether we all tend to agree on who is pretty and who is not.

Who's Pretty?

The first research study ever conducted by one of your current authors (Rowland Miller) involved physical attractiveness. When I was an undergraduate at Cornell University, I needed photographs depicting attractive and unattractive women, so I got a school yearbook from another campus and carefully selected pictures of the people I thought were the most and least desirable of the bunch. I was startled to find, when I solicited the opinions of friends and classmates, that some of the women I thought were gorgeous got low ratings from some men, and some women I considered quite unattractive were appealing to other fellows. I did get a subset of photos on which there was unanimous agreement, but I've never forgotten that surprising idiosyncrasy in judgments of attractiveness.

Now, (too many!) years later, several studies have shown that, to a limited extent, beauty is indeed in the "eye of the beholder" (e.g., Diener, Wolsic, & Fujita, 1995). If you ask several men and several women to sit down, take a close look at each other, and rate everyone else's physical attractiveness, you'll get some mild disagreement among the observers as each one sees things, to some degree, his or her own way (Marcus & Miller, 2003).

However, diverse observers still agree in their perceptions of beauty much more than they disagree. Despite some variability from person to person, people generally share the same notions of who is and who isn't pretty (Marcus & Miller, 2003). Moreover, this consensus exists across ethnic groups; Asians, Hispanics, and black and white Americans all tend to agree with each other about the attractiveness of women from all four groups (Cunningham et al.,

There is remarkable agreement from one culture to the next about who is, and who is not, attractive. People who are judged to be lovely in other countries will typically be attractive to us, as well.

1995). Even more striking is the finding that newborn infants exhibit prefer-ences for faces like those that adults find attractive, too (Slater et al., 1998); when they are much too young to be affected by social norms, babies spend more time gazing at attractive than unattractive faces.

What faces are those? There's little doubt that women are more attractive if they have "baby-faced" features such as large eyes, a small nose, a small chin, and full lips (Jones, 1995). The point is not to look childish, however, but to appear feminine and youthful (Cunningham, Druen, & Barbee, 1997); beautiful women combine those baby-faced features with signs of maturity such as promi-nent cheekbones, narrow cheeks, and a broad smile (Cunningham, Barbee, & Philhower, 2002). Women who present all these features are thought to be attractive all over the world (Jones, 1995).

Male attractiveness may be more complex. Men who have strong jaws and broad foreheads—who look strong and dominant—are usually thought to be handsome (Cunningham, Barbee, & Pike, 1990). (Envision George Clooney.) On the other hand, when average male faces are made slightly more feminine and baby-faced through computer imaging, the "feminized" faces—which look warm and friendly—are attractive, too (Perrett et al., 1998). (Envision Tobey Maguire.) Remarkably, which facial style is more attractive to women may depend on their menstrual cycles; they may find rugged, manly features more

Which of these two faces is most appealing to you? They are composite images of the *same* face that have been altered to include feminine or masculine facial features, and if you're a woman, your answer may depend on the current phase of your menstrual cycle. Most women find the more masculine face on the right to be more attractive when they are fertile, but they consider the more feminine face on the left to be more appealing during the rest of the month.
Left: 50% feminized male composite; *right:* 50% masculinized male composite. From: Little, A. C., Penton-Voak, I. S., Burt, M., & Perrett, D. I. (2002). Evolution and individual differences in the perception of attractiveness: How cyclic hormonal changes and self-perceived attractiveness influence female preferences for male faces. In G. Rhodes & L. A. Zebrowitz (Eds.), *Facial attractiveness: Evolutionary, cognitive and social perspectives* (pp. 59–90). Westport, CT: Ablex.
Source: Little, Penton-Voak, Burt, & Perrett, 2002.

appealing when they are ovulating and fertile, but be more attracted to youthful boyishness the rest of the month (Little et al., 2002; Penton-Voak & Perrett, 2000).

In any case, good-looking faces in both sexes have features that are neither too large nor too small. Indeed, they are quite average. If you use a computer to create composite images that combine the features of individual faces, the "average" faces that result are more attractive than nearly all of the faces that make up the composite (Langlois, 2004; Rubenstein, Langlois, & Roggman, 2002). This is true not only in the United States but in China, Nigeria, India, and Japan as well (Pollard, 1995; Rhodes et al., 2002).

However, this doesn't mean that gorgeous people have bland, ordinary looks. The images that result from this averaging process are actually rather unusual. Their features are all proportional to one another; no nose is too big, and no eyes are too small, and there is nothing about such faces that is exaggerated, underdeveloped, or odd. Averaged faces are also *symmetrical*, with the two sides of the face being mirror images of one another; the eyes are the same size, the cheeks are the same width, and so on. Facial symmetry is attractive in its own right, whether or not a face is "average" (Grammer & Thornhill, 1994). In fact, if you take a close look at identical twins, whose faces are very similar, you'll probably think that the twin with the more symmetric face is the more attractive of the two (Mealey, Bridgstock, & Townsend, 1999). Apparently, symmetry and "averageness" each make their own contribution to facial beauty; even in a group of symmetrical images, faces are more appealing the more average they become (Rhodes, Sumich, & Byatt, 1999). Thus, beautiful faces seem to combine the best features of individual faces in a balanced, well-proportioned whole (Perrett et al., 1999).

Of course, some bodies are more attractive than others, too. Men find women's shapes most alluring when they are of normal weight, neither too

Look what happens when 2, 8, or 32 real faces are morphed together into composite images. When more faces are combined, the resulting image portrays a face that is not odd or idiosyncratic in any way, and that has features and dimensions that are more and more typical of the human race. The result is a more attractive image. "Average" faces are attractive faces.

Source: Rubenstein, Langlois, & Roggman, 2002.

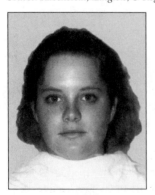 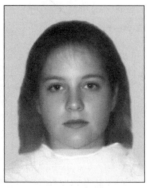 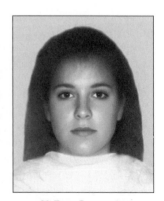

2-Face Composite   8-Face Composite   32-Face Composite

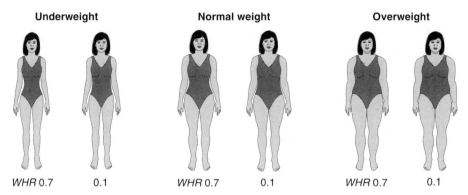

Underweight   **Normal weight**   **Overweight**

WHR 0.7   0.1   WHR 0.7   0.1   WHR 0.7   0.1

FIGURE 3.3. Waist-to-hip ratios.
These six figures differ in two different ways. Two of them depict women who are thinner than normal, two depict women who are heavier than normal, and the remaining two portray women of normal weight. In addition, three of the figures depict women whose waists have a circumference that is 70 percent that of their hips (so that their waist-to-hip ratios are 0.7), whereas the other three have waists that are the same circumference as their hips. When men rated these drawings, the figures with the smaller waist-to-hip ratios were always preferred to those who were less curvy, and the 0.7 figure of normal weight was liked best of all.
Source: Singh, 1993.

heavy nor too slender, and their waists are noticeably narrower than their hips (Forestell, Humphrey, & Stewart, 2004). The most attractive **waist-to-hip ratio,** or WHR, is a curvy 0.7 in which the waist is 30 percent smaller than the hips (see Figure 3.3); this shape appeals to men around the world (Furnham, McClell, & Omer, 2003; Singh & Luis, 1995). In the United States, women make better impressions when they're underweight rather than overweight, but skinny women are *not* as attractive to men as they would be if they put on a few pounds. Normal weight is clearly the most attractive of all (Barber, 1999; Singh, 1993). Men also like larger, as opposed to smaller, breasts, but only if a woman has a low WHR; larger breasts don't enhance a woman's appeal if they are paired with a stocky body (Furnham, Dias, & McClelland, 1998).

Once again, male attractiveness is more complex. Men's bodies are most attractive when their waists are only slightly narrower than their hips, with a WHR of 0.9. However, a nice shape doesn't attract a woman to a man unless he has other resources as well; a man's WHR only affects women's evaluations of him when he earns a healthy salary (Singh, 1995). A man is not all that attractive to women if he is handsome but poor.

Judgments of attractiveness are evidently multi-faceted, and there are still other characteristics that influence those perceptions. Both men and women tend to prefer heterosexual partnerships in which he is taller than she is (Hensley, 1994; Pierce, 1996), so tall men get more responses to their personal advertisements than short men do (Lynn & Shurgot, 1984). Tall people also get more respect and higher incomes at work than shorter people do; independently of a person's age or sex, each inch of height amounts to $789 more in pay, on average, in the United States and Great Britain each year (Judge & Cable, 2004). Across various occupations, for instance, men who are 6'1" earn $3,156 more each year than do men who are 5'9".

A potential partner's smell matters more to women than to men (Herz & Inzlicht, 2002). Nevertheless, men prefer the natural scents of pretty women to those of women who are less attractive (Thornhill et al., 2003). In a typical study of this sort, people sleep in the same t-shirt for several nights without using any cologne or perfume. Then, research participants who have never met those people take a big whiff of those shirts and select the scents that are most appealing to them. Symmetrical, attractive people evidently smell better than asymmetrical, less attractive people do, because strangers prefer the aromas of attractive people to the smells of those who are more plain (Thornhill et al., 2003). Finally, men prefer longer hair to shorter hair on women (Fazzone, Kline, & Peeler, 2003), and black men prefer fairer, as opposed to darker, skin tones on black women (Hill, 2002).

An Evolutionary Perspective on Physical Attractiveness

We've just mentioned a lot of details, so you may not have noticed, but people's preferences for prettiness generally fit the assumptions of evolutionary psychology. Consider these patterns:

- Despite striking cultural differences, people all over the world tend to agree on who is and who is not attractive (Cunningham et al., 1995; Jones, 1995; Pollard, 1995). That's one reason why the winners of international beauty pageants usually seem gorgeous no matter where they're from.
- Babies appear to be born with preferences for the same faces that adults find attractive (Langlois, 2004). Some reactions to good looks may be inherited.
- People with symmetrical faces also tend to have symmetrical bodies and to enjoy better mental and physical health—and therefore make better mates—than do people with asymmetrical faces (Shackelford & Larsen, 1997). Faces that are free of odd proportions—the symmetrical faces that we find attractive—are associated with good health (Hume & Montgomerie, 2001).
- Hormones influence waist-to-hip ratios by affecting the distribution of fat on people's bodies. With their particular mix of estradiol and progesterone, women with WHRs near the attractive norm of 0.7 get pregnant more easily and tend to enjoy better physical health than do women with fewer curves (Henderson, 2004; Singh, 1994). A man with an attractive WHR of 0.9 is likely to be in better health than another man with a plump belly (Singh, 1995). So, both sexes are most attracted to the physical shapes that signal the highest likelihood of good health in the other sex.
- Younger women are more likely than older women to have long hair, and hair quality is correlated with physical health. So, the long hair that men prefer is associated with qualities that make a woman a good mate (Hinsz, Matz, & Patience, 2001).

- Everybody likes good looks, but physical attractiveness matters most to people who live in equatorial regions of the world where there are many parasites and pathogens that can endanger good health (Gangestad & Buss, 1993). In such areas, unblemished beauty may be an especially good sign that someone is in better health—and will make a better mate—than someone whose face is in some way imperfect (Fink, Grammer, & Thornhill, 2001).

- There are subtle but provocative changes in women's preferences that accompany their monthly menstrual cycles (Gangestad & Cousins, 2001). Women are only fertile for the few days that precede their ovulation each month, and during that period women find some characteristics in men to be more appealing than they seem during the rest of the month (see Figure 3.4). When they are fertile, women prefer more masculine faces, the scents of more symmetrical men, and bolder, more charismatic behavior than they do when they are infertile (Gangestad, 2004; Gangestad et al., 2004). Thus, women are attracted to assertive, cocky men when they are most likely to conceive a child, but they prefer warmer, less pushy men the rest of the month.

FIGURE 3.4. Women's probability of conception during the menstrual cycle. Women are fertile during the few days just before they ovulate at the end of the follicular phase of their menstrual cycles. During that period, they prefer more masculine faces and bolder, more cocky behavior in men than they do during the rest of the month.

Source: From Jöchle, 1973. Total N = 1800.

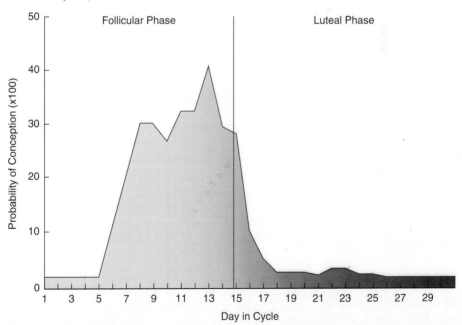

These patterns convince some theorists that standards of physical beauty have an evolutionary basis (e.g., Buss, 2004; Thornhill & Grammer, 1999). Presumably, early humans who successfully sought fertile, robust, and healthy mates were more likely to reproduce successfully than were those who simply mated at random. As a result, the common preference of modern men for symmetrical, baby-faced, low-WHR partners, and of modern women for symmetrical, masculine, and dynamic men, may be evolved inclinations that are rooted more in their human natures than in their particular cultural heritage.

Culture Matters, Too

On the other hand, there's no doubt that standards of attractiveness are also affected by changing economic and cultural conditions. For instance, fashions tend to change as a culture's sex ratio does. When the sex ratio is low and there are too few men, women wear shorter skirts (Barber, 1999), and when the ratio is high and there are too few women, men sport more mustaches and beards (Barber, 2001). And have you seen those Renaissance paintings of women who look fat by modern standards? During hard times, when a culture's food supply is unreliable, slender women are actually *less* desirable than heavy women are (Anderson et al., 1992). Only during times of plenty are slender women considered to be attractive. Indeed, as economic prosperity spread through the United States during the twentieth century, women were expected to be slimmer and slimmer (Barber, 1998), so that *Playboy* Playmates and Miss America contestants are now skinnier, on average, than they were when you were born (Pettijohn & Jungeberg, 2004). In fact, the average Playmate is now so slender she meets the weight criterion for having an eating disorder (Owen & Laurel-Seller, 2000).

Norms can differ across ethnic groups as well (influenced in part, perhaps, by different patterns of economic well-being). Black women in America are more likely to be obese than white women are (Kuczmarski et al., 1994), but they are also more likely to be satisfied with their weight (Stevens, Kumanyika, & Keil, 1994). White women consider obesity to be unattractive, but black women do not (Hebl & Heatherton, 1998; Vaughn et al., 2003). (But watch out: Black men like heavier women than white men do [Siciliani & Pride, 2003], but they still prefer the same curvaceous 0.7 WHR that is universally appealing to men [Singh & Luis, 1995]).

These findings suggest the possibility that human nature and environmental conditions work together to shape our collective judgments of who is and who isn't pretty. Nothing is certain; although we expect people with attractive faces to be especially healthy, it doesn't always turn out that way (Kalick et al., 1998). Still, beauty is not just in the eye of the beholder. There is remarkable agreement about who's gorgeous and who's ugly around the world.

Who Has a Bias for Beauty?

Still, we should note that some people do care more about physical attractiveness than others do (Livingston, 2001). How important are others' looks to you?

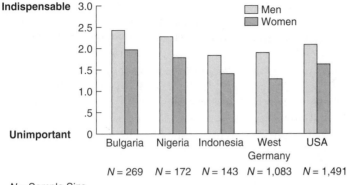

FIGURE 3.5. Desire for physical attractiveness in a romantic partner. From Buss, D. M., & Schmitt, D. P. (1993). Sexual strategies theory: An evolutionary perspective on human mating. *Psychological Review*, 100, 204–232. Copyright © 1993 by the American Psychological Association. Adapted with permission.

Your answer may depend on whether you are a man or a woman. All over the world, men report higher interest in having a physically attractive romantic partner than women do (see Figure 3.5). If they run a personal ad seeking a partner, for instance, men are more likely than women to come right out and specify that they're looking for an attractive mate (Feingold, 1990).

But don't get the wrong impression: Women do care about men's looks. When college students meet each other, physical attractiveness is one of the most powerful—if not *the* most potent—influences on how much the two sexes will initially like each other (Sprecher, 1989). In one compelling example of this effect, researchers at the University of Minnesota created 376 blind dates when they invited freshmen students to a "computer dance" at which the students expected to meet a compatible partner who had been selected for them by computer (Walster et al., 1966). The students had filled out a variety of scales that assessed their personalities and attitudes, but the researchers paired them off at random to see what would happen. Two hours later, after these young adults had gotten a chance to know one another, what do you think determined how much they liked each other? Similar backgrounds? Shared interests? Compatible personalities? Of all the variables measured by the researchers, there was only one influence that mattered: physical attractiveness. The better-looking the students were, the more their partners liked them.

Overall, a partner's physical attractiveness is more important to men than to women. That may be why 86 percent of the cosmetic surgery performed in the United States in 2003 was done on women (Barrett, 2004); women know that men are judging them by their looks. However, women are also attracted to a handsome man, and physical attractiveness may be the single most important influence on early attraction among both men and women.

Nevertheless, the bias for beauty is stronger in some people than others, as research on the personality trait of **self-monitoring** shows. Self-monitoring refers to people's tendency to regulate their social behavior to meet the demands of different social situations (Gangestad & Snyder, 2000). High self-monitors are ready, willing, and able to tailor their behavior to make a good impression on others. In contrast, low self-monitors strive to be true to their private beliefs and desires and are more consistent across situations. (You can assess your own standing on this trait with the Self-Monitoring Scale in chapter 4.)

Men who are high self-monitors—who are sensitive to the impressions they make on others—are especially interested in having good-looking dating partners. In fact, if they have to choose between (a) a date with an attractive woman who has an ugly personality and (b) a date with an unattractive woman who has a lovely personality, they'll pick the gorgeous shrew (Snyder, Berscheid, & Glick, 1985). Even more remarkably, if they're asked to pick a new employee, high self-monitoring men hire women who are beautiful but incompetent over women who are talented but plain (Snyder, Berscheid, & Matwychuk, 1988). Appearance is obviously very important to such men. In contrast, men who are low self-monitors are more attracted to substance than style. They select dates with desirable personalities and employees with talent over better-looking competitors who are less friendly or skilled.

So personalities matter, too. The studies just mentioned required men to make difficult choices, and the preferences of high and low self-monitoring men are not so starkly different when you allow them to rate many different partners (Shaffer & Bazzini, 1997). Nevertheless, both men and women may find outward appearances to be especially important to them if they are high self-monitors (Snyder & DeBono, 1985).

The Interactive Costs and Benefits of Beauty

People obviously notice the physical attractiveness of those they meet, and some of us are consistently considered to be more attractive than others. What effects do our looks have on our interactions with others? To adequately answer that question, we need to examine various interactions with diverse partners on varied occasions, and several studies have done just that. Physical attractiveness *is* influential.

As you might expect, beautiful women get more dates than plain women do (Reis, Nezlek, & Wheeler, 1980). Moreover, people tend to enjoy their interactions with attractive women; they talk more and are more involved, and they feel that the interactions are of higher quality (Garcia et al., 1991). Handsome men fare well, too, receiving more smiles, talk, and positive feelings from others than unattractive men do (Garcia et al., 1991; Stiles et al., 1996).

However, men's attractiveness may play an even larger part in influencing their access to the other sex than women's looks do (Reis et al., 1982). There is actually no correlation overall between a woman's beauty and the amount of time she spends interacting with men. Attractive women get more dates, as we noted, but plain women spend plenty of time interacting with men in group settings where others are present. In contrast, men's looks *are* correlated with the number and length of the interactions they have with women. Unattractive men have fewer interactions of any sort with fewer women than good-looking guys do. In this sense, then, physical attractiveness has a bigger effect on the social lives of men than it does on women.

Being more popular, attractive people tend to be less lonely, more socially skilled, and a little happier than the rest of us (Diener, Wolsic, & Fujita, 1995; Feingold, 1992b). One study even suggested that physical attractiveness accounts for about 10 percent of the variability in people's adjustment and well-being over their lifetimes (Burns & Farina, 1992). The lives of beautiful people aren't as rosy as the "beautiful is good" stereotype would suggest, however, because there are disadvantages to being attractive as well. For one thing, others lie to pretty people more often. People are more willing to misrepresent their interests, personalities, and incomes to get a date with an attractive person than they are to fabricate an image for a plain partner (Rowatt, Cunningham, & Druen, 1999). As a result, realizing that others are often "brown-nosing," or trying to ingratiate themselves, gorgeous people may cautiously begin mistrusting or discounting some of the praise they receive from others.

Consider this clever study: Attractive or unattractive people receive a written evaluation of their work from a person of the other sex who either does or does not know what they look like (Major, Carrington, & Carnevale, 1984). In every case, each participant receives a flattering, complimentary evaluation. (Indeed, everyone gets exactly the same praise.) How did the recipients react to this good news? Attractive men and women trusted the praise more and assumed that it was more sincere when it came from someone who didn't know they were good-looking. They were evidently used to getting insincere compliments from people who were impressed by their looks. On the other hand, unattractive people found the praise more compelling when the evaluator did know they were plain; sadly, they probably weren't used to compliments from people who were aware of their unappealing appearances.

So, gorgeous people are used to pleasant interactions with others, but they may not trust other people as much as less attractive people do (Reis et al., 1982). In particular, others' praise may be ambiguous. If you're very attractive, you may never be sure whether people are complimenting you because they respect your abilities or because they like your looks. Over time, this may not be good for your self-confidence (Satterfield & Muehlenhard, 1997).

There even seem to be various costs and benefits for those of us who merely associate with other very attractive people. On the plus side, for most of us, it feels good to gaze at handsome or lovely people of the other sex; simply looking at them puts us in a good mood (Kenrick et al., 1993). On the other hand, when we encounter gorgeous people of the same sex, we often feel worse, probably because we suffer by comparison. People create different—and poorer—evaluations of their own looks when they compare themselves to attractive others than when they compare themselves to ordinary folks (Thornton & Moore, 1993). This is an example of a **contrast effect,** a perceptual phenomenon in which a given object is perceived differently depending on the other objects to which it is compared. If we compare ourselves to supermodels, for instance, we can seem quite frumpy, although we may actually be rather appealing compared to most people.

A similar contrast effect can influence our perceptions of other people, too. If people examine very attractive models from *Playboy* or *Penthouse* magazines, they then give lower ratings to pictures of nude women of average attractiveness (Kenrick & Gutierres, 1989). Worse, men who view such models feel less sexual attraction and love for their own lovers (Kenrick & Gutierres, 1989)! Women's ratings of their lovers are not affected in this manner. Nevertheless, both men and women tend to underestimate the attractiveness of average people when they use unusually attractive people as a standard of comparison. These findings raise the disturbing possibility that our popular culture leaves us ill-equipped to appreciate the beauty of the real people we're likely to meet. Stop a moment and consider the media you consume each day; the TV you watch, the magazines you read, and the websites you visit probably all present an endless parade of very attractive people, who are prettier than the people who sit next to you in class. The danger is that you may be doing your class-mates a disservice, thinking that they're not especially attractive because you're using an unrealistic, artificially high standard of attractiveness based on a select group of people that you'll never actually meet!

Still, despite these various pros and cons, the bottom line is that good looks make someone attractive to others. Beauty is aesthetically pleasing and puts us in a good mood, and we usually assume that beautiful people possess a variety of other desirable traits as well. Thus, the effects of physical attractiveness, like proximity, are consistent with the reward model of interpersonal attraction.

Matching in Physical Attractiveness

We've spent several pages discussing physical attractiveness—which is an indi-cation of its importance in relationship research—but there is one last point to make about its influence at the beginning of a relationship. People may want gorgeous partners, but they're likely to end up paired off with others who are only about as attractive as they are (Feingold, 1988). Partners in established re-lationships tend to have similar levels of physical attractiveness; that is, their looks are well-matched. This phenomenon is known as **matching.**

Matching helps determine whether partners ever get together in the first place. The relationships that get started typically involve two people who are a reasonably good match in physical attractiveness, and the more similar their looks, the further their relationship is likely to progress (Folkes, 1982).

Indeed, the more serious and committed a relationship becomes, the more obvious matching usually is. People sometimes share casual dates with others who are not as good-looking as they, but they are unlikely to go steady with, or be-come engaged to, someone who is "out of their league" (White, 1980b). What this means is that, even if everybody wants a physically attractive partner, only those who are also good-looking are likely to get them. None of the really good-looking people want to pair off with us folks of average looks, and we, in turn, don't want partners who are "beneath us," either (Carli, Ganley, & Pierce-Otay, 1991).

Thus, it's not very romantic, but similarity in physical attractiveness may operate as a screening device. If people generally value good looks, matching will occur as they settle for the best-looking partner who will have them in return (Kalick & Hamilton, 1986). As a result, husbands and wives tend to be noticeably similar in physical attractiveness (Price & Vandenberg, 1979). And trouble may loom if that match fades away. A leading cause of sexual difficulty among married men is the perception that—although *they* still "look good"—their wives have "let themselves go" and are less attractive than they used to be (Margolin & White, 1987).

RECIPROCITY: LIKING THOSE WHO LIKE US

The matching phenomenon suggests that, to enjoy the most success in the relationship marketplace, we should pursue partners who are likely to return our interest. In fact, most people do just that. When we ponder possible partners, most of us rate our realistic interest in others—and the likelihood that we will approach them and try to start a relationship—using a formula like this (Shanteau & Nagy, 1979):

Desirability = Physical Attractiveness × Probability of Acceptance

Everything else being equal, the better-looking people are, the more desirable they are. However, this formula suggests that physical attractiveness is multiplied by our judgments of how likely it is that someone will like us in return to determine a particular person's overall appeal. Do the math. If someone likes us a lot but is rather ugly, that person probably won't be our first choice for a date. If someone else is gorgeous but doesn't like us back, we won't waste our time. The most appealing potential partner is often someone who is moderately attractive and who seems to offer a reasonably good chance of accepting us (perhaps *because* he or she isn't gorgeous [Huston, 1973]).

Not everyone follows this formula—some people just think desirability equals physical attractiveness (Shanteau & Nagy, 1979)—but a high likelihood of acceptance from others appears to be an important consideration for most of us. For instance, surveys of men at the University of Wisconsin and Texas A&M University found that, if they found a woman attractive, very few of them—only 3 percent—would offer her a date if they had no idea what she would say in response (Muehlenhard & Miller, 1988). Almost all of the men reported that they would either bide their time and look for signs of reciprocal interest or simply give up and do nothing at all if they weren't confident, before they even asked, that a potential date would say yes.

Obviously, people are usually reluctant to risk rejection. Another demonstration of this point emerged from a clever study in which college men had to choose where to sit to watch a movie (Bernstein et al., 1983). They had two choices: squeeze into a small cubicle next to a very attractive woman, or sit in an adjacent cubicle—alone—where there was plenty of room. The key point is that some of the men believed that the *same* movie was playing on both monitors, whereas other men believed that *different* movies were showing on the two screens. Let's consider the guys' dilemma. Presumably, most of them wanted to become acquainted with the beautiful woman. However, when only one movie was available, squeezing in next to her entailed some risk of rejection; their intentions would be obvious, and there was some chance that the woman would tell them to "back off." However, when two different movies were available, they were on safer ground. Sitting next to the woman could mean that they just wanted to see that particular movie, not that they were attracted to her, and a rebuff from her would be rude. In fact, only 25 percent of the men dared to sit next to the woman when the same movie was on both monitors, but 75 percent did so when two movies were available and their intentions were more ambiguous. Moreover, we can be sure that the men were taking advantage of the uncertain situation to move in on the woman—instead of really wanting to see that particular movie—because the experimenters kept changing which movie played on which screen. Three-fourths of the men squeezed in with the gorgeous woman no matter which movie was playing there!

In general, then, people seem to take heed of the likelihood that they will be accepted and liked by others, and they are more likely to approach those who offer acceptance than rejection. Indeed, everything else being equal, it's hard *not* to like those who like us (Curtis & Miller, 1986). Imagine that the first thing you hear about a new transfer student is that he or she has noticed you and really likes you; don't you feel positively toward him or her in return?

Obviously, this tendency to like those who like us is consistent with the reward model of attraction. It also fits another perspective known as **balance theory** that suggests that people desire consistency among their thoughts, feelings, and social relationships (Heider, 1958). When two people like each other, their feelings fit together well and can be said to be "balanced." This is also true when two people dislike each other, but not when a person likes someone else but is disliked in return. What happens when there are three people involved? In one study that addressed this question, college students encountered an experimenter who was either pleasant or rude to them (Aronson & Cope, 1968). After that, the experimenter's supervisor walked in and was either pleasant or rude to the experimenter! The students then had an opportunity to do a favor for the supervisor. How did they react? The students were more generous toward the supervisor when he or she had been either nice to the pleasant experimenter or mean to the unpleasant experimenter—that is, when the two interactions seemed balanced. This study and the rest of the research evidence generally support the notion that we prefer balance among our relationships. For that reason, then, before we ever meet them, we often expect that our enemies' enemies will be our friends.

SIMILARITY: LIKING THOSE WHO ARE LIKE US

It's rewarding to meet people who like us. It's also enjoyable to find others who are *just* like us and who share the same background, interests, and tastes. Indeed, one of the most basic principles of interpersonal attraction is the rule of similarity: Like attracts like. The old cliché that "birds of a feather flock together" is absolutely correct (McPherson, Smith-Lovin, & Cook, 2001). Few other aspects of attraction have been as thoroughly and extensively documented. Consider these examples:

- At the University of Michigan, male transfer students were given free rooms in a boardinghouse in exchange for their participation in a study of developing friendships among the previously unacquainted men (Newcomb, 1961). At the end of the semester, the men's closest friendships were with those housemates with whom they had the most in common.
- At Purdue University, researchers intentionally created blind dates between men and women who held either similar social and political attitudes or dissimilar views (Byrne, Ervin, & Lamberth, 1970). Each couple spent 45 minutes at the student union getting to know each other over soft drinks.

BOX 3.2
What's a Good Opening Line?

You're shopping for groceries, and you keep crossing paths with an attractive person you've seen somewhere on campus who smiles at you warmly when your eyes meet. You'd like to meet him or her. What should you say? You need to do more than just say, "Hi," and wait for a response, don't you? Perhaps some clever food-related witticism is the way to go: "Is your dad a baker? You've sure got a nice set of buns."

Common sense suggests that such attempts at humor are good opening lines. Indeed, various books invite you to use their funny pickup lines to increase your chances of getting a date (e.g., Allen & Ferrari, 1997; Dweck & Ivey, 1998). Be careful with such purchases, however; they may lead you astray. Careful research has compared the effectiveness of three different types of opening lines, and a cute or flippant remark may be the *worst* thing to say. Let's distinguish cute lines from "innocuous" openers (such as just saying, "Hi" or "How're you doing?") and "direct" lines that honestly communicate your interest (such as "Hi, I'm a

little embarrassed about this, but I'd like to get to know you"). When women evaluate lines like these by watching videotapes of men who use them, they like the cute lines much less than the other two types (Kleinke & Dean, 1990). More importantly, when a guy actually uses one of these lines on a woman in a singles bar, the innocuous and direct openers get a favorable response 70 percent of the time, compared to a success rate of only 24 percent for the cute lines (Cunningham, 1989). There's no comparison: Simply saying hello is a much smarter strategy than trying to be cute.

Why, then, do people write books full of flippant pickup lines? Because they're men. When a *woman* uses a cute line on a *man* in a singles bar, she gets a favorable response 90 percent of the time. In fact, any opening line from a woman works well with a man; in Cunningham's (1989) study, saying "Hi" succeeded every time. Men don't seem to care what opening lines women use, and this may lead them to overestimate women's liking for cute openers in return.

After the "dates," similar couples liked each other more than dissimilar couples did.

- At Kansas State University, 13 men spent 10 days jammed together in a simulated fallout shelter (Griffit & Veitch, 1974). Their feelings about each other were assessed along the way. The men got along fine with those with whom they had a lot in common, but would have thrown out of the shelter, if they could, those who were the least similar to themselves.

As these examples suggest, similarity is attractive.

What Kind of Similarity?

But what kinds of similarities are we talking about? Well, almost any kind. Whether they are lovers or friends, happy relationship partners resemble each other more than random strangers do on almost any measure. First, there's *demographic* similarity in age, sex, race, education, religion, and social class (Buss, 1985). Remember your best friends from high school? Most of them were probably of the same age, sex, and race (Kandel, 1978). In romantic couples, people tend to pair off with others of similar weight (Schafer & Keith, 1990), and they're even more likely than we'd expect to marry someone whose last name begins with the same last letter as their own (Jones et al., 2003)!

Then there's similarity in *attitudes and values*. As Figure 3.6 shows, there is a straightforward link between the proportion of the attitudes two people share and their attraction to each other: the more agreement, the more liking (Byrne & Nelson, 1965a). Take note of this pattern. Attraction doesn't level off after a certain amount of similarity is reached, and there's no danger in having "too much in common." Instead, where attitudes are concerned, the more similar two people are, the more they like each other. Think again about your high school

Attraction is strongly influenced by similarity. People who are similar in background characteristics, personality, physical attractiveness, and attitudes are more likely to be attracted to each other than are those who are dissimilar.

FIGURE 3.6. The relationship between attitude similarity and attraction.

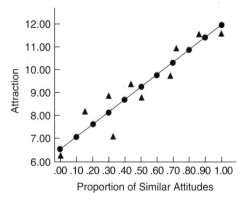

friends: Your alcohol and drug use was probably similar to that of your friends (Kandel, 1978), you probably got similar grades (Kubitschek & Hallinan, 1998), and if you were a virgin, your best friend probably was, too (Billy & Udry, 1985).

Finally, partners may have similar *personalities*. People with similar styles and traits like each other better, especially as time goes by (Botwin, Buss, & Schackelford, 1997; Tesser et al., 1998). In particular, husbands and wives with similar personalities have happier marriages than do spouses with different styles (Caspi & Herbener, 1990). What's notable about this is that if you have some undesirable personality traits, you may be more content with someone who shares those liabilities than with someone who offers no such drawbacks. If you're a fretful, anxious person, you may want to seek out another nervous type. Happy people like to associate with other happy people, of course, but gloomy people are actually more attracted to other gloomy people than to those with brighter moods (Locke & Horowitz, 1990). And people like others with similar attachment styles, too (Frazier et al., 1996; Klohnen & Luo, 2003); secure people prefer other secure people, whereas anxious people actually prefer others who are also anxious.

Do Opposites Attract?

The more similar two people are to one another, the more they like each other. Why, then, do many people believe "opposites attract?" Are there instances in which people become more attracted to each other the less they have in common? In general, the answer is no. With perhaps just one exception (which we'll mention later), there is no evidence that people are routinely more content with dissimilar, rather than similar, partners. However, there are several important subtleties in the way similarity operates that may mislead people into thinking that opposites do sometimes attract.

Matching Is a Broad Process

We've already seen that people tend to pair off with others who are similar to them in physical attractiveness. On the other hand, notable mismatches in looks sometimes occur—as in 1993, when Anna Nicole Smith, a 26-year-old *Playboy* Playmate of the Year, married J. Howard Marshall II, an 89-year-old billionaire. In such cases, the partners are dissimilar in specific ways, and "opposites" may seem to attract. That's an unsophisticated view, however, because such partners are really just matching in a broader sense, trading looks for money and vice versa (Elder, 1969). They may have different assets, but such partners are still seeking good matches with others who have similar standing overall in the interpersonal marketplace. People usually end up with others of similar *mate value*, or overall attractiveness as a marriage partner (Brase & Guy, 2004), but the specific rewards they offer each other may be quite different (Shackelford & Buss, 1997b).

This sort of thing goes on all the time. Among heterosexuals, high-income men who advertise for romantic partners (in personal ads or at dating services) are likely to stipulate that they are seeking an attractive woman, whereas attractive women are likely to announce that they want a well-to-do man (Green, Buchanan, & Heuer, 1984; Koestner & Wheeler, 1988). Among homosexuals, men

Here are the happy newlyweds, Anna Nicole Smith and J. Howard Marshall II, back in 1993. Matching is a broad process. They may have dissimilar assets to offer each other, but people usually pair off with partners of similar overall mate value.

who are not infected with HIV (the virus that causes AIDS) are picky, requesting higher status, more attractive partners in their personal ads than do men who are infected with HIV (Hatala, Baack, & Parmenter, 1998). It doesn't seem very romantic, but fame, wealth, health, talent, and looks all appear to be commodities that people use to attract more desirable partners than they might otherwise entice. If we think of matching as a broad process that involves both physical attractiveness and various other assets and traits, it's evident that people usually pair off with others of similar status, and like attracts like.

In fact, trade-offs like these are central ideas in evolutionary psychology. Because men are more likely to reproduce successfully when they mate with healthy, fertile women, natural selection has presumably promoted men's interest in youthful and beautiful partners (Buss, 2004). Youth is important because women are no longer fertile after they reach menopause in middle age. Beauty is meaningful because it is roughly correlated with some aspects of good health (Thornhill & Grammer, 1999). Thus, men especially value good looks in women (see Figure 3.5), and, as they age, they marry women who are increasingly younger than themselves (Kenrick & Keefe, 1992): Men who marry in their twenties pair off with women who are two years younger than they are, on average, but if a man marries in his fifties, his wife is likely to be 15 years younger than he.

Women don't need to be as concerned about their partners' youth because men normally retain their capacity for reproduction as long as they live. Instead,

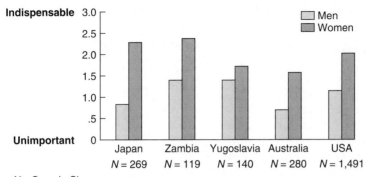

FIGURE 3.7. Desire for good financial prospects in a romantic partner. From Buss, D. M., & Schmitt, D. P. (1993). Sexual strategies theory: An evolutionary perspective on human mating. *Psychological Review, 100,* 204–232. Copyright © 1993 by the American Psychological Association. Adapted with permission.

according to the parental investment model, women should seek mates who can shelter and protect them during the long period of pregnancy and nursing (Feingold, 1992a); they should prefer powerful, high-status men with resources that can contribute to the well-being of mother and child. In fact, as Figure 3.7 illustrates, women *do* care more about their partners' financial prospects than men do (Buss & Schmitt, 1993). Furthermore, women's preferences for the age of their mates do not change as they age; women prefer to marry men who are a few years older throughout their entire lives (Buunk et al., 2001).

BOX 3.3
Interethnic Relationships

Most of our intimate relationships are likely to be with others of the same race. Nevertheless, marriages between spouses from different ethnic groups are much more common than they used to be (Saluter, 1996). About 7 percent of the married couples in the U.S. are of mixed race or ethnicity (Armas, 2003), and those couples raise an interesting question: If similarity attracts, what's going on? The answer is actually straightforward: Nothing special. If you ignore the fact of their dissimilar ethnicity, interethnic couples appear to be influenced by the same motives that guide everyone else. The partners tend to be similar in age, education, and attractiveness (Kouri & Lasswell, 1993; Lewis, Yancey, & Bletzer, 1997), and their relationships, like most, are based on common interests and personal compatibility (Shibazaki & Brennan, 1998). Circumstances may matter; compared to other people, those in interethnic relationships report that they had a larger number of potential partners of other ethnicities available to them (Shibazaki & Brennan, 1998). In general, however, interethnic couples are just like any others: Two people who are more alike than different decide to stay together because they fall in love (Porterfield, 1982).

Thus, matching based on the exchange of feminine youth and beauty for masculine status and resources is commonplace. Indeed, it occurs around the world (Buss, 1989b; Koziel & Pawlowski, 2003). Still, is it the result of evolutionary pressures? Homosexual men and women have age preferences for their partners that are like those of heterosexual men and women, which is a bit difficult for an evolutionary model to explain (Kenrick et al., 1995). In addition, advocates of the cultural perspective argue that women pursue desirable resources through their partners because they have been denied direct access to political and economic power on their own (Eagly & Wood, 1999). On the other hand, when women do have high-status jobs, they're even more (not less) likely to be attracted to resourceful, powerful men (Leone, Robins, & Connell, 2003). And when such women marry at middle age, they don't typically seek much younger spouses as men do (Kenrick & Keefe, 1992). Even when women attain professional positions of high prestige, they do not exhibit preferences like those of high-status men.

So, the origins of the feminine-beauty-for-masculine-money tradeoff remain uncertain. Different possibilities exist. But in any case, the bottom line here is that matching is a broad process that involves multiple resources and traits. When "opposites" seem to attract, people may be trading one asset for another in order to obtain partners of similar social status, and it's their similar mate values, not any apparent "opposites," that make them attractive to each other.

Discovering Similarities Takes Time

Another source of confusion lies in the fact that it takes a while for two people to get to know each other well enough to understand fully what they do and do not have in common. For one thing, various misplaced hopes and expectations can get in the way. Even when they know nothing else about her, for instance, men assume they have more in common with an attractive woman than with one who is plain (Marks & Miller, 1982). Initial attraction for any reason, such as physical attractiveness or demographic similarity, can lead us to expect that someone has attitudes and values similar to ours. If we're mistaken, correcting such misperceptions can take time.

This process was evident in Newcomb's (1961) study of developing friendships among transfer students sharing a boardinghouse. Soon after they met, the men liked best the housemates who they thought were most like them; at first, their friendships were influenced mostly by **perceived similarity.** As the semester progressed, however, the actual similarities the men shared with each other played a larger and larger role in their friendships. When they got to know each other better, the men clearly preferred those who really were similar to them, although this was not always the case at first.

Even when we feel we know our partners well, there may be surprises ahead. According to Bernard Murstein's (1987) **stimulus-value-role** theory, there are three different types of information we gain about a new partner that influence developing relationships. When partners first meet, their attraction to each other is primarily based on "stimulus" information involving obvious attributes such as age, sex, and physical appearance. Thereafter, during the

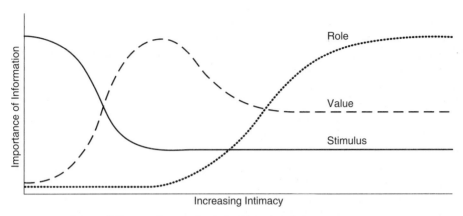

FIGURE 3.8. Three different phases of relationship development.
Murstein's (1987) Stimulus-Value-Role theory suggests that developing relationships are influenced by three different types of information as time goes by and the partners learn more about each other.
Source: Murstein, 1987.

"value" stage, attraction depends on similarity in attitudes and beliefs, as people learn whether they like the same kinds of pizzas, movies, and vacations (see Figure 3.8). Only later does "role" compatibility become important as partners finally find out if they agree on the basics of parenting, careers, and housecleaning, among other life tasks. The point is that partners can be perfectly content with each other's tastes in politics and entertainment without ever realizing that they disagree fundamentally about where they'd like to live and how many kids—if any!—they want to have. Important dissimilarities sometimes become apparent only after couples have married; such spouses may stay together despite their differences, but it's not because opposites attract.

The influence of time and experience is also apparent in **fatal attractions** (Felmlee, 1998, 2001). These occur when a quality that initially attracts one person to another gradually becomes one of the most obnoxious, irritating things about that partner. For instance, partners who initially seem spontaneous and fun may later seem irresponsible and foolish, and those who appear strong may later seem domineering. Those who initially welcome a partner's high level of attention and devotion may come to resent such behavior when it later seems too possessive. In such cases, the annoying trait is no secret, but people fail to appreciate how their judgments of it will change with time. Importantly, such fatal qualities are often different from one's own; they may seem admirable and desirable at first, but over time people realize that such opposites aren't attractive (Felmlee & Flynn, 2004).

Perceived versus Real Similarity: Misperception Lingers

A third subtlety lies in the fact that we rarely get to know our partners as well as we think we do. The real similarities people share exert considerable influence on their relationships as time goes by. Even after years of marriage, however, spouses usually think they have more in common with each other than they really do. They overestimate the similarity that really exists. What makes this provocative is that there is a higher correlation between perceived similarity and marital satisfaction than there is between real similarity and marital bliss (Byrne & Blaylock, 1963; Levinger & Breedlove, 1966). To some degree, people seem to be married to illusory images of their partners that portray them as similar soulmates—they're in love with the people they *think* their partners are (Montoya & Horton, 2004)—and they might be disappointed to learn the true extent of their disagreements about various issues.

This tendency to form pleasant images of our partners can help maintain relationships, as we'll see in chapter 4. On the other hand, to the extent that it involves any misperception, it can also help explain why opposites sometimes seem to attract. If they try hard enough, people may perceive similarity where it does not exist and be attracted to others who are actually quite different from them. Perceived similarity can bring people together, at least for a while, even when their dissimilarity is apparent to everyone else.

You May Be the Person I Want to Become

People also admire those who possess skills and talents they wish they had. Another nuance in the operation of similarity lies in our attraction to others who are the sorts of people we want to become. We tend to like those who are similar to our *ideal selves*, that is, who exhibit desirable qualities that we want to, but may not yet, possess. This tendency is complex because it's threatening and unpleasant when people surpass our ideals and make us look bad by comparison (Herbst, Gaertner, & Insko, 2003). However, as long as others are only a little better than us—so that they offer us implicit encouragement instead of humiliation—we may be attracted to those who are actually a little different from us (for now) (Klohnen & Luo, 2003). Let's not overstate this subtlety. The most appealing partners of all may be those who are similar to us in most dimensions but who fit our attainable ideals in others (Luo & Klohnen, 2003). Such people are hardly our "opposites." But as long as the differences are not too great, we may prefer a partner who is someone we'd like to become to one who more closely resembles who we really are now.

Dissimilarity May Decrease Over Time

Moreover, relationships do sometimes change people (Ruvolo & Ruvolo, 2000). As time goes by, the members of a couple may come to share increasingly similar attitudes (Acitelli, Kenny, & Weiner, 2001) and emotional reactions (Anderson, Keltner, & John, 2003) to the events they encounter. Some of this decrease in dissimilarity probably occurs automatically as a couple shares compelling experiences, but some of it also occurs as the partners consciously seek compatibility and contentment (Davis & Rusbult, 2001). Thus, opposites don't attract, but some opposites may gradually fade if a couple stays together for some other reason. And over time, newfound similarity may help keep partners together even when they didn't start off having much in common.

Maybe It's Dissimilarity, Not Similarity, that Matters

Not all researchers agree that similarity is attractive; instead, some argue that *dissimilarity* is *un*attractive and leads us to avoid others (Rosenbaum, 1986). In this view, we keep our distance from others who seem different from us, but we do not like others better the more similar they become. Such a process would mean that once we screen out those who are clearly unlike us, similarity has little effect on our choices of partners. As a result, people may pair off with others who are only somewhat like them, and opposites may seem to attract.

Indeed, romantic partners may not assess the similarity of their lovers as carefully as friends do. People may feel romantic infatuation for a wide variety of other people, including some with whom they have little in common (Lykken & Tellegen, 1993). On the other hand, real similarity improves romantic relationships (Hendrick, 1981), and it is plainly at work in most friendships (e.g., Carli, Ganley, & Pierce-Otay, 1991). The best conclusion appears to be that both similarity and dissimilarity are influential (Singh & Teoh, 1999; Tan & Singh, 1995); people first avoid dissimilar others and then are more attracted to everyone else the more similar they seem to be (Byrne, Clore, & Smeaton, 1986).

One Way "Opposites" May Attract: Complementarity

Finally, there may be one particular way in which different types of behavior can fit together well. We like responses from others that help us reach our goals. When two partners have different skills, each is usually happy to allow the other to take the lead on those tasks at which the other is more talented (Beach et al., 2001). Such behavior is said to *complement* our own, and **complementarity**—reactions that provide a good fit to our own—can be attractive. Most complementary behaviors are actually similar actions; people who are warm and agreeable, for instance, are happiest when they are met with warmth and good humor in return. However, one reliable form of complementarity involves different behaviors from two partners: dominance and submission. When people feel very sure of themselves, they want their partners to heed their advice; on other occasions, when people need help and advice, they want their partners to give it (Markey, Funder, & Ozer, 2003). In this manner, "opposites" may occasionally attract.

We shouldn't overstate this case. People like others who have similar personalities much more than they like those who are different (Richard, Wakefield, & Lewak, 1990), and even dominant people like other assertive folks more than they like those who are chronically servile and submissive (Dryer & Horowitz, 1997). On the other hand, when you really want something, it's nice when your partner lets you have your way. (And if you're both generous, understanding, and self-confident enough, you can take turns rewarding each other in this fashion.) The important thing to remember is that similar partners probably supply us what we want more often than anyone else can.

Why Is Similarity Attractive?

It's usually reassuring to meet others who are just like us. Encountering similarity in others can be comforting, reminding us that we're okay the way we are (Byrne & Clore, 1970). Similar others are also more likely to like us, so we anticipate pleasant, friendly interaction with such people (Baxter & West, 2003; Condon & Crano, 1988). Then, when we give it a try, we usually do have smooth, relatively effortless interactions with those who are a lot like us (Davis, 1981); there are fewer points of disagreement and conflict, and more things we can happily do together. As we've seen, there are several reasons why opposites may seem to attract, but in fact birds of a feather do flock together. Similarity is rewarding; opposition is not.

BARRIERS: LIKING THOSE WE CANNOT HAVE

A final influence on attraction involves the common tendency for people to struggle to overcome barriers that keep them from what they want. The theory of psychological **reactance** states that when people lose their freedom of action or choice, they strive to regain that freedom (Brehm & Brehm, 1981). As a result, we may want something more if we are threatened with losing it.

This principle can apparently affect our feelings about our partners in relationships. Among unmarried couples, researchers sometimes observe an interesting pattern called the **Romeo and Juliet effect:** The more their parents interfere with their romances, the more love people feel for their partners (Driscoll, Davis, & Lipetz, 1972). This may be more than just a simple correlation; over time, parental interference may play an active role in increasing the ardor young lovers feel for each other (Driscoll et al., 1972). This pattern doesn't occur all the time (Leslie, Huston, & Johnson, 1986), but it does suggest that parents should think twice before they forbid their teenagers to see certain partners. If they create a state of reactance, the parents may unintentionally make the forbidden partners seem more attractive than they are. The best course of action in such cases may be for the parents to express their displeasure mildly or even to do nothing at all.

Another kind of barrier occurs every night when bars close and everybody has to go home. If you're looking for a late-night date, you may find that the potential partners in a bar seem more and more attractive as closing time approaches and you face the prospect of leaving alone. In fact, when time is running out, unattached bar patrons consider the available members of the other sex to be better-looking than they seemed to be earlier in the evening (Olson et al., 2004; Pennebaker et al., 1979). This phenomenon doesn't involve "beer goggles," or intoxication; it occurs even if people haven't been drinking (Gladue & Delaney, 1990). However, it only occurs among those who are seeking company they don't yet have; those who are already committed to close relationships don't exhibit this pattern (Madey et al., 1996). Thus, the "closing time effect" appears to be another case of desired-but-forbidden fruit seeming especially sweet.

SO, WHAT DO MEN AND WOMEN WANT?

We are nearly at the end of our survey of major influences on attraction, but one important point remains. As we mentioned, men and women differ in the value they place on a partner's physical attractiveness and income. We don't want those results to leave you with the wrong impression, however, because despite those differences, men and women generally seek the same qualities in their relational partners (Buss et al., 2001). Let's look more closely at what men and women want.

Around the world, there are three themes in the criteria with which people evaluate potential mates (Fletcher, 2002). If we had our way, almost all of us would have partners who offered

- *warmth and loyalty,* being kind, supportive, understanding, and considerate;
- *attractiveness and vitality,* being good-looking, sexy, and outgoing; and
- *status and resources,* being financially secure and living well.

All of these characteristics are desirable, but they're not of equal importance, and their prominence depends on whether we're seeking a relatively casual, short-term fling or a more committed long-term romance.

Both men and women are less picky when they're evaluating partners for short-term liaisons than for lasting unions (Fletcher et al., 2004). For instance, both sexes will accept lower intelligence, warmth, and earning potential in a lover with whom they have a casual fling than they would require in a spouse (Buunk et al., 2002; Stewart, Stinnett, & Rosenfeld, 2000). In particular, when they are contemplating short-term affairs, women will accept men who aren't especially kind, dependable, or understanding, as long as their lovers are muscular (Frederick & Haselton, 2004), sexy, and "hot" (Scheib, 2001).

In contrast, when they are picking husbands, women consider a man's good character to be more important than his good looks. A man's warmth and loyalty are more influential than his physical attractiveness when he's being considered as a long-term mate (Urbaniak & Kilmann, 2003). Indeed, when they are pondering a lasting relationship, women attach more importance to the criteria of warmth and loyalty and status and resources than to the criterion of attractiveness and vitality (Fletcher et al., 2004). If she can't have it all, the average woman prefers a man who is kind and understanding and well-to-do—but not particularly handsome—to one who is good-looking but poor, or good-looking and rich but cold and disloyal (Li et al., 2002; Scheib, 2001).

Men have different priorities. Like women, they value warmth and loyalty, but unlike women they attach more importance to attractiveness and vitality in a long-term partner than to status and resources (Fletcher et al., 2004). The average fellow prefers a kind, beautiful woman without any money to wealthy women who are gorgeous grouches or sweet but ugly (Li et al., 2002).

Of course, we typically have to accept some trade-offs like these when we're seeking intimate partners. Fulfilling all of our diverse desires by finding (and winning!) the perfect mate is hard to do. If we insist that our partners be kind and understanding *and* gorgeous *and* rich, we're likely to stay frustrated for a long time (Tolmacz, 2004). So, when they're evaluating potential mates, men typically check first to make sure that a woman has at least average looks, and then they seek as much warmth, kindness, honesty, openness, stability, humor, and intelligence as they can get (Li et al., 2002; Sprecher & Regan, 2002). Great beauty is desirable to men, but it's not as important as high levels of warmth and loyalty are (with status and resources coming in a distant third). Women usually check first to make sure that a man has at least some money or prospects, and then they, too, seek as much warmth, kindness, honesty, openness, stability, humor, and intelligence as they can get (Li et al., 2002; Sprecher & Regan, 2002). Wealth is desirable to women, but it's not as important as high levels of warmth and loyalty are, and a man's looks are in third place.

So, add all this up, and attraction isn't so mysterious after all. Men attend to looks and women attend to resources, but everybody seems to want partners who are amiable, agreeable, loving, and kind, and men and women do not differ in this regard. As long as she's moderately pretty and he has some money, both sexes want as much warmth and loyalty as they can get. To the extent there is any surprise here, it's in the news that women don't simply want strong, dominant men; they want their fellows to be warm and kind and capable of commitment, too (Jensen-Campbell, Graziano, & West, 1995; Simpson, 2004). If you're an unemotional, macho male, take note: Women will be more impressed if you develop some affectionate warmth to go with your strength and power.

FOR YOUR CONSIDERATION

Rasheed introduced himself to Rebecca because she was really hot, and he was mildly disappointed when she turned out to be a little suspicious, self-centered, and vain. On the other hand, she was really hot, so he asked her out anyway. Because she was impressed with his designer clothes and bold style, Rebecca was intrigued by Rasheed, but after a few minutes she thought him a little pushy and arrogant. Still, he had tickets to an expensive concert, so she accepted his invitation to go out on a date.

In your opinion, what does the date—and the future—hold for Rebecca and Rasheed? Why?

CHAPTER SUMMARY

The Fundamental Basis of Attraction: A Matter of Rewards

According to most theories, we are attracted to people whose presence is rewarding to us. Two major types of reward influence attraction: direct rewards produced by someone (rewarding behaviors, rewarding characteristics, access to external rewards) and rewarding associations in which we connect the presence of another person with other positive experiences. Attraction is an interactive process involving personal needs, another's perceived characteristics, and the situation.

Proximity: Liking Those Near Us

Proximity provides the opportunity for social interactions but does not determine the quality of these interactions. We select our friends, and our enemies, from those around us.

Convenience: Proximity Is Rewarding, Distance Is Costly. Relationships with distant partners are ordinarily less satisfying than they would be if the partners were nearby, because long-distance interaction offers fewer rewards but requires more costs.

Familiarity: Repeated Contact. In general, familiarity breeds attraction. Even brief, *mere exposure* to others usually increases our liking for them.

The Power of Proximity. Close proximity accentuates our feelings about others. We like most people better when they're nearby, but repeated contact with someone we do not like can increase hostility instead.

Physical Attractiveness: Liking Those Who Are Lovely

In general, people are attracted to others who are physically attractive.

The Bias for Beauty: "What Is Beautiful Is Good". Widespread stereotypes lead us to assume that attractive people have other desirable personal characteristics, but the specific beliefs about good-looking people vary from one culture to the next.

Who's Pretty? People all over the world have similar standards of physical beauty. Symmetrical faces with features that approximate the mathematical average of individual faces are especially beautiful. *Waist-to-hip ratios* of 0.7 are very appealing in women, whereas a WHR of 0.9 is attractive in a man, if he has money. Both men and women prefer partnerships in which he is taller than she is.

An Evolutionary Perspective on Physical Attractiveness. The cross-cultural agreement about beauty, the increased importance of attractiveness in areas prone to parasites, and the link between attractive waist-to-hip ratios and good health are all consistent with the assumptions of evolutionary psychology. In addition, cyclical variations in women's preferences make healthy, dominant men more attractive to women when they are ovulating than when they are not.

Culture Matters, Too. On the other hand, standards of beauty fluctuate with changing economic and cultural conditions. Sex ratios seem to influence fashion, and prosperous cultures require women to be more slender than poor cultures do.

Who Has a Bias for Beauty? Men care about the physical attractiveness of a potential partner more than women do, but looks are one of the most important influences on initial attraction for both men and women. People who are high in the personality trait of *self-monitoring* place particular emphasis on the physical attractiveness of others.

The Interactive Costs and Benefits of Beauty. Physical attractiveness has a larger influence on men's interactions than on women's; unattractive men have less contact with women than attractive men do. However, there are disadvantages to being beautiful; attractive people doubt the praise they receive from others, and are lied to more often. Still, attractive people tend to have pleasant interactions with others, and are generally a little happier than unattractive people are.

Comparing ourselves and others to exceptionally attractive models can lead us to underestimate our own and others' attractiveness. The media may do us a disservice by creating artificially high standards of beauty.

Matching in Physical Attractiveness. People tend to pair off with others of similar beauty. Physical attractiveness may operate as a filter with which people seek the most attractive partners who will have them in return.

Reciprocity: Liking Those Who Like Us

People are reluctant to risk rejection. We like those who offer a high probability of accepting us in return, and rarely offer dates to people whose acceptance is uncertain. Indeed, most people seem to calculate others' global desirability by multiplying their physical attractiveness by their probability of reciprocal liking.

These findings are consistent with balance theory, which holds that people desire consistency among their thoughts, feelings, and relationships. A preference for balance encourages us to like our friends' friends and our enemies' enemies.

Similarity: Liking Those Who Are Like Us

Birds of a feather flock together. People like those who are similar to them.

What Kind of Similarity? Happy relationship partners resemble each other on almost any measure. They come from similar demographic groups, share similar attitudes and values, and have similar personality traits.

Do Opposites Attract? Differences among people generally do not increase their attraction to each other. However, the belief that "opposites attract" may persist for several reasons. First, matching is a broad process in which people of similar social status sometimes offer each other different assets; fame, wealth, health, talent, and looks are all commodities people use to attract others. In particular, matching based on the exchange of women's youth and beauty for men's status and resources is commonplace.

Second, it takes time for *perceived similarity* to be replaced by a more accurate understanding of the attributes we share with others. The *stimulus-value-role* model suggests that there are three different types of information that influence developing relationships as time goes by. And time and experience can change people's perceptions of *fatal attractions*, characteristics of a new partner that are initially appealing but later aggravating. Still, misperception can linger. Even long-term partners usually think they have more in common than they really do.

People are also attracted to those who are mildly different from them but similar to their ideal selves. Such people are not "opposites," but they are somewhat dissimilar in some ways. People also tend to become more similar over time, sharing more attitudes and emotions than they used to, so some opposites may fade if a couple stays together long enough for some other reason.

Finally, even though we may avoid those who seem dissimilar to us, we may occasionally appreciate behavior from a partner that differs from our own but that complements our actions and helps us to reach our goals. Submissive responses to our attempts at dominance are an example of this.

Why Is Similarity Attractive? Similarity in others is reassuring. We also assume similar others will like us, and we usually enjoy pleasant interaction with those who are a lot like us.

Barriers: Liking the Ones We Cannot Have

The theory of psychological *reactance* suggests that people strive to restore lost freedom. The theory provides an explanation for the *Romeo and Juliet effect*, which occurs when parental interference increases the intensity of teenage romance. It may also influence the tendency for potential partners to get more attractive at closing time.

So, What Do Men and Women Want?

People evaluate potential partners with regard to three types of traits: (a) warmth and loyalty, (b) attractiveness and vitality, and (c) status and resources. Men and women are less selective when they choose short-term mates, and for short affairs women value good looks more than warmth and kindness. For lasting romance, however, women want men who are very warm and kind and who are not poor, and men want women who are warm and kind and who are not unattractive. Thus, everybody wants intimate partners who are amiable, agreeable, and loving.

CHAPTER 4

Social Cognition

Imagine that you're home in bed, sick with a killer flu, and your lover doesn't call you during the day to see how you're doing. You're disappointed. Why didn't your partner call? Does he or she not love you enough? Is this just another frustrating example of his or her self-centered lack of compassion? Or is it more likely that your loving, considerate partner didn't want to risk waking you from a nap? There are several possible explanations, and you can choose a forgiving rationale, a blaming one, or something in between. And importantly, the choice may really be up to you; the facts of the case may allow several different interpretations. But whatever you decide, your judgments are likely to be consequential. At the end of the day, your perceptions will have either sustained or undermined the happiness of your relationship.

 We'll focus on judgments like these in this chapter on **social cognition,** a term that refers generally to the processes of perception and judgment with which we make sense of our social worlds (Kunda, 1999). Our primary concern will be with the way we *think* about our relationships. We'll explore how our judgments of our partners and their behavior set the stage for the events that follow. We'll consider our own efforts to influence and control what our partners think of us. And we'll ponder just how well two people are likely to know each other, even in an intimate relationship. Throughout the chapter, we'll emphasize the fact that our perceptions and interpretations of our partnerships are of enormous importance: What we think helps to determine what we *feel,* and then how we *act.* This wouldn't be a problem if our judgments were always correct. However, there are usually a variety of reasonable ways to interpret an event (as our opening example suggests), and we can make mistakes, even when we're confident that we have arrived at the truth. Indeed, some of those mistakes may begin the moment we meet someone, as studies of first impressions reveal.

FIRST IMPRESSIONS (AND BEYOND)

First impressions matter. The judgments we form of others after a brief first meeting often have enormous staying power, with our initial perceptions continuing to be influential months later. This fact may be obvious if we dislike someone so much after an initial interaction that we avoid any further contact with him or her; in such cases, our first impressions are the only impressions we ever get, and they are clearly the source of our lasting evaluations of that person. However, first impressions continue to be influential even when we do see more of a new acquaintance. When researchers formally arranged get-acquainted conversations between new classmates, the initial impressions the students formed continued to influence their feelings about each other nine weeks later (Sunnafrank & Ramirez, 2004).

Conceivably, some first impressions may last because they are discerning and correct. Sometimes it doesn't take us long to accurately decide who's nice and who's not, and if we're right, we may never need to revise our initial perceptions. On the other hand, first impressions can be remarkably persistent even when they're erroneous. Right or wrong, first impressions linger, and that's why they matter so much. Let's consider how they operate.

Whether or not we realize it, we start judging people from the moment we meet them. Everyone we meet, for instance, fits some category of people about whom we already hold stereotyped first impressions. This may sound like a daring assertion, but it really isn't. Think about it: Everyone is either male or female, and (as we saw in chapter 1), gender-role stereotypes lead us to expect different behavior from men and women. Further, at a glance, we can tell if someone is beautiful or plain, and (as we saw in chapter 3), we assume that pretty people are likeable people. There are dozens of other distinctions that may come into play—young/old, black/white, pierced/unpierced, country/urban, and many more. The specifics of these stereotypes may vary from one perceiver to the next, but they operate similarly in anyone: Stereotypes supply us with preconceptions about what people are like. Moreover, we don't decide to use stereotypes; they influence us automatically, even when we are unaware of using them (Devine & Monteith, 1999). So, some initial feelings about others may spring up unbidden even when we want to be impartial and open-minded.

Then, if we do interact with someone, we form preliminary impressions of them rapidly. Please take a moment to form a quick judgment of someone who is

envious, stubborn, critical, impulsive, industrious, and intelligent.

Would you want this person as a coworker? Probably not much. Now, please take another moment to size up someone else who is

intelligent, industrious, impulsive, critical, stubborn, and envious.

More impressive, yes? This person isn't perfect, but he or she seems competent and ambitious. The point, of course, is that the two descriptions offer the same information in a different *order*, and that's enough to engender two different

When we meet others for the first time, we rarely form impressions of them in an unbiased, even-handed manner. Instead, various stereotypes and primacy effects influence our interpretations of the behavior we observe.

impressions (Asch, 1946). Our judgments of others are influenced by a **primacy effect,** a tendency for the first information we receive about others to carry special weight, along with our stereotypes, in shaping our overall impressions of them.

Primacy effects provide one important indication of why first impressions matter so much: Regardless of their source, our quick first judgments of others influence our interpretations of the later information we encounter. Once a judgment forms, it affects how we use the data that follows—often in subtle ways that are difficult to detect. John Darley and Paget Gross (1983) demonstrated this when they showed Princeton students a videotape that established the social class of a young girl named "Hannah." Two different videos were prepared, and some people learned that Hannah was rather poor, whereas others found that she was pretty rich; she either played in a deteriorating, paved schoolyard and returned home to a dingy, small duplex, or played on expansive, grassy fields and went home to a large, lovely house. The good news is that when Darley and Gross asked the participants to guess how well Hannah was doing in school, they did not assume the rich kid was smarter than the poor kid; the two groups both assumed she was getting average grades

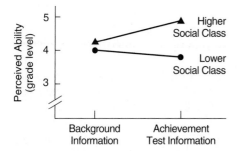

FIGURE 4.1. Our preconceptions control our
interpretations of information about others.
People equipped with different expectations
about the social class of a fourth-grade girl
drew very different conclusions about her
performance on an achievement test, even
though they all witnessed the very *same*
performance.
Source: Darley & Gross, 1983.

(see Figure 4.1). After that, however, the researchers showed the participants a
tape of Hannah taking an aptitude test and doing an inconsistent job, answering some difficult questions correctly but blowing some easy ones. Everyone
saw the same tape, but—and here's the bad news—they interpreted it very differently depending on their impressions of her social class. People who thought
that Hannah was poor cited her mistakes and judged her as performing *below*
average, whereas those who thought she was rich noted her successes and rated
her as considerably *better* than average. Perceivers equipped with different preconceptions about Hannah's social class interpreted the *same* sample of her behavior in very different ways and came to very different conclusions. And note
how subtle this process was: They didn't leap to biased assumptions about
Hannah simply by knowing her social class, making a mistake that might easily
be noticed. But their knowledge of her social class clearly lingered in their
minds and contaminated their interpretations of her later actions. And they
probably made their biased judgments with confidence, feeling fair and impartial. Both groups could point to a portion of her test performance—the part that
fit their preconceptions— and feel perfectly justified in making the judgments
they did, never realizing that people with other first impressions were watching
the same videotape and reaching contradictory conclusions.

Thus, first impressions affect our interpretations of the subsequent information we encounter about others. They also affect our choices of the new information we seek. When we want to test a first impression about someone,
we're more likely to pursue information that will confirm that belief than to
inquire after data that could prove it wrong. That is, people ordinarily display a
confirmation bias: They seek information that will prove them right more often
than they look for examples that would prove them wrong (Snyder, 1981). For
instance, imagine that you're instructed to interview a fellow student to find out

if he or she is a sociable extravert, and you're handed a list of possible questions to ask. Some of the questions are neutral (e.g., "What are the good and bad points of acting friendly and open?") but others are slanted toward eliciting introverted responses (e.g., "What do you dislike about loud parties?"), while still others are likely to get extraverted answers (e.g., "What do you do when you want to liven things up at a party?"). How would you conduct the interview? If you're like most people, you'd select questions that probe for evidence that your expectation is correct.

That's just what happened when researchers asked some people to find out if a stranger was extraverted, but asked others to find out if the person was introverted (Snyder & Swann, 1978b). The two groups of interviewers adopted two very different lines of investigation, asking questions that made it likely that they'd get examples of the behaviors they expected to find. In fact, the interviews were so biased that audiences listening to them on tape actually believed that the strangers really were rather extraverted or introverted, depending on the interviewers' preconceptions. Moreover, participants in this study continued to display confirmation biases even when they were given a $25 incentive to be as accurate as possible.

The problem with confirmatory strategies is that they elicit one-sided information about others that fits our preconceptions—and as a result, we too rarely confront unequivocal evidence that our first impressions are wrong. Thus, not only may we cling to snap judgments that are incorrect, we may also think we're right about others more often than we are. Indeed, most people are **overconfident** in their beliefs about others, making more mistakes than they realize. Here's an example. After you begin dating a new romantic partner, you're likely to become confident that you understand his or her sexual history as time goes by. You'll probably feel increasingly certain, for instance, that you know how many other lovers your partner has had, or whether or not he or she has a sexually transmitted infection. Remarkably, however, you're not likely to be as well-informed as you think. Studies at the University of Texas at Austin found that people could not estimate the risk that a new acquaintance was HIV-positive as well as they thought they could (Swann, Silvera, & Proske, 1995). They were overconfident when a new relationship began, and as the relationship developed, they only got *worse* (Swann & Gill, 1997). With greater familiarity, they became more certain that they understood their new partners well, but their accuracy did not change (see Figure 4.2).

Altogether, then, two reasons first impressions matter are because the first things we learn (a) direct our attention to certain types of new information, and (b) influence our interpretations of the new facts we get later. The net result is that we do not process information about others in an unbiased, evenhanded manner. Instead, our existing notions, whether they're simple stereotypes or quick first impressions, affect how we access and use the new data we encounter. We are usually unaware of how readily we overlook evidence that we could be wrong. We're not tentative. Armed with only some of the facts—those that tend to support our case—we put misplaced faith in our judgments of others, being wrong more often than we realize.

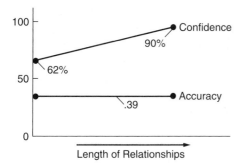

FIGURE 4.2. Accuracy and (over) confidence
in developing relationships.
At the beginning of their relationships, people felt
that they knew more about the sexual histories of
their new partners than they really did. Then, as
time went by, they became quite certain that they
were familiar with all the facts, when in truth, their
actual accuracy did not improve.
Data from Swann & Gill, 1997.

Now, of course, we come to know our partners better with time and experience. One of the hallmarks of intimacy is personal knowledge about a partner,
and first impressions certainly change as people gain familiarity with each
other. However—and this is the fundamental point we wish to make—*existing
beliefs are influential* at every stage of a relationship. Even flimsy first impressions typically change less easily than they logically should, because of the
manner in which they influence subsequent thinking. And what happens when
a relationship develops and you have a lot of information about an intimate
partner? These patterns continue. People may see what they want to see and
hold confident judgments that aren't always right.

Indeed, existing beliefs about lovers and friends are undoubtedly even
more powerful than first impressions about new acquaintances. The stakes are
higher, because interdependent intimacy means that emotions will be involved
(Berscheid & Ammazzalorso, 2001), and that makes things complex. In a close
relationship, each partner may be the other's "most knowledgeable *and* least
objective observer" (Sillars, 1985, p. 280). Despite knowing more about each
other than outsiders do, intimate partners' hopes and dreams may sometimes
make it hard for them to admit the truth.

For instance, who are the better judges of how long your current romantic
relationship will last, you or your parents? Remarkably, when university students, their roommates, and their parents were all asked to forecast the future of
the students' dating relationships, the parents made better predictions than the
students themselves, and the roommates did better still (MacDonald & Ross,
1999). You'd think that people would be the best judges of their own relationships, but the students focused on the strengths of their relationships and
ignored the weaknesses; as a result, they confidently and optimistically

predicted that the relationships would last longer than they usually did. Parents and roommates were more dispassionate and evenhanded, and although they were less confident in their predictions, they were more accurate in predicting what the future would hold. In fact, the most accurate predictions of all regarding the future of a heterosexual relationship often come from the friends of the woman involved (Loving, 2004). If her friends approve of a partnership, it's likely to continue (Sprecher & Felmlee, 2000), but if they think the relationship is doomed, it probably is (Agnew et al., 2001).

Thus, the same overconfidence, confirmatory biases, and preconceptions that complicate our perceptions of new acquaintances operate in established relationships as well. Obviously, we're not clueless about our relationships. When we thoughtfully evaluate our partnerships with a deliberate, cautious frame of mind, we make more accurate predictions about their futures than we do when we're in a romantic mood (Gagné & Lydon, 2001a). But it's hard to be dispassionate when we're devoted to a relationship and want it to continue (Gagné & Lydon, 2001b). When people are trying to keep their relationships intact, they are particularly prone to confirmation biases that support their optimistic misperceptions of their partners (Wilson et al., 2002).

So, our perceptions of our relationships are often less detached and straightforwardly accurate than we think they are. (See Box 4.1). And, for better or for worse, they have considerable impact on our subsequent feelings and behavior in our relationships, as we'll see in the section that follows.

BOX 4.1
Haste Makes Waste in Social Cognition

An important characteristic of social cognition in relationships is that a lot of it is done in a hurry, while we're engaged in interaction with others. People are at their best, making their most accurate judgments of others, when they can stop and think and analyze the available data in a deliberate, cautious way (Gilbert & Osborne, 1989). We make more mistakes when we hastily form snap judgments and then— because we are busy or distracted—we fail to double-check our reasoning (Gilbert, Krull, & Pelham, 1988). Unfortunately, social interaction is just the sort of task that can prevent people from carefully critiquing, and correcting, their erroneous impressions of others.

When we're thinking of what to say next, we're not wondering just how accurate our perceptions are, and mistakes in judgment can go unnoticed (Osborne & Gilbert, 1992). There's a big difference between being caught up in the middle of the action and standing off to the side, thoughtfully analyzing what's going on (Pontaria & Schlenker, 2000), and those in the middle of things may make more hurried errors. Thus, another reason why your roommates and friends are likely to be astute critics of your current relationship is because they may be pondering the interactions they witness between you and your partner more carefully than you do much of the time.

THE POWER OF PERCEPTIONS

Our judgments of our relationships and our partners seem to come to us naturally, as if there were only one reasonable way to view the situations we encounter. Little do we realize that we're often *choosing* to adopt the perspectives we use, and we facilitate or inhibit our satisfaction with our relationships by the choices we make.

Idealizing Our Partners

What are you looking for in an ideal romantic relationship? As we saw in chapter 3, most of us would like to have a partner who is warm and trustworthy, loyal and passionate, attractive and exciting, and rich and powerful, and our satisfaction with a lover depends on how well he or she approaches those ideals (Fletcher, 2002). What we usually get, however, is something less. How, then, do we ever stay happy with the real people we attract?

One way is to construct charitable, generous perceptions of our partners that emphasize their virtues and minimize their faults. People often judge their lovers with **positive illusions** that portray their partners in the best possible light (Holmes, 2004). Such "illusions" are a mix of realistic knowledge about a partner and an idealized vision of who a perfect partner should be. They do not ignore a partner's real liabilities; they just consider such faults to be less significant than other people perceive them to be (Murray & Holmes, 1999). For instance, satisfied spouses perceive their partners' deficiencies as circumscribed, specific drawbacks that are less important and influential than their many assets and advantages are (Neff & Karney, 2002, 2003). They also consider their partners' positive qualities to be rarer and more unique than their deficiencies, which are judged to be commonplace and routine (Goodfriend, 2004). So, committed lovers tend to have all the facts, but they interpret them differently than everyone else (Gagné & Lydon, 2003). They idealize their partners, judging them more positively than other people do, and even more positively than the partners judge themselves (Murray, Holmes, & Griffin, 1996a).

Isn't it a little dangerous to hold a lover in such high esteem? Won't people inevitably be disappointed when their partners fail to fulfill such positive perceptions? The answers may depend on just how unrealistic our positive illusions are. If we're genuinely fooling ourselves, imagining desirable qualities in a partner that he or she does not possess, we may be dooming ourselves to disillusionment (Miller, 1997b). Newlyweds do grow dissatisfied if they become aware that their new spouses fall too far short of their standards for an ideal spouse (Ruvolo & Veroff, 1997). On the other hand, if we're aware of all the facts but are merely interpreting them in a kind, benevolent fashion, such "illusions" can be very beneficial. When we idealize our partners, we're predisposed to judge their behavior in positive ways, and we are more willing to commit ourselves to maintaining the relationship (Murray, Holmes, & Griffin, 1996b; Gulliford et al., 2002). It bolsters our self-esteem to be loved by others who we perceive to be so desirable (Murray, Holmes, & Griffin, 2000). And we can slowly convince our partners that they actually are the wonderful people we believe them to be, as our high regard improves their self-esteem, too (Murray et al., 1996b). Add it all up, and idealized images of romantic partners are associated with greater satisfaction, love, and trust, and longer-lasting relationships as time goes by (Murray & Holmes, 1997).

In addition, there's a clever way in which we protect ourselves from disillusionment: Over time, as we come to know our partners well, we tend to revise our opinions of what we want in an ideal partner so that they fit the partners we've got (Fletcher, Simpson, & Thomas, 2000a). To a degree, we conveniently decide that the qualities our partners have are the ones we want.

Thus, by choosing to look on the bright side—perceiving our partners as the best they can be—and by editing our ideals and hopes so that they fit the realities we face, we can increase the chances that we'll be happy with our present partners. Our delight or distress is also affected by the manner in which we choose to explain the things our partners do, as we'll see next.

Attributional Processes

The explanations we generate for why things happen—and in particular why a person did or did not do something—are called **attributions.** An attribution identifies the causes of an event, emphasizing the impact of some influences and minimizing the role of others. Studies of such judgments are important, because there are usually several possible explanations for most events in our lives, and they can differ in meaningful ways. We can emphasize influences that are either *internal* to someone, such as the person's personality, ability, or effort, or *external*, implicating the situation or circumstances the person faces. For instance (as you've probably noticed), students who do well on exams typically attribute their success to internal causes (such as their preparation and talent), whereas those who do poorly blame their grades more on external factors (such as a tricky, unfair test) (Forsyth & Schlenker, 1977). The causes of events may also be rather *stable* and lasting, as our abilities are, or *unstable* and transient, such as moods that come and go. Even further, causes can be said to be *global*, affecting many situations in our lives, or *specific*, affecting only a few. With all of these distinctions in play, diverse explanations for a given event may be plausible. And in a close relationship, in which interdependent partners may *both* be partly responsible for much of what occurs, judgments of cause and effect can be especially complicated.

Nevertheless, three broad patterns routinely emerge from studies of attributions in relationships. First, despite their intimate knowledge of each other, partners are affected by robust **actor/observer effects:** They generate different explanations for their own behavior than they do for the similar actions they observe in their partners. This is a common phenomenon in social life (Krueger, Ham, & Linford, 1996). People are often acutely aware of the external pressures that have shaped their own behavior, so they make external attributions for themselves, but then they overlook how the same circumstances affect others, attributing others' behavior to internal sources such as their intentions and personality. What makes this phenomenon provocative in close relationships is that it leads the partners to overlook how *they* often personally provoke the behavior they observe in each other. During an argument, if one partner thinks, "she infuriates me so when she does that," the other is likely to be thinking, "he's so temperamental. He needs to learn to control himself." This bias is so pervasive, two people in almost any interaction are reasonably likely to agree about what each of them did but to disagree about why each of them did it (Robins et al., 2004). And to complicate things further, the two partners are unlikely to be aware of the discrepancies in their attributions; each person is likely to believe that the other sees things his or her way (Harvey, Wells, & Alvarez, 1978). When partners make a conscious effort to try to understand the other's point of view, the actor/observer discrepancy gets smaller (Arriaga & Rusbult, 1998), but it rarely vanishes completely (Malle & Pearce, 2001). The safest strategy is to assume that even your closest partners seldom comprehend all your reasons for doing what you do.

Second, despite genuine affection for each other, partners are also likely to display **self-serving biases** in which they try to take credit for their successes but avoid the blame for their failures. People like to feel responsible for the good things that happen to them, but they prefer external excuses when things go wrong. Thus, although they may not admit it to each other (Miller & Schlenker, 1985), partners are likely to believe that they personally deserve much of the credit when their relationships are going well, but they're not much to blame if a partnership is faltering (Thompson & Kelley, 1981). One quality that makes this phenomenon interesting is that people expect others to be self-serving, but they don't feel that they are themselves (Kruger & Gilovich, 1999). Most of us readily recognize overreaching ownership of success and flimsy excuses for failure when they come from other people, but we think that our own similar, self-serving perceptions are sensible and accurate (Pronin, Lin, & Ross, 2002). This occurs in part because we are aware of—and we give ourselves credit for—our own good intentions, even when we fail to follow through on them, but we judge other people only by what they do, and not what they may have intended to do (Kruger & Gilovich, 2004).

This is a provocative phenomenon, so let's consider how it works. Imagine that Fred goes to sleep thinking, "I bet Wilma would like breakfast in bed in the morning." He intends to do something special for her, and he proudly gives himself credit for being a thoughtful partner. But when he oversleeps and has to dash off to work without actually having done anything generous, he's likely to continue feeling good about himself: After all, he had kind intentions. In contrast, Wilma can only judge Fred by his actions; she's not a party to what he was thinking, and she has no evidence in this instance that he was thoughtful at all. Their different sources of information may lead Fred to consider himself a better, more considerate partner than Wilma (or anyone else) perceives him to be. (Remember those thank-you notes you were intending to write but never did? You probably give yourself some credit for wanting to get around to them, but all your disappointed grandmother knows is that she never got thanked and that you're behaving like an impolite ingrate!)

Subtle processes like these make self-serving explanations of events routine in social life. It's true that when they consider themselves a close couple, loving partners are less self-serving toward each other than they are with other people (Sedikides, et al., 1998). Nevertheless, self-serving biases exist even in contented relationships. In particular, when they fight with each other, spouses tend to believe that the argument is mostly their partner's fault (Schutz, 1999). And if they have extramarital affairs, people usually consider their own affairs to be innocuous dalliances, but they consider their spouse's affairs to be grievously hurtful (Buunk, 1987).

Thus, partners' idiosyncratic perspectives allow them to feel that they have better excuses for their mistakes than their friends and lovers do. They also tend to believe that their partners are the source of most disagreements and conflict. Most of us feel that *we're* pretty easy to live with, but *they're* hard to put up with sometimes. Such perceptions are undoubtedly influential, and, indeed, a third important pattern is that the general pattern of a couple's attributions helps determine how satisfied they will be with their relationship (Fincham, Harold, & Gano-Phillips, 2000). Happy people make attributions for their partners' behavior that are *relationship-enhancing*. Positive actions by the partner are judged to be intentional, habitual, and indicative of the partner's behavior in other situations; that is, happy couples make internal, stable, and global attributions for each other's positive behavior. They also tend to discount one another's transgressions, seeing them as accidental, unusual, and delimited; thus, negative behavior is excused with external, unstable, and specific attributions.

Through such attributions, satisfied partners magnify their partner's kindnesses and minimize their cruelties. But dissatisfied partners do just the opposite, exaggerating the bad and minimizing the good (Fincham, 2001). Unhappy people make *distress-maintaining* attributions that regard a partner's negative actions as deliberate and routine and positive behavior as unintended and accidental. (See Figure 4.3.) Thus, whereas satisfied partners judge each other in benevolent ways that are likely to keep them happy, distressed couples perceive each other in ways that may keep them dissatisfied no matter how each behaves. When distressed partners *are* nice to one another, each is likely to write off the other's thoughtfulness as a temporary, uncharacteristic lull in the negative routine (Holtzworth-Munroe & Jacobson, 1985). When kindnesses seem accidental and hurts seem deliberate, satisfaction is hard to come by.

Where does such a self-defeating pattern come from? People who are high in neuroticism are more likely than others to make distress-maintaining attributions, but disappointments of various sorts may cause anyone to gradually adopt a pessimistic perspective (Karney & Bradbury, 2000). One thing is clear: Maladaptive attributions can lead to cantankerous behavior and ineffective problem-solving (Bradbury & Fincham, 1992), and they can cause dissatisfaction that would not have occurred otherwise (Fincham & Bradbury, 1993; Horneffer & Fincham, 1996). Trust and contentment in a relationship lead partners to adopt relationship-enhancing attributions, but, in turn, such attributions also help produce greater trust and contentment (Fincham et al., 2000; Miller & Rempel, 2004). With various points of view at their disposal, people can choose

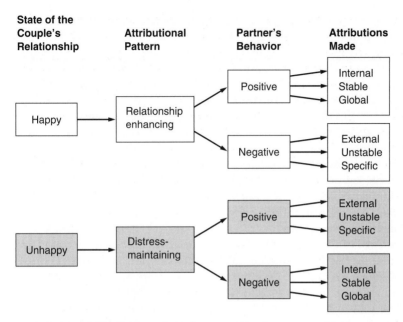

State of the Couple's Relationship	Attributional Pattern	Partner's Behavior	Attributions Made

FIGURE 4.3. Attributions made by happy and unhappy couples.
Source: Brehm & Kassin, 1990.

to explain a partner's behavior in ways that are endearing and forgiving, or pessimistic and pejorative—and the success of their relationship may ultimately hang in the balance.

Memories

Our perceptions of the current events in our relationships are obviously influential. So are our memories of the things that have happened in the past.

Most of us undoubtedly feel that our memories are faithful representations of past events. In particular, we're likely to trust vivid recollections because they seem so certain and detailed. But years of research (see Schacter, 1996) have clearly demonstrated that we edit and update even vivid memories as new events unfold, so that what we remember about the past is always a mix of what happened then and what we know now. Psychologists use the term **reconstructive memory** to describe the manner in which our memories are continually revised and rewritten as new information is obtained (Aronson, Wilson, & Akert, 2005).

Reconstructive memory influences our relationships. For one thing, partners' current feelings about each other influence what they remember about their shared past (McFarland & Ross, 1987). If they're presently happy, people tend to forget past disappointments; but if they're unhappy and their relationship is failing, they underestimate how happy and loving they used to be. These tricks of memory help us adjust to the situations we encounter, but they often leave us feeling that our relationships have always been more stable and predictable than they really were—and that can promote damaging overconfidence.

The good news is that by misremembering their past, partners can remain optimistic about their future. At any given point in time, contented lovers are likely to recall that they have had some problems in the past but that things have recently gotten better, so they are happier now than they used to be (Karney & Frye, 2002), and the future seems bright (Newby-Clark & Ross, 2003). What's notable about this pattern is that, if you follow couples over time, they'll tell you this over and over even when their satisfaction with each other is gradually eroding instead of increasing (Frye & Karney, 2004). Evidently, by remembering recent improvement in their partnerships that has not occurred, people remain happier than they might otherwise be.

In (re)constructing histories like these, partners in close relationships typically *work together* to construct vivid stories about their shared past that are richer and more detailed than the memories of either of them alone (Wegner, Erber, & Raymond, 1991). Each of them may be entrusted with the details of certain events, and their shared recollections may be quite extensive.

And those memories also set the stage for their joint reactions to new events. The stories partners tell about their history as a couple influence their interpretations of their subsequent real-life interactions (McGregor & Holmes, 1999). Remarkably, for instance, close inspection of partners' memories of their past together allowed researchers in one study (Buehlman, Gottman, & Katz, 1992) to accurately predict who would be divorced three years later! Those whose partnerships were in peril remembered the early years of their relationships less fondly than did those who were likely to stay together; they recalled more tumultuous courtships, less mutuality, and bigger disappointments when they finally married. Such memories probably reflected pasts that really were more difficult and less rewarding. Nevertheless, by rehearsing such memories *now*, those couples were clearly setting themselves up for further frustration in the future (McGregor & Holmes, 1999). Like other perceptions, the stories we recount and the memories we rehearse influence subsequent interpretations, emotions, and behavior in close relationships.

Relationship Beliefs

People also enter their partnerships with established beliefs about what relationships are like. These are organized in mental structures called *schemas* that provide a filing system for our knowledge about relationships and that, importantly, provide us with coherent assumptions about how they work (Baldwin, 1995). One set of interrelated beliefs that is often influential in our relationship schemas is **romanticism,** the view that love should be the most important basis for choosing a mate (Weaver & Ganong, 2004). Romanticism has several facets, and four of them can be found on a Romantic Beliefs Scale created by Susan Sprecher and Sandra Metts (1989): People high in romanticism believe that (a) their loves will be perfect; (b) each of us has only one perfect, "true" love;

TABLE 4.1. The Romantic Beliefs Scale

How romantic are you? Rate how much you agree or disagree with each of these statements by using this scale:

$$1 \quad 2 \quad 3 \quad 4 \quad 5 \quad 6 \quad 7$$

Strongly disagree   *Strongly agree*

1. I need to know someone for a period of time before I fall in love with him or her.

2. If I were in love with someone, I would commit myself to him or her even if my parents and friends disapproved of the relationship.

3. Once I experience "true love," I could never experience it again, to the same degree, with another person.

4. I believe that to be truly in love is to be in love forever.

5. If I love someone, I know I can make the relationship work, despite any obstacles.

6. When I find my "true love," I will probably know it soon after we meet.

7. I'm sure that every new thing I learn about the person I choose for a long-term commitment will please me.

8. The relationship I will have with my "true love" will be nearly perfect.

9. If I love someone, I will find a way for us to be together regardless of any opposition to the relationship, physical distance between us, or any other barrier.

10. There will be only one real love for me.

11. If a relationship I have was meant to be, any obstacle (such as lack of money, physical distance, or career conflicts) can be overcome.

12. I am likely to fall in love almost immediately if I meet the right person.

13. I expect that in my relationship, romantic love will really last; it won't fade with time.

14. The person I love will make a perfect romantic partner; for example, he/she will be completely accepting, loving, and understanding.

15. I believe if another person and I love each other we can overcome any differences and problems that may arise.

To get your score, *reverse* the rating you gave to Question 1. If you chose 2, change it to a 6; if you chose 3, make it a 5, and so on. (4 stays the same.) Then determine the *average* of your responses by adding them up and dividing by 15. The mean score for men (4.8) is higher than the mean for women (4.6), but typical scores range a point above and below those averages for each sex. If you're a man and your average rating is 5.8 or higher, you have a very romantic outlook; if your average is 3.8 or lower, you're less romantic than the average guy. For women, the similar scores are 5.6 and 3.6, respectively. From Sprecher & Metts, 1989.

(c) true love will find a way to overcome any obstacle; and (d) love is possible at first sight (see Table 4.1).

High scorers on the Romantic Beliefs Scale tend to experience more love, satisfaction, and commitment in their romantic relationships than low scorers do, but romanticism does not predict which relationships are likely to last over a four-year span (Sprecher & Metts, 1999). That's probably a good thing, because romanticism declines as the years go by, even in couples that stay together—and it drops a lot in partners who break up (Sprecher & Metts, 1999).

Romantic beliefs apparently provide a rosy glow that makes a partnership seem special, but they do not play a significant role in affecting the partners' behavior in their relationship.

The same cannot be said for some other beliefs that are clearly disadvantageous. Certain beliefs that people have about the nature of relationships are *dysfunctional*; that is, they appear to have adverse effects on the quality of relationships, making it less likely that the partners will be satisfied (Goodwin & Gaines, 2004). What ideas could people have that could have such deleterious effects? Here are six:

- Disagreements Are Destructive—Disagreements mean that my partner doesn't love me enough. If we loved each other sufficiently, we would never fight about anything.
- "Mindreading" Is Essential—People who really care about each other ought to be able to intuit each other's needs and preferences without being told what they are. My partner doesn't love me enough if I have to tell him or her what I want or need.
- Partners Cannot Change—Once things go wrong, they'll stay that way. If a lover hurts you once, he or she will hurt you again.
- Sex Should Be Perfect Every Time—Sex should always be wonderful and fulfilling if our love is pure. We should always want, and be ready for, sex.
- Men and Women Are Different—The personalities and needs of men and women are so dissimilar, you really can't understand someone of the other sex.
- Great Relationships Just Happen—You don't need to work at maintaining a good relationship. People are either compatible with each other and destined to be happy together or they're not.

Most of these beliefs were identified by Roy Eidelson and Norman Epstein (1982; Epstein & Eidelson, 1981) years ago, and since then several studies have shown that they put people at risk for distress and dissatisfaction in close relationships (Crohan, 1992; Fitzpatrick & Sollie, 1999b; Knee, 1998). They're unrealistic. They may even be "immature" (Noller, 1996). When disagreements do occur—as they always do—they seem momentous to people who hold these views (Cramer, 2004). Any dispute implies that their love is imperfect. Worse, people with these perspectives do not behave constructively when problems arise. Believing that people can't change and that true loves just happen, they don't try to solve problems, they just avoid them (Franiuk, Cohen, & Pomerantz, 2002), and they report more interest in ending the relationship than in making an effort to repair it (Knee, 1998).

In their work on relationship beliefs, Chip Knee and his colleagues refer to perspectives like these as **destiny** beliefs because they assume that two people are either well-suited for each other and destined to live happily ever after, or they're not (Knee, Patrick, & Lonsbary, 2003). Destiny beliefs take an inflexible view of intimate partnerships. They suggest that if two people are meant to be happy, they'll know it as soon as they meet; they'll not encounter early doubts or difficulties, and once two soulmates find each other, a happy future is assured.

BOX 4.2

Attachment Styles and Perceptions of Partners

Relationship beliefs may vary a lot from person to person, and another individual difference that's closely tied to the way people think about their partnerships is attachment style (Whisman & Allan, 1996). People with different attachment styles are thought to have different "mental models" of relationships; they hold different beliefs about what relationships are like, expect different behavior from their partners, and form different judgments of what their partners do. In particular, people with secure styles are less likely than avoidant or anxious/ambivalent people to hold maladaptive relationship beliefs (Stackert & Bursik, 2003), and they're more likely to employ relationship-enhancing attributions (Sümer & Cozzarelli, 2004). Secure people trust their partners more (Mikulincer, 1998), believe that their partners are more supportive (Collins & Feeney, 2004), and have more positive expectations about what the future holds (Rowe & Carnelley, 2003); they're also

more likely than insecure people to remember positive things that have happened in the past (Miller & Noirot, 1999). Secure people form positive judgments of others more readily than avoidant people do, but they're also less likely to jump to conclusions about others than anxious people are (Zhang & Hazan, 2002). In general, then, people with secure styles are more generous, optimistic, and kindly in their judgments of others than insecure people are.

Attachment styles *can* change, as we noted in chapter 1, but no matter what style people have, they tend to remember past events and their past perspectives on relationships as being consistent with what they're thinking *now* (Feeney & Cassidy, 2003; Scharfe & Bartholomew, 1998). Happily, if positive experiences in a rewarding relationship help us gradually develop a more relaxed and trusting outlook on intimacy with others, we may slowly forget that we ever felt any other way.

Alternative perspectives known as **growth** beliefs take a different view (Knee et al., 2003). Growth beliefs assume that happy relationships are the result of hard work. Good relationships are believed to develop gradually as the partners work at surmounting challenges and overcoming obstacles, and a basic presumption is that with enough effort, almost any relationship can succeed.

As you might expect, these different views of relationships generate different outcomes when difficulties arise. When couples argue or a partner misbehaves, people who hold growth beliefs remain more committed to the relationship and more optimistic that any damage can be repaired than do those who do not hold such views (Knee et al., 2004; Lomore & Cohen, 2002). And people who hold growth beliefs can discuss their lovers' imperfections with equanimity; in contrast, people who hold destiny beliefs get hostile when they are asked to confront their partners' deficiencies (Knee et al., 2001).

Clearly, some relationship beliefs are more adaptive than others (Fitzpatrick & Sollie, 1999b). Left to themselves, these perspectives tend to be stable and lasting (Franiuk et al., 2002), but they can change with education and insight

(Sharp & Ganong, 2000). Indeed, if you recognize any of your own views in the preceding list of destiny-related beliefs, we hope that these data are enlightening. Unrealistic assumptions can be so idealistic and starry-eyed that no relationship measures up to them, and distress and disappointment are certain to follow.

Expectations

Relationship beliefs are global assumptions about the nature of intimate partnerships, and when they're false (as dysfunctional relationship beliefs are), they *stay* false. In contrast, people can also have more specific expectations about the behavior of others that are initially false but that become true (Madon et al., 2003; Rosenthal, 2003). We're referring here to **self-fulfilling prophecies,** which are false predictions that become true because they lead people to behave in ways that make the erroneous expectations come true. Self-fulfilling prophecies are extraordinary examples of the power of perceptions, because the events that result from them occur only because people expect them to, and then act as if they will.

Let's examine Figure 4.4 together to detail how this process works. In a first step in a self-fulfilling prophecy, a person who we'll call the *perceiver forms an expectancy* about someone else—the *target*—that predicts how the target will behave. Various information about the target, such as his or her age, sex, race, physical attractiveness, or social class may affect the perceiver's judgments in ways of which the perceiver is unaware.

Then, in an important second step, the *perceiver acts,* usually in a fashion that is in accord with his or her expectations. Indeed, it may be hard for the perceiver to avoid subtly communicating what he or she really thinks about the target (Biesanz et al., 2001). Perceivers with favorable expectations, for instance, interact longer and more often with their targets, sharing more eye contact, sitting closer, smiling more, asking more questions, and encouraging more responses than do perceivers who have less positive expectations (Harris & Rosenthal, 1985).

The recipient of the perceiver's behavior is likely to notice all of this, and the *target's interpretation* will influence his or her response (Stukas & Snyder, 2002). In most cases, however, when the *target responds* in the fourth step, it will be in a manner that is similar to the perceiver's behavior toward him or her. Enthusiasm is usually met with interest (Snyder, Tanke, & Berscheid, 1977), hostility with counterattacks (Snyder & Swann, 1978a), and flirtatiousness with allurement (Ridge & Reber, 2002). Thus, the perceiver usually elicits from the target the behavior he or she expected, and that may be nothing like the way the target would have behaved if the perceiver hadn't gone looking for it.

But such is the nature of a self-fulfilling prophecy that, as the *perceiver interprets* the target's response in the last step in the process, the perceiver is unlikely to recognize the role that he or she played in producing it (McNulty & Karney, 2002). The actor-observer effect will lead the perceiver to attribute the target's behavior to the target's personality or mood. And after all, the perceiver found in the target the behavior he or she expected; what better evidence is there that the perceiver's expectations were correct? (This is another reason why we tend

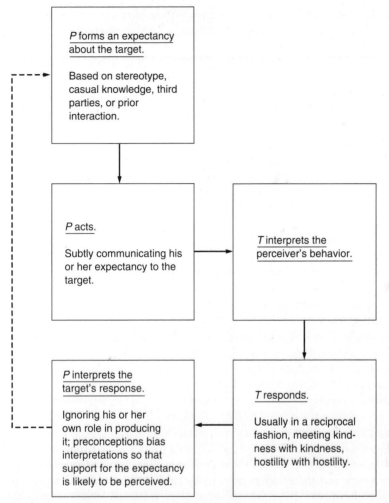

FIGURE 4.4. A self-fulfilling prophecy.
Originally false expectations in a perceiver (*P*) can seem to come true
when he or she interacts with the target (*T*).
Source: Leary & Miller, 1986.

to be overconfident in our judgments of others; when we make our false expectations come true, we never realize that we were ever wrong.)

Here, then, is another fundamental reason why our perceptions of others are so influential. They not only influence our interpretations of the information we gain, they guide our behavior toward others, too. We often get what we expect from others, and that is sometimes behavior that would not have occurred without our prompting—but we're rarely aware of how our expectations have created their own realities.

Mark Snyder and his colleagues (1977) provided an elegant example of this when they led men at the University of Minnesota to believe that they were chatting on the phone with women who were either very attractive or quite unattractive. The experimenters gave each man a fake photograph of the woman with whom he'd be getting acquainted and then recorded the ensuing conversations to see what happened. The men had higher expectations when they thought they'd be talking to gorgeous women than they did when they anticipated a conversation with a plain partner, and they were much more eager and interested when the interactions began; listeners rated them, for instance, as more sociable, warm, outgoing, bold, and socially adept. The men's (often erroneous) judgments of the women were clearly reflected in their behavior toward them. How did the women respond to such treatment? They had no knowledge of having been labeled as gorgeous or homely, but they did know that they were talking to a man who sounded either enthusiastic or aloof. As a result, the men got what they expected: The women who were presumed to be attractive really did sound more alluring, reacting to their obviously interested partners with warmth and appeal of their own. By comparison, the women who talked with the relatively detached men who thought they were unattractive sounded pretty drab. In both cases, the men got out of the women the behavior they expected, whether or not their expectations were accurate.

Because they guide our actions toward others, our expectations are not inert. Another fascinating example of this was obtained when researchers sent people to chat with strangers after leading them to expect that the strangers would probably either like or dislike them (Curtis & Miller, 1986). Participants in the study were told that, in order to study different types of interactions, the researchers had given a stranger bogus advance information about them, and they could anticipate either a friendly or unfriendly reaction from the stranger when they met. In truth, however, none of the strangers had been told anything at all about the participants, and the false expectations that the interaction would go well or poorly existed only in the minds of the participants themselves. (Imagine yourself in this intriguing position: You *think* someone you're about to meet already likes or dislikes you, but the other person really doesn't know anything about you at all.) What happened? People got what they expected. Expecting to be liked, people greeted others in an engaging, open, positive way—they behaved in a likeable manner—and really *were* liked by the strangers they met. However, those who expected to be disliked were cautious and defensive and were much less forthcoming, and they actually got their partners to dislike them. Once again, false expectations created their own behavioral reality—and positive expectations were beneficial and advantageous, but negative expectations were not.

Indeed, over time, people who chronically hold different sorts of expectations about others may create different sorts of social worlds for themselves (Reich, 2004). For instance, a program of research by Geraldine Downey has demonstrated that people who tend to worry about rejection from others often behave in ways that make such rejection more likely (Levy, Ayduk, & Downey, 2001). People who are high in *rejection sensitivity* tend to anxiously perceive snubs from others when none are intended (Downey et al., 1998). Then they overreact, fearfully displaying more hostility (Ayduk et al., 1999) and resorting to more aggression (Downey, Feldman, & Ayduk, 2000) than others would.

BOX 4.3

Nonconscious Social Cognition

If we stop and think, we can recognize most of the elements of social cognition that we have discussed so far. Some attributions, beliefs, and expectations may be habitual so that they operate almost automatically without any deliberation or contemplation. But they are still conscious processes: If we turn our attention to them, we can identify them, and we know they're at work.

Our close relationships can have some effects on us, however, of which we are completely unaware. We can learn lessons from our intimate connections to others that influence our actions later on in ways that we may never notice (Andersen & Chen, 2002).

For instance, particular relationships with others are sometimes characterized by recurring themes; your father, for example, may have constantly urged you to get good grades in school. Now, if something subtly reminds you of your father (and you like him), you may persevere longer at a difficult task than you would have had you not been reminded of him (Fitzsimons & Bargh, 2003). You may act as if your father were standing behind you, urging you on. What makes this provocative is that the "reminder" can be his name flashed in front of your eyes so quickly that you cannot be sure what you saw (Shah, 2003). In such a case, you may have no conscious thought of your Dad and may

not realize that you've been subliminally reminded of him, but your past experiences with him may guide your present behavior, nevertheless.

We can unwittingly import old experiences into our new relationships, too. When the new people we meet resemble past partners who treated us badly, we may unintentionally behave more coolly toward them without realizing it. Those actions may elicit less friendly reactions from our new acquaintances, and we may begin to create another unpleasant relationship that resembles our unhappy past experience without our past partners ever coming consciously to mind (Berk & Andersen, 2000).

Happily, nonconscious influences can work for us, too. If a new acquaintance resembles someone with whom you shared good times, your interactions may get off to an especially good start. Although you may not consciously be reminded of your prior partner, you may, without meaning to, be warmer, more cheerful, and more sociable than you usually are (Chen & Andersen, 2003).

Thus, we're not aware of all the ways that our memories and expectations can influence our social outcomes. Without our knowledge, some events can trigger nonconscious tendencies learned in past relationships that we do not even know to exist.

Their behavior is obnoxious, and as a result, both they and their partners tend to be dissatisfied with their close relationships (Downey & Feldman, 1996).

Misplaced expectations can even prevent relationships from ever getting started. When people want to initiate a romantic relationship but are shyly reluctant to make the first move, they're usually painfully aware of their own fear of rejection that keeps them from acting. However, if their potential partners behave in exactly the same way and wait for them to act, they assume that the others' passivity indicates a lack of interest in developing a relationship with them (Vorauer & Ratner, 1996). The occasional result is that nobody makes the first move, although both potential partners secretly wish the other would. Evidently, false expectations that others won't like us are especially likely to come true.

With time and experience, we undoubtedly learn the truth about some of our false expectations about others. In particular, some prophecies that initially fulfill themselves can dissipate over time as people become more familiar with each other (Smith, Jussim, & Eccles, 1999). On the other hand, some self-fulfilling prophecies can persist for years if people continue to act in accord with their early expectations (Smith et al., 1999). Altogether, then, our perceptions of our partners, the attributions we make, and the beliefs and expectations we bring to our relationships may exert a powerful influence on the events that follow. Our judgments of each other matter (Holmes, 2002). And those of us who expect others to be trustworthy, generous, and loving may find that others actually *are* good to us more often than those with more pessimistic perspectives find others being kind to them.

Self-Perceptions

A last example of the power of our perceptions lies in the judgments we form of *ourselves*. Our discussion of self-esteem in chapter 1 noted that our self-evaluations are potent influences on our interactions. People who have high self-esteem are usually confident that their friendly overtures toward others will be met with warmth in return, but people with low self-esteem are less certain that they can get others to like them (Baldwin & Keelan, 1999). Consequently, people who doubt themselves tend to doubt their intimate partners, and they are typically less secure in their relationships than are people with higher self-esteem (Murray et al., 1998).

But self-esteem is just one part of our broader **self-concepts,** which encompass all of the beliefs and feelings we have about ourselves. Our self-concepts include a wide array of self-knowledge along with our self-esteem, and all the components of the self-concept are intimately tied to our relationships with others.

During social interaction, our self-concepts try to fulfill two different functions (Sedikides & Strube, 1997). On the one hand, people seek feedback from others that will *enhance* their self-concepts and allow them to think of themselves as desirable, attractive, competent people. We like to hear good things about ourselves, and we try to associate with others who will help us support positive self-images.

On the other hand, because it's unsettling to encounter information that contradicts our beliefs, we also want feedback that sustains our existing self-concepts (Swann, 1997). For better or worse, our self-concepts play vital roles in organizing our views of the world; they make life predictable and support coherent expectations about what each day will bring. Without a stable, steady self-concept, social life would be a confusing, chaotic jumble, and being constantly confronted with information that contradicts our self-images would be unnerving. For that reason, people also seek feedback from others that is consistent with what they already think about themselves and that *verifies* their existing self-concepts (Sanitioso & Wlodarski, 2004).

These two motives, **self-enhancement** and **self-verification,** go hand-in-hand for people who like themselves and have positive self-concepts. When such people associate with others who compliment and praise them, they receive feedback that is simultaneously self-enhancing and self-verifying. But life is more complex for people who genuinely consider themselves to be unskilled and unlovable. Positive evaluations from others make them feel good but threaten their negative self-images; negative feedback and criticism affirm their self-concepts but feel bad.

How do both motives coexist in people with negative self-concepts? One answer is that people with poor self-concepts like praise for specific talents that are important to them, but they prefer self-verifying feedback about their general worth (Bosson & Swann, 2001; Neff & Karney, 2002). People seem to like uplifting compliments here and there as long as they don't contradict people's broader self-conceptions. Self-enhancement also appears to be an automatic, relatively nonconscious response that is primarily emotional, whereas self-verification emerges from deliberate and conscious cognition. What this means is that people with poor self-concepts *like* praise and compliments from others, but once they get a chance to *think* about them, they don't believe or trust such feedback (Swann et al., 1990).

Okay, so what? The relevance of these phenomena to the study of relationships lies in the fact that if people are choosing relationship partners carefully, they'll seek intimate partners who *support their existing self-concepts,* good or bad (Katz & Joiner, 2002). Here's an example: Imagine that after a semester of sharing a double room in a college dorm, you're asked if you want to change roommates. You have a positive self-concept, and your roommate likes you and tells you so. Do you want to leave? Probably not. But if your roommate *dis*liked you and constantly disparaged you, you'd probably want out. You'd not want to live with someone who disagreed with you about who you are because it would be wearying and unpleasant to have to face such a contrary point of view all the time.

Now imagine that you have a lousy self-concept and you're paired with a roommate who compliments you all the time. Such praise is self-enhancing and feels great, and you want more, right? Wrong. The motive to protect and maintain our existing self-concepts is so strong that people with negative self-concepts want to *escape* roommates who like and approve of them; they'd rather have roommates who dislike them (Swann & Pelham, 2002). Such disapproval is unpleasant, but at least it reassures the recipients that the world is a predictable place.

Things get more complicated in romantic relationships. When people choose dating partners, self-enhancement is an important motive; everybody seeks partners who like and accept them. Thus, even people with poor self-concepts pursue casual partners who provide positive feedback (Katz & Beach, 2000; Swann, Bosson, & Pelham, 2002). However, in more interdependent, committed relationships such as marriage, self-verification rises to the fore—a phenomenon called the *marriage shift*—and people want feedback that supports their self-concepts (Swann, De La Ronde, & Hixon, 1994). If people with negative self-images find themselves married to spouses who praise and appreciate them, they'll gradually find ways to avoid their spouses as much as possible:

> Imagine a man who receives what he construes to be undeserved praise from his wife. Although such praise may make him feel optimistic and happy at first, the positive glow will recede if he concludes that his wife could not possibly believe what she said. . . . [or] he may decide that she is a fool. In either case, overly favorably evaluations from someone who knows one well may foster a sense of uneasiness, inauthenticity, and distrust of the person who delivered them. (*Swann, 1996, p. 118*)

BOX 4.4
Narcissism and Relationships

A negative self-concept can evidently have an adverse impact on one's relationships, but an overly positive self-concept can be problematic, too. Narcissists possess highly inflated, unrealistic perceptions of their talents, desirability, and self-worth. Their self-perceptions are grandiose (Rhodewalt & Sorrow, 2003), and they exhibit patterns of social cognition that have important implications for their relationships.

First, they're prone to strong self-serving biases (Stucke, 2003); if things go well, they want all the credit, but if things go wrong, they will accept none of the blame. They also have biased memories of others' reactions to them; they remember more acceptance and approval than they actually received (Rhodewalt & Eddings, 2002), but still tend to think that others don't treat them as well as they should (McCullough et al., 2003). Indeed, rejection from others is particularly hard for them to tolerate; their excessive pride leads them to overreact to imagined slights from others. Being full of themselves, they feel cruelly wronged when they judge that people are disrespectful or uncaring, so they react more angrily and aggressively than others would

(Twenge & Campbell, 2003). Male narcissists are also more approving than other men of the idea of raping a woman who changes her mind and turns them down (Bushman et al., 2003).

Furthermore, when they enter close relationships, they are chronically less committed to their romantic partners than other people are (Campbell, Foster, & Finkel, 2002). Their arrogant sense of entitlement leads them to stay on the prowl, looking for more desirable partners than the ones they have (Campbell & Foster, 2002). They work less hard to please their current partners and constantly think they deserve "better."

Narcissists obviously make rather poor partners, but it is sometimes surprisingly hard for all the rest of us to see that at first (Hotchkiss, 2003). Early on, their self-assurance may be appealing, and it often takes time to realize how selfish and exploitative and touchy they really are. Thus, narcissism often takes the form of a "fatal attraction;" it may be attractive at first but deadly in the long run (Brunell et al., 2004), and it presents a challenge to us to be as discerning and perceptive in our judgments of potential partners as we can possibly be.

On the other hand, if their spouses belittle them, people with negative self-concepts will stay close at hand. (And of course, it's the other way around for those who have positive self-concepts.)

Overall, then, our self-concepts help direct our choices of intimate partners. Approval and acceptance from others is always pleasant, but in meaningful relationships over the long haul, people prefer reactions from others that confirm what they think of themselves. And that means that although most of us will be most content with spouses who uplift us, people with negative self-concepts will not.[1]

IMPRESSION MANAGEMENT

Others' impressions of us are obviously very important. And because they are, we often try to control the information that others receive about us. We sometimes try to make deliberate impressions on others, choosing our words, our apparel, our settings, and even our associates carefully to present a certain public image. On other occasions, when we're not consciously pursuing a particular impression, we often fall into habitual patterns of behavior that portray us in ways that have elicited desirable responses from others in the past (Schlenker, 2003). So, whether or not we're thinking about it, we're often engaging in **impression management,** trying to influence the impressions of us that others form.

This is a significant idea for at least two reasons. First, nearly anything we do in the presence of others may be strategically regulated in the service of impression management. People are much more likely to wash their hands in a public restroom when others are present than they are when they believe they are completely alone (Munger & Harris, 1989). Women will eat less on a date with an attractive man than they would have eaten had they been out with their girlfriends (Pliner & Chaiken, 1990). Both men (Morier & Seroy, 1994) and women (Zanna & Pack, 1975) will edit what they say about themselves to appear compatible with an attractive member of the other sex, but they won't go to such trouble for undesirable people who they're not trying to impress. And because people like to advertise their association with winners, college students often wear school insignia to class on Mondays if their football team wins its game on the previous Saturday—but those clothes stay at home if the team loses (Cialdini et al., 1976).

A second reason why impression management is an important concept is that it is a pervasive influence on social life. Others' evaluations of us are eventful, and when we are in the presence of others, we are rarely unconcerned about

[1]Of course, self-concepts can change, and the ease with which they do depends on the certainty with which they are held (Swann & Ely, 1984). The good news is that if you suspect you're a nincompoop but aren't really sure, positive feedback from an adoring lover may change your self-image rather quickly as you enjoy, and come to believe, what your partner says. The bad news is that if you're quite sure you're unworthy, you'll feel more at home around those who know you well enough to take you as you are—that is, those who *agree* that you're unworthy.

what they may be thinking of us (Miller, 1996). By providing a means with which we can influence others' judgments, impression management increases our chances of accomplishing our interpersonal objectives. And there's rarely anything dishonest going on; impression management is seldom deceitful or duplicitous. To the contrary, although people do occasionally misrepresent themselves through lying and pretense, most impression management involves revealing—perhaps in a selective fashion—one's real attributes to others (Leary, 1995; Schlenker, 2003). By announcing some of their attitudes but not mentioning others, for example, people may appear to have something in common with almost anyone they meet; this simple tactic of impression management facilitates graceful and rewarding social interaction and does not involve untruthfulness at all. Because frauds and cheats are rejected by others, people seldom pretend to be things they are not.

Strategies of Impression Management

Nevertheless, because most of us have diverse interests and talents, there may be many distinct impressions we can honestly attempt to create, and we may seek different images in different situations. Indeed, there are four different strategies of impression management people routinely use (Jones & Pittman, 1982). We use **ingratiation** when we seek acceptance and liking from others; we do favors, pay compliments, mention areas of agreement, describe ourselves in desirable ways, and are generally charming in order to get others to like us. Ingratiation is a common form of impression management in developing romances (Honeycutt et al., 1998; Pataki & Clark, 2004), and as long as such efforts are not transparently manipulative or "slimy" (Marchand & Vonk, 2004; Vonk, 1998), they usually do elicit favorable reactions from others (Gordon, 1996).

On other occasions, when we wish our abilities to be recognized and respected by others, we may engage in **self-promotion,** recounting our accomplishments or strategically arranging public demonstrations of our skills. Self-promotion is a preferred strategy of impression management during job interviews (Stevens & Kristof, 1995), but even in settings like those, vigorous self-promotion can be risky for women because it makes them seem "unladylike" (Rudman, 1998). Indeed, men boast about their accomplishments to their friends more than women do (Dolgin & Minowa, 1997), but both men and women tend to be more modest among friends than they are around strangers (Tice et al., 1995).

Both ingratiation and self-promotion create socially desirable impressions, but other strategies create *un*desirable images. Through **intimidation,** people portray themselves as ruthless, dangerous, and menacing so that others will do their bidding. Such behavior is obnoxious and tends to drive others away, but if it's used only occasionally—or if the recipients are children or impoverished spouses with no place else to go—intimidation may get people what they want. Finally, using the strategy of **supplication,** people sometimes present themselves as inept or infirm in order to avoid obligations and elicit help and support from others. People who claim that they're "just too tired" to do the dishes after a "hard day at work" are engaging in supplication. Most people avoid using intimidation and supplication if the other strategies work for them because most of us prefer to be liked and respected rather than feared or pitied. But almost everyone uses intimidation and supplication occasionally. If you've ever made a point of showing a partner that you were angry about something, or sad about something else, in order to get your way, you were using intimidation and supplication, respectively (Clark, Pataki, & Carver, 1996).

Impression Management in Close Relationships

There are three specific features of impression management with intimate partners that are worthy of mention. First, although the impressions we make on our friends and lovers are much more influential than the images we create for acquaintances or strangers, we usually go to *less* trouble to maintain favorable images for our intimate partners than we do for others. We worry less about how we're coming across, and try less hard to appear likeable and competent all the time (Guerrero, 1997; Leary et al., 1994). For instance, the longer people have known their partners, the less time they spend preening and grooming themselves in the restroom during a dinner date (Daly et al., 1983). In general, we tend to the images we present to intimate partners less attentively than we do to the impressions we make on others, and there may be several reasons why (Leary & Miller, 2000). For one thing, we know our friends and lovers like us, so there's less motivation to be charming to win their approval. Also, because they know us well, there's less we can do to have much effect on what they think. However, it's also likely that people simply get lazy. Being on one's best behavior requires concentration and effort. Polite behavior usually involves some form of self-restraint. We can relax around those who already know and love us, but that means that people are often much cruder with intimate partners than they are with anyone else they know (Miller, 1997b). People who are very decorous early in a relationship—who would never show up for breakfast without being showered and dressed—often become spouses who sit at the table in their underwear, unwashed, scratching and picking, pilfering the last doughnut. This is ironic. Having behaved beautifully to win the love of a romantic partner, some of us never work at being so charming to that lover ever again. (And this may be a big problem in many relationships, as we'll see in chapter 6.)

A second interesting aspect of impression management, once a relationship develops, is that people often take pains to create desired public images of their *partners.* For instance, imagine that you are describing a friend to someone of the other sex who your friend finds very attractive, and you know this person's preferences for what he or she is looking for in an ideal date. What would you say about your friend? Faced with this situation, most people describe their friends in a way that fits the preferences of the attractive listener (Pontari & Dockery, 2004). On the other hand, if the listener is *un*attractive, people helpfully describe a friend as being *in*compatible with the listener, implicitly suggesting that the friend is "not your type" (Schlenker & Britt, 1999). In general, the closer a relationship, the more people treat their partners' images as if they were their own, taking the time to make their partners look good whenever possible (Pontari & Schlenker, 2004).

People may also go to some lengths to present a particular image of their relationships to others. Early on, the big decision is often whether or not to admit that a relationship even exists; college students are especially likely to conceal a relationship from their parents, usually because they wish to avoid comments and criticism (Baxter & Widenmann, 1993). Thereafter, once their partnership is established and acknowledged, the partners may collaborate to construct a particular public image of their relationship. One common example is the effort to hide spats and squabbles from others; couples who have bickered all the way to a party may "put on a happy face" and pretend to be perfectly happy once they arrive. People seem generally aware that the public images of their partners and their relationships do reflect on their own personal images to some extent.

Finally, there are individual differences in people's motives to manage their impressions that may have meaningful effects on the patterns of their relationships (Nezlek & Leary, 2002). As we saw in chapter 3, for instance, people who are high in the trait of **self-monitoring** are adept at adjusting their behavior to fit the varying norms of different situations (Gangestad & Snyder, 2000). By comparison, low self-monitors seem less attentive to social norms and are less flexible, making the same stable impressions even when they're not appropriate to the situation. Thus, high self-monitors are more changeable and energetic impression managers.

These different styles lead to different networks of friends. Because they can deftly switch images from one audience to the next, high self-monitors tend to have more friends than low self-monitors do, but they have less in common with each of them.[2] High self-monitors often surround themselves with "activity specialists," partners who are great companions for some particular pleasure—such as a "tennis buddy" or "ballet friend"—but with whom they are not compatible in other respects (Snyder, Gangestad, & Simpson, 1983). High self-monitors are skilled at steering clear of the topics that would cause dispute, and the specialist friends allow them to really enjoy those activities—but if they threw a party and invited all those friends, very different people who have little in common with each other would show up. By comparison, low self-monitors must search harder for partners with whom they are more similar across the board. If low self-monitors had all their friends over, relatively few people would come, but they'd all be a lot alike.

These differences in style appear to be consequential as time goes by. When they first meet others, high self-monitors enjoy interactions of higher intimacy than low self-monitors do; they're skilled at finding common ground for a conversation and are good at small talk (Snyder & Simpson, 1984). They can also feign interest in other people better than low self-monitors can (Leck &

---

[2]We should note that this and the following distinctions between high and low self-monitors are based on comparisons of the *highest* self-monitors, the 25 percent of us with the very highest scores, to the *lowest* self-monitors, the 25 percent of us with the lowest scores. Researchers sometimes do this to study the possible effects of a personality trait as plainly as possible, but you should recognize that half of us, those with scores ranging from somewhat below average to somewhat above, fall in between the examples being described here.

Simpson, 1999). Being able impression managers seems to help them to interact comfortably with a wide variety of people. On the other hand, they invest less of their time in each of their friends, so that they tend to have shorter, somewhat less committed relationships than low self-monitors do (Snyder & Simpson, 1987). The interactive advantage enjoyed by high self-monitors when a relationship is just beginning may become a small liability once the relationship is well established.

Altogether, then, the greater attentiveness to social images shown by high self-monitors seems to influence the partners they choose (see chapter 3) and the relationships they form. Would you rather be high or low on this trait? You can determine your own self-monitoring score using the scale in Table 4.2. Just remember that only very high and very low scorers closely fit the portraits we've drawn here.

TABLE 4.2. The Self-Monitoring Scale

Is each of the following statements true or false?

1. I find it hard to imitate the behavior of other people.
2. At parties or social gatherings, I do not attempt to say or do things that others will like.
3. I can only argue for ideas that I already believe.
4. I can make impromptu speeches even on topics about which I have almost no information.
5. I guess I put on a show to impress or entertain others.
6. I would probably make a good actor.
7. In a group I am rarely the center of attention.
8. In different situations and with different people I often act like very different persons.
9. I am not particularly good at making other people like me.
10. I'm not always the person I appear to be.
11. I would not change my opinions (or the way I do things) in order to please someone.
12. I have considered being an entertainer.
13. I have never been good at games like charades or improvisational acting.
14. I have trouble changing my behavior to suit different people and different situations.
15. At a party I let others keep the jokes and stories going.
16. I feel a bit awkward in public and do not show up quite as well as I should.
17. I can look anyone in the eye and tell a lie (if for a right end).
18. I may deceive people by being friendly when I really dislike them.

Give yourself a point for each of these statements that were *true* of you: 4, 5, 6, 8, 10, 12, 17, 18.
Then give yourself a point for each of these statements that were *false*: 1, 2, 3, 7, 9, 11, 13, 14, 15, 16.
What's your total score? If it's 13 or higher, you're a relatively high self-monitor. If it's 7 or lower, you're a relatively low self-monitor (Snyder, 1987). Scores between 7 and 13 are average.

Source for scale: Snyder, M., & Gangestad, S. (1986). On the nature of self-monitoring: Matters of assessment, matters of validity. *Journal of Personality and Social Psychology, 51,* 125–139.

SO, JUST HOW WELL DO WE KNOW OUR PARTNERS?

Let's add up the elements of social cognition we've encountered in this chapter. In a close relationship, partners may hold idealized but overconfident perceptions of each other, and when they act in accord with those judgments, they may elicit behavior from each other that fits their expectations but which would not have otherwise occurred. Moreover, right or wrong, they are likely to interpret one another's actions in ways that fit their existing preconceptions. Combined with all this are the partners' efforts to adjust their behavior so that they make the impressions on each other that they want to make. Evidently, there are various processes at work in intimate partnerships that cause us to see in our partners those attributes and motives that we expect or want (or that *they* want us) to see. How accurate, then, are our perceptions of our partners? How well do we know them?

The simple answer is, "not as well as we think we do" (Sillars, 1998). We often accurately recognize traits in our partners that have big effects on our relationships (Gill & Swann, 2004), but as we saw in chapter 3, we routinely perceive our partners to be more like us than they really are. We believe that they agree with us more often than they really do (Kenny & Acitelli, 2001; Sillars et al., 1994), and we overestimate how similar their personality traits are to our own (Murray et al., 2000; Watson, 2000). As a result, we feel that we understand them, and they understand us, more than is actually the case (Acitelli, Kenny, & Weiner, 2001; Pronin, Gilovich, & Ross, 2004). Such misperceptions are not disadvantageous. Indeed, the more similarity and understanding we perceive in our partners, the more satisfying our relationships with them tend to be (Murray et al., 2000). Still, we misunderstand our partners more than we realize. To a degree, our perceptions of our partners are fictions that portray our partners as people they are not.

There are several factors that determine just how (in)accurate our judgments are. Interpersonal perception depends both on the people involved and on the situation they face.

Knowledge

The conclusion that we don't know our partners as well as we think we do isn't inconsistent with the fact that intimate partners have a great deal of factual knowledge about one another. As their relationship develops and they spend more time together, two people do come to understand each other better (Colvin, Vogt, & Ickes, 1997; Kurtz & Sherker, 2003). Married people perceive each other more accurately than dating couples or friends do (Watson et al., 2000b), and acquaintances judge each other more accurately than strangers do (Funder, Kolar, & Blackman, 1995). Intimate partners interact often and have detailed knowledge about each other—and, as we saw in chapter 3, they really are likely to have a lot in common—and all of these influences may contribute to accuracy (Stinson & Ickes, 1992).

Motivation

However, our perceptions of others don't necessarily become more accurate as time goes by (Park, Kraus, & Ryan, 1997). One study found that the length of time two people had known each other didn't predict how accurate they would be, but the length of time they had been living together did (Bernieri et al., 1994). Furthermore, other studies have found that spouses who have been married for *shorter* lengths of time do better at inferring what their partners are thinking than more experienced spouses do (Kilpatrick, Bissonnette, & Rusbult, 2002; Thomas, Fletcher, & Lange, 1997). Evidently, the interest and motivation with which we try to figure each other out help determine how insightful and accurate we will be (Graham & Ickes, 1997; Thomas & Fletcher, 1997), and people who have recently moved in with each other (who are presumably highly motivated to understand each other) may understand each other as well as they ever will. But longer periods of very close contact, such as marriage, seem to gradually result in less, not more, accuracy as time goes by (Ickes, 2003).

In general, women spend more time thinking carefully about their relationships than men do (Acitelli & Young, 1996). Both men and women may analyze their new relationships carefully, but women tend to ponder their partnerships more thoughtfully once they are established (Acitelli, 2001). And remarkably, they may be more astute during certain phases of their menstrual cycles: Women judge the strength and dominance of men more quickly and effortlessly when they are fertile—that is, just before they ovulate each month—than when they are not (Macrae et al., 2002).

But are women generally better judges of others than men are? The evidence bearing on this question is mixed (Ickes, 2003). Women often read others' thoughts and feelings more accurately than men do, but that may be because they are usually more highly motivated to understand other people; if men merely shared women's motivation to be intuitive, they might do just as well. Indeed, when Kristi Klein and Sara Hodges (2001) offered to *pay* people for accurate inferences about others, both sexes were more insightful and discerning than usual, and there was no difference in the performances of men and women at all.

Finally, no matter how long people have known each other, their judgments and evaluations of each other may depend in part on the moods they're in. Transient frames of mind affect people's perceptions of their partners and their relationships; when they're in a good mood, both are perceived more positively than when more surly, irascible moods prevail (Forgas, Levinger, & Moylan, 1994).

Partner Legibility

Some of the traits people have are more visible than others—that is, they impel behavior that is observable and obvious—and the more evident a trait is, the more accurately it will be perceived (Watson, 2000). People who are sociable and extraverted, for instance, are likely to be accurately perceived as gregarious and affable, but high neuroticism is harder to detect (Ambady, Hallahan, &

Rosenthal, 1995). Moreover, some people are generally easier to judge correctly than others are. People who are taciturn and reserved can be very hard to figure out, simply because they don't give observers many clues about what they're feeling; even the friends and lovers of such people may not often be able to tell what they're thinking (Hancock & Ickes, 1996).

Perceiver Ability

Some people may be hard to judge, but some judges are better than others. People who are intelligent and open-minded tend to perceive others more accurately than dogmatic, narrow-minded people do (Thomas, 2000). To judge others well, perceivers have to note, weigh, and combine diverse and often conflicting sources of information (such as a partner's behavior, facial expression, tone of voice, and vocabulary), and integrating all these pieces can be a complicated task. People who are flexible, complex thinkers seem to do this more capably than more rigid, less sophisticated people can (Davis & Kraus, 1997).

Attachment styles also appear to be important in this regard. Perceivers who have a secure style understand their partners better than insecure people do (Mikulincer, Orbach, & Iavnieli, 1998; Tucker & Anders, 1999). In particular, anxious-ambivalent people are especially likely to overestimate how much they have in common with their romantic partners (Mikulincer et al., 1998).

There may be unsettling consequences of being a poor judge of others. When William Schweinle and William Ickes (2002) asked married men to watch videotapes of women discussing their divorces, they found (as you might expect) that some men read the women's thoughts and feelings better than others. The videos were highly charged and full of emotion, and the men had never met the women they were watching, but men who could accurately tell when the women were really mad or bitter tended to be satisfied with their own marriages. In contrast, other men considered the women to be more hostile than they really were; these men perceived criticism and rejection in the women's remarks that was not apparent to other perceivers. And those men were more likely to beat their own wives (Schweinle, Ickes, & Bernstein, 2002). A thin-skinned tendency to perceive antagonism from female strangers that did not exist was correlated with mistreatment of one's own spouse.

Happily, training and practice can improve people's abilities to understand their partners. In one study, participants in a 10-hour empathy training program were able to understand their partners' thoughts and feelings more accurately six months later. Their partners were also more satisfied with their relationship (Long et al., 1999).

Threatening Perceptions

Intimate partners typically understand each other much better than they understand mere acquaintances, but they may not want to on those occasions when a partner's feelings or behavior are distressing or ominous. When accurate perceptions would be worrisome, intimate partners may actually be motivated to be *in*accurate in order to fend off doubts about their relationship (Ickes & Simpson, 2001). And that's a good thing, because relationships suffer when people correctly perceive unwanted, threatening feelings in their partners (Simpson, Oriña, & Ickes, 2003). Imagine this situation: You and your romantic partner are asked to examine and discuss several pictures of very attractive people your partner may be meeting later. Afterwards, while watching a videotape of the two of you discussing the pictures, you try to discern exactly what your partner was thinking when he was inspecting the pictures of gorgeous women (or she was inspecting the pictures of handsome men) that could be potential rivals for you. How astute would you be? Would you really want to know that your partner found one of the pictures to be especially compelling and was really looking forward to meeting that person? Not if you're like most people. The more attractive (and thereby threatening) the photos were, and the closer their relationship was, the *less* accurately dating partners perceived each other's thoughts and feelings in this situation (Simpson, Ickes, & Blackstone, 1995). Most people understood a partner's reactions to unattractive photos reasonably well, but they somehow remained relatively clueless about a partner's reactions to attractive pictures. They were inattentive to news they did not want to hear.

But not everyone successfully managed threatening perceptions in this manner. People with an anxious-ambivalent attachment style were actually *more* accurate in judging their partners when the partners inspected the attractive photos (Simpson, Ickes, & Grich, 1999). They were unsettled by their perceptions, however, and they evaluated their relationships less favorably as a result. Anxious-ambivalent people were like moths drawn to a flame; they were especially good at intuiting their partners' feelings in just those situations in which accuracy was disconcerting and costly. Such sensitivity may be one reason why such people *are* chronically anxious and ambivalent about their relationships.

Perceiver Influence

Finally, we should remember that people are not passive judges of others. In a close relationship, they are engaged in continual interaction with their partners, behaving in accord with their expectations and reacting to the perceptions they construct. If they come to realize that their partners are not the people they wish they were, they may try to *change* their partners by encouraging some behaviors and impeding others. In a sense, people are sometimes like sculptors who try to construct the partners they want from the raw material a real partner provides (Drigotas et al., 1999). If our partners seem dispirited, we may try to cheer them up. Or, if they're too pompous and pretentious, we may try to bring them back to earth (De La Ronde & Swann, 1998). Because intimate partners are continually shaping and molding each other's behavior, perceptions that are initially inaccurate may become more correct as we induce our partners to become the people we want them to be.

Summary

With all these influences at work, our perceptions of our partners can range from outright fantasy to pinpoint correctness. We certainly know our partners better as a relationship develops, but motivation and attentiveness can come and go, and some people are easier to read than others. Some of us are more astute perceivers than others, too. In addition, even if you know your partner well, there may be occasions for which *in*attention is profitable, helping you avoid doubt and distress. And partners influence each other, so perceptions can become either more or less accurate as time goes by. In general, we usually understand our partners less than we think we do, but our accuracy may vary with necessity, our moods, and the stage of our relationship.

Our important closing point is that our perceptions of our partners are clearly influential (Kurdek, 2003). Right or wrong, our judgments of our lovers and friends can either support or undermine our contentment in our relationships. Some of us look on the bright side, thinking well of our partners, using relationship-enhancing attributions, and expecting kindness and generosity—and that's what we get. Others of us, however, doubt our partners and expect the worst—and thereby make it more likely that our relationships will fail.

FOR YOUR CONSIDERATION

Martha looked forward to meeting Gale, because those who knew her said that she was friendly, outgoing, and bright. But their paths happened to cross when Gale was suffering from a bad case of poison ivy; she was uncomfortable from the endless itching and drowsy from the allergy medicine, and altogether, she was having a really bad day. So, things did not go well when Martha said hello and introduced herself. Martha came away from their brief interaction thinking that Gale was really rather cold and unsociable.

After Gale recovered and was back in her usual spirits, she encountered Martha again and greeted her warmly but was surprised when Martha seemed distant and wary. What do you think the future holds for Martha and Gale. Why?

CHAPTER SUMMARY

Social cognition includes all the processes of perception and thought with which we make sense of our social worlds. This chapter focuses on the way we think about our relationships.

First Impressions (And Beyond)

When we first meet others, stereotypes and *primacy effects* (which cause us to attach particular importance to the first information we acquire about others) are especially influential in shaping our overall impressions. Early impressions matter because any existing judgment is likely to influence our interpretations of the later information we encounter. People with different preconceptions may draw very different conclusions about others from the same information.

First impressions also affect our selection of subsequent data. People ordinarily display a *confirmation bias,* seeking information that will confirm their beliefs with more interest and energy than they look for examples that will prove them wrong. As a result, we rarely confront unequivocal evidence that our impressions of others are incorrect. This leads to *overconfidence* that leads people to put unwarranted faith in their judgments. Most people make more mistakes in judging others than they realize.

Overconfidence, confirmation biases, and preconceptions operate in established relationships as well. As a result, outsiders such as parents and friends who are not personally involved in a relationship can sometimes judge it more accurately than the participants can.

The Power of Perceptions

There are often a variety of ways to interpret a given event in a close relationship, and the partners' perspectives can be very consequential.

Idealizing Our Partners. Happy partners construct charitable, generous perceptions known as *positive illusions* that emphasize their partners' virtues and minimize their faults. Although highly unrealistic positive illusions may be risky, we tend to revise our opinions of what we want in a partner so that they fit the real partners we have. The resulting idealized perspectives—which perceive our partners as the best they can be—usually lead to good feelings and positive interpretations of a partner's behavior that result in greater satisfaction with a relationship.

Attributional Processes. The explanations we generate for why things happen are called *attributions.* We can emphasize influences that are internal or external to a person, stable or unstable, or global or specific, but such judgments may be especially complex in close relationships, where both partners may be partly responsible for a given event.

Despite their intimate knowledge of each other, partners are affected by *actor/observer effects:* They generate different explanations for their own behavior than they do for actions they observe in their partners. Whereas people are typically aware of the external pressures that have influenced their own behavior, they attribute their partners' behavior to internal sources in similar situations. This leads people to overlook how they have personally provoked the behavior they observe in each other, a problem that persists because partners are rarely aware of the discrepancies in their perspectives.

People also tend to be *self-serving;* they gladly take personal credit for their successes but try to avoid blame for their failures. In relationships, this leads partners to perceive problems as typically being the other person's fault. Most of us feel that we're pretty easy to live with, but our partners are hard to put up with sometimes.

Patterns of attribution can be either *relationship-enhancing,* giving a partner credit for his or her positive actions and excusing the partner's transgressions, or *distress-maintaining*, regarding a partner's negative actions as deliberate and routine. Relationship-enhancing attributions promote relationship satisfaction, but distress-maintaining attributions may keep people dissatisfied no matter what their partners do.

Memories. We edit and update our memories as time goes by so that what we remember is always a mix of what happened in the past and what we know now. This process of *reconstructive memory* helps couples stay optimistic about their futures; happy partners typically recall that they have had problems in the past but that things have recently improved, so they are happier now than they used to be.

Partners also work together to construct vivid stories about their shared past that set the stage for their reactions to new events. The partners' current feelings about each other influence what they are likely to remember, and if their memories are predominantly negative, their relationship may be at risk.

Relationship Beliefs. People enter their partnerships with established beliefs about what relationships are like. One such set of beliefs is *romanticism*, the view that love should be the most important basis for choosing a mate. People high in romanticism believe that (a) their loves will be perfect, (b) each of us has only one perfect, "true" love, (c) true love will find a way to overcome any obstacle, and (d) love is possible at first sight. Such beliefs apparently provide a rosy glow that makes a partnership seem special.

By comparison, *dysfunctional relationship beliefs* are clearly disadvantageous. People who believe that "disagreements are destructive," "mindreading is essential," "partners cannot change," "sex should be perfect every time," "men and women are different," or that "great relationships just happen" don't try to solve problems, they just avoid them. All of these are *destiny* beliefs that assume that two people are either compatible and destined to live happily ever after, or they're not.

In contrast, *growth* beliefs assume that good relationships result from hard work and perseverance. People who hold growth beliefs tend to be more committed to their partners than are people who hold destiny beliefs.

Expectations. Our expectations about others can become *self-fulfilling prophecies*, false predictions that make themselves come true. This happens because expectations guide our behavior toward others; people typically act in ways that fit their expectations, and they can elicit reactions from others that would not have occurred had the perceivers not created them. When this occurs, people are very unlikely to recognize their role in producing the reactions they obtained. Thus, men who think they are conversing with attractive women are likely to find that their partners actually sound quite appealing, and people who expect that others will dislike them typically *are* disliked. Some self-fulfilling prophecies dissipate over time, but others do not; they may persist for years if people continue to act in accord with their initial expectations.

Self-Perceptions. Our self-concepts encompass all of the beliefs and feelings we have about ourselves. During interaction, we seek reactions from others that are self-enhancing and complimentary *and* that are consistent with what we already think of ourselves. *Self-enhancement* is an automatic, specific, emotional motive whereas *self-verification* is deliberate, cognitive, and global—and these different spheres of operation explain how both motives coexist in people with negative self-concepts, who like praise but don't believe it.

People ordinarily seek intimate partners who support their existing self-concepts. Although people with negative self-concepts often date and appreciate casual partners who compliment and praise them, they prefer spouses who tell them that they are undesirable, deficient people.

Impression Management

Because others' impressions are so important, people often engage in *impression management*, trying to influence the impressions of them that others form. Nearly anything we do in the presence of others may be strategically regulated in the service of impression management, and the motive to control the information that others receive about us is a pervasive influence on social life.

Strategies of Impression Management. Four different strategies of impression management are commonplace. With *ingratiation*, people seek acceptance and liking from others, and with *self-promotion*, they seek respect. In contrast, people portray themselves as dangerous and menacing through *intimidation* or as helpless and needy through *supplication*.

Impression Management in Close Relationships. Although our intimate partners mean much more to us than other people do, we work less hard to present favorable images to them than to others. We worry less about how we're coming across, and we try less hard to appear likable and competent all the time. Simple laziness may be involved, because being on our best behavior requires concentration and effort, and both may wane over time.

People often take pains to create desirable images for their partners as well as for themselves. They also go to great lengths to present particular images of their relationships to others. When a relationship is new, this often involves denying that it exists, especially to one's parents.

Individual differences in *self-monitoring* are influential because high self-monitors surround themselves with activity specialists, friends who are good companions for a particular pleasure but little else. Low self-monitors have fewer friends, but have more in common with each of them. Low self-monitors also are more committed to their romantic partners but do not enjoy as much intimacy with others at the beginning of their relationships as high self-monitors do.

So, Just How Well Do We Know Our Partners?

We generally do not understand our partners as well as we think we do, but there are several influences that determine just how accurate (or inaccurate) our perceptions of our partners will be.

Knowledge. As a relationship develops and partners spend more time together, they acquire detailed knowledge about each other and typically do understand each other better.

Motivation. The interest and motivation with which people try to figure each other out help determine how insightful and accurate they will be. Women spend more time thinking about established relationships than men do, but men are just as accurate in their judgments of others as women are when they are paid to do well. Moods are also influential; when people are in good moods, they perceive their partners more positively than they do when they're grumpy.

Partner Legibility. Some personality traits, such as extraversion, are more visible than others. In addition, some people are chronically easier to judge than others are.

Perceiver Ability. Some judges are better than others, too. People who are intelligent and open-minded tend to perceive others more accurately than dogmatic, narrow-minded people do. In addition, perceivers who have a secure style understand their partners better than insecure people do. Poor ability seems to impair relationships; men who perceive antagonism from women where none exists are more likely than other men to abuse their wives.

Threatening Perceptions. However, when accurate perceptions would be worrisome, intimate partners may actually be motivated to be inaccurate in order to fend off doubts about their relationship. Research participants who watched their romantic partners evaluate attractive photos of potential rivals intuited their partners' thoughts less accurately than did those who watched their partners evaluate less threatening photographs—unless the perceivers had an anxious-ambivalent attachment style. Anxious-ambivalent people could tell what their partners were thinking but were disconcerted as a result.

Perceiver Influence. People are sometimes like sculptors who try to construct the partners they want from the raw material a real partner provides. Because intimate partners are continually shaping and molding each other's behavior, perceptions that are initially inaccurate may become more correct as we induce our partners to become the people we want them to be.

Summary. Our perceptions of our partners are clearly influential. Right or wrong, our judgments of our lovers and friends can either support or undermine our contentment in our relationships.

CHAPTER 5

Communication

NONVERBAL COMMUNICATION ◆ Components of Nonverbal Communication ◆ Nonverbal Sensitivity ◆ Sex Differences in Nonverbal Communication ◆ VERBAL COMMUNICATION ◆ Self-Disclosure ◆ Gender Differences in Verbal Communication ◆ DYSFUNCTIONAL COMMUNICATION AND WHAT TO DO ABOUT IT ◆ Miscommunication ◆ Saying What We Mean ◆ Active Listening ◆ Being Polite and Staying Cool ◆ The Power of Respect and Validation ◆ FOR YOUR CONSIDERATION ◆ CHAPTER SUMMARY

Imagine that you and your romantic partner are seated alone in a comfortable room, discussing the topic of your last disagreement. Your conversation is more structured than most, because before you say anything to your partner you record a quick rating of what you intend to say next. You rate the intended impact of your message by pushing one of five buttons with labels ranging from *super negative* through *neutral* to *super positive*. Then, after you speak, your partner quickly rates his or her perception of your message in the same way before replying to you. This process continues as you take turns voicing your views and listening to what your partner says in return. You're engaging in a procedure called the *talk table* that allows researchers to get a record of both your private thoughts and your public actions. The notable point is that if you're dissatisfied with your relationship, you may not *intend* to annoy or belittle your lover, but you're likely to do so, anyway. Unhappy couples don't differ on average from happy, contented couples in what they are trying to say to each other, but the impact of their messages—what their partners think they hear—is more critical and disrespectful nonetheless (Gottman et al., 1976). And this is consequential because this single afternoon at the talk table predicts how happy the two of you will be later on; regardless of how satisfied they were originally, couples whose communications were frustrating were less happily married five years later (Markman, 1981).

Communication is incredibly important in intimate relationships. And it's more complex than we usually realize. Let's consider the simple model of communication shown in Figure 5.1. Communication begins with the sender's intentions, the message that the sender wishes to convey. The problem is that the sender's intentions are private and known only to him or her. In order for them to be communicated to the listener, they must be encoded into verbal and nonverbal actions that are public and observable. A variety of factors, such as the sender's mood or social skill, or noisy distractions in the surrounding

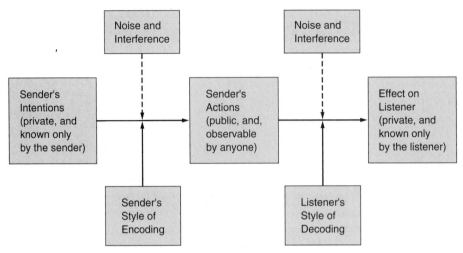

FIGURE 5.1. A simple model of interpersonal communication.
Adapted from Gottman, Notarius, Gonso, & Markman, 1976.

environment, can influence or interfere with this process. Then, the receiver must decode the speaker's actions, and interference can occur here as well (Albright et al., 2004). The final result is an effect on the receiver that is again private and known only to him or her.

The point here is that getting from one person's intentions to the impact of that person's message on a listener involves several steps at which error and misunderstanding may occur. We usually assume that our messages have the impact that we intended, but we rarely *know* that they do (Sillars et al., 1994). More often than we realize (Keysar & Henly, 2002), we face an **interpersonal gap** in which the sender's intentions differ from the effect on the receiver (Gottman et al., 1976). And, as studies with the talk table show, such gaps are related to present and future dissatisfaction in close relationships.

This chapter examines communication in relationships, and we'll do what we can to help you close your own interpersonal gaps. But we'll start not with what people say in interaction but with what they do. Accompanying the spoken word in communication is a remarkable range of nonverbal actions that also carry many messages, whether you intend them or not.

NONVERBAL COMMUNICATION

Imagine that as part of a research study, you put on a cap that identifies you as a member of either an admired or disliked group, and you walk around town with it on, shopping, eating lunch, and applying for some jobs. You've put on the cap without looking at it, and you *don't know* what you're wearing. Would you be able to tell what sort of cap you have on by watching others' reactions to you? You might (Hebl et al., 2000). If you're wearing an obnoxious cap, your waitress may not be as warm and cheerful as usual. People you pass at the mall may glance at you and display a quick expression of distaste or disgust. Even if no one mentions your cap, others' behavior may clearly indicate that they do not like what they see. In fact, because you'd be curious and alert to how others responded, their sentiments might be unmistakably plain.

In such a situation, you'd probably notice the remarkable amount of information carried by nonverbal behavior, which includes all of the things people do in interaction except for their spoken words and syntax. Indeed, although we don't always notice, nonverbal behavior can serve several functions in our transactions with others. Table 5.1 lists six such functions that have been identified by Miles Patterson (1988, 1990). We'll take particular note of three of them.

First, nonverbal behavior **provides information** about people's moods or about what they really mean by what they say. If you playfully tease someone,

TABLE 5.1. Functions of Nonverbal Behavior in Relationships

Category	Description	Example
Providing information	A person's behavior allows others to make inferences about his or her intentions, feelings, traits, and meaning	A husband's facial expression leads his wife to judge that he is upset
Regulating information	Nonverbal behavior provides cues that regulate the efficient give-and-take of smooth conversations and other interactions	A woman looks at her partner and holds her gaze as the tone of her voice gets lower on her last word, and he starts speaking because he knows she's done
Defining the nature of relationships	The type of partnership two people share may be evident in their nonverbal behavior	Lovers stand closer to each other, touch more, and look at each other more than less intimate partners do
Social control	Goal-oriented behavior designed to influence someone else	As a person requests a favor from his friend, he leans forward, touches him on the arm, and gazes intently
Presentational function	Nonverbal behavior that is managed by a person, or a couple, to create or enhance a particular image	A couple may quarrel on the way to a party but then hold hands and pretend to be happy with each other once they arrive
Service-task function	Patterns of nonverbal involvement are determined primarily by service or task-oriented goals in an interaction	The close approach and touching initiated by a physician is part of her job and is not intended to suggest liking or intimacy

Source: From Patterson, 1988.

for instance, your facial expression and the sound of your voice may be the only way listeners can tell that you don't intend to be antagonistic. This function is so important that we have had to invent emoticons, the imitation facial expressions people put in e-mail messages, so that readers can correctly interpret our written messages.

Nonverbal behavior also plays a vital part in **regulating interaction.** Nonverbal displays of interest often determine whether or not interaction ever begins, and, thereafter, subtle nonverbal cues allow people to take turns in a conversation seamlessly and gracefully.

Finally, by expressing intimacy and carrying signals of power and status, nonverbal behavior helps **define the relationships** we share with others. People who are intimate with each other act differently toward one another than acquaintances do, and dominant, high-status people act differently than subordinates do. Without a word being spoken, observers may be able to tell who likes whom and who's the boss.

How are these functions carried out? The answer involves all of the diverse components of nonverbal communication, so we'll survey them next.

Components of Nonverbal Communication

One clue to the enormous power of nonverbal communication is the number of different channels through which information can be transmitted. We'll describe six.

Facial Expression

People's facial expressions signal their moods and emotions (Horstmann, 2003) in a manner that's similar anywhere you go (Ekman, 2003). Even if you don't speak the language in a foreign country, for example, you'll be able to tell if others are happy: If they are, the muscles in their cheeks will pull up the corners of their mouths, and the skin alongside their eyes will crinkle into folds. Obviously, they're *smiling,* and happiness, like several other emotions—sadness, fear, anger, disgust, and surprise—engenders a unique facial expression that's the same all over the world. Other emotions, such as embarrassment, involve sequences of facial actions and expressions that are also unmistakable (Keltner & Shiota, 2003). In fact, the universality of these expressions suggests that they are hard-wired into our species. People don't *learn* to smile when they're happy—they're born to do it. People who have been blind all their lives, for instance, display the same facial expressions all the rest of us do (Galati, Scherer, & Ricci-Bitti, 1997). We do a little better identifying emotions that are expressed by others from our own cultural groups than we do in recognizing the expressions of people from elsewhere in the world (Elfenbein & Ambady, 2003). Nevertheless, accurate recognition of others' emotions from their facial expressions is almost an automatic process; American college students can recognize happiness, sadness, anger, disgust, and surprise in three-quarters of a second or less (Tracy & Robins, 2004).

  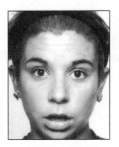 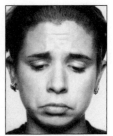

Here are examples of the basic facial expressions of happiness, sadness, fear, and surprise. You've never seen this woman before, but can you tell which emotion each photo depicts? We bet you can.

So, the universal meanings of facial expressions make them extremely informative—when they're authentic. Unfortunately, because facial expressions do figure so prominently in nonverbal communication, people sometimes try to deliberately manage them to disguise their true emotions (DePaulo, 1992). On occasion, this occurs due to **display rules,** cultural norms that dictate what emotions are appropriate in particular situations (Andersen & Guerrero, 1998; Zaalberg, Manstead, & Fischer, 2004). There are at least four ways we may try to modify our expressions of emotion to follow these rules. First, we may *intensify* our expressions, exaggerating them so that we appear to be experiencing stronger feelings than we really are. If you're only mildly pleased by a gift you've just opened, for example, you should try to appear happier than you feel if the donor is present. Second, we sometimes *minimize* our expressions, trying to seem less emotional than we really are. Because Western culture assumes that "big boys don't cry," a man may stoically try not to seem too affected by a sad movie. Third, we may *neutralize* our expressions, trying to withhold our true feelings altogether. Good poker players try to do this so that they give no hint of what their cards may be. Finally, we can *mask* our real feelings by replacing them with an entirely different apparent emotion. A first runner-up in a beauty pageant who looks so thrilled when the other contestant actually wins the pageant is almost certainly masking her true feelings.

However, even when people try to control their expressions, the truth may leak out. First, feigned expressions often differ in subtle ways from authentic expressions. For instance, people can easily pull up the corners of their mouths when they want to fake a smile, but they have a harder time voluntarily crinkling the skin around their eyes; as a result, the difference between a real and fake smile is often apparent to an attentive viewer (Miles, 2003). Second, despite our efforts, authentic flashes of real emotion, or *microexpressions,* can be visible during momentary lapses of control. If you watched the network television news anchors carefully during the 1976 and 1984 U.S. presidential campaigns, for example, it was apparent which candidate each one secretly supported; despite their posed professional detachment, they all revealed their preferences through favorable or unfavorable brief expressions during their reports about candidates (Friedman, DiMatteo, & Mertz, 1980; Mullen et al., 1986).

Gazing Behavior

Obviously, facial expressions provide meaningful information about a partner's feelings. Gazing, the direction and amount of a person's eye contact, is also influential. For one thing, looking at someone communicates interest, and that can determine whether or not two strangers begin talking with each other (Cary, 1978). If you find someone glancing at you in a singles bar and you don't want to talk to him or her, look away and don't look back.

Gazing also helps define the relationship two people share once interaction begins. Lovers really do spend more time looking at each other than friends do, and friends look more than acquaintances do (Kleinke, 1986). Moreover, when strangers spend time gazing into each other's eyes, they end up liking each other more than they would have if they'd spent the time together looking someplace else (Kellerman, Lewis, & Laird, 1989). A lot of looking can evidently communicate affection as well as simple interest.

But it can communicate dominance, too. In ordinary interaction, people usually look at their conversational partners more when they're listening (gazing at the speaker about 60 percent of the time, on average) than when they're speaking (looking at the listener about 40 percent of the time). However, powerful, high-status people tend to depart from these norms—they look more while speaking but less while listening than the average person does (Ellyson, Dovidio, & Brown, 1992). Researchers summarize these patterns in a **visual dominance ratio** (VDR) that compares "look-speak" (the percentage of time a speaker gazes at a listener) to "look-listen." A high-power pattern of gazing turns the typical ratio of 40/60 on its head, producing a high VDR of 60/40 (Dovidio et al., 1988). Dominant partners in an interaction can insist, "Look at me when I'm talking to you!" but they often do not offer as much visual attention in return.

Body Movement

So far, we've only been describing nonverbal communication from the neck up, but the whole body is involved. Body movements routinely accompany and support our verbal communication, making it easier for us to convey what we mean—try describing the size of a fish you caught without using your hands (Rauscher, Krauss, & Chen, 1996)—but they can also replace spoken words entirely, in the form of gestures that are widely understood. (A good example in North America, for better or worse, is a gesture in which one holds up one's hand with one's middle finger extended. The recipient of the gesture will probably know what it means.) The problem with gestures is that, unlike facial expressions, they vary widely from culture to culture (Archer, 1997). For instance, in the United States, touching your thumb to your index finger and extending the other fingers is a gesture that means "okay," or "good." However, in France it means "zero," in Japan it means "money," and in the Middle East it's an obscene insult (just like the American middle finger). The language of the face needs no interpreter, but that's not true of the language of gestures (Axtell, 1991).

Less specific, but still useful information can be conveyed by the posture or motion of the body. For instance, the impressions observers get from brief (10-second) silent videotapes allow them to predict the teaching evaluations college professors will get from their students (Ambady & Rosenthal, 1993), and, even more remarkably, the sexual orientation of total strangers (Ambady, Hallahan, & Conner, 1999) at levels noticeably better than chance. Only 60 seconds of observation allow strangers to make reasonably accurate judgments about our personality traits (Carney, Colvin, & Hall, 2004). One reason why body language is informative is that it's harder to control than facial expressions are; it's "leakier," which means that it's more likely to indicate what our true feelings are (Babad, Bernieri, & Rosenthal, 1989). United States customs inspectors, for example, use bodily signs of restlessness and anxiety, not facial expressions, to decide whether or not to search travelers' luggage for contraband (Kraut & Poe, 1980).

Body postures can also signal status. High-status people tend to adopt open, asymmetric postures in which the two halves of the body assume different positions (Leffler, Gillespie, & Conaty, 1982). They take up a lot of space. In contrast, low-status people use closed, symmetric postures that are relatively compact. If a powerful boss is talking with a subordinate seated across from him or her, you can usually tell who's who just by watching them.

Touch

Physical contact with another person can also have various meanings. In many cultures, people may touch each other by shaking hands when they first meet, and—just as common sense suggests—there is useful information to be gained from the strength and vigor and fullness of grip with which someone shakes your hand. Several personality traits are related to handshaking behavior; people with firm, full, long handshakes tend to be more extraverted and open to experience, and less neurotic, than people with wimpy handshakes are. Women with strong handshakes also tend to be more agreeable (Chaplin et al., 2000).

So, touch may be informative from the moment two people meet. Thereafter, two people tend to touch each other more as their relationship becomes more intimate (Emmers & Dindia, 1995). Touch clearly conveys closeness and affection. However, uninvited touch can also be an implicit signal of dominance that establishes one's place in a status hierarchy (Major & Heslin, 1982). In fact, when two people differ in status, touch tends to be a one-way street; high-status people are more likely to touch those of lower status than vice versa. Think about it: If you ask a question of your instructor during an exam, it would not be bizarre for him or her to rest a hand on your shoulder as he or she bends over your seat to talk to you. However, if you go to the front of the room to ask your question, it would be quite odd for you to touch your instructor in the same way.

The potential mixed message of touch may be the reason why men and women tend to respond differently to touches from strangers. When they are touched briefly by others on the hand or arm, women usually respond positively, but most men do not. Sheryl Whitcher and Jeffrey Fisher (1979) provided a compelling demonstration of this in a study in which a nurse touched some hospital patients, but not others, when she was giving them instructions the night before their surgery. The nurse rested her hand on the patient's arm for about a minute, an action that could be construed as comforting. That's how women reacted; the touch calmed them and lowered their blood pressure. In contrast, the touch made men *more* anxious and actually made their blood pressure go up.

Perhaps because of this sex difference, men tend to touch women more than women touch men (Major, Schmidlin, & Williams, 1990), particularly among younger couples (Hall & Veccia, 1990). In fact, women who touch men during casual interaction are not evaluated favorably by observers unless the women are clearly of higher status than their male counterparts (Storrs & Kleinke, 1990).

Interpersonal Distance

One aspect of touching that makes it momentous is that people have to be located very close to each other for touching to occur. That means that the two partners are typically in a region of interpersonal distance—the physical space that separates two people—that is usually reserved for relatively intimate interactions. The **intimate zone** of interpersonal distance extends out from the front of our chests about a foot-and-a-half (Hall, 1966). If two people are standing face-to-face that close to each other, their interaction is probably quite loving or quite hostile. More interactions occur at greater distances, in a **personal zone** that ranges from $1^1/_2$ to 4 feet away from us. Within this range, friends are likely to interact at smaller distances, acquaintances at larger ones, so distancing behavior helps to define the relationships people share. Even further away, in a **social zone** (4 to 12 feet), interactions tend to be more businesslike. When you sit across a desk from an interviewer or a professor, you're in the social zone, and the distance seems appropriate; however, it would seem quite odd to stand five feet away from a good friend to hold a personal conversation. Beyond 12 feet, interactions tend to be quite formal. This is the **public zone,** which is used for structured interaction like that between an instructor and his or her students in a lecture class.

These distances describe the general patterns of interactions among North Americans, but they tend to be larger than those used by many other peoples of the world (Burgoon, Buller, & Woodall, 1989). French, Latin, and Arabic cultures prefer distances smaller than these. A person's sex and status also affect distancing behavior (Holland et al., 2004). Men tend to use somewhat larger distances than women do, and people usually stand further away from high-status partners than from those of lower power and prestige. Whatever one's preferences, however, spacing behavior is a subtle way to calibrate the desired intimacy of an interaction, and it may even be an indirect measure of the quality of a relationship: Spouses who are unhappy choose to maintain larger distances between each other than do spouses who are currently content (Crane et al., 1987).

Paralanguage

The final component of nonverbal communication isn't silent like the others can be. Paralanguage includes all the variations in a person's voice other than the

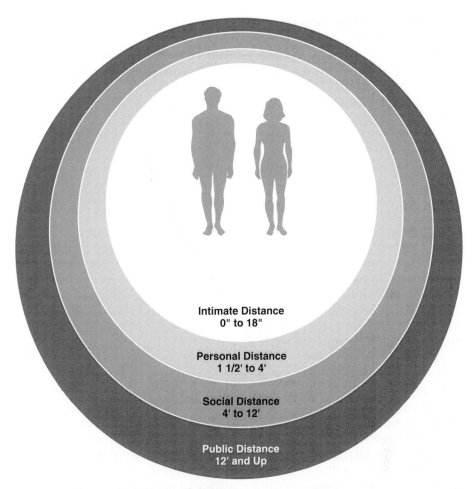

FIGURE 5.2. Zones of interpersonal distance.
Researchers recognize four discrete regions of space in which different kinds of social interaction are likely to occur.

actual words he or she uses, such as rhythm, pitch, loudness, and rate. Thus, paralanguage doesn't involve *what* people say, but *how* they say it. A good example of distinctive paralanguage is "baby talk," the vocal style that is marked by variable intonation, high pitch, and unique rhythms. On the one hand, baby talk communicates affection; people use it with their lovers (Bombar & Littig, 1996), babies, and pets (DePaulo & Friedman, 1998). On the other hand, it can also mean that the speaker believes that the listener is incapable or infirm; people sometimes use baby talk to address people who are mentally retarded or institutionalized in nursing homes. Interestingly, if the elderly residents of nursing homes *are* ailing or feeble, they like being addressed this way, but the more competent they are, the less they like it (Caporael, Lukaszewski, & Culbertson, 1983).

Paralanguage helps define relationships, because lovers tend to talk to each other with different rhythms than friends use. Lovers tolerate longer delays in responding, are silent more often, and say less overall (Guerrero, 1997). The sound of a woman's voice can also tell eavesdropping strangers whether she's talking to an intimate or casual male friend; women sound more submissive and scatterbrained when they're conversing with their boyfriends than they do when they're talking to other men (Montepare & Vega, 1988). In fact, women often use more submissive paralanguage in mixed-sex interactions than men do (Berger, 1994).

Combining the Components

We have introduced the components of nonverbal communication as if they are independent, discrete sources of information, and, in one sense, they are: Each of them can have its own effects on interaction (Rashotte, 2002). Usually, however, they reinforce each other, working together to convey consistent information about a person's sentiments and intentions. When you're face-to-face with someone, all of these components are in play, and together, they often tell you what people really mean by what they say. Consider sarcasm, for instance, when people say one thing but mean another: Their true intent is conveyed not in their words but in their actions and paralanguage. Most of the time, our nonverbal behavior communicates the same message as our words. But when there *is* a discrepancy between people's words and actions, the truth behind their words usually lies in their nonverbal, not their verbal, communication (Burgoon, 1994).

These various nonverbal actions also allow us to fine-tune the intimacy of our interactions to establish a comfortable level of closeness (Patterson, 1990). Imagine that you're seated next to an acquaintance on a two-person couch when the conversation takes a serious turn and your acquaintance mentions an intimate personal problem. If this development makes you uncomfortable—if that's more than you needed to hear—you can adjust the perceived intimacy of your interaction by nonverbally "backing off." You can turn away and lean back to get more distance. You can avert your gaze. And you can signal your discomfort through less animated paralanguage and a less pleasant facial expression, all without saying a word (Andersen, 2001). Nonverbal communication serves several important functions in interaction and is the source of useful subtlety in social life.

Nonverbal Sensitivity

Given all this, you might expect that it's advantageous for couples to do well at nonverbal communication, and you'd be right. The sensitivity and accuracy with which couples communicate nonverbally predict how happy their relationship will be (Carton, Kessler, & Pape, 1999). In particular, husbands and wives who do poorly at nonverbal communication tend to be dissatisfied with their marriages. Moreover, when such problems occur, it's usually the husband's fault (Noller, 1987).

What? How can researchers arrive at such a conclusion? Well, when nonverbal exchanges fail, there may be errors in encoding or decoding, or both: The sender may enact a confusing message that is difficult to read (that's poor

---

BOX 5.1
Flirting

A great example of nonverbal communication—and the misunderstandings that can result from it—is the way people behave when they intentionally want to attract attention and to communicate their interest in others (Egland, Spitzberg, & Zormeier, 1996). When people flirt, they tend to smile more, move closer, gaze longer, and touch their partners more often than they do when they are less eager to stimulate others' interest (Koeppel et al., 1993). Their speech is more animated, involving fewer silences and more laughter, and their voices sound warmer (Coker & Burgoon, 1987). And coupled with these signals of interest and immediacy may be particular expressions and postures such as a head cant, pouting mouth, and coy look that are fairly unique (Simpson, Gangestad, & Biek, 1993). Together, these actions clearly signal one's desire for continued interaction with the person to whom they are directed (Abrahams, 1994).

Behavior that is merely flirtatious differs from behavior that is straightforwardly seductive. Actions that are intended to convey sexual interest involve even more eye contact, smiling, and touching, more intimate paralanguage, and smaller interpersonal distances than friendly flirtatiousness does (Koeppel et al., 1993). But the distinction is often lost on men, who tend to see sexual overtones in the friendly behavior they receive from women (Abbey, 1982; Saal, Johnson, & Weber, 1989). Men are more likely than women to read sexual motives or intentions into flirtatious behavior, and women who intend their actions to be fun, frivolous, and festive (but nothing more) run a constant risk of being misunderstood (Henningsen, 2004).

---

encoding), or the receiver may fail to correctly interpret a message that is clear to anyone else (and that's poor decoding). Women typically start with an advantage at both tasks because, if no deception is involved, women are both better encoders and more astute decoders than men are on average (Hall, 1998; Hall & Matsumoto, 2004). (There's no difference in men's and women's abilities to detect deception, as we'll see in chapter 10.) Thus, the old stereotype about "women's intuition" actually has a basis in fact; more than men, women tend to attentively use subtle but real nonverbal cues to discern what's really going on. Women may not possess better nonverbal abilities than men do, but they do work harder, and thereby perform better, at nonverbal communication (Ickes, 2003). (Keep this distinction between ability and effort in mind; we'll return to it shortly.)

Researchers can assess husbands' and wives' encoding and decoding skills by asking them to send specific nonverbal messages that are then decoded by the other spouse. The messages are statements that can have several different meanings, depending on how they are nonverbally enacted; for instance, the phrase, "I'm cold, aren't you?" could be an affectionate invitation ("Come snuggle with me, you cute thing"), a spiteful complaint ("Turn up the damn heat, you cheapskate!"), or something else. In research on nonverbal sensitivity, a spouse is assigned a particular meaning to convey and is videotaped sending the message. Then, impartial strangers are used as a control group. If they can't figure out what the spouse is trying to communicate, the spouse's encoding is assumed to be faulty. On the other hand, if they *can* read the message but the other spouse *can't*, the partner's decoding skill is implicated.

In the first ingenious study of this sort, Patricia Noller (1980) found that husbands in unhappy marriages sent more confusing messages and made more decoding errors than happy husbands did. There were no such differences among the wives, so the poorer communication Noller observed in the distressed marriages appeared to be the husbands' fault. Men in troubled marriages were misinterpreting communications from their wives that were clearly legible to total strangers. Other researchers observed this pattern, too (Gottman & Porterfield, 1981). Even worse, such husbands were completely clueless about their mistakes; they assumed that they were doing a fine job communicating with their wives, and were confident that they understood their wives and that their wives understood them (Noller & Venardos, 1986). The men were doing a poor job communicating and didn't know it, and that's why they seemed to be at fault.

On the other hand, to be fair, marital miscommunication in the nonverbal domain is not entirely due to husbands' shortcomings. In another study, Noller (1981) compared spouses' accuracy in decoding the other's messages to their accuracy in decoding communications from strangers. In unhappy marriages, *both* the husbands and wives understood strangers better than they understood each other. Moreover, the greater their dissatisfaction, the greater the disparity between their inaccuracy with each other and their accuracy with strangers. Evidently, distressed husbands and wives were both miscommunicating despite being capable of adequate nonverbal communication with others.

This is a key point because, based on Noller's findings, there are at least two possible ways nonverbal communication and relationship satisfaction could affect each other:

1. Nonverbal skills may determine how satisfying relationships are. Poor skills may lead to poor relationships, and good skills may lead to good relationships. Alternatively,
2. Relationship satisfaction may determine how hard people work to communicate well. Poor relationships may engender poor communication, and good relationships may foster good communication.

Actually, both of these propositions are probably correct. It's likely that nonverbal insensitivity makes someone a less rewarding partner than he or she otherwise would be. But once partners grow dissatisfied for any reason, they may start tuning each other out and communicate less adeptly than they could if they really tried (Noller & Feeney, 1994; Sabatelli, Buck, & Dreyer, 1980, 1982). In this fashion, nonverbal insensitivity and dissatisfaction can become a vicious cycle, with each exacerbating the other.

In any case, people's problems with communication may stem from either skill deficits or performance deficits, and the distinction is an important one. If miscommunication results from a skill deficit—a person does not know how to communicate clearly—then we can improve that person's relationships by teaching the skill. If, on the other hand, the problem is a performance deficit— the person knows how to communicate clearly but doesn't do so with a partic- ular partner—then efforts to improve the skill will probably have no effect on that relationship.

Some people do appear to have nonverbal skill deficits, and they are provocative (and a little eerie). For instance, convicted rapists are especially poor at identifying negative feelings such as distaste and displeasure when they are expressed by women (Lipton, McDonel, & McFall, 1987). Abusive mothers have trouble identifying signs of distress in infants; they even tend to see nega- tive emotions as positive ones (Kropp & Haynes, 1987). Both of these results suggest the possibility that skill deficits can give people blind spots that make them insensitive to nonverbal reactions from others that would inhibit unlaw- ful behavior in all the rest of us (although, because these were correlational studies, we don't know that for sure).

For most of us, however, the likely cause of any nonverbal insensitivity will be a performance deficit born of a lack of attention and a lack of effort. Most of us are reasonably skilled and can interpret others' nonverbal messages accu- rately when we look and listen and put our minds to it. Indeed, differences in the accuracy of men's and women's judgments of others disappear when the sexes are equally motivated to get them right (Klein & Hodges, 2001). But too often, we overestimate how cleverly we are decoding others (Realo et al., 2004), and inattention and laziness can lead us to frustrate our partners by sending mixed messages and misunderstanding their moods and meanings. And there lies an almost certain path to less happiness and relationship satisfaction than we otherwise could have had (Noller, 1987).

Sex Differences in Nonverbal Communication

We just noted that women ordinarily do better at nonverbal communication than men do (Hall, 1998), and we mentioned in passing that there are specific differences between the sexes in paralanguage (Berger, 1994), interpersonal dis- tancing (Burgoon et al., 1989), and touching (Major et al., 1990), as well. What we haven't yet mentioned is that there are sex differences in all of the other com- ponents of nonverbal communication, too. Women smile more than men do, even when they're not particularly happy (LaFrance, Hecht, & Paluck, 2003), and they display lower visual dominance ratios when they're interacting with men than men display toward them in return (Bente, Donaghy, & Suwelack, 1998; Ellyson et al., 1992). They also tend to adopt postures that are less open and more symmetrical than those used by men (Cashdan, 1998). Take a look at Figure 5.3 and you'll see what we mean.

Individually, these sex differences aren't remarkable, and each is open to various interpretations. A simple explanation for the difference in postures, for instance, is the different apparel men and women often wear; if men were wearing dresses (or kilts), they probably wouldn't adopt postures like the one

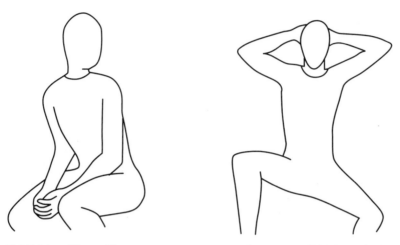

FIGURE 5.3. These silhouettes portray a man and a woman. Which is which?
Adapted from Frieze et al., 1978, p. 330.

TABLE 5.2. Sex and Status Differences in Nonverbal Behavior

Nonverbal Behavior	Women	Men	Low-Status Person	High-Status Person
Smiling	more	less	more	less
Gazing	low VDR	high VDR	low VDR	high VDR
Posture	closed, symmetric	open, asymmetric	closed, symmetric	open, asymmetric
Touch	less	more	less	more
Distance	less	more	less	more
Paralanguage	submissive	assertive	submissive	assertive
Nonverbal Sensitivity	more	less	more	less

Note: The table lists patterns in the behavior of men and women in mixed-sex, but not same-sex, interactions. When women are interacting with other women, they do not display all of the styles listed here. Similarly, the table lists patterns that distinguish high- and low-status people in interactions where status differentials exist. People generally do not display these styles with others of equal status.

in Figure 5.3! Collectively, however, these sex differences are rather striking: In each instance, the behavior of women who are interacting with men mirrors the behavior of low-status people who are interacting with their superiors (Burgoon & Bacue, 2003). This pattern, which is documented in Table 5.2, was first noticed by Nancy Henley (1977), who argued that one reason people often consider women to be less powerful than men is that women constantly communicate that they are less forceful and decisive through their nonverbal behavior. In fact, as Table 5.2 shows, women often do interact with men using a style that is less assertive and powerful than that displayed by the men in return.

However, the question of why this occurs has many possible answers (Ickes, 2003). Sex is merely correlated with nonverbal behavior, and that leaves things ambiguous. One fact is clear: When women occupy positions of power and interact with their subordinates, these sex differences disappear. Moreover, anyone, male or female, is likely to behave in the relatively deferential manner described in Table 5.2 when he or she interacts with others of higher status (Snodgrass, 1985, 1992).

Thus, nonverbal behavior tends to change as people play different roles in different settings. Nevertheless, the pattern remains: Around men of similar status, women often act as if they were of lower status than their male partners. And because cultural expectations are involved, such habits may be surprisingly resistant to change. If you're a woman, try using the male style of behavior listed in Table 5.2, and see what people think; you'll probably come across as "pushy" or "brazen" (Morrow & Cikara, 2004). Our nonverbal behavior may be influential in perpetuating unspoken and unwanted stereotypes about what it means to be a man or woman.

VERBAL COMMUNICATION

If nonverbal communication is so important, what about the things we actually say to each other? They are probably even more consequential, of course (Dindia & Fitzpatrick, 1985). Verbal communication is a vital part of close relationships, and it is extensively involved in the development of intimacy in the first place (Dindia & Timmerman, 2003; Sprecher & Duck, 1994).

Self-Disclosure

Imagine that as part of a psychology experiment you meet a stranger and engage in tasks that lead you to gradually reveal more and more personal information about yourself. For instance, you describe your relationship with your mother, an embarrassing moment, or a deep regret. The stranger does the same thing, and 45 minutes later, you know a lot of personal details about each other. What would happen? Would you like the stranger more than you would have if the two of you had just shared small talk for the same amount of time? In most cases, the answer is definitely yes. An experience like this usually generates immediate closeness between the participants. People who open up to each other, even when they're just following researchers' instructions, like each other more than do couples who do not reveal as much (Aron et al., 1997).

The process of revealing personal information to someone else is called **self-disclosure.** It is one of the defining characteristics of intimacy: Two people cannot be said to be intimate with each other if they do not share some personal, relatively confidential information with one another (Laurenceau, Barrett, & Pietromonaco, 1998; Parks & Floyd, 1996).

The Theory of Social Penetration

Of course, in real life, meaningful self-disclosure takes longer than 45 minutes. Most relationships begin with the exchange of superficial information—"small talk"—and only gradually move to more meaningful revelations. The manner in which this occurs is the subject of **social penetration theory,** which holds that the development of a relationship is closely tied to systematic changes in communication (Altman & Taylor, 1973). People who have just met may feel free to talk with each other about only a few, impersonal topics: "Where are you from?" "What's your major?" But if this superficial conversation is rewarding, they're likely to move closer to each other by increasing two aspects of their communication:

1. Its *breadth:* the variety of topics they discuss, and
2. Its *depth:* the personal significance of the topics they discuss.

According to the theory, if we diagram all the things there are to know about someone, interaction with a new relationship partner is likely to take the form of a wedge that's both narrow (only a few different topics are being discussed) and shallow (only impersonal information is being revealed). (See Figure 5.4.) As the relationship develops, however, the wedge should become broader (with more topics being discussed) and deeper (with more topics of personal significance being revealed).

In general, that is what happens. Ordinarily, however, breadth and depth don't change at the same rate. As you can see in Figure 5.5, breadth usually increases faster than depth at the beginning of a relationship. People talk about a wide variety of superficial topics before they get to the real personal stuff, and the wedge becomes broader before it becomes deeper. Then, intimate self-disclosure grows faster: The wedge becomes deeper without much change in breadth (Hornstein & Truesdell, 1988).

In addition, early encounters between acquaintances usually involve obvious *reciprocity* in self-disclosure. New partners tend to match each other's level of openness, disclosing more as the other person does, and disclosing less if the other person's self-disclosure declines (Dindia, 2000b). Just how

FIGURE 5.4. Altman and Taylor's wedge of social penetration.

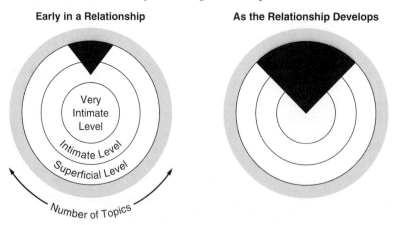

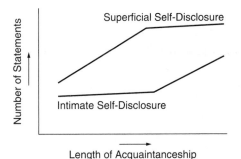

FIGURE 5.5. Changes in the rate of
self-disclosure over time.

much people reveal about themselves, then, tends to depend on the specific partner and may vary considerably from relationship to relationship (Dindia, Fitzpatrick, & Kenny, 1997).

Once a relationship is well established, however, obvious reciprocity occurs less often (Altman, 1973; Derlega, Wilson, & Chaikin, 1976). A partner who discloses some rather personal information may not receive a similar disclosure in return for some time. Instead of reciprocity, sustained intimacy seems to hinge on *responsiveness* from a partner (Reis, 2004; Reis & Patrick, 1996); that is, people want to feel loved and valued, so they want their self-disclosures to be met with apparent understanding, caring, support, and respect (Laurenceau et al., 1998). When we reveal some private confidence to a close friend or lover, we don't need a similar secret in exchange, but we do want our honesty to engender sympathy, tolerance, and acceptance (Sprecher et al., 1995).

It's also likely that, even in the closest partnerships, we'll keep some things to ourselves (Mathews et al., 2004). Social penetration is almost never total, and it probably shouldn't be because partners like and need some privacy, too (Petronio, 2002). No relationship is likely to be able to sustain total openness and intimacy over long periods of time (Dindia, 2000), and it may be a mistake to even try: Both intimate self-disclosure *and* selective secrecy contribute to marital satisfaction (Finkenauer & Hazam, 2000). Some privacy is desirable even in a close, intimate relationship. (We're reminded of a recent cover story in *Cosmopolitan* magazine that asked, if you've had an affair, "Should You Ever Tell?" Their answer, after much discussion, was "probably not.") In the long run, it may be a healthy balance between self-disclosure and respect for privacy that sustains an intimate attachment (Baxter & Montgomery, 1997).

There are also important issues that many close partners simply don't want to talk about. Explicitly or implicitly, partners may agree to steer clear of **taboo topics,** sensitive matters that, in the opinion of the partners, may threaten the quality of their relationship. Curiously, the most common taboo topic is the state of the relationship itself; in one survey, 68 percent of the respondents acknowledged that the current or future state of their romantic relationships was a subject that was better off not being mentioned (Baxter & Wilmot, 1985).

BOX 5.2

Are You a High "Opener?"

Some people are especially good at eliciting self-disclosure from others. Lynn Miller, John Berg, and Rick Archer (1983) developed the Opener Scale to assess this ability, and people who get high scores really do draw out more intimate information from others than do people who receive low scores on the scale. They do this through both verbal and nonverbal channels: High openers appear more attentive during conversation—gazing and nodding more, and looking comfortable and interested—and they verbally express more interest in what others are saying (Purvis, Dabbs, & Hopper, 1984). They seem to enjoy their conversations and to be absorbed by what others have to say (Pegalis, Shaffer, Bazzini, & Greenier, 1994). As a result, they tend to be very good interviewers (Shaffer, Ruammake, & Pegalis, 1990).

Women tend to be better openers than men (Miller et al., 1983). The average score for women on the Opener Scale is 31, whereas 28 is typical for men. If your own score is 5 points higher than average, you're a fairly high opener, but if it's 5 points lower, your score is rather low. You can figure your score by rating yourself on each item using this scale:

0	1	2	3	4
Strongly disagree	Disagree	Neither agree nor disagree	Agree	Strongly agree

The Opener Scale

1. People frequently tell me about themselves.
2. I've been told that I'm a very good listener.
3. I'm very accepting of others.
4. People trust me with their secrets.
5. I easily get people to "open up."
6. People feel relaxed around me.
7. I enjoy listening to people.
8. I'm sympathetic to people's problems.
9. I encourage people to tell me how they are feeling.
10. I can keep people talking about themselves.

(Other common taboos involved current relationships with *other* partners, avoided by 31 percent of the respondents, and past relationships [25 percent].) People are often keenly interested in the likely future of their partnerships and are eager to learn their partners' expectations and intentions, but they don't ask. Instead, romantic partners may create *secret tests* of their lovers' fidelity and devotion (Baxter & Wilmot, 1984). They watch closely to see how their lovers respond to other attractive people (that's a "triangle test"); they contrive difficulties that the lover must overcome in order to demonstrate his or her devotion (an "endurance test"); and they find reasons to be apart to see how enthusiastically their lovers welcome their return (a "separation test"). This all seems like a lot of trouble when they could simply ask the partner what he or she is thinking—and they *do* often ask the partner's *friends*—but in many relationships, such matters seem too delicate to be discussed openly. In general, the more taboo topics there are in a relationship, the less satisfied the partners are, unless they are highly committed to each other; taboo topics are not related to adverse outcomes when people feel that they're in their relationships to stay (Roloff & Ifert, 1998).

Finally, let's note that two different patterns of social *de*penetration often occur when relationships are in trouble. For some couples, both breadth and depth decrease as partners gradually withdraw from their relationship and their interaction returns to a superficial level (Baxter, 1987). For others, breadth contracts as satisfaction declines, but the depth of self-disclosure actually increases, stimulated by the barrage of negative feelings that the unhappy partners express to each other (Tolstedt & Stokes, 1984). In this case, self-disclosure in a distressed relationship does not resemble the sliver of a superficial relationship or the wedge of a satisfying intimate relationship, but rather a long, thin dagger of words designed to hurt.

Is It Always Gradual?

The theory of social penetration describes a gradual process of communication change and relationship development. But not all relationships develop gradually. Sometimes, people meet each other and quickly bare their souls and tell all. There seem to be two major types of these "quick revelation encounters." The first is the legendary stranger-on-the-plane phenomenon. Settling down next to a stranger while embarking on a long journey, you may find yourself telling the stranger things you have never mentioned to very good friends. Does this phenomenon contradict social penetration theory? The authors of the theory, Irwin Altman and Dalmas Taylor, think not. They believe that this kind of "intimacy" only occurs because you know you will never see the other person again. The stranger doesn't know any of your friends and can't reveal your secrets, so such circumstances let you talk over your concerns without having to worry about any long-term consequences (Derlega & Chaiken, 1977). And, because thinking through your problems and confiding in others improves people's psychological and physical health (Pennebaker, 1997), the stranger-on-the-plane phenomenon offers an opportunity to obtain a real benefit at virtually no cost.

But then there's love, and self-revelation, at first sight. People who quickly self-disclose a great deal sometimes have every intention of creating a long-lasting relationship. In such cases, instant openness can be exhilarating, but it is also risky. When people say too much too soon, they are likely to violate their partners' expectations and be evaluated less positively than they would have had their self-disclosures been more gradual (Berger et al., 1976). They may even put the futures of their relationships at risk; in one study, college roommates who reported high levels of self-disclosure after living together for only two weeks reported *less* liking for each other six months later.

On the other hand, lasting friendships are sometimes created quickly (Hays, 1985). On occasion, intimate self-disclosure takes place very rapidly without becoming excessive. In general, as long as you stay within your comfort zone and both you and your partner are opening up to the same degree, the best strategy may be to play it by ear, judging the appropriateness of self-disclosure by taking the context and the partner into account (Miller, 1990).

Self-Disclosure and Relationship Satisfaction

The bottom line is that self-disclosure that fits the situation breeds liking and contentment in close relationships. The more spouses self-disclose to each other, for instance, the more happily married they tend to be (Hendrick, 1981; Meeks, Hendrick, & Hendrick, 1998). Indeed, happy spouses talk to each other differently than less intimate partners do. For one thing, they are likely to have their own idiosyncratic codes and figures of speech that allow them to communicate in a manner that is not transparent to others. They use pet phrases and specialized vocabulary, or **idioms,** whose meaning is known only to them, and the more idioms they use, the happier their marriages tend to be (Bell, Buerkel-Rothfuss, & Gore, 1987; Bruess & Pearson, 1993). The resulting interactions are so distinctive that strangers who listen to the conversations of couples in research studies can usually tell whether the speakers are close friends or just acquaintances (Planalp & Benson, 1992). The conversations of intimate partners are marked by more obvious knowledge of the other person, more personal self-disclosure, and greater relaxation than occurs in the interactions of people who are not intimate.

There are several reasons why self-disclosure is linked to liking (Collins & Miller, 1994). First, we tend to reveal more personal information to those we like. If we're attracted to others, we tend to be more open with them. However, we also tend to like others more *because* we have self-disclosed to them. Everything else being equal, opening up to others causes us to like them more. Finally, and perhaps most importantly, it's rewarding to be entrusted with self-disclosures from others. People who engage in intimate disclosures are liked more by others than are those who say less about themselves (Sprecher, 1987). And reciprocal self-disclosure builds trust. Thus, it feels good to give and to receive self-disclosures, and this aspect of verbal communication is an essential building block of close relationships. Try it yourself for 45 minutes, and you'll probably make a new friend (Aron et al., 1997).

Gender Differences in Verbal Communication

People have made a lot of money writing books that describe men and women as different species that come from different planets and speak different languages. We've tried to combat that simple-minded way of thinking throughout this book because the sexes really are more similar than they are different. However, men and women do tend to use different styles of nonverbal communication when they interact with each other, as we saw in Table 5.2. What about verbal communication? Some differences exist there, too. As we'll see, men and

---

BOX 5.3

Communication and the Internet

This may be hard to believe, but back in a more primitive time, your parents often had to use a phone and talk to only one person at a time when they wanted to chat with distant friends! Now, of course, you can communicate with several people at once in an Internet chat room and/or conduct simultaneous one-on-one interactions with partners who may either be next door or in another hemisphere. If you remember the old days, this is remarkable, and this new technology has changed how we communicate with others and with whom we interact (McKenna & Bargh, 2000).

The nature and pace of interactions on the Net is quite different than talking on the phone, and that's one reason people like them. We can take our time to consider what we want to say, and because no "leaky" paralanguage is involved, we have more control over the messages we send. Typing those messages takes work, however, so we often develop idioms, acronyms (such as BRB for "be right back"), and code words that constitute a unique language and that may distinguish special online relationships from more casual interactions (Ruane, 1999).

Internet chat can also be (or at least seem to be) much more anonymous than other conversation, and that apparent anonymity may have several important effects. First, influences such as physical attractiveness that have enormous impact on other forms of social interaction are much less important online. Second, people may feel freer to reveal intimate information about themselves (Griffiths, 2001); some of the personal details that "bloggers" post in their Web diaries are quite intimate, indeed (Fisher, 2004). But, there may also be more misinformation passed back and forth online; people may say more about themselves that is exaggerated or simply untrue simply because such deception is harder to detect (Whitty & Gavin, 2001).

As a result, there's little doubt that some relationships that would never have even begun through face-to-face interaction may thrive, at least temporarily, online (Orr, 2004). Add up these influences, and, remarkably, randomly paired young adults are more likely to like each other if they chat via online messages than if they talk face-to-face (McKenna, Green, & Gleason, 2002), especially if their newfound acquaintances are members of the other sex (Cahn & Cheng, 2004). The Web is evidently a unique platform for the development of close relationships, a fact that is drawing increasing attention from relationship researchers (e.g., Whitty, 2004).

---

women don't speak different languages, but they tend to talk about different things.

Topics of Conversation

If you read a transcript of a conversation between two friends, would you be able to tell if the participants were men or women? You might. Among themselves, women are more likely than men to discuss their feelings about their close relationships and other personal aspects of their lives (Clark, 1998). They're also more likely to gossip, critiquing other people and coming to more negative conclusions than positive ones (Leaper & Holliday, 1995). Feelings and people figure prominently in the conversations, and the e-mail messages, of women (Boneva, Kraut, & Frolich, 2001). In contrast, men tend to stick to more impersonal matters, discussing objects and actions such as cars and sports, and seeking a few laughs instead of support and counsel (Clark, 1998; Martin, 1997). As a result, the conversations men have with each other tend to be less intimate and personal than the conversations women share (Reis, 1998).

Styles of Conversation

Women also tend to speak with less forcefulness than men do (Berger, 1994). Their style of speech is more indirect and tentative. For instance, women use more hedges that soften their assertions—"We're kind of interested"—and employ more verbs that express uncertainty—"It seems to be that way" (Mulac, 1998). More often than men, they ask questions in conversation and make statements in a questioning tone with a rising inflection at the end (Lakoff, 1975). This manner of speech—"I skipped class, um, on Thursday?"—is much less commanding than men's usual style, which seems more certain and knowledgeable. Women are also less profane (Martin, 1997).

Moreover, in conversations with women, men do most of the talking (Haas, 1979), and despite hackneyed stereotypes about women being more talkative than men, we're apparently used to this pattern. When people listen to recordings of conversations, they think it's more disrespectful and assertive for a woman to interrupt a man than vice versa (LaFrance, 1992).

Self-Disclosure

In established relationships, women are more self-disclosing than men are, and in keeping with their higher scores on the "Opener" scale (see Box 5.2), they elicit more self-disclosure as well (Dindia & Allen, 1992). However, men and women do not differ in their self-disclosures to acquaintances and strangers, so it's clear that gender differences in self-disclosure depend on the nature of a relationship and the sex of one's partner (Miller, 1990). In particular, men offer less intimate self-disclosures to their male partners (such as their best friends) than to their female partners in close relationships. As we noted above, topics of conversation among men tend to be relatively impersonal, so they say less about their personal feelings and private thoughts to other men than they do to women. As a result, interactions that involve a woman tend to be more intimate and meaningful than are interactions that involve only men (Reis, 1998). Men open up to women, and women are open among themselves, but men disclose less to other men.

An important consequence of all this is that men are often more dependent on women for emotional warmth and intimacy than women are on them in return (Wheeler, Reis, & Nezlek, 1983): Whereas women may have intimate, open, supportive connections with partners of both sexes, men are likely to share their most meaningful intimacy only with women. Consequently, a man may need a woman in his life to keep him from being lonely, but women don't usually need men in this way (see chapter 14).

BOX 5.4
Attachment Styles and Communication

The global orientations toward relationships that we label as attachment styles are also evident in communicative behavior. Compared to avoidant people, those with secure styles generally exhibit warmer, more expressive nonverbal behavior involving more laughter, smiling, gazing, and touching; their greater comfort with intimacy and closeness is apparent in their actions (Tucker & Anders, 1998). Secure people also engage in more self-disclosure (Bradford, Feeney, & Campbell, 2002), keep fewer secrets (Vrij et al., 2003), and express their emotions more honestly (Kafetsios, 2004) than insecure people do. Secure people are thus more open with their intimate partners than insecure people are, and that's one reason why their marriages tend to be more satisfying as the years go by (Feeney, 1999a).

This pattern of lower intimacy among men in the United States is almost certainly the result of sociocultural influences because it does not occur in countries with different traditions (Reis, 1998). For instance, in Jordan, a country that encourages same-sex bonding among men, there's no difference at all in the meaningfulness of the interactions men share with women or other men. Moreover, even in the U.S., men can have very intimate conversations with their male best friends when they are following researchers' instructions to do so (Reis, Senchak, & Solomon, 1985). Thus, the communicative styles of men and women appear to have more to do with learned habits and preferences than with any actual differences in ability.

Instrumentality Versus Expressivity

Indeed, the differences between men and women we have described in this section are *gender* differences that are more closely associated with their gender roles than with their biological sex. Women engage in intimate verbal communication with trusted partners because they tend to be high in expressivity and are comfortable talking about their feelings. However, this also comes naturally to men who are high in expressivity, as androgynous men are, and such men tend to have meaningful, intimate interactions with both sexes just like women do (Aube et al., 1995). So, to refine the point we made previously, it's really just traditional, macho men who have superficial conversations with their best friends and who need relationships with women to keep from being lonely. More than other men, macho guys shut out their male friends (Shaffer, Pegalis, & Bazzini, 1996) and tend to be sad and lonely when they do not have a female romantic partner (Wheeler et al., 1983). In contrast, androgynous men (who are both assertive *and* warm) self-disclose readily to both sexes and enjoy meaningful interactions with all their friends; as a result, they tend not to be lonely, and they spend more time interacting with women than less expressive, traditional men do (Reis, 1986).

Given this, it's silly to think that men and women speak different languages and come from different planets. Many men *are* more taciturn than the average woman, but there are also men who are more open and self-disclosing than most women are. The typical intimacy of a person's interactions is tied to his or her level of expressivity, and once you take that into account, it doesn't much matter whether the person is a man or woman. Moreover, expressivity is a trait that ranges from low to high in both women and men, so it makes more sense to take note of individual differences in communicative style than to lump all men together and treat them as a group distinct from women.

Nevertheless, it's true that about half of all men are sex-typed, which means that they're high in instrumentality and low in expressivity, and such macho men are much less expressive than most women are. Thus, they are likely to display a style of emotional communication that is rather different from that of most women. Whereas women tend to be open with their feelings, such men are likely to be comparatively close-mouthed. As a result, many wives get into the habit of thinking that if their husbands don't complain about anything, then everything's okay; the wives interpret a lack of hostility as an indication of continued love. In contrast, most husbands seem to think that if their wives don't express obvious affection for them, then everything's not okay; the husbands interpret a lack of overt love as a sign of hostility (Gaelick, Bodenhausen, & Wyer, 1985). This means that men and women tend to differ in their reactions to neutral interactions that are devoid of either affection or animosity: A woman is likely to think things are fine, but a man may start worrying that she doesn't love him anymore. It's also especially risky for a close-mouthed man to pair off with a talkative woman who criticizes him a lot (Swann, Rentfrow, & Gosling, 2003). When such couples have affectionate thoughts about each other, they're less likely to share them with one another than other couples are, so they enjoy their relationships less (Hammes & Swann, 2004). Gender differences in communication can evidently be problematic.

A closing note: Men value instrumental communication skills such as the ability to give clear instructions and directions more than women do. And women value expressive communication skills such as expressing affection and feelings more than men do. But both men and women consider expressive skills to be more important in close relationships than instrumental skills are (Burleson et al., 1996). Although they are sometimes caricatured as speaking different languages, men and women agree that the ability to adequately communicate one's love, respect, and regard for one's partner is indispensable in close relationships.

DYSFUNCTIONAL COMMUNICATION AND WHAT TO DO ABOUT IT

As we've seen, the more open and self-disclosing spouses are to one another, the more happily married they tend to be (Meeks et al., 1998). But not all our efforts to speak our minds and communicate with our partners have positive results. More often than we realize, we face an interpersonal gap that causes misunderstanding or confusion in those who hear what we have to say. And the nature and consequences of miscommunication are very apparent in relationships in which the partners are distressed and dissatisfied. The verbal communications of unhappy partners often just perpetuate their discontent and make things worse instead of better.

Miscommunication

Indeed, we can gain valuable insights about what we shouldn't do when we talk with others by carefully comparing the communicative behaviors of happy lovers to those of unhappy partners. John Gottman and his colleagues at the University of Washington have been doing this for over 30 years, and they have observed several important patterns. First, unhappy people do a poor job of *saying what they mean* (Gottman, 1994b). When they have a complaint, they are rarely precise; instead, they're prone to **kitchen-sinking,** in which they tend to address several topics at once (so that everything but the "kitchen sink" gets dragged into the conversation). This usually causes their primary concern to get lost in the barrage of frustrations that are announced at the same time. If they're annoyed by late fees at the video store, for instance, they may say, "It's not just your carelessness, it's those friends you hang out with, and your lousy attitude about helping out around the house." As a result, their conversations frequently drift **off-beam,** wandering from topic to topic so that the conversation never stays on one problem long enough to resolve it: "You never do what I ask. You're just as hard-headed as your mother, and you always take her side." Flitting from problem to problem on a long list of concerns makes it almost certain that none of them will be fixed.

Second, unhappy partners do a poor job of *hearing each other.* They rarely try to patiently double-check their understanding of their partners' messages. Instead, they jump to conclusions (often assuming the worst) and head off on tangents based on what they presume their partners really mean. One aspect of this is **mindreading,** which occurs when people assume that they understand their partners' thoughts, feelings, and opinions without asking. All intimate couples mindread to some extent, but distressed couples do so in critical and hostile ways; they tend to perceive unpleasant motives where neutral or positive ones actually exist: "You just said that to make me mad, to get back at me for yesterday." Unhappy partners also **interrupt** each other in negative ways more than contented couples do. Not all interruptions are obnoxious. People who interrupt their partners to express agreement or ask for clarification may actually be communicating happily and well. But people who interrupt to express disagreement or to change the topic are likely to leave their partners feeling disregarded and unappreciated (Daigen & Holmes, 2000).

Distressed couples also listen poorly by finding something wrong or unworkable with anything their partners say. This is **yes-butting,** and it communicates constant criticism of the others' points of view: "Yeah, we could try that, but it won't work because . . ." Unhappy partners also engage in **cross-complaining** that fails to acknowledge others' concerns; instead of expressing interest in what their partners have to say, they just respond to a complaint with one of their own:

> *"I hate the way you let the dishes pile up in the sink."*
> *"Well, I hate the way you leave your clothes lying around on the floor."*

Finally, unhappy partners too often display *negative affect* when they talk with each other (Gottman & Levenson, 1992). They often react to their partner's complaints with sarcastic disregard that is demeaning and scornful, and instead of mending their problems, they often make them worse. Damaging interactions like these typically begin with **criticism** that attacks a partner's personality or character instead of identifying a specific behavior that is causing concern. For instance, instead of delineating a particular frustration ("I get annoyed when you leave your wet towels on the floor"), a critic may inflame the interaction by making a global accusation of a character flaw ("You are such a slob!"). **Contempt** in the form of insults, mockery, or hostile humor is often involved as well. The partners' common response to such attacks is **defensiveness;** instead of treating the clumsy complaint as legitimate and reasonable, the partners seek to protect themselves from the perceived attack by making excuses or by cross-complaining, hurling counterattacks of their own. **Stonewalling** may follow, particularly in men, as a partner "clams up" and reacts to the messy situation by withdrawing into a stony silence (Heavy, Layne, & Christensen, 1993). People may believe they're helping the situation by refusing to argue further, but their lack of responsiveness can be infuriating (Zadro & Williams, 2000). Instead of demonstrating appropriate acknowledgement and concern for a partner's complaints, stonewalling typically communicates "disapproval, icy distance, and smugness" (Gottman, 1994b, p. 94). Ultimately, destructive **belligerence** may occur, with one partner aggressively rejecting the other altogether ("So what? What are you gonna do about it?").

When communication routinely degenerates into these contentious patterns, the outlook for the relationship is grim (Gottman et al., 1998). In fact, videotapes of just the first three minutes of a marital conflict enable researchers to predict with 83 percent accuracy who will be divorced six years later (Carrère & Gottman, 1999). Couples whose marriages are doomed display noticeably more contempt, defensiveness, and belligerence than do those who will stay together. And among those who stay together, spouses who communicate well are happier and more content than those who suffer frequent misunderstanding (Feeney, 1994).

The challenge, of course, is that it's not always easy to avoid these problems. When we're angry, resentful, or anxious, we may find ourselves cross-complaining, kitchen-sinking, and all the rest. How can we avoid these traps? Depending on the situation, we may need to send clearer, less inflammatory messages, listen better, or stay polite and calm, and sometimes we need to do all three.

Saying What We Mean

Complaints that criticize a partner's personality or character disparage the partner and often make mountains out of molehills, portraying problems as huge, intractable dilemmas that cannot be easily solved. (Given some of the broad complaints we throw at our partners, it's no wonder that they sometimes get defensive.) It's much more sensible—and accurate—to identify as plainly and concretely as possible a specific behavior that annoyed us. This is **behavior description,** and it not only tells our partners what's on our minds, it focuses the conversation on discrete, manageable behaviors that, unlike personalities, can often be readily changed. A good behavior description specifies a particular event and does not involve generalities; thus, words such as *always* or *never* should never be used. This is *not* a good behavior description: "You're always interrupting me! You never let me finish!"

We should also use **I-statements** that specify our feelings. I-statements start with "I" and then describe a distinct emotional reaction. They force us to identify our feelings, which can be useful both to us and our partners. They also help us to "own" our feelings and acknowledge them instead of keeping the entire

---

BOX 5.5
Communicating Sympathy and Concern

Few of us know what to say when we encounter bereaved others who are suffering from the loss of a loved one. We want to express sympathy and support, but our words often seem inadequate to the task. However, grief, and others' reactions to it, have been studied by relationship researchers (Lehman, Ellard, & Wortman, 1986), and we can offer some advice about this important kind of communication. First, you *should* mention the person's loss (Okonski, 1996). The death of a beloved is a huge loss, something that the person will never forget. Assuming that the person's pain has ended or is no longer salient to him or her, even months later, is simply insensitive (Martin, 1997). Talking about the lost partner acknowledges the person's distress and communicates caring and concern.

What should you say? Something simple. Try "I'm so sorry," or "I feel so sad for you" and then *stop.* Do not try to comfort the person with optimistic projections about the future. Do not imply that the loss is not the most tragic, awful thing that has ever happened. And do

not offer advice about how the person can put his or her life back together. Such efforts may spring from kind intentions, but each of them ultimately demeans the person's current suffering. Offer heartfelt sympathy and nothing more. Just nod your head and be a good listener and be nonjudgmental.

Thus, offering welcome comfort to others is more straightforward than you may have thought, as long as you avoid the pitfalls of saying too much. With this in mind, can you see what's wrong with the following dumb remarks? Each is a quote from someone who was probably trying—and failing—to be kind (Landers, 1997; Martin, 1997; Lehman et al., 1986):

"The sooner you let go, the better."

"You'll get over it."

"He should have been wearing a seat belt."

"She's with God now."

"You're young, you can have other children."

"You have many good years left."

focus on the partner. Thus, instead of saying, "You really piss me off," one should say, "I feel pretty angry right now."

A handy way to use both behavior descriptions and I-statements to communicate more clearly and accurately is to integrate them into **XYZ statements.** Such statements follow the form of "When you do **X** in situation **Y**" (that's a good behavior description), "I feel **Z**" (an I-statement). Listen to yourself next time you complain to your partner. Are you saying something like this:

"You're so inconsiderate! You never let me finish what I'm saying!"

Or, are you being precise and accurate and saying what you mean:

"When you interrupted me just now, I felt annoyed."

There's a big difference. One of those statements is likely to get a thoughtful, apologetic response from a loving partner, but the other probably won't.

Active Listening

We have two vital tasks when we're on the receiving end of others' messages. The first is to accurately understand what our partners are trying to say, and the second is to communicate that attention and comprehension to our partners so that they know we care about what they've said. Both tasks can be accomplished by **paraphrasing** a message, repeating it in our own words and giving the sender a chance to agree that that's what he or she actually meant. When people use paraphrasing, they don't assume that they understood their partners and issue an immediate reply. Instead, they take a moment to check their comprehension by rephrasing the message and repeating it back. This sounds awkward, but it is a terrific way to avoid arguments and conflict that would otherwise result from misunderstanding and mistakes. Whenever a conversation begins to get heated, paraphrasing can keep it from getting out of hand. Look what's wrong here:

WILMA: (sighing) I'm so glad your mother decided not to come visit us next week.
FRED: (irate) What's wrong with my mother? You've always been on her case, and I think you're an ungrateful witch!

Perhaps before Fred flew off the handle, some paraphrasing would have been helpful:

WILMA: (sighing) I'm so glad your mother decided not to come visit us next week.
FRED: (irate) Are you saying you don't like her to be here?
WILMA: (surprised) No, she's always welcome. I just have my paper due in my relationships class and won't have much time then.
FRED: (mollified) Oh.

Another valuable listening skill is **perception checking,** which is the opposite of mindreading. In perception checking, people assess the accuracy of their inferences about a partner's feelings by asking the partner for clarification. This communicates one's attentiveness and interest, and it encourages the partner to be more open: "You seem pretty upset by what I said, is that right?"

Cathy is trying to engage in active listening, but she's not getting very far.
CATHY © 1983 Cathy Guisewite. Reprinted with permission of UNIVERSAL PRESS SYNDICATE.

Listeners who paraphrase and check their perceptions make an *active* effort to understand their partners, and that care and consideration is usually much appreciated. Active listening is also likely to help smooth the inevitable rough spots any relationship encounters. Indeed, people who practice these techniques typically report happier marriages than do those who simply assume that they understand what their partners mean by what they say (Markman, Stanley, & Blumberg, 1994).

Being Polite and Staying Cool

Still, even the most accurate sending and receiving may not do much good if our conversations are too often surly and antagonistic. It's hard to remain mild and relaxed when we encounter contempt and belligerence from others, and people who deride or disdain their partners often get irascible, irritated reactions in return. Indeed, dissatisfied spouses spend more time than contented lovers do locked into patterns of *negative affect reciprocity* in which they're contemptuous of each other, with each being scornful of what the other has to say (Levenson, Carstensen, & Gottman, 1994). Happy couples behave this way, too—there are probably periods of acrimonious disregard in most relationships—but they break out of these ugly cycles more quickly than unhappy partners do (Burman, Margolin, & John, 1993).

In fact, defusing cycles of increasing cantankerousness when they begin may be very beneficial, but it may not be easy. Although XYZ statements and active listening skills can help prevent surly interactions altogether, Gottman and his colleagues argue that people rarely have the presence of mind to use them once they get angry (Gottman et al., 2000). It can be difficult or even "impossible to make 'I-statements' when you are in the 'hating-my-partner, wanting revenge, feeling-stung-and-needing-to-sting-back' state of mind" (Wile, 1995, p. 2).

Thus, being able to stay cool when you're provoked by a partner, and being able to calm down when you begin to get angry, are very valuable skills. You'll be better able to do this if you construe anger as just one way of thinking about

Unhappy partners often have difficulty saying what they mean, hearing each other, and staying polite and calm when disagreements arise.

a problem. Anger results from the perception that others are causing us illegitimate, unfair, avoidable grief. Use a different point of view and anger is reduced or prevented altogether (Tavris, 1989; Zillman, 1993). Instead of thinking, "S/he has no right to say that to me!," it's more adaptive to think, "Hmm. Contrary statements from someone who loves me. I wonder why?"

Of course, it can be hard to maintain such a placid stream of thought when one is provoked. So it's also a good idea to (try to) reduce the number of provocations you encounter by agreeing in advance to be polite to each other whenever possible (Gottman, 1994b). You may wish to schedule regular meetings at which you and your partner (politely) air your grievances; knowing that a problem will be addressed makes it easier to be pleasant to your partner the rest of the week (Markman et al., 1994). And under no circumstances should the two of you continue an interaction in which you're just hurling insults and sarcasm back and forth at each other. If you find yourself in such a pattern of negative affect reciprocity, take a temporary *time out* to stop the cycle. Ask for a short break—"Honey, I'm too angry to think straight. Let me take 10 minutes to calm down"—and then return to the issue when you're less aroused (Markman et al., 1994). Get off by yourself and take no more than six long, slow, deep breaths per minute, and you will calm down, faster than you think (Tavris, 1989).

The Power of Respect and Validation

The central ingredients in all of these components of good communication— our conscious efforts to send clear, straightforward messages, to listen carefully and well, and to be polite and nonaggressive even when disagreements occur— are the indications we provide that we care about and respect our partners' points of view. We expect such concern and regard from our intimate partners, and distress and resentment build when we think we're disrespected (Reis & Patrick, 1996). Thus, **validation** of our partners that acknowledges the legitimacy of their opinions and communicates respect for their positions is always a desirable goal in intimate interaction.

Validation does not mean that you agree with someone. You can communicate appropriate respect and recognition of a partner's point of view without agreeing with it. Consider the following three responses to Barney's complaint:

	BARNEY: I hate it when you act that way.
Cross-complaining	BETTY: And I hate it when you get drunk with Fred.
Agreement	BETTY: Yeah, I agree. It's not a nice way to act, and I'll try to change.
Validation	BETTY: Yeah, I can see how you'd feel that way. You've got a point. But I'd like you to try to understand what I'm feeling, too.

Only the last response, which concedes the legitimacy of Barney's point of view but allows Betty her own feelings, invites an open, honest dialogue. We need not be inauthentic or nonassertive to respect our partners' opinions, even when we disagree with them.

Indeed, validating our partners will often make disagreement much more tolerable. All of the skills we have mentioned here support an atmosphere of responsive care and concern that can reduce the intensity and impact of disputes with our partners (Huston & Chorost, 1994). You may even be able to set a troubled relationship on a more promising path by rehearsing these skills and pledging to be polite and respectful to one another when difficulties arise (Stanley, Bradbury, & Markman, 2000).

FOR YOUR CONSIDERATION

James loved deer hunting season. He liked to sit shivering in a deer blind in the chill before dawn, sipping coffee, and waiting for what the day would bring. But his wife Judy always dreaded that time of year. James would be gone for several weekends in a row, and each time he returned he'd either be grumpy because he was empty-handed or he would have lots of venison—and extra work—for her to handle. The costs of his permit and lease were also substantial, and the expense kept them from enjoying an occasional weekend at that bed-and-breakfast at the lake she liked so much.

So, when Judy handed James a thermos of hot coffee and walked with him to the door at 4:30 in the morning on the first day of deer season, she was already feeling melancholy and lonely. She looked at him and tried to be cheerful, but her smile was forced and her expression downcast as she said in a plaintive tone, "Have a nice time, dear." James happily replied, "Okay, thanks, hon. See you Sunday night!" and was gone.

What do you think the future holds for James and Judy? Why?

CHAPTER SUMMARY

Communication is an important factor in the development and quality of relationships. Research using the "talk table" demonstrates that unhappy partners frustrate and annoy each other through miscommunication more often than happy partners do. When a sender's intentions differ from the impact that a message has on the recipient, a couple faces an *interpersonal gap.*

Nonverbal Communication

A clue to the power of nonverbal communication lies in the number of channels through which it is transmitted.

Nonverbal communication serves vital functions, *providing information, regulating interaction,* and *defining the nature of the relationship* two people share.

Components of Nonverbal Communication

Facial expression. Several basic facial expressions, such as happiness, sadness, fear, anger, disgust, and surprise, appear to be inborn; people all over the world display the same expressions when they experience those emotions. As a result, facial expressions are good guides to others' moods. Following *display rules,* cultural norms that dictate what emotions are appropriate in particular situations, people often try to control their expressions. Nonetheless, subtle indications of their real feelings often leak out.

Gazing behavior. The direction and amount of a person's looking is important in defining relationships and in regulating interaction. In particular, high-status people use a higher *visual dominance ratio,* looking at others more when they are speaking, and less when they are listening, than low-status people do.

Body movement. Small elements of body movement such as gestures vary widely across cultures, but the posture and motion of the entire body is informative as well. Customs agents use body movement to decide whether or not to search a traveler's luggage.

Touch. Men and women tend to respond differently to touches from strangers, with women responding positively, men negatively. As a result, men touch women more than women touch men.

Interpersonal distance. We use different zones of personal space—the *intimate, personal, social,* and *public* zones—for different kinds of interactions. Preferred distances vary with culture, sex, and status.

Paralanguage. Paralanguage involves all the variations in a person's voice, such as rhythm, rate, and loudness, other than the words he or she uses. A good example is baby talk, which is often used to address lovers, elderly people, and pets, as well as babies.

Combining the components. Together, these nonverbal actions are very informative. When there is a discrepancy between people's words and actions, the truth usually lies in their nonverbal, not their verbal, communication. Nonverbal actions also allow us to fine-tune the intimacy of our interactions in subtle but real ways.

Nonverbal Sensitivity. Nonverbal accuracy predicts relationship satisfaction. Unhappy spouses, especially husbands, do a poor job at nonverbal communication. Either skill or performance deficits may be involved in such problems, but no matter why it occurs, nonverbal insensitivity probably makes one an unrewarding partner.

Sex Differences in Nonverbal Communication. When they interact with men, women display deferential patterns of nonverbal behavior that resemble those of low-status people interacting with those of higher status. The reason why is unclear, but such behavior may be influential in perpetuating unwanted stereotypes.

Verbal Communication

Self-Disclosure. Two people cannot be said to be intimate with one another unless they have revealed personal information about themselves to their partners.

The theory of social penetration. As a relationship develops, both the breadth and depth of self-disclosure increase. Participants discuss more topics and reveal more personally meaningful information. However, breadth increases faster than depth does at first. Reciprocity in self-disclosure is also more common between strangers than between intimates.

Both self-disclosure and selective secrecy contribute to relationship satisfaction. Partners try to avoid talking about *taboo topics* such as the state of their relationship, but they may resort to a variety of secret tests to assess their partners' commitment. When their relationships are failing, some couples decrease the breadth but increase the depth of their self-disclosure, reflecting the intense negative emotions expressed during conflict.

Is it always gradual? Sometimes people disclose highly personal information soon after they first meet. In the "stranger-on-the-plane" phenomenon, quick self-disclosure is usually safe because people don't expect to meet again. But where an enduring relationship is possible, premature self-disclosure may damage the long-term prospects of the relationship. The best strategy is to judge the appropriateness of self-disclosure by taking both the context and the partner into account.

Self-disclosure and relationship satisfaction. Appropriate self-disclosure breeds liking and contentment because we reveal more personal information to those we like, like others more because we have self-disclosed to them, and like to be entrusted with self-disclosures from others.

Gender Differences in Verbal Communication. Men and women are more similar to each other than different, but there are some gender differences in communicative style.

Topics of conversation. Among themselves, women are more likely than men to discuss feelings and people, whereas men are more likely to seek a few laughs and talk about more impersonal matters.

Styles of conversation. When they are conversing with men, women also tend to speak less often and with less forcefulness than men do. Men are more profane.

Self-disclosure. On average, women self-disclose more than men in close relationships, but there are no such differences in more casual relationships. Men self-disclose relatively little to other men even when they are friends, and thus they are likely to share their most meaningful intimacy only with women. This is not true in some other countries, so this pattern appears to be a learned preference that is influenced by cultural norms.

Instrumentality versus expressivity. Intimate self-disclosure is linked to expressivity, so traditional, macho men (who are low in expressivity) need relationships with women to keep from being lonely. In contrast, androgynous men, who are more expressive, enjoy more meaningful interactions with all their friends.

However, because so many men are sex-typed and are close-mouthed about their feelings, wives often interpret a lack of hostility from their husbands as a sign of love. Men, on the other hand, tend to interpret a lack of overt love as a sign of hostility. In this manner, gender differences in communication can be problematic. In any case, both men and women agree that communication of affectionate feelings is indispensable in close relationships.

Dysfunctional Communication and What to Do about It

The impact of miscommunication is obvious in unhappy relationships, where conversation often makes things worse instead of better.

Miscommunication. Distressed couples have trouble saying what they mean. They're prone to *kitchen-sinking* as they clumsily address several topics at once, and their conversations frequently drift *off-beam*, straying from topic to topic. They also do a poor job of hearing each other. They engage in *mindreading* and *interrupt* each other disagreeably, finding fault with what the other says. Worst of all, they display negative affect and say things that are *critical, contemptuous,* and *defensive;* they may also *stonewall* each other and become *belligerent.* Such behavior is very destructive, and too much of it may doom spouses to divorce.

Saying What We Mean. When they are complaining about something, skillful senders focus on specific, concrete actions instead of personalities. They also make their feelings clear with *I-statements*, often integrating them into *XYZ statements* that identify discrete events they found annoying.

Active Listening. Good listeners make an effort to understand their partners, often *paraphrasing* a sender's message to double-check its meaning. They also use *perception checking* to assess the accuracy of their inferences by asking whether their judgments are correct.

Being Polite and Staying Cool. Happy couples also avoid extended periods of negative affect reciprocity, but this is sometimes hard to do. Anger can be defused with adaptive mental scripts and slow breathing, but it's a good idea for couples to agree in advance to be polite to each other whenever possible. Regular meetings that address problems can be helpful in this regard.

The Power of Respect and Validation. Finally, even when they disagree, partners should strive to *validate* each other by communicating respect and recognition of the other's point of view. Such actions reduce the impact of disputes, and they may even save troubled relationships.

Interdependency

If you've been in a relationship for a while, why are you staying in that relationship? Are you obligated to continue it for some reason? Do you consider it your duty? Or are you simply waiting for something better to come along? Hopefully, all of your current relationships have been so rewarding that none of these questions will apply. However, all of them provide the focus for this chapter, which will take an *economic* view of our dealings with others.

Our subject will be interdependency, our reliance on others, and they on us, for valuable interpersonal rewards. We'll examine why we stay in some relationships and leave others, and we will ponder the nature of lasting relationships. We'll say nothing about love, which is the topic of another chapter. Instead, here we will ponder the balance sheets with which we tally the profits and losses of our interactions with others. You may not yet have thought of yourself as an interpersonal accountant, but doing so provides powerful insights into the workings of close relationships.

SOCIAL EXCHANGE

Interdependency theories assume that people are like shoppers who are browsing at an interpersonal shopping mall. We're all looking for good buys. We seek interactions with others that provide maximum reward at minimum cost, and we only stay with those partners who provide sufficient profit (Rusbult, Arriaga, & Agnew, 2001). However, because everybody behaves this way, both partners in a relationship must be profiting to their satisfaction or the relationship is unlikely to continue.

From this perspective, social life entails the mutual exchange of desirable rewards with others, a process called **social exchange** (Blau, 1964; Homans,

1961). There are several different social exchange theories, but the ideas introduced by John Thibaut and Harold Kelley (1959; Kelley, 1979; Kelley & Thibaut, 1978)—now known as *interdependence theory*—are most often used by relationship scientists, so we'll feature them here. Let's first consider the central elements of social exchange.

Rewards and Costs

The rewards of interactions are the gratifying experiences and commodities we obtain through our contact with others. They come in very different forms, ranging from impersonal benefits, such as the directions you can get from strangers when you're lost, to personal intimacies, such as acceptance and support from someone you love. We'll use the term *reward* to refer to anything within an interaction that is desirable and welcome and that brings enjoyment or fulfillment to the recipient.

In contrast, *costs* are punishing, undesirable experiences. They can involve financial expenditures, such as buying dinner for your date, or actual injuries, such as split lips and blackened eyes. However, some of the most important costs of intimate interaction are psychological burdens: uncertainty about where a relationship is headed, frustration over your partner's imperfections, and regret about all the things you don't get to do because you're in that relationship (Sedikides, Oliver, & Campbell, 1994). All of the diverse consequences of interaction that are frustrating or distressing are costs.

We'll summarize the rewards and costs associated with a particular interaction with the term **outcome,** which describes the net profit or loss a person encounters, all things considered. Adding up all the rewards and costs involved,

$$\text{Outcome} = \text{Rewards} - \text{Costs}$$

Obviously, if an interaction is more rewarding than punishing, a positive outcome results. But remember, the social exchange perspective asserts that people want the *best possible* outcomes. The simple fact that your interactions are profitable doesn't mean that they are good enough to keep you coming back to that partner. Indeed, one of the major insights of interdependence theory is its suggestion that whether your outcomes are positive or negative isn't nearly as important as where they stand compared to two criteria with which we evaluate the outcomes we receive. The first criterion involves our expectations, and the second involves our perceptions of how well we could manage without our current partner.

What Do We Expect from Our Relationships?

Interdependence theory assumes that each of us has an idiosyncratic **comparison level** (which we'll abbreviate as **CL**), that describes the value of the outcomes that we believe we deserve in our dealings with others. Our CLs are based on our past experiences. People who have a history of highly rewarding partnerships are likely to have high CLs, meaning that they expect, and feel they deserve, very good outcomes now. In contrast, people who have had troublesome relationships in the past are likely to expect less and have lower CLs.

A person's comparison level represents his or her neutral point on a continuum that ranges all the way from abject misery to ecstatic delight. Our CLs are the standards by which our *satisfaction* with a relationship is measured. If the outcomes you receive exceed your CL, you're happy; you're getting more than the minimum payoff you expect from interaction with others. Just how happy you are depends on the extent to which your outcomes surpass your expectations; if your outcomes are considerably higher than your CL, you'll be very satisfied. On the other hand, if your outcomes fall below your CL, you're dissatisfied, even if your outcomes are still pretty good and you're doing better than most people. This is a significant point: Even if you are still making a profit on your transactions with others, you may not be happy if the profit isn't big enough to meet your expectations. If you're a rich, spoiled celebrity, for instance, you may have an unusually high CL and be rather dissatisfied with a fabulous partner who would bedazzle the rest of us.

So, satisfaction in close relationships doesn't depend simply on how good in an absolute sense our outcomes are; instead, satisfaction derives from how our outcomes compare to our comparison levels, like this:

$$\text{Outcomes} - \text{CL} = \text{Satisfaction or Dissatisfaction}$$

How Well Could We Do Elsewhere?

However, another important assumption of interdependence theory is that satisfaction is not the only, or even the major, influence that determines how long relationships last. Whether or not we're happy, we use a second criterion, a **comparison level for alternatives** (or **CL_{alt}**), to determine if we could be doing even better somewhere else. Our CL_{alt}s describe the outcomes we can receive by leaving our current relationships and moving to the best alternative partnerships or situations we have available. And if you're a good accountant, you can see that our CL_{alt}s are also the lowest levels of outcome we will tolerate from our present partners. Here's why: If other relationships promise better profits than we currently receive, we're likely to leave our present partners and pursue those bigger payoffs even if we're satisfied with what we already have. (Remember, we want the best possible deal we can get.) On the other hand, even if we are dissatisfied with our current relationships, we are unlikely to leave them unless a better alternative presents itself. This is a very important point, which helps explain why people stay in relationships that make them miserable: even though they're unhappy where they are, they think they'd be worse off if they left. If they thought a better situation awaited them elsewhere, they'd go (Choice & Lamke, 1999; Heaton & Albrecht, 1991). This idea—that our contentment with a relationship is not the major determinant of whether we stay in it or leave—is one of interdependence theory's most interesting insights.

Thus, our CL_{alt}s determine our *dependence* on our relationships. Whether or not we're satisfied, if we believe that we're already doing as well as we possibly can, we are dependent upon our present partners and are unlikely to leave them (Ellis, Simpson, & Campbell, 2002). Moreover, the greater the gap between our current outcomes and our poorer alternatives, the more dependent we are. If our current outcomes are only a little better than those that await us elsewhere, we don't need our current partners very much and may leave if our alternatives improve.

But would people really leave relationships in which they're already happy? Presumably, they would, if their CL_{alt}s are genuinely better than what they're getting now. To keep things simple when you consider this, think of a CL_{alt} as the global outcome, the net profit or loss, that a person believes will result from switching partners, all things considered (Kelley, 2002). If the whole process of ending a present partnership and moving to an alternative promises better outcomes, a person should move. It's just economic good sense.

A problem, of course, is that these are difficult calculations to make. There's a lot to consider. On the one hand, there are the new external attractions that can lure us away from our present partners. We need to assess the desirability and availability of alternative partners, and solitude—being alone—is also an option to ponder. When other partners or simple solitude seem attractive, our CL_{alt}s go up. However, there may also be a variety of costs that we will incur by leaving an existing relationship, and they can dramatically affect the net profit to be gained by moving elsewhere (Levinger, 1999). For instance, social psychologist Caryl Rusbult has demonstrated that one's **investments** in a present relationship, the things one would lose if the relationship were to end, are also important influences on one's decision to stay or go (e.g., Rusbult, Drigotas, & Verette, 1994). The investments a person leaves behind can either be tangible goods, such as furniture and dishes you have to split with an ex-spouse, or intangible psychological benefits, such as love and respect from in-laws and friends (Goodfriend & Agnew, 2004). An unhappy spouse may refrain from filing for divorce, for example, not because she has no other options but because she doesn't want to accept the potential costs of confused children, a bitter ex-spouse, disappointed parents, and befuddled friends (Goodfriend & Agnew, 2002). All of these would reduce the global desirability of leaving, and thus reduce one's CL_{alt}.

Another complication is that a person's CL_{alt} is what he or she *thinks* it is, and a variety of factors can influence people's perceptions of their alternatives. Self-esteem, for one. When people don't like themselves, they're unlikely to think that others will find them desirable (Kiesler & Baral, 1970), and they may underestimate their prospects with other partners. Learned helplessness may also be influential (Strube, 1988). If people get stuck in a bad relationship for too long, they may lose hope and glumly underestimate their chances of doing better elsewhere. And access to information may affect one's CL_{alt}, too. If you become a stay-at-home parent who doesn't work, you'll probably have much more limited information about potential alternatives than you would have if you went to work in a large city every day (Rusbult & Martz, 1995); as a result, you'll probably have a lower CL_{alt} than you would have if you got out and looked around.

Indeed, desirable alternatives will only enhance your CL_{alt} if you are aware of them, and if you're content with your current partners you may not pay much attention to people who could be compelling rivals to your existing relationships. In fact, people who are satisfied with their existing relationships do report less interest in looking around to see how they could be doing elsewhere; as a result, they also think they have lower CL_{alt}s than do those who pay more attention to their alternatives (Miller, 1997a). This may be important. College students who keep track of their options and monitor their alternatives with care switch romantic partners more often than do those who pay their alternatives less heed (Miller, 1997a).

These results mean that although interdependence theory treats satisfaction and dependence as relatively independent components of relationships, they are actually correlated. As an old cliché suggests, the grass may be greener in other relationships, but if you're happy with your current partner, you're less likely to notice. Still, there's wisdom in remembering that satisfaction with a relationship has only a limited role in a person's decision to stay in it or go. Consider the usual trajectory of a divorce: Spouses who divorce have usually been unhappy for quite some time before they decide to separate. What finally prompts them to act? Something changes: Their CL_{alt}s finally come to exceed their current outcomes (Albrecht & Kunz, 1980). Things may get so bad that their outcomes in the marriage slip below those that are available in alternative options that used to seem inadequate. Or, the apparent costs of ending the marriage decrease (which raises one's CL_{alt}); because the spouses have been unhappy for so long, for instance, their kids, parents, and pastor may change their minds and support a divorce for the first time. Or, the apparent rewards of leaving increase, perhaps because they have saved some money or found an alternative partner. (This also raises one's CL_{alt}.) The bottom line is that people don't divorce when they get unhappy; they divorce when, one way or the other, their prospects finally seem brighter elsewhere.

So, if we remember that CL_{alt} is a multifaceted judgment encompassing both the costs of leaving—such as lost investments—and the enticements offered by others, we get:

$$\text{Outcomes} - CL_{alt} = \text{Dependence or Independence}$$

In summary, the three key elements of social exchange are people's *outcomes, comparison levels* (CL), and *comparison levels for alternatives* (CL_{alt}). The net profits or losses people receive from interaction are their outcomes. When their outcomes exceed their expectations, or CLs, they are satisfied; however, if they are not doing as well as they expect (that is, when their outcomes are lower than their CLs), they are dissatisfied. In addition, when people's current outcomes are better than those they could get elsewhere (that is, when their outcomes exceed their CL_{alt}s), they are dependent on their current partners and are unlikely to leave. However, if their outcomes from their current partners get worse than those that can be readily obtained elsewhere (and their outcomes fall below their CL_{alt}s), they will be independent and will be likely to depart.

Four Types of Relationships

Now that we understand CLs and CL_{alt}s, let's see how they work together to define the types of relationships people encounter. CLs, CL_{alt}s, and the outcomes people experience can all range from low to high along a continuum of outcome quality. Interdependence theory suggests that when we consider all three of these factors simultaneously, four different broad types of relationships result.

Consider what happens when people's outcomes exceed both their CLs and their CL_{alt}s. They're getting more from their partners than they expect *and* they believe they're doing better than they could anywhere else. So, they're happy and (as far as they're concerned) their relationships are stable. They're not going anywhere. This pleasant situation is depicted in Figure 6.1 in two different ways. In one case, a person's CL is higher than his or her CL_{alt}, whereas in the other case the reverse is true. In these and all the other examples we'll explain, the specific amount of satisfaction or dependence a person feels depends on the extent to which CL and CL_{alt} differ from the person's current outcomes. So, in graph A_1, the person is more satisfied than dependent, whereas in graph A_2, the person is more dependent than satisfied. However, in both cases—and this is the point we wish to make—the person is in a happy, stable relationship. We showed you both graphs A_1 and A_2 to demonstrate that, in terms of the simple classifications illustrated in Figure 6.1, it doesn't matter whether CL is higher than CL_{alt} or vice versa. Even if they're exactly the same, the same broad category will apply; if the person's current outcomes surpass both CL and CL_{alt}, that person will be content and unlikely to leave.

FIGURE 6.1. Types of relationships in interdependence theory.

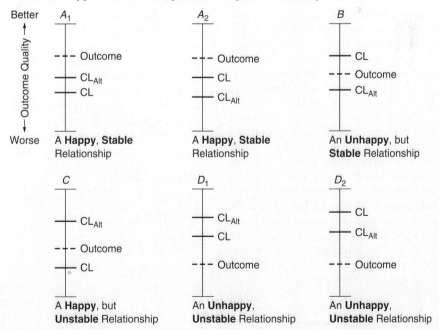

Contrast that situation with what happens when people's outcomes fall below their CLs but are still higher than their CL_{alt}s (in graph *B*). These folks are dissatisfied. They're getting less than they expect and feel they deserve, but they're still doing better than they think they can elsewhere. They're in an unhappy but stable relationship that they will not leave. Hopefully, you've never encountered such a situation yourself, but if you've ever had a lousy, low-paying job that you disliked but couldn't leave because it was the best job available at the time, you know what we're talking about. That's the sort of fix these folks are in.

BOX 6.1
Power and (In)Dependence

Figure 6.1 portrays the situations that may face one member of a couple, but a relationship involves two people. How might their CL_{alt}s influence their interactions with each other? Let's assume a romantic couple, Betty and Barney, receive similar outcomes from their relationship, and each is dependent on the other, but Barney's CL_{alt} is lower than Betty's. That would mean that Barney needs Betty more than she needs him; if the relationship ended, he would lose more by moving to his next best option than she would. Because neither of them wants to leave their partnership, this might seem like a trivial matter, but, in fact, this disparity in dependence gives her more *power* than he has.

As we'll see in chapter 11, power is the ability to influence another person's behavior. A nuance of social exchange, the **principle of lesser interest,** suggests that the partner who is less dependent on a relationship has more power in that relationship (Waller & Hill, 1951). Or, the person with less to lose by ending a desired partnership gets to call the shots. In fact, when it comes to winning arguments and getting one's way, the principle seems to be accurate; the more independent member of a romantic relationship is usually acknowledged by

both partners to be the more dominant of the two (Berman & Bennett, 1982).

If the difference in Betty's and Barney's dependence on each other is too great, there may be trouble ahead. People generally do not like relationships that involve an inequality of dependence as much as those in which the partners need each other to a similar degree (Le & Agnew, 2001; Lehmiller, Agnew, & Etcheverry, 2004). Nevertheless, for as long as it lasts, Betty's higher CL_{alt} is likely to mean that she's the boss.

FIGURE 6.2. In this situation, Betty and Barney are dependent on each other, and neither is likely to leave. Nevertheless, Betty's alternatives are better than Barney's, and that gives her more power in their relationship.

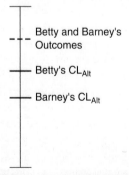

Betty and Barney's Outcomes

Betty's CL_{Alt}

Barney's CL_{Alt}

By comparison, if people's CL_{alt}s are higher than their outcomes but their CLs are lower, they're in a much more favorable situation (graph C). They're satisfied with their present partners but believe that they have even more attractive outcomes, all things considered, awaiting them somewhere else. Their current relationships are happy but unstable because they're not likely to stay where they are. In an analogous situation in the workplace, you'd face this situation if you liked your existing job but you got an even better offer from another employer. If you added it all up—including the friends you'd leave behind, the costs of relocating, and the uncertainties of your new position—and thought you'd be better off by leaving, you would leave, wouldn't you?

Finally, people's outcomes may be lower than both their CLs and CL_{alt}s. Again, at this level of analysis, it wouldn't matter whether their CLs were lower than their CL_{alt}s (graph D_1) or vice versa (graph D_2); as long as their present outcomes were lower than both of them, they'd be in an unhappy and unstable relationship that probably wouldn't last much longer.

In real relationships, of course, a huge variety of configurations are possible as people's CLs, CL_{alt}s, and outcomes all range from excellent to poor. These four types of relationships are only meant to be general guides to diverse possibilities. CLs, CL_{alt}s, and outcomes may all change over time as well. In fact, changes in these variables lead to further interesting nuances of interdependence theory.

CL and CL_{alt} as Time Goes By

Imagine you find the perfect relationship. Your partner is loving, gorgeous, smart, rich, generous, and tireless, and is an award-winning chef, accomplished masseuse, expert auto mechanic, and computer programmer. He or she provides you outcomes that exceed your wildest dreams. When you get home each night, your partner has something exquisite for you to eat after you get your welcome-home massage and pedicure. Would you be satisfied? Of course you would. But what's likely to happen after you've enjoyed several straight months of this bliss?

You might get home one evening to find no massage and no supper because your partner has been delayed by traffic. "Hey," you might think, "where's my gourmet meal? Where's my backrub?" You've come to expect such marvelous treatment, which means your comparison level has risen. But if your CL goes up and your outcomes remain the same, satisfaction goes down (see Box 6.2). Once you get used to your perfect partner, you may find that you derive less pleasure from his or her pampering than you used to.

Indeed, interdependence theory predicts such a pattern. Because they are based on our experiences, our CLs tend to fluctuate along with the outcomes we receive. When we first encounter excellent outcomes, we're delighted, but our pleasure may slowly dwindle as we come to take such benefits for granted and our CLs rise. In this manner, rewarding relationships can gradually become less and less satisfying even though nothing (but our expectations) has changed.

That's a problem. Worse, since you were born, sociocultural influences may have caused our expectations to creep up and up. Blessed with economic

---

BOX 6.2
Comparison Levels in Lottery Winners

Most people think that they'd be pretty happy if they just had a few thousand dollars more than they have now, so they think that they'd be *really* happy if they won a big lottery and became rich (Myers & Diener, 1995). Are they correct? You may find this surprising, but the answer is "not really." For a time, lottery winners are often delighted with their improved standard of living. Getting rich can be a lot of fun at first. But remarkably soon after they win, they begin to get used to their newfound riches. They adapt to their changed circumstances, start to take them for granted, and feel less and less delighted as their expectations change (Diener, 2000). They may live better, but they tend to be just as frustrated as you and I. Whereas we get frustrated when the video store is sold out of the new release we wanted to rent, the rich get frustrated at their crummy seats at the Cannes Film Festival, and they're just as frustrated as we are. Typical lottery winners end up a year later no happier, on average, than they were before they won.

In the terms of interdependence theory, their global comparison levels, what they expect out of life, have gone up. Satisfaction results from the *discrepancy* between people's CLs and the outcomes they receive, and if their expectations are almost as high as their outcomes, they won't be very happy no matter how high those outcomes are. Rich people may have very high outcomes, but if they expect them and take them for granted, they may derive little satisfaction from them (Houston, 1981). So, in fact, the usual trajectory for lottery winners is initial delight that gradually fades as they adjust to their new lives and their CLs rise.

Is finding a wonderful relationship partner anything like winning a lottery? Yes. A longitudinal study of over 24,000 people in Germany demonstrated that getting married made most people happier but only for a while (Lucas et al., 2003). Two years later, most of them were only as happy as they had been before they wed. Neither winning a lottery nor finding that perfect partner is likely to make you happy forever.

---

prosperity, Americans have more disposable income than ever before, and they now expect a standard of living that used to be thought luxurious (Myers, 2000). In the view of some observers, a similar sense of entitlement has crept into our expectations for our relationships (Attridge & Berscheid, 1994). We expect our romances to be magical rather than merely pleasant, and it's hard to be happy when we expect so much (see Box 6.2 again). In fact, on average, American marriages are less happy than they were 30 years ago, and our higher CLs may be partly responsible (Glenn, 1996).

Cultural changes may also have caused widespread increases in our CL$_{alt}$s. The sex ratio has been climbing in recent years, so women have had more men to pick from (see chapter 1). Women's increased participation in the workforce has also provided them more financial freedom (South & Lloyd, 1995). People are more mobile than ever before, changing residences and traveling at unprecedented rates (Putnam, 2000). And legal, religious, and social barriers against divorce have gradually eroded (Berscheid & Lopes, 1997). No-fault divorce legislation that has made it easier for spouses to get divorces, for exam-ple, may be directly responsible for thousands of divorces that might not have otherwise occurred (Rodgers, Nakonezny, & Shull, 1999). Altogether, the costs of departing a marriage have declined even as, in many cases, people have found more options and more partners available to them. We may even have entered an era of "permanent availability," in which people remain on the mar-riage market—continuing to size up the people they meet as potential future mates—even after they're married (Farber, 1987)! If you add up these influences and look back at Figure 6.1, maybe we shouldn't be surprised that the American divorce rate has risen sharply since 1960; when CLs and CL$_{alt}$s are both high, people are more likely to find themselves in unhappy and unstable relation-ships (White & Booth, 1991).

THE ECONOMIES OF RELATIONSHIPS

As you can see, interdependence theory and its cousins take an unromantic view of close relationships. We even likened a happy, stable relationship to a de-sirable job with good benefits in describing some of the nuances of this ap-proach. But can the success or failure of close relationships really be reduced to nothing more than the profits or losses on an interaction spreadsheet? Are re-wards and costs, or the size of your "salary," everything that matter? The an-swer, of course, is no. Too specific a focus on the rewards and costs of a couple's interactions can lead us to overlook important influences that can make or break a partnership. For instance, your ultimate success in an important rela-tionship may someday depend on how well you adapt to external stresses that you cannot control (Karney & Bradbury, 1995).

On the other hand, interdependence theory's businesslike emphasis on the outcomes people derive from interaction is enormously important. Counting up the rewards and costs of a relationship provides extraordinary information about its current state and likely future (see Bradbury, 1998). And the picture of normal intimacy that emerges from studies of this sort is a bit surprising. The stereotype of intimate relations is that they are generous and loving, and, sure enough, couples who are nice to each other are more likely to stay together over time than are those who provide each other fewer rewards (e.g., Bui, Peplau, & Hill, 1996; Fitzpatrick & Sollie, 1999a). In one study, for instance, measures of generosity, affection, and self-disclosure administered at the very beginning of a dating relationship were quite accurate at predicting whether the couples would still be together four months later (Berg & McQuinn, 1986).

But costs are informative, too, and the surprise is that a lot of unpleasantness actually occurs in many relationships. On any given day, 44 percent of us are likely to be annoyed by a lover or friend (Averill, 1982). Each week, college stu-dents report an average of 8.7 aggravating hassles in their romantic relationships, a rate of more than one frustrating nuisance per day (Perlman, 1989). Most young adults complain that their lovers were overly critical, stubborn, selfish, *and* unreliable at least once during the past week (Perlman, 1989). Typical spouses report one or two unpleasant disagreements in their marriages each month

(McGonagle, Kessler, & Schilling, 1992). Long-term intimacy with another person apparently involves more irritation and exasperation than some of us may expect. Indeed, during their lives together, married people are likely to be meaner to each other than to anyone else they know (Miller, 1997b). This does *not* mean that close relationships are more punishing than rewarding overall; that's not true (in many cases) at all. However, on those (hopefully rare) occasions when intimates are at their worst, they're likely to be more tactless, impolite, sullen, selfish, and insensitive with each other than they would be with total strangers.

In fact, research has compared the manners in which people interact with their spouses and with total strangers on a problem-solving task (Vincent, Weiss, & Birchler, 1975). When they were discussing issues with others they did not know well, people were polite and congenial; they withheld criticism, swallowed any disapproval, and suppressed signs of frustration. In contrast, with their spouses, people were much more obnoxious. They interrupted their lovers, disparaged their points of view, and openly disagreed. Intimacy and interdependence seemed to give people permission to be impolite instead of courteous and considerate.

Does this matter? You bet it does. Over time, irritating or moody behavior from a spouse puts a marriage at risk (Caughlin, Huston, & Houts, 2000; Karney & Bradbury, 1997). Outright hostility is even worse (Matthews, Wickrama, & Conger, 1996). When people seek a divorce, they usually have a list of several recurring aggravations that have caused them grief (Amato & Rogers, 1997). And even a few frustrations may be influential because negative behaviors in a close relationship seem to carry more psychological weight than similar amounts of positive behavior do (e.g., Pasch & Bradbury, 1998). That is, "bad is stronger than good" (Baumeister et al., 2001).

Here's an example of what we mean. Imagine that you're walking down a sidewalk when a $20 bill blows into your path. There's no one else around, and it's obviously yours to keep. Does finding the money feel good? Of course it does. But now imagine that on another occasion you reach into a pocket where you put a $20 bill and find nothing but a hole. That's a disappointment. But which has the stronger effect on your mood, finding the new money or losing the money you already had? The answer is that losses usually affect us more than equivalent gains do; we hate losses but we merely like gains (Kahneman & Tversky, 1982).

In a similar fashion, undesirable events in close relationships are more noticeable and influential than logically equivalent desirable events are (Baumeister et al., 2001). If you get one compliment and one criticism from your lover during an evening at home, for instance, they probably won't cancel each other out; the compliment will help soften the blow of the criticism, but the combination will leave you somewhat distressed. Bad is stronger than good.

In fact, in order to stay satisfied with a close relationship, we may need to maintain a rewards-to-costs ratio of at least 5-to-1. That figure comes from research by John Gottman and Robert Levenson (1992), who observed married couples who were revisiting the topic of their last argument. They carefully coded the partners' behavior during their discussion, giving each spouse a point for each attempt at warmth, collaboration, or compromise, and subtracting a point for each display of anger, defensiveness, criticism, or contempt. Some of the couples were able to disagree with each other in a manner that communicated respect and regard for each other, and the longer their conversations went on, the more positive their scores became. These couples, who were said to be at low risk of divorce by Gottman and Levenson, were maintaining a ratio of positive to negative exchanges of 5:1 or better. (See Figure 6.3.) However, other

FIGURE 6.3. The interactions of couples at low and high risk of divorce. (Pos-Neg = number of positive vs. negative exchanges.) *Adapted from Gottman & Levenson, 1992.*

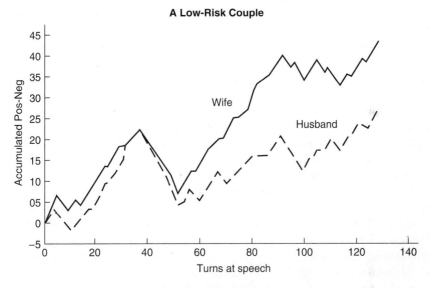

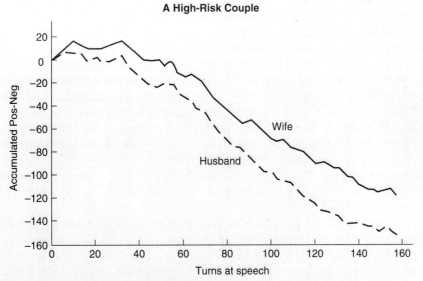

couples disagreed with sarcasm and disdain, and in those cases, the longer they talked, the worse their scores got. When the researchers compared the two groups at the time of the study, the low-risk couples were more satisfied with their marriages than the other couples were. No surprise there. More impressively, however, more than half (56 percent) of the high-risk couples were divorced or separated only four years later, whereas just under a quarter (24 percent) of the low-risk couples had split up. A short discussion on a single afternoon clearly provided meaningful information about the chances that a marriage would last. And couples who did not maintain a substantial surfeit of positive exchanges faced twice the risk that their marriages would fail.

So, both rewards and costs are important influences on relationship satisfaction and stability, and there may need to be many more of the former than the latter if a relationship is to thrive. On the surface, this is a pretty obvious conclusion; we'd expect happy relationships to be more rewarding than punishing. In another study, for instance, 93 percent of the happily married couples reported making love more often than they argued, whereas none of the unhappily married couples did (Howard & Dawes, 1976). But if it's so obvious, why are there so many unhappy relationships? One possibility is that the partners disagree about the meaning and the value of the rewards they try to provide one another (see Box 6.3). Some of the well-intentioned things that partners do for each other may not seem particularly thoughtful or affectionate to their partners. In addition, romantic partners simply don't notice all of the loving and affectionate behaviors their lovers provide; one study that tracked partners' perceptions for four weeks found that both men and women failed to notice about one quarter of the positive behaviors that their partners said they performed (Gable, Reis, & Downey, 2003). Husbands and wives with avoidant attachment styles are especially likely to miss some of the positive, loving things their spouses do for them (Carmichael, Gable, & Reis, 2003). (This suggests the intriguing possibility that one reason why such people are less comfortable with interdependent intimacy is that they don't fully realize how pleasant it can be!)

Another more subtle answer is that rewards and costs have different, separate effects on our well-being in relationships, and this creates confusing complexity. Theorists Shelly Gable and Harry Reis (2001) suggest that people have two distinct motivations. First, we seek positive outcomes; we have an appetite for desirable experiences that Gable and Reis term an **appetitive** motivation. Second, we try to avoid negative outcomes, and this is an **aversive** urge. But the pleasure that results from fulfilling our appetitive needs is not just the opposite of the pain that results from failing to fulfill our aversive desires. Instead, pleasure and pain are presumed to operate independently, involving different brain mechanisms and causing distinct emotions and behaviors (Cacioppo & Gardner, 1999). The provocative result is that pleasure and pain can coexist, or both may be absent, in any relationship.

The appetitive and aversive dimensions are pictured in Figure 6.4. Relationships that are full of positive events are exciting and invigorating, whereas those that offer few positive outcomes are unfulfilling and stagnant. Importantly, dull relationships aren't unpleasant, they're just not fun. And whether or not they're

---

BOX 6.3

"To Show You I Love You, I Washed Your Car":
Sex Differences in the Evaluation of Relationship Rewards

There are no price tags on the various commodities and rewards people exchange in their relationships, and partners sometimes disagree about what an exchange is worth. In a study by Wills, Weiss, and Patterson (1974), seven married couples kept track of their behavioral exchanges for two weeks. The rewards they exchanged either involved tasks and responsibilities (such as taking out the garbage) or emotion and affection (such as saying, "I love you"). When the spouses rated their pleasure with their partners' behavior, wives particularly appreciated their husbands' affectionate behavior, whereas husbands liked their wives' task-oriented help. The sexes apparently attached different values to such actions as doing the dishes and expressing warmth and love. The consequences of this sex difference were revealed when, toward the end of the study, the husbands were asked to increase their affectionate behavior toward their wives. Most did, but they also engaged in more task-oriented helping, which suggests that they were confusing the two. One husband was no more affectionate than usual but was annoyed when he was asked why; he had washed his wife's car, and he thought that was a perfectly

good way to communicate his affection for her. She didn't see it that way.

This study used a very small sample, so we shouldn't make too much of it. However, there are some differences in the rewards men and women extract from intimate relationships. For instance, men are more likely than women to describe sexual gratification as a substantial benefit, whereas women are more likely to say that a relationship has increased their self-confidence and self-esteem (Sedikides et al., 1994). Men also think that their partners' sexual faithfulness is more valuable and important than their own, whereas women attach equal value to their own and their partners' fidelity (Regan & Sprecher, 1995). These results offer the useful lesson that although the language of social exchange sounds straightforward—rewards and costs, gains and losses—the reality is more complex. Exchanges with others involve a *psychological* arithmetic in which people's motives, beliefs, and emotions affect their perceptions of the outcomes they receive. What matters to me may not matter as much to you, and those differing perceptions add complexity to our quest for mutually satisfying interaction.

---

rewarding, some relationships are full of conflict and danger, whereas others are more placid. However, just because a partnership is safe and has no negatives doesn't necessarily mean it *is* fun. As Reis and Gable (2003, p. 142) assert, "the absence of conflict and criticism in a relationship need not imply the presence of joy and fulfillment, just as the presence of joy and fulfillment need not denote the absence of conflict and criticism."

So, why do we care, exactly? There are several reasons. First, people differ in the strength of their appetitive and aversive motivations (Gable, Reis, & Elliot,

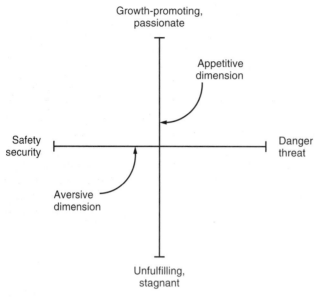

FIGURE 6.4. Appetitive and aversive processes in relationships. People seek rewards and want to avoid costs, but these may be two different motivations that combine to influence our feelings in close relationships. When aversive motivations are fulfilled, people avoid costs but are not necessarily happy. When appetitive motivations are fulfilled, people feel engaged and excited but may not feel safe and secure. Only when both motivations are fulfilled simultaneously are people wholly content.
Figure adapted from Reis & Gable, 2003.

2003). Bad is generally stronger than good, for instance, but some people are very sensitive to negative events that wouldn't much ruffle others of us—and such people may feel especially threatened by disagreements or conflict with their partners. Second, this approach acknowledges that people can have mixed feelings about their relationships (Bissonnette & Lipkus, 2002). We may love the good times and hate the bad times, but sometimes they're the *same* times. Finally, and most importantly, being happy may involve different strategies than what not being unhappy entails. If we wish our relationships to prosper and be fulfilling, we need to do more than simply avoid any unpleasantries. We must also find and invent ways to play and have fun (Aune & Wong, 2002), and we must consistently strive to provide our partners joyous, passionate, exciting experiences (Strong & Aron, 2004).

With all this in mind, a final reason why so many relationships are unhappy may be that couples begin their relationships when their interactions are rewarding, but things change with time. Indeed, despite the partners' best intentions, many relationships gradually become less satisfying as time goes by. Let's take a look at how rewards and costs change as relationships develop.

Rewards and Costs as Time Goes By

Here's the situation: You've just started dating a new partner with many appealing qualities, and your initial interactions have been reasonably rewarding. Can you predict at this point what the future holds? Will the relationship prosper or will it ultimately fail? Every partnership may have its unique qualities, but there are still some common patterns in situations like this. Roy Eidelson (1981) studied these questions by asking young adults to keep track of the specific rewards and costs they encountered in new relationships, and he found *no difference* between the number of rewards offered by relationships that would thrive and by those that would founder. When they began, relationships that would succeed were no more rewarding than those that would not (see Figure 6.5). However, there *was* a difference in the number of costs people encountered in the two types of relationships. Doomed partnerships were more costly from the moment they started. People reported more frustrations and annoyances in relationships that would fail than in those that would succeed.

This is interesting. Evidently, there's a lot to like in partnerships that will not work out. The only difference between successful and unsuccessful relationships at the start is in the number of costs they exact. But what happens next is intriguing, too. Even in relationships that will ultimately succeed, costs typically *rise* as the partners spend more time together. Eidelson explained this by suggesting that there are pros and cons to investing time and effort in a new relationship. On the one hand, intimate partners exchange more valuable rewards, but on the other, they lose some independence and freedom. Instead of waiting to be asked out on a date, for instance, a new partner may start *assuming* that you'll get together this weekend, and your loss of autonomy can be disconcerting. In prosperous relationships, rewards rise, too, but the increasing costs can cause a lull in the amount of satisfaction people feel. Take a look at Figure 6.6; Eidelson (1980) found that as successful relationships developed, people routinely experienced a sharp increase in satisfaction that was followed by a lull—perhaps a period of reflection and reevaluation as they came to grips with the costs of increased interdependency. After that, however, costs

FIGURE 6.5. Rewards and costs in beginning relationships.
Adapted from Eidelson, 1981.

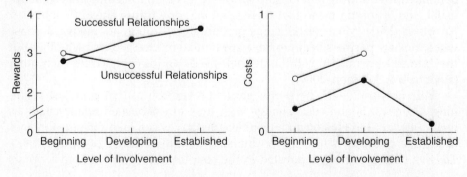

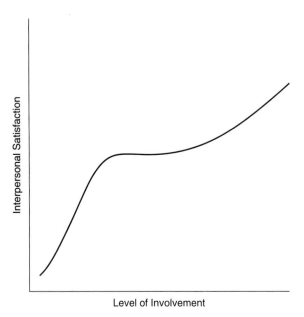

FIGURE 6.6. Satisfaction in beginning relationships.
Adapted from Eidelson, 1980.

decreased as people adjusted to the limitations imposed by the new partner. This resulted in a new but more gradual increase in satisfaction as the relationship continued to develop.

What happened in those relationships that did not continue? Eidelson found that their costs also increased but their rewards did not (Figure 6.5). As a result, the partner's outcomes fell and the relationships ended. This took time to unfold, however, so the only way to distinguish successful and unsuccessful relationships at the start was by a careful accounting of their costs.

There may be some valuable lessons here. First, thoughtful consumers of relationships should pay heed to their doubts about new partners. There are more such doubts and irritations in relationships that will fail, and they will only get worse. On the other hand, we shouldn't be surprised when our increasing delight with a budding relationship suddenly levels off for a time; that's not unusual, and it doesn't mean that there's not a happy future ahead (Solomon & Knobloch, 2001). Most relationships probably go through an awkward phase when the new partners begin to have substantial influence over each other but they are still learning to coordinate their needs and accommodate each other (Knobloch & Solomon, 2004).

Still, Eidelson (1980, 1981) only studied relationships that were just beginning. Do rewards and costs change with time in established relationships as well? They do. Ted Huston and his colleagues have been following the fortunes of a large group of spouses who married in 1981 (Huston & Houts, 1998). They've been especially interested in the couples that divorced (and 13 years

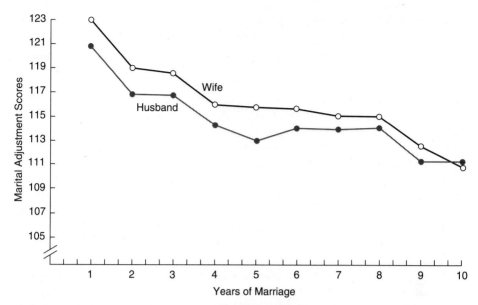

FIGURE 6.7. The average trajectory of marital satisfaction.
Many people presume that their marriages will get better and better as time goes by,
but most marriages actually feel less wonderful as time passes.
Data from Kurdek, 1999.

later, 35 percent of them had; Huston, 1999). In general, the problems the couples faced did not change over time; the complaints the spouses had were
known to them when they decided to get married in the first place. But marriage did not make those costs seem more manageable; to the contrary, existing
problems became more obnoxious once people were wed. Worse, the rewards
of their relationships fell once they married and moved in with each other. In
particular, acts of kindness and expressions of affection dropped by half within
their first two years as husband and wife. As a result, with the spouses' costs rising and rewards dropping, Huston observed a pattern that is also a routine result in other studies (e.g., Karney & Bradbury, 1997; Kurdek, 1999; Leonard &
Roberts, 1997): Relationship satisfaction declines in the first few years after people are married, as Figure 6.7 illustrates.

   This is bad news. Interdependence theory suggests that satisfaction can
wane as people's CLs rise, but the research data actually reveal that outcomes
fall, too. Why does this occur? We can suggest several reasons (Miller, 1997b).
First, we all know how to be polite and thoughtful, and we can behave that way
when we want to (Vincent et al., 1975), but it takes work. Once a courtship is
over and a partner is won, for instance, people may stop trying so hard to be
consistently charming. The same people who would never fart noisily on a
blind date may become spouses who fart at will at the dinner table, perhaps
dismissing their lack of propriety by saying, "Sorry, I couldn't help it." The
point is that they *could* help it if they wanted to—they just didn't go to the
trouble to do so (Miller, 2001).

Second, interdependency magnifies conflict and friction. We spend lots of time with our intimate partners and depend on them for unique, especially valuable rewards, and that means that they are certain to cause us more frustration— even inadvertently—than anyone else can. For instance, we're more affected by the moods (Caughlin et al., 2000) or work stress (Chan & Margolin, 1994) of intimate partners than by the similar difficulties of others. Frequent interaction also means that trivial annoyances may gradually cause real grief through sheer repetition, in the same way that the light tapping of a slowly dripping faucet can drive you mad when you're trying to sleep at night (Cunningham, 2004).

Third, intimacy means that others know your secrets, foibles, and weaknesses. That gives them ammunition with which to wound and tease us when conflict occurs. But even when they have no wish to do us harm, their access to sensitive information practically guarantees that they will accidentally reveal some secret (Petronio, Olson, & Dollar, 1989), hurt our feelings (Kowalski, 2003), or embarrass us (Miller, 1996) sometime or other. They can unintentionally hurt us in ways others can't.

Fourth, even if people are usually aware of most of their incompatibilities and problems before they marry, there will almost always be some surprises ahead. These tend to be of two general types. First, there's learning the truth about things we thought we knew. A good example of this are the "fatal attractions" we mentioned in chapter 3. You may know and even like the fact that your lover is fun-loving and spontaneous, but you may not appreciate how irresponsible, flighty, and unreliable that same behavior may seem after a few years of marriage when you have a mortgage and babies to contend with. Speaking of babies, the other type of unwelcome surprise is learning undesired things that you didn't know at all, and the real facts of parenthood are often good examples. If you don't have kids, you might assume that parenthood will be fun, your kids will be invariably adorable, and raising children will bring you and your partner closer together. The reality, however (as you know if you do have kids), is that "after the birth of a child the prognosis for the course of the marital relationship is unequivocally grim" (Stafford & Dainton, 1994, p. 270). We can safely say that parenthood is an extraordinary and often marvelous adventure, but it is unquestionably hard on the relationship between the parents; children are endless work, and most parents experience a steep and unexpected decline in the time they spend having fun together (Kurdek, 1993). When babies arrive, conflict increases, and satisfaction with the marriage (and love for one's partner) decrease, especially among women (Belsky, 1990; Rholes et al., 2001). If the parents don't expect such difficulties, they're going to be surprised.

Finally, all of this means that close relationships are often much different from the blissful, intimate idylls we want them to be, and the difference between what we expected and what we get can leave us feeling cheated and disappointed, sometimes unnecessarily so (Attridge & Berscheid, 1994). To the extent that great relationships still involve hard work and sacrifice, people with misplaced, glorified expectations about relationships may end up disappointed in their outcomes even when they're doing better than everyone else. (Remember, satisfaction derives from the difference between the outcomes we receive and our CLs—our expectations.)

So, through (a) **lack of effort;** because (b) **interdependency is a magnifying glass;** and through (c) **access to weaponry;** (d) **unwelcome surprises;** and (e) **unrealistic expectations,** people usually fail to maintain the outcomes that lead them to marry (Miller, 1997b), and satisfaction actually declines during the first years of marriage. There are certainly some valuable lessons here, too. Ted Huston's (1999) work demonstrates that existing problems and incompatibilities do not gradually disappear after people marry; to the contrary, if anything, they are accentuated. We should not naively hope that our problems will just fade away. And marriage does not increase the spouses' delight with one another; if anything, their contentment is likely to decrease somewhat. There may be several reasons why, but we suspect that the impact of all of them can be minimized if people are better informed and know what to expect about the usual trajectories of marital intimacy. On average, people who begin their marriages with the highest expectations of how special and wonderful wedlock will be are the *least* happy spouses a few years down the road. James McNulty and Ben Karney (2004) followed 82 newlywed couples across the first four years of their marriages and found that, over time, the happiest couples were those who had had the most realistic outlooks about what wedded life would be like; in particular, spouses who had unrealistically positive expectations tended to be disappointed once the honeymoon was over. (In fact, over one fifth of the couples followed by McNulty and Karney were divorced after only four years.) As advice columnist "Dear Prudence" suggested, "Prudie has a shock for you, so please sit down. The intensity and the honeymoon phase ALWAYS end" when reality settles in (Howard, 2003, p. B6).

This may seem gloomy, but we don't want this analysis to seem pessimistic at all! To the contrary, we suspect that a thorough understanding of these issues can help people to avoid needless disappointment, and it may even help them to forestall or avoid the creeping decline in outcomes that would otherwise occur. We think there's more danger in naïve optimism than in informed caution.

And importantly, if nothing else, this perspective reminds us of our constant responsibility to be as pleasant as possible to those whose company we value. We want great outcomes, but so do they, and even if they like us, they'll go elsewhere if we don't give them enough reward. This is a consequential idea, and it leads to some subtleties of the social exchange perspective that we have not yet considered.

ARE WE REALLY THIS GREEDY?

So far in this chapter, we have portrayed people as greedy hedonists who are only concerned with their own outcomes. That's not a complimentary portrayal, but it is useful because rewards and costs matter enormously in close relations. The research data support the basic precepts of interdependence theory quite well. Nevertheless, at this point, our portrait is incomplete. There are good reasons why people will usually want their partners to prosper as well.

The Nature of Interdependency

Okay, you've got the idea: According to interdependence theory, people want maximum reward at minimum cost, and always want the best interpersonal deals they can get. Everybody behaves this way. But what happens when they get a good deal? Then they're dependent on their partners and don't want to leave them. That's significant, because it means that they have an important stake in *keeping their partners happy*, so that their partners will continue providing those desired rewards. If you want to keep valued relationships going, it's to your advantage to ensure that your partners are just as dependent on you as you are on them, and a straightforward way to do that is to provide them high outcomes that make them want to stay.

Pursuing this strategy can influence the value of many transactions with a desired partner. Actions that would be costly if enacted with a stranger can actually be rewarding in a close relationship because they give pleasure to one's partner and increase the likelihood that one will receive valuable rewards in return (Kelley, 1979). Providing good outcomes to one's partner, even when it involves effort and sacrifice, can ultimately be self-serving if it causes a desirable relationship to continue. Indeed, even greedy people should be generous to others if it increases their own profits!

So, interdependence theory suggests that in the quest for high outcomes, individuals will often be magnanimous to those on whom they depend because

People (and cats) are usually generous to those on whom they depend.

it is reasonable (and valuable) to do so. And if both partners in a relationship want it to continue, both of them should thoughtfully protect and maintain the other's well-being. If people need each other, it can be advantageous to be positively philanthropic to each other, increasing the partner's profits to keep him or her around. Thus, even if people are greedy, there is likely to be plenty of compassionate thoughtfulness and magnanimity in interdependent relationships.

Exchange versus Communal Relationships

Indeed, when people seek closeness with others, they are often generous from the moment they meet those new partners (Berg & Clark, 1986). We seem to realize that rewarding interdependency is more likely to develop when we're *not* greedily pursuing instant profit. With this in mind, Margaret Clark and Judson Mills (1979, 1993) proposed a distinction between partnerships that are clearly governed by explicit norms of even exchange and other, more generous, relationships that are characterized by obvious concern for the partner's welfare. **Exchange** relationships are governed by the desire for and expectation of immediate repayment for benefits given. Thus, any costs should be quickly offset by compensating rewards, and the overall balance should remain at zero. As Table 6.1 shows, people in exchange relationships don't like to be in one another's debt; they track each other's contributions to joint endeavors; they monitor the other person's needs only when they think there's a chance for personal gain; and they don't feel badly if they refuse to help the other person. As you might expect, exchange relationships are typified by superficial, often brief, relatively task-oriented encounters between strangers or acquaintances.

In contrast, **communal** relationships are governed by the desire for and expectation of mutual responsiveness to the other's needs (Mills & Clark, 2001). People who seek a communal relationship avoid strict cost accounting, and they are obviously concerned for their partners' welfare. They do not prefer to have their favors quickly repaid; they do not make a clear distinction between their work and that of their partners; they monitor their partners' needs even when they see no opportunity for personal gain; and they feel better about themselves when they help their partners. People often make small sacrifices on behalf of their partners in communal relationships, such as going to a movie they don't want to see, just to please their partners, but they enjoy higher quality relationships as a result (Clark & Grote, 1998). People like marriages to operate this way (Clark, Graham, & Grote, 2002), and meaningful romantic attachments typically are communal relationships, but communal and exchange norms are about equally likely to apply to friendships, which may be of either type (Clark & Mills, 1993).

Indeed, the extent of our generosity in response to our partners' needs can vary from relationship to relationship, and Mills and Clark and their colleagues (Mills et al., 2004) have developed a short scale to measure *communal strength*, the motivation to be responsive to a particular partner's needs

TABLE 6.1. Differences between Exchange and Communal Relationships

Situation	Exchange Relationships	Communal Relationships
When we do others a favor	We prefer those who pay us back immediately.	We don't prefer those who repay us immediately.
When others do us a favor	We prefer those who ask for immediate repayment.	We prefer those who do not ask for immediate repayment.
When we are working with others on a joint task	We try to ensure that our contributions are distinguished from those of others.	We don't make any clear distinction between others' work and our own.
When others may need help	We keep track of the others' needs only when they can return any favors.	We keep track of the others' needs even when they will be unable to return any favors.
When we help others	Our moods and self-evaluations change only slightly.	Our moods brighten and our self-evaluations improve.
When we don't help others	Our moods do not change.	Our moods get worse.
When we express our emotions and show others how we feel	Our partners like us less.	Our partners like us more.

Source: Clark, 1984; Clark, 2002; Clark et al., 2004; Clark & Mills, 1979; Clark, Mills, & Corcoran, 1989; Clark, Mills, & Powell, 1986; Clark & Waddell, 1985; Williamson & Clark, 1989; and Williamson, et al., 1996.

(see Table 6.2). As their feelings of communal strength increase, people work harder to provide more help to their friends, and their spouses are more satisfied with their marriages (Mills et al., 2004). Thoughtful concern for the well-being of one's partner is clearly connected to closeness and contentment in intimate partnerships.

But does the lack of apparent greed in communal relationships indicate that the principles of exchange we've been discussing do not apply there? Not at all. For one thing, tit-for-tat exchanges are probably also taking place in communal partnerships, but in a manner that involves more diverse rewards across a longer span of time (Clark, 1981). In more businesslike relationships, exchanges are expected to occur quickly, so that debts are rapidly repaid. They should also be comparable, so that you pay for what you get. In more intimate relationships, there's more versatility. What we do to meet a partner's needs may involve very different actions from what the partner did to meet our own needs. We can also wait longer to be repaid because we trust our partners and expect the relationship to continue. In this sense, both exchange and communal partnerships are "exchange" relationships in which people expect to receive benefits that fit those they provide, but the exchanges take different forms and are less obvious in communal relationships.

TABLE 6.2. A Measure of Communal Strength

You can compare the communal strength of your relationships with different partners by answering these questions more than once. For each relationship, fill in your partner's initials in the blank. Then answer each question by writing down your rating from the scale below:

0	1	2	3	4	5	6	7	8	9	10
not at all										extremely

1. How far would you be willing to go to visit _____?
2. How happy do you feel when doing something that helps _____?
3. How large a benefit would you be likely to give _____?
4. How large a cost would you incur to meet a need of _____?
5. How readily can you put the needs of _____ out of your thoughts?
6. How high a priority for you is meeting the needs of _____?
7. How reluctant would you be to sacrifice for _____?
8. How much would you be willing to give up to benefit _____?
9. How far would you go out of your way to do something for _____?
10. How easily could you accept not helping _____?

To determine your score, reverse the rating you gave to questions 5, 7, and 10. If your rating was 0, change it to 10; a 1 becomes a 9; 2 changes to 8; and so on. Then add up your ratings. Your sum is the strength of your communal motivation toward that particular partner.

Source: Mills et al., 2004.

In addition, the exchange perspective may not seem to describe intimate relationships because, when they are healthy, the partners enjoy an "economy of surplus" and seem unconcerned with how well they're doing (Levinger, 1979). Both partners are prospering, and there seems to be little need to "sweat the small stuff" by explicitly quantifying their respective rewards and costs. People in happy and stable relationships, for instance, probably haven't been wondering "what has my partner done for me lately?" both because the partner has done plenty and because they're happy enough not to care. However, if their outcomes start falling and their heady profits evaporate, even intimate partners in (what were) communal relationships may begin paying close attention to the processes of exchange (Clark et al., 2002; Grote & Clark, 2001). Indeed, when dissatisfaction sets in, people in (what were) communal relationships often become very sensitive to minute injustices in the outcomes they receive (Jacobson, Follette, & McDonald, 1982). In a sense, they start balancing their "checkbooks" and counting every "penny."

So, a distinction between exchange and communal relationships isn't incompatible with interdependency theory at all. However, the workings of communal relationships do demonstrate how readily people provide benefits to those with whom they wish to develop close relationships and how quickly people begin to take others' welfare under consideration once interaction begins (Berg & Clark, 1986). Most people seem to recognize, as interdependency theory suggests, that if you want others to be nice to you, you've got to be nice to them.

Equitable Relationships

Another point of view argues that you not only have to be nice, you have to be *fair*. **Equity** theorists extend the framework of social exchange to assert that people are most satisfied in relationships in which there is *proportional justice*, which means that each partner gains benefits from the relationship that are proportional to his or her contributions to it (Hatfield, 1983; Sprecher & Schwartz, 1994). A relationship is equitable when the ratio of your outcomes to your contributions is similar to that of your partner, or when

$$\frac{\text{Your outcomes}}{\text{Your contributions}} = \frac{\text{Your partner's outcomes}}{\text{Your partner's contributions}}$$

Note that equity does not require that two partners gain equal rewards from their interaction; in fact, if their contributions are different, equality would be inequitable. A relationship is fair, according to equity theory, only when a partner who is contributing more is receiving more as well.

Let's look at some examples. Here are three equitable relationships, with outcomes and contributions rated on a 0-to-100-point scale:

	Partner X		Partner Y
(a)	80/50	=	80/50
(b)	20/100	=	20/100
(c)	50/25	=	100/50

In relationships (a) and (b), both partners are receiving equal outcomes and making equal contributions, but the quality of outcomes is much higher for the partners in relationship (a) than for those in relationship (b). Equity theory emphasizes fairness, not the overall amount of rewards people receive, and because both (a) and (b) are fair, they should both be satisfying to the partners. (Do you think they would be? We'll return to this point later.) Relationship (c) is also equitable, even though the partners do not make equal contributions or derive equal outcomes. Partner Y is working harder to maintain the relationship than partner X is, but both of them are receiving outcomes that are proportional to their contributions—each is getting two units of benefit for every unit he or she contributes, so Y's higher outcomes are fair.

In contrast, in inequitable relationships, the two ratios of outcomes to contributions are not equal. Consider these examples:

	Partner X		Partner Y
(d)	80/50	≠	60/50
(e)	80/50	≠	80/30

In relationship (d), the partners are working equally hard to maintain the relationship, but one of them is receiving better outcomes than the other. In (e), their outcomes are the same, but their contributions are different. In either case, the partners are likely to be distressed—even if they're getting good outcomes—because the relationship isn't fair. In such situations, one partner is **"overbenefited,"** receiving better outcomes than he or she deserves, and the other is **"underbenefited,"** receiving less than he or she should. Does that matter? Interdependence theory says it shouldn't, much, as long as both partners are prospering, but equity theory says it does.

The Distress of Inequity

One of the most interesting aspects of equity theory is its assertion that everybody is nervous in inequitable relationships. It's easy to see why underbenefited partners would be unhappy; they're being cheated and exploited, and they may feel angry and resentful. On the other hand, overbenefited partners are doing too well, and they may feel somewhat guilty. It's better to be over- than underbenefited, of course, but equity theory proposes that everybody is most content when both partners receive fair outcomes. Any departure from an equitable relationship is thought to cause some discomfort, if only because such situations are inherently unstable: People are presumed to dislike unfairness and will want to change or escape it (Iida, Bolger, & Shrout, 2004), especially if they're underbenefited. So, according to this perspective, the most satisfactory situation is an equitable division of outcomes; equity theory predicts that overbenefited people will be somewhat less content than those who have equitable relationships, and underbenefited people will be *much* less satisfied (Hatfield, 1983).

Ways to Restore Equity

If you're underbenefited, what can you do? First, you can try to restore *actual equity* by changing your (or your partner's) contributions or outcomes (Canary & Stafford, 2001). You can request better treatment so that your outcomes will improve—"it's your turn to cook dinner while I relax"—or you can reduce your contributions, hoping that your outcomes stay about the same. You could even sabotage your partner, reducing his or her outcomes so that they're no longer out of line (Hammock et al., 1989).

If these efforts fail, you can try to restore *psychological equity*, changing your perceptions of the relationship and convincing yourself it really is equitable after all. You could talk yourself into thinking that your partner is someone special who deserves the better deal (McDonald, 1981). Or, you could start doubting yourself and decide that you deserve your lousy outcomes.

Finally, as a last resort, you could *abandon the relationship* to seek fairness elsewhere. You could actually leave your partner, or perhaps just have an affair (Prins, Buunk, & VanYperen, 1993).

In any case, as all these examples suggest, equity theory argues that people are motivated to redress inequity when it occurs. That certainly makes sense if you're underbenefited. But would you really want to change things if you're overbenefited? Let's see what the data have to say.

How Much Is Enough? Equity versus Overbenefit

Several studies that have assessed the satisfaction of spouses and other romantic couples have obtained results that fit the predictions of equity theory very nicely (e.g., Davidson, 1984; Sprecher, 1986, 1992; Walster, Walster, & Traupmann, 1978): Partners who were overbenefited were less relaxed and content than were those whose outcomes were equitable, and people who were underbenefited were less happy still. However, most of these studies used cross-sectional designs that compared people who were overbenefited to those in equitable situations at one point in time. In addition, few of them assessed the participants' comparison levels or otherwise took note of just how good their outcomes were. (Remember, you can be overbenefited relative to how your partner is doing and still be getting crummy outcomes that could cause some dissatisfaction.) A different picture could emerge when equity is compared to the overall quality of outcomes people receive; fairness may not matter much if everybody's prospering.

Indeed, some more recent investigations have tracked couples over long periods of time (often for several years) using a broader array of measures, and they provide less support for the particulars of equity theory (e.g., Sprecher, 1998a, 1999, 2001). Nobody likes being underbenefited—all studies agree on that—but being overbenefited is not always associated with reduced satisfaction. In fact, some people who are overbenefited like it just fine (Sprecher, 2001), especially when they have been underbenefited in the past (Buunk & Mutsaers, 1999). Moreover, several studies that assessed the quality of partners' outcomes found that—just as interdependence theory asserts—the overall amount of reward that people receive is a better predictor of their satisfaction than is the level of equity they encounter (Cate, Lloyd, & Henton, 1985; Cate et al., 1982; Cate, Lloyd, & Long, 1988). In these studies, it didn't matter what one's partner gave or got as long as one's own benefits were high enough, and the more rewards people said they received from a relationship, the better they felt about it.

There's complexity here. Some studies suggest that fairness is an important factor in the workings of intimate relationships, and some do not. One reason for these conflicting results may be that some people are more concerned with fairness in interpersonal relations than other people are. Across relationships, some people consistently value equity more than others do, and they, unlike other people, are more satisfied when equity exists than when it does not (Buunk & VanYperen, 1991; Donaghue & Fallon, 2003). Curiously, however, such people tend to be less satisfied overall with their relationships than are people who are less concerned with equity (Buunk & VanYperen, 1991). They may be paying too much attention to a careful accounting of their rewards and costs!

Nevertheless, no matter who we are, equity may be more important in some domains than in others. Two sensitive areas in which equity appears to be advisable are in the allocation of household tasks and child care: When these chores are divided fairly, spouses are more satisfied with their marriages (Grote, Frieze, & Stone, 1996; Lavee & Katz, 2002). Unfortunately, equitable allocation of these duties is often difficult for women to obtain (Feeney & Noller, 2002). Even when they have similar job responsibilities outside the home, working mothers tend to do twice as many household chores as their husbands do (Huppe & Cyr, 1997), and this inequity can produce considerable strain on the relationship. Indeed, one general admonition offered by marriage researchers to modern couples is for men "to do more housework, child care, and affectional maintenance if they wish to have a happy wife" (Gottman & Carrère, 1994, p. 225). Equity in these conspicuous domains may be much more influential than similar fairness applied to other areas of a couple's interactions.

A third possible reason why research results are mixed may be that equity is a salient issue when people are dissatisfied, but it's only a minor issue when people are content (Holmes & Levinger, 1994). When rewards are in good supply, equity may not matter. People who are prospering in their relationships may spend little time monitoring their exchanges and may casually dismiss any imbalances they do notice. (They might also tend to report that their partnerships are "fair" when researchers ask.) But if costs rise and rewards fall, people may begin tracking their exchanges much more carefully, displaying concern about who deserves to get what. And no matter what the truth is, people who are very dissatisfied are likely to perceive that they are being underbenefited by their partners (Grote & Clark, 2001). In this sense, then, inequity may not cause people to become dissatisfied; instead, being dissatisfied could lead people to think they're being treated unfairly.

Finally, it's also likely that people apply different rules for allocating outcomes to different situations or to different relationships (Clark & Chrisman, 1994). Whereas a business relationship had better be equitable at all times, for instance, communal relationships often seem to involve episodes of compassionate sacrifice and generosity. As we noted earlier, people may only make investments like this when they expect the partnership to provide substantial benefits in the long run, so such behavior may not be altruistic at all. Nevertheless, some close relationships may be inequitable for long periods without causing much distress.

Overall, the best conclusion appears to be that both the global quality of outcomes people receive *and* underbenefit, when it occurs, play important roles in predicting how satisfactory and enduring a relationship will be (Feeney, Peterson, & Noller, 1994; Sprecher, 1999; 2001). Overbenefit doesn't seem to bother people much, and equity doesn't seem to improve a relationship if it is already highly rewarding. In contrast, the inequity that accompanies deprivation and exploitation—underbenefit—is indicative of distress (Kuijer et al., 2002; Ybema et al., 2002). Still, the bottom line is that outcome level is probably a more important factor than inequity is; if our outcomes are poor and unsatisfactory, it isn't much consolation if they're fair, and if our outcomes are wonderful, inequity isn't a major concern.

Summing Up

So, what's the final answer? Is simple greed a good description of people's behavior in intimate relationships? The answer offered by relationship science is a qualified yes. People are happiest when their rewards are high and their costs (and expectations) are low. But because we are dependent on others for the rewards we seek in intimate relationships, we have a stake in satisfying them, too. We readily protect the well-being of our intimate partners and rarely exploit them if we want those relationships to continue. Such behavior may be encouraged by selfish motives, but it is still thoughtful, generous, and often loving. So, even if it is ultimately greedy behavior, it's not undesirable or exploitative.

THE NATURE OF COMMITMENT

The good news is that happy dependence on an intimate partner leads to **commitment,** the intention to continue the relationship. People who both need their partners and are content associate the concept of commitment with positive qualities such as sharing, supportiveness, honesty, faithfulness, and trust (Fehr, 1999a; 2001); they are affectionate and respectful, and they look forward happily to what the future brings (Weigel & Ballard-Reisch, 2002; Weigel

TABLE 6.3. Arriaga and Agnew's Commitment Scale

Answer each of the questions that follow using this scale:

1	2	3	4	5
not at all true	slightly true	moderately true	very true	extremely true

1. I feel very strongly linked to my partner—very attached to our relationship.
2. It pains me to see my partner suffer.
3. I am very affected when things are not going well in my relationship.
4. In all honesty, my family and friends are more important to me than this relationship.
5. I am oriented toward the long-term future of this relationship (e.g., I imagine being with my partner several years from now).
6. My partner and I joke about what things will be like when we are old.
7. I find it difficult to imagine myself with my partner in the distant future.
8. When I make plans about future events in my life, I think about the impact of my decisions on our relationship.
9. I intend to stay in this relationship.
10. I want to maintain our relationship.
11. I feel inclined to keep our relationship going.
12. My gut feeling is to continue in this relationship.

To determine your total commitment score, reverse the rating you used for questions 4 and 7. If you answered 1, change it to 5; 2 becomes 4; 4 becomes 2; and so on. Then add up your ratings. The higher your score, the greater your commitment.

Source: Arriaga & Agnew, 2001.

et al., 2003). (You can see why these people are staying put.) The bad news is that unhappy people can be committed to their relationships, too, not because they want to stay where they are but because they feel they *must*. For these people, commitment is probably experienced more as burdensome entrapment than as a positive feeling.

Different components of commitment are apparent in a handy commitment scale developed by Ximena Arriaga and Christopher Agnew (2001) that contains three themes. First, committed partners expect their relationship to continue. They also hold a long-term view, foreseeing a future that involves their partners. And finally, they are psychologically attached to each other so that they are happier when their partners are happy, too. Each of these themes is represented by four questions on the commitment scale; take a look at Table 6.3 to see if you can tell which theme applies to each question.

This portrayal of commitment as a multifaceted decision is consistent with a well-known conceptualization of commitment developed by Caryl Rusbult and her colleagues known as the *investment model*. According to the investment model, commitment emerges from all of the elements of social exchange that are associated with people's CLs and CL$_{alt}$s (e.g., Rusbult et al., 2001; Rusbult et al., 1999). First, satisfaction increases commitment. People generally wish to continue the partnerships that make them happy. However, alternatives of high quality are also influential, and they *decrease* commitment. People who have enticing alternatives luring them away from their present partners are less likely to stay in their existing relationships. But people don't always pursue such alternatives even when they're available, if the costs of leaving their current relationships are too high. Thus, a third determinant of commitment is the size of one's investments in the existing relationship. High investments increase commitment, regardless of the quality of one's alternatives and whether or not one is happy.

Altogether, then, the investment model suggests that people will wish to remain with their present partners when they're happy, or when there's no other desirable place for them to go, or when they won't leave because it would cost too much (see Figure 6.8). These influences are presumed to be equally

FIGURE 6.8. The investment model of commitment.
From Rusbult, Drigotas, & Verette, 1994.

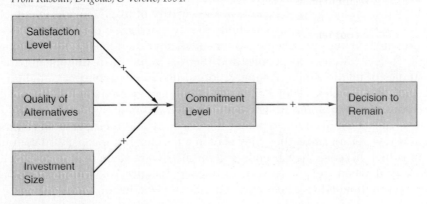

important, and commitment emerges from the complex combination of all three. Thus, as people's circumstances change, relationships often survive periods in which one or both partners are dissatisfied, tempted by alluring alternatives, or free to walk out at any time. Episodes like these may stress the relationship and weaken the partners' commitment, but the partnership may persist if the other components of commitment are holding it together.

In general, research results support the investment model quite well (Le & Agnew, 2003). Satisfaction, the quality of one's alternatives, and the size of one's investments each tell us something useful about how committed a person is likely to be, and the model applies equally well to men and women (Bui et al., 1996), heterosexuals and homosexuals (Kurdek, 1992), and people in both the Netherlands (Van Lange et al., 1997) and Taiwan (Lin & Rusbult, 1995), as well as the United States. Moreover, the usefulness of the investment model provides general support for an exchange perspective on intimate relationships. The economic assessments involved in the investment model do a very good job of predicting how long relationships will last (Drigotas & Rusbult, 1992), whether or not the partners will be faithful to each other (Drigotas, Safstrom, & Gentilia, 1999), and even if battered wives will try to escape their abusive husbands (Rusbult & Martz, 1995).

However, the investment model treats commitment as a unitary concept—that is, there's really only one kind of commitment—and other theorists argue that commitment not only springs from different sources, it comes in different forms (Cate, Levin, & Richmond, 2002). For instance, sociologist Michael Johnson (1999) asserts that there are actually three types of commitment. The first, **personal commitment,** occurs when people *want* to continue a relationship because they are attracted to their partners and the relationship is satisfying. In contrast, the second type, **constraint commitment,** occurs when people feel they *have* to continue a relationship because it would be too costly for them to leave. In constraint commitment, people fear the social and financial consequences of ending their partnerships, and they continue them even when they wish they could depart. Finally, the third type of commitment, **moral commitment,** derives from a sense of moral obligation to one's partner or one's relationship. Here, people feel they *ought* to continue the relationship because it would be improper to end it and break their promises or vows. Spouses who are morally committed tend to believe in the sanctity of marriage and may feel a solemn social or religious responsibility to stay married no matter what.

Research using this scheme demonstrates that the three types of commitment do feel different to people, and there is value in distinguishing them in studies of relationships (Adams & Jones, 1997, 1999; Johnson, Caughlin, & Huston, 1999; Kurdek, 2000). Personal commitment is often the strongest of the three, but constraint commitment and moral commitment can be influential, too (Cate et al., 2002). Even when people are unhappy and their personal commitment is low, for instance, they may stay in a partnership if constraint commitment is high because their friends and families want them to stay (Cox et al., 1997). And when people embark on a long-distance romantic relationship, moral commitment does a better job of predicting whether or not the partnership will survive the period of separation than personal commitment does (Lydon, Pierce, & O'Regan, 1997). Evidently, moral commitment can keep a relationship going even when one's enthusiasm for the relationship wanes.

The Consequences of Commitment

Nevertheless, whatever its origins or nature, commitment substantially affects the relationships in which it occurs (Rusbult et al., 1999). The long-term orientation that characterizes commitment reduces the pain that would otherwise accompany rough spots in the relationship. When people feel that they're in a relationship for the long haul, they may be better able to tolerate episodes of high cost and low reward in much the same way that investors with a long-range outlook will hold on to shares of stock during periods of low earnings. In addition, commitment can lead people to think of themselves and their partners as a single entity, as "us" instead of "him" and "me" (Agnew, 2003). This may substantially reduce the costs of sacrifices that benefit the partner, as events that please one's partner produce indirect benefits for oneself as well.

Perhaps the most important consequence of commitment, however, is that it leads people to take action to protect and maintain a relationship, even when it is costly for them to do so (Rusbult et al., 2001). Committed people engage in a variety of behavioral and cognitive maneuvers that both preserve and enhance the relationship and reinforce their commitment to it (Burton et al., 2002; Etcheverry & Le, 2004). These *relationship maintenance mechanisms* will be described in detail in chapter 15. However, to close this chapter, we'll give you a brief preview of that material.

As one example, commitment promotes **accommodative behavior** in which people refrain from responding to provocation from their partners with similar ire of their own (Rusbult et al., 1998; Rusbult et al., 1991). Accommodating people tolerate destructive behavior from their partners without fighting back; they swallow insults, sarcasm, or selfishness without retaliating. By so doing, they avoid quarrels and altercations and help dispel, rather than perpetuate, their partners' bad moods. That's usually good for the relationship. Such behavior may involve considerable self-restraint, but it is not motivated by weakness; instead, accommodation often involves a conscious effort to protect the partnership from harm.

Committed people also display greater **willingness to sacrifice** their own self-interests for the good of the relationship (Van Lange et al., 1997). They do things they wouldn't do if they were on their own, and they do not do things they would have liked to do, in order to benefit their partners and enhance their relationships.

As a final example, commitment changes people's perceptions of their partnerships. Committed people exhibit **perceived superiority**—they think their relationships are better than those of other people (Buunk & van der Eijnden, 1997; Van Lange & Rusbult, 1995). In particular, they think that they enjoy more rewards and suffer fewer costs than other people encounter with their partners (Broemer & Diehl, 2003).

There are other mechanisms with which people maintain their relationships, but these three sufficiently illustrate the manner in which commitment motivates thoughts and actions that preserve partnerships. People seek maximum reward at minimum cost in their interactions with others, but dependency on a partner leads them to behave in ways that take the partner's well-being into account. As a result, committed partners often make sacrifices and accommodate their partners, doing things that are not in their immediate self-interest, to promote their relationships.

If people did these things indiscriminately, they would often be self-defeating. However, when they occur in interdependent relationships, and when both partners behave this way, such actions provide powerful means of protecting and enhancing desired connections to others (Drigotas, Rusbult, & Verette, 1999). In this manner, even if we are basically greedy at heart, we are often unselfish, considerate, and caring to those we befriend and love.

FOR YOUR CONSIDERATION

One of the things Jack liked about Karen was that she was a great cook. When she would have him over to dinner, she would serve elaborate, delicious meals that were much more appealing than the fast food he often ate on his own. He liked to keep things tidy and neat, and he noticed that her apartment was always disheveled and cluttered, but he didn't much care because she was an exciting, desirable companion. However, once they were married, Karen cooked less often; they both worked, and she frequently called him before he came home to ask him to pick up take-out meals for dinner. He also became annoyed by her slovenly housekeeping. He did his fair share of housework, but a pile of unfolded laundry constantly occupied their living room couch, and they had to push it aside to sit together to watch television. She seemed not to notice just how scattered and disorganized her belongings were, and Jack began to feel resentful.

What do you think the future holds for Jack and Karen? Why?

CHAPTER SUMMARY

Social Exchange

The economic view of social interaction offered by interdependence theory suggests that people seek relationships that provide maximum reward at minimum cost.

Rewards and Costs. Rewards are gratifying and costs are punishing. The net profit or loss from an interaction is its *"outcome."*

What Do We Expect from Our Relationships? People have *comparison levels* (CLs) that reflect their expectations for their interactions with others.

When the outcomes they receive exceed their CLs, they're satisfied, but if their outcomes fall below their CLs, they're discontented.

How Well Could We Do Elsewhere? People also compare their outcomes to those available elsewhere using a *comparison level for alternatives* (CL_{alt}). When the outcomes they receive exceed their CL_{alt}s, they're dependent on their current partners. Both the external rewards awaiting us outside our current relationships and the *investments* we would lose by leaving influence the calculation of our CL_{alt}s. However, these are complicated judgments, and they depend on whether we're paying attention to our alternatives or are relatively heedless of them.

Four Types of Relationships. Comparing people's CLs and CL_{alt}s with their outcomes yields four different relationship states: happy and stable; happy and unstable; unhappy and stable; and unhappy and unstable.

CL and CL_{alt} as Time Goes By. People adapt to the outcomes they receive, and relationships can become less satisfying as the partners' CLs rise. Cultural influences shape both our expectations and our CL_{alt}s and may have put more pressure on relationships in recent years than in years past.

The Economies of Relationships

Counting up the rewards and costs of a relationship provides extraordinary information about its current state and likely future. A lot of unpleasantness occurs in many relationships. This is influential because negative events carry more psychological impact than similar positive events do. As a result, a ratio of at least five rewards to every one cost may be needed to maintain a satisfactory partnership.

Rewards and costs may have independent effects on relationships. An *appetitive* motivation leads us to seek rewards, and an *aversive* motivation leads us to avoid costs. Either or both motivations may be fulfilled, but in very unhappy relationships, neither may be.

Rewards and Costs as Time Goes By. When they begin, relationships that will succeed are no more rewarding than those that will quickly fail. Their rewards increase over time, but so do their costs, leading to a lull in increasing satisfaction as they develop. Costs also rise in unsuccessful relationships, but their rewards drop, and the unpleasant combination brings the faltering relationships to an end.

Marital satisfaction actually decreases over the first years of marriage. This may be due to the partners' *lack of effort* and to the manner in which interdependence magnifies small irritations, and to other routine influences such as *unwelcome surprises* and *unrealistic expectations*. Insight may forestall or prevent these problems.

Are We Really This Greedy?

The Nature of Interdependency. Interdependent partners have a stake in keeping each other happy. As a result, generosity toward one's partner is often beneficial to oneself.

Exchange versus Communal Relationships. *Exchange* relationships are governed by the desire for immediate repayment of favors, whereas *communal* relationships are governed by the expectation of mutual responsiveness to another's needs. Communal partners do not seem to keep track of their rewards and costs, but they usually resume careful accounting if they become dissatisfied.

Equitable Relationships. *Equity* occurs when both partners gain benefits from a relationship that are proportional to their contributions to it. People are overbenefited if they receive better outcomes than they deserve, and underbenefited if they get less than they should.

The distress of inequity. According to equity theory, people dislike inequity and are motivated to change or escape it.

Ways to restore equity. Manipulation of one's outcomes or effort can sometimes restore equity. If not, people may change their perceptions of the relationship in order to convince themselves that it is equitable anyway. If all these efforts fail, people may abandon the relationship.

How much is enough? Equity versus overbenefit. Recent studies suggest that overbenefit is not always associated with reduced satisfaction with a relationship, although underbenefit is. Variable research results may be due to differences among people in their desire for equity and the possibility that equity doesn't matter much when one's outcomes are good. People probably apply different rules for the allocation of rewards to different types of relationships as well.

Summing Up. Altogether, both the quality of outcomes one receives and underbenefit, when it occurs, appear to play meaningful roles in determining how happy and stable a relationship will be.

The Nature of Commitment

Commitment is the intention to continue a relationship. The investment model of commitment asserts that satisfaction, the quality of one's alternatives, and the size of one's investments determine how committed one will be. However, there may be three different kinds of commitment that are based on attraction to a relationship, the costs of leaving it, and moral obligation to the relationship.

The Consequences of Commitment. Committed people tend to adopt a long-term orientation to their relationships and think of themselves and their partners as a collective whole. They also take action to protect and maintain their relationships, being accommodating, making sacrifices willingly, and considering their relationships to be better than those of other people. When both partners behave this way, commitment exerts a powerful influence on the stability of relationships.

PART THREE

Friendship and Intimacy

CHAPTER 7

Friendship

THE NATURE OF FRIENDSHIP ◆ Attributes of Friendships ◆ The Rules
of Friendship ◆ FRIENDSHIP ACROSS THE LIFE CYCLE ◆ Infancy ◆ Childhood
◆ Adolescence ◆ Young Adulthood ◆ Midlife ◆ Old Age ◆ DIFFERENCES
IN FRIENDSHIP ◆ Gender Differences in Same-Sex Friendships ◆ Individual
Differences in Friendship ◆ FOR YOUR CONSIDERATION ◆ CHAPTER SUMMARY

> Without friendship life is not worth living. *Cicero*
> Friendship is the only cement that will ever hold the world together. *Woodrow
> Wilson*
> Each friend represents a world in us, a world possibly not born until they
> arrive, and it is only by this meeting that a new world is born. *Anais Nin*
> I get by with a little help from my friends. *John Lennon*

Take a moment and think about your two best friends. Why are they such close
companions? Why do you think of them as friends? It's likely that you *like* but
don't *love* them. (Or, at least, you're not "in love" with them, or you'd probably
think of them as more than just "friends.") You've probably shared a lot of good
times with them, and you feel comfortable around them; you know that they like
you, too, and you feel that you can count on them to help you when you need it.

Indeed, the positive sentiments you feel toward your friends may actually
be rather varied and complex. They annoy you sometimes, but you're fond of
them, and, because they're best friends, they know things about you that no one
else may know. You like to do things with them, and you expect your relationship to continue indefinitely. In fact, if you look back at the features that define
intimacy (on page 4, in chapter 1), you may find that your connections to your
best friends are quite intimate, indeed. You may have substantial knowledge of
them, and you probably feel high levels of trust and commitment toward them;
you may not experience as much caring, interdependence, and mutuality as
you do with a romantic partner, but all three are present, nonetheless.

So, are friendships the same as, but just less intimate than, our romantic
partnerships? Yes and no. Friendships are based on the same building blocks
of intimacy as romances are, but the mix of components is usually different.
Romances also have some ingredients that friendships typically lack, so their
recipes do differ. But many of the elements of friendships and romances are
quite similar, and this chapter will set the stage for our consideration of love (in
chapter 8) by detailing what it means to *like* an intimate partner. Among other

topics, we'll describe various features of friendship and question whether men and women can be "just friends."

THE NATURE OF FRIENDSHIP

Our friendships are indispensable sources of pleasure and support. A study of students at the University of Minnesota found that over one third of them (36 percent) considered a friendship to be their "closest, deepest, most involved, and most intimate" current relationship (Berscheid, Snyder, & Omoto, 1989). A larger proportion (47 percent) identified a romantic relationship as their most important partnerships, and none of the students were married, but friendships were obviously significant connections to others. And they remain so, even after people marry. Another study that used an experience-sampling proce-dure[1] to track people's interactions found that the participants were generally having more fun when they were with friends than when they were alone or with family members, including their spouses. The best times occurred when both their spouses and their friends were present, but if it was one or the other, people derived more enjoyment and excitement from the presence of a friend than from the presence of a spouse (Larson & Bradney, 1988). Why? What's so great about friendship?

Attributes of Friendships

A variety of attributes come to mind when people think about their friends. When professional men and women living in Boston, New York, and Los Angeles were asked to complete the sentence "A friend is someone. . . .", they reported (in order from the most to least frequent mentions) that a friend is someone (Sapadin, 1988)

> With whom we are intimate,
>
> Whom we trust,
>
> On whom we can depend,
>
> Who shares,
>
> Who is accepting,
>
> Who is caring,
>
> With whom we are close, and
>
> Whom we enjoy.

Evidently, people feel that they can count on their friends to treat them fairly and to like them in return. Friends are also reliable sources of comforting regard and, when it's needed, help.

---

[1]If a reminder about experience-sampling will be helpful, look back at page 62 in chapter 2. In this study, participants wore pagers that prompted them to record what they were doing and who they were with every two hours during the day.

Other work has identified further attributes of friendship. In addition to the *acceptance, support, enjoyment, caring, knowledge,* and *trust* that emerge from the list above, prototypical friendships include *equality,* with both partners' preferences being valued; *authenticity,* with people feeling free to be themselves without pretense; and *respect,* with each valuing the other's talents and judgment (Davis & Todd, 1985). Theorists have summarized these various characteristics by distilling them into three broad themes, with friendships being thought to involve *affective, communal,* and *sociable* elements. The affective component refers to

> The sharing of personal thoughts and feelings (i.e., self-disclosure) and other related expressions of intimacy, appreciation, and affection (including respect and feelings of warmth, care, and love). Additionally, friends are described as providing encouragement, emotional support, empathy, and bolstering one's self-concept, all of which are made possible by an underlying sense of trust, loyalty, and commitment. *(deVries, 1996, p. 252)*

The communal aspect of friendship refers to participating in common activities, similarity, and giving and receiving practical assistance. The sociability theme presents friends as "sources of amusement, fun, and recreation" (p. 253). All of this led Beverly Fehr (1996, p. 7) to define **friendship** as "a voluntary, personal relationship, typically providing intimacy and assistance, in which the two parties like one another and seek each other's company."

Differences between Friendship and Love

How, then, is friendship different from romantic attraction? As we'll see in chapter 8 when we consider love in detail, love involves more complex feelings than liking does. Both liking and loving involve positive and warm evaluations of one's partner (Rubin, 1973), but romantic love includes fascination with one's partner, sexual desire, and a greater desire for exclusiveness than friendship does. Love relationships also involve more stringent standards of conduct; we're supposed to be more loyal to, and even more willing to help, our lovers than our friends (Davis & Todd, 1985). The social norms that regulate friendship are less confining than those that govern romantic relationships, and friendships are easier to dissolve (Fehr, 1996). In addition, friendships are less likely to involve overt expressions of positive emotion, and friends, as a general rule, spend less of their free time together than romantic partners do.

Of course, because most romantic relationships involve partners of different sexes but most friendships do not, we could wonder if the difference between friendship and romantic relationships partially reflects the difference between same-sex and other-sex relationships. One study that shed light on this asked 1,755 junior-high school students living in Toronto to describe both their friendships and romantic relationships with people of the other sex (Connolly et al., 1999). The friendships were said to be less passionate and less committed than the romances were, so differences between friendship and love don't appear to be due solely to the sexes of the people involved.

All in all, it's clear that friendships entail fewer obligations and are usually less emotionally intense and less exclusive than romantic relationships are. And friendships typically do not involve sexual intimacy, whereas romantic relationships frequently do (see chapter 9). So, they are typically less passionate than romances, but rich friendships still contain all the other components that characterize rewarding intimacy. Let's mention several of those next.

Respect

When people respect others, they admire them and hold them in high esteem. The specific traits that seem to make a relationship partner worthy of respect include commendable moral qualities, consideration for others, acceptance of others, honesty, and willingness to listen to others (Frei & Shaver, 2002). We generally like those whom we respect (Frei & Shaver, 2002), and the more we respect a friend or lover, the more satisfying our relationship with that person tends to be (Hendrick & Hendrick, 2004). Our closest friendships tend to be with others whom we respect.

Trust

We trust our partners when we are confident that they will behave benevolently toward us, selflessly taking our best interests into account (Rempel, Ross, & Holmes, 2001). Such confidence takes time to cultivate, but it is likely to develop when someone is alert to our wishes and reliably behaves unselfishly toward us (Wieselquist et al., 1999). Trust is invaluable in any close relationship because it makes interdependency more palatable; it increases our willingness to invest in a relationship, and it promotes efforts to protect and maintain the partnership (Wieselquist et al., 1999). Trust allows people to be comfortable and relaxed in their friendships, and those who do not fully trust their partners tend to be guarded and cautious and less content (Rempel et al., 2001). And the loss of trust has corrosive effects on a close relationship (Miller & Rempel, 2004); those who have been betrayed by a partner (see chapter 10) sometimes find trust, and their satisfaction with their relationship, hard to recover (Mitchell & Sugar, 2003).

Responsiveness

Most of the time, our friends are also interested in who we are and what we have to say. They pay attention to us, and thereby communicate that they value their relationships with us. They are also usually warm and supportive, and that leaves us feeling understood and cared for. This combination of attentive and supportive recognition of our needs and interests is known as *responsiveness*, and it is powerfully rewarding (Reis, Clark, & Holmes, 2004). Responsive partners obviously appreciate us, and their responsiveness leads us to feel valued, validated, and understood (Reis & Patrick, 1996). Responsiveness thus promotes intimacy; a friend's attention and support encourages self-disclosure, trust, and interdependency, and people typically feel much closer to responsive partners than to those who seem uninterested (Reis, 2004). (See Box 7.1.)

Capitalization

Good friends also tend to enhance, rather than diminish, our delight when we share good news or events with them. We don't always receive enthusiastic

---

BOX 7.1

Responsiveness in Action

One of the most successful relationship self-help books of all time is 70 years old and still going strong. Dale Carnegie published *How to Win Friends and Influence People* in 1936, long before relationship scientists began studying the interactive effects of responsiveness, but he firmly believed that the road to financial and interpersonal success lay in behaving toward others in a manner that made them feel important and appreciated. Carnegie suggested six straightforward ways to get others to like us, and the enduring popularity of his homespun advice helps demonstrate why responsiveness from a friend is so uplifting. Here are Carnegie's rules (p. 110):

1. Become genuinely interested in other people.

2. Smile.

3. Remember that a man's name is to him the sweetest and most important sound in any language.

4. Be a good listener. Encourage others to talk about themselves.

5. Talk in terms of the other man's interest.

6. Make the other person feel important—and do it sincerely.

All of these actions help communicate the attention and support that constitute responsiveness, and Carnegie was right: These are good ways to make people feel valued, and our best friends do them frequently.

---

congratulations from others when we encounter good fortune; on occasion, we get bland best wishes, and sometimes others are simply uninterested. But good friends are usually pleased by our successes, and their excitement can increase our enjoyment of the event (Strachman & Gable, 2005). So, in a pattern of interaction known as capitalization (Gable, 2005), we often share good news with friends and receive positive, rewarding responses that are good for close relationships: We feel closer to those who enthusiastically enhance our happiness than to those who respond to our good fortune with apathy or indifference, and relationships in which capitalization routinely occurs are more satisfying than those in which it is infrequent (Gable et al., 2004).

Social Support

Finally, we can count on good friends to provide assistance when we need it. There are several ways in which people can provide us help and encouragement (Drach-Zahavy, 2004), and studies of the aid, or *social support*, we receive from others typically identify three broad types of assistance. We rely on our friends for *emotional support* in the form of affection and acceptance, *advice support* in the form of information and guidance, and *material support* in the form of money and goods (Berscheid & Reis, 1998). A partner who tries to reassure you when you're nervous about an upcoming exam is providing emotional support, whereas a friend who loans you her car is providing material support.

Don't take these distinctions too seriously, however, because these types of aid can and do overlap; because her generous concern would be touching, a friend who offers a loan of her car as soon as she learns that yours isn't running could be said to be providing emotional as well as material support.

Social support can be of enormous value, but there are several complexities involved in the manner in which it operates in close relationships. Consider these points:

- Emotional support has real physiological effects. People who have affectionate partners have chronically lower blood pressures, cholesterol levels, and stress hormone levels than do those who receive lesser amounts of encouragement and caring from others (Seeman et al., 2002). In lab procedures, they even experience less pain when they submerge their arms in ice-cold water (Brown et al., 2003). And when people are under stress, just thinking about a supportive friend tends to reduce their heart rates and blood pressures (Smith, Ruiz, & Uchino, 2004).

- Social support also leads people to feel closer to those who provide it (Gleason, Bolger, & Shrout, 2005). Sensitive, responsive support from others increases our happiness, self-esteem, and optimism about the future (Feeney, 2004), and all of these have beneficial effects on close relationships.

- But some people are better providers of social support than others are. Women provide more emotional support to their partners than men do, on average (Fritz, Nagurney, & Helgeson, 2003), and when people are asked to give difficult impromptu speeches, support from a woman reduces their cardiovascular stress, whereas support from a man does not (Glynn, Christenfeld, & Gerin, 1999). Men tend to give advice, not emotional support (Fritz et al., 2003). Nevertheless, whatever its type, the quality of the support a person provides depends in part on his or her attachment style. Secure people, who readily accept interdependent intimacy with others, tend to provide effective support that reassures and bolsters the recipient, and they do so for altruistic, compassionate reasons (Mikulincer & Shaver, 2005). In contrast, insecure people are more self-serving, tending to provide help out of obligation or for the promise of reward. Moreover, their support tends to be less effective, either because (in the case of avoidant people) they provide less help than secure people do, or because (in the case of anxious-ambivalent people) their help is intrusive and controlling (Feeney & Collins, 2001, 2003).

- Indeed, not all social support is wholly beneficial to its recipients. Even when supportive friends are well-intentioned and altruistic, their efforts to help may threaten our self-esteem or be intrusive, and unwelcome indebtedness can occur when we accept such help. So, social support sometimes comes with emotional costs, and for that reason, the best help may occasionally be *invisible support* that actually goes unnoticed by the recipient (Bolger, Zuckerman, & Kessler, 2000). When cohabiting couples kept diaries of the support they gave and received during a stressful period in which one of them was preparing for a bar examination, the support that was most effective in reducing the test-taker's anxiety was aid the partner said was given but that the test-taker didn't report receiving (Bolger et al., 2000). Sometimes, the best way to help a friend is to do so unobtrusively in a manner that does not add to their woes.

- Nevertheless, although invisible support has its uses, one of the most important patterns in studies of social support is that it's not what people do for us but what we *think* they do for us that matters in the long run. The support we perceive is often only a rough match for the support we actually get (Lakey et al., 2002), and people become distressed when they believe that their partners are unsupportive, whether or not their partners really are (Lakey et al., 2004). In fact, perceived support has more to do with our satisfaction with a partner than with the amount of aid he or she actually provides: When we're content with our friends and lovers, we perceive them to be supportive, but when we're dissatisfied, we perceive them to be neglectful and unhelpful (Kaul & Lakey, 2003). Our judgments aren't totally unrealistic; the more support our partners provide us, the more supportive we usually perceive them to be (Collins & Feeney, 2000). Still, we're more likely to notice and appreciate their aid and assistance when we trust them and we're content with them, so that satisfaction may enhance perceived support at the same time that perceived support is increasing satisfaction (Collins & Feeney, 2000). In general, then, our judgments of the aid we receive from others "are likely to possess both a kernel of truth and a shell of motivated elaboration" (Reis et al., 2004, p. 214).

Finally, our personal characteristics also affect our perceptions of social support (Lakey & Scoboria, 2005). People who doubt others' care and concern for them tend to take a biased, and undeservedly critical, view of others' efforts to aid them. In particular, people who have low self-esteem (Gracia & Herrero, 2004) or insecure attachment styles (Collins & Feeney, 2004) judge the social support they receive to be less considerate and less helpful than do those who hold more favorable, more confident views of themselves and their relationships. Remarkably, even when their friends are being genuinely supportive, insecure people are likely to consider their partners' assistance and encouragement to be insufficient (Kane et al., 2005).

Overall, then, we rely on our friends and lovers for invaluable support, but the amount and quality of sustenance we (feel we) receive is affected by both our and our partners' characteristics. The social support we perceive is also greatly influenced by the quality of our relationships; in general, partners who make us happy seem more supportive than do those with whom we share less satisfying friendships. But good friends are obviously important, vital figures in our lives; add up all the attributes of friendship, such as support, respect, trust, responsiveness, and capitalization, and it's clear that friends can supply us with potent interpersonal rewards.

The Rules of Friendship

Good friends can also be counted on to play by the rules. We don't often explicate our expectations about what it means to be a friend, but most of us nevertheless

TABLE 7.1. The Rules of Friendship

Volunteer help in time of need
Respect the friend's privacy
Keep confidences
Trust and confide in each other
Stand up for the other person in their absence
Don't criticize each other in public
Show emotional support
Look him/her in the eye during conversation
Strive to make him/her happy while in each other's company
Don't be jealous or critical of each other's relationships
Be tolerant of each other's friends
Share news of success with the other
Ask for personal advice
Don't nag
Engage in joking or teasing with the friend
Seek to repay debts and favors and compliments
Disclose personal feelings or problems to the friend

Source: Argyle & Henderson, 1985.

have **rules for relationships** that are shared cultural beliefs about what behaviors friends should (or should not) perform. These standards of conduct help relationships operate more smoothly. We learn the rules during childhood, and one of the things we learn is that when the rules are broken, disapproval and turmoil result. For instance, in a seminal study, British researchers generated a large set of possible friendships rules and asked adults in Britain, Italy, Hong Kong, and Japan which of the rules they would endorse (Argyle & Henderson, 1984). Several rules for conducting friendships appeared to be universal, and they're listed in Table 7.1. These rules pertain to such things as giving help, disclosure and privacy, third parties, and things to avoid (e.g., publicly criticizing or nagging).

The rules are dictates about what we should and shouldn't do, but people don't always follow the rules of friendship. When they were asked to judge the proportion of people who honor a variety of different relationship rules, students at two San Francisco universities estimated that most rules are followed only 50 percent of the time (Gambrill, Florian, & Thomas, 1999). But that doesn't mean the rules are unimportant. When people compare their current friendships to past partnerships that have failed, they remember following the rules of friendship less regularly in their failed friendships (Argyle & Henderson, 1984). Furthermore, people usually realize that their failure to honor various rules helped cause the end of those friendships. Thus, whether or not we consciously think about them, there appear to be standards of behavior in friendships—the social rules of relationships—that can make or break our friendships.

FRIENDSHIP ACROSS THE LIFE CYCLE

There are various types of friendships. They vary in terms of the social context in which they are maintained (for instance, whether your friends are colleagues at work versus neighbors at home), the degree of closeness or intimacy involved, and in the age and sex of the participants (Fehr, 1996). We'll now examine some of the ways friendships change and are intermingled with other types of relationships across the life cycle.

Infancy

The moment they're born, babies have a particular interest in the human face (Mondloch et al., 1999). At two months of age, babies will smile spontaneously at any human face, and, if the recipient responds, they'll usually make happy noises. So, although children may later begin manifesting anxiety in the presence of strangers (at around seven months of age), humans appear to be social animals virtually from birth.

But when do friendships first emerge? Children who are frequently together are capable of simple complementary and reciprocal interactions when they are just over a year old (Howes, 1996). And before their second birthdays, pairs of children sometimes gravitate toward one another; their play becomes more associative and cooperative, and they take evident pleasure in each other's company. Older preschoolers may be found working together with blocks, talking about which block should go where, and trying to build structures jointly, and at those ages (between three and five), rudimentary friendships may be apparent. It's also during the preschool years that children first label playmates as friends. As one three-year-old put it: "We're friends now because we know each other's names" (Rubin, 1980).

Childhood

After infancy, the enormous changes that children encounter as they grow and mature are mirrored in their friendships, which gradually grow richer and more complex (Blieszner & Roberto, 2004). One change in children's friendships is rooted in their cognitive development; as they age, children are increasingly able to take others' perspectives and to understand their wishes and points of view. The development of this ability led Robert Selman (1981) to suggest that childhood friendships go through several stages that are increasingly sophisticated.

Before the age of ten, for instance, Selman suggested that children's friendships are characterized by *fair-weather cooperation*. They are starting to fathom their friends' points of view, and they recognize that conflicts are more easily resolved when both parties' interests are served, but they construe friendship as serving self-interests rather than mutual interests. Their temporal perspectives are also limited, so if conflicts aren't solved when they occur, the participants are likely to feel that their relationship is over.

Thereafter, in middle school, children enter a stage of *intimate-mutual sharing* (Selman, 1981). Friendship is seen as a collaboration that serves everyone's interests, but it is also seen as an exclusive and possessive relationship: Children will be hurt and offended if their invitation for a friend to play at their house is rejected because the friend is already playing with someone else. But at this stage, children recognize that relationships can withstand occasional turbulence, and they begin to expect loyalty and commitment in their friendships. Trust assumes significance, and talking things through is considered a key way of resolving conflicts.

Finally, in their teen years, adolescents enter a final level of development, *autonomous interdependence*. At this stage, they recognize that a particular friendship cannot fulfill all emotional and psychological needs, and friends are allowed to develop independent relationships with others. Adolescents also believe that relationships are dynamic rather than fixed; as the people involved change, so too does their friendship.

Accompanying this increasing cognitive sophistication are changes in the interpersonal needs that are preeminent as children age. According to Duane Buhrmester and Wyndol Furman (1986), these key needs are *acceptance* in the early elementary years, *intimacy* in preadolescence, and *sexuality* during the teen years. Presumably, new needs are added on top of old ones at each stage, so that older children have more needs to satisfy than younger children do. And the successful resolution of each stage requires the development of specific competencies that affect the way a child handles later stages; if those skills aren't acquired, problems occur.

For instance, when children enter elementary school, the companionship of, and *acceptance* by, other children becomes increasingly important. Elementary students learn about differences among their peers and about the status hierarchies that exist among people, and, increasingly, those who are not accepted by their peers feel ostracized and excluded.

Later, in preadolescence, children develop a need for *intimacy* that typically focuses on a friend who is similar to them in age, background, and interests. This is when full-blown friendships that are characterized by intense closeness and extensive self-disclosure first emerge. During this period, children develop the skills of perspective taking, empathy, and altruism that are the foundation for close adult relationships. Children who were not previously accepted by others may overcome their sense of isolation or rejection, but if they cannot, they may experience true loneliness for the first time.

Thereafter, *sexuality* erupts, and the typical adolescent develops an interest in the other sex. Most adolescents initially have difficulty establishing relationships that will satisfy their new emerging needs, but most manage to form sensitive, caring, and open sexual relationships later on.

Overall, then, theorists generally agree that our relationships change as we grow older. The rich, sophisticated ways in which adults conduct their friendships are years in the making. And, to some degree, success in childhood friendships may pave the way for better adult outcomes. Children who are rejected by their peers tend to encounter a variety of difficulties, such as dropping out of school, criminal arrests, and psychological maladjustment, at higher rates than do those who are well-liked by others (Bukowski & Cillessen, 1998; Kupersmidt, Coie, & Dodge, 1990). Relationship scientists can't do experiments on peer rejection—no one would randomly assign a child to be chronically disliked by others—so the correlation between peer rejection and subsequent maladjustment allows several possibilities. In particular, we don't know whether peer rejection *causes* such problems or is instead a symptom of other influences that are actually at fault. Nevertheless, whatever the case, interventions that teach social skills tend to enhance children's acceptance by their peers, and that reduces their risk of later maladjustment (Waas & Graczyk, 1998).

Adolescence

There are several other ways in which friendships change during the teen years. First, teens spend less and less time with their families and more and more time with their peers. A time-sampling study in Chicago found that children in fifth grade spent 35 percent of their time with family members, whereas adolescents in twelfth grade were with their families only 14 percent of the time (Larson et al., 1996). Time spent with peers without any family members present increases for both boys and girls throughout junior high and high school, and the change is especially notable for girls (increasing in another study [Larson & Richards, 1991] from 18 percent in fifth grade to 34 percent in ninth grade). Some of this time, adolescents are with romantic partners, and the amount of time they spend with such partners also increases as they get older, often at the expense of time they would otherwise spend with friends (Zimmer-Gembeck, 1999). But time spent alone increases, too, so the amount of time spent with family drops appreciably.

A second change is that adolescents increasingly turn to their friends for the satisfaction of important attachment needs (Fraley & Davis, 1997). Attachment theorists identify four components of attachment (Hazan & Zeifman, 1994): (a) *Proximity Seeking*, which involves approaching, staying near, or making contact with an attachment figure; (b) *Separation Protest*, in which people resist being separated from a partner and are distressed by separation from him or her; (c) *Safe Haven*, turning to an attachment figure as a source of comfort and support in times of stress; and (d) *Secure Base*, using a partner as a foundation for exploration of novel environments and other daring exploits. All of these components of attachment can be found in the relationships young children have with their parents, but, as they grow older, adolescents gradually shift their primary attachments from their parents to their peers in a component-by-component fashion (Hazan & Zeifman, 1994).

For instance, around the ages of eleven to fourteen, young adolescents often shift the location of their safe haven from their parents to their peers; if something upsets them, they'll seek out their friends before they approach their parents. Older adolescents who are fifteen to seventeen years old still mention their parents most frequently as their secure base, and they continue to feel some distress when they are separated from their parents, but peers are increasingly

---

BOX 7.2
What's a Best Friend?

People usually have a lot of friendly acquaintances, a number of casual friends, a few close friends, and just one or two *best* friends, with whom they share especially rich relationships. What's so special about a best friend? What distinguishes a best friend from all of the other people who are important to us?

The simple answer is that it's all a matter of degree (Fehr, 1996). Best friendships are more intimate than common friendships are, and all of the components of intimacy are involved. Consider *knowledge:* Best friends are usually our closest confidants. They often know secrets about us that are known to no one else, including our spouses! Consider *trust:* We typically expect a very high level of support from our best friends, so that a best friend is "someone who is there for you, no matter what" (Yager, 1997, p. 18). Con-

sider *interdependence:* When our best friends are nearby and available to us, we try to see more of them than our other friends; we interact with them more often and in a wider range of situations than we do with lesser buddies. And finally, consider *commitment:* We ordinarily expect that a best friend will be a friend forever. Because such a person "is *the* friend, before all others," best friendships routinely withstand "the tests of time and conflict, major changes such as moving, or status changes, such as marrying or having a child" (Yager, 1997, p. 18).

In general, then, best friendships are not distinctly different relationships of some unique type (Fehr, 1996). Instead, they are simply more intimate than other friendships—involving richer, more rewarding, and more personal connections to others—and that's why they are so prized.

---

used for these functions, too. Indeed, a number of older teens (41 percent) identify a peer, rather than a parent, as their primary attachment figure. (Most of the time, however, that person is a romantic partner rather than a friend [Hazan & Zeifman, 1994].)

So, peers gradually replace parents in people's lives, but even young adults may still rely on their parents for some components of attachment. College students are most likely to seek proximity with their friends, and they tend to turn to friends as a safe haven, but they remain relatively unlikely to rely on friends as a secure base (Fraley & Davis, 1997). That's a role still often reserved for Mom or Dad. When people are moving to new locales, taking new jobs, and training for new professions, it's still comforting for most of them to know that they can return home for a visit, clean laundry, and free meals when they want to.

The social networks in which friendships operate also tend to change over time. As adolescents age, their peer groups usually become more complex, moving through five different stages (Dunphy, 1963). Think back to sixth or seventh grade: That's Stage One, where interaction occurs in same-sex *cliques* (or small groups of individuals who hang around with each other). At Stage

Two, occasional group-level interaction between boy and girl cliques occurs, but any interaction on an individual basis is still rare and is perceived as rather daring. At Stage Three, upper-status members of same-sex cliques initiate heterosexual interactions that lead to the formation of crowds that subsume male, female, and mixed-sex cliques. (Remember ninth grade?) During the next stage, the intersecting same-sex and cross-sex cliques re-form to comprise separate mixed-sex cliques that associate in a crowd. And finally, in Stage Five, the crowd begins to disintegrate into loosely associated groups of couples. Thus, as adolescents go from the middle school years to the end of high school, their peer groups are constantly evolving, and the number of friendships they share with the other sex are gradually increasing (Hartup, 1993).

Adolescent friendships can also involve notable amounts of argument, teasing, competition, and other forms of conflict. Discord and conflict are prevalent in adolescence; on average, adolescents report seven disagreements with others each day (Laursen & Collins, 1994). Some of this conflict is with their parents, but the frequency of parent-child conflict actually declines during the teen years (Laursen, Coy, & Collins, 1998), and much of the conflict adolescents encounter is in partnerships with their peers. Discord in teen friendships is usually less intense than conflict in family relationships (Laursen & Collins, 1994), but roughly one fifth of best friendships in adolescence appear to be characterized by both positive feelings and high conflict (Way et al., 2001). These friendships are apparently desirable, however, because the participants typically enjoy better self-esteem and family relations and lower depression than do those whose closest friendships lack either intimacy or strong conflict. For some adolescents, conflict with friends is undoubtedly a source of tension, but for many teens, conflict may simply be a part of honest, authentic relationships.

Finally, adolescent friendships involve peer pressure that reaches a peak around the age of fifteen (Berndt, 1996), influencing a person's choice of clothing, academic performance, drinking behavior, smoking, sexual behavior, and more. Friends often behave similarly because they naturally have a lot in common (Remember chapter 3?), but peer influence matters, too. On occasion, friends may coerce a partner to do what they want, but most peer pressure is probably more innocuous than that (Berndt, 1996). Friends often discuss issues freely until they reach a consensus, using reasoning, offers of rewards, or teasing to persuade each other. These influences can be either negative or positive, but they are probably only rarely coercive and obnoxious.

Young Adulthood

During their late teens and twenties, people enter young adulthood. Intimacy is an important aspect of social support in adolescent relationships (Berndt, 1996), but many developmental researchers believe that intimacy is even more consequential in young adulthood. For instance, Erik Erikson (1950), a historically prominent theorist, believed that the central task of a person's late teen years and early twenties was working through the developmental stage of "intimacy versus isolation." From this vantage point, intimacy does not necessarily involve sexuality, but it does involve sensitivity to the aspirations, needs, and wishes of one's partner.

This search for intimacy is often undertaken in a novel environment—when many North Americans leave home to attend college. When people move away from home, new friends help compensate for any old friends that are lost, but in general, "the transition to university has deleterious effects on friendships" (Fehr, 1999b, p. 269). A year-long survey of a freshman class at the University of Denver demonstrated that the friendships the students had at home tended to erode and to be replaced by new relationships as the year went by (Shaver, Furman, & Buhrmester, 1985). This didn't happen immediately, however, and the students' satisfaction with their friendship networks was lowest in the fall and winter after they arrived at college. Almost all (97 percent) of the incoming students quickly found a new "close" friend, but few of these relationships retained their prominence for long; only about a third of them were still designated as best friendships in the spring. The students were evidently shuffling and reshuffling their social networks, and those who were outgoing and self-disclosing had an easier time of it; during their freshman year, socially skilled students were more satisfied with their relationships than were those who were less socially skilled. By the close of the study in the spring, the students had generally regained their satisfaction with their social networks, but they did so by relying less on their families and by forming new friendships; as the year went on, family relationships had less and less to do with how satisfied people were.

How do things change after college? In one impressive study, 113 young adults kept dairies of their social interactions for a couple of weeks on two separate occasions, once when they were still in college and again six years after they had graduated (Reis et al., 1993). Overall, the participants spent less time interacting with others after they graduated than they did when they were in college. In particular, the amount of time spent with same-sex friends and groups of three or more people declined. The total amount of time spent with partners of the other sex increased, but the number of other-sex partners with whom that time was spent decreased, especially for men. Still, just as developmental theorists would suggest, the average intimacy levels of the participants' interactions increased during their twenties. In general, the data suggest that after college, people tend to interact with fewer friends, but they have deeper, more interdependent relationships with the friends they have.

Midlife

What happens when people settle down with a primary romantic partner? The connection between people's friendships and their romances is very clear: When people become involved with a romantic partner, they typically spend less time with their families and friends. A pattern of **dyadic withdrawal** occurs as intimacy grows in a blossoming romantic relationship; as people see more and more of a lover, they see less and less of their friends (Fehr, 1999b). One study found that people usually spent two hours per day with good friends when they were casually dating someone, but they saw their friends for less than 30 minutes per day once they became engaged (Milardo, Johnson, & Huston, 1983). Romantic couples do tend to increase their contact with friends they have in common, but this doesn't offset declines in the total number of friends they have and the amount of time they spend with them. Moreover, because heterosexual couples in the United States tend to socialize more often with *his* friends than with *her* friends, women's friendships with other women are especially likely to be affected by dyadic withdrawal (Fehr, 1999b).

The erosion of people's friendships doesn't stop once they get married. Friendships with members of the other sex are especially affected; people tend to see much less of friends who could be construed by a spouse to be potential romantic rivals (Werking, 1997). Still, even though they see less of their friends, spouses often have larger social networks than they did when they were single because they see a lot more of their in-laws (Milardo et al., 1983). (Make no mistake about this, and beware if you don't like your lover's family: You will see a lot more of them if you marry!)

Thus, people's social lives don't wither away completely when they commit themselves to a spouse and kids, but the focus of their socializing does shift from their personal friends to friends and family they share with their husbands or wives. There are two other notable patterns as well. If people have children, their friendships with other parents may prosper. The number of close friends people have may also rebound when their children leave home and they have more free time (deVries, 1991).

Old Age

Ultimately, elderly people have smaller social networks and fewer friends than younger people do (Carstensen, Isaacowitz, & Charles, 1999). This pattern is less pronounced among women than among men because older women are better able to make and keep friends than older men are (Adams & Blieszner, 1995). But both men and women tend to focus their interpersonal energies on a small number of special friends in old age; they have just as many close friends as they did when they were younger, but they spend less time with casual friends and other peripheral social partners (Fung, Carstensen, & Lang, 2001).

Why are seniors less sociable, overall? One possibility is that older people desire the same social contact as anyone else, but their social participation is impeded by a variety of **barriers** younger people don't have to overcome (Havighurst, 1961). Such barriers might include mandatory retirement, poor transportation, the death of friends, and subtle discrimination against the elderly. In fact, practical matters of mobility and health sometimes do complicate seniors' social lives. However, older adults often bypass opportunities for social participation that are freely available (Lansford, Sherman, & Antonucci, 1998). In addition, if older people were blocked from having relationships they desired, you'd expect them to be dissatisfied with their social networks; to the contrary, however, "older people express great satisfaction with their social relationships" (Lang & Carstensen, 1994, p. 315), a fact that makes the "barrier" perspective on seniors' sociability suspect.

BOX 7.3

Can Pets be Our Friends?

There are over 140 million pet dogs and cats in the United States (Allen 2003); that's nearly one pet for every two people in the whole country. Moreover, big majorities of pet owners consider their companion animals to be cherished members of the family, and we've all heard that "a dog is a man's best friend." Can a pet be a friend?

People certainly behave as if that's the case: The presence of a beloved pet can help someone manage stressful situations even better than a human friend can. In one study of this effect (Allen, Blascovich, & Mendes, 2002), people were asked to work a mental math problem for five minutes—rapidly counting backwards by threes from 7,654—when they were (a) alone, (b) with their spouses, or (c) with their pets and no one else. The presence of a pet was soothing; the difficult task caused only slight arousal when people were with their pets, but their heart rates and blood pressures went up substantially when they were alone, and their cardiovascular readings soared when their spouses

were present. A human audience, even a loving partner, made the potentially embarrassing task more stressful, but a companion animal made it less taxing.

These results are intriguing, but they could be due to idiosyncrasies in the people who choose to have pets. So, in another test of this effect (Allen, Shykoff, & Izzo, 2001), businessmen who lived alone were *randomly assigned* either to adopt pets from an animal shelter or to continue to live alone. When they were then put under stress, the new pet owners displayed increases in blood pressure that were only half as large as those that occurred among those without pets. Moreover, the fewer friends the men had, the greater the benefits of owning a pet.

Obviously, a dog or a cat cannot supply the same responsiveness, respect, or trust that human friends can. But people take great pleasure in the companionship that pets provide, and the support that pets can supply is genuinely beneficial. Sure, as long as we use the term loosely, pets can be our friends.

Another possibility is offered by the **disengagement perspective,** which holds that older people voluntarily socialize less as a normal, inevitable part of aging (Cumming & Henry, 1961). Proponents of this view suggest that decreases in activity levels lead seniors to become more passive, and lower sociability is a result of a less energetic approach to social life. Arguing against this possibility is the fact that elderly people disengage from some types of relationships but not from others; although they do tend to drop their casual partners as they advance in years, the number of close friends in their networks remains about the same (Fung et al., 2001).

A third, more subtle possibility is that aging changes the basic motivations that direct social behavior (Lang, 2004). **Socioemotional selectivity theory** argues that seniors have different interpersonal goals than younger people do (Löckenhoff & Carstensen, 2004). With a long life stretching out before them, young adults are presumed to pursue future-oriented goals aimed at acquiring information that will be useful later in life. (That's presumably what you're doing now that you're in college.) With such ends in mind, young people seek relatively large social networks that include diverse social partners. However, when people age and their futures seem more and more finite, they presumably become oriented more toward the present than toward the future, and they emphasize emotional fulfillment to a greater extent (Fung & Carstensen, 2004). The idea is that as their time perspective shrinks, people "systematically hone their social networks such that available social partners satisfy emotional needs" (Carstensen et al., 1999, p. 173). And that's why seniors let casual relationships lapse; they're aiming for quality, not quantity, in their friendships.

An intriguing prediction of socioemotional selectivity theory is that anyone who considers his or her future to be limited will also choose to spend more time with a small number of close friends instead of a wider variety of more casual buddies—and that's exactly what happens in younger adults whose time orientation is changed by contracting HIV (Carstensen et al., 1999). Given its conceptual sophistication and empirical support, socioemotional selectivity theory seems to be a reasonable explanation for age-related declines in sociability.

Finally, let's note that the social support provided by friends may be especially important when we're older and somewhat less able. A 10-year longitudinal study of 2,812 seniors in Connecticut found that frequent interactions with friends reduced the risk that one would develop a disability (such as not being able to dress oneself, bathe oneself, or walk across a room) (Mendes de Leon et al., 1999). Moreover, if a disability did develop, close friendships were linked to a higher rate of recovery. Overall, elderly people who have good friends live longer, healthier lives than do those who are less connected to others (Sabin, 1993). Friendships are invaluable for as long as we live.

DIFFERENCES IN FRIENDSHIP

Friendships don't just differ across the life cycle, they also differ from person to person and from partner to partner. In this last section of the chapter, we'll consider how the nature of friendships is intertwined with gender and other individual differences.

Gender Differences in Same-Sex Friendships

Consider these descriptions of two same-sex friendships:

Wilma and Betty are very close friends. Often, they stay up half the night talking about love and life. In times of trouble, the other is always there for support and counsel. When they experience any problems in their romantic relationships, they immediately get on the phone with each other, asking for, and getting, all the advice and consolation they need. Wilma and Betty feel that they know everything about each other.

Fred and Barney are very close friends. Often, they stay up half the night playing cards or tinkering with Fred's beloved 1960 Chevy, which is constantly breaking down. In times of trouble, they always help each other out. Fred will loan Barney money whenever he runs short; Barney will give Fred a ride home from work whenever their best efforts fail to revive Fred's old car. They go everywhere together—to the bars, to play basketball, on double dates. Barney and Fred feel they are the best of buddies.

Do these two descriptions sound familiar? Based on your own experience and your observations of others, do you believe that women's friendships tend to be like Wilma and Betty's, while men's friendships tend to be like Fred and Barney's? If so, you agree with a good deal of research that shows that women's friendships are usually characterized by **emotional sharing** and self-disclosure, whereas men's friendships revolve around **shared activities,** companionship, and fun (Fehr, 1996; Winstead, Derlega, & Rose, 1997; Wright, 1998). It's an oversimplification, but a pithy phrase coined years ago by Wright (1982) is still serviceable today: Women's friendships are *"face-to-face,"* whereas men's are *"side-by-side"*.[2]

This difference emerges from several specific patterns in same-sex friendships (Fehr, 1996):

- women spend more time talking to friends on the phone;
- men and women talk about different topics; women are more likely to talk about relationships and personal issues, whereas men are more likely to talk about impersonal interests such as sports;
- women self-disclose more than men do;
- women provide their friends more emotional support than men do; and
- women express more feelings of love and affection in their friendships than men do.

Add all this up, and women's same-sex friendships tend to be closer and more intimate than men's are. The net result is that women typically have partners outside their romantic relationships to whom they can turn for sensitive, sympathetic understanding and support, but men often do not. For instance, ponder this provocative question (Rubin, 1986, p. 170): "Who would you turn to if you came home one night and your wife [or husband or lover] announced she [or he] was leaving you?" When research participants actually considered this question, nearly every woman readily named a same-sex friend, but only a few men did (Rubin, 1986). (In fact, most men could not come up with anyone to whom they could turn for solace if their lovers left them.)

Why are men's same-sex friendships less intimate than women's partnerships? Are men less capable of forming close friendships with each other, or are they just less willing? In most cases, it appears that they are less willing; most men can be as expressive and close as women are, but they simply choose not

---

[2]This clever statement is oversimplified because it implies that women just talk and men just play, and of course that isn't true. Women share enjoyable activities with their friends about as often as men do (Fehr, 1996). However, men are more reluctant than women to share their feelings and fears with their friends, so emotional sharing does distinguish women's friendships from those of men, on average (Wright, 1998).

to be (Fehr, 1996). In particular, men seem to be fully capable of forming intimate friendships with other men when the circumstances support such closeness—but they generally choose not to do so because such intimacy is less socially acceptable among men than among women (Reis et al., 1985). When social norms make it appropriate, men actually self-disclose *more* than women do (Derlega et al., 1985). Further, gender differences in the intimacy of friendship are commonplace in cultures (such as the United States) in which expressions of affection and intimacy between men are discouraged, but the differences disappear in societies (such as the Middle East) where expressive male friendships are encouraged (Reis, 1998).

So, why don't North American norms support more intimacy in men's friendships? There are at least three reasons why (Bank & Hansford, 2000). First, *gender roles* play a part. A traditional upbringing encourages men to be instrumental, but not expressive,[3] and (as we noted in chapter 5) a person's expressivity predicts how self-disclosing he or she will be (Aube et al., 1995). Androgynous men tend to have closer friendships than traditional, sex-typed men do, but more men are sex-typed than androgynous. Second, in keeping with typical gender roles, men are expected to display more *emotional constraint* than women do. Social norms lead men to be more reluctant than women to express their worries and emotions to others. Finally, men's same-sex friendships are more influenced by *homophobia,* a fear of homosexuality and a dread of being perceived to be homosexual. In general, it appears that if men felt as free as women to admit that they cared for their friends, they would do so (Bank & Hansford, 2000).

Thus, the lower intimacy of men's friendships probably isn't due to an inability to share meaningful, close attachments to other men. Instead, it's a choice that is supported by cultural pressures that play "an important role in shaping men's reluctance to engage in intimate interactions with one another" (Reis, 1998, p. 225). Many men would probably have closer same-sex friendships if Western cultures did not discourage psychological intimacy with other men.

Individual Differences in Friendship

In addition to the effects of gender, there are several other differences from person to person that influence the friendships we form. One of these is **self-monitoring,** which we discussed in chapter 4. (Look back at pages 136–137.) High self-monitors tend to construct broad social networks of companions who are "activity specialists," partners with whom they share a particular pleasure, but not much else. As a result, high self-monitors tend to be less invested in their friendships than low self-monitors are; low self-monitors have fewer friends, but they tend to have more in common with each of them, and their friendships are more intimate, on average (Snyder & Simpson, 1987).

---

[3]Would you like a quick reminder about the nature of instrumentality and expressivity? Look back at page 24 in chapter 1.

BOX 7.4

Can Men and Women be Close Friends?

Of course. They often are. Most people have had a close friendship with a member of the other sex (Sapadin, 1988), and such relationships are commonplace among college students (Rose, 1985). However, once they leave college, most people no longer maintain intimate cross-sex friendships (Wright, 1989). Why? What's going on?

The first thing to note is that men and women become friends for the same reasons they grow close to their same-sex friends: "companionship, good times, conversation, and laughter" (Blescke-Rechec & Buss, 2001, p. 1320). The same respect, trust, and social support are involved. And because they are dealing with women instead of other men, men are often more open and expressive with their female friends than with their male companions (Fehr, 1996).

However, cross-sex friendships face challenges that same-sex partnerships do not ordinarily encounter (O'Meara, 1989). One hurdle is determining whether the relationship is a friendship or a romance. Friendships are typically non-exclusive, non-sexual, equal partnerships that differ from standard romances (which are exclusive, sexual relationships in which the partners assume different roles), and people may find themselves in unfamiliar territory as they try to negotiate an intimate friendship with someone of the other sex (Werking, 1997). A big question is whether the partners—who, after all, are very close—will have sex. This issue is unimportant when one (or both) of the partners is homosexual, but it is a frequent stumbling block among heterosexuals; in one survey (Sapadin, 1988), one fifth of the women and one quarter of the men reported that "sexual

tension" was the thing they disliked most about their cross-sex friendships.

On the other hand, sexual titillation is sometimes one of the things people like best about their friendships with the other sex (Sapadin, 1988), and about half of the young adults in one study reported that they had had sex with at least one friend who they did not consider to be a romantic partner (Afifi & Faulkner, 2000). In most cases (about two thirds of the time), the respondents said that the sex had improved the relationship, bringing the partners closer together, without transforming their friendship into a romantic liaison. (Thus, they evidently became "friends with benefits".)

Nevertheless, sex among friends is sometimes problematic; it can cause confusion and complicate the partnership (Werking, 2000), and most cross-sex friendships never become sexual (Afifi & Faulkner, 2000). Indeed, most of the time, people do not want to turn their cross-sex friendships into romances (Reeder, 2000), and they actually strive to keep their partnerships platonic. There may be several reasons why (Messman, Canary, & Hause, 2000). Sometimes, people do not want to risk losing a rewarding relationship by changing it into something else. As one research participant reported (Werking, 1997, p. 102): "I really like her friendship. And if we became boyfriend-girlfriend, that might be fine. But then we might lose a friendship." In other cases, a sexual spark is missing and there is insufficient sexual attraction, and in still other instances, there are third parties involved (such as a romantic partner) who would object.

Indeed, cross-sex friendships can be tricky when the partners are married to others. Arguably, close friends who provide companionship and caring outside of one's marriage can reduce the emotional burden placed on one's spouse (Werking, 1997). However, a spouse may be threatened by one's close connection to a potential rival even when no sex is involved (as we make clear in chapter 10). As a result, married people are less likely than singles to have close cross-sex friendships, and that's a major reason why such relationships become less common after people finish their schooling.

Need for Intimacy

People also take different approaches to friendship on the basis of their personal needs. Consider, for example, the **need for intimacy,** or N_{int}. "The intimacy motive," according to Dan McAdams (1985, p. 87), "is a recurrent preference or readiness for warm, close, and communicative exchange with others—an interpersonal interaction perceived as an end in itself rather than as a means to another end." The need for intimacy is associated with social behavior that emphasizes the depth and quality of social relations. Those with a high N_{int} are more trusting, and they confide more to their partners than do those who have lower needs for intimacy (McAdams, Healy, & Krause, 1984). They also tend to enjoy better mental health (McAdams & Bryant, 1987).

A need for intimacy may play a particularly important role in close friendships. The friendships of individuals high in the need for intimacy involve high levels of self-disclosure and loyalty that do not occur to the same extent in the friendships of people with low N_{int}. And people high in N_{int} behave kindly toward their friends. They share more personal information and listen more, and if conflict occurs, they blame their partners less and are more likely to reconcile with them (McAdams, 1985).

High need for intimacy may even promote positive life outcomes over the long haul. In a longitudinal study, McAdams and Vaillant (1982) found that the social motives of men at age 30 predicted how well-adjusted they would be almost twenty years later. Those who were high in N_{int} as young adults were better adjusted in middle age. These findings reinforce the conclusion that emerges from studies of friendships among the elderly: In the long run, the quality of one's friendships substantially affect one's well-being.

Depression

If N_{int} has a salutary role in friendships, are there personal attributes that can have a detrimental role? The answer is yes, and one candidate is depression. In general, when people experience the gloomy, dour moods of depression, others don't like them much (Segrin et al., 2003), and that seems to be because depressed people interact with others in an impoverished manner that is unrewarding for their partners. In particular, they (Gotlib & Whiffen, 1991)

speak more slowly and more monotonously,

take longer to respond to others' statements,

maintain less eye contact,

are more self-focused and pessimistic, and

are less skillful at solving interpersonal problems.

They also engage in an obnoxious pattern of *excessive reassurance seeking:* They persistently probe for assurances that others like and accept them but doubt the sincerity of such declarations when they are received (Joiner & Metalsky, 2001). Discontent and anxious, they continue to seek more convincing comfort and gradually wear out their partners' patience (Shaver, Schachner, & Mikulincer, 2005).

This dreary style of interaction tends to be off-putting. It undermines others' contentment (Beach et al., 2003) and leaves depressed people with fewer close friends and smaller and less supportive social networks than those enjoyed by happier people (Gotlib & Whiffen, 1991). So, the link between depression and friendship appears to be a two-way street (Davila, 2001). One reason people sometimes get depressed is that they are rejected by others; they don't have enough friends and they don't get enough social support, and that leaves them disheartened and dejected (Nolan, Flynn, & Garber, 2003). But once they become gloomy and glum, they behave in an unfriendly manner that makes it even harder to attract the friends they need. Studies of depression remind us just how important friendship is: We are much, much poorer without it.

FOR YOUR CONSIDERATION

Don and Teddi became best friends when they went through graduate school together. They started their studies the same year and took the same classes, and they worked together on several projects outside of class. They learned that they were both conscientious and clever, and they came to respect and trust each other completely. Each learned the other's most intimate secrets. They also had great fun playing together. They were both nonconformists, and they shared a wry and offbeat sense of humor; they would frequently laugh at jokes that nobody else seemed to get. The night that Teddi finished her doctoral dissertation, they got drunk and almost had sex, but they were interrupted and the moment passed. And soon thereafter, they graduated and took jobs in different parts of the country; he moved to California and she went to Minnesota. Now, six years later, they have both married, and they see each other only every year or so at professional meetings.

What do you think the future holds for Don's and Teddi's friendship? Why?

CHAPTER SUMMARY

The Nature of Friendship

Friendships are based on the same building blocks of intimacy as romances are, but the mix of components is usually different.

Attributes of Friendships. Our friendships are indispensable sources of pleasure and support. Close friendships are genuinely intimate relationships that involve acceptance, support, enjoyment, caring, knowledge, and trust. Equality and authenticity are also involved. Thus, friendship is a "voluntary, personal relationship, typically providing intimacy and assistance, in which the two parties like one another and seek each other's company" (Fehr, 1996, p. 7).

Friendships differ from romantic relationships in a variety of ways: Romantic love includes fascination with one's partner, sexual desire, and a greater desire for exclusiveness than friendship does. Nevertheless, all of the components of enjoyable intimacy are present in close friendships, including

- *Respect.* People usually admire their friends and hold them in high esteem.
- *Trust.* People are usually confident that their friends will behave benevolently toward them, selflessly taking their best interests into account.
- *Responsiveness.* Friends provide attentive and supportive recognition of our needs and interests.
- *Capitalization.* Friends usually respond eagerly and energetically to our happy outcomes, sharing our delight and reinforcing our pleasure.
- *Social Support.* This comes in various forms, including affection, advice, and material assistance. Social support is valuable to the recipient, but some people are better providers of social support than others are; people with secure attachment styles tend to provide effective support. Invisible support that goes unnoticed by the recipient is sometimes very beneficial, but perceived support is very important; it's not what people do for us but what we *think* they do for us that matters in the long run. But people with low self-esteem or insecure attachment styles tend to underestimate the amount of support they receive from others.

The Rules of Friendship. Friendships also have rules, which are shared beliefs among members of a culture about what behaviors friends should (or should not) perform. These standards of conduct help relationships operate more smoothly.

Friendship across the Life Cycle

Infancy. Toddlers play together cooperatively and take evident pleasure in each other's company. They can be said to have rudimentary friendships.

Childhood. As children grow and mature, their friendships gradually grow richer and more complex. Some changes are rooted in cognitive development; as they age, children are increasingly able to take others' perspectives and to understand their wishes and points of view. Selman suggested that child-hood friendships go through several stages: fair-weather cooperation, intimate-mutual sharing, and autonomous interdependence. Different interpersonal needs may be preeminent at different ages: acceptance in the early elementary years, intimacy in preadolescence, and sexuality during the teen years. Overall, theorists generally agree the sophisticated ways in which adults conduct their friendships are years in the making.

Adolescence. During the teen years, adolescents spend less and less time with their families and more and more time with their peers. They also increasingly turn to their friends for the satisfaction of important attachment needs; if something upsets them, they'll seek out their friends before they ap-proach their parents. The social networks in which friendships operate also tend to change over time; the same-sex cliques of middle school are gradually replaced with the romantic partnerships of high school. Finally, adolescent friendships involve peer pressure that reaches a peak around the age of fifteen.

Young Adulthood. After college, people tend to interact with fewer friends, but they have deeper, more interdependent relationships with the friends they have.

Midlife. *Dyadic withdrawal* occurs when people settle into a primary romantic relationship; as people see more and more of a lover, they see less and less of their friends. Friendships with members of the other sex are especially affected, but spouses often have larger social networks than they did when they were single because they see a lot more of their in-laws.

Old Age. Elderly people tend to focus their interpersonal energies on a small number of special friends in old age; they have just as many close friends as they did when they were younger, but they spend less time with casual friends and other peripheral social partners. Why are seniors less sociable, over-all? They may desire more social contact but be impeded by a variety of *barriers* younger people don't have to overcome. Alternatively, a *disengagement perspec-tive* holds that older people voluntarily socialize less as decreases in activity lev-els lead them to become more passive. But *socioemotional selectivity theory*, which argues that seniors have different interpersonal goals than younger people do, enjoys the best support. Presumably, when people age and their futures seem more and more finite, they become oriented more toward the present than toward the future and they emphasize emotional fulfillment to a greater extent; as a result, they aim for quality, not quantity, in their friendships.

Differences in Friendship

Gender Differences in Same-Sex Friendships. Women's friendships are usually characterized by *emotional sharing* and self-disclosure, whereas men's friendships revolve around *shared activities*, companionship, and fun. As a result, women typically have partners outside their romantic relationships to whom they can turn for sensitive, sympathetic understanding and support, but men do not. Why are men's same-sex friendships less intimate than women's partnerships? Men seem to be fully capable of forming intimate friendships with other men when the circumstances support such closeness, but they generally choose not to do so when, as in Western cultures, such intimacy is discouraged. Traditional gender roles, social norms encouraging emotional constraint, and homophobia discourage intimacy in men's friendships in the United States.

Individual Differences in Friendship. Low *self-monitors* have fewer friends than high self-monitors do, but they tend to have more in common with their friends, and their friendships are typically more intimate. *Need for intimacy* is a social motive that prompts individuals to seek out warm, close contact with others. The intimacy motive is associated with social behavior that emphasizes the depth and quality of social relations, and it may contribute to long-term adjustment. *Depression*, on the other hand, is associated with social rejection. Depressed people interact with others in an impoverished manner; in particular, they engage in an obnoxious pattern of excessive reassurance seeking. This dreary style of interaction tends to be off-putting, making it hard for depressed people to attract the friends they need.

CHAPTER 8

Love

A Brief History of Love ◆ Types of Love ◆ The Triangular Theory of Love ◆
Romantic, Passionate Love ◆ Companionate Love ◆ Styles of Loving ◆
Individual Differences in Love ◆ Attachment Styles ◆ Age ◆ Men and
Women ◆ Does Love Last? ◆ Why Doesn't Romantic Love Last? ◆
So, What Does the Future Hold? ◆ For Your Consideration ◆
Chapter Summary

Here's an interesting question: If someone had all the other qualities you desired in a spouse, would you marry that person if you were not in love with him or her? Most people reading this text would say no. At the end of the twentieth century, huge majorities of American men and women considered romantic love to be necessary for marriage (Simpson, Campbell, & Berscheid, 1986). Along with all the other characteristics people want in a spouse—such as warmth, physical attractiveness, and dependability—young adults in Western cultures insist on romance and passion as a condition for marriage. What makes this remarkable is that it's such a new thing. Throughout history, the choice of a spouse has usually had little to do with romantic love (Ackerman, 1994; de Rougemont, 1956); people married each other for political, economic, practical, and family reasons, but they did not marry because they were in love with each other. Even in North America, people have only recently begun to feel that marriage requires love. In 1967, 76 percent of women and 35 percent of men *would* have married an otherwise perfect partner whom they did not love (Kephart, 1967). Now, most people would refuse such a marriage.

In a sense, then, we have embarked on a bold experiment. Never before has a culture considered love to be an essential reason to marry. People experience romantic passion all over the world (Hamon & Ingoldsby, 2003; Jankowiak & Fischer, 1992), but most cultures still do not consider it a precondition for marriage (Dion & Dion, 1996). North Americans use romance as a reason to marry to an unprecedented degree (Sprecher et al., 1994). Is this a good idea? If there are various, overlapping types of "love" and different types of lovers—and worse, if passion and romance decline over time—marriages based on love may often be prone to confusion and, perhaps, disappointment.

In this chapter, we will examine these possibilities and try to avoid those problems by examining what social scientists have to say about love. We'll start with a brief history of love and then ponder different varieties of love and different types of lovers. Then, we'll finish with a question of substantial interest:

244

Does love last? By the time you're done with this chapter, you'll have a much better understanding of the complexities of love.

A BRIEF HISTORY OF LOVE

Our modern belief that spouses should love one another is just one of many perspectives with which different cultures have viewed the experience of love (de Rougemont, 1956; Hunt, 1959). Over the ages, attitudes toward love have varied on at least four dimensions:

- *Cultural value:* Is love a desirable or undesirable state?
- *Sexuality:* Should love be sexual or nonsexual?
- *Sexual orientation:* Should love involve homosexual or heterosexual partners?
- *Marital status:* Should we love our spouses, or is love reserved for others?

Different societies have drawn upon these dimensions to create some strikingly different patterns of what love is, or should be.

In ancient Greece, for instance, passionate attraction to another person was considered a form of madness that had nothing to do with marriage or family life. Instead, the Greeks admired platonic love, the nonsexual adoration of a beloved person that was epitomized by love between two men.

In ancient Egypt, people of royal blood often married their siblings, and in ancient Rome, "the purpose of marriage was to produce children, make favorable alliances, and establish a bloodline . . . it was hoped that husband and wife would be friends and get on amiably. Happiness was not part of the deal, nor was pleasure. Sex was for creating babies" (Ackerman, 1994, p. 37).

Heterosexual love took on more positive connotations in the concept of "courtly love" in the twelfth century. Courtly love required knights to seek love as a noble quest, diligently devoting themselves to an aristocratic lady love. It was very idealistic, very elegant, and—at least in theory—nonsexual. It was also explicitly adulterous. In courtly love, the male partner was expected to be unmarried and the female partner married—to someone else! In the Middle Ages, marriage was not expected to be romantic; in contrast, it was a deadly serious matter of politics and property. Indeed, passionate, erotic desire for someone was thought to be "dangerous, a trapdoor leading to hell, which was not even to be condoned between husband and wife" (Ackerman, 1994, p. 46).

Over the next 500 years, people came to believe that passionate love could be desirable and ennobling but that it was usually doomed. Either the lovers would be prevented from being with each other (often because they were married to other people), or death would overtake one or the other (or both) before their love could be fulfilled. It was not until the seventeenth and eighteenth centuries that Europeans, especially the English, began to believe that romantic passion could occasionally result in a "happy ending." Still, the notion that one *ought* to feel passion and romance for one's husband or wife was not a widespread idea.

Even now, the assumption that romantic love should be linked to marriage is the exception rather than the rule (Xiaohe & Whyte, 1990). Nevertheless, as a reader of this book, you probably do think love and marriage go together. Why should your beliefs be different from those of most people throughout history? Why has the acceptance of and enthusiasm for marrying for love been most complete in North America (Hamon & Ingoldsby, 2003)? Probably because of America's individualism and economic prosperity (which allow most young adults to live away from home and choose their own marital partners) and its lack of a caste system or ruling class. The notion that individuals (instead of families) should choose marriage partners because of emotional attachments (not economic concerns) makes more sense to Americans than it does to many other peoples of the world.

In any case, let's consider all the different views of love we just encountered:

- Love is madness.
- Love has little to do with marriage.
- The best love occurs among people of the same sex.
- Love need not involve sexual contact.
- Love is a noble quest.
- Love is doomed.
- Love can be happy and fulfilling.
- Love and marriage go together.

Some of these distinctions simply reflect ordinary cultural and historical variations (Hatfield & Rapson, 2002; Sternberg, 1998). However, these different views may also reflect an important fact: There may be diverse forms of love. In the next section, we consider the various types of love that have been explored in recent theory and research.

TYPES OF LOVE

Advice columnist Ann Landers was once contacted by a woman who was perplexed because her consuming passion for her lover fizzled soon after they were married. Ms. Landers suggested that what the woman had called "the love affair of the century" was "not love at all. It was one set of glands calling to another" (Landers, 1982, p. 2). There was a big distinction, Ms. Landers asserted, between horny infatuation and real love, which was deeper and richer than mere passion. Love was based in tolerance, care, and communication, Landers argued; it was "friendship that has caught fire" (p. 12).

Does that phrase characterize your experiences with romantic love? Is there a difference between romantic love and infatuation? According to a leading theory of love experiences, the answer to both questions is probably yes.

The Triangular Theory of Love

Robert Sternberg (1986, 1987) proposed that three different building blocks combine to form different types of love. The first component of love is **intimacy.**

It includes the feelings of warmth, understanding, communication, support, and sharing that often characterize loving relationships. The second component is **passion,** which is characterized by physical arousal and desire. Passion often takes the form of sexual longing, but any strong emotional need that is satisfied by one's partner fits this category. The final ingredient of love is **commitment,** which includes the decisions to devote oneself to a relationship and to work to maintain it. Commitment is mainly cognitive in nature, whereas intimacy is emotional and passion is a motive, or drive. The "heat" in loving relationships is assumed to come from passion, and the warmth from intimacy; in contrast, commitment reflects a decision that may not be emotional or temperamental at all.

In Sternberg's theory, each of these three components is said to be one side of a triangle that describes the love two people share. Each component can vary in intensity from low to high so that triangles of various sizes and shapes are possible. In fact, countless numbers of shapes can occur, so to keep things simple, we'll consider the relatively pure categories of love that result when one or more of the three ingredients is plentiful but the others are very low. As we proceed, you should remember that pure experiences that are this clearly defined may not be routine in real life.

> *Nonlove.* If intimacy, passion, and commitment are all absent, love does not exist. Instead, you have a casual, superficial, uncommitted relationship between people who are probably just acquaintances, not friends.
>
> *Liking.* Liking occurs when intimacy is high but passion and commitment are very low. Liking occurs in friendships with real closeness and warmth that do not arouse passion or the expectation that you will spend the rest of your life with that person. If a friend *does* arouse passion or is missed terribly when he or she is gone, the relationship has gone beyond liking and has become something else.
>
> *Infatuation.* Strong passion in the absence of intimacy or commitment is infatuation, which is what people experience when they are aroused by others they barely know. Sternberg (1987) admits that he was painfully preoccupied with a girl in his tenth-grade biology class whom he rarely talked to; he pined away for her but never got up the courage to get to know her. This, he now acknowledges, was nothing but passion. He was infatuated with her.
>
> *Empty love.* Commitment without intimacy or passion is empty love. In Western cultures, this type of love can be seen in burned-out relationships in which the warmth and passion have died, and the decision to stay is the only thing that remains. However, in other cultures in which marriages are arranged, empty love may be the first, rather than final, stage in the spouses' lives together.

None of the categories mentioned so far may seem much like love to you. That's probably because each is missing some important ingredient that we associate with being in love—and that is precisely Sternberg's point. Love is a multifaceted experience, and that becomes clear when we combine the three components of love to create more complex states.

Love can last a lifetime. But companionate love seems
to endure longer than passionate love for most people.

Romantic love. When high intimacy and passion occur together, people
experience romantic love. Thus, one way to think about romantic love is as
a combination of liking and infatuation. People often become committed to
their romances, but Sternberg argues that commitment is not a defining
characteristic of romantic love. A summer love affair can be very romantic,
for instance, even when both lovers know that it is going to end when the
summer is over.

Companionate love. Intimacy and commitment combine to form love for a
close companion, or companionate love. Here, closeness, communication,
and sharing are coupled with substantial investment in the relationship as
the partners work to maintain a deep, long-term friendship. This type of
love is epitomized by a long, happy marriage in which the couple's youthful passion has gradually died down.

Fatuous love. Passion and commitment in the absence of intimacy create a foolish experience called fatuous love. This type of love can occur in whirlwind courtships in which two partners marry quickly on the basis of overwhelming passion but don't know (or necessarily like) each other very well. In a sense, such lovers invest a lot in an infatuation—a risky business.

Consummate love. Finally, when intimacy, passion, and commitment are all present to a substantial degree, people experience "complete," or consummate, love. This is the type of love many people seek, but Sternberg (1987) suggests that it's a lot like losing weight: easy to do for a while, but hard to maintain over time.

Thus, according to the triangular theory of love, diverse experiences can underlie the simple expression, "I love you." (The different types of love are summarized in Table 8.1.) Another complication that makes love tricky is that the three components can change over time, so that people may encounter various types of love in a given relationship (Sternberg, 1986). Of the three, however, passion is assumed to be the most variable by far. It is also the least controllable, so that we may find our desire for others soaring and then evaporating rapidly in changes we cannot consciously control.

Is the theory right? Are these assertions accurate? Consider that, if the triangular theory's characterization of romantic love is correct, one of its major ingredients is a high level of passion that simply may not last. There's much to consider in wondering whether love lasts, however, so we'll put that off until the end of the chapter. For now, let's note that the three components of intimacy, passion, and commitment do all appear to be important aspects of loving relationships (Aron & Westbay, 1996; Bonner, Franiuk, & Logli, 2004); in particular, each of the three components makes a loving relationship more satisfying, and the most rewarding romances contain big servings of all three ingredients (Nathan, Logan, & Andersen, 2002).

TABLE 8.1. The Triangular Theory of Love: Types of Relationships

	Intimacy	Passion	Commitment
Nonlove	Low	Low	Low
Liking	High	Low	Low
Infatuated love	Low	High	Low
Empty love	Low	Low	High
Romantic love	High	High	Low
Companionate love	High	Low	High
Fatuous love	Low	High	High
Consummate love	High	High	High

Source: Based on Sternberg, 1986.

However, the theory seems to be correct in suggesting that we don't always experience all three components at the same time. The neurochemical pathways that regulate our sexual desire for others are in different regions of the brain than those from which feelings of attachment and commitment to our lovers emerge (Diamond, 2004). In some state-of-the-art studies of love, researchers are examining people's brain functions and hormone levels as they look at pictures of their lovers, and passion activates different areas of the brain than affection and commitment do (Bartels & Zeki, 2000; Aron et al., 2004). Thus, it should not be surprising that we sometimes feel strong desire for those we do not love and occasionally feel little passion for those to whom we are happily attached (Diamond, 2004).

On the other hand, intimacy, passion, and commitment are clearly inter-related in many loving relationships (Whitley, 1993). When men become sexually aroused by inspecting sexually explicit material, they report more love for their romantic partners than they do when they're not "turned on" (Dermer & Pyszczynski, 1978; Stephan, Berscheid, & Walster, 1971), and, as Sternberg (1987) admits, it is probably easier to feel long-lived passion for someone with whom you also share substantial intimacy.

As a result, as we warned you earlier, the clearly defined categories offered by the triangular theory may not seem so distinct in real life. People's actual experiences of love appear to be complex. For instance, a sister's love for her brother is likely to revolve around the central feature of intimacy, as the theory suggests, but it is also likely to include a variety of other mixed feelings (Fehr & Russell, 1991). A father's love for his son is likely to resemble his love for his own father, but the two feelings are also likely to differ in subtle, idiosyncratic ways that the triangular theory does not readily explain. Different types of love probably overlap in a messier, more confusing way than the theory implies (Fehr, 1994).

Nevertheless, the theory offers a very useful framework for addressing different types of love, and whether or not it is entirely correct it identifies two types of love that may be especially likely to occur in many marriages. Let's examine each of them more closely.

Romantic, Passionate Love

Has anyone ever told you, "I love you, but I'm not *in* love with you"? If so, it was probably bad news. As you probably knew, they were trying to say that, "I like you, I care about you, I think you're a marvelous person with wonderful qualities and so forth, but I don't find you sexually desirable" (Myers & Berscheid, 1997, p. 360). Just as the triangular theory of love proposes, sexual attraction (or "passion") appears to be one of the defining characteristics of romantic love (Regan, 2003; Regan, Kocan, & Whitlock, 1998). So, it's disappointing if your romantic partner says, "I just want us to be friends."

The fact that romantic love involves passion is important. Remarkably, *any* form of strong emotion, good or bad, can influence our feelings of romantic love.

Arousal

A provocative analysis of romantic love by Elaine Hatfield and Ellen Berscheid proposed that passionate attraction is rooted in two factors: (1) physiological arousal such as a fast heart beat that is coupled with (2) the belief that another person is the cause of your arousal (Berscheid & Walster, 1974). According to this two-factor perspective, romantic love is produced, or at least intensified, when feelings of arousal are attributed to the presence of another attractive person.

If that other person actually is the reason for our excitement, our romantic attraction to him or her is appropriate. But the two-factor idea also allows the interesting possibility that we can make occasional mistakes, or **misattributions,** in interpreting our feelings and thereby feel attraction to others that is exaggerated or misplaced. Sometimes, in a process called **excitation transfer** (Zillmann, 1978, 1984), arousal caused by one event combines with additional arousal elicited by a second event, but the first event is ignored. Our combined feelings are then thought to be caused only by the second event, which seems more influential than it really is.

Imagine this situation: You're in a park in North Vancouver, British Columbia, starting across a long, narrow bridge made of wooden planks that are suspended by wire, hanging hundreds of feet over a deep gorge. The bridge has a low wire railing that only comes up to your waist, and it bounces and tilts and sways as you walk across it. Far, far below is a rocky creek, and (because you're like most people) you can't help but feel some nervous excitement (or perhaps outright fear) as you make your way across. But, then, right in the middle of the precarious bridge, you encounter an attractive person of the other sex who asks you to answer a few questions. You're shown a picture and asked to make up a story, and your interviewer thanks you warmly and invites you to call later if you have any questions. How attracted would you be to the person you met on the bridge?

This is just the question that was asked in a famous experiment by Dutton and Aron (1974), who sent research assistants to interview unaccompanied young men (between 19 and 35 years of age) either in the middle of the spooky suspension bridge or on another bridge that was wide and stable and just a few feet off the ground in another part of the park. The picture that the men wrote a story about was from the Thematic Apperception Test, and it was possible to score each story in terms of sexual imagery. Dutton and Aron found that the men who met a woman on the swaying suspension bridge used more sexual imagery than did other men. In addition, those men were more likely to call the assistant later at her home. They were more attracted to her, and the arousal—or fear—caused by the dangerous bridge had evidently fueled their interest in her. Other men who encountered the same woman in a less dramatic place found her less attractive. On the precarious bridge, fear had apparently fueled attraction.

Or had it? Could nervous excitement really be mistaken, at least in part, for romantic attraction to someone else? Well, try this procedure: You're a young man who runs in place for either two minutes or fifteen seconds, so your pulse rate is high and you're breathing hard, or you're just a little more aroused than

TABLE 8.2. Arousal and Attraction

	Attractiveness of the Woman	
Arousal of the Men	High	Low
Low	26.1	15.1
High	32.4	9.4

The higher the scores, the more desirable the men judged the woman to be. The physically attractive woman was always judged to be more desirable than the unattractive woman was, but a faster heart beat accentuated this effect, making an attractive woman seem more compelling and an unattractive woman seem even less desirable.

Source: White, Fishbein, & Rutstein, 1981.

normal. Flushed with high or low arousal, you move to another room and inspect a videotape of a young woman whom you think you're about to meet. You and other men all see the same woman, but, through the wonders of makeup, she looks either quite attractive or rather unattractive. What do you think of her? When real research participants reported their reactions, it was clear that high arousal intensified the men's ordinary responses to the woman (White, Fishbein, & Rutstein, 1981). The attractive version of the woman was always preferred to the unattractive version, of course, but as you can see in Table 8.2, the men liked the attractive model even more—and liked the unattractive model even less—when they were aroused than when they were calm. High arousal magnified the fellows' responses, so that men who encountered an attractive woman when their pulses were racing thought that she was *really* hot.

Moreover, the effects of arousal on attraction do not depend on the type of arousal that is produced. In another study (White et al., 1981), men listened to one of three tapes:

- *Negatively arousing.* A description of the brutal mutilation and killing of a missionary while his family watched.
- *Positively arousing.* Selections from Steve Martin's comedy album, *A Wild and Crazy Guy.*
- *Neutral.* A boring description of the circulatory system of a frog.

Thereafter, as before, the men viewed a videotape of an attractive or unattractive woman and provided their impressions of her. Arousal again fueled attraction, and it didn't matter what type of arousal it was. When the men had experienced strong emotion—whether by laughing hard at the funny material or by being disgusted by the gory material—they were more attracted to the appealing woman and less attracted to the unappealing woman than they were when they had listened to the boring biology tape.

Taken together, these studies demonstrate that adrenaline fuels love. High arousal of various types, including simple exertion and the emotional states of fear, disgust, and amusement, all seem to be able to enhance our feelings of romantic attraction to desirable potential partners. Genuine misunderstanding of the source of our activation in the form of misattributions isn't necessary for these effects to occur because arousal increases attraction even when the source of the arousal is unambiguous (Foster et al., 1998); that is, even if men on the suspension bridge consciously realized that the bridge was unnerving them, their fearful activation was likely to increase their attraction to the woman they met. On the other hand, arousal has a stronger effect on attraction when we don't know *why* we're keyed up (Foster et al., 1998). If we're aroused for some reason that we're not noticing and we misattribute our stimulation to a desirable partner, we're likely to find ourselves being very attracted to that person.

So, there's little doubt that arousal from an unrelated source can intensify our emotional reactions. Consider the implications: Have you ever had a screaming argument with a lover and then found that it was especially sweet to "kiss and make up" a few minutes later? Might your anger have fueled your subsequent passion? Is that what being "in love" is like?

To some degree, it is. One useful measure of the passion component of romantic love is the Passionate Love Scale (Hatfield & Rapson, 1987). The short form of the scale is reprinted in Table 8.3; as you can see, the scale assesses fascination and preoccupation with, high desire for, and strong emotions about the object of one's love. Scores on the Passionate Love Scale increase as someone falls deeper and deeper into love with someone else, only leveling off when the partners become engaged or start living together (Hatfield & Sprecher, 1986). (Note that—as we mentioned earlier—American couples decide to marry or live together when their passion is at a peak.) Interestingly, although there are no differences between men's and women's average passion later on, men report higher passion than women do when they first start dating. As we saw in chapter 4, men tend to be more romantic than women are, and they also tend to "fall in love" more easily than women do (Hatfield & Sprecher, 1986).

In any case, the vision of romantic love that emerges from the Passionate Love Scale is one of need and desire—ecstasy when one is loved in return and agony when one is rejected—and these are clearly responses that burn brighter when one is aroused than when one is calm and relaxed. One researcher has even argued that there is a chemical basis for the elation and excitement of romantic passion (Liebowitz, 1983): We feel passion when our bodies produce increased quantities of phenylethylamine (or PEA), a substance that is chemically related to amphetamines and has similar effects on our moods and energy. "PEA whips the brain into a frenzy of excitement, which is why lovers feel euphoric, rejuvenated, optimistic, and energized, happy to sit up talking all night or making love for hours on end" (Ackerman, 1994, p. 165). From this perspective, romantic passion *is* a form of physical activation and arousal, so arousal and love are closely connected. Moreover, the emotional crash that can follow the end of a romantic love affair is thought to be much like the lethargy and despondency that accompanies withdrawal from amphetamines.

So, one aspect of romantic love is the exhilaration and euphoria of high arousal, and various events that excite us may increase our feelings of love for our partners. Romance is more than just passion, however. It also involves our thoughts.

TABLE 8.3. The Passionate Love Scale (Short Form)

This questionnaire asks you to describe how you feel when you are passionately in love. Some common terms for this feeling are: passionate love, infatuation, love sickness, or obsessive love. Please think of the person whom you love most passionately *right now*. If you are not in love right now, please think of the last person you loved passionately. If you have never been in love, think of the person whom you came closest to caring for in that way. Keep this person in mind as you complete this questionnaire. (The person you choose should be of the opposite sex if you are heterosexual or of the same sex if you are homosexual.) Try to tell us how you felt at the time when your feelings were the most intense.

Answer each item using this scale:

1	2	3	4	5	6	7	8	9
Not at all true				Moderately true				Definitely true

1. I would feel deep despair if _____ left me.
2. Sometimes I feel I can't control my thoughts; they are obsessively on _____.
3. I feel happy when I am doing something to make _____ happy.
4. I would rather be with _____ than anyone else.
5. I'd get jealous if I thought _____ were falling in love with someone else.
6. I yearn to know all about _____.
7. I want _____ physically, emotionally, mentally.
8. I have an endless appetite for affection from _____.
9. For me, _____ is the perfect romantic partner.
10. I sense my body responding when _____ touches me.
11. _____ always seems to be on my mind.
12. I want _____ to know me—my thoughts, my fears, and my hopes.
13. I eagerly look for signs indicating _____'s desire for me.
14. I possess a powerful attraction for _____.
15. I get extremely depressed when things don't go right in my relationship with _____.

Higher scores on the PLS indicate greater passionate love. Across all 15 items, the average rating per item—add up all your ratings and divide by 15—for both men and women is 7.15.

Source: Hatfield & Sprecher, 1986.

Thought

The two-factor theory of passionate love emphasizes the role of our thoughts and beliefs in accounting for arousal. Thoughts may also be linked to romance in other ways. In particular, romantic lovers are likely to think about each other in ways that differ from the ways they think about their friends. Some of these distinctions are apparent in the contents of a Love Scale and a Liking Scale created by Zick Rubin in 1973. Years before Hatfield and Sprecher

TABLE 8.4. Rubin's (1973) Love and Liking Scales: Some Example Items

Rubin's Love Scale

1. I feel that I can confide in my partner about virtually anything.

2. If I could never be with my partner, I would be miserable.

3. I would do almost anything for my partner.

Rubin's Liking Scale

1. My partner is one of the most likable people I know.

2. My partner is the sort of person that I would like to be.

3. I think that my partner is unusually well-adjusted.

created the Passionate Love Scale, Rubin created dozens of statements that reflected a wide range of interpersonal attitudes and asked people to use them to describe both a lover and a friend. The handful of items that epitomized people's romances ended up on a Love Scale that gives a partial indication of what lovers are thinking.

One theme in the items on the Love Scale is *intimacy*, just as the triangular theory of love defines it. Romance is characterized by openness, communication, and trust (see item 1 in Table 8.4). A second theme, in Rubin's (1973) terminology, is needy *attachment* (see item 2 in Table 8.4). The attachment items describe longing for contact with one's partner that has much in common with the passion we discussed. A last theme on the Love Scale, however, describes feelings that are not mentioned by the triangular theory: *caring*. Romantic lovers report concern for the welfare and well-being of their partners (see item 3). They want to take care of their partners and keep them happy.

Thus, like other efforts to characterize love (e.g., Fehr, 1994; Regan et al., 1998), the Love Scale portrays romantic love as a multifaceted experience that involves both giving (i.e., caring) and taking (i.e., attachment). If you're in love with someone, it's probably partly selfish—you love your partner because of how that person makes you feel—and partly generous; you genuinely care for your partner and will work to satisfy and protect him or her. (In fact, the compassionate concern for those we love is drawing increased attention from relationship researchers. See Box 8.1.) In addition, these diverse sentiments are experienced with relative intensity and urgency: You'd do *anything* for your partner and be *miserable* without him or her.

Compare those thoughts and feelings to the sorts of things people say about their friends. As you can see in Table 8.4, the Liking Scale seems bland by comparison. People say they like their friends because their friends are nice, well-adjusted, likable people. But they love their lovers because they need them and would do anything the lover asks. There's a fervor to the thoughts that characterize romantic love that is lacking when we just like someone.

BOX 8.1
Caring for Others: Compassionate Love

Sternberg's (1987) triangular theory of love does not assert that considerate caring for other people is a specific component of love, but perhaps it should. Rubin's (1973) work with his Love Scale showed that people consider *caring* to be a meaningful aspect of love, and more recent research is replicating those results. Researchers are finding that lovers often have distinct feelings of *compassionate love* that lead them to have altruistic care and concern for the well-being of their partners (Mikulincer & Shaver, 2005). (Now before we go any further, let's take a moment and examine the label "compassionate" love; it sounds something like both romantic, passionate love [which obviously involves passion] and companionate love [which comes from the word "companion"], but it is different from either one. Compassion involves the benevolent

wish to aid those who are in need of help.)

People who feel compassionate love say that when they see others feeling sad, they feel a need to reach out to them. They say that it is easy for them to feel the pain or joy that their loved ones experience, and they would rather suffer than to allow someone close to them to be hurt (Sprecher & Fehr, 2005). Caring for others, trust, understanding, and support are all central features of compassionate love (Fehr & Sprecher, 2004), and importantly, these are feelings that are correlated with, but are nevertheless different from, the feelings that define romantic love and companionate love. Careful analysis of compassionate love has just begun, but researchers are already pondering procedures that may help increase the altruism and kindness we feel for others (Mikulincer & Shaver, 2005).

Indeed, preoccupation and obsessive thinking about one's partner is part of the passion component of romantic love (Hatfield & Rapson, 1987). Interestingly, however, the connection between love and thought seems to work both ways; if we spend a lot of time thinking about our partners, we may come to feel we love them more than we would have if we hadn't thought about them so much. For instance, on two occasions two weeks apart, researchers asked unmarried young adults how much they thought about and loved their dating partners (Tesser & Paulus, 1976). The study showed that the more people loved their partners, the more they thought about them. That's no surprise, but the reverse was true, too: The more people thought about their partners, the more they came to love them later on.

The specific judgments people make of their partners are important, too. As we saw in chapter 4, people tend to hold rosy views of their relationship partners, and their tendency to idealize and glorify their lovers is probably at a peak when they are most in love. In fact, the moment romance enters the picture, people start ignoring or reinterpreting undesirable information about potential partners. Imagine that you're a male college student who is asked to play the role of a restaurant owner who is evaluating the work of a woman who is pitching you an advertising campaign (Goodwin et al., 2002). You watch a videotape of

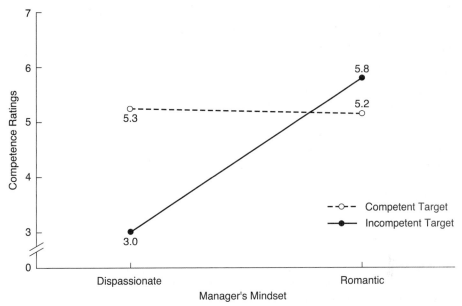

FIGURE 8.1. Love is blind.
When men expected to date a woman, they thought her lousy work was much better than it really was.
Source: Goodwin et al., 2002.

her presentation, which is either coherent and clever or clumsy and inept. Would you be able to tell the difference between the competent and incompetent work? Of course you would. But what if you knew that you'd be going out on a date with the woman on Friday? Would the possibility of a romance influence your judgment? You may not think so, but when men really participated in a procedure like this, a romantic orientation had a big effect, as Figure 8.1 illustrates. The upcoming date obviously contaminated the men's judgment, magically transforming lousy work into material of much higher quality. The poor work was not perceived to be better than the competent work—that difference was not statistically significant—but any distinction between the good and bad work disappeared entirely when the possibility of romance was in play.

The results of this and other studies (e.g., Gold, Ryckman, & Mosley, 1984) suggest that, in a real way, "love is blind": People underestimate or ignore their lovers' faults. They hold idealized images of their lovers that may differ in meaningful ways from the concrete realities they face. In fact, a major difference between love and friendship may be our imaginations—our lovers are fascinating, mysterious, and appealing in ways our friends are not (Aron et al., 1989).

Finally, even our thoughts about ourselves can change when we fall in love. Arthur and Elaine Aron, a husband-wife team of social psychologists, suggest that love causes our self-concepts to expand and change (Aron & Aron, 2000). Romantic partners bring us new experiences and new roles, and we gradually learn things about ourselves that we didn't know before. One of the things we usually learn is that a desirable person likes us in return, and that's both rewarding and exciting (Aron et al., 1989). As a result, our self-concepts become more diversified and our self-esteem goes up (Aron, Paris, & Aron, 1995).

All of this is potent stuff. The arousal and cognition that characterize romantic, passionate love involve surging emotion, imagination and idealization, and occasional obsession (Lamm & Wiesmann, 1997; Shaver, Morgan, & Wu, 1996). And it is the presence of this complex, hectic state that leads most North Americans to consider marriage. However, romantic passion may not be the reason they stay married in the years that follow. The longevity of a relationship may have more to do with companionate love.

Companionate Love

Because it does not depend on passion, companionate love is a more settled state than romantic love is. The triangular theory suggests that it is a combination of intimacy and commitment, but we can characterize it more fully as a "comfortable, affectionate, trusting love for a likable partner, based on a deep sense of friendship and involving companionship and the enjoyment of common activities, mutual interests, and shared laughter" (Grote & Frieze, 1994, p. 275). It takes the form of a rich, committed friendship with someone with whom our lives are intertwined (Walster & Walster, 1978).

Sounds pleasant, but isn't it a bit bland compared to the ecstasies of romantic passion? Perhaps so, but you may want to get used to it. When hundreds of couples who had been married at least fifteen years were asked why their marriages had lasted, they *didn't* say that they'd do anything for their spouses

TABLE 8.5. The Friendship-Based Love Scale

Think about your closest current relationship, and then rate your agreement or disagreement with each of these questions on the following scale:

1	2	3	4	5
strongly disagree				strongly agree

1. I feel our love is based on a deep and abiding friendship.
2. I express my love for my partner through the enjoyment of common activities and mutual interests.
3. My love for my partner involves solid, deep affection.
4. An important factor in my love for my partner is that we laugh together.
5. My partner is one of the most likable people I know.
6. The companionship I share with my partner is an important part of my love for him or her.

The average total score for married men is 25.2, and the average total for married women is 26.4. Scores on the scale are more highly correlated with relationship satisfaction and duration than scores on the Passionate Love Scale are.

Source: Grote & Frieze, 1994.

or be miserable without them, like romantic lovers do (Lauer & Lauer, 1985). Instead, for both men and women, the two most frequent reasons were (1) "My spouse is my best friend," and (2) "I like my spouse as a person." Long-lasting, satisfying marriages seem to include a lot of companionate love.

A useful measure of companionate love is the Friendship-Based Love Scale created by Nancy Grote and Irene Frieze (1994). As you can see in Table 8.5, the feelings described by the scale are very different than those that accompany passionate love; friendship and companionship are much more in evidence on the Friendship-Based Love Scale than they are on measures of romantic love.

Of course, deep friendships also occur often in the context of romantic love. In one study, 44 percent of the young adults in premarital relationships reported that their romantic partner was also their closest friend (Hendrick & Hendrick, 1993). However, when they are a part of romantic love, friendships are combined (and sometimes confused) with sexual arousal and passion. The predominant importance of friendship in creating the experience is easier to

---

BOX 8.2

A Type of Love You May **Not** *Want to Experience*
Unrequited Love

Have you ever loved someone who did not love you back? You probably have. Depending on the sample, 80 percent (Aron, Aron, & Allen, 1998) to 90 percent of young adults (Baumeister, Wotman, & Stillwell, 1993) report that they have experienced unrequited love: romantic, passionate attraction to someone who did not return that love. It's a common experience that seems to be most frequent in one's late teens, between the ages of 16 and 20 (Hill, Blakemore, & Drumm, 1997). Still, it doesn't strike everybody; it happens to more men than women (Hill et al., 1997) and is more likely to befall people with an anxious/ambivalent attachment style than those with secure or avoidant styles (Aron et al., 1998).

Why do we experience such loves? Several factors may be involved. First, would-be lovers are very attracted to their unwilling targets, and they assume that relationships with them are worth working and waiting for. Second, they optimistically overestimate how much

they are liked in return (Aron et al., 1998). And third, perhaps most importantly, as painful as it is, unrequited love has its rewards. Along with their frustration, would-be lovers experience the real thrill, elation, and excitement of being in love (Baumeister et al., 1993).

It's actually worse to be the target of someone's unwanted adoration. Sure, it's nice to be wanted, but those on the receiving end of unrequited love often find their pursuers' persistence to be intrusive and annoying, and they usually feel guilty when they turn their ardent pursuers down. They are usually nice, "well-meaning people who find themselves caught up in another person's emotional whirlwind and who themselves often suffer acutely as a result" (Baumeister & Wotman, 1992, p. 203). As distressing as it was to gradually realize that the objects of our affection would not become our steady partners, we may have made it harder on them when we fell into unrequited love.

detect in companionate love, when intimacy is paired with commitment, than in romantic love, when intimacy is paired with passion.

Still, as we noted earlier, we may only rarely encounter pure categories of these experiences that are comprised of just two of the components of love and none of the third. Companionate lovers can and do experience passion, and romantic lovers can and do feel commitment. As we experience them, the distinctions between romantic and companionate love are much fuzzier than this discussion may have implied (Fehr, 1994). Nevertheless, if we're willing to tolerate some ambiguity, we can conclude that there appear to be two major types of love that frequently occur in American marriages: a love that's full of passion that leads people to marry, and a love that's full of friendship that underlies marriages that last. Over time, companionate love is typically stronger in enduring relationships than romantic, passionate love is, and it is more highly correlated with the satisfaction people enjoy (Fehr, 2001). We'll return to this point at the end of the chapter.

Styles of Loving

Another scheme for distinguishing different types of love experiences was offered by sociologist John Alan Lee (1977, 1988), who used Greek and Latin words to describe six styles of love that differ in the intensity of the loving experience, commitment to the beloved, desired characteristics of the beloved, and expectations about being loved in return. (See Table 8.6.) A first style is **eros,** from which the word *erotic* comes. Eros has a strong physical component, and erotic lovers are likely to be heavily influenced by physical appearance and to believe in love at first sight.

The second style, **ludus** (pronounced loo-dus), treats love as an uncommitted game. Ludic lovers are often fickle and (try to) have several different partners at once. In contrast, the third style, **storge,** (store-gay) leads people to de-emphasize strong emotion and seek genuine friendships that gradually lead to real commitment.

TABLE 8.6. Styles of Loving

Eros	The erotic lover searches for a person with the right physical appearance and is eager for an intense relationship.
Ludus	The ludic lover is playful in love and likes to play the field.
Storge	The storgic lover prefers slowly developing attachments that lead to lasting commitment.
Mania	The manic lover is demanding and possessive toward the beloved and has a feeling of being "out of control."
Agape	The agapic lover is altruistic, loving without concern for receiving anything in return.
Pragma	The pragmatic lover searches for a person with the proper vital statistics: job, age, religion, etc.

Source: Based on Lee, 1977, 1988. Reprinted from Brehm & Kassin, 1990.

The fourth style, **mania,** is demanding and possessive and full of vivid fantasy and obsession. The fifth style, **agape** (ah-gaa-pay), is giving, altruistic, and selfless, and treats love as a duty. Finally, the last style, **pragma,** is practical and pragmatic. Pragma leads people to dispassionately seek partners who will logically be a good match for them.

How useful are these distinctions? Instead of thinking of them as six additional types of love, it may make more sense to consider them as six themes in love experiences that overlap and are differentially related to the types of love identified by Sternberg's triangular theory (Woll, 1989). For instance, romantic love appears to be positively related to eros and agape (remember, it's love as giving *and* love as taking), and negatively related to ludus (which means it's serious business) (Levy & Davis, 1988). Clyde and Susan Hendrick, another husband-wife research team, have developed a Love Attitudes Scale to measure people's endorsement of the six styles, and they have found that men score higher on ludus than women do, whereas women are more storgic and pragmatic than men (Hendrick & Hendrick, 2003; Hendrick, Hendrick, & Dicke, 1998). Other researchers have detected a tendency for people to pair off with others who share similar attitudes toward love (Davis & Latty-Mann, 1987; Morrow, Clark, & Brock, 1995). In general, the love styles remind us of meaningful influences on love (such as practicality) that are sometimes overlooked. Also, differentiating the styles allows researchers to fine-tune their analyses of the diverse experiences people have with love.

INDIVIDUAL DIFFERENCES IN LOVE

Obviously, there are a variety of different feelings people may be experiencing when they say, "I love you." To make things even more complicated, certain people may be more likely than others to experience certain types of love. In this section, we consider relatively enduring differences among individuals that are linked to love. We'll begin by revisiting an idea we introduced in chapter 1: People have global orientations toward close relationships that result from, and subsequently influence, their intimate partnerships.

Attachment Styles

When relationship scientists (e.g., Hazan & Shaver, 1987) began to study attachment styles, they used the same three categories of attachment that had been identified in children by developmental researchers. Thus, as you may remember from chapter 1, early studies distinguished among **secure, avoidant,** and **anxious/ambivalent** orientations to close relationships. Secure people were said to be comfortable with emotional intimacy and interdependency, whereas avoidant people disliked dependency and closeness. Anxious/ambivalent people were said to be clingy, possessive folks who sought more intimacy and reassurance than others were generally willing to provide.

As a wave of studies quickly showed, attachment researchers were on to something. People who had a secure style tended to be more trusting, committed, and satisfied in their romantic relationships than avoidant or anxious people were. They also experienced more positive and fewer negative emotions in their relationships than insecure (i.e., avoidant or anxious/ambivalent) people. On the whole, secure people tended to have more contented, more interdependent, and more intimate romantic relationships than people with insecure styles did (Simpson, 1990).

In particular, it became clear that attachment styles were associated with the manner in which people tried to handle unpleasant emotions (Fuendeling, 1998). When something distressed them, secure people turned to others for comfort and support, and they remained relatively calm. In contrast, avoidant people withdrew from their partners and became hostile, and anxious people (as the name implies) became excessively anxious and fretful (Kobak & Sceery, 1988; Simpson, Rholes, & Nelligan, 1992).

When it came to love, researchers found that a secure style was positively correlated with all three of the components of love; secure people tended to experience high intimacy, passion, and commitment. Secure attachment was also linked to higher levels of the love styles of eros and agape, and lower levels of ludus (Levy & Davis, 1988). Altogether, then, secure attachment was associated with richer experiences of both romantic and companionate love. By comparison, insecure people experienced lower intimacy, passion, and commitment. Avoidant attachment was positively correlated with ludus, reflecting the lower commitment and interdependency of avoidant people, and anxious ambivalence was positively associated with the emotional extremes of mania (Levy & Davis, 1988; Shaver & Hazan, 1988).

A New Conceptualization of Attachment

As you can see, early studies of adults' attachment styles demonstrated that there were meaningful differences among people in the types of love they were likely to have. Results like these attracted attention, and attachment research soon became one of the most active areas of relationship science (see Cassidy & Shaver, 1999). But there were problems: Researchers began to worry that a usual means of assessing attachment styles—asking people which of three paragraphs described them best (look back at Table 1.1 on page 16)—was a little simplistic. In addition, attachment expert Kim Bartholomew (1990; Bartholomew & Horowitz, 1991) thought that avoidant attachment was more complex than most researchers realized. Bartholomew suggested that there were two ways that people could seem to be avoidant. In one case, people could want relationships with others but be wary of them, fearing rejection and mistrusting others. In the other case, people could be independent and self-reliant, genuinely preferring autonomy and freedom to closeness with others.

Thus, Bartholomew (1990) proposed four general categories of attachment style (see Table 8.7). The first, a **secure** style, remained the same as the secure style in the original three categories of attachment. The second, a **preoccupied** style, was a new name for anxious/ambivalence. Bartholomew renamed the category to reflect the fact that, because they nervously depended on others' approval to feel good about themselves, such people greedily sought acceptance and were preoccupied with their relationships.

TABLE 8.7. Examples of Bartholomew's (1990) Four Categories of Attachment Style

Secure	It is easy for me to become emotionally close to others. I am comfortable depending on others and having others depend on me. I don't worry about being alone or having others not accept me.
Preoccupied	I want to be completely emotionally intimate with others, but I often find that others are reluctant to get as close as I would like. I am uncomfortable being without close relationships, but I sometimes worry that others don't value me as much as I value them.
Fearful	I am uncomfortable getting close to others. I want emotionally close relationships, but I find it difficult to trust others completely, or to depend on them. I worry that I will be hurt if I allow myself to become too close to others.
Dismissing	I am comfortable without close emotional relationships. It is very important to me to feel independent and self-sufficient, and I prefer not to depend on others or have others depend on me.

Source: Bartholomew, 1990.

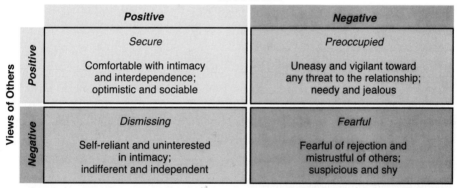

FIGURE 8.2. A model of adult attachment.
Note. Adapted from Bartholomew, 1990.

The third and fourth styles emerged from the old avoidant category, with one of them, a **fearful** style, retaining much of the flavor of that old category. Fearful people avoided intimacy with others because of their fears of rejection. Although they wanted others to like them, they worried about the risks of relying on others. In contrast, people with the last style, a **dismissing** style, felt that intimacy with others just wasn't worth the trouble. Dismissing people felt self-sufficient, and they rejected interdependency with others, not really caring much whether others liked them or not.

Bartholomew (1990) described these four revised styles as separate categories of attachment (just as the original three had been), but, in an important theoretical insight, she suggested that they could be arranged along two dimensions that differentiated them. As Figure 8.2 shows, Bartholomew proposed that people's global judgments of themselves and of others could both be relatively positive or rather negative, and the combination of the two created the four different categories. Secure people were thought to hold favorable opinions of both themselves and others; as a result, they happily pursued intimacy with other people. In contrast, fearful people held negative views of themselves and others, leading them to expect the worst from their relationships. Preoccupied people liked others but doubted themselves, causing them to be overly dependent on others, whereas dismissing people liked themselves but didn't respect others very much.

Researchers have determined that Bartholomew's predictions about the links between attachment styles and self-esteem are generally correct (e.g., Brennan & Morris, 1997; Diehl et al., 1998). However, it's now widely accepted (see Brennan, Clark, & Shaver, 1998; Sanford, 1997) that it's useful to think about the "self" and "other" dimensions in terms of their interpersonal effects. (See Figure 8.3.) People's judgments of others describe their *avoidance of intimacy,* which affects the ease and trust with which a person can accept interdependent intimacy with others. People who are comfortable and relaxed in close relationships are low in avoidance, whereas those who feel uneasy when others get close to them are high in avoidance. Further, people's judgments of themselves influence their *anxiety over abandonment,* their dread that others will find them unworthy and leave them. Secure people take great comfort in closeness with others and do not worry that others will mistreat them; as a result they gladly seek intimate, interdependent relationships. In contrast, with all three of the other styles, people are burdened with anxiety or discomfort that leaves them less at ease in close relationships. Preoccupied people want closeness but anxiously fear rejection. Dismissing people don't worry about rejection but don't like closeness. And fearful people get it from both sides, being uncomfortable with intimacy *and* worrying it won't last.

FIGURE 8.3. The dimensions underlying attachment styles.
Note. Adapted from Brennan, Clark, & Shaver, 1998.

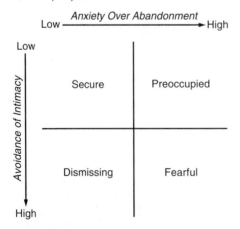

Importantly, the two themes of avoidance of intimacy and anxiety over abandonment are *continuous* dimensions that range from low to high. This means that, although it's convenient to talk about the four styles as if they were discrete, pure categories that do not overlap, it's not really accurate to do so (Fraley & Waller, 1998). This is the same subtlety we encountered when we discussed Sternberg's (1987) triangular theory of love; different types of love were easy to distinguish when intimacy, passion, and commitment were all very high or very low, but real emotions are more complex than that. Sternberg's classification scheme gets muddy, and some different types of love overlap, when the three components of love are all present to a moderate degree. So it is with attachment style. When they are simply asked to pick which one of the four paragraphs in Table 8.7 fits them best, most people, usually around 60 percent, describe themselves as being securely attached (Mickelson, Kessler, & Shaver, 1997). However, if someone has moderate anxiety over abandonment and middling avoidance of intimacy, which category fits him or her best? The use of any of the four categories is rather arbitrary in the middle range of anxiety and avoidance, where the boundaries of the categories meet (Bartholomew & Shaver, 1998).

So don't treat the neat classifications in Figure 8.3 too seriously. The better, more sophisticated way to think about attachment is that there seem to be two important themes that shape people's global orientations toward relationships with others. Each is important, and if you compare high scorers on either dimension to low scorers on that dimension, you're likely to see meaningful differences in the manner in which those people conduct their relationships. On the other hand, small differences on either dimension may not be important, even if they would lead you, for instance, to label some people as secure and others as dismissing. Indeed, some recent studies of attachment have deemphasized the use of the four distinct style names, describing people with regard to their relative standing on the two dimensions of anxiety and comfort instead of labeling them as secure, preoccupied, fearful, or dismissing (e.g., Feeney, 1999; Feeney, Noller, & Roberts, 2000). Samples of the items that are currently used to measure anxiety and avoidance are provided in Table 8.8.

Nevertheless, the four labels are so concise that they are still widely used, so keep your wits about you. Before 1990, researchers spoke of only three attachment styles: secure, avoidant, and anxious/ambivalent. Now they routinely speak of four styles, but they treat them as convenient labels for sets of anxiety and avoidance scores, not as distinctly different categories that have nothing in common. The biggest distinction may be between people who are "secure" and those who are not (who have high anxiety over abandonment or high avoidance of intimacy, or both).

And attachment styles are worth studying. Anxiety over abandonment and avoidance of intimacy are associated with a wide range of behaviors and characteristics that have big effects on our relationships:

- *Beliefs, expectations, and memories.* People with secure attachment styles generally view others as trustworthy, dependable, and kind, whereas those who are insecure are more wary of others. In particular, people who are

TABLE 8.8. Measuring Attachment Style

Researchers often use items like these to assess *anxiety over abandonment* and *avoidance of intimacy* (Fraley, Waller, & Brennan, 2000). Respondents are asked to describe how they generally experience relationships by rating their agreement or disagreement with these statements:

Anxiety

I worry about being abandoned.

I need a lot of reassurance that I am loved by my partner.

I worry a fair amount about losing my partner.

My desire to be very close sometimes scares people away.

Avoidance

I prefer not to show a partner how I feel deep down.

I get uncomfortable when a romantic partner wants to be very close.

I try to avoid getting too close to my partner.

I feel comfortable sharing my private thoughts and feelings with my partner.

(Disagreement with the last item would be indicative of higher avoidance.)

Source: Brennan, Clark, & Shaver, 1998.

high in avoidance typically view others with suspicion, perceiving them to be dishonest and undependable (Collins & Allard, 2001). Moreover, when they remember their childhoods, secure people retrieve happy, uplifting memories more readily than they recall negative, distressing events, whereas avoidant and anxious people remember negative events more easily (Mikulincer, 1998).

- *Communication.* Secure people are more open with their partners, happily engaging in more self-disclosure than anxious or avoidant people do (Keelan, Dion, & Dion, 1998). Avoidant spouses are particularly likely to be close-mouthed, telling their partners relatively little about their feelings and desires (Feeney et al., 2000).
- *Coping and Caregiving.* When their partners are nervous and need support, insecure people provide less reassurance than secure people do, leaving their partners less at ease (Collins & Feeney, 2000; Simpson et al., 2002). In particular, people who are high in avoidance behave more negatively, and sometimes get angry, when they are asked to provide comfort and consolation to a needy partner (Campwell et al., 2001; Rholes, Simpson, & Oriña, 1999). And secure people seek help more effectively than insecure people do (Collins & Feeney, 2000). In fact, when they are stressed out, secure people relax when they just think about a close partner, whereas similar thoughts make those who are high in anxiety over abandonment even more distressed (McGowan, 2002).

These influences may be especially important when partners become parents (Feeney et al., 2003). A wide variety of adjustments and changes accompany the transition to parenthood, and preoccupied women who do not obtain all the support they seek from their husbands tend to become more depressed, less satisfied with their marriages, and more anxious over abandonment than they were before giving birth (Simpson & Rholes, 2002; Simpson et al., 2003). In contrast, new mothers who seek less support and whose husbands are high in avoidance of intimacy become more avoidant themselves (Simpson, et al., 2003).

- *Sexual Behavior.* People who are high in avoidance tend not to have sex to foster closeness with, and to celebrate their intimacy with, their partners (Davis, Shaver, & Vernon, 2004). Instead, in part because they tend to approve of casual sex between uncommitted partners (Gentzler & Kerns, 2004), avoidant people often have sex to impress their friends, to have something to brag about, and to feel better about themselves (Schachner & Shaver, 2004). By comparison, people who are high in attachment anxiety have more passionate, needier sex that springs from a desire to feel accepted and to please their partners (Davis et al., 2004; Tracy et al., 2003). There's nothing wrong with passion, but to avoid displeasing their partners anxious people are also less likely to use condoms and to refuse to do things they don't want to do (Feeney & Noller, 2004). And with their endless appetites for reassurance, married men who are anxious about abandonment are more likely to have extramarital affairs (Lokey & Schmidt, 2000). All things considered, the greatest sexual self-confidence, best communication, and most satisfaction with sex seems to be enjoyed by people with secure attachment styles (Feeney & Noller, 2004).

- *Personal Well-Being.* In general, secure people have lower levels of psychological distress and better mental health than insecure people do (Meyers & Landsberger, 2002; Neria et al., 2001). They have more self-confidence (Diehl et al., 1998), are less afraid of failure (Elliot & Reis, 2003), and are less likely to become addicted to various substances (Van Leeuwen, 2003), and secure men even have higher testosterone levels than anxious or avoidant men do (Hwang & Dabbs, 2002). In particular, higher anxiety over abandonment is associated with more discontent about one's physical appearance (Cash, Thériault, & Annis, 2004), more depression (Strodl & Noller, 2003), and poorer, less restful sleep (Carmichael & Reis, 2004).

- *Relationship Satisfaction.* Finally, as you'd probably expect from all of this, people who are low in avoidance and anxiety tend to enjoy more contentment and satisfaction in both heterosexual (Banse, 2004) and homosexual (Elizur & Mintzer, 2003) relationships. Day by day, secure people have more intimate, more positive, and more satisfying interactions with both their lovers and friends than insecure people do (Feeney, 2002; Kafetsios & Nezlek, 2002).

Altogether, with their greater self-confidence, openness, fidelity, and supportiveness, secure people may be easier to love than insecure people are. Certainly, as we noted above, secure people experience more intense romantic and companionate love than insecure people do (Levy & Davis, 1988).

But, importantly, people also typically have several different partners, such as lovers, parents, and friends, who are important attachment figures at any one time, and they may be relatively secure in some of those relationships and somewhat insecure in others (Trinke & Bartholomew, 1997). Lurking within the global orientations towards relationships that we label as attachment styles may be several different sets of feelings about specific partners (Overall, Fletcher, & Friesen, 2003), so that a person's attachment quality can vary from partner to partner (Cook, 2000). People who are relatively anxious about abandonment by one partner, for instance, may trust another partner wholeheartedly (Ross & Spinner, 2001). So, attachment varies from relationship to relationship as well as from person to person, making attachment styles in loving partnerships rather complex (McCreary & Branscum, 2004).

Still, the global attitudes we have described here are important. Varying levels of avoidance of intimacy and anxiety over abandonment characterize relationships all over the world (Ijzendoorn & Sagi, 1999). And they clearly set the stage for our dealings with others. Teenagers who avoid intimacy with others tend to have comparatively unsatisfying close relationships years later as adults (Collins et al., 2002). Not only are there different types of loves, there are also different kinds of lovers.

Age

Another slowly changing personal characteristic that may affect love is one's age. As we suggested in chapter 2, age can be a tricky variable to study because it's usually confounded with experience and history. As people age, they may have (a) relationships of longer duration and (b) more relationships overall. So if love does seem to change with age, it may be because age makes a difference or because of the length of people's relationships, the extent of their previous romantic experience, or some combination of all three.

Nevertheless, one thing seems clear about age: Most people mellow. When researchers compared spouses in their sixties to those in their forties, they found that the older couples interacted with more good cheer, but less physical arousal. Their emotions were less intense, but more positive on the whole, even in marriages that were not particularly happy at the time (Levenson, Carstensen, & Gottman, 1994). Some of the burning, urgent, emotional intensity that leads young people to marry seems to dwindle with time, to be replaced with a more genial and more mature outlook on love.

Men and Women

A potentially important individual difference that does not change with time is one's sex. On the whole, men and women are more similar than different when it comes to love (Canary & Emmers-Sommer, 1997; Hendrick & Hendrick, 1995). They experience the various types of love similarly, and there are few differences in the proportions of men and women who have each attachment style (Feeney & Noller, 1990; Fehr, 1994); men tend to be more dismissing than women are, but the difference is rather small (Schmitt et al., 2003). Women do experience more intense and more volatile emotions than men do, on average (Brody & Hall, 1993); nevertheless, studies rarely find any differences between men and women on measures of romantic feelings such as the Love Scale (Rubin, 1973) and the Passionate Love Scale (Hatfield & Sprecher, 1986). Evidently, as we have noted before, it's just plain silly to think that men come from one planet and women come from another.

On the other hand, as we saw in chapter 4, men tend to possess more romantic attitudes than women do. Men are more likely than women to think that if you just love someone enough, nothing else matters (Sprecher & Metts, 1989). They're also more likely to believe that it's possible to experience "love at first sight," and that may be why they tend to fall in love faster than women do (Hatfield & Sprecher, 1986). In fact, if you combine these trends with the sex differences in love styles we mentioned—remember, women are more pragmatic than men are, and men are more likely to treat love as a game (Hendrick et al., 1998)—you may find, as researchers have, that women tend to be more cautious than men when it comes to love. Women tend to be more selective about *whom* they love, feeling passion more slowly and limiting their affection to partners of relatively higher intelligence, status, and other desirable qualities (Kenrick et al., 1990). Men tend to be less discriminating, a fact that is reflected by their greater acceptance, on average, of casual sex (Hendrick et al., 1998). (All of these patterns, we should remind you, are consistent with the evolutionary model, which predicts that women *should* be cautious about whom they love because their parental investments in any offspring are so much greater than men's [Buss, 2004]. In contrast, the sociocultural model attributes women's greater selectivity to their traditionally lower status in many societies; according to this perspective, careful selection of a high-status mate is one of the few means available to women to obtain resources that are more accessible to men [Eagly & Wood, 1999]. Which explanation do you find more convincing?)

Men also seem to put more stock in passion. Men and women agree that love should be affectionate and committed, but men also think it should be more passionate than women do (Fehr & Broughton, 2001). Indeed, of the three components of love, passion is most highly associated with men's satisfaction with their relationships, whereas commitment is the best predictor of satisfaction for women (Nathan et al., 2002). This puts men in the position of relying on the component of love that, according to Sternberg's (1986) triangular theory, is the least stable and reliable as time goes by.

DOES LOVE LAST?

So, how does the passage of time affect love? Does love last? This is a difficult question to answer conclusively because, as we've seen, there are different types of loves and idiosyncratic types of lovers. Your experiences with love through the years may differ from those of another person reading this book. Nevertheless, the prototypical North American marriage occurs when people in their twenties who are flushed with romantic passion pledge to spend the rest of their lives together, probably expecting their passion to last. Will it? Despite the couples' good intentions, the best answer relationship science can provide is, probably not, at least not to the extent the partners expect.

The simple truth is that romantic love decreases after people marry (Sprecher & Regan, 1998). Scores on romantic and passionate love scales go down as the years go by (Acker & Davis, 1992; Tucker & Aron, 1993), and that's among couples who manage to stay married! After several years, husbands and wives are no longer claiming to the same degree that they'd do anything for each other or that they melt when they look into each other's eyes. Figure 8.4 provides an interesting example of this in a study conducted in India that compared couples who chose to marry for love—like most North Americans do—to couples whose marriages were arranged for them by their families (Gupta & Singh, 1982). Romantic couples who were still married after ten years reported much lower scores on Rubin's (1973) Love Scale than did those who had only been married for a year or two. (Couples who divorced and were not married that long were not included in the data you see in Figure 8.4. What do you think their love scores would be?)

FIGURE 8.4. Romantic love decreases after people marry for love.
A study in India compared arranged marriages to those in which the spouses married because they were in love. Just as in the average American marriage, romantic love decreased substantially as the years went by after people married for love.

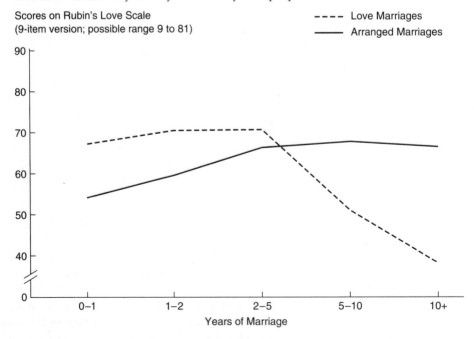

What's more, the decrease in a couple's romantic love may sometimes be quite rapid. After only two years of marriage, average spouses express affection for each other only half as often as they did when they were newlyweds (Huston & Chorost, 1994). Worldwide, divorces occur more frequently in the fourth year of marriage than at any other time (Fisher, 1995). Many, if not most, couples fail to maintain the urgent longing for each other that leads them to marry in the first place.

Why Doesn't Romantic Love Last?

In fact, if we consider it carefully, there may be several reasons why we should expect romantic love to decline over time (Walster & Walster, 1978). First, **fantasy** enhances romance. As we noted earlier, love is blind to some degree. Flushed with passion, lovers tend to idealize their partners and minimize or ignore information that should give them pause. In one study, men who learned that they had little in common with a woman were not attracted to her before they actually met her; however, if they did share a brief interaction, the men shrugged off their knowledge that they were incompatible and found her desirable anyway (Gold et al., 1984). Imagination, hope, and flights of fancy can make people who are quite different from us seem appealing, at least temporarily. The problem, of course, is that fantasy erodes with time and experience. To the extent that romance is enhanced by idealized glorification of one's partner, we should expect it to decline when people begin living together and reality slowly intrudes. "Ideals are easily tarnished, spells broken, sleights of hand exposed . . . romance fades over time because familiarity provides a more realistic, 'warts and all' view of the other; the harsh sunlight of the morning after dispels the enchantment of the moonlight" (Mitchell, 2002, p. 94).

In addition, sheer **novelty** adds excitement and energy to new loves. A first kiss is often much more thrilling than most of the thousands that follow, and when people are invigorated and fascinated by a new partner, they may be unable to appreciate how familiar and routine that same lover may seem 30 years later. Indeed, novelty causes sexual arousal in other species. For instance, if a male rat is caged with a female in estrus, he'll mate with her repeatedly until he appears to be sexually exhausted; however, if the first female is then replaced with another receptive female, the male will mount her with renewed interest and vigor. By continuing to replace an old partner with a new one, researchers can elicit two to three times as many ejaculations from the male as would have occurred with only the single female (Dewsbury, 1981). Researchers call this effect of novelty on arousal the *Coolidge effect*, referring to an old story that may or may not be true. Supposedly, President Calvin Coolidge and his wife were once touring a chicken farm when Mrs. Coolidge noticed a rooster covering one hen after another. Impressed with the rooster's prowess, she asked the guide to mention the rooster to the president. When he heard about the rooster's stamina, Coolidge is said to have reflected a moment and then replied, "Please tell Mrs. Coolidge that there is more than one hen" (Walster & Walster, 1978).

Does novelty have similar effects on people? It might. Engaging in novel, arousing activities together gets romantic couples to feel more in love with each other (Aron et al., 2002). Further, Roy Baumeister and Ellen Bratslavsky (1999) have suggested that romantic passion is directly related to changes in our relationships. When we're falling in love, everything is new and intimacy is increasing, and passion is likely to be very high. However, once a relationship is established, and novelty is lost, passion slowly subsides (Vohs & Baumeister, 2004). Some support for this view is found in the results of a broad survey of American sexuality that showed that an average couple's frequency of intercourse (one measure of their passion for each other) declines continually over the course of their marriage (Call, Sprecher, & Schwartz, 1995). (A similar pattern occurs in Germany as well [Klusmann, 2002].) This decline is obviously confounded with age, as Figure 8.5 shows. However, people who remarry and change partners increase their frequency of sex, at least for a while, so aging does not seem to be wholly responsible for the decline of passion with time. Arguably, "romance thrives on novelty, mystery, and danger; it is dispersed by familiarity. Enduring romance is therefore a contradiction in terms" (Mitchell, 2002, p. 27).

Finally, as Figure 8.5 also implies, **arousal** fades as time goes by. As we've seen, there's no question that physical arousal—such as a rapid pulse rate and fast, shallow breathing—fuels passion (Foster et al., 1998). But it's impossible to stay keyed up forever! In the case of romantic love, the brain may gradually habituate to high levels of PEA, the natural stimulant that is associated with romantic passion, so that even if your partner arouses you as much as ever, which is unlikely, you don't feel it as intensely (Liebowitz, 1983). In any case, for whatever reason, the passion component of love changes more rapidly than

FIGURE 8.5. Frequency of sexual intercourse by age.
Data from Call, Sprecher, & Schwartz, 1995.

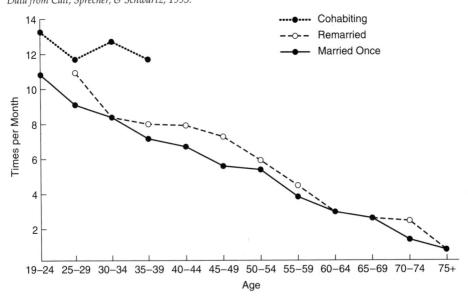

either intimacy or commitment (Acker & Davis, 1992), and that means that romantic love will change as well.

So, What Does the Future Hold?

Because three important influences on romantic passion—fantasy, novelty, and arousal—tend to dwindle over the years, romantic love decreases, too (Walster & Walster, 1978). In many relationships, it doesn't vanish entirely, of course, but it does tend to drop well below the levels that got a couple to marry in the first place. This is obviously a surprise for many couples, and it helps explain why the American divorce rate is so high: A common complaint is that the "magic" has died (see chapter 13).

However, we really don't want this news to be depressing! To the contrary, we think it offers important advice about how marriages can succeed. Often, the love that encourages people to marry is not the love that keeps them together decades later. Intimacy is more stable than passion. Thus, companionate love is more stable than romantic love is (Sprecher & Regan, 1998). And, as we noted earlier, people who have been happily married for a long time typically express a lot of companionate love for their spouses (Lauer & Lauer, 1985). Such people are often genuinely happy, too: Although it does not rely on passion, companionate love is very satisfying to those who experience it (Hecht, Marston, & Larkey, 1994). And because intimacy and passion are correlated (Whitley, 1993), being good friends may help to keep your passion alive.

Perhaps, then, we can distill some suggestions from all this. Enjoy passion, but don't make it the foundation of the relationships that you hope will last. Nurture a friendship with your lover. Try to stay fresh; grab every opportunity to enjoy novel adventures with your spouse (Aron et al., 2002). And don't be surprised or disappointed if your urgent desires gradually resolve into placid but deep affection for your beloved. That happy result is likely to make you a lucky lover.

FOR YOUR CONSIDERATION

Before David and Catherine met, neither of them had been in love, so they were both excited when their dating relationship gradually developed into a more intimate love affair. Each was the other's first lover, and they found sex to be both awkward and thrilling, and, within a few weeks, flushed with more romantic feelings than either of them had known, they decided to marry. But David soon became annoyed by Catherine's apparent desire to know everything about his day. She would call him every morning and afternoon when he was at work, just to "be in touch," and she would start to fret if he met clients over lunch or was out of the office running errands. For her part, Catherine was troubled by David's apparent reluctance to tell her what was on his mind. He prided himself on his self-sufficiency and didn't feel that it was necessary to tell her everything, and he began to feel crowded by her insistent probing.

What do you think the future holds for David and Catherine? Why?

CHAPTER SUMMARY

A Brief History of Love

Different societies have taken very different perspectives on love. Four dimensions on which views of love differ are cultural value, sexuality, sexual orientation, and marital status. The ancient Greeks took a negative view of love, seeing it as a kind of madness that had nothing to do with marriage. In medieval times, courtly love between an unmarried knight and a married lady was viewed as an idealistic, nonsexual quest. Modern ideas about love and marriage began to emerge in the seventeenth century, when, for the first time, love and marriage were viewed as compatible. Today, the belief that people should marry for love is widely accepted in North America, where most young adults say that they would not marry an otherwise perfect partner if they were not in love with him or her.

Types of Love

The Triangular Theory of Love. The triangular theory of love suggests that *intimacy, passion,* and *commitment* combine to produce eight different types of love. Of the three components, passion is thought to be the most variable and the least controllable.

Romantic, Passionate Love. Intimacy and passion combine to form romantic love, the experience people have in mind when they say they are "in love" with someone. A two-factor theory of passionate love holds that it occurs when physical arousal is attributed to the presence of a beloved person. In some circumstances, arousal can be *misattributed* to the wrong source, intensifying unrelated emotions through a process of *excitation transfer.* In excitation transfer, arousal caused by one stimulus is added to that caused by a second stimulus, making the second influence seem more powerful than it really is. Excitation transfer accounts for the fact that impersonal sources of arousal (such as fear of heights, or exercise) can enhance romantic attraction. Indeed, passion increases when a person becomes aroused for any reason. There may even be a chemical basis for these effects; our bodies may produce greater quantities of an amphetamine-like substance when we're in love.

Romantic love is also characterized by idealized evaluations of one's partner. In a sense, love is "blind"; objectivity and dispassion seem to decrease when romance enters the picture. Romantic love also tends to influence people's self-evaluations, leading them to develop more diversified self-concepts and increased self-esteem.

Companionate Love. Intimacy and commitment combine to form companionate love, a deep friendship with someone with whom one's life is intertwined. Spouses who have stayed married for more than fifteen years describe friendship as the primary reason their marriages have lasted.

Styles of Loving. Six themes in love experiences that are differentially correlated with the various types of love have also been identified. People tend to pair off with others who share their attitudes toward love.

Individual Differences in Love

Individual differences are relatively enduring characteristics of people that exert an influence across different situations.

Attachment Styles. The *secure, avoidant,* and *anxious/ambivalent* styles of attachment originally described by developmental researchers have been revised and expanded in studies of adult relationships. Four styles—*secure, preoccupied, fearful,* and *dismissing*—are now recognized. They differ from each other along continuous dimensions that describe a person's avoidance of intimacy and anxiety over abandonment. These dimensions seem to influence people's beliefs and expectations, communication, caregiving, sexual behavior, and personal well-being, and people with a secure style, who relish closeness with others and who are not anxious about interdependency, enjoy stronger experiences of romantic and companionate love than insecure people do.

Age. People mellow with age, experiencing less intense love as time goes by.

Men and Women. Men and women are more similar than different when it comes to love. However, women are more selective than men are; they pick their lovers more carefully and fall in love less quickly than men do.

Does Love Last?

In general, romantic love decreases after people marry, sometimes quite rapidly.

Why Doesn't Romantic Love Last? Romance and passion involve *fantasy, novelty,* and *arousal,* and each fades with time. Novelty causes sexual arousal in other species—a phenomenon called the Coolidge effect—and it may fuel human passion as well. One theory links passion to changes in our relationships, so that a developing relationship often causes considerable passion that gradually evaporates after the relationship is established.

So, What Does the Future Hold? Companionate love is very satisfying and is more stable than romantic love is. If lovers are good friends and understand the usual course of romance, they may improve their chances for a long, contented relationship.

Sexuality

We have two questions for you. First, if a mischievous genie offered you a lifetime supply of compelling orgasms but required that you experience them alone and never again have sex with another person, would you accept the offer? Second, if you discovered on your honeymoon that your new spouse had been secretly taking a drug like Viagra to enhance his or her sexual response to you, would you be hurt?

Different people will undoubtedly answer these questions in different ways. Those who have not had sex with an intimate romantic partner for a long time may find compelling orgasms, even solitary ones, an attractive option. But we suspect that most people would be reluctant to give up a potential future of physical connections with a lover or lovers. Most of us would be disappointed were we no longer able to share sex with someone we love. And we want our lovers to find *us* compelling and to want us in return. So, it may be hurtful to learn that a partner's apparent desire for us is the result, at least in part, of some drug (Morgentaler, 2003).

As these questions may imply, there's a lot more to human sexuality than great orgasms. For some people, at least, sex need not always involve romantic intimacy, but for most people romantic intimacy involves sex. Our close romantic relationships often have a sexual component, and our sexual behavior and sexual satisfaction are often dependent on the nature, and health, of those relationships. This chapter considers a variety of questions: What kinds of attitudes do we have about sexuality in and out of relationships? How is sexual behavior affected by one's relationship status? What relationship factors influence feelings of sexual satisfaction? Who wants more sex, men or women? How do partners communicate with one another about sex? As we'll see, all of the answers highlight the close connection between sexuality and intimate relationships.

SEXUAL ATTITUDES

Attitudes about Casual Sex

Times have changed, and you're probably more accepting of premarital sexual intercourse[1] than your grandparents were. When your parents were born, most people disapproved of sex "before marriage" (Hunt, 1974), but in 1998 only 35 percent of a large U.S. sample felt that premarital sex was "always or almost always wrong" (Davis, Smith, & Marsden, 2002). Some people still believe that intercourse should only occur when partners are married, but most people now feel that sex outside of marriage can be unobjectionable. The circumstances matter. Most people still generally disapprove of sexual intercourse between people who are not committed to each other (Willetts, Sprecher, & Beck, 2004) and of sex with more than one person in a short span of time (Gentry, 1998). People who are sexually active are viewed more positively when they are in a "serious" rather than a "casual" relationship (Bettor, Hendrick, & Hendrick, 1995), and most people also prefer their own spouses to have had limited sexual experience (Sprecher et al., 1997). Thus, we seem to endorse a "permissiveness-with-affection" standard (Reiss, 1967); we believe that sexual activity among people who are not married is acceptable as long as it is in the context of a committed relationship. So while people are no longer expected to "save themselves for marriage" as our grandmothers were supposed to, there is clearly an accepted prerequisite of relational attachment and affection as the most appropriate context for sexual activity.

Do men and women differ in their sexual opinions? On average, they do: Men hold more permissive sexual values and attitudes (Oliver & Hyde, 1993; Somers & Paulson, 2000), although the difference is shrinking over time, and how big it is depends on the particular attitude being measured. One of the largest sex differences is in attitudes toward casual premarital sex (Oliver & Hyde, 1993); men are more likely than women to enjoy sex without intimacy, whereas women prefer sexual activities to be part of a psychologically intimate relationship (Bailey et al., 2000). To a lesser extent, men also have more permissive attitudes towards extramarital sex than women do (Glass & Wright, 1992; Oliver & Hyde, 1993), although, in general, most Americans strongly disapprove of a married person having sex with someone besides his or her spouse (Willetts et al., 2004).

A person's sex may be involved in other sexual attitudes, as well. Traditionally, women have been judged more harshly than men for being sexually experienced or permissive. Whereas women who have multiple sexual partners may be dismissed as "sluts," men with the same number of partners may be admired as "studs." This asymmetry is known as the *sexual double standard*, and it has been studied extensively. Forty years ago, a double standard may have been robust, but it appears to be more subtle today. For example, men may *like*

---

[1] We recognize that not all people will marry, but "premarital" is a more familiar, more convenient term than "unmarried" is.

BOX 9.1

Love and Lust

Rob and Nancy are college students who have been dating for about 6 months. They spend quite a bit of time together, and both enjoy rollerblading and going to the movies. Rob and Nancy feel strong sexual desires for one another, and in fact, they have sex three or four times a week. If you had to guess, how happy would you say Rob and Nancy are with each other? How much in love? How committed? And would you guess differently if you had been told instead that they didn't have much sexual desire for one another and had not had sex?

If you are like most people, your answer to the last question would be yes. Pamela Regan (1998) conducted a study in which she described Rob and Nancy as feeling either high or low desire for each other and as either having or not having intercourse. College students judged the couple to be more in love, more committed, happier, and more satisfied when they were hot for each other than was the case when they felt little lust. The presence or absence of desire clearly influenced people's perceptions of the relationship, but, interestingly, whether or not Rob and Nancy were actually having sex did not. Whether or not it was being fulfilled, lust led people to assume that love was at work, and Regan (1998) also found the connection to run in the other direction: Couples who were said to be in love were assumed to also desire each other sexually.

Regan's research demonstrates that people consider lust and love to go hand-in-hand. We want our romantic partners to feel sexual desire for us, and we want to feel it for them (Regan, 2004). And these results also suggest why any decline in passion as the years go by can be worrisome: If love and lust go together, partners may view declining lust as a sign of waning love.

---

their dating partners to be sexually permissive but prefer their potential spouses to be less experienced (Oliver & Sedikides, 1992). Another study found that although Canadian women believed that most people judge sexually experienced women more harshly than sexually experienced men, the women themselves did not endorse this belief (Milhausen & Herold, 1999). Yet another investigation found that sexually active women were seen as more liberal and assertive, but no less desirable, than women who were not sexually active (Gentry, 1998). A strong sexual double standard no longer seems to exist, but some studies (e.g., Sprecher, McKinney & Orbuch, 1987) do suggest that a person's sex still influences people's evaluations of his or her sexual experiences.

Attitudes about Same-Sex Sexuality

So far our discussion of sexual attitudes has focused exclusively on heterosexual sex. Attitudes about same-sex sexuality are decidedly more negative than attitudes towards premarital sex, with 62 percent of adult Americans feeling that "sexual relations between adults of the same sex" are always or almost always wrong (Davis et al., 2002). Americans are becoming more tolerant of homosexuality as time goes by (Loftus, 2001), but homosexuality still engenders disregard.

People's attitudes about same-sex sexuality often extend beyond beliefs about sex per se. Most Americans object to what they consider to be the "homosexual lifestyle" (Turque, 1992). Gay and lesbian relationships are often assumed to be dysfunctional and unhappy (Testa, Kinder & Ironson, 1987), despite research evidence that suggests that homosexual relationships are quite similar to heterosexual partnerships (Peplau, Fingerhut, & Beals, 2004). Negative stereotypes and hate crimes against gays and lesbians are still all too common.

On the other hand, there is reason to expect that heterosexuals' attitudes about gays and lesbians will slowly continue to become more positive. There are many more gay and lesbian characters visible in the media now than in the past, and knowing someone who is gay or lesbian seems to promote more positive attitudes toward homosexuality. The more contact people have with gays and lesbians, the more favorable their feelings toward homosexuals tend to be (Herek & Glunt, 1993). This may occur for at least two reasons. Gays and lesbians are probably more likely to disclose their sexuality to heterosexuals who already have generally positive attitudes, but it's also likely that dispassionate contact with homosexuals usually results in more positive attitudes. Such processes may foreshadow increasingly positive attitudes toward homosexuality over time.

Cultural Differences in Sexual Attitudes

As we've seen, many sexual attitudes have become more permissive over time. And given the amount of pornographic spam you have to clear out of your e-mail accounts, you may be tempted to think of Western cultures, particularly the United States, as being more permissive than most. But you'd be wrong. In fact, the sexual attitudes of Americans look surprisingly conservative when compared to the opinions expressed by people in other countries. Table 9.1 shows the percentages of people in several countries surveyed in one study (Widmer, Treas, & Newcomb, 1998) who felt that different forms of nonmarital sex were "always wrong." While there was some agreement across cultures (for instance, all countries tended to disapprove of extramarital sex), you can see that the United States was consistently among the most conservative countries with regard to beliefs about sex before marriage, sex before age 16, extramarital sex, and homosexual sex. Canada was more permissive than the U.S. on all of the measures, particularly with regard to homosexual sex. These cultural differences are not simply regional, then; countries that are close neighbors do not necessarily share the same sexual attitudes. There are a variety of possible explanations for the differences observed in Table 9.1, including cultural, historical, religious, and political factors, but there is clear evidence that despite a trend over time towards more permissive sexual attitudes, Americans still hold relatively conservative sexual attitudes.

TABLE 9.1. Attitudes towards Nonmarital Sex by Country

Countries	Sex before marriage	Sex before Age 16	Extramarital sex	Homosexual sex
Australia	13	61	59	55
Canada	12	55	68	39
Germany	5	34	55	42
Great Britain	12	67	67	58
Israel	19	67	73	57
Japan	19	60	58	65
Netherlands	7	45	63	19
Russia	13	45	36	57
Spain	20	59	76	45
Sweden	4	32	68	56
USA	29	71	80	70

Note: Numbers represent the percentage of respondents who felt this type of sex was always **wrong**.
Source: Widmer, Treas, & Newcomb, 1998.

SEXUAL BEHAVIOR

It's one thing to ask what people are thinking and another to find out what they're actually doing. Studies of sexual behavior are intriguing because we can put our own sexual behavior into context: How many people are still virgins by the time they are 20? How many times a week does the average couple have sex, and how does that compare to one's own sexual frequency? How common is it for a person to cheat on his or her relationship partner? An understanding of general trends in sexual behavior allows us to determine whether our own behavior is "normal." Remember, however, as you read about these trends that the broad descriptions of sexual behavior patterns reported in this section mask enormous variability in people's experiences. And behavior that is common is not necessarily more desirable or appropriate than sexual behavior that is less typical. We'll find that what is perhaps most important about sexual behavior in relationships is that it is desired by and satisfying for both partners.

Premarital Sex

When do most people engage in sex for the first time? Assuming that we are talking about heterosexual intercourse, the average age of first intercourse—the age at which half of the people surveyed have had sex and half have not—is 15 for African-American men, 16 for Latinos, and 17 for white men. African-American women typically remain virgins until they are nearly 17, and Latinas and white women wait until they are nearly 18 (Michael, Gagnon, & Kolata, 1994). Large majorities of Americans have sex before they turn 20.

Adolescents provide diverse reasons to explain their sexual activity (Metts, 2004). Some young adults have sex because they want to express their love or affection for their partners (e.g., Hill & Preston, 1996). Others are curious and want to experience the physical pleasure of sex. Other reasons focus on external factors, such as succumbing to peer pressure or wanting to please their partners. On the whole, however, the reasons offered by adolescents for engaging in their first sexual intercourse are similar to the sexual motives reported by people more generally; love, pleasure, conformity, and social recognition were all motives offered by older college students for having sex (Browning et al., 2000). Thus, many key motives for engaging in sex are relational, highlighting the importance of relationships in most people's sexual experiences.

What factors predict *when* an individual will engage in sex for the first time? In general, a person's values and attitudes are the best predictors of premarital sexual behavior. Premarital sexual activity is more likely among teenagers who view dating as important in their lives and who express strong desires for a partner (Newcomb, Huba, & Bentler, 1986). In turn, the importance teens attach to dating is associated with (1) confidence about being popular with and attractive to the other sex, (2) positive self-esteem, and (3) more experiences involving stressful physical or family-related events. Thus, one key predictor of premarital sexual activity, the desire to have a dating partner, is correlated with both positive factors (social and personal confidence) and negative experiences (stress). Similar findings are obtained in research on pregnancies among adolescents (Robbins, Kaplan, & Martin, 1985). The likelihood of becoming a parent out of marriage is greater for teens whose parents have a lower socioeconomic status, who have more difficulties in school, and who are more popular among their peers. It appears, then, that socially successful teenagers who face stressful life circumstances may be more likely than others to become sexually active and to run the risk of unplanned pregnancies.

Another set of predictors of premarital sexual activity revolve around a desire for achieving "adult" status. Teenagers who engage in sex at an early age place greater value on independence (Jessor et al., 1983) and early autonomy (Rosenthal, Smith, & de Visser, 1999). Adolescent males who engage in earlier sexual activity are more physically mature and are more likely to use drugs than are those who engage in sex at a later age (Rosenthal et al., 1999). Lack of self-restraint (such as agreeing with statements like, "People who get me angry need to watch out") is also a predictor of early sexual activity for girls. Evidently, "the desire to achieve the transition to adulthood at an earlier age than their peers . . . constitutes a powerful incentive for young people to become sexually active" (Rosenthal et al., 1999, p. 332).

Family structure is also related to premarital sexual activity. Adolescents who live in single-parent homes tend to have sex earlier than do those who live with two parents, and there may be several reasons why (Willetts et al., 2004). On the one hand, overtaxed single parents may supervise their teens less closely than two parents do, and on the other, the teens may simply be emulating the dating behavior they witness in their parents. Imitation may matter: Teens who have an older brother who is sexually active tend to have sex at a younger age than do those without such a role model (Widmer, 1997).

Sex in Committed Relationships

How often do people in relationships typically have sex? It depends. Sexual frequency is linked to a number of factors, including the nature of one's relationship. Couples who are living together, but not married, have sex about three times per week, on average, whereas those who are married have sex about two times per week (Call et al., 1995; Laumann et al., 1994). Couples in both kinds of relationships, however, have sex more often than those who are single (Laumann et al., 1994), which is probably due to the fact that singles are less likely to have consistent access to a sexual partner. Married people may sometimes envy the swinging life of singles, but they usually get more sex than singles do.

Another important factor influencing sexual frequency is a person's age (Blumstein & Schwartz, 1983; Call et al., 1995). Look back at Figure 8.5 on page 272: Older people generally have sex much less frequently than younger people do. It's likely that physical changes associated with aging are influential in this regard (Call et al., 1995): Decreased hormone levels in older women may result in less vaginal lubrication, and decreased circulation in men may affect the ability to maintain an erection. Declines in physical health may also erode one's vigor, so we shouldn't be surprised that sexual desire wanes some over the years. In couples that have been together for a long time, however, there is another, more subtle possibility: The passion long-term partners feel for one another may simmer down as each becomes a familiar and routine sexual partner and the thrill of discovery and novelty is lost (Vohs & Baumeister, 2004). As we noted in chapter 8, this may be one reason why romantic love becomes less intense as relationships age, and the size of this effect (see Figure 8.5) leads us to offer this cautionary note: If you're a young adult who's staying in a relationship (at least in part) because of great, hot sex, it's simply silly to expect that your passion, desire, and need for that partner will never change. Of course it will.

A final factor associated with sexual frequency is sexual orientation. When their relationships are young, gay men have more sex with their partners than lesbians or heterosexuals do (Blumstein & Schwartz, 1983). (Keep this pattern in mind when we discuss sexual desire a few pages from now.) After ten years together, everybody has sex less often, but the drop in frequency is greater for gays, and they end up having sex less frequently than heterosexual couples do. (See Figure 9.1.) On the other hand, regardless of the duration of the relationship, lesbians have sex less often than any other relationship group. When it's just up to them, women have sex much less frequently than they do when there is a man involved.

Monogamy

Most people around the world have a decidedly negative view of someone who is in a committed relationship engaging in **extradyadic sex** (that is, having sex outside the dyad, or couple, with someone other than one's partner) (Widmer

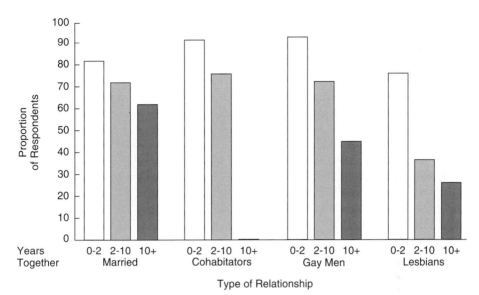

FIGURE 9.1. Differences in sexual frequency by type and length of relationship.
The figure displays the proportion of couples in each type of relationship who reported
having sex at least once a week. There is no value provided for cohabiting relationships
that lasted for more than 10 years because there were not enough couples in this
category to provide a reliable estimate.
Source: Blumstein & Schwartz, 1983.

et al., 1998). Thus, we might expect that sexual infidelity would be relatively
rare. But is it? A compilation of 28 different investigations involving more than
58,000 participants, most of them in the U.S. and most of them married, found
that 21 percent of the women and 32 percent of the men had been sexually unfaithful to their romantic partners at least once. Most husbands and wives never
have sex with other people after they marry, but about one out of every five
wives and one out of three husbands do (Tafoya & Spitzberg, in press).

Who cheats? What circumstances or personal characteristics distinguish
those who cheat on their partners from those who do not? Whether one is a man
or woman is one important predictor: Compared to women, men hold more
favorable attitudes toward extramarital sex (Seal, Agostinelli, & Hannett, 1994)
and are more likely to have extramarital affairs (Tafoya & Spitzberg, in press).
Moreover, among those spouses who do cheat, men are likely to have a greater
number of outside sexual partners than women do (Blumstein & Schwartz,
1983).

The same-sex relationships of gay and lesbian couples provide an interesting comparison of male and female fidelity free of the influence of the other sex.
Given men's greater acceptance of and interest in extradyadic sex, we'd expect
more extradyadic behavior among gay men than among lesbian women, and
that's exactly what seems to occur (Peplau et al., 2004). In fact, gay men seem
to be much more likely than heterosexual men to engage in extradyadic sex.

BOX 9.2

Men Report More Sexual Partners than Women Do. How?

The best, most comprehensive surveys of sex in the United States paint somewhat different pictures of the sexual behavior of men and women. In particular, the National Life and Social Health Survey found that the average middle-aged man had had six sexual partners during his lifetime whereas the average woman had had only two (Laumann et al., 1994). Men also report having sex more often than women do (Oliver & Hyde, 1993). Why don't these figures agree? One would think that each time a man has sex with a new partner, that partner does, too. So, why is this sex difference routinely found?

There are several possible reasons (Willetts, Sprecher, & Beck, 2004), and they bear on issues we've encountered before. One possibility is that men may be having a lot of sex with other men. There are about twice as many gay men as lesbian women, and gays have sex more often than lesbians do (Laumann et al., 1994), so differences in homosexual behavior probably do account for some of the discrepancy. On the other hand, only 5 percent of adult men have homosexual experiences, so same-sex sexuality is only a small influence (Baumeister & Tice, 2001).

A more important issue has to do with the procedures used by sex researchers. Despite their careful sampling techniques, surveys usually fail to include representative numbers of those particular women—prostitutes—who have sex with many men (if for no other reason than that they're not home at night when the surveys are usually conducted). When researchers make special efforts to include prostitutes in their samples, the average numbers of partners reported by men and women are more similar (Kanouse et al., 1999).

Men and women also tend to define "sex" differently. If a heterosexual couple engages only in oral sex, for instance, he is more likely to say that they've had "sex" than she is (Sanders & Reinisch, 1999). The sexes agree completely that vaginal intercourse is "sex", but men are more likely than women to count as "sex partners" lovers with whom intercourse did not occur.

Still, it's probable that the most important source of the discrepancy is a tendency for men to exaggerate, and for women to minimize, the number of partners they've had (Willetts et al., 2004). Men tend to estimate their number of partners, and they tend to give generous estimates, so that men who have had many partners almost always answer researchers' inquiries with round numbers, such as "30"; they almost never provide seemingly exact counts such as 26 or 27 (Brown & Sinclair, 1999). In contrast, women seem to count their partners more accurately and then subtract a partner or two from their announced totals (Wiederman, 2004). Self-reports like these are thus prone to biases that result both from impression management and reconstructive memory, topics we covered back in chapter 4, and they speak to some of the difficulties researchers face in studying intimate behavior.

One more point: When college students are asked how many sex partners they would like to have over the rest of their lives, the typical response from an overwhelming majority of both men and women is "one" (Pedersen et al., 2002). A tiny minority of men hopes to have many more partners, and there are more such men than women, but almost all people hope to settle into a rewarding sexual relationship with just one special partner for the foreseeable future.

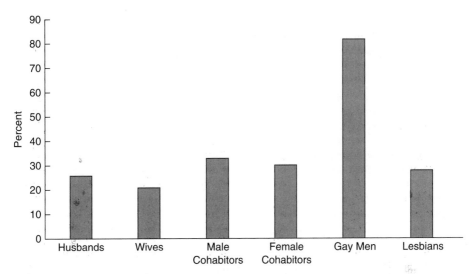

FIGURE 9.2. Percentages of individuals reporting any instance(s) of nonmonogamy since the beginning of their relationship.
From Blumstein & Schwartz, 1983.

Figure 9.2 depicts the results of a large survey of Americans back in the early 1980s that obtained data on spouses, cohabiting couples, and gay and lesbian couples (Blumstein & Schwartz, 1983), and as you can see, gay men were more likely than anyone else to have had sex outside their primary relationships. We don't know exactly why this difference occurred, but we should note that in many cases, the gay men had such sex with the permission (if not the encouragement) of their partners (Peplau et al., 2004). Some observers have speculated that some heterosexual men would also behave this way were their greater permissiveness not checked by the more conservative attitudes of their female lovers (Peplau, 2003).

Certainly, however, not all men are promiscuous and not all women are chaste, and researchers have also examined individual differences that describe people who are likely to engage in extradyadic sex. For some of us, sex is connected to love and commitment: It's not especially rewarding to have sex with people we don't know well or don't care much about, and we have casual sex with acquaintances or strangers rarely, if at all. For others of us, however, sex has little to do with love and commitment; we think that "sex without love is OK," and we're content to have sex with people for whom we have no particular feelings. These different approaches to sex emerge from our **sociosexual orientations,** the trait-like collections of beliefs and behaviors that describe our feelings about sex (Simpson, Wilson, & Winterheld, 2004). Individual differences in *sociosexuality* were discovered by Jeff Simpson and Steve Gangestad (1991), who used the measure in Box 9.3 to measure respondent's sociosexual orientations. People who were generally willing to have sex only in the context of a committed and affectionate relationship were said to have a "restricted" sociosexual orientation, whereas those who did not seek much closeness or commitment before pursuing sex were said to have "unrestricted" sociosexuality.

BOX 9.3
Measuring Sociosexuality

Sociosexuality describes the degree to which a person is comfortable having sex in the absence of any love or commitment. Jeff Simpson and Steve Gangestad (1991) developed this brief measure, the Sociosexual Orientation Inventory, to assess sociosexuality. Respondents are asked to answer these questions as honestly as possible:

1. With how many different partners have you had sex (sexual intercourse) within the past year?

   _____

2. How many different partners do you foresee yourself having sex with during the next five years? (Please give a *specific, realistic* estimate). _____

3. With how many different partners have you had sex on *one and only one* occasion? _____

4. How often do you fantasize about having sex with someone other than your current dating partner? (Circle one).

   1. never
   2. once every two or three months
   3. once a month
   4. once every two weeks
   5. once a week
   6. a few times each week
   7. nearly every day
   8. at least once a day

5. Sex without love is OK.

1	2	3	4	5	6	7	8	9

   I strongly disagree   I strongly agree

6. I can imagine myself being comfortable and enjoying "casual" sex with different partners.

1	2	3	4	5	6	7	8	9

   I strongly disagree   I strongly agree

7. I would have to be closely attached to someone (both emotionally and psychologically) before I could feel comfortable and fully enjoy having sex with him or her.

1	2	3	4	5	6	7	8	9

   I strongly disagree   I strongly agree

Responses to the last item (#7) are reverse scored, and a total score is computed by weighing the scores of some items more heavily than others. In general, higher numbers on each question (and for the total score) reflect an *unrestricted* sexual orientation, and lower numbers reflect a *restricted* orientation. Compared to those with a restricted orientation, people with an unrestricted orientation "typically engage in sex earlier in their romantic relationships, are more likely to engage in sex with more than one partner at a time, and tend to be involved in sexual relationships characterized by less expressed investment, less commitment, and weaker affectional ties" (Simpson & Gangestad, 1991, p. 879). Sociosexuality is a good example of how characteristics of individuals have a powerful impact on the nature of sexual interactions.

People with unrestricted orientations—those who get high scores on the Sociosexual Orientation Inventory in Box 9.3—tend to be dynamic, flirtatious people who are on the prowl for new partners (Simeon & Miller, 2005; Simpson et al., 2004). They're sociable and extraverted, and they drink a lot of alcohol (Clark, 2004; Wright & Riese, 1997). But they're also less likely than those with restricted orientations to have secure attachment styles; they are relatively uncomfortable with intimacy, and they're less committed to their romantic partners (Simeon & Miller, 2005). And as you might expect, men are more unrestricted on average than women are (Simpson & Gangestad, 1991).

Given all this, it probably won't surprise you to learn that sociosexuality is associated with the likelihood that people will have extradyadic sex (Bailey et al., 2000). Over their lifetimes, compared to those with more restricted orientations, unrestricted people have a greater number of sexual partners and are more likely to cheat on their primary lovers (Ostovich & Sabini, 2004). David Seal and his colleagues (1994) shed light on this pattern in a clever study of heterosexual college students who were currently in dating relationships. Participants were asked to evaluate a computer dating video in which an attractive member of the other sex described him- or herself. After viewing the tape, participants were told they could enter a drawing to win a free date with the person in the video by filling out a card with their name and phone number. They were then asked to imagine that they had actually won the free date and that they had gone on the date and had a good time; then, they were invited to indicate how willing they would be to engage in a series of physically intimate behaviors with the date. The researchers found that 36 percent of those who were unrestricted in their sociosexuality entered the drawing for a free date, whereas only 4 percent of those who were restricted did. (Remember, all the participants were currently involved in existing relationships!) In addition, unrestricted individuals were more interested in having sex with their new dates than restricted individuals were. Finally, unrestricted people were equally interested in the new date whether or not they were committed to their current partners; the more committed restricted people were, the less likely they were to pursue the new partner, but that wasn't true of people with unrestricted sociosexual orientations. Add it all up, and sociosexuality is one meaningful characteristic that distinguishes those who are likely to cheat from those who are not.

Other attempts to predict patterns of extradyadic sex have focused on qualities of a person's relationship. Levels of relationship satisfaction and commitment are both important in ways that probably won't surprise you: In general, those who are unhappy with their relationships are more likely to have engaged in recent acts of sexual infidelity (Treas & Giesen, 2000), and those who feel committed to their partnerships are less likely to stray (Drigotas, Safstrom, & Gentilia, 1999). In particular, because cohabiting partners typically feel less commitment to their relationship than spouses do, they are more likely to have extradyadic sex than are those who are married (Forste & Tanfer, 1996; Treas & Giesen, 2000).

The principles of equity theory have also proven useful for identifying particular relationship factors that are associated with sexual infidelity. As you may recall[2], equity theory emphasizes that relationships are most stable and satisfying when people derive benefits from a relationship that are proportional to the effort they invest to maintain the partnership. A relationship is unfair and inequitable when one member is getting more out of it than he or she deserves, and in such cases, that partner is being *overbenefited* while his or her mate is being *underbenefited*. Walster, Traupmann, and Walster (1978) used these concepts in examining extradyadic sex in a sample of 2,000 men and women who were married or cohabiting, and found that underbenefited partners reported a greater number of extradyadic relationships than did either those who were overbenefited or those who felt their relationship was equitable. Moreover, among those who had cheated, underbenefited people had their first affair earlier in their relationships (after an average of nine to eleven years) than did those who were fairly treated or overbenefited (twelve to fifteen years). A lack of equity may be one prominent reason why people have affairs, especially for wives (Prins, Buunk, & VanYperen, 1993): In general, people who feel they are not getting the benefits to which they feel entitled are the ones most likely to turn, and to turn earlier, to other relationships.

Sexual Desire

Men's higher sociosexuality scores and more frequent infidelity may be results, in part, of another, broader difference between the sexes. On average, men have higher **sex drives** than women do. They experience more frequent and more intense sexual desires and are routinely more motivated to engage in sexual activity than women are (Vohs, Catanese, & Baumeister, 2004). As we examine this sex difference, remember that there are sizable individual differences among men and among women, and there are certainly many men who are chronically less horny than many women are. Nevertheless, a wide array of facts demonstrates that men have higher sex drives than women do:

- Men masturbate more often. Almost half of all men who have a regular sexual partner still masturbate more than once a week, whereas only 16 percent of women who are in sexual relationships masturbate as frequently (Klusmann, 2002).
- Men want sex more often than women do, and they are more likely than women to feel dissatisfied with the amount of sex they get (Sprecher, 2002).
- In developing relationships, men typically want to begin having sex sooner than women do (Sprecher, Barbee, & Schwartz, 1995). As a result, women are usually the "gatekeepers" who decide when sex begins in a new relationship; on average, when he first wants to have sex, he has to wait, but when she wants to have sex, they do.
- Men fantasize about sex more often than women do (Leitenberg & Henning, 1995).
- Men spend more money on sex, buying more sex toys and porn (Laumann et al., 1994). In particular, men sometimes pay to obtain sex—in one study

[2]Need a reminder? Equity theory is described on pages 206–207.

in Australia, 23 percent of men had paid for sex at least once—but women almost never do (Pitts et al., 2004).

- Finally, as we have already mentioned, men are more accepting of casual sex, on average, than women are (Ostovich & Sabini, 2004).

Add up these patterns, and the sex difference in sex drive may be no small matter. To a greater or lesser degree, each of these patterns may lead to misunderstanding or annoyance as heterosexual couples negotiate their sexual interactions. Some husbands may be chronically frustrated by getting less sex than they want at the same time that their wives are irritated by their frequent insistence for more. (We're reminded, in this regard, of a clever bit in the movie *Annie Hall*, which beat *Star Wars* to win the Academy Award for Best Picture for 1977: On a split screen, both members of a romantic couple are visiting their therapists, who have asked how often they have sex; he laments, "Hardly ever, maybe three times a week," as she complains, "Constantly, I'd say three times a week.") And consider a wife who discovers her husband masturbating: Even if she is getting all the sex she wants, she may still be hurt to find him pleasuring himself without her. The typical sex difference in sex drive means that some couples will encounter mismatches in sexual desire, and difficulty may result.

Other more subtle consequences may result from men wanting more sex than women do. As the gatekeepers who decide when sex occurs, women may find men willing to offer various concessions in exchange for sex (Vohs et al., 2004). Men's greater interest in sex may put the principle of lesser interest[3] in action: Women's control over access to something that they have and that men want may give them power with which to influence their men. In some relationships, sex may be "a valued good for which there is a marketplace in which women act as sellers and men as buyers" (Baumeister & Vohs, 2004, p. 359).

This sounds pretty tacky, but partners need not be consciously aware of this pattern for it to affect their interactions. Instead, without ever thinking about it, people may just take it for granted that a woman who, over a period of time, accepts a series of gifts from a man—such as expensive dates and other desirable entertainments—should feel some obligation to increase the intimacy of the relationship (or else she should stop accepting the gifts) (Catanese, Vohs, & Baumeister, 2004). A dark consequence of this pattern is that some men may feel justified in pressuring or coercing women to have sex when they feel that the women "owe it" to them.

Preventing Pregnancy and Sexually Transmitted Infections

Social scientists have also focused significant attention on the issues of pregnancy and sexually transmitted disease prevention. The social and personal costs of teen pregnancy, combined with the frightening incidence of sexually transmitted infections, such as HIV[4] and chlamydia, point to a pressing need for

---

[3]Do you need to refresh your understanding of the principle of lesser interest? Look back at page 188.

[4]The Human Immunodeficiency Virus, the virus that causes AIDS.

more responsible sexual behavior. Although pregnancy and disease can and do occur outside the context of relationships, they are nonetheless relationship issues; both the prevention and, if prevention efforts fail, the consequences of pregnancy and sexually transmitted disease raise questions for relationship partners, past, present, and future.

We know from the experience of the gay male community that sexual behavior can be modified. Among older gay and bisexual males, "AIDS education and prevention campaigns have resulted in the most profound modification of personal health-related behaviors ever recorded" (Stall, Coates, & Hoff, 1988, p. 878). On the other hand, efforts to promote the safe-sex use of condoms among intravenous drug users appear to have met with little success, and there is growing concern that younger gay males may be engaging in risky sexual practices too often (Griggs, 1990; Lemp et al., 1994).

These concerns are not limited to gay men: Among a sample of largely heterosexual college students, Carroll (1988) found that there was more talk than action in response to the fear of AIDS. Although more than 40 percent of sexually active respondents said that they had modified their sexual behavior because of concerns about AIDS, their reports of actual sexual behavior failed to confirm these claims. Another study of heterosexuals found that only 30 percent had used a condom the last time they had had sex (Campbell, Peplau, & DeBro, 1992). Worse yet, the more sexual partners people have had, the less likely they say they are to use a condom in the future (Gerrard & Warner, 1994)! So, those most at risk may be least likely to engage in risk-reducing behaviors. Other studies have reported essentially the same pattern: At best, heterosexuals have changed their behavior only minimally in the face of the AIDS threat (Catania et al., 1993).

This is a particularly frightening notion, given that many young adults engage in casual sex, at least occasionally. Surveys suggest that most college students—about three fourths—have had **hookups,** or sexual interactions with brief acquaintances or strangers that usually last one night and that do not involve any expectation of a lasting relationship (McGinn, 2004; Paul, McManus & Hayes, 2000). Hookups sometimes just involve kissing and heavy petting, but about half of them include oral sex or intercourse (especially if people have been drinking), and when sex occurs, condoms are used only about half of the time (Paul & Hayes, 2002). One of the striking things about hookups is that they are not as popular as most people, including the participants, think they are. Both men and women do not enjoy hookups as much as they think other people do, and, in particular, women who have experienced hookups are *un*comfortable with the idea of hookups that involve intercourse or oral sex (Lambert, Kahn, & Apple, 2003). Nevertheless, most students believe that *other* students generally approve of such behavior, and they therefore feel some social pressure to do the same (Hines, Saris, & Throckmorton-Belzer, 2002).

These studies raise a crucial question: Why is it that among well-educated, young Americans, considerable high-risk sex still occurs? There is, of course, no easy answer, but research has suggested some possibilities. First, even if condoms are the method of choice for preventing the transmission of sexually transmitted diseases, people who don't like condoms may not use them, even if they "know better." Some people don't use condoms because they claim that they are unpleasant or uncomfortable, for example (Montano et al., 2001).

This simple statement belies the complexity of people's attitudes about condoms, however. Research has identified a number of different components to these attitudes, and not all components are equally important for understanding who is likely to practice safer sex and who isn't. Susan Campbell and her colleagues (1992) developed a measure that assessed four aspects of condom attitudes: the comfort and convenience of condoms, the effectiveness of condoms for birth control and disease prevention, the interpersonal aspects of condom use, and the effects of condoms on sexual sensation. They found that the college students in their sample were already convinced that condoms were effective for the prevention of pregnancy and disease. Knowing that condoms were effective was not, however, associated with using condoms reliably. Instead, it was the interpersonal dimension that predicted college students' willingness to use a condom. If students believed that using a condom would be embarrassing or would somehow "spoil the mood," they were less likely to intend to use condoms in the future (Campbell et al., 1992). Interpersonal issues are clearly involved in condom use; in particular, young adults tend to think their relationships are closer and more meaningful when they don't use condoms than when they do (Conley & Rabinowitz, 2004). For all of these reasons, experts have argued that condoms need to be viewed as more than a "necessary evil" of sexual relations; further attempts should be made to portray condoms as an expected, desirable part of ordinary sexual interaction (Kyes, Brown, & Pollack, 1991).

A second reason why people often don't use condoms when they should revolves around the potent mixture of sex and alcohol that is commonplace among college populations. When people get drunk, they're less likely to use condoms when they have sex (Morris, 2001), in part because intoxication makes them think that having sex, regardless of the consequences, isn't such a bad idea (MacDonald et al., 2000). This is an example of a phenomenon known as **alcohol myopia,** which involves the reduction of people's abilities to think about and process all of the information available to them when they are drunk (Steele & Josephs, 1990). This limited capacity means that they are able to focus only on the most immediate and salient environmental cues. An attractive partner, then, becomes a cue that elicits sexual arousal, and people who are drunk may not be able to focus on anything but their own arousal, thereby forgetting their own good intentions to use condoms (MacDonald et al., 2000). People who want to avoid high-risk sexual behavior should avoid mixing sex with alcohol.

Another influence on condom use is the **illusion of unique vulnerability**—believing that bad things are more likely to happen to others than to you (Burger & Burns, 1988). This illusion keeps people from taking sensible precautions that would prevent foreseeable dangers because they underestimate their personal risks of victimization. Thus, the less likely people think they are to get infected with HIV, the less likely they are to use condoms (Gerrard & Warner, 1994). This outlook would make some sense if these judgments were accurate, but they typically are not: In general, the *less* people know about HIV and AIDS, the lower they perceive their risks to be, and the less likely they are to protect themselves.

Finally, people's general attitudes influence their practices of safe or unsafe sex. Negative reactions to sex—such as guilt, anxiety, and negative evaluations of sexual situations—seem to make people less likely to use contraceptives (Byrne & Fisher, 1983). Note the irony of these findings. People with negative attitudes toward sex are less likely to have sex, but if they do, they are more likely to have unsafe sex (Fisher, 1986). Why? One reason is that people who are uncomfortable with sex know less about safe-sex practices (Goldfarb et al., 1988); they actively avoid such information, and that puts them at risk. It is also likely that the tendency for men to rely on women to use contraception (Geis & Gerrard, 1984) creates an impression-management problem for women. Women with negative attitudes and feelings toward sex may fear that if they practice contraception or ask a man to use a condom, they will appear overly experienced and eager (Marecek, 1987). Unfortunately, for some people the need to appear sexually naïve may take precedence over their wish to avoid an unwanted pregnancy or a deadly disease.

SEXUAL SATISFACTION

As interesting as it is to consider all the things people *do* in their sexual relationships, it is arguably more important to consider how people *feel* about their sexual relationships. After all, a wife who is having frequent sex with her husband is not likely to be very happy about her sex life if she feels that her specific sexual needs are not being met. How do we assess whether a person is satisfied with his or her sexual relationship? One way is simply to ask people how much physical pleasure they experience with their partners. When asked whether they were "*extremely* physically satisfied with their sexual relationship," nearly half of both the male and female respondents to the National Health and Social Life Survey said they were (Michael et al., 1994). Interestingly, these numbers were somewhat higher for married respondents, particularly married men, than for unmarried men and women. If we include those who reported their sex lives to be at least "*very* physically satisfying," the numbers rise to almost 90 percent (Michael et al., 1994). Other studies have also found married couples to be quite satisfied with the sexual aspects of their relationship (Sprecher & Cate, 2004), suggesting that the stereotype of boring, routine married sex may not be terribly accurate! As we noted earlier, married couples have less frequent sex as time goes by, and their sexual satisfaction tends to decline some in longer relationships, too; happily, however, the decrease in satisfaction is not nearly as dramatic as is the decrease in frequency (Laumann et al., 1994). Indeed, even when intercourse becomes infrequent, couples may engage in other forms of sexual activity that keep them content (Hinchliff & Gott, 2004). Married couples are certainly not the only happy lovers out there, either: Byers, Demmons, and Lawrance (1998) reported very high levels of sexual satisfaction among heterosexual dating couples, and

Kurdek (1991) found that the sexual satisfaction of gay, lesbian, and heterosexual cohabiting couples did not differ from that of married couples.

Sexual Frequency and Satisfaction

Average ratings of sexual satisfaction in relationships are high, but some people are clearly more satisfied than others. What distinguishes those people who have fulfilling sexual relationships from those who don't? You might guess that people who have sex more often are happier with their sex lives, and in general, you'd be right. Sexual satisfaction is closely tied to sexual frequency (Call et al., 1995; Laumann et al., 1994). In one study, 89 percent of husbands and wives who had sex three times a week or more reported that they were satisfied with the quality of their sex lives, whereas only 32 percent of spouses having sex once a month or less felt the same sexual satisfaction (Blumstein & Schwartz, 1983). The same pattern was found among cohabiting heterosexuals, gays, and lesbians, too.

Of course, a positive correlation between frequent sex and sexual satisfaction does not necessarily indicate that having more frequent sex *causes* people to be more satisfied. There are several possibilities, and it's just as likely that people who find sex satisfying choose to have sex more often as it is that frequent sex increases one's sexual satisfaction. Other influences may be at work, as well. Perhaps those who have strong sex drives or permissive sexual attitudes are also more likely *both* to have more frequent sex and to be happy with their sex lives.

Still, it's clear that for most couples, the quality of their sexual interactions is an important feature of the relationship. And while frequent sex is a likely contributor to sexual satisfaction, it's also clear that contentment comes from more than the sexual act itself. This view was echoed by a lesbian woman describing the value of sexual intimacy for herself and her partner:

> It is very important because it is one way of keeping in touch, feeling affectionate, keeping close, staying close. . . . It is not so much the orgasm itself, although I feel this is a wonderful experience. It is the actual being close to each other and touching each other, feeling taken care of and taking care of someone else. (Blumstein & Schwartz, 1983, p. 490)

Sex and Relationship Satisfaction

This woman's comment on the importance of sex as a "relational" experience is echoed by research evidence. Many studies have demonstrated that couples who are happy with their sex lives tend to be happy with their relationships, as well (Sprecher & Cate, 2004). Whether they are married or cohabiting, heterosexual or homosexual, couples who are satisfied with their sexual interactions are also more satisfied with, and committed to, their relationships and more in love with their partners (Kurdek, 1991; Sprecher, 2002).

The relationship between sexual satisfaction and relationship satisfaction is almost certainly bidirectional (Sprecher, 2002). That is, fulfilling sex probably makes a partnership more gratifying, and love for a partner makes sex more rewarding in return. But sexual contentment may also just be a reflection, in part, of a broader friendly compatibility that makes a relationship rewarding in other ways, as well (Sprecher & Cate, 2004). Couples who report higher frequencies of sexual interaction are also likely to share more frequent leisure-time activities such as sports, hobbies, and social events (Birchler & Webb, 1977). Having great sex may have a lot in common with liking to play golf with each other: People who enjoy doing things together (including having sex!) are likely to be happier than those who don't.

In any case, it's clear that, with regard to sex, "overall relationship quality is associated with whether couples have it, how often they have it, and how satisfied they are with it. The amount of time couples engage in genital sexual activity may be very little compared to the time they spend doing other activities together (watching television, eating, sharing household tasks, etc.), but the quality of this time together can impact the rest of the relationship" (Sprecher & Cate, 2004, p. 252).

Interdependency Theory and Sexual Satisfaction

We should also acknowledge that, like any relationship, sex is probably never perfect. There will almost always be some features you really like, some aspects you wish were better, and perhaps a thing or two that you'll want to avoid the next time. In this regard, sex is comprised of a mixture of specific rewards and costs, just like relationships in general, and our global reactions may be determined by comparison levels and comparison levels for alternatives[5] that are similar to the standards with which we evaluate our relationship as a whole (Sprecher, 1998c). Indeed, Kelli-An Lawrance and Sandra Byers (1995) developed an Interpersonal Exchange Model of Sexual Satisfaction that makes just this point. Experiencing more sexual rewards, fewer sexual costs, and having one's expectations favorably met or exceeded are all likely to result in feelings of sexual satisfaction (Byers et al., 1998; Lawrance & Byers, 1995). (Inspect Box 9.4 for a description of some of the sexual rewards and costs identified by women and men). In particular, sexual interactions are more satisfying when they are pleasing and desirable for both participants. Just as we saw in chapter 6, people may be greedy and interested in having their own needs met, but they enjoy sex more when their partners profit, too.

The principles of equity theory have also been used to explain sexual satisfaction. People who perceive their developing relationships to be fair and equitable have sex sooner, and consider their sex to be more rewarding, than do those who feel either underbenefited or overbenefited (Walster, Walster, & Traupmann, 1978). It's better to be overbenefited than underbenefited, of

---

[5]These concepts are detailed back in chapter 6 on pages 183–186.

BOX 9.4
Sexual Costs and Rewards

Interdependency theorists emphasize the importance of costs and rewards for understanding how satisfied people are in their relationships, and the approach applies to sexual satisfaction, as well. Lawrance and Byers (1995) asked men and women in long-term heterosexual relationships to consider a variety of possible rewards and costs from sexual interactions and to indicate which they had experienced with their sexual partner.

What were the most commonly identified sexual rewards? More than 90 percent of both men and women reported that the degree of comfort they felt with their partner was an important reward. Other commonly reported rewards were: "how you feel about yourself during/after sex," "the physical sensations from caressing and hugging," and "the extent to which sexual interactions make you feel secure about the total relationship with your partner" (Lawrance & Byers, 1995). These rewards are interesting because they highlight the multi-faceted nature of sexual experiences, involving an individual's own psychological and physical sensations, as well as the nature of the relationship.

What constitutes a sexual cost? Having sex when you or your partner is not in the mood is a frequently mentioned cost for both women and men. The amount of spontaneity (or lack of it) in sexual activity is another common

cost. The frequency of sexual activity and the amount of time spent in sexual activities were costs reported by many women and men, although whether people were frustrated by getting too much or too little sex was unclear. Regardless, the theme of these costs seems to be mismatched sexual desire and availability, a difficulty that may emerge from sex differences in sexual desire (Lawrance & Byers, 1995).

Men and women were equally likely to report experiencing all of the rewards and costs described thus far. However, the researchers did report some significant sex differences. Women were more likely than men to say that the following constituted sexual rewards for them: "how your partner treats you during sex," "being with the same partner each time you have sex," "how your partner responds to your sexual advances," and "oral sex: your partner stimulates you." Women were also more likely to report experiencing sexual costs such as "how easily you reach orgasm" and "engaging in sexual activities that you dislike, but your partner enjoys" (Lawrance & Byers, 1995). Some of these concerns probably emerge from the more general differences in the sexual attitudes and behaviors of women and men that we have already discussed, and they may provide some clues about how to be a more fulfilling sexual partner.

---

course, and people (especially men) who are profiting too much from their relationships are often quite satisfied with the sex they're having. Nevertheless, on the whole, the greatest sexual contentment is reported by those who feel that both they and their partners are prospering to an extent that is just, reasonable, and fair (Hatfield et al., 1982).

Overall, then, studies of sexual satisfaction point out that the amount and frequency of the sex partners share is not some kind of magical ingredient that automatically makes a relationship fulfilling. Good sex also seems to depend on:

- Each person having his or her needs met by a partner who respects the other's specific sexual desires.
- Having the proper balance of positive and negative interactions (sexual and nonsexual) in the relationship, so that there are more positives than negatives.
- Enjoying being with each other, in bed and out of it.

SEXUAL COMMUNICATION

There is clearly a close connection between sex and relationship quality and functioning. And like other relationship issues, sex that is satisfying and meaningful for both partners requires honest and trusting communication. But sexual communication often presents couples with special problems. Many of us are not very comfortable talking about sex. Too many children are taught that sexual language and terminology is "dirty," and many adults avoid extensive or detailed sexual discussions with children. So we often grow up without a comfortable vocabulary for talking openly about sex. And things are made even more complicated by our concern about how a partner will respond to sexual talk. Will he or she be offended by an attempt at sexual communication? If a couple hasn't yet had sex, bringing up the issue of sex risks the embarrassment of discovering that one's partner isn't even interested (de Graaf & Sandfort, 2004).

Communicating Desire

Perhaps the most basic aspect of sexual communication involves conveying sexual desire to one's partner. Because sexual desire can be communicated effectively without words (e.g., by initiating a kiss or unbuttoning a partner's clothes), it may be the most common form of sexual communication (Metts, Sprecher & Regan, 2000). The meaning of some nonverbal strategies is fairly clear, while others may be somewhat ambiguous. One study found that 60 percent of couples reported using fairly direct nonverbal techniques such as kissing or touching to communicate their desire for sex (Brown & Auerback, 1981). Another study asked college students to describe how they communicate sexual intent and interest to a partner, and responses included much less direct nonverbal strategies, such as good grooming and dressing attractively (Greer & Buss, 1994). The disadvantage of such strategies is obvious: what may be intended to convey sexual interest may be interpreted as neatness and an eye for fashion!

Of course, being direct about our sexual feelings requires that we *know* how we feel—and sometimes we may not be sure of our own desires, or we may not have strong feelings one way or the other. Most people experience ambivalence about engaging in sexual activity at one time or another, and they deal with it in various ways (O'Sullivan & Gaines, 1998). Some straightforwardly tell their partners that they're not sure they want to have sex. More often, however, people either feign interest in having sex or reject their partner's advances, despite their uncertainty about their own feelings (O'Sullivan & Gaines, 1998). The fact that people often avoid telling potential partners exactly how they feel is probably a measure of how vulnerable people are in sexual situations: We opt for indirect communication because we don't want to risk rejection or risk hurting our partner's feelings.

Vulnerable or not, men are more likely than women to initiate sexual activity (Impett & Peplau, 2003), and after a move is made, it is up to the other partner to indicate his or her consent (or lack of consent). How is consent communicated? This type of sexual communication can be a simple matter—all that's required is a straightforward "Yes, I'd like to have sex"—but research suggests that these communications are often fairly complex. Young adults report a wide variety of strategies for communicating sexual consent, but the most common strategy for both sexes is just to not resist a partner's initiation; in other words, instead of conveying consent by saying yes, people often just don't say no (Hickman & Muehlenhard, 1999). Some strategies are more likely to be used by one sex than the other. Women are more likely to use indirect verbal strategies, such as asking a partner if he has a condom, whereas men are more likely to use indirect nonverbal strategies, such as kissing or touching a partner. These stylistic differences are fairly small, however, and men and women generally tend to communicate consent, without saying anything, in similar ways (Hickman & Muehlenhard, 1999).

Communicating about sex sometimes requires that we do more than let a partner know whether or not we're interested. Sometimes we need to discuss particular sexual issues: "Would you like to try a different position?" "How many sexual partners have you had?" or "Do you like oral sex?" Not surprisingly, research confirms that people often have difficulty discussing such things (Fisher et al., 1980). Most young adults do discuss sexual issues now and then, but they say less to their partners about their sexual tastes and histories than they disclose about non-sexual preferences (Byers & Demmons, 1999). Still, sexual self-disclosure is just like other forms of self-disclosure in being fuller and more intimate when it is reciprocated by one's partner. People are most comfortable talking honestly about sex if their partners do the same (Byers & Demmons, 1999).

Sexual Communication and Satisfaction

Well, do we really need to talk about sex? Can't we just rely on prolonged eye contact or an appropriately-timed moan to communicate with a sexual partner? Indirect strategies like these may seem easier in the short run, but it's wasteful if we never talk honestly, fearlessly, and openly with our partners about our sexual likes and dislikes, for one very big reason: Clear communication about sex is associated with greater satisfaction with sex (Sprecher & Cate, 2004). People who talk candidly about sex have more fulfilling sexual interactions with their partners than do those who just grunt and moan now and then.

The famous sex researchers William Masters and Virginia Johnson (1970) highlighted the importance of good sexual communication in a provocative study that compared the sexual experiences of heterosexuals and homosexuals. The researchers observed couples having sex, interviewed them extensively, and concluded that the subjective quality of the sexual experience—including psychological involvement, responsiveness to the needs and desires of the partner, and enjoyment of each aspect of the sexual experience—was actually greater for gays and lesbians than it was for heterosexuals. Homosexuals were having better sex. Masters and Johnson noted that one advantage of the sexual interactions shared by gays and lesbians was that both participants were of the same sex; as a result, knowing what they liked themselves, homosexuals could reasonably predict what their partners might like, too. However, Masters and Johnson argued that the primary foundation for the rewarding, high-quality sex shared by homosexuals was good communication. Gays and lesbians talked more easily and openly about their sexual feelings than heterosexuals did. They would ask each other what was desired, provide feedback on what felt good, and generally guide their lovers on how to please them. In contrast, heterosexual couples exhibited a "persistent neglect of the vital communicative exchange" and a "potentially self-destructive lack of intellectual curiosity about the partner" (Masters & Johnson, 1970, p. 219).

Better communication may also help people manage situations in which they do not want to have sex and their intentions are being misunderstood. You may have already learned the hard way that women and men sometimes interpret sexual situations differently, and frustration or antagonism can result (de Graaf & Sandfort, 2004). Men have stronger sexual desires than women do, and they're literally thinking about sex more often than women are, so they tend to read sexual interest into innocent behavior from women who have no sexual intentions (Haselton, 2002). This was first demonstrated in a classic study by Antonia Abbey (1982), who invited men and women to get acquainted with each other, chatting one-on-one, while another man and another woman observed their conversation. Both the men participating in the interactions and those watching them tended to interpret friendliness from the women as signs of sexual interest, even when the women, both those doing the talking and those looking on, had no wish to be sexually provocative. The men literally perceived signs of sexual flirtatiousness that were not intended and that probably did not exist.

Men are more prone to make such mistakes when they have been drinking (Jacques et al., 2004), but consider the implications. Imagine that Barney and Betty are out together for the first time. They've had a couple of beers, and Barney believes that the way Betty is glancing up at his face, playing with her hair, and "accidentally" brushing his arm with hers is Betty's way of communicating sexual desire. Betty, on the other hand, is preoccupied with the piece of spinach she just noticed in Barney's teeth, she's having trouble with the piece of hair that keeps falling into her face, and she is chastising herself for clumsily bumping into him. Barney's misreading of her signals could lead to awkward or unpleasant consequences. And, as we'll see in the next section, these differences in interpretation may conceivably contribute to sexual violence, especially date rape. Even if the consequences are not so severe, however, there's no question that people and their relationships benefit from honest, forthright communication about sexual desires and intentions.

SEXUAL AGGRESSION

We have focused thus far almost exclusively on the positive aspects of sexual interaction. But, of course, not all sexual experiences are satisfying, or even wanted. Sadly, unwanted sexual experiences are all too common. Exact statistics differ from study to study depending in part on the questions asked and the samples studied, but Cate and Lloyd (1992, p. 99) concluded that "fully one half to three fourths of college women report experiencing some type of sexual aggression in dating relationships."

What forms does sexual aggression take? In a meta-analysis of 120 studies involving over 100,000 participants, Spitzberg (1999) examined five different types of sexual aggression. These were:

- *Rape:* Penile penetration via the use or threat of force;
- *Attempted rape:* unsuccessful rape attempts;
- *Sexual assault:* use of objects such as the penis or tongue to penetrate any orifices (oral, anal, vaginal) via force or threat of force;
- *Sexual contact:* unwanted sexual play, kissing, rubbing, disrobing and the like (but not penetration) obtained through force, threat of force, continued arguments or authority; and
- *Sexual coercion:* intercourse obtained by "symbolic means" such as authority or persistent arguments.

Overall (see Table 9.2), about 13 percent of the women and 3 percent of the men in these various studies reported having been raped; 18 percent of women and 6 percent of men said they had been the victims of a rape attempt; and

TABLE 9.2. Statistical Summary of Sexual Aggression Estimates across 120 Different Studies

	Female Victimization	Female Perpetration	Male Victimization	Male Perpetration
	Mean Percent	Mean Percent	Mean Percent	Mean Percent
Rape	12.9	3	3.3	4.7
Attempted Rape	18.3	—	5.6	10.8
Sexual Assault	22.0	6.0	14.2	8.9
Sexual Contact	24.0	8.8	7.9	13.4
Sexual Coercion	25.0	29.0	23.2	24.1

Note: No value is listed for a woman's attempted rape of a man because no study examined that behavior.
Source: Spitzberg, 1999.

22 percent of women and 14 percent of men reported having been sexually assaulted. And close inspection of Table 9.2 supports three general conclusions. First, men were more likely than women to report having engaged in sexually aggressive behavior. Second, women were more often victims than perpetrators. And third, on most of the measures, the percentage of women who said they had been victims of aggression was higher than the percentage of men who acknowledged having been perpetrators. It is possible that a small number of men are coercive toward a larger number of women, but it's more likely that this difference is one instance of a common pattern: Perpetrators underestimate the force they use and the harm they do (Baumeister & Tice, 2001).

Because men initiate sexual activity more often than women do, and because people often signal sexual consent indirectly (sometimes by not saying anything, yes or no!), men often face the tricky judgment of whether their partners are really accepting their invitations. And a regrettable complication is that women sometimes offer token resistance to sex by initially saying no when they really mean yes; one survey of hundreds of undergraduate women found that more than a third of them had engaged in token resistance at least once in the past (Muehlenhard & Hollabaugh, 1988). In such cases, their partners may have been rewarded if they ignored the women's apparent reluctance and persisted in their pursuit of sex. Now, of course, on any one occasion, the vast majority of women (and men) who say no really mean no, and they do not want sex to occur (Muehlenhard & Rodgers, 1998). Nevertheless, cultural pressures, including the sexual double standard, sometimes encourage men to continue to press for sex even when their partners seem hesitant.

And the lack of sufficient communication that pervades our sexual interactions promotes misunderstanding. There is nothing subtle about rape. When a person is confronted with a gun, a knife, or a fist and told to submit sexually, this is clearly rape, whether it occurs on a date, in a marriage, or in a back alley. But coercion is not always so clear-cut, and miscommunication makes things worse. A woman can feel physically forced when the man believes he is only being appropriately assertive. And a man can believe that a woman has "led him on" to a point where he should not be expected to stop. Or perhaps he really believes that she has communicated her desire for sex, even if she hasn't. A serious problem on many college campuses today, date rape, sometimes results, in part, from genuine confusion and misunderstanding.

We certainly do not wish to characterize rape as a mere problem of communication gone awry. On the other hand, there is no doubt that better sexual communication and decision making can only help to decrease the risk of sexual aggression. If you put two young people with healthy sexual appetites together with some alcohol, inadequate understanding of each other's concerns, and a fair amount of insecurity about their own self-worth, you may have a situation ready-made for date rape. But what if we change that scenario? What if both people agree in advance that each of them has veto power over sex? Could date rape be reduced if dating partners fully accepted that no really does mean no and puts an end to the discussion? Perhaps so. Open communication about a woman's preferences decreases the likelihood that men will pressure her for sexual activity (Muehlenhard, Andres, & Beal, 1995). However, so long as we regard male sexual activity as a form of conquest, encourage women to "play" hard-to-get, and feel embarrassed by honest talk with a sexual partner, it will be difficult to disentangle problems of power and violence from issues of sexual communication and responsibility.

FOR YOUR CONSIDERATION

Chad was in love with Jennifer. He felt a lot of sexual desire for her, and he always enjoyed having sex with her, but he still felt something was missing. She was usually glad to have sex, and she seemed to enjoy it, too, but she rarely took any initiative and he typically did all the work. She usually just lay there, and he wanted her to be more active and take the lead now and then. He wished that she would be more inventive, and he wanted her to work him over occasionally. Nevertheless, he didn't say anything. Their sex was good, if not great, and he worried that any complaints would make things worse, not better, between them.

What do you think the future holds for Chad and Jennifer? Why?

CHAPTER SUMMARY

Sexual Attitudes

Attitudes about Casual Sex. People's attitudes about sex have generally become more permissive over time. Today, most people endorse a "permissiveness-with-affection" standard that is accepting of nonmarital sex in the context of an affectionate relationship. Men are somewhat more likely than women to approve of sex outside of such a relationship, but this difference has decreased over time. Still, there may be an enduring tendency, a *sexual double standard*, to judge women's sexuality more harshly than men's.

Attitudes about Same-Sex Sexuality. Americans are becoming more tolerant of homosexuality as time goes by, but their attitudes about homosexuality are more negative than their attitudes about casual sex. Nevertheless, the more contact people have with gays and lesbians, the more favorable their feelings toward homosexuals tend to be.

Cultural Differences in Sexual Attitudes. Despite increasing permissiveness among Americans, sexual attitudes in the United States are relatively conservative compared to those expressed by people in other countries. This is true for attitudes about sex before marriage, sex before the age of sixteen, extramarital sex, and homosexual sex.

Sexual Behavior

Premarital Sex. Large majorities of American men and women have sex before they turn 20. Young people have many different motives for engaging in and avoiding sexual activity, and many of these reasons are tied to the nature of their relationships (e.g., wanting to please a partner or express their love and affection). Researchers have identified a number of predictors of the age at which adolescents first engage in sex, including an individual's values, a desire to become more "adult," and family structure, among others.

Sex in Committed Relationships. The frequency with which people have sex depends on several factors. Relationship status, age, sexual orientation, and duration of the relationship may all be influential. Spouses have sex more often than singles do, but the frequency with which people have sex drops sharply as people age.

Monogamy. Despite general disapproval of extradyadic sex, a sizable minority of people—about one out of every five wives and one out of three husbands—cheat on their primary partners during their lifetimes. Men are more likely than women, and gay men are more likely than heterosexual men, to have extradyadic sex. One's *sociosexual orientation*, which describes one's comfort with casual sex, also predicts who will cheat and who will not, and people who feel that their relationships are fair are less likely to be unfaithful.

Sexual Desire. Men have higher *sex drives* than women do. They experience more frequent and more intense sexual desires, and are routinely more motivated to engage in sexual activity than women are. This may lead to misunderstanding or annoyance as heterosexual couples negotiate their sexual interactions. It also puts women into the position of being the gatekeepers who decide when sex occurs.

Preventing Pregnancy and Sexually Transmitted Infections. *Hookups* are common on college campuses, and participants use condoms only about half the time when intercourse occurs. Whether or not people practice safer sex is influenced by interpersonal obstacles to condom use, the influence of alcohol on sexual decision making, beliefs of personal invulnerability, and negative attitudes about sex.

Sexual Satisfaction

Sexual Frequency and Satisfaction. Most people report generally high levels of sexual satisfaction, and this is particularly true for people who have sex more often.

Sex and Relationship Satisfaction. Partners who are satisfied with their sex lives tend to be more satisfied with their relationships, in general. The relationship between sexual satisfaction and relationship satisfaction is almost certainly bidirectional. That is, fulfilling sex probably makes a partnership more gratifying, and love for a partner makes sex more rewarding in return.

Interdependency Theory and Sexual Satisfaction. An Interpersonal Exchange Model of Sexual Satisfaction focuses on an individual's sexual costs, rewards, and expectations as predictors of sexual satisfaction. Equity theory predicts that a lack of equity (especially if one is the underbenefited partner) is associated with less sexual satisfaction, and indeed, most people are happiest when their partners are satisfied, too.

Sexual Communication

Communicating Desire. Communication of sexual desire is often nonverbal and indirect. Men are more likely than women to initiate sex, and both sexes use a variety of strategies to indicate a willingness to engage in sexual activity. Talking about specific sexual issues, particularly sexual problems and tastes, is often difficult for sexual partners. As a result, the most common strategy for both sexes is just to not resist a partner's initiation; in other words, instead of conveying consent by saying yes, people often just don't say no.

Sexual Communication and Satisfaction. Direct and honest sexual communication is associated with greater relationship and sexual satisfaction. Because homosexuals often talk more easily and openly about their preferences than heterosexuals do, they often enjoy sex that is more gratifying and rewarding than that shared by heterosexuals.

Sexual Aggression

Sexual violence is frighteningly common. Researchers have identified a variety of forms of sexual aggression, and women are more likely than men to be the victims of such aggression. There is debate about whether sexual miscommunication plays a role in the incidence of sexual aggression, but there is no doubt that men tend to read sexual interest into innocent behavior from women who have no sexual intentions.

PART FOUR

Relationship Issues

CHAPTER 10

Stresses and Strains

RELATIONAL EVALUATION ◆ HURT FEELINGS ◆ OSTRACISM ◆ JEALOUSY ◆ Two Types of Jealousy? ◆ Who's Prone to Jealousy? ◆ Who Gets Us Jealous? ◆ What Gets Us Jealous? ◆ Responses to Jealousy ◆ Coping Constructively with Jealousy ◆ DECEPTION AND LYING ◆ Lying in Close and Casual Relationships ◆ Lies and Liars ◆ So, How Well Can We Detect a Partner's Deception? ◆ BETRAYAL ◆ Individual Differences in Betrayal ◆ The Two Sides to Every Betrayal ◆ Coping with Betrayal ◆ FORGIVENESS ◆ FOR YOUR CONSIDERATION ◆ CHAPTER SUMMARY

Let's pause for a moment and take stock. In previous chapters, we have discussed adaptive and maladaptive cognition, good and bad communication, and rewarding and unrewarding social exchange. Until now, we have given equal time to both beneficial and disadvantageous influences on close relationships. But not here. In this chapter, we'll concentrate on various pitfalls, stumbling blocks, and hazards that cause wear and tear in relationships. And importantly, the stresses and strains we cover here—hurt feelings, ostracism, jealousy, lying, and betrayal—are commonplace events that occur in most relationships somewhere along the way. We've all had our feelings hurt (Vangelisti, 2004), and sooner or later, almost everyone lies to their intimate partners (DePaulo et al., 1996). Even outright betrayals of one sort or another are surprisingly widespread and hard to avoid (Baxter et al., 1997).

However, the fact that these incidents are commonplace doesn't mean they are inconsequential. Negative events like these can be just as influential as—and sometimes even more powerful than—the rewards people get from their relationships (Rook, 1998). They help explain why most of us report having had a very troublesome relationship within the last five years (Levitt et al., 1996). And despite their idiosyncrasies, all of these unhappy events may share a common theme (Leary & Springer, 2001): They suggest that we are not as well-liked or well-respected as we wish we were.

RELATIONAL EVALUATION

Fueled by our need to belong,[1] most of us care deeply about what our intimate partners think of us. We want them to want us. We want them to value our company and to consider their partnerships with us to be valuable and important.

[1]Need a reminder about the human need to belong? Look back at p. 6 in chapter 1.

TABLE 10.1. Degrees of Acceptance and Rejection

Being accepted or rejected by others is not an all-or-nothing event. People can desire our company to greater or lesser degrees, and researchers use these labels to describe the different extents to which we may be included or excluded by others.

Maximal inclusion	Others seek us out and go out of their way to interact with us
Active inclusion	Others welcome us but do not seek us out
Passive inclusion	Others allow us to be included
Ambivalence	Others do not care whether we are included or not
Passive exclusion	Others ignore us but do not avoid us
Active exclusion	Others avoid us, tolerating our presence only when necessary
Maximal exclusion	Others banish us, sending us away, or abandon us

Note. Adapted from Leary, 1990.

We want our partners to evaluate their relationships with us positively, and sometimes, we want that relationship to be very meaningful and close. As a result, according to theorist Mark Leary (2002), it's painful to perceive that others' **relational evaluation**—that is, the degree to which they consider their relationships with us to be valuable, important, or close—is lower than we would like it to be.

Over time, we're likely to encounter various degrees of acceptance and rejection in our dealings with others, and Leary (2001b) has suggested that they can be arranged along the continuum described in Table 10.1. At the extreme of *maximal inclusion*, people seek our company and don't want to have a party unless we can come. They are somewhat less accepting, but still positively inclined toward us, when they offer us *active inclusion*: They invite us to the party and are glad we can come. However, their acceptance is more passive when they don't invite us to the party but admit us if we show up, and they are *ambivalent*, neither accepting nor rejecting, when they genuinely don't care one way or the other whether we show up or not.

If we want others to like us and want us, noncommittal ambivalence from them may be bad enough, but things can get worse. We encounter *passive exclusion* when others ignore us and wish we were elsewhere, and we suffer *active exclusion* when others go out of their way to avoid us altogether. However, the worst rejection occurs when, in *maximal exclusion*, others order us to leave their parties when they find us there. In such instances, merely avoiding us won't do; they want us gone.

Our emotional reactions to such experiences depend on how much we want to be accepted by particular others, and just what their acceptance or rejection of us means (Leary & Rice, 2004). On occasion, people exclude us because they regard us positively, and rejections like those are much less painful than are exclusions that result from our deficiencies or faults. Consider the game show, *Survivor*: Contestants sometimes try to vote the most skilled, most able competitors off the island to increase their personal chances of winning the game. Being excluded because you're better than everyone else may not hurt much, but rejection that suggests that you're inept, insufficient, or inadequate usually does (Leary & Rice, 2004).

In addition, it's not much of a blow to be excluded from a party you didn't want to attend in the first place. Exclusion is much more painful when we want to be accepted by others than when we don't much care what they think of us. Indeed, it's also possible to be accepted and liked by others but be hurt because they don't like us as much as we want them to. This is what unrequited love (Baumeister & Dhavale, 2001; see Box 8.2) is often like; those for whom we feel unrequited love may be fond of us in return, but if we want to be loved instead of merely liked, their mildness is painful.

All of these possibilities suggest that there is only a rough connection between the objective acceptance or rejection we receive from others and our *feelings* of acceptance or rejection that result, so we will focus on the *perception that others value their relationships with us less than we want them to* as a core ingredient of the stresses and strains that we will inspect in this chapter (Leary, 2001b). We feel hurt when the relational evaluations we perceive from others are lower than we wish they were.

HURT FEELINGS

In fact, the feelings of acceptance or rejection we experience in our dealings with others is related to their evaluations of us in a complex way: Maximal exclusion doesn't feel much worse than simple ambivalence does (Buckley, Winkel, & Leary, 2004). Take a careful look at Figure 10.1. The graph depicts people's reactions to evaluations from others that vary across a 10-point scale. Maximal exclusion is described by the worst possible evaluation, a 1, and maximal inclusion is described by the best possible evaluation, a 10; ambivalence, the point at which others don't care about us one way or the other, is the 5 at the midpoint of the scale. The graph demonstrates that once we find that others don't want us around, it hardly matters whether they dislike us a little or a lot: Our momentary judgments of our self-worth bottom out when people reject us to any extent (that is, when their evaluations range from 4 down to 1).

On the other hand, when it comes to acceptance, being completely adored doesn't improve our self-esteem beyond the boost we get from being very well-liked. Instead, we appear to be more sensitive to small differences in regard from others that range from ambivalence at the low end to active inclusion at the high end. As people like us more and more, we feel better and better about ourselves until their positive regard for us is fully assured. This all makes sense from an evolutionary perspective (Leary et al., 1998); carefully discerning degrees of acceptance that might allow access to resources and mates is more useful than monitoring the enmity of one's enemies. (After all, when it comes to reactions from potential mates, there are usually few practical differences between mild distaste and outright disgust!)

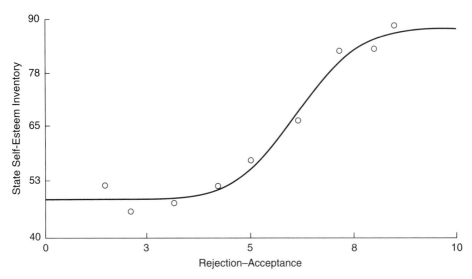

FIGURE 10.1. Reactions to acceptance and rejection.
This curve describes how our momentary feelings about ourselves map onto the treatment we receive from others. Self-esteem increases sharply as people move from being ambivalent about us to wanting us around, but any rejection at all causes our self-esteem to bottom out. When people prefer to ignore us, we feel nearly as badly about ourselves as we do when they order us to leave or throw us out.
Source: Leary, Haupt, Strausser, & Chokel, 1998.

So, mild rejection from others usually feels just as bad as more extreme rejection does. But *increases* in any rejection we receive from others may have a greater impact, particularly when they occur in that range between ambivalence and active inclusion—that is, when people who liked us once appear to like us less now (Leary & Rice, 2004). Mark Leary and his colleagues demonstrated the potent impact of decreases in acceptance when they manipulated the evaluations research participants received from new acquaintances (Buckley et al., 2004). As young adults talked about themselves to another person over an intercom system, they received intermittent approval ratings on a computer screen (see Figure 10.2); the ratings supposedly came from their conversation partner, but they were actually controlled by the experimenters, who provided one of four patterns of feedback. Some people received consistent acceptance, receiving only 5's and 6's, whereas others encountered constant rejection, receiving only 2's and 3's. It's painful to be disliked by others, so of course, those who were accepted by the unseen acquaintance were happier and felt better about themselves than those who were rejected. But other people received evaluations that changed over time, starting poorly and getting better, or starting well and getting worse. In the latter case, over a span of 5 minutes, the research participants received successive ratings of 6, 5, 3, 3, and 2; apparently, as the new acquaintance got to know them better, the less they were liked.

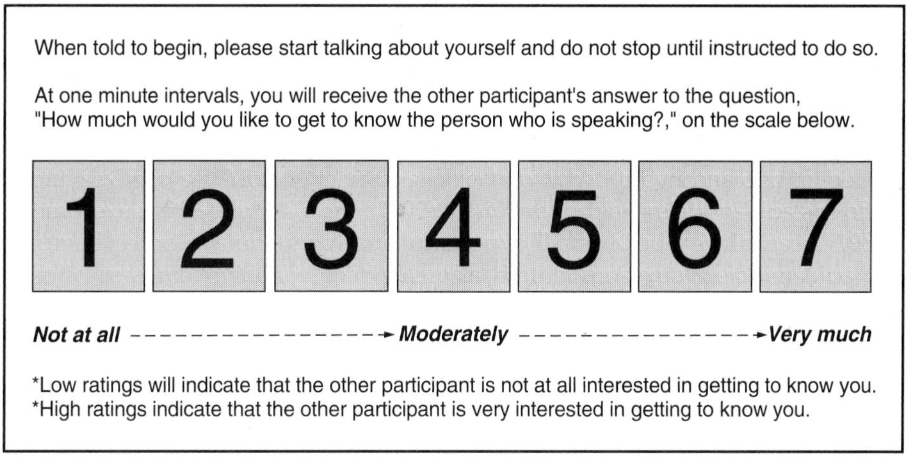

When told to begin, please start talking about yourself and do not stop until instructed to do so.

At one minute intervals, you will receive the other participant's answer to the question, "How much would you like to get to know the person who is speaking?," on the scale below.

| 1 | 2 | 3 | 4 | 5 | 6 | 7 |

Not at all ----------------→ **Moderately** ---------------→**Very much**

*Low ratings will indicate that the other participant is not at all interested in getting to know you.
*High ratings indicate that the other participant is very interested in getting to know you.

FIGURE 10.2. Relational devaluation in the lab.
Imagine that as you describe yourself to someone in another room, you receive evaluations that start high, but get worse and worse over time. After five minutes, the other person is giving you a "2" that indicates that he or she is quite uninterested in meeting you. How would you feel?
Source: Leary, 2004.

The pattern of increasing rejection was particularly painful, causing more negative reactions than even constant rejection did (Buckley et al., 2004). Evidently, it's especially awful to experience **relational devaluation**—that is, apparent decreases in others' regard for us—and it causes a variety of unhappy emotions. When their partners turned against them, people felt sad, angry, and *hurt*, with the latter emotion being a particular sensation that is uniquely associated with low relational evaluation (Leary, 2003). A variety of studies have examined hurt feelings, and they generally agree that such feelings are much like the emotions that accompany physical pain (Eisenberger, Lieberman, & Williams, 2003; Vangelisti, 2004); when people's feelings are hurt, they feel psychologically wounded and despondent. People who are hurt often also experience other emotions such as anger and anxiety, but the sense of injury that characterize hurt feelings—the feeling that one has been damaged, shattered, cut, or stabbed—makes hurt feelings a distinct emotional experience (Feeney, 2005).

When relational devaluation occurs, some people experience more hurt than others do. People who have high levels of anxiety over abandonment,[2] who nervously fret that others don't want them, experience more hurt in response to a decrease in acceptance than those with lower anxiety do. And people who are high in avoidance of intimacy experience less hurt when others withdraw; exclusion hurts less when you don't want to be close to others to begin with (Feeney, 2005). People's levels of self-esteem matter, too: People with

[2]Remember the two dimensions that shape attachment styles? Look back at p. 264 in chapter 8.

low self-esteem get their feelings hurt more easily than those with higher self-regard do (Nezlek et al., 1997).

In fact, self-esteem may be an important predictor of how people respond to potent experiences of rejection, such as ostracism. We can also detail the interpersonal effects of hurt feelings more fully when we examine what happens when people are ignored or given the "silent treatment."

OSTRACISM

A specific form of rejection that often occurs even in close relationships is **ostracism,** in which people are given the "cold shoulder" and ignored by those around them. When the silent treatment is intentional, ostracizers deliberately refrain from responding to others, sometimes pretending that their targets are not even present. Most of us have experienced ostracism; in one broad survey, 67 percent of Americans admitted that they had given an intimate partner the cold shoulder, and 75 percent reported that they had received such treatment from a loved one (Williams, 2001).

Why do people sometimes intentionally ignore their partners? Ostracizers usually justify their actions as an effective way to punish their partners, to avoid confrontation, or to calm down and cool off following a conflict, and they usually believe that the ostracism was beneficial in helping them achieve their goals (Sommer et al., 2001). But by its very nature, ostracism often leaves its targets wondering why they are being ignored (Williams, 2001). Only rarely is an explanation offered when a partner remains silent, and the victims of ostracism often have no idea why it is happening. They only know that they are being rejected, and they are more often angry, frustrated, and hurt than guilty and contrite (Sommer et al., 2001). As a result, the targets of ostracism typically do not consider their partners' withdrawal to be a kind or effective way to behave, and they rarely believe that the ostracism has improved their relationships.

Indeed, people often become defensive and antagonistic when they are ostracized. Interpersonal rejection causes people to derogate those who exclude them, so that we tend to dismiss the opinions of those who ostracize us as unfounded, illegitimate, and dim-witted (Bourgeois & Leary, 2001). Worse, rejection also sometimes causes people to become less generous and charitable toward others in general, so that those who feel excluded are more often surly and aggressive (even toward innocent bystanders) than cowed and compliant (Tice, Twenge, & Schmeichel, 2002). In fact, instances of ostracism or romantic rejection precede most of the awful cases in which students take guns to school and shoot their classmates (Leary et al., 2003). Victims of ostracism do not always lash out at others; sometimes they work hard to regain others' regard, being compliant and doing what their ostracizers want (Williams, 2001). But if they feel that there is little chance that others will ever accept them, aggression is a likely outcome.

Researchers who study ostracism have developed a variety of ingenious procedures to create potent experiences of rejection in the lab. After short introductions to strangers, people have learned that no one wanted to work with them (Leary, 2002), and others have been ignored in face-to-face discussions or Internet chat rooms run by research assistants (Williams, 2001). But an inspired procedure created by Kipling Williams and his colleagues that involves a simple game of catch is especially nefarious (Williams & Zadro, 2001). If you encounter this procedure, you'll find yourself sitting for five minutes with two other people who begin playfully tossing and bouncing a racquetball back and forth. You've all just met, and you're all just passing time, waiting for an experimenter to return; so, the first minute of play, in which you frequently receive the ball, is pretty lighthearted. But then things change. Over the next four minutes, nobody tosses you the ball. The two other people gleefully toss the ball between themselves and completely ignore you, neither looking your way nor acknowledging any protest. It's as if you have ceased to exist.

Researchers have even conducted studies of ostracism online, and thousands of people around the world have now encountered a variation of the ball-tossing procedure on the Web (Williams, Cheung, & Choi, 2000). In this version, people believe that they are online with two other people, represented by screen icons, who are sending a Cyberball back and forth by clicking each other's icons. What happens next is all controlled by the computer program and there really aren't any other people involved, but as in real life, after a few warm-up throws, participants are partially or fully excluded from the "tossing" of the ball. What's striking is that this Internet ostracism is quite painful even when it is (apparently) dispensed by strangers one will never meet. In fact, even after people learn that their exclusion is controlled by the computer and that no real interpersonal evaluation is even remotely involved, they still get their feelings hurt when the computer program fails to toss them the ball (Zadro, Williams, & Richardson, 2004)! Our species seems to be quite sensitive to even the merest hint of social rejection.

Studies of this sort have demonstrated that rejection is painful because it threatens basic social needs (Williams, 2001). In undermining our attachments to others, the silent treatment threatens the need to belong, damages feelings of self-worth, and reduces our perceived control over our interactions. And when they face interpersonal rejection, people become stupid, selfish, and impulsive (Baumeister, Twenge, & Ciarocco, 2002). They do more poorly on intelligence tests (Baumeister, Twenge, & Nuss, 2002) and make poorer, more self-defeating choices (Twenge, Catanese, & Baumeister, 2002). Time even seems to slow down and pass more slowly; in one study in which they were asked to estimate how much time had passed during a 40-second interval, people who felt accepted by others offered an average (and quite accurate) estimate of 42 seconds, whereas those who felt rejected believed that 64 seconds had passed (Twenge, Catanese, & Baumeister, 2003). In general, it appears that rejection causes people to enter a lethargic state of mind in which rational planning and complex thought is reduced.

So, ostracism is an obnoxious, unpleasant experience that is just as likely to engender hostility as compliance. And people with high self-esteem are relatively unlikely to put up with it. When they encounter a cold shoulder, people with high self-regard are more likely than those with lower self-esteem to end their relationships with their ostracizers and to seek new partners who will treat them better—and perhaps as a result, they get the silent treatment less often (Sommer, 2001). In comparison, people with low self-esteem experience more ostracism, and they are more likely to carry a grudge and to ostracize others in return (Sommer, 2001). Instead of leaving those who ostracize them, people with low self-regard are more likely to hang around but be spiteful.

In sum, then, we are likely to feel sadness, anger, and hurt when others ostracize us, and a core ingredient in such experiences seems to be the perception that those others do not value their relationships with us as much as we wish they did. Let's turn now to the special kind of relational devaluation that occurs when we believe that a romantic rival is luring a beloved partner away.

JEALOUSY

A different kind of negative emotional experience results from the potential loss of a valued relationship to a real or imagined rival (Salovey, 1991). **Jealousy** often involves a variety of feelings, ranging all the way from sad dejection to actual pride that one's partner is desirable to others, but the three feelings that define jealousy best are *hurt, anger,* and *fear* (Guerrero, 2004; Guerrero & Andersen, 1998b).[3]

Hurt follows from the perception that our partners do not value us enough to honor their commitments to our relationships, and fear and anxiety result from the dreadful prospect of abandonment and loss (Guerrero & Andersen, 1998a). But it's not just the painful loss of a rewarding partnership that creates jealousy; people suffer when they lose a relationship for any reason, ranging from a partner's move overseas to take a wonderful job, to the partner's accidental death. The unique element in jealousy is the romantic rival who threatens to lure a partner away: "To be jealous, one must have a relationship to lose and a rival to whom to lose it" (DeSteno & Salovey, 1994, p. 220). It's being cast aside for someone else that gets people angry (Mathes, Adams, & Davies, 1985), and unless the rival is a friend who is also thought to be guilty of a personal betrayal, most of that anger is directed at the partner who is beginning to stray (Paul, Foss, & Galloway, 1993). Sometimes that anger turns violent; 13 percent of all the murders in the United States result from one spouse killing another, and when that occurs, jealousy is the most common motive (Buss, 2000).

Obviously, jealousy is an unhappy experience. It appears to be a common experience around the world, however (Buss et al., 1999), and it has even been

---

[3]Jealousy is sometimes confused with envy, but the two are quite different (Parrott & Smith, 1993). We envy someone when we wish we had what they have; envy is characterized by a humiliating longing for another person's possessions. In contrast, jealousy is the confused state of hurt, anger, and fear that results from the threat of losing what we already have, a relationship that we do not wish to give up.

observed in children under two years of age (when their mothers ignored them to play with other children; Masciuch & Kienapple, 1993). Moreover, our cultural reactions to jealousy are not always negative. An analysis of magazine articles from 1945 to 1985 demonstrated that back in the 1950s and 1960s, jealousy was usually considered to prove one's love and to be good for a marriage (Clanton, 1989). In the 1970s and 1980s, the typical view changed to depict jealousy as an improper, unhealthy state born of insecurity and personality defects. In the twenty-first century, our ambivalence continues, with jealousy seeming to be "a two-edged sword—an expression of love on the one hand, of perceived paranoia on the other" (Guerrero & Andersen, 1998a, p. 40). Remarkably, most people still think that a man who hits or abuses his wife out of jealousy loves her just as much as one who never abuses his wife at all (Puente & Cohen, 2003). And if anything, people may be more prone to jealousy than they used to be. In the 1990s, both homosexual and heterosexual men reported more jealousy at the thought of a lover having sex with someone else than did men surveyed 12 years earlier (Bringle, 1995).

Given that, here's an interesting question: How would you feel if you *couldn't* make your lover jealous? Would you be disappointed if nothing you did gave your partner a jealous twinge? Most people probably would be, but whether or not that's a sensible point of view may depend on what type of jealousy we're talking about, why your partner is jealous, and what your partner does in response to his or her jealousy. Let's explore those factors.

Two Types of Jealousy

Reactive jealousy occurs when someone becomes aware of an actual threat to a valued relationship (Bringle & Buunk, 1991; Parrott, 1991). The troubling threat may not be a current event; it may have occurred in the past, or it may be anticipated in the near future (if, for instance, one's partner expresses the intention to date someone else), but reactive jealousy always occurs in response to a realistic danger. A variety of behaviors from one's partner can cause concern; people all over the world become jealous if their partners have sex with someone else (Hupka et al., 1985; Mullen & Martin, 1994), but even just fantasizing about or flirting with someone else is considered "unfaithful" by young adults in the United States (Yarab, Allgeier, & Sensibaugh, 1999). Unfortunately, there may be a lot to be jealous about. In one survey of nearly 700 American college students, most young adults reported having dated, kissed, fondled, or slept with someone else at some time while they were in a serious dating relationship with a romantic partner (Wiederman & Hurd, 1999). Two-thirds of the men and half of the women said they had kissed and fondled someone else, and half of the men and a third of the women said they had had intercourse with a rival (most of them more than once).

In contrast, **suspicious jealousy** occurs when one's partner *hasn't* misbehaved and one's suspicions do not fit the facts at hand (Bringle & Buunk, 1991). Suspicious jealousy results in worried and mistrustful vigilance and snooping as the jealous partner seeks to confirm his or her suspicions, and it can range from outright paranoia to a mildly overactive imagination. In all cases, however, suspicious jealousy can be said to be unfounded; it results from situations that would not trouble a more secure and more trusting partner.

The distinction between the two types of jealousy is meaningful because almost everybody feels reactive jealousy when they realize that their partners have been unfaithful (Bringle & Buunk, 1991; Buss, 2000), but people vary a lot in their tendencies to feel suspicious jealousy in the absence of any provocation. Nevertheless, the distinction between the two isn't quite as sharp as it may seem. A jealous reaction to a partner's affair may linger on as suspicious jealousy years later, as trust, once lost, is never fully regained. Reactive jealousy may create suspicious jealousy that had not been present earlier. And people may differ in their judgments of what constitutes a real threat to their relationship (Buunk & Hupka, 1987). Knowledge that a partner is merely fantasizing about someone else may not trouble a secure partner who is not much prone to jealousy, but it may cause reactive jealousy in a partner who is insecure. What is reactive jealousy in one person may seem like suspicious jealousy to another. So, the boundary between them can be vague, and as we explore individual differences in susceptibility to jealousy in our next section, we'll ask a generic question that refers to both types of jealousy.

Who's Prone to Jealousy?

On the whole, men and women do not differ in their jealous tendencies (Buunk, 1995), but there are individual differences in susceptibility to jealousy that lead some people to feel jealous more readily and more intensely than other people do. One obvious precursor of jealousy is *dependence* on a relationship (Buunk, 1982). When people feel that they need a particular partner because their alternatives are poor—that is, when people have a low CL_{alt}—any threat to their relationship is especially menacing. In contrast, people who have desirable alternatives tend to be less jealous because they have less to lose if the relationship ends (Hansen, 1985b).

Jealousy also increases with feelings of *inadequacy* in a relationship (White, 1981a, 1981b). People who worry that they can't measure up to their partners' expectations, or who fret that they're not what their lovers are looking for, are less certain that their relationships will last, and they are more prone to jealousy than are people who feel certain they can keep their partners satisfied (Knobloch, Solomon, & Cruz, 2001). Self-confidence in a relationship is undoubtedly affected by a person's global sense of self-worth, but people with high self-esteem are not always less jealous than those with low self-esteem (Guerrero & Andersen, 1998a). Instead, it's a person's perceptions of his or her adequacy as a partner in the relationship that matters, and that depends more on how much your partner likes and needs you than on how much you like yourself. Even people with generally high self-esteem can be prone to jealousy if they doubt their ability to fulfill a beloved partner.

One of the ingredients in such doubt is a discrepancy in the mate value each person brings to the relationship (Buss, 2000). If one partner is more desirable than the other, possessing (for example) more physical attractiveness, wealth, or talent, the less desirable partner is a less valuable mate, and that's a potential problem. The less desirable partner is likely to be aware that others could be a better match for his or her lover, and that may cause a sense of inadequacy that does not exist in other areas of his or her life (or with other partners). Here is another reason, then, why "matching" occurs, with people pairing off with others of similar mate value (see chapter 3): Most of us want the most desirable partners we can get, but it can be threatening to realize that our partners could do better if they really wanted to.

In any case, consider the perilous situation that faces people who feel both dependent on and inadequate in their current relationships: They need their partners but worry that they're not good enough to keep them. It's no wonder that they react strongly to real or imagined signs that a romantic rival has entered the scene.

Attachment styles influence jealousy, too, and to some extent, people with a preoccupied style routinely find themselves in a similar fix: They greedily seek closeness with others, but they remain chronically worried that their partners don't love them enough in return. That's a recipe for jealousy, and sure enough, preoccupied people experience more jealousy than do those with the other three styles (Buunk, 1997; Sharpsteen & Kirkpatrick, 1997). People with a fearful style share the same anxiety over abandonment that preoccupied people do (remember Figure 8.3 back on p. 264), so they experience similar worry and suspicion in jealousy-provoking situations, but with their higher avoidance of intimacy, they tend not to be as sad or scared by competition with a rival (Guerrero, 1998). By comparison, people with secure or dismissing styles don't worry about being abandoned by others, so they tend to be less prone to jealousy than preoccupied or fearful people are (Karakurt, Sheese, & Graziano, 2004). However, secure people do tend to experience more fear than dismissing people do when a valued relationship is imperiled (Guerrero, 1998). Add all this up, and the folks who are least affected across the board when a relationship is threatened are typically those with a dismissing style of attachment. Feeling self-sufficient and trying not to depend on others is apparently one way to stay relatively immune to jealousy.

Personality traits are also involved. People who are high in neuroticism, who tend to worry about a lot of things, are particularly prone to jealousy. On the other hand, agreeable people, who tend to be cooperative and trusting, are less likely than others to become jealous (Gehl & Watson, 2003).

Other personal characteristics also promote jealousy. People who value *sexual exclusivity*, who want and expect their partners to be monogamous, are likely to experience high levels of reactive jealousy if their partners have affairs (White, 1981a, 1981b). On the other hand, if their partners share their desire for sexual exclusivity and are being faithful, such people tend to experience less suspicious jealousy than others because a sexual betrayal seems unlikely (Pines & Aronson, 1983). By comparison, people who have had (or are planning) affairs of their own tend to be less jealous when their partners stray (Buunk, 1982), but they also tend to worry more that their partners *will* stray in the future

Jealousy is the negative emotional experience—a combination of hurt, anger, and fear—that results from the potential loss of a valued relationship to a real or imagined rival.

(Guerrero & Andersen, 1998b). Overall, then, people who do not value sexual exclusivity tend to experience less reactive jealousy but more suspicious jealousy than do people who emphasize monogamy.

Traditional gender roles also make jealousy more likely (Hansen, 1985a, 1985b). Macho men and feminine women experience more jealousy than androgynous people do, perhaps because the rules of traditional relationships tend to be quite strict. With their rigid expectations, there's little room for idiosyncrasy in traditional partnerships, and that causes greater dismay if the partners break the rules by, for instance, forming a friendship with a coworker of the other sex at work.

Who Gets Us Jealous?

Learning that our partners are interested in someone else can evoke jealousy, but not all rivals are created equal. It's particularly obnoxious when our friends start horning in on our romantic relationships; rivalry from a friend is more upsetting than is similar behavior from a stranger (Bleske & Shackelford, 2001). It's also especially painful when our partners start expressing renewed interest in their former lovers (Cann & Baucom, 2004). But no matter who they are, romantic rivals who have high mate value and who make us look bad by comparison are worrisome threats to our relationships, and they arouse more jealousy than do rivals who are milder competition. The particular talents of a rival matter, too. A rival who surpasses us in accomplishments we care about—who has achieved things we wish we had—is especially galling (DeSteno & Salovey, 1996b).

A rival who is attractive to our partners is particularly disturbing. And what kind of rival is that? It depends on whether a partner is male or female. As we saw in chapter 3, men are particularly interested in women's looks, whereas women are particularly interested in men's resources. The worst rival is one who can beat us at our own game, and men are more jealous of other men who are self-confident, dominant, and assertive (which are traits that suggest one is resourceful) than they are of rivals who are simply very handsome (Dijkstra & Buunk, 1998, 2002). In contrast, women are more jealous of other women who are pretty than they are of rivals who are self-confident and dominant. This pattern has been observed in the Netherlands and Korea as well as in the U.S. (Buss et al., 2000). Thus, both men and women typically experience more jealousy when they encounter rivals who are good at giving the other sex what it wants, but for women the threatening comparison is physical attractiveness, and for men it's dominance.

You might remember that this pattern is consistent with evolutionary psychology's assumption—emerging from the parental investment model—that men seek youth and fertility (thus, beauty) in their partners, whereas women seek resources (thus, dominance) in their men. Evolutionary psychology has also stimulated study of another, more arguable, difference between men and women in the misbehavior from their partners that threatens them most.

What Gets Us Jealous?

An evolutionary perspective suggests that jealousy evolved to motivate behavior designed to protect our close relationships from the interference of others (Buss, 1999, 2000). Presumably, early humans who reacted strongly to interlopers—being vigilant to outside interference, fending off rivals, and working hard to satisfy and fulfill their current partners—maintained their relationships and reproduced more successfully than did those who were blasé about meddlesome rivals. This perspective thus suggests that, because it offered reproductive advantages in the past, jealousy is now a natural, ingrained reaction that is hard to avoid (Buss, 2000). More provocatively, it also suggests that men and women should be especially sensitive to different sorts of infidelity in their romantic partners.

As you may recall (from chapter 1), men face a reproductive problem that women do not have: paternity uncertainty. A woman always knows whether or

BOX 10.1

Mate Poaching

The good news with regard to romantic rivalries is that huge majorities—99 percent!—of American college students say that they want to settle down with a mutually monogamous sexual partner at some point in their lives (Pederson et al., 2002). Most of us expect to be faithful to one special person sometime down the road. However, the bad news is that *mate poaching*, behavior that is intended to attract someone who is already in a romantic relationship, is commonplace. Around the world, about 60 percent of men and 40 percent of women have tried to poach someone else's partner, and about four fifths of them have succeeded at least once (Schmitt et al., 2004). Moreover, about 70 percent of us have encountered a poacher's efforts to lure us away from our partners (at least for one night), and most men (60 percent) and half of all women who have been pursued have succumbed to a poaching attempt (Schmitt et al., 2004).

What sort of person pursues someone else's mate? In general, mate poachers are horny, extraverted people who are low in agreeableness and conscientiousness and who approve of adulterous promiscuity (Schmitt & Buss, 2001); they also tend to have avoidant attachment styles, so they are relatively disinterested in trusting intimacy with others (Schachner & Shaver, 2002). Nevertheless, the more attractive they are, the more successful their poaching attempts tend to be (Schmitt et al., 2004). Their success may lie in the fact that those who succumb to poaching attempts tend to resemble their pursuers; people who are lured away by poachers tend to be sexually attractive, horny, extraverted people who are open to experience and who do not much value sexual fidelity (Schmitt et al., 2004).

The poaching tactics used by men and women tend to differ. When they are trying to entice someone else's mate, women advertise their good looks and sexual availability, whereas men publicize their power and their willingness to provide their lovers desirable resources (Schmitt & Buss, 2001). The sexes also tend to adopt different approaches when they want to be poached and they wish to communicate to potential poachers that they are available. In such cases, women flaunt their beauty, promise access to sex, and complain about their current partners, whereas men offer compliments and are overly generous to those whose attention they seek (Schmitt & Shackelford, 2003).

Presumably, people succumb to poaching when poachers offer benefits that are not currently available from their present partners (Greiling & Buss, 2000). In the long run, however, they may not be doing themselves a favor. Relationships that result from mate poaching inevitably begin with betrayal, and the partnerships that follow do not seem to be as satisfying and committed, on average, as those in which poaching does not occur (Foster, Shrira, & Campbell, 2004). To some degree, people get poached because they are looking around for something better, and such people tend to *keep* looking around even after they start new relationships with their poachers. Having been unfaithful once, they tend to be unfaithful again (Foster et al., 2004).

not a particular child is hers, but, unless he is completely confident that his mate hasn't had sex with other men, a man can't be certain (without using some advanced technology) that he is a child's father. And being cuckolded and raising another man's offspring is an evolutionary dead end; the human race did not descend from ancestors who raised other people's children and had none of their own! Indeed, the potential evolutionary costs of failing to detect a partner's infidelity are so great that natural selection may have favored men who were *too* suspicious of their partners' faithfulness over those who were not suspicious enough (Haselton & Buss, 2000). Unwarranted doubt about a part-ner's fidelity is divisive and painful, but it may not be as costly and dangerous to men, in an evolutionary sense, as being too trusting and failing to detect infidelity when it occurs. Thus, today, men have more extramarital affairs than women do (Buss, 1994), but husbands tend to be less certain than wives are that their spouses have been totally faithful to them (Paul et al., 1993). Paternity uncertainty may cause men to be more vigilant than women are about the threat of sexual infidelity. (And in a surprising number of cases, vigilance may be sen-sible; genetic studies suggest that about 10 percent of the children in North America are being raised by men who do not know that the children were fathered by another man [Cerda-Flores et al., 1999; vos Savant, 2004].)

For their part, women presumably enjoyed more success raising their chil-dren when they were sensitive to any signs that a man might withdraw the re-sources that were protecting and sheltering them and their children. Assuming that men were committed to them when the men in fact were not would have been risky for women, so natural selection may have favored those who were usually skeptical of men's declarations of true love. Unfairly doubting a man's commitment may be obnoxious and self-defeating, but believing that a mate was devoted and committed when he was not may have been more costly still. In our ancestral past, women who frequently and naïvely mated with men who then abandoned them probably did not reproduce as successfully as did women who insisted on more proof that a fellow was there to stay. Thus, mod-ern women are probably the "descendants of ancestral mothers who erred in the direction of being cautious," who tended to prudently underestimate the commitment of their men (Haselton & Buss, 2000, p. 83).

As a result of all this, men may experience the most jealousy at the thought of *sexual* infidelity in their mates, whereas women react more to the threat of *emotional* infidelity, the possibility that their partners are falling in love with someone else. Either type of infidelity can provoke jealousy in either sex, but they differ in their evolutionary implications. For a man, it's not a partner's love for someone else that's the bigger threat to his reproductive success, it's the *sex*; his children may still thrive if his mate loves another man, but he certainly does not want to raise the other man's children. For a woman, it's not a partner's sex with someone else that's more dangerous, it's the *love*; as long as he continues to provide needed resources, her children may still thrive even if he impreg-nates other women, but if he falls in love and moves out entirely, her kids' future may be imperiled.

This reasoning led David Buss and his colleagues (Buss et al., 1992, p. 252) to pose this compelling question to research participants:

> Please think of a serious committed romantic relationship that you have had in the past, that you currently have, or that you would like to have. Imagine that you discover that the person with whom you've been seriously involved became interested in someone else. What would distress or upset you more (*please pick only one*):
>
> (A) Imagining your partner forming a deep emotional attachment to that person.
>
> (B) Imagining your partner enjoying passionate sexual intercourse with that other person.

Which one would you pick? Most of the men—60 percent—said the sex would upset them more, but only 17 percent of the women chose that option; instead, a sizable majority of the women—83 percent—reported that they would be more distressed by a partner's emotional attachment to a rival. Moreover, a follow-up study demonstrated that men and women differed in their physiological reactions to these choices (Buss et al., 1992). Men displayed more autonomic changes indicative of emotional arousal when they imagined a partner's sexual, rather than emotional, infidelity, but the reverse was true for women.

On the surface, these results are consistent with an evolutionary perspective. However, they have been challenged by critics who suggested that they are less convincing than they seem. One straightforward complaint is methodological. The use of a "forced-choice" question in which research participants have to pick one option or the other can exaggerate a subtle and relatively minor sex difference (DeSteno et al., 2002; Harris, 2003). If men find sexual infidelity only slightly more threatening than women do, a forced-choice question could yield the striking results Buss et al. (1992) obtained even if the actual difference in men's and women's outlooks was rather trivial.

More importantly, men and women may differ in their judgments of the meanings of emotional and sexual infidelity (DeSteno & Salovey, 1996a; Harris & Christenfeld, 1996). If women routinely assume that men can have sex with someone without loving that partner, sexual infidelity may be just that: casual sex. However, if women also assume that when a man is in love with someone else, he's having (or wants to have) sex with her, a man's emotional infidelity would imply that sexual infidelity is occurring as well. Thus, if women think that men's sexual infidelity often occurs by itself, but emotional and sexual infidelity always go together, it would be reasonable for them to consider emotional infidelity the bigger threat. For their part, if men assume that women often love someone without having sex, but usually love those with whom they do have sex, sexual infidelity would seem the more momentous threat to them.

In fact, people do tend to assume that a person conducting an extramarital affair is more likely to be emotionally attached to the illicit lover, and more committed to the extramarital relationship, if the cheating spouse is a woman instead of a man (Sprecher, Regan, & McKinney, 1998). People think that sex and love are more closely connected for women than for men (Glass & Wright, 1992), so the choice between the two types of infidelity probably does mean different things for men than for women.

There are other possible problems with the results obtained by Buss et al. (1992). Other researchers have had trouble getting the same patterns of physiological responses (Grice & Seely, 2000); men do respond with more arousal to imagined scenes of sexual, rather than emotional, infidelity, but they're also affected by *any* scenes with sexual content, whether or not infidelity is involved (Harris, 2000). Even the basic finding that men dread sexual infidelity more than women do may pertain more to hypothetical than to real events; no difference between men and women was found in a study in which people recalled their actual experiences with a mate's real infidelity (Harris, 2002).

Nevertheless, when people contemplate infidelity, a sex difference usually results, and it has now been replicated in Sweden (Wiederman & Kendall, 1999), the Netherlands and Germany (Buunk et al., 1996), and Korea and Japan (Buss et al., 1999). Overall, the extent to which people react jealously to sexual infidelity varies from culture to culture, but men routinely find it more distressing than women do. Moreover, the sex difference still results when people are asked to pick the infidelity that bothers them most after *both* infidelities have occurred (Buss et al., 1999), a finding that answers the criticism that they mean different things to the different sexes. The sex difference is also obtained in most (Buunk & Dijkstra, 2004)—but not all (Harris, 2003)—studies when people rate their distress in response to the two infidelities instead of just picking the one that bothers them most; the pattern doesn't just depend on how you ask the question.

Moreover, the sex difference disappears when parents are asked to envision the infidelity of a daughter-in-law or son-in-law. Grandmothers face the same challenges to their reproductive success as grandfathers do, so an evolutionary perspective suggests that they should not differ in their reactions to infidelity from a child's partner. And indeed, when they imagine their sons or daughters having a cheating spouse, both mothers and fathers regard sexual infidelity to be more worrisome when it is committed by a daughter-in-law, and emotional infidelity to be more distressing when it is committed by a son-in-law (Fenigstein & Peltz, 2002).

The most reasonable conclusion from all these studies is that everybody hates both types of infidelity. Here, as in so many other cases, the sexes are more similar to each other than different. Still, to the extent that they differ at all, women are likely to perceive a partner's emotional attachment to a rival as more perilous than men do (e.g., Sagarin et al., 2003). This pattern is consistent with evolutionary assumptions, but it doesn't prove that they are correct; there may be other influences at work, including the simple possibility that—consistent with their predominant gender roles—women are more attuned to their partners' feelings about things than men are (Harris, 2000). In any case, it's clear that the threat of infidelity is a salient, jealousy-provoking event for both men and women (see Box 10.2), and evolutionary psychology offers a fascinating, if arguable, explanation of men's and women's reactions to it.

BOX 10.2

Cues to Infidelity

The extent of people's sensitivity to the threat of infidelity from a romantic partner is apparent in the number of different cues they consider to be warning signs of potential unfaithfulness. Todd Shackelford and David Buss (1997a) asked a large group of college students to nominate events that would lead them to suspect sexual or emotional infidelity, and the students identified 170 of them! These diverse cues reflected 14 different broad categories of events, and most of them were believed to be more indicative of one type of infidelity than the other. As you can see, the cues ranged from uncharacteristic anger and inconsiderateness to exaggerated displays of affection, so they covered a lot of ground. Have you noticed any of these in your romantic partner?

CUES MORE DIAGNOSTIC
OF SEXUAL INFIDELITY

Revelation of an affair: Finding a partner in bed with a rival, or being told by friends;

Physical clues: Encountering an unexpected sexually transmitted infection;

Sexual disinterest or boredom: Finding a partner to be strangely unresponsive;

Changes in the normal routine: New and unusual sexual positions, or changes in sleeping, eating, or clothing habits; and

Exaggerated sexual interest or affection: Sudden, suspicious increases in sexual appetite or affectionate behavior.

CUES MORE DIAGNOSTIC OF
EMOTIONAL INFIDELITY

Dissatisfaction with the relationship: Suggestions that you break up or begin seeing others;

Emotional disengagement: Forgetting anniversaries, or neglecting to say "I love you";

Acting guilty or anxious: Being unusually apologetic or avoiding eye contact;

Reluctance to discuss someone: Avoiding talk or acting nervous about some other person;

Avoiding the relationship: Ducking dates, or offering fewer invitations to spend time together;

Increased anger and criticism: Becoming less tolerant and more argumentative; and

Increased inconsiderateness: Becoming rude or less gentle.

CUES EQUALLY DIAGNOSTIC
OF EITHER INFIDELITY

Spending time with a rival: Wearing something belonging to a rival, or calling you by a rival's name; and

Acting apathetic: Spending less time on appearance, or becoming less excited to see you.

Interestingly, when they really are trying to hide an affair, women often behave more romantically and offer more sex to the men they seek to deceive, whereas men become more attentive and share more "quality time" with the women they're fooling (Schmitt & Shackelford, 2003). So the list above is only partially accurate, and many of these cues—particularly those thought to signal emotional infidelity—are quite ambiguous. We hope that people do not inadvertently poison their relationships by assuming the worst when such conclusions are unwarranted.

Responses to Jealousy

People may react to the hurt, anger, and fear of jealousy in ways that have either beneficial or destructive effects on their relationships (Dindia & Timmerman, 2003). On occasion, jealous people lash out in ways that are unequivocally harmful, retaliating against their partners with violent behavior or verbal antagonism, or with efforts to make them jealous in return (Guerrero & Andersen, 1998a). On other occasions, people respond in ways that may be intended to protect the relationship but that often undermine it further: spying on their partners, restricting their partners' freedom, or derogating or threatening their rivals. There are times, however, when people respond positively to jealousy by straightforwardly expressing their concerns and trying to work things out with their partners, or by making themselves or their relationships more desirable (by, for instance, improving their appearance, sending the partner gifts, or doing more housework) (Guerrero & Andersen, 1998b).

Attachment styles help determine what people will do. When they become jealous, people who are relatively comfortable with closeness—those with secure or preoccupied attachment styles—are more likely to express their concerns and to try to repair their relationships than are those with more avoidant styles (Guerrero, 1998). By comparison, people who are dismissing or fearful are more likely to avoid the issue or deny their distress by pretending nothing is wrong or by acting like they don't care.

Men and women often differ in their responses to jealousy, too, with consequences that can complicate heterosexual relationships. Imagine yourself in this situation: At a party, you leave your romantic partner sitting on a couch when you go to refill your drinks. While you're gone, your partner's old boyfriend or girlfriend happens by and sits for a moment, and they share a light kiss of greeting just as you return with the drinks. What would you do? When researchers showed people videotapes of a scenario like this and measured their intentions, men and women responded differently (Shettel-Neuber, Bryson, & Young, 1978). Women said they would react to the rival's interference by seeking to *improve the relationship*; they intended to put on a show of indifference but compete with the rival by making themselves more attractive to their partners. In contrast, men said they would strive to *protect their egos*; they planned to get drunk, confront and threaten the rival, and pursue other women. Whereas women seemed to focus on preserving the existing relationship, men considered leaving it and salving their wounded pride with conquests of new partners.

Sex differences like these have also been obtained in other studies (Guerrero & Reiter, 1998), and one thing that makes them worrisome is that women are much more likely than men to *try* to get their partners jealous (White, 1980a). When they induce jealousy—usually by discussing or exaggerating their attraction to other men, sometimes by flirting with or dating them—they typically seek to test the relationship (to see how much he cares) or try to elicit more attention and commitment from their partners (White, 1980a). They evidently want their men to respond the way they do when they get jealous, with greater effort to protect and maintain the relationship. The problem, of course, is that that's not the way men typically react. Women who seek to improve their relationships by inducing jealousy in their men may succeed only in driving their partners away.

Coping Constructively with Jealousy

So, near the end of our discussion, would you still be disappointed if you couldn't make your partner jealous? It's an unhappy mixture of hurt, anger, and fear that occurs when your partner wants you but isn't sure he or she can keep you. It sometimes seems to be the glue that keeps people together, but it can also be "the explosive force that destroys the couple and alienates the persons from each other" (Bringle & Buunk, 1991, p. 149). It may be a natural thing for humans to feel, but it's often an ugly, awful feeling that results in terribly destructive behavior (Buss, 2000). Someday, you may find yourself wishing that you could feel it less intensely, and limit its effects. What can be done?

There are no easy and certain answers to this question, but many of those who have considered this issue have emphasized two major themes. First, we have to do away with the notion that jealousy is a sign of "true love." In fact, jealousy is a sign of dependency and is a reflection of our own desires, our own self-interest. Jealousy isn't based in generous concern for the well-being of our partners, it's inherently selfish. The first step in controlling jealousy is to learn to recognize it for what it is.

A second step is to work on reducing the connection between the exclusivity of a relationship and our sense of self-worth. Finding that someone we love is attracted to a rival can be painful. However, it does not mean that your partner is a horrible, worthless person, or that you are. We react irrationally when we act as though our self-worth totally depended on a particular relationship.

In fact, when they succeed in reducing unwanted jealousy, people tend to use two techniques that help them to maintain a sense of independence and self-worth (Salovey & Rodin, 1988). The first is *self-reliance,* which involves efforts to "stay cool" and avoid feeling angry or embarrassed by refusing to dwell on the unfairness of the situation. The second is *self-bolstering,* giving a boost to one's self-esteem by doing something nice for oneself and thinking about one's good qualities. Maintaining a sense of self-confidence about one's ability to act, and to survive, independently apparently helps keep jealousy at manageable levels.

When people are unable to do that on their own, formal therapy can help. Clinical approaches to the treatment of jealousy usually try to (a) reduce irrational, catastrophic thinking that exaggerates either the threat to the relationship or the harm that its loss would entail; (b) enhance the self-esteem of the jealous partner; (c) improve communication skills, so the partners can clarify their expectations and agree on limits that prevent jealous misunderstandings; and (d) increase satisfaction and fairness in the relationship (White & Mullen, 1989; Pines, 1998). Most of us don't need therapy to cope with jealousy. But it might help some of us if romantic relationships came with a warning label:

> WARNING: It may be dangerous to your and your partner's health if you do not know beyond doubt that you are a valuable and worthwhile human being with *or* without your partner's love.

DECEPTION AND LYING

The last two sources of stress and strain we'll cover in this chapter can certainly cause jealousy when they involve romantic rivals, but they involve rivals only now and then and occur much more often than jealousy does. Indeed, the hazards we'll consider in this section of the chapter, lying and other forms of deception, occur so often in social life that they are commonplace, whether we realize it or not (McCornack, 1997). As we'll see, deception of some sort or another occurs regularly even in intimate relationships that are based on openness and trust (Metts, 1989).

Deception is intentional behavior that creates an impression in the recipient that the deceiver knows is false (Buller & Burgoon, 1994). Outright lying in which people fabricate information and make statements that contradict the truth is the most straightforward example of deceptive behavior, but there are various other ways to convey misleading impressions without coming right out and saying things that are untrue (Buller & Burgoon, 1994). For instance, people may simply *conceal* information and not mention details that would communicate the truth, or they may *divert attention* from vital facts, abruptly changing topics to avoid the discussion of touchy subjects. On other occasions, they may mix truthful and deceptive information into *half-truths* that are misleading. We'll focus on lies in the following discussion because they have been studied much more extensively than other forms of deception, but we'll only be scratching the surface of the various ways intimate partners mislead each other.

Lying in Close and Casual Relationships

Research by Bella DePaulo (2004) and her colleagues has painted a remarkable portrait of lying in everyday life. College students who keep diaries of their interactions with others report telling two lies a day on average, lying to one out of every three (34 percent) of the people with whom they interact (DePaulo et al., 1996). Adults off campus tell fewer lies, about one per day, lying in one of every five interactions. Very few people, only 5 percent, report having told no lies at all in a given week. Most of these lies are casual, spontaneous events that are not considered to be serious by those who tell them, and most of them are successful; the liars are confident that their lies are accepted 59 percent of the time, but they feel sure that they've been caught lying only 19 percent of the time. (On other occasions, they aren't sure of the result.)

In most interactions, the most common type of lie is one that benefits the liar, warding off embarrassment, guilt, or inconvenience, or seeking approval or material gain. However, one fourth of all lies are told to benefit others, protecting their feelings or advancing their interests, and when women interact with other women, such lies are as common as self-centered ones are (DePaulo et al., 1996). People are especially likely to misrepresent the truth when brutal honesty would hurt the feelings of someone who is highly invested in the issue at hand. Imagine, for instance, that you really dislike a painting, but are describing your feelings about it to an art student who may have painted it. Would you be totally honest? In just such a situation, no one was (DePaulo & Bell, 1996). People typically admitted that the painting wasn't one of their favorites, but they were much less critical than they had been in prior written evaluations of the piece.

Some lies are obviously undertaken to promote polite, friendly interaction with others. We often claim to agree with others when in fact we do not, and we often say that we are more pleased with events than we really are. Most lies in close relationships, where we expect our partners to be generous and honest, are benevolent, small lies like these (DePaulo & Kashy, 1998). People tell fewer self-serving, greedy lies—and fewer lies overall—to their lovers and friends than to acquaintances and strangers. In particular, spouses are more likely to conceal information, and less likely to make explicitly false statements, than are partners in other relationships (Metts, 1989).

These patterns make lying sound rather innocuous in close relationships. However, people still tell a lot of lies to their intimate partners, and when they do tell serious lies about topics that could destroy their reputations or relationships, they tell them more often to their closest partners than to anyone else (DePaulo et al., 2004). The biggest deceptions we undertake occur more often in our intimate relationships than anywhere else.

In addition, lies can be consequential even when they go undetected. In general, people consider interactions in which they tell a lie for any reason to be less pleasant and less intimate than interactions in which they are totally honest, and lying to a close partner makes them particularly uncomfortable (DePaulo & Kashy, 1998; Lee, 2002). Despite its prevalence in social life, most of us judge lying harshly (Gordon & Miller, 2000), and people evidently know they're living dangerously when they lie to others. Moreover, lying in close relationships undermines the liar's trust in the partner who receives the lie (Sagarin, Rhoads, & Cialdini, 1998). This is a phenomenon known as **deceiver's distrust;** when people lie to others, they may begin to perceive the recipients of the lies as less honest and trustworthy as a result. This seems to occur both because liars assume that other people are just like them, so they assume that others share their own deceitful motives, and because they feel better about themselves when they believe their faults are shared by others (Sagarin et al., 1998). In either case, lying can sully a relationship even when the liar is the only one who knows that any lying has taken place.

Liars are also likely to think that their lies are more harmless and inoffensive than the recipients do (Gordon & Miller, 2000). This is a common pattern when someone misbehaves in a partnership, and we'll see it again at the end of this chapter when we discuss betrayals: The recipient (or victim) of a partner's wrongdoing almost always considers it more informative and influential than the perpetrator does (e.g., Mikula, et al., 1998). When lies are discovered, the recipients usually think them more worrisome and momentous than the liars do (McCornack & Levine, 1990a); what liars consider to be a small fib may be considered to be a harmful and duplicitous deceit by others. But that begs the question, how often do liars get caught? As we'll see, the answer is, "it depends."

Lies and Liars

Some people do lie more than others do (Kashy & DePaulo, 1996). Those who are gregarious and sociable, and those who are more concerned with the impressions they make on others, tell more lies than do those who are less outgoing. In addition, people who have insecure attachment styles tell more lies to their lovers than secure partners do; both avoidance of intimacy and anxiety over abandonment are positively correlated with lying (Cole, 2001).

However, frequent liars are not necessarily more successful liars. High social skill makes people more convincing (Burgoon & Bacue, 2003), but a liar's performance also depends on the level of motivation (and guilt and fear) with which he or she enacts the lie (Zuckerman, DePaulo, & Rosenthal, 1981). Lies are typically shorter and less detailed than truths are (Newman et al., 2003), unless the lie is important and the liar is highly motivated to get away with the lie; when liars care enough to send their very best, they create scripts that are more convincing than those authored by liars who are less highly motivated (DePaulo, Lanier, & Davis, 1983). However, when they deliver their lies, motivated liars do a poorer, more suspicious job than do those who have less to lose and who are more spontaneous and relaxed (Forrest & Feldman, 2000). People who really want to get away with a lie tend to be more obvious than they would be if they didn't care so much. In particular, people who are lying to make good impressions on attractive people of the other sex tend to be quite transparent, both to the recipients of their lies and to anyone else who's watching (DePaulo, Stone, & Lassiter, 1985)! People who are lying to unattractive targets, or to members of their own sex, are harder to detect.

What goes wrong when lies are detected? The liar's nonverbal behavior gives him or her away (DePaulo et al., 2003). When people are lying, they often speak hesitantly in a higher pitch and make more grammatical errors and slips of the tongue than they do when they're telling the truth (Vrij, Edward, & Bull, 2001). In addition, their pupils dilate and they blink more often (DePaulo, 1994). Except for brief flashes ("microexpressions") of honesty when they're gaining control (Ekman & O'Sullivan, 1991), their facial expressions usually don't give them away; people know they're supposed to look sincere and to look others directly in the eye when they're trying to seem honest, and they are usually able to do so. But there tend to be discrepancies and mismatches between their tones of voice and their facial expressions that arouse suspicion (Zuckerman, Driver, & Koestner, 1982). None of these cues is certain evidence of lying all by itself; "there is no one cue that always indicates that a person is lying" (DePaulo, 1994, p. 85). However, the global pattern of a person's paralanguage and physical tension often indicates that he or she is lying, and this takes place in a manner that is equally obvious in both men and women (Burgoon et al., 1998).

So, How Well Can We Detect a Partner's Deception?

The problem is that the specific reactions that indicate that a person is lying may be quite idiosyncratic. People differ in their mannerisms. Some of us speak hesitantly most of the time, whereas others are more verbally assertive; some people engage in frequent eye contact, whereas others rarely look us in the eye. Lying is usually apparent in changes in a person's ordinary demeanor, but to notice those changes, one may need some prior familiarity with the person's style (DePaulo, 1994). Moreover, deceptive behavior may change in the middle of an interaction as deceivers adjust their actions and adapt to the recipients' reactions to their lies; the longer a deceptive interaction goes on, the less apparent a person's lying may become (Burgoon et al., 1999). The detection of deception is actually a complex process that requires attention to a complicated array

---

BOX 10.3

Lying Online

The remarkable reach of the Web allows us to interact with lots of interesting people we would not otherwise meet, but it also allows those people to lie to us with relative impunity. With whom are we chatting when we send instant messages to a stranger online? It's often hard to say. The information we receive from new acquaintances on the Web may result from some mixture of illusion, variable social skills, outright falsehoods, and truth (Orr, 2004). Men are likely to lie about their financial status (Whitty, 2002), women are likely to lie about their physical attractiveness (Benz, Miller, & Anderson, 2004), and people of both sexes may even pretend to be the other sex online (Barnes, 2001)!

Faced with occasional fictions and frauds, people tend to be cautiously suspicious when they interact online. We expect others to be less trustworthy (Okdie et al., 2004), and if anything seems implausible, if people seem "too good to be true," most of us assume the worst (Cornetto, 2001). However, people we already know may actually be more honest with us online than they are over the phone or in person. When college students kept diaries of their communications with others for a week, they reported telling a lie in 37 percent of their phone calls and 27 percent of their face-to-face conversations, but in only 21 percent of their instant messages and 14 percent of their e-mails (Hancock, Thom-Santelli, & Ritchie, 2004). Conceivably, people lie more reluctantly whenever their remarks are written down and can be more easily checked later for accuracy. Thus, although they may sometimes tell huge lies to those who do not know them well, people tend to be more truthful online than when they're face-to-face (Okdie et al., 2004).

of information. People can learn to detect deception in others: When research participants get repeated opportunities to judge whether or not someone is lying—and are given continuing feedback about the accuracy of their judgments—they do become better judges of that person's truthfulness. However, their improvement is limited to that particular person, and they're no better at detecting lying in anyone else (Zuckerman, Koestner, & Alton, 1984)!

Intimate partners have personal, idiosyncratic knowledge of each other that should allow them to be sensitive judges of each other's behavior. But they also *trust* each other (or their relationship probably isn't very intimate), and that leads them to exhibit a **truth bias** in which they assume that their partners are usually telling the truth (Levine & McCornack, 1992). And believing that one's partner is generally trustworthy and honest seems to make it harder to recognize when the partner is dishonest (O'Sullivan, 2003). The net result is that intimate partners make very confident judgments of each other's veracity, but their confidence has nothing whatsoever to do with how accurate they are (DePaulo et al., 1997). This means that people are sometimes certain that their partners are telling the truth when their partners are actually lying.

There is some evidence that, early in a developing relationship, women (but not men) get better at detecting deception in their partners as they spend more time together (Anderson et al., 1999). And as we saw in chapter 5, women decode others' nonverbal behavior better than men do, so it wouldn't be surprising if they were more proficient at catching lies (McCornack & Parks, 1990). On the other hand, women are more trusting than men are (Rosenthal & DePaulo, 1979), and people are relatively unlikely to notice deception when they are not suspiciously looking for it (McCornack & Levine, 1990b). The bottom line, then, is that on the whole women do not seem to be better lie detectors than men (Rosenthal & DePaulo, 1979).

In fact, as relationships become intimate and trust increases, the partners' accuracy in detecting deception in each other doesn't improve, it declines (McCornack & Parks, 1990). Mere practice doesn't seem to be of much use where lie detection is concerned (Anderson, DePaulo, & Ansfield, 2002). Indeed, experienced customs inspectors (Kraut & Poe, 1980), agents of the FBI, CIA, or National Security Agency, and psychiatrists (Ekman & O'Sullivan, 1991) all do no better than laypersons do at detecting lies told (or powder smuggled) by strangers. And that means they're not doing well at all. Federal law enforcement officers studied by DePaulo and Pfeifer (1986) correctly identified 52 percent of the lies they encountered in videotaped statements, but because half of the statements they judged were truthful and half were lies, they should have gotten 50 percent right if they were just flipping a coin! Neither their performance nor that of a comparison group of college students (who got 54 percent right) was reliably different than just random guessing.

Now, some people—including some Secret Service agents and some clinical psychologists—*can* catch liars readily (Ekman, O'Sullivan, & Frank, 1999). And if anyone routinely knows when *you're* lying, your intimate partners probably do. However, any belief that our partners are completely transparent to us is probably misplaced. People tend not to be very skilled lie detectors, and despite our considerable experience with our close friends and lovers, we usually do a poorer job of distinguishing their fact from fancy than we realize (DePaulo et al., 1997). In fact, when we're lying, the chances that we'll be caught are usually lower than we think they are (Gilovich, Savitsky, & Medvec, 1998).

Thus, people tell lots of lies, even in close relationships, and they get away with most of them. However, don't pat yourself on the back if you're currently deceiving a partner. Most people think that they're better at deceiving their partners than their partners are at deceiving them (Boon & McLeod, 2001), so your partner may be secretly proud about fooling you, too. And consider the big picture. People tell fewer lies in the relationships they find most rewarding, in part because lying violates shared expectations of honesty and trust. Keeping secrets isn't easy (see Box 10.4). And even if your lies go undetected, they may poison the atmosphere in your relationship, contributing to unwarranted suspicion and doubt. And you run the risk that if they are detected, your lies may seem to your partner to be a despicable example of this chapter's last topic: betrayal of an intimate partner.

BOX 10.4

Keeping Secrets

Sometimes, people interact with others when they are aware of information that they think it best to keep secret. Research by Daniel Wegner and his colleagues has shown that this isn't always easy to do (Wegner & Lane, 1995). Secrecy has consequences that people rarely anticipate. For one thing, it takes effort. In order to keep a secret successfully, we have to monitor our behavior mindfully, carefully checking for any signs that the unwanted information is about to slip out. Ironically, this keeps the forbidden knowledge in the back of our minds so that, if we become tired or distracted and let down our guard, it's actually more likely to intrude on our thoughts than it would have been if we hadn't been trying to keep it secret at all (Lane & Wegner, 1994, 1995). People who are keeping secrets often become preoccupied with the clandestine knowledge they're trying to put behind

them, so they constantly run the risk that it could be revealed at any time (Wegner & Gold, 1995).

Moreover, there's a special allure to secret relationships. In one study in Wegner's lab, a man and a woman who were previously unacquainted followed the researchers' instructions to secretly play "footsie" under a table (keeping their feet in contact) while they were talking with two other strangers who were not covertly carrying on (Wegner, Lane, & Dimitri, 1994). Other couples played footsie publicly, with the knowledge of everyone involved. Afterwards, the partners who had been touching each other secretly were more attracted to each other than were those who had been touching openly. Secret loves not only tend to occupy our thoughts, they sometimes seem sweeter than they would be if they were public and everyone knew about them.

BETRAYAL

People don't always do what we want or expect them to do. Some of the surprises our partners spring on us are pleasant ones (Afifi & Metts, 1998). But sometimes, our partners do harmful things (or fail to do desirable things) that violate the expectations we hold for close confidants. Such acts are **betrayals,** disagreeable, hurtful actions by people we trusted and from whom we reasonably did not expect such treachery (Couch, Jones, & Moore, 1999). Sexual and emotional infidelity and lying are common examples of betrayal, but any behavior that violates the norms of benevolence, loyalty, respect, and trustworthiness that support intimate relationships may be considered treasonous to some degree (Schratter, 2001). People who reveal secrets about their partners, gossip about them behind their backs, tease in hurtful ways, break important promises, fail to support their partners, spend too much time elsewhere, or simply abandon a relationship are often thought to have betrayed their partners (Bollmer et al., 2003; Metts, 1994).

All of these actions involve relational devaluation. When we are victimized by intimate partners, their betrayals demonstrate that they do not value their relationships with us as much as we had believed, or else, from our point of view, they would not have behaved as they did (Fitness, 2001). The sad irony is that for relational devaluation of this sort to occur, we must have (or think we have) a desired relationship that is injured; thus, casual acquaintances cannot betray us as thoroughly and hurtfully as trusted intimates can (Jones & Burdette, 1994). We're not always hurt by the ones we love, but the ones we love *can* hurt us in ways that no one else can (Miller, 1997b).

In fact, when our feelings get hurt in everyday life, it's usually our close friends or romantic partners who cause us distress (Leary & Springer, 2001). Those partners are rarely being intentionally malicious—which is fortunate because it's very painful to believe that our partners intended to hurt us (Vangelisti & Young, 2000)—but they often disappoint us anyway. Almost all of us have betrayed someone, and have been betrayed by someone else, in a close relationship at some time or another, and a betrayal has occurred in about half of the relationships we have now (Jones et al., 2001). Betrayal is a common event in close relationships.

Because caring and trust are integral aspects of intimacy, this may be surprising, but perhaps it shouldn't be. Most of us are close in some way to more than one person, and when people try to be loyal simultaneously to several different relationships, competing demands are inescapable. When obligations overlap, occasional violations of the norms in a given relationship may be unavoidable (Baxter et al., 1997). If two of your close friends scheduled their weddings in different cities on the same day, for instance, you'd have to disappoint one of them, even without wanting to. Moreover, we occasionally face competing demands within a given relationship, finding ourselves unable to appropriately honor all of the responsibilities of a caring friend or lover. One of your authors (who, in this case, we will not single out!) once learned that the ex-wife of a good friend was now sleeping with the friend's best friend.

Honesty and openness required that your author inform the friend of his other friend's—and, arguably, the ex-wife's—betrayal. However, caring and compassion suggested that the friend not be burdened with painful, embarrassing news he could do nothing about. It was a no-win situation. Your author, seeking to protect the friend's feelings, decided not to tell him about his other friend's betrayal, but when he later learned the truth, he was hurt and disappointed that your author had kept such a secret from him. Perceived betrayals sometimes occur when people have the best intentions but simply cannot honor all of the overlapping and competing demands that intimacy and interdependency may make.

Individual Differences in Betrayal

Nevertheless, some of us betray our partners more often than others do. Using a scale designed to assess the frequency with which people engage in various acts of betrayal, Warren Jones and his colleagues at the University of Tennessee have found that betrayal scores are higher among college students majoring in the social sciences, education, business, and the humanities, and lower among those studying the physical sciences, engineering, and other technical fields (Jones & Burdette, 1994). (You can examine the Interpersonal Betrayal Scale for yourself; it's reprinted in Table 10.2.) Off-campus, white people betray others more often than other folks do, but betrayal is less frequent among those who are older, better educated, and religious. More importantly, those who report repeated betrayals of others tend to be unhappy and maladjusted. Betrayers tend to be resentful, vengeful, and suspicious people. They're prone to jealousy and cynicism, have a higher incidence of psychiatric problems, and are more likely than others to come from broken homes. They also tend to be lonely (Jones, 2000). Overall, betrayers do not trust others much, perhaps because they wrongly attribute to others the same motives they recognize in themselves (Couch & Jones, 1997).

Men and women do not differ in their tendencies to betray others, but they do differ in the targets of their most frequent betrayals (Jones & Burdette, 1994). Men are more likely to betray their romantic partners and business associates than women are, whereas women betray their friends and family members more often than men do. Whether one is at particular risk for betrayal from a man or woman seems to depend on the part one plays in his or her life.

The Two Sides to Every Betrayal

Those who betray their intimate partners usually underestimate the harm they do. As we saw in chapter 4, it's normal for people to perceive their actions in self-serving ways, but when it comes to betrayal, this tendency leads people to excuse and minimize actions that their partners may find quite harmful (Cameron, Ross, & Holmes, 2002). Betrayers often consider their behavior to be inconsequential and innocuous, and they are quick to describe mitigating circumstances that vindicate their actions (Stillwell & Baumeister, 1997). However,

TABLE 10.2. The Interpersonal Betrayal Scale

How often have you done each of these things? Read each item and respond to it using this scale:

> 1 = I have never done this.
>
> 2 = I have done this once.
>
> 3 = I have done this a few times.
>
> 4 = I have done this several times.
>
> 5 = I have done this many times.

___ 1. Snubbing a friend when you are with a group you want to impress.

___ 2. Breaking a promise without good reason.

___ 3. Agreeing with people you really disagree with so that they will accept you.

___ 4. Pretending to like someone you detest.

___ 5. Gossiping about a friend behind his or her back.

___ 6. Making a promise to a friend with no intention of keeping it.

___ 7. Failing to stand up for what you believe in because you want to be accepted by the "in" crowd.

___ 8. Complaining to others about your friends or family members.

___ 9. Telling others information given to you in confidence.

___10. Lying to a friend.

___11. Making a promise to a family member with no intention of keeping it.

___12. Failing to stand up for a friend when he or she is being criticized or belittled by others.

___13. Taking family members for granted.

___14. Lying to your parents or spouse about your activities.

___15. Wishing that something bad would happen to someone you dislike.

Calculate your score by adding up your answers. The average score for college men and women is 36. The average for adult men and women off campus is 35. However, in a sample of elderly people over age 65, the average score was 27.6. The standard deviation of the scores people get on the scale is eight points, so if your own score is 44 or higher, your betrayal score is higher than average. On the other hand, if your score is 28 or lower, you betray others less often than most other people do.

Source: Jones & Burdette, 1994.

their victims rarely share those views. Those who are betrayed routinely judge the transgression to be more severe (Kowalski, 2000; Kowalski et al., 2003) and more memorable (Van Lange et al., 1999) than the betrayers do.

These two different perspectives lead to disparate perceptions of the harm that is done. People who are betrayed almost never believe that such events

---

BOX 10.5

A Practical Guide to Getting Away with It

Deception is corrosive and forgiveness is good for people, so we hesitate to offer advice about how to get away with betraying your partners. Nevertheless, we're here to present relationship science to you as objectively as possible, so here goes. Relationships are more adversely affected, and forgiveness is harder to obtain, if our partners catch us in an act of betrayal or learn of it from some third party than if we tell them of it ourselves when they ask (Afifi, Falato, & Weiner, 2001). (The least damaging mode of discovery, if our partners do learn of our betrayal, is for us to admit our wrongdoing without being asked, but that's not the point of this box.)

So, admitting a wrong is better than being caught red-handed, but just what we say is important, too. When you're asked about a transgression you've committed, you shouldn't deny it outright, because your bold lie will compound your sins if (when?) the truth comes out. Instead, equivocate (Champion & Kelly,

2004). Make your response as truthful as possible, and don't contradict the truth. A crafty strategy is to confess to a less serious offense; that often seems more trustworthy than claiming to be entirely innocent, and it avoids the consequences of admitting the more serious wrong (Sternglanz, 2004).

We are *not* encouraging you either to betray or to deceive your partners. If you follow the guidelines presented here, you will be behaving disreputably. However, you will be in well-known company. When President Bill Clinton claimed, "I did not have sexual relations with that woman, Miss Lewinsky," he was equivocating (DePaulo, 2004); his statement was technically correct, if you take "sexual relations" to mean intercourse, and it allowed many listeners to continue to think him entirely innocent, without him saying so, until more information became available. Even when his equivocation was discovered, some people did not think it much of a lie.

---

have no effect on their relationships; 93 percent of the time, they feel that a betrayal damages the partnership, leading to lower satisfaction and lingering suspicion and doubt (Jones & Burdette, 1994). In contrast, the perpetrators acknowledge that their behavior was harmful only about half the time. They even think that the relationship has *improved* as a result of their transgression in one of every five cases. Such judgments are clearly ill-advised. We may feel better believing that our occasional betrayals are relatively benign, but it may be smarter to face the facts: Betrayals almost always have a negative, and sometimes lasting, effect on a relationship (Amato & Rogers, 1997). Indeed, they are routinely the central complaint of spouses seeking therapy or a divorce (Geiss & O'Leary, 1981).

Coping with Betrayal

Betrayal can be tough to take, and betrayals typically have adverse effects on the quality of a relationship. Still, when such events occur, some responses are more helpful than others. When they think back to past betrayals, college students report less anxiety and better coping when they say they tried to (a) face up to the betrayal instead of denying that it happened; (b) reinterpret the event in a positive light and use it as an impetus for personal growth; and (c) rely on their friends for support (Ferguson-Isaac, Ralston, & Couch, 1999). People seem to fare less well when they try to pretend it didn't happen, wallow in negative emotions such as bitterness and spite, and resort to drugs and alcohol to blot out the pain. Women often respond more constructively than men do; women are more likely than men to seek support from others and to (try to) think positively about the situation, whereas men are more likely than women to get intoxicated to blunt their distress (Couch, Rogers, & Howard, 2000).

However, victims of both sexes sometimes feel that they want to exact some form of painful revenge (Haden et al., 2004). When they are wronged, some people are more vengeful than others; vengefulness is related to the angry belief that retaliation is often appropriate and needed in social life because a lot of other people are malevolent and hostile. Vengeful people tend to think that mistreatment from others should be repaid in kind, so that "if someone important to you does something negative to you, you should do something even more negative to them" (Eisenberger et al., 2004, p. 789). This seems to be a rather sour outlook, and, indeed, vengeful people tend to ruminate about the wrongs they have encountered and to be generally less happy with life than those who are less prone to vengeance; they also tend to be high in neuroticism and low in agreeableness (McCullough et al., 2001).

Thus, partners who have been betrayed sometimes take hurtful action. They withdraw, destroy old letters and gifts, pursue other relationships, and defame their partners to others (Yoshimura, 2004). None of this is good for a partnership of course, so let's end our look at painful stresses and strains by focusing on the healing process that can help a relationship survive a partner's misbehavior.

FORGIVENESS

If a relationship is to continue to thrive after a painful incident of betrayal, forgiveness may be necessary (Fincham, 2000). Forgiveness is "a decision to give up your perceived or actual right to get even with, or hold in debt, someone who has wronged you" (Markman, Stanley, & Blumberg, 1994, p. 217). When you forgive someone, you discard the desire to retaliate (Kearns & Fincham, 2004); you don't condone a partner's misbehavior, but you do communicate your "willingness to exit from a potential cycle of abuse and recrimination" (Fincham & Beach, 2002, p. 240), and that sets the stage for possible reconciliation and relationship repair.

It's not always easy to forgive someone, and it comes more readily to some people than to others. Attachment style matters. Secure people are more forgiving than insecure people are (Couch & Olson, 2004) because anxiety over abandonment and avoidance of intimacy both seem to make people less forgiving

(Kachadourian, Fincham, & Davila, 2004). And those who are high in agreeableness forgive others relatively easily (Ross et al., 2004), perhaps because they are better than other people at separating blame from anger; they can hold wrong-doers responsible for their misbehavior without getting angry and hostile toward them, and that is hard for less agreeable people to do (Meier & Robinson, 2004).

Still, no matter who we are, forgiveness takes effort (McCullough, 2000). But it does come more readily when two important ingredients exist. The first is an *apology*. Victims are more likely to forgive those who betray them when the offenders admit to doing wrong and offer a sincere apology (Zechmeister et al., 2004). Forgiveness is less likely to occur when excuses are given, an apology seems insincere, or the betrayer simply begs for understanding and mercy (Couch et al., 1999). If you have misbehaved and a relationship is suffering, you might do well to recognize that your behavior was harmful, and apologize. A second component to forgiveness is *empathy* on the part of the victim (Fincham, Paleari, & Regalia, 2002). People who can imagine why their partners behaved the way they did and who are able to feel some compassion for those partners are much more likely to forgive them than are those in whom empathy is lacking (Batson et al., 2003).

Fortunately, forgiveness is more likely to occur in close, committed relationships than in those that are less committed (Finkel et al., 2002), both because empathy occurs more easily and because the betrayers are more likely to apologize (Couch et al., 1999). And forgiveness usually improves the relationships in which it occurs. Retribution rarely gets our partners to reform and behave better, but forgiveness can (Kelln & Ellard, 1999). And perhaps more importantly, people who are able to forgive their intimate partners enjoy more well-being—that is more self-esteem, less hostility, more satisfaction with life, and less distress—than do those from whom forgiveness is less forthcoming (Berman & Frazier, 2004; Karremans et al., 2003). There's no question that, within intimate relationships, forgiveness is more desirable and beneficial to those who wield it than is vengeance.

Ultimately, the stakes are higher in intimate partnerships. It's more painful when our partners misbehave, but there's more reason to work to repair any damage that is done. Intimacy offers the potential for both invaluable, irreplaceable rewards and excruciating costs.

FOR YOUR CONSIDERATION

When Ann returned from her business trip, she described her weekend as pretty dull and uneventful, so Greg was surprised when he found pictures on her digital camera of a raucous dinner at which she and some guys had obviously been drinking and carrying on. A picture of her sitting at a table beaming with pleasure as two good-looking men hugged her and kissed her cheeks really rattled him. Stung and unhappy, he became sullen and distant. He started giving her the cold shoulder and began to ponder how to "pay her back." Ann knew that she had been too flirtatious, but she was secretly titillated by one of the guys in the picture who was now e-mailing her with veiled suggestions about their next meeting. In addition, Ann wasn't sure what Greg knew or suspected, but she was beginning to resent his petulance.

What do you think the future holds for Ann and Greg? Why?

CHAPTER SUMMARY

Some hazards are surprisingly common in close relationships. Hurt feelings, ostracism, jealousy, lying, and even betrayal occur regularly, and may be very influential.

Relational Evaluation

We encounter various amounts of acceptance and rejection from others that communicate their *relational evaluation*, the degree to which they consider their relationships with us to be valuable, important, or close. Their treatment of us can range from maximal inclusion all the way down to maximal exclusion, and our perception that they value their relationships with us less than we want them to is a core ingredient of the stresses and strains covered in this chapter.

Hurt Feelings

Mild rejection from others usually feels just as bad as more extreme rejection does, but we are very sensitive to *relational devaluation*, or apparent decreases in others' regard for us. Relational devaluation causes hurt feelings, leaving us psychologically wounded and despondent.

Ostracism

People sometimes give their partners the "silent treatment," ignoring them in order to achieve some goal, but the recipients of such ostracism usually resent it. In the lab, people who are excluded by others become stupid, selfish, and impulsive, making bad choices and behaving in uncharitable ways. People with high self-esteem tend not to put up with it; they are more likely than those with low self-esteem to end the relationship and seek new partners when they are ostracized.

Jealousy

When people face the potential loss of a valued relationship to a real or imagined rival, they often experience *jealousy*, a negative emotional experience that is a combination of hurt, anger, and fear. The unique element that distinguishes jealousy from other states, such as envy or the sadness that follows a lost relationship, is the rival who threatens to lure a partner away. Our cultural reactions to jealousy are often mixed; to some people, jealousy may seem to prove one's love, whereas others may consider it an improper sign of insecurity.

Two Types of Jealousy.   When people get jealous in response to a real threat to their relationships, *reactive jealousy* is said to occur. In contrast, *suspicious jealousy* occurs when one's partner has not misbehaved and one's suspicions do not fit the facts at hand. The distinction between the two types of jealousy is important, because almost everybody feels reactive jealousy in response to a partner's unfaithfulness, but people vary considerably in their tendency to feel suspicious jealousy in the absence of any provocation.

Who's Prone to Jealousy?   Some people feel jealous more readily and more intensely than other people do. Those who are dependent on a particular partner tend to be more jealous. So are those who feel inadequate and uncertain that they can keep their partners satisfied. Needing someone but worrying that you're not good enough to keep that person is a recipe for jealousy.

Personality traits and attachment styles influence jealousy, too. Neuroticism increases, and agreeableness decreases, jealousy. People with a preoccupied style are especially prone to jealousy, whereas people with a dismissing style are not. In addition, people who value sexual exclusivity experience less suspicious jealousy—but more reactive jealousy after infidelity occurs—than do those who value monogamy less. Finally, androgynous people experience less jealousy than do those who adhere to traditional gender roles.

Who Gets Us Jealous?   Not all rivals are created equal. A rival who surpasses us in accomplishments we care about is especially galling. A rival who is attractive to our partners is disturbing, too. Both men and women experience more jealousy when they encounter rivals who are good at giving the other sex what it wants, but for women the threatening comparison is physical attractiveness, and for men it's dominance.

What Gets Us Jealous?   An evolutionary perspective suggests that men and women should be sensitive to different kinds of infidelity in their romantic partners. For men, who face the problem of paternity uncertainty, the evolutionary costs of failing to detect a partner's sexual infidelity are so great that natural selection may have favored men who were too suspicious of their partners' faithfulness over those who were not suspicious enough. For a man, it's not a partner's love for someone else that's the bigger threat to his reproductive success, it's the sex. For their part, women presumably became sensitive to any signs that a man might withdraw the resources that were protecting their children. Natural selection may have favored those who were usually skeptical of men's declarations of true love, because a man's emotional infidelity conceivably endangers his female partner's reproductive success more than his sexual infidelity does.

In fact, most men do say that a partner's sexual infidelity would trouble them more than her emotional infidelity would, whereas the reverse is true for women. This finding has engendered criticism, but it has also been replicated in diverse cultures and does not seem to depend on how researchers ask the question. Men and women hate both types of infidelity, but women perceive a partner's emotional attachment to a rival as more worrisome than men do.

Responses to Jealousy. People may react to jealousy in ways that either hurt or help their relationships. People who have secure or preoccupied attachment styles tend to express their concerns and try to repair their relationships, but people who are dismissing or fearful more often pretend that they just don't care. Men and women often differ in their responses to jealousy, too. Women typically seek to improve and repair their relationships, whereas men strive to protect their egos by getting drunk and pursuing other women. Women are more likely than men to try to induce jealousy in their partners, but this is a dangerous strategy: Women who seek to improve their relationships by inducing jealousy in their men may succeed only in driving their partners away.

Coping Constructively with Jealousy. To keep jealousy at manageable levels, we may have to do away with the notion that it is a sign of true love. Jealousy isn't based on generous concern for the well-being of our partners, it's inherently selfish. We may also have to reduce the connection between the exclusivity of a relationship and a personal sense of self-worth. Indeed, people who succeed in reducing unwanted jealousy on their own often practice self-reliance and self-bolstering, maintaining a sense of self-confidence about their ability to act and survive independently. Formal therapies usually try to reduce catastrophic thinking, improve communication skills, enhance the jealous partner's self-esteem, and increase the fairness of the troubled relationship.

Deception and Lying

Deception is intentional behavior that creates an impression in the recipient that the deceiver knows is false. Some deception involves attempts to conceal information or divert attention from the truth, and people sometimes tell half-truths, but outright lying is the most straightforward example of deceptive behavior.

Lying in Close and Casual Relationships. There's a lot of lying in everyday life. College students report lying to one out of every three of the people with whom they interact. Most lies are self-serving, but people also tell many lies that are intended to benefit others. Lies of the latter sort are especially common in close relationships.

However, when people tell lies about serious matters, they tell them more often to their intimate partners than to anyone else. Lies also engender *deceiver's distrust*, which leads liars to perceive the recipients of their lies as untrustworthy. In addition, if lies are discovered, the recipients usually consider them to be more injurious than the liars do.

Lies and Liars. People who are extraverted and who are concerned with the impressions they make on others lie more often than others do. But practice doesn't make perfect. A liar's performance depends on the motivation with which he or she enacts the lie; people who really want to get away with a lie tend to be more transparent than they would be if the lie were less important.

Liars make more speech errors, speak in a higher pitch, and blink often. They often look sincere, however, and no single cue always indicates that a person is lying. Instead, the global pattern of a person's physical tension and paralanguage—and discrepancies between the person's tone of voice and facial expression—usually indicate whether or not he or she is lying.

So, How Well Can We Detect a Partner's Deception? The reactions that indicate that a person is lying may be quite idiosyncratic. People can learn to detect deception in a certain partner, but such success is usually limited to that person. Intimate partners have detailed knowledge of each other, but they also exhibit a *truth bias* that leads them to assume that their partners are being honest with them. In fact, as relationships become more intimate, the partners' accuracy in detecting deception in each other usually declines.

People tend not to be very skilled lie detectors, and liars get away with most of their lies. Nevertheless, lies have poisonous effects on close relationships even when they go undetected, and they are inherently risky.

Betrayal

Betrayals are hurtful actions by people we trusted and from whom we did not expect such misbehavior. In order for a meaningful betrayal to occur, we must have a desired relationship to be injured. Indeed, when our feelings get hurt, it's usually our friends or lovers who cause us distress, and such incidents may be hard to avoid; most people are close to more than one person, and when people try to be loyal simultaneously to several different relationships, competing demands are inescapable.

Individual Differences in Betrayal. Men and women do not differ in their tendencies to betray others, but white people betray others more often than other ethnic groups do, and betrayal is less frequent among those who are older, better educated, and religious. Frequent betrayers tend to be unhappy and maladjusted people who are resentful, vengeful, and suspicious of others.

The Two Sides to Every Betrayal. Betrayers often consider their behavior to be inconsequential and innocuous, but their victims rarely share those views. In almost every case, victims feel that a betrayal damaged their relationship. Perpetrators are much less likely to recognize the harmfulness of their actions.

Coping with Betrayal. Victims who face up to a betrayal, reinterpret it positively, and rely on friends for support, cope more constructively than do those who try to pretend it didn't happen and ignore their distress. Women are more likely than men to respond constructively to betrayal.

However, victims of betrayal sometimes want revenge. Vengeful people tend to have a sour outlook that leads to the desire to "pay back" those who have wronged them.

Forgiveness

Forgiveness entails giving up one's right to retaliate for wrongdoing from others. It occurs more readily when the betrayers apologize for their actions and the victims are able to empathize with the offenders, and secure people offer forgiveness more readily than insecure people do. Forgiveness usually improves the relationships in which it occurs, so it's fortunate that forgiveness is more likely to occur in close, committed relationships than in those that are less committed.

CHAPTER 11

Power

POWER AND INTERDEPENDENCY THEORY ◆ Sources of Power ◆ Types
of Resources ◆ The Process of Power ◆ The Outcome of Power ◆
THE TWO SIDES OF POWER ◆ FOR YOUR CONSIDERATION ◆
CHAPTER SUMMARY

Who calls the shots in your relationship? Do you usually get your way? Or do you and your partner trade the lead, with each of you getting some of what you want? Most people say that an ideal relationship would be an equal partnership, with both partners sharing the ability to make important decisions and to influence one another; in one study, 95 percent of women and 87 percent of men said they believed that dating partners should have "exactly equal say" in the relationship (Hill et al., 1979). In addition, people prefer friendships in which the partners share similar amounts of power to friendships in which one of the partners is typically the boss (Veniegas & Peplau, 1997). This may not surprise you, but this preference for sharing power is an enormous departure from the traditional model endorsed by previous generations, in which men were the dominant partners in heterosexual relationships, making all the important decisions and calling all the shots. These days, few people explicitly announce that they want to emulate this old-fashioned model, but figuring out how to achieve equality in a relationship can be much more complicated than it sounds. Consider one aspect of power in close relationships, the ability to make decisions about what the partners will do. How should decision-making work in an egalitarian relationship? Should the partners make all decisions together? Or does each partner take responsibility for making exactly half the decisions? Does it matter which decisions are important and which ones aren't? Endorsing equality in a relationship is a simple matter, but making it a reality is a much greater challenge.

This chapter will explore the ways in which social power operates in intimate relationships. Social **power** is the ability to influence the behavior of others and to resist their influence on us (Huston, 2002). It affects all kinds of relationships—between friends as well as lovers, at work as well as in the family, in superficial as well as close encounters. We will identify some of the basic factors that contribute to relational power, the ways in which people exercise power in their relationships, and the consequences of power for individuals and couples.

POWER AND INTERDEPENDENCY THEORY

There are different ways to analyze social power, but the most widely adopted perspective is that of interdependency theory (Thibaut & Kelley, 1959), which we examined in chapter 6. In this chapter, we'll use interdependency ideas to describe the bases on which power is built, the processes by which power is wielded, and the outcomes that are produced by its use.

Sources of Power

From an interdependency perspective, power is based on the control of valuable resources. If Wilma controls access to something Fred wants, Fred will be motivated to comply with Wilma's wishes so that she will allow him to get what he wants. Wilma will then have power over Fred; she'll be able, at least temporarily to get him to do what *she* wants. This is a simple idea, but (as you might expect) there are various subtleties involved in this view of social power.

First, the person who has power does not have to possess the desired resources; it is enough that he or she controls access to them. Imagine that you are shopping with a friend at a flea market and you discover the rare imported bootleg concert DVD that you have spent months looking for; better yet, it's half price! But you don't have enough money with you, and you need a loan from your friend to buy the elusive disc. Your friend doesn't actually have the object you desire, but his or her power in this situation will come from controlling your ability to get it. In a similar fashion, relationship partners can control our access to valuable interpersonal rewards—such as self-disclosure and physical affection—and thereby have power over us.

Of course, one only derives power from controlling a resource if other people want it, and the greater their need or desire, the greater one's power. The example of the rare DVD is an illustration of this: If you have only a mild interest in the disc, a friend with the money to buy it has only a little power over you. But if you want the disc desperately, your friend has more power, and will be able to ask for a sizeable favor in return.

We encountered an example of one person's desire fueling another person's power back in Box 6.1 (on page 188) when we introduced the **principle of lesser interest:** In any partnership, the person who has less interest in continuing and maintaining the relationship has more power in that partnership (Waller & Hill, 1951). If your partner loves and needs you more than you love him or her, you'll get to do what you want more often than not. This sounds cold-blooded, but it is true; in romantic relationships, the partner who is less emotionally involved in the relationship usually has more power (Sprecher & Felmlee, 1997). An example of this was obtained in a study of second marriages (Pyke, 1994) that found that women who had been reluctant to marry a second time were more likely than those who remarried quickly to have egalitarian second marriages in which they had a lot of power. One woman explained that she had not wanted to remarry unless she could find a second husband who would behave like her father: He "loves my mother so much that she has him wrapped around her finger . . . She can get him to do anything. And he loves her so much that he'll do it." (Pyke, 1994, p. 87). Indeed, whenever we want something badly (be it a rare DVD or interpersonal intimacy) and believe we cannot get it elsewhere, the person who has what we want is able to exert control over us.

We mentioned another example of this pattern in chapter 8, when we noted that men want more sex, on average, than women do. Men's greater interest in sex gives women power; it's quite unromantic, but rather enlightening, to think of sex as a valuable resource that women can exchange for various benefits from men (Baumeister & Vohs, 2004). This arrangement is explicit in the case of prostitution, when women trade sex for money, but it often also operates in more subtle ways in many romantic relationships. It's not uncommon, for instance, for a woman to wait for a declaration of affection and emerging commitment from a man before allowing him access to sex.

Of course, if something we want is readily available elsewhere, we can just go there to get it, and the availability of alternative sources of desired resources is another critical factor in an interdependency perspective on power. If there is another friend at the flea market who could lend you the money you need, the first friend has less power over you. And if there are many people who would loan you the money, then you are not very dependent on any one of them, and not one of them has much power over you at all.

In the same fashion, the availability of alternatives influences the balance of power in an intimate relationship. Those with few alternatives to their existing partnerships (who therefore have low $CL_{alt}s$) will be more dependent on their relationships than will those with many other other potential partners (who thereby have high $CL_{alt}s$). And as we have just seen, being more dependent means having less power. If one partner has few alternatives and the other has many, there will be a larger imbalance of power than would be the case if they needed each other to similar degrees (Gephart & Agnew, 1997).

In fact, differences in available alternatives may be one reason why men are typically more powerful than women in traditional marriages. When husbands work outside the home and their wives do not, they often have higher $CL_{alt}s$ for at least two important reasons. First, they may encounter larger numbers of other potential partners, and second, they're more likely to have the money to pursue them if they wish. In contrast, stay-at-home wives may not meet many other interesting men, and even if they do, they're likely to be economically dependent on their husbands, having little money of their own (Levinger, 1976). Thus, the balance of power in a marriage sometimes changes when a wife enters the work force and gains new friends and money of her own (Fitch & Ruggles, 2000).

There are two more broad points to make about the interdependence perspective on power. First, interdependence theory recognizes two different broad types of power. On occasion, one can control a partner's outcomes no matter what the partner does; in such cases, one has a form of power known as **fate control:** One can autocratically determine what outcomes a partner receives, thereby controlling the other's fate. When she is his only option, a woman who refuses to have sex with her husband is exercising fate control; she can unilaterally determine whether or not sex occurs. A second, more subtle, type of power is **behavior control.** This occurs when, by changing one's own behavior, one encourages a partner to alter his or her actions in a desirable direction, too. If a woman offers to provide a special backrub if her partner cleans the garage, she's engaging in behavior control.

Of course, in almost all relationships, the partners *both* have power over each other, and the last, and perhaps most essential, point of an interdependency perspective is that the interactions of two partners emerge from their mutual influence on one another. One partner's power over the other may be matched by the other's *counterpower* over the one, so that both partners are able to get each other to do what they want some of the time. For instance, a woman may have fate control over whether or not her husband has sex, but he probably has some behavior control over her in return; by cajoling her, pleasing her, or worse, threatening her, he may be able to get her to do what he wants. Two partners' abilities to influence one another may be diverse and variable, being strong in some situations and weak in others, but both of them will routinely have some control over what the other does.

Types of Resources

If power is based on the resources we possess, what kinds of resources are involved? Table 11.1 lists six bases of power first identified by French and Raven (1959); this scheme has been applied to all kinds of interactions, including those that occur in intimate relationships. The first two types, **reward power** and **coercion power,** refer to a person's ability to bestow various rewards and punishments on someone else. The benefits and costs involved can be physical or material goods, such as a pleasant gift or a painful slap, or intangible, interpersonal gains and losses, such as reassuring approval or hurtful disdain (Raven, 2001). For example, if a husband craves a shoulder massage from his wife, she has reward power over him: She can rub his back or not, supplying or withholding a physical reward. But in return, he may have coercion power over her: If he doesn't get his massage, he may sulk and be less affectionate, imposing intangible costs.

The capabilities to provide desired benefits or to impose aversive costs on our partners are very important and very influential, but there are other ways to influence people, too. **Legitimate power** exists when our partners believe that we have a reasonable right to tell them what to do, and they have an obligation to comply. In some cultures, for instance, a husband really is thought to be the boss, and a wife is supposed not only to love and honor him, but to *obey* him as well, doing whatever he asks. This form of legitimate power comes from being in a position of authority, but potent social norms can also impart legitimate power to requests that come from anyone (Raven, 2001). The norm of *reciprocity* encourages us to do unto others as they have done unto us, and if someone who has already done you a favor asks for some kindness in return, the norm obligates you to repay the good deed. *Equity* is also normative, and if your partner has done extra housework lately, an invitation to fold some laundry might be

TABLE 11.1. **Types of Resource Power**

Type of Power	Resource	Gets People to Do What You Want Them to Do Because:
Reward power	Rewards	You can give them something they like or take away something they don't like.
Coercive power	Punishments	You can do something to them they don't like or take away something they do like.
Legitimate power	Authority or norms of equity, reciprocity, or social responsibility	They recognize your authority to tell them what to do.
Referent power	Respect and/or love	They identify with you, feeling attracted and wanting to remain close.
Expert power	Expertise	You have the broad understanding they desire.
Informational power	Information	You possess some specific knowledge they desire.

Source: Based on Raven, 2001.

difficult to decline. Finally, a norm of *social responsibility* urges us to be generous to those who depend on us—to help those who cannot help themselves—and if your partner is sick in bed with the flu, a request for some juice may be hard to turn down. Any of these norms can impart power to a partner's desires, making them very influential, at least temporarily.

We have **referent power** over our partners when they adore us and wish to do what we want because they feel connected to us. Our wishes may change our partners' preferences about what they want to do when they love us and want to stay close to us. **Expert power** exists when our partners recognize our superior knowledge and experience and are influenced by us because we know more than they do. When a wife is a better cook than her husband, for instance, he'll often follow her advice and instructions without question when it's his turn to prepare dinner. Finally, we have **informational power** when we have specific pieces of information that influence our partners' behavior; our partners may do what we want if we offer to share a juicy bit of gossip with them.

How are these resources used in your relationships? Many cultures are still governed by a norm of patriarchy that expects men to have higher levels of expert and legitimate power than women, and women to have higher levels of referent power than men (Carli, 1999). It's often taken for granted that men have wider domains of competence and authority than women do, and that puts women at a disadvantage when they try to influence others by drawing on their abilities and expertise. In particular, when women are in positions of leadership, they're often evaluated more harshly than men are when they straightforwardly tell others what to do (Carli, 2001). On the other hand, if they try to influence others by being charming and likable—if they use referent power—women receive favorable evaluations but seem less authoritative (Carli, 1995). Cultural norms evidently shape our judgments of what bases of power are most appropriate for each sex.

People also often assume that women and men have expertise in different domains, so that women may get their way regarding household matters and children, with men calling the shots with regard to money (Harvey et al., 2002). Even if a man is presumed to be the household boss, he may routinely yield to his female partner on issues that are traditionally associated with "women's work" (Carli, 2001).

We should also note that, whereas some types of power can have desirable effects on relationships, others do not. In general, it's more pleasant to be enticed to do something that will obtain some reward than it is to feel pressured to do something to avoid a painful cost, and, as a result, the use of coercive power often leaves one's partner feeling less content than reward power does. In particular, husbands who rely on coercive strategies such as the threat of violence to get their way tend to have dissatisfied wives (Frieze & McHugh, 1992). This makes coercion a poor long-term strategy from an interdependency perspective because the lower one's outcomes become, the less likely one will be to remain in that relationship. Other types of power have less corrosive effects, but the use of coercive power can gradually undermine one's influence and ruin relationships.

So, what does all this mean for the balance of power in heterosexual relationships? Is it possible for equal power to be based on the control of different resources? Conceivably, women's greater referent power could balance out men's greater legitimate power and control of economic resources. In practice, however, the issue is complex. Some resources that provide people power can be used more flexibly than others can. Theorists describe some resources (such as money) as *universalistic* and others (such as love) as *particularistic* (Foa et al., 1993). Universalistic resources can be exchanged with almost anyone in a wide variety of situations, and whoever controls them has considerable freedom in deciding what to do with them (and with whom to do it). Particularistic resources are valuable in some situations and not in others, and they may confer power to their owner only with particular partners. A partner's love for you may give you referent power over him or her and no one else, whereas a large pile of cash may provide you reward power over almost everyone you meet.

Then there is the matter of ultimate control over the resource. The ownership of money is clear-cut. The person who has it controls it. The vulnerability of money is also obvious; it can be stolen or taken away by superior force. Love, in contrast, is far more complicated. It cannot be taken by force: "We cannot force others to give us their approval, regardless of how much power we have over them, because coercing them to express this admiration or praise would make their expression worthless" (Blau, 1964, p. 17). The power of love is that it must be given spontaneously.

On the other hand, love, like any other resource, must be valued to be effective in creating power. Our love is only powerful when another person wants our affection and regard, and the value of love may thus be more variable than that of money. Basing one's power in a relationship on the give and take of love can be precarious. Thus, if men control more universalistic resources that are widely influential in social life, and women control more particularistic resources, it shouldn't surprise us to find men being more influential than women in many relationships.

The Process of Power

Another major consideration is the manner in which power is expressed. People often announce their preferences directly, but power can also be expressed indirectly, through hints and other implications, or nonverbally, with a glower or a slap. (See Box 11.1.) The behaviors with which we seek to get our way are influenced both by the resources we control and by cultural norms that suggest how we should behave. And as we'll see, those behaviors tend to differ for men and women.

BOX 11.1
Influencing a Partner to Use a Condom

You'd think that it'd be taken for granted these days that people would expect to have safe sex when they begin having sex in a new relationship. Unfortunately, too often, one partner still needs to convince the other to use a condom. How do such negotiations proceed? The most common strategy is to straightforwardly announce one's wish to use a condom (Lam, Mak, & Lindsay, 2004) and to back up one's request with reward power, coercive power, or informational power (De Bro, Campbell, & Peplau, 1994). Promised rewards often include the increased respect and closeness that compliance will bring, threatened costs include the discontent or withholding of sex that resistance will produce, and persuasive information often describes the risks that will be avoided by making the smart choice to employ a condom.

But people also make their wishes known through other means that do not involve explicit discussion (Lam et al., 2004). One effective tactic is to simply produce a condom and begin putting it on. Without saying a word, one can demonstrate that condom use is expected and appreciated. The reluctant partner may protest that such precautions aren't needed, but his or her objections probably won't last long if the proactive partner persists.

Indeed, when people *don't* want to use a condom, they usually don't mention their preference. Instead, they typically try to seduce their partners, getting them so turned on that sex proceeds without a pause for protection (De Bro et al., 1994). Thus, it may be useful, if you seek safe sex, to keep your wits about you and to remember that, with the force of supportive social norms behind you, your preference is likely to be more powerful than any defense your partner can deploy.

Language

Our use of language and our style of paralanguage may be two of the most subtle and pervasive processes of power. The conversations two people share may be strongly influenced by the balance of power between them. And for better or for worse, women tend not to speak to men with the same implicit strength and power that they display toward other women. As we noted in chapter 5, all you have to do is listen carefully to find that women often speak more tentatively and less forcefully when they are talking to men than they do when they are talking with other women.

In fact, Zimmerman and West (1975) surreptitiously recorded conversations of college students in public places (obtaining permission to analyze the recordings after the conversations were done) and then compared the language and paralanguage of same-sex dyads to those in which men and women talked to each other. There were no important differences between the conversations of the same-sex couples; women and men behaved similarly when they were talking to others of the same sex. However, distinctive patterns emerged in interactions with the other sex. First, men interrupted their female partners much more often than their female partners interrupted them. Interrupting someone is one way to display one's social power, and it's more common for high-status people to interrupt those of low status than vice versa (Kollock, Blumstein, & Schwartz, 1985). Second, women talked less than the men did. More often than the men, they were interrupted before they were done speaking, or, if they did finish, they received a minimal response (such as "um"). Given this, women's lower rates of speaking are not surprising: What's the point in talking if he isn't interested?

In a second study, West and Zimmerman (1983) examined the cross-sex conversations of unacquainted couples in a laboratory setting, and again, even when they had just met, men interrupted women more often than women interrupted men. It's evident, then, that whether or not they know each other, men tend to have more active control over their conversations than women do (LaFrance, 1992). The topic of conversation matters; women dominate the discussion when traditionally feminine topics are being discussed, but men lead discussion of traditionally masculine topics *and* neutral ones (Brown, Dovidio, & Ellyson, 1990).

Indeed, when women speak too forcefully to men, they may actually be less influential than they are when they are more tentative. Women who speak assertively to men make poorer impressions on them than do women who are less direct, and the men are often less likely to heed what they say (Carli, 1990). Assertive women are influential with other women but less powerful with men, and tentative, "feminine" styles of speech may actually be more successful with many men. Altogether, men who use styles of speech that command respect are more likely to get what they want from both men and women, but women are more influential when they use different styles for different audiences.

Nonverbal Behavior

Dominance and power are also communicated to others nonverbally (Aguinis, Simonsen, & Pierce, 1998). Take a look back at Table 5.2 on page 160.

Accompanying the assertive paralanguage of high-status people are patterns of eye contact, body movement, and touch that clearly differ from those of people with lower social power. And as we mentioned in chapter 5, women tend *not* to display these high-status styles of behavior when they are interacting with men.

There may be a good reason why. Women may actually be less influential when they use dominant nonverbal behavior with men. Linda Carli and her colleagues (1995) demonstrated this when they trained research assistants to deliver a persuasive message (about changing the student meal plan) using different nonverbal styles. One style involved behaviors that conveyed calm confidence and competence: rapid, fluent speech, moderately high eye contact, an upright posture, and modest hand gestures. It was a style that seemed authoritative and knowledgeable, and men who used it tended to be very persuasive. Women were also convincing when they used this style with other women, but they were less successful when they used it with men. Instead, women persuaded more men when they used a friendlier, more likable presentation that involved more smiling, slower speech, and more demure behavior. Thus, studies of both language and nonverbal behavior support the same conclusion: Women tend to get their way when they use authoritative behavior with other women, but they enjoy less success when they direct such behavior toward men.

Nonverbal Sensitivity

Remember, too, that women are generally more accurate judges of others' emotions and meaning than men are. Women decode others' nonverbal communications more accurately than men do (Hall, 1998), and they are usually more aware of what others are feeling (Ciarrochi, Hynes, & Crittenden, 2005). This skill is a tremendous asset because (as we discussed in chapter 5) the sensitivity and accuracy with which a couple communicates nonverbally predicts how satisfied with each other they are likely to be (Carton et al., 1999).

On the other hand, a person's nonverbal sensitivity also has something to do with how powerful he or she is. When two people differ in status, it's typically the job of the subordinate to keep track of what the boss is feeling, and not the other way around (Miller, 1976). When there's a big difference in power, bosses don't have to care what their subordinates are feeling; underlings are supposed to do what a boss wants whether they like it or not. In contrast, subordinates can increase their own (limited) power when they carefully monitor their supervisors' moods; if they make requests when their bosses are in good moods (and stay out of sight when the bosses are cranky), they're more likely to get what they want. (Remember back in fifth grade when you had to tell a parent about some misbehavior at school? You were probably very alert and careful to deliver your news when your parent was in a good mood; you knew that things would go worse if you dropped your bomb when your parent was already grumpy. You were better off if you—the low-status party—were able to astutely decode the nonverbal moods of your parent—the boss.)

Thus, in being adept users of nonverbal communication, women gain valuable information that can make them more pleasing partners and that can

BORN LOSER® by Art and Chip Sansom

When a difference in status exists, it's usually up to the subordinate to understand what the boss is feeling, rather than vice versa.
Reprinted by permission of United Media.

increase their influence over men. On the other hand, they also behave as subordinates do when they are dealing with people of higher status. Ironically, a useful and desirable talent may perpetuate a stereotypical pattern in which women behave as if they are the minions of men.

Styles of Power

Just what strategies, then, do men and women use in their efforts to influence each other? Toni Falbo and Anne Peplau (1980) addressed this question in a classic study that asked 50 lesbians, 50 gay men, 50 heterosexual women, and 50 heterosexual men to describe "how I get [my partner] to do what I want." Two themes characterized the participants' replies. First, the researchers found that partners sometimes explicitly asked for what they wanted, straightforwardly announcing their wishes or making unambiguous requests. Their efforts to influence their partners were overt and *direct*, and their preferences were plain. On other occasions, however, people's actions were more *indirect*; they hinted at what they wanted or pouted when their wishes were unfulfilled, but they never came right out and said what they wanted. Importantly, the more satisfied people were with their relationships, the more likely they were to use direct strategies. Among other possibilities, this could mean that when people have rewarding partnerships, they feel safe enough to be honest and forthright with their partners. On the other hand, it could also mean that people whose desires are expressed indirectly and ambiguously are less adept at getting what they want, and they're likely to be dissatisfied as a result. What's your guess? Does indirectness lead to dissatisfaction or follow from it? (Remember, it could be both.)

The second theme that distinguished different strategies described the extent to which people sought their goals through interaction with their partners (as opposed to doing what they wanted on their own). Sometimes, people reasoned or bargained with their partners in efforts to persuade them to provide some desired outcome; in such cases, people sought cooperation or collaboration from their partners, and their strategies were *bilateral*, involving both members of the couple. In contrast, on other occasions, people took independent *unilateral* action, doing what they wanted without involving their partners.

Importantly, people who reported that they were more powerful than their partners said that they made frequent use of bilateral strategies, whereas those who were less powerful were more likely to use unilateral strategies. Thus, people who were able to influence their partners successfully did just that, reasoning and negotiating with them to gain their compliance. In contrast, those possessed of low power were less likely to seek their partners' cooperation; they just went off and did their own thing.

Falbo and Peplau found that, overall, the strategies used by homosexuals did not differ from those employed by heterosexuals. Further, gay men and lesbian women did not differ in their influence attempts. There were differences, however, between the strategies employed by heterosexual men and women; on average, heterosexual men reported more extensive use of direct and bilateral styles, whereas heterosexual women used more indirect and unilateral strategies. Thus, when they were dealing with their romantic partners, heterosexual men tended to use styles of influence that are characteristic of people who are satisfied and powerful, whereas women adopted styles typically used by those who are powerless and discontent.

Wow. Is it true, then, that heterosexual men typically behave in a mature and assertive fashion in their romantic partnerships, asking for what they want and reasoning logically with their lovers, while their partners pout, get moody, and become cold and distant without ever saying what they want? Well, yes, to a degree. That statement is obviously too sweeping, but it is fair to say that in heterosexual relationships men tend to be more openly assertive than women, whereas women tend to be more timid and tentative than men. Moreover, this tends to be true from the moment a relationship begins. When they want to start a relationship, men use more direct strategies, such as asking a woman for a date, whereas women more often use indirect strategies, such as trying to seem friendly and waiting to be asked (Clark, Shaver, & Abrahams, 1999).

However, it's also clear that it's not a person's sex, per se, that is correlated with his or her use of power. Further research has demonstrated that Falbo and Peplau's (1980) results emerged from two other influences that tend to be linked to one's biological sex. The first of these is a person's *gender role*[1]. Whether they are male or female, people who are high in instrumentality—who are, after all, assertive, self-confident people—tend to use direct, bilateral styles of power. By comparison, feminine people (who are high in expressivity but low in instrumentality) tend to use indirect, unilateral styles (Falbo, 1982). And as we saw in chapter 1, more men than women tend to be high in instrumentality.

The second influence, a person's *status*, is even more important than his or her gender (Sagrestano, 1992b). No matter who people are, they are unlikely to behave authoritatively and assertively in situations in which they have lower status than the others they are trying to influence. Lynda Sagrestano (1992a) demonstrated this when she asked men and women to respond to scenarios in which they were either experts with more power than their partners or novices

---

[1]If a reminder about just what we mean by "instrumentality" and "expressivity" will be helpful, revisit pages 23–24 back in chapter 1.

with lower power; both men and women used direct strategies of power when they were experts but indirect strategies when they were novices, and the sexes did not differ in the styles they selected. In addition, teens of both sexes use indirect and unilateral styles in dealing with their parents, especially their fathers, but they use more direct and bilateral strategies in dealing with their friends (Cowan, Drinkard, & MacGavin, 1984). Finally, recall that there are no differences between the sexes in the ways that gays and lesbians seek to influence their partners (Falbo & Peplau, 1980).

Add all this up, and it appears that the different styles of influence exhibited by heterosexual men and women in their romantic relationships are products of the typical balance of power and status in those partnerships. Men and women do not differ in their power preferences in their same-sex partnerships, and women can be just as direct as men when that style pays off for them (Carothers & Allen, 1999), but men have traditionally held more power than women, both in and out of the home. Historically, women have had lower status than men, even in their romantic partnerships, and indirect styles of power have been the result. This may be changing. These days, each new generation of American women is higher in instrumentality than the one before (Twenge, 1997), and both men and women are becoming more egalitarian in their views of marriage (Bryant, 2003). Men probably have less automatic authority in their intimate relationships than they used to, and that may be a good thing: Spouses who feel relatively powerless tend to be dissatisfied with their marriages (Wilkie, Ferree, & Ratcliff, 1998). People who have to hint and pout to get (some of) what they want tend to be less content than are those who can come right out and ask for what they desire.

The Outcome of Power

So, who wins when men and women try to influence each other? The answer is a bit complicated because it depends on whom you ask. Husbands' and wives' self-reports about how much power each has in the relationship often do not agree (Olson & Cromwell, 1975). In particular, because we are aware of the many compromises and sacrifices we make to please our partners—and because our partners' similar concessions may be less obvious to us—we often underestimate just how powerful we are (Turk & Bell, 1972).

Specifically, because social norms still tend to lead us to expect that husbands will be the heads of their households, wives are often more powerful than they think they are. A study of marital power in new marriages (Corrales, 1975) provided a good illustration of this. As Table 11.2 shows, husbands and wives both reported that the husbands made most of the decisions around the house. But when researchers watched the couples complete a decision-making task in the laboratory, it was evident that the wives had a great deal more power than the couple believed. The husbands were more influential in some decisions, but the wives were more influential in others, and they made egalitarian decisions almost half the time. Despite the couples' expectations, the wives' power was very similar to that of their husbands.

TABLE 11.2. Who's in Charge Here?

	Self-Reports of Who Usually Decides	
	Husbands' Reports	Wives' Reports
Husband-dominated	58%	62%
Egalitarian	31	32
Wife-dominated	11	6

	Observed Interactions in the Laboratory
Husband-dominated	29%
Egalitarian	47
Wife-dominated	24

Source: Data from Corrales, 1975.

On the other hand, we can overestimate our influence if we just count up the number of relational decisions we make each day, particularly if our partners are delegating those decisions to us and letting us make them. Decision-makers don't have that much power if a higher authority can veto their decisions at any time. In one investigation, for instance, Japanese-American wives in Hawaii reported that they routinely made many more decisions regarding the care and feeding of their families than their husbands did (Johnson, 1975). As Table 11.3 shows, they did acknowledge that their husbands were influential in major decisions, but even those choices seemed egalitarian to them. However, when the women were interviewed in detail about how decisions were made in their families, their responses (as coded by judges) revealed that things usually went their husbands' way (see Table 11.3). Most of the time, the wives made relatively minor, everyday decisions the way their husbands wanted them to, and the husbands retained the larger amount of power in their relationships; had the wives made decisions with which their husbands disagreed, they would have found their influence to be weaker than they believed.

Female Dominance: A Taboo?

It seems, then, that in most heterosexual relationships, the partners either share fairly equal power or the men call most of the shots. When there are *im*balances of power, men are more influential than women are.

Why does female dominance not often occur? Why are women not the more powerful partners in their relationships just as often as men are? One reason is that both men and women are less satisfied in female-dominated relationships than they are in either egalitarian or male-dominated relationships (Corrales, 1975; Gray-Little & Burks, 1983). In fact, obvious displays of female dominance may put partnerships at risk. In an ambitious study that tracked dating couples over five years, researchers regularly interviewed the participants and, without their knowledge, counted the number of times one partner interrupted another (Filsinger & Thoma, 1988). (As we noted earlier,

TABLE 11.3. Decision-Making is not the Same Thing as Authority

	Daily Decisions (Based on Wives' Questionnaire Responses)		
	Wife-Dominated	Egalitarian	Husband-Dominated
Financial	45%	18%	37%
Social	28	60	12
Child rearing	58	40	2
Major decisions (e.g., changing jobs or residences)	2	50	48

	Authority in the Home (Based on In-Depth Interviews)
Wife-dominated	7%
Egalitarian	39
Husband-dominated	54

Source: Data from Johnson, 1975.

people with high status and power interrupt those of lesser standing more often than they are interrupted in return.) Then, the researchers simply distinguished those couples in which the man interrupted the woman more often than she barged in on him (which is the usual pattern) from those couples in which she interrupted him more than vice versa (which is unusual [Anderson & Leaper, 1998]). Over the course of the study, 80 percent of the latter couples—those in which the woman was verbally dominant—broke up, whereas only 20 percent of the more typical partnerships failed. Moreover, among those couples that were still together, most of them now married, the more often the woman interrupted her man, the less satisfied both partners were with their relationship.

Evidently, heterosexual relationships in which the woman publicly displays dominance are particularly vulnerable to dissatisfaction and dissolution. Are our expectations and perceptions of proper conduct still bound by a patriarchal past? Despite the increasing acceptance of an egalitarian norm for heterosexual relationships (Bryant, 2003), many people are still more comfortable with male dominance than with female dominance.

THE TWO SIDES OF POWER

There's both good news and bad news with which to finish this chapter. In some men, the need for power takes the form of a *Don Juan syndrome* (named for the literary figure who used the sexual conquest of women to prove his manhood and to flaunt his power) (Winter, 1973). Power is important to such men, and the higher their need for power, the less love they feel for their partners and the less satisfied they and their partners are. They are less likely to marry than other men are, but when they do, they try to maintain control over their wives. Their wives are less likely to have full-time careers than are the wives of men who have lower needs for power, and they inflict more physical abuse on their wives than other men do (Mason & Blankenship, 1987). They tend to be narcissistic (Campbell et al., 2002), and they are prone to disruptive behaviors such as drinking, drug use, aggression, and gambling (Winter, 1988).

Obviously, there's a dark side to the need for power. Some people actively seek to be the top dogs in their relationships, and they tend to be controlling, domineering people who have partners who are relatively discontented. That's the bad news. (You probably guessed that!) But there's another side to power, and the good news is that power does not always lead to the greedy exploitation of one's partners. Indeed, when people adopt communal orientations[2] in committed romantic relationships, they typically use their power for the benefit of their partners and their relationships, not for selfish ends (Gardner & Seeley, 2001). When people care for each other and want to maintain a rewarding relationship, they become benevolent; they display concern for the welfare of their partners, and they use their influence to enhance the other's well-being as well as their own (Chen, Lee-Chai, & Bargh, 2001). Moreover, there are probably some people who are chronically high in communal strength[3] who are routinely generous towards their partners and who become even more magnanimous when they hold positions of power (Lee-Chai, Chen, & Chartrand, 2001).

Thus, because it can be used either for good or for ill, power is neither malevolent nor benevolent in and of itself (Pratto & Walker, 2001). An old cliché asserts that "power corrupts," implying that people inevitably become greedy and selfish when they are able to get others to do what they want. But in interdependent, intimate relationships in which both partners want the desirable outcomes the other can provide, power need not be a corrosive, deleterious thing. Instead, committed, happy lovers often use their influence to benefit their partners and to enhance, rather than undermine, their mutual contentment.

FOR YOUR CONSIDERATION

During their first year of marriage, Amanda and Deion fell into a pattern in which he balanced the checkbook and paid all their bills each month. She was still a senior in college and didn't have a job, but he was working and earning just enough money for them to live on each month if they were careful. He took pride in his prudent management of money, but both of them were glad when she graduated and got a great job that actually paid her a little more than Deion's did.

He was surprised, however, when she announced that she wanted to maintain her own checking and savings accounts. She suggested that they each put half of their earnings into a joint account that would pay the bills and then keep

[2]Need a refresher on the distinction between communal and exchange orientations? Take a look back at p. 203 in chapter 6.
[3]Look back at Table 6.2 on p. 205.

the rest of their money for their own use. He was hurt that she did not want to merge their monies and join financial forces, and he was annoyed when he realized that, if they each kept half their money, she would have a lot more money than he would after a few years. But she argued that she wanted to be allowed to do what she wanted with her extra earnings, spending or investing them as she saw fit, and she thought that separate accounts would actually avoid disagreements and conflict.

What do you think the future holds for Amanda and Deion? Why?

CHAPTER SUMMARY

Social power is the ability to influence the behavior of others and to resist their influence on us. People often say that they want relationships in which they and their lovers have equal power, but maintaining an egalitarian partnership may be surprisingly complex.

Power and Interdependency Theory

Sources of Power. From an interdependency perspective, power is based on the control of valuable resources. A powerful person does not need to have direct control over these resources; he or she need only control access to them. But such control increases one's power only to the extent that one's partner values the resource. If the partner can easily do without the resource, one's power will be slim.

Resource power also depends on the availability of alternative sources of the resource. The more alternatives you have, the less dependent you are on any one person and the less power any one person has over you. The *principle of lesser interest* states that in a dyadic relationship, power and dependency are inversely related: The one who is more dependent has less power.

There are two different broad types of power. With *fate control*, one partner can determine what happens to the other no matter what that other partner does. *Behavior control* is less absolute; it exists when one partner can encourage, but not compel, the other to do what he or she wants. In almost all relationships, both partners have some power over each other, with each being able to influence the other some of the time.

Types of Resources. There are six resources that provide people power. *Reward power* and *coercion power* refer to one's ability to bestow rewards and punishments, respectively, on someone else. *Legitimate power* exists when one partner has a reasonable right—by dint of authority, reciprocity, equity, or social responsibility—to tell the other what to do. A partner's love and affection provides the other *referent power*, knowledge and expertise creates *expert power*, and specific pieces of information lend one *informational power*.

Traditional norms lead us to expect men to have higher levels of expert and legitimate power than women, and women to have higher levels of referent power than men. Indeed, if women try to influence men by being charming and likable, they are evaluated more favorably than they are when they straightfor-wardly tell men what to do.

The balance of power in close relationships is also affected by the univer-salistic or particularistic nature of the resources one controls. Universalistic resources can be exchanged with almost anyone in a wide variety of situations, whereas particularistic resources confer power to their owner only with partic-ular partners. Love is a particularistic resource; our affection is only influential when another person wants it.

The Process of Power. The process of power refers to the manner in which power is expressed. Language and paralanguage are involved here, with men tending to interrupt women more than vice versa. Dominance and power are also expressed through assertive patterns of eye contact, body movement, and touch, but when women adopt such styles of behavior, they make better im-pressions on other women than on men. Subordinates also tend to be astute judges of their supervisors' feelings.

Influence tactics may be overt and direct or indirect and implicit, and they may be bilateral, involving both members of a couple in negotiation and bar-gaining, or unilateral, with individuals doing what they want without involv-ing their partners. There are no differences in the tactics used by women and men in same-sex partnerships, but men tend to be more direct and bilateral, and women more indirect and unilateral, in heterosexual relationships.

Men and women differ in this manner for two reasons. First, masculine people tend to be more direct and bilateral than feminine people are. Second, and more importantly, traditional norms accord husbands more status than wives, and high-status people are more direct and bilateral than people of lower status are.

The Outcome of Power. Husbands and wives often disagree about the extent of their power, but wives often have more power than they think they do. Nevertheless, people can overestimate their influence if they simply count up the number of decisions they make each day, particularly if their partners are delegating those decisions to them and can veto them at any time. On the whole, when there is an imbalance of power in a heterosexual relationship, men are usually more influential than women are. One reason for this is that many people are still more comfortable with male dominance than with female dominance.

The Two Sides of Power

In some men, the need for power takes the form of a *Don Juan syndrome:* The higher their need for power, the less love they feel for their partners and the less satisfied they and their partners are. However, when they are committed to a relationship, many people use power benevolently, generously enhancing their partners' well-being as well as their own. Thus, power is neither malevolent nor benevolent in and of itself. Committed, happy lovers often use their influence to benefit their partners and to enhance, rather than undermine, their mutual contentment.

Conflict and Violence

Does your romantic partner always do everything you want, when you want it? Of course not. It's hard to imagine an intimate relationship that does not involve occasional friction and incompatibility in the desires, opinions, and actions of the two partners. No matter how much two people care for each other, no matter how well-suited they are to each other, dispute and disagreement will occur (Canary, 2003). And the more interdependent they are—the more time they spend together and the wider the variety of activities and tasks they try to coordinate—the more likely occasional conflict becomes (Miller, 1997b). Conflict is inevitable in close relationships.

It's also very influential. Over time, the manner in which two partners manage their conflicts may either enhance or erode their love and regard for each other. In this chapter, then, we'll examine the nature and sources of this sometimes frustrating, sometimes fulfilling, but ultimately unavoidable aspect of intimate relationships. We'll look at how conflicts unfold, how they escalate, and how people respond to them. We'll discuss how people can more effectively cope with conflicts and whether conflict can be beneficial to relationships. We'll also consider a dark side of conflict: the violence that sometimes occurs in marital and dating relationships.

THE NATURE OF CONFLICT

What Is Conflict?

Interpersonal conflict occurs whenever one person's motives, goals, beliefs, opinions, or behavior interfere with, or are incompatible with, those of another.

Conflict is born of dissimilarity, which may be passing in the form of moods, or lasting in the form of beliefs and personality. Two people always differ in important ways, but we favor a definition of conflict that involves active inter- ference with another's goals (Dal Cin, Holmes, & Young, 2005): Conflict occurs when one's wishes or actions actually obstruct or impede those of someone else. Thus, if partners differ in their political preferences, the potential for conflict certainly exists; but if they privately vote for different candidates without making their disagreement known, actual conflict may not occur. If, recognizing their differences, people thoughtfully keep their disagreements to themselves and allow their partners to do as they wish, they may avoid conflict that would otherwise occur if they confronted each other with their differences. On the other hand, if people have to give up something that they want because of their partners' influence, conflict exists. Anger and hostility aren't necessary; we make some sacrifices to accommodate our partners generously and happily. And not all conflicts are overt; one partner is sometimes unaware of the diffi- culties he or she is causing the other (Fincham & Beach, 1999). It's enough that someone knowingly or unknowingly prevents another from getting or doing everything he or she wants.

Conflict is inescapable for two reasons. First, any two people will occasion- ally differ in their moods and preferences. Intermittent incompatibilities between two partners' goals and behaviors will inevitably arise. For instance, even if both members of a couple are highly extraverted, hard-partying social animals, there will be times when one of them is disappointed by the other's wish to leave a party before it's over; a case of the flu or an upcoming exam in a close relationships class might make one of the partners, but not the other, unwilling to stay late.

Second, conflict is unavoidable because there are certain tensions that are woven into the fabric of close relationships that will, sooner or later, always cause some strain. When they devote themselves to an intimate relationship, people often experience opposing motivations called dialectics that can never be entirely satisfied because they contradict each other (Baxter, 2004). Fulfilling one goal may endanger another, so partners must engage in a delicate balancing act that leaves them drawn in different directions at different times. And with each partner vacillating between the pursuit of these opposing goals, occasional conflict between their predominant individual motives is inescapable (Erbert, 2000).

For instance, one potent dialectic in close relationships is the continual ten- sion between personal *autonomy and connection* to others. On one hand, people often want to be free to do what they want, so they value their independence and autonomy. On the other hand, they also seek warm, close connections to others that can make them dependent on particular partners. So, which do they pursue? Intimacy or freedom? Independence or belonging? It's reasonable to assume that most people want some of both, but embracing one of them can mean denying the other. So people's preferences may swing back and forth as they come to be more influenced by whichever motive has lately been less ful- filled. One motive may typically be more compelling than the other (Eidelson,

1980), and the average strength of each motive will vary from person to person (McAdams, 1985), so people experience contradiction from the simultaneous operation of drives for both autonomy and connection to varying degrees. Nevertheless, we can't simultaneously maintain high *in*dependence from a romantic partner and high *inter*dependence with him or her, so something's got to give. And conflict between the partners may occur as they strive to fulfill opposing motives at different rates and at different times.

Another powerful dialectic is the tension between *openness and closedness*. Intimacy involves self-disclosure, and intimate partners are expected to share their thoughts and feelings with one another. However, people also like their privacy, and there are some things that prudent partners want to keep to themselves (Petronio, 2002). On the one hand, there's candor and transparent authenticity, and on the other hand, there's discretion and restraint.

There's also friction between *stability and change*. People with pleasant partnerships will want to maintain and protect them, keeping things the way they are. But people also relish novelty and excitement (Aron et al., 2002). Too much stagnant predictability becomes mundane and monotonous. So, people are attracted to both the familiar and the new, and occasional indecision and conflict may result.

Finally, there's dialectic tension between *integration* with *and separation* from others outside one's partnership. Would you rather go to that party with your friends or stay home and snuggle with your sweetheart tonight? Will you travel to your in-law's home for Thanksgiving again this year or stay home and begin your own family tradition? One's motive to stay involved with other people is sometimes at odds with the wish to devote oneself to a romantic partnership. For instance, people see less of their friends when they invest time and effort into a romantic relationship (Milardo et al., 1983), and finding a satisfying ratio of time spent with and time apart from other people can be difficult.

Altogether, these four dialectics—autonomy versus connection, openness versus closedness, stability versus change, and integration versus separation—accounted for more than one third of the recent fights and arguments reported by married couples in one study (Erbert, 2000). And what's important is that these tensions typically continue to some degree throughout the entire life of a relationship (Sahlstein & Baxter, 2001). The dilemmas posed by fluctuating, opposing motives in close relationships never end. Sooner or later, conflict occurs.

The Frequency of Conflict

How often do partners engage in conflict? Frequently, but the answer varies with the population studied and the way in which conflict is defined and assessed. Little children and their parents are often at odds; one study determined that some conflict occurred every 3.6 minutes in conversations between four-year-olds and their mothers (Eisenberg, 1992)! When families eat together, 3.3 disputes occur per meal (Vuchinich, 1987). Adolescents encounter an average of seven disagreements per day in their various relationships (Laursen & Collins,

---

BOX 12.1

Enemies

Relationships that Result from Conflict

However rich or powerful a man may be, it is the height of folly to make personal enemies — LYTTETON

What might be called "enemyships" are relationships between antagonists that have resulted from conflict in which negative feelings and actions are central features. There have not been many studies of enemies, but after intensive interviews with 140 adults, Wiseman and Duck (1995) found that enemies came from three common groups: others that people hardly knew, co-workers, and former friends and lovers. Respondents thought former friends and lovers to be especially dangerous enemies because they had confidential information that they could use to do harm. When people became enemies, they did so suddenly and unexpectedly, usually (at least in the respondents' minds) because of the other person's actions. Enemy conduct involved actions that let respondents down, betrayed their trust, broke agreements, or were embarrassing or

offensive. These acts tended to baffle the targets, who typically believed that they had done nothing to deserve such treatment, so a sense of injustice prevailed.

The dominant strategy people said they used for dealing with antagonistic relationships was to avoid their enemies. Working to improve enemyships was rare. Neither counterattack nor retaliation were common, but people usually felt uncomfortable and tense around their enemies, so a key goal was to get one's enemies out of one's life.

Wiseman and Duck concluded that having an enemy is not simply the opposite of having a friend. Friendships evolve over time, whereas enemyships tend to erupt suddenly. There are different degrees of friendship, but enemyship tends to be a categorical distinction; people are either our enemies or they are not. Friendships sometimes fade with time, but once others become our enemies, they tend to remain our anatagonists. Overall, then, enemyships are relatively unique, long-lasting, problematic relationships.

1994), and dating couples report 2.3 conflicts per week when they keep diaries of their interactions (Lloyd, 1987). A broad sample of spouses experienced one or two "unpleasant disagreements" each month, and that was a rate that didn't change over a span of three years (McGonagle, Kessler, & Schilling, 1992). And, importantly, many conflicts are never addressed; in one investigation, Northwestern University students did not mention to their partners 40 percent of the conflicts and irritations they identified in their dating relationships (Roloff & Cloven, 1990). Not only is conflict common in close relationships, it also probably occurs more often than we realize.

However, as you might expect, some people experience more conflict than other people do. There are a variety of influences that are correlated with the conflict we encounter:

Personality. People who are high in neuroticism worry a lot and are impulsive and prone to anger—and they have more unhappy disagreements with others than people of low neuroticism do (McGonagle et al., 1992). In contrast, people high in agreeableness, who are good-natured, cooperative, and generally easy to get along with, probably experience fewer conflicts because they compromise easily. If conflict does occur, they also react more constructively than people of low agreeableness do (Jensen-Campbell & Graziano, 2001).

Attachment style. People who are anxious over abandonment tend to fret that their partners may leave them, and—perhaps because they nervously expect the worst—they think that there is more conflict in their relationships than their partners do. In addition, when conflict does occur, they consider it to be more damaging to the relationship than their partners do (Campbell et al., 2005). Attachment anxiety apparently leads people to perceive danger and threat where it does not exist, and, ironically, their apprehension may gradually create the disputes and tension they fear (Kirkpatrick & Davis, 1994).

Stage of Life. Stereotypes suggests that teenagers have a lot of conflict with their parents, but the frequency of conflict between parents and their children actually declines as adolescents grow older (Laursen, Coy, & Collins, 1998). The conflicts that do occur during mid-adolescence tend to be more heated than those that occurred earlier, but there are fewer of them.

Older married couples also tend to have fewer disagreements than middle-aged couples do. A comparison of California couples in their forties to some in their sixties found that the younger couples experienced more conflict, especially in the areas of children, money, recreation, and religion (Levenson, Carstensen, & Gottman, 1993).

Similarity. Conflict emerges from incompatibility, so it's not surprising that the less similar dating partners are, the more conflict they experience (Surra & Longstreth, 1990). Then, if people marry, this pattern continues; spouses who share similar tastes and expectations encounter less conflict and enjoy happier marriages than do those who have less in common (Huston & Houts, 1998). (Anybody who really believes that "opposites attract" should try living with someone who is notably different from them. Dissimilarity fuels friction, not smooth sailing.)

Alcohol. Finally, lest there's any doubt, alcohol does not make people more agreeable and courteous; instead, intoxication exacerbates conflict. An intriguing study of alcohol's effects invited men who were either sober or intoxicated to revisit a recent romantic conflict (MacDonald, Zanna, & Holmes, 2000). Drunkenness made the men more sour and surly; in response to events of the same average intensity, intoxicated men were more hostile and blaming than sober men were. Adding alcohol to a frustrating disagreement is a bit like adding fuel to a fire.

THE COURSE OF CONFLICT

Instigating Events

So, what events cause conflict? A wide-ranging review of conflict studies by Donald Peterson (2002, p. 367) concluded that couples may disagree about almost any issue: "how to spend time together, how to manage money, how to deal with in-laws, frequency and mode of sexual intercourse, who did which chores, insufficient expressions of affect (not enough affection), exaggerated expressions of affect (moodiness, anger), personal habits, political views, religious beliefs, jealousies toward other men and women, relatives, and the couples' own children." You name it, and some couple somewhere is quarreling over it. After David Buss (1989a) asked students at the University of Michigan to specify things that men do that upset women (and vice versa), he grouped their answers into 147 distinct sources of conflict. It's obvious that the interdependency that characterizes an intimate relationship provides "abundant opportunities for dispute" (Peterson, 2002, p. 367).

To make sense of this variety, Peterson (2002) classified the events that instigate conflicts into four common categories: criticism, illegitimate demands, rebuffs, and cumulative annoyances. **Criticism** involves verbal or nonverbal acts that are perceived as demeaning or derogatory. It doesn't matter what the actor intends by his or her remark or behavior; what matters is that the target interprets the action as being unjustly critical. A mild suggestion about how to load the dishwasher to fit more stuff in may injure one's partner and engender conflict if the suggestion is judged to be needless criticism.

Illegitimate demands involve requests that seem unjust because they exceed the normal expectations that the partners hold for each other. Even when one partner is frantically completing a major project, for instance, the other may be upset by being asked to fix dinner *and* do the dishes three nights in a row.

Rebuffs involve situations in which "one person appeals to another for a desired reaction, and the other person fails to respond as expected" (p. 371). Someone whose partner rolls over and goes to sleep after receiving an implicit invitation to have sex is likely to feel rebuffed.

Finally, **cumulative annoyances** are relatively trivial events that become irritating with repetition. Such events often take the form of *social allergies* (Cunningham et al., 2005): Through repeated exposure to small recurring nuisances, people may develop hypersensitive reactions of disgust and exasperation that seem out of proportion to any particular provocation. Women are especially likely to become annoyed with men's uncouth habits, such as belching at the dinner table, and men are likely to grow irritated with women's lack of consideration, such as being late for appointments and shopping too long (Cunningham et al., 2005).

Evolutionary psychology makes its own intriguing predictions about conflict in close relationships (Buss, 2004). From an evolutionary perspective, some conflict in heterosexual relationships flows naturally from differences in the partners' reproductive interests. Presumably, given their lower parental investment in any babies that may result, men can afford to be more interested in casual, uncommitted sex than women are; by comparison, women should be more prudent, offering access to sex only in return for meaningful commitment from a man. And in fact, the frustrations that men and women usually encounter early in a romantic relationship run right along these lines: "Women, far more than men, become angry and upset by those who want sex sooner, more frequently, and more persistently than they want. Men, far more than women, become angry and upset by those who delay sex or thwart their sexual advances"

(Buss, 2000, p. 38). Sexual conflict seems to decline after people settle into established monogamous relationships—dating partners are more often upset by sexual aggression or unfaithfulness than newlyweds are (Buss, 1989a)—but individual differences in sexual tastes and drives can remain a source of distressing rebuffs as long as a relationship lasts (Schwartz, 2000).

We can also note that there may be a few differences in the sore points routinely encountered by gay, lesbian, and heterosexual couples. Lawrence Kurdek (1994a) examined the sources of conflict in couples of all three types who had been together for several years, and found that heterosexuals disagreed about social issues, such as political attitudes, more than the homosexual couples did. Trust was a more frequent source of conflict for gay and lesbian couples than for heterosexuals, perhaps because gays and lesbians were more likely to retain previous lovers in their networks of friends, making issues of trust more salient. On the whole, the conflicts experienced by the three types of couples were more similar than different; the couples did not differ, for instance, with regard to conflicts over power, intimacy, and a partner's personal flaws. Still, Kurdek's work provides a valuable reminder that the events that instigate conflict may be idiosyncratic, varying from couple to couple.

Attributions

The differing perspectives that any two people bring to their interaction will often be another source of exasperating disagreement. *Actor-observer effects* guarantee that partners will have slightly different explanations for their actions than anyone else does, and *self-serving biases* lead them to judge their own actions more favorably than others do.[1] In particular, although people readily recognize self-serving attributions in others' judgments of events, they usually consider their own similarly biased perceptions to be fair and impartial (Pronin et al., 2002). As a result, two partners' attributions routinely differ, and this can create conflict in two different ways. First, frustrating misunderstanding can result if people fail to appreciate that their partners always have their own individual points of view. And second, if those differing views come to light, the partners may engage in **attributional conflict,** fighting over whose explanation is right and whose account is wrong (Orvis, Kelley, & Butler, 1976). Partners may agree entirely about what one of them did but simultaneously disagree completely about why that person did it. Attributional arguments are often hard to resolve because there's usually no single explanation for an event that is objectively and conclusively correct. People who (may have) behaved selfishly, for instance, will often have difficulty realizing that they were greedy, while others will tend to be blind to the manner in which their own selfishness may have elicited similar temporary thoughtlessness in return. The interactions two partners share may be affected by so many subtle influences that reasonable people can, and often will, disagree about why things turn out the way they do.

---

[1]If a reminder about these attributional patterns will come in handy, take a look back at pages 118–119 in chapter 4.

BOX 12.2

Mastering Our Anger

A lot of people seem to believe that, when they are cruelly provoked, their anger is something that just happens to them that is beyond their control. Even worse, popular notions suggest that once we get angry, it's dangerous to bottle it up; when we get "hot," we have to "vent," or we'll suffer high blood pressure and continuing stress. However, there are two huge problems with such beliefs: First, they're wrong (Tice & Baumeister, 1993), and second, they promote behavior that may actually cause *higher* stress that lasts for longer periods of time.

Because it takes effort to control and manage angry emotion, people often "blow off steam" by directing furious, fuming behavior at their adversaries (or, occasionally, at innocent third parties). Releasing our ire is supposed to make us feel better, but that simple-minded notion ignores the interpersonal consequences of surly behavior. "When you 'let out' an emotion it usually lands on somebody else, and how you feel—relieved, angrier, depressed—is going to depend on what the other person does" (Tavris, 1982, p. 145). Sometimes, the targets of our wrath are chastened by our anger, and, being contrite, they accept our anger, apologize, and strive to remediate their sins. But in close relationships, where people expect generous and tolerant treatment from their partners, aggressive displays of anger often just get one's partners angry in return. And then there may be *two* irate people fussing and sniping at each other in a churlish interaction that perpetuates, rather than reduces, the anger in the air.

The bottom line is that "expressing anger *while you feel angry* nearly always makes you feel angrier" (Tavris, 1982,

p. 223), and it is the presence of anger, rather than its absence, that gradually erodes our health (Tice & Baumeister, 1993). People who lash out at their partners in the heat of anger often stay angry longer and suffer more cardiovascular stress than they would if they behaved more moderately. By comparison, those who gain control of their anger and then voice their complaints in an assertive but less heated fashion are more likely to get understanding and cooperation from their partners; they are more likely to get what they want.

So, how can we manage our anger? Because irritation and resentment are signs that something is wrong, we shouldn't ignore anger and pretend that it doesn't exist. But it's usually worthwhile to reduce the venom and fury we dump on our partners, and there are several ways to do this (Tice & Baumeister, 1993). First, we can *think differently.* Anger is inflamed by perceptions that our partners acted negligently or maliciously, so the attributions with which we explain some annoyance are key. When you feel yourself beginning to get angry, taking the time to consider why your partner may have behaved that way without wishing to injure or annoy you can keep your indignation in check. Second, if you do get angry, *chill out.* Don't engage in infuriated interaction. Leave the room, take a walk, breathe slowly and deeply, and count to ten (or ten thousand). You will calm down, and you'll do so quicker than you think if you breathe slowly, relax your muscles, and stop rehearsing the injustice in your mind. Finally, find *humor* where you can. It's impossible to feel jocular and angry at the same time, so anything that lightens your mood will decrease your anger.

All of this is easier said than done, and some people will need to "practice, practice, and practice alternative responses" to their anger before they can reform their angry habits (Notarius, Lashley, & Sullivan, 1997, p. 245). The time to rehearse is when small annoyances occur, and it's very helpful when both partners are involved. And the good news is that destructive anger can be overcome; "if you each try to help the other person master a new way of dealing with anger, and do this repeatedly, you will find the old patterns giving way to change" (Notarius et al., 1997, p. 246).

Then, when any conflict occurs, the explanations with which intimate partners account for the frustrations they encounter have a huge influence on how distressed they feel and how angrily they respond. (See Box 12.2.) If a partner's misbehavior is construed to be an unintentional accident, being attributed to external and unstable causes, the partner will seem relatively blameless, and strong emotion (and retribution) will be inappropriate. In contrast, if a partner's misdeeds are attributed to internal and stable sources, the misdeeds seem intentional and the partner seems malicious, selfish, indecent, or inept—and in such circumstances, one's inconvenience seems unjust, and one's anger fitting (Canary, 2003). It's no accident then, that happy couples are less likely than unhappy couples to regard their partners as selfishly motivated and as behaving with negative intent. Benevolent attributions paint a partner in a favorable light and make it seem likely that conflicts can be resolved, and that's one reason why such attributions promote continued satisfaction with a relationship (Fincham et al., 2000).

Engagement and Escalation

Once an instigating event occurs, partners must decide either to engage in conflict or to avoid the issue and let it drop. This decision is the first choice point in Peterson's (2002) general model of conflict, which appears in Figure 12.1. (At first glance, you may find the figure a little daunting, but be patient; it cleverly illustrates several different manners in which conflict can unfold. Trace some of the paths and see.) *Avoidance* occurs only when both partners wish to evade the issue, and it presumably transpires either when the event is seen as insufficient to warrant active dispute or when the issue seems intractable and conflict will do no good (Roloff & Ifert, 2000).

Otherwise, the issue is addressed and conflict is engaged. In some cases, the couple enters into *negotiation* and seeks to resolve the conflict through rational problem-solving. However, in other cases, *escalation* occurs and the conflict heats up. Escalation often involves the dysfunctional forms of communication we described in chapter 5. Other issues may get dragged into the interaction, scornful disregard of the partner may be expressed, and belligerent demands and threats may be made. Angry fighting may ensue.

An analysis of intimate combat by Dan Canary (2003) made two points: First, partners sometimes say mean and nasty things to each other when they're

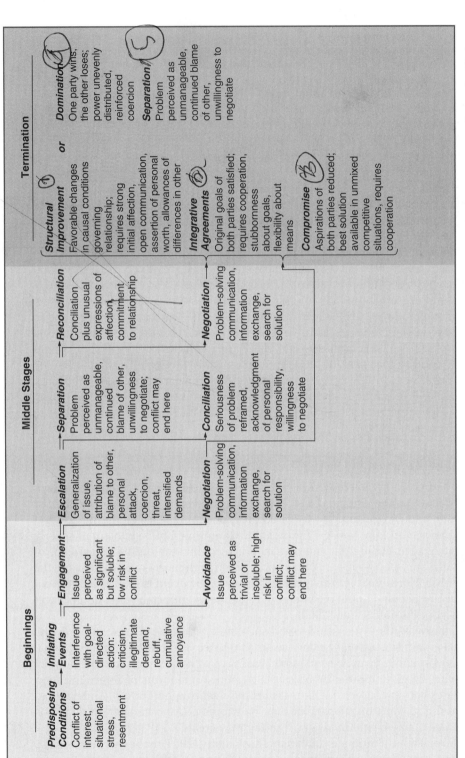

FIGURE 12.1. The possible courses of conflict from its beginnings, through its middle stages, to its termination. Arrows indicate the likely sequences, ending with avoidance, separation, or any of four other possible terminations of the conflict.
Source: Peterson, 2002.

fighting, and second, nasty remarks may be of two types. <u>*Direct*</u> tactics explicitly challenge one's partner; they're "in one's face." Direct tactics include (a) accusations that criticize the partner and attribute negative qualities to him or her; (b) hostile commands for compliance that sometimes involve threats of physical or emotional harm; (c) antagonistic questions; and (d) surly or sarcastic put-downs that communicate disgust or disapproval (including argumentative interruptions and shouting down one's partner). *Indirect* nasty tactics manage the conflict in a less straightforward manner; one's displeasure is veiled, and one's intentions are less explicit. Indirect tactics include (a) condescension or implied negativity that hints at animosity or arrogance; (b) dysphoric affect, such as melancholy, dejection, or whining; (c) attempts to change topics preemptively, and (d) evasive remarks that fail to acknowledge the partner or that fail to recognize the conflict. All of these behaviors are obnoxious to some degree, and they tend to inflame, rather than to resolve conflict. Satisfied partners engage in these behaviors less often than discontented, disgruntled partners do, and married couples who routinely fight in such a manner are much more likely to divorce than are those who rarely act this way (Gottman et al., 1998).

The Demand/Withdraw Pattern

Another unpleasant pattern of interaction that exacerbates conflict is the demand/withdraw pattern, in which "one member (the demander) criticizes, nags, and makes demands of the other, while the partner (the withdrawer) avoids confrontation, withdraws, and becomes defensive" (Eldridge & Christensen, 2002, p. 289). The pattern is objectionable in part because it is self-perpetuating. Frustrated by the withdrawer's retreat, the demander is likely to become more insistent that the issue be addressed; however, this increased pressure tends to make the withdrawer even more resistant and close-lipped, and the pattern continues. It's a dysfunctional way to manage conflict, and over time, it undermines a couple's satisfaction with their relationship (Caughlin & Huston, 2002).

Men and women do not differ much in their other responses to conflict (Gayle, Preiss, & Allen, 2002), but in this case, women tend to be the demanders and men the withdrawers more often than not (Christensen & Heavey, 1993). (Take a look at Table 12.1 to examine questions that are used in research that studies this phenomenon.) Why do women demand and men withdraw? Various explanations have been suggested. One possibility is that the pattern emerges from the usual *gender differences* that distinguish men and women (Eldridge & Christensen, 2002). Women are encouraged to be communal and expressive, whereas men are encouraged to be independent and autonomous, and the demand/withdraw pattern is presumed to result from the woman seeking closeness and the man defending his autonomy. When anything's wrong in a relationship, women want to fix it, and their desire for renewed closeness makes them demanding. By comparison, men, who are already less at ease in emotional, intimate domains, want to maintain more independence and self-sufficiency, and they resist women's calls for self-expression.

TABLE 12.1. Short Self-Report Measure of Demand/Withdraw Interaction

	Very Unlikely							Very Likely
When some problem in the relationship arises:								
Woman tries to start a discussion while man tries to avoid a discussion.	1 2 3 4 5 6 7 8 9							
During a discussion of a relationship problem:								
Woman nags and demands while man withdraws, becomes silent, or refuses to discuss the matter further.	1 2 3 4 5 6 7 8 9							
Woman criticizes while man defends himself.	1 2 3 4 5 6 7 8 9							
When some problem in the relationship arises:								
Man tries to start a discussion while woman tries to avoid a discussion.	1 2 3 4 5 6 7 8 9							
During a discussion of a relationship problem:								
Man nags and demands while woman withdraws, becomes silent, or refuses to discuss the matter further.	1 2 3 4 5 6 7 8 9							
Man criticizes while woman defends herself.	1 2 3 4 5 6 7 8 9							

Another explanation, the *social structure* hypothesis, argues that the demand/withdraw pattern results from pervasive differences in the power of men and women in society and marriage alike (Eldridge & Christensen, 2002). As we saw in chapter 11, men tend to have more power in heterosexual relationships than women do, and if you're getting your way, you're likely to resist change. On the other hand, if they're underbenefited, women are likely to press for changes that make their partnerships more equitable. Consider housework. Women who realize that they're doing more than their fair share (as most of them are [Huppe & Cyr, 1997]) may agitate for change, nagging their men to do more. But if they avoid such discussions and put off any showdown, men can lazily continue to goof off; they won't be pleasing their wives, but by withdrawing from such conflicts they can continue to get what they want.

Researchers have developed a clever way to study such issues by asking couples to have two discussions, one in which the woman wants change and another in which the man wants change (e.g., Christensen & Heavy, 1993). In some investigations, the demand/withdraw pattern depends entirely on who's asking; when she's asking, she demands and he withdraws, but when he's asking, he demands and she withdraws (Klinetob & Smith, 1996). Overall, however, results support both the gender differences (Caughlin & Vangelisti, 2000) and the social structure (Vogel & Karney, 2002) points of view. Women are generally more likely to press for desired change in a relationship no matter whose issue is at hand, and imbalances of power affect who's more likely to withdraw.

Negotiation and Accommodation

Not all conflicts turn heated or ugly, and those that do ultimately simmer down. And when loving partners are finally cool-headed, *negotiation* usually occurs. The partners announce their positions and work toward a solution in a sensible manner. In a best-case scenario, each is responsive to the other and each feels validated by the other's responses.[2]

Dan Canary's (2003) analysis of conflict tactics identified several ways in which partners can be nice to each other during their negotiations. Again, some of these are *direct,* openly addressing the issue, and another is *indirect,* skirting the issue but defusing ill feeling. Nice direct tactics include (a) showing a willingness to deal with the problem by accepting responsibility or by offering concessions or a compromise; (b) exhibiting support for the other's point of view through paraphrasing; (c) offering self-disclosure with "I-statements"; and (d) providing approval and affection. An indirect tactic is friendly, non-sarcastic humor that lightens the mood. Some problems are easier to solve than others, of course, but the use of kind tactics like these during conflict helps to protect and maintain a relationship (Gottman et al., 1998).

Obviously, some responses to conflict are destructive, undermining a relationship, and others are constructive, helping to sustain it. Add this distinction to the difference between engaging a conflict and avoiding it that we mentioned earlier, and you've got four different types of reponses to conflict and dissatisfaction in a relationship that have been identified by Caryl Rusbult (1987). Examine Figure 12.2; the four categories differ in being either *active* or *passive* and in being either *constructive* or *destructive:*

1. **Voice**—behaving in an active, constructive manner by trying to improve the situation by discussing matters with the partner, changing one's behavior in an effort to solve the problem, or obtaining advice from a friend or therapist;
2. **Loyalty**—behaving in a passive but constructive manner by optimistically waiting for conditions to improve;
3. **Exit**—behaving in an actively destructive manner by leaving the partner, threatening to end the relationship, or engaging in abusive acts such as yelling or hitting; or
4. **Neglect**—behaving in a passive but destructive manner by avoiding discussion of critical issues and reducing interdependence with the partner. When one is neglectful, one stands aside and just lets things get worse.

If a relationship has been satisfying and their investments in it are high, people are more likely to employ the constructive responses of voice and loyalty than to neglect the relationship or exit from it (Rusbult, Zembrodt, & Gunn, 1982). We typically seek to maintain relationships to which we are committed. On the other hand, when difficulties arise, the presence of attractive alternative

---

[2]For a refresher on what we mean by *responsiveness* and *validation,* we invite you to look back at p. 222 in chapter 7 and p. 177 in chapter 5, respectively.

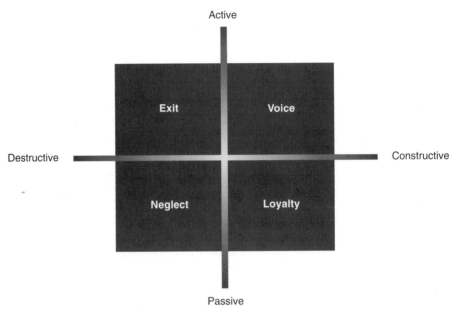

FIGURE 12.2. A typology of responses to dissatisfaction in close relationships.
Source: Adapted from Rusbult, 1987.

partners encourages exit; people are more likely to bail out of a struggling relationship than to work to sustain it when tempting alternatives exist (Rusbult
et al., 1982). A variety of personal characteristics also influence the strategies
people select. People who are high in the attachment dimension of avoidance of
intimacy (that is, those who have dismissing or fearful attachment styles) tend to
be more passive than active, and more destructive than constructive, when they
grow discontent. Thus, they often sit back and let their relationships deteriorate
through neglect instead of striving to repair them. By comparison, people who
are more comfortable with closeness (who have secure or preoccupied attachment styles) are more likely to voice complaints in an active effort to overcome
problems (Johnston, Fabrigar, & Wilson, 2005). Masculine people such as
macho males are more likely to engage in destructive exit or neglect than in
constructive responses, but the reverse is true of feminine people (Rusbult,
Zembrodt, & Iwaniszek, 1986). And, similarly, people from individualistic
cultures such as the United States tend to engage in more destructive exit and
neglect, and less voice and loyalty, than people from collectivist cultures do
(Yum, 2004).

Relationships are at risk when both partners choose destructive responses
to conflict (Rusbult, Johnson, & Morrow, 1986), so the ability to remain constructive in the face of a lover's temporary disregard, which we identified as
accommodation back in chapter 6 (on page 213), is a valuable gift. When
partners behave destructively, accommodation involves inhibiting the impulse
to fight fire with fire and striving to react instead with constructive voice or
loyalty. We'll mention accommodation again in chapter 15; for now, we'll simply
note that couples who are able to swallow occasional provocation from each

other without responding in kind tend to be happier than are those who are less tolerant and who always bite back (Rusbult et al., 1998).

Dealing with Conflict: Four Types of Couples

Does the desirability of accommodation mean that you and your partner should avoid arguing with each other? Not at all. Even heated arguments can be constructive, and some couples who engage in forceful, robust arguments appear to have stable, satisfying marriages. There appear to be two key influences that determine whether arguments support or erode a couple's satisfaction; the first is the similarity of the partners' preferences, and the second is the manner in which arguments are conducted.

Marriage researcher John Gottman (1993, 1994a, 1999) has studied conflict for years. In a typical procedure, he invites couples to discuss a continuing disagreement and then carefully inspects videotapes of the resulting interactions. His results have led him to suggest that there are three discrete approaches to conflict that can lead to stable and enduring marriages. (Box 12.3 provides a simple measure of these different styles; before you read further, we invite you to assess your own conflict type.)

Volatile couples have frequent and passionate arguments. They plunge into fiery efforts to persaude and influence each other, and they often display high levels of negative affect, but they temper their anger with plenty of wit and evident fondness for each other.

Validators fight more politely. They tend to be calmer than volatile couples are, and they behave more like collaborators than like antagonists as they work through their problems. Their discussions may become heated, but they frequently validate each other by expressing empathy for, and understanding of, the other's point of view.

In contrast to volatiles and validators, avoiders rarely argue. They avoid confrontation, and if they do discuss their conflicts, they do so mildly and gingerly. As Gottman (1993, p. 10) reported:

> The interviewer had a great deal of difficulty setting up the conflict discussion. . . . Once each person has stated his or her case, they tend to see the discussion as close to an end. They consider accepting these differences as a complete discussion. Once they understand their differences, they feel that the common ground and values they share overwhelm these differences and make them unimportant and easy to accept. Hence, there is very little give and take and little attempt to persuade one another. The discussion has very little emotion, either positive or negative. Often the proposed solutions to issues are quite nonspecific.

Rather than discuss a conflict with their partners, avoiders often just try to fix it on their own or wait it out, hoping that the passage of time will solve the problem.

Although they are very different, Gottman asserts that all three types of couples can last because they all maintain a high ratio of rewards to costs in their approaches to conflict. Volatile couples exchange a lot of negative emotion,

---

BOX 12.3

Assessing Your Couple Conflict Type

Following are descriptions of how people in four different types of relationships handle conflict. Which type most closely describes how you and your partner deal with conflict in your relationship? For each description, indicate how often it applies to your conflicts:

A. In our relationship, conflicts may be fought on a grand scale, and that is okay, since our making up is even grander. We have volcanic arguments, but they are just a small part of a warm and loving relationship. Although we argue, we are still able to resolve our differences. In fact, our passion and zest for fighting actually leads to a better relationship with a lot of making up, laughing, and affection.

1 = Never
2 = Rarely
3 = Sometimes
4 = Often
5 = Very Often

B. In our relationship, conflict is minimized. We think it is better to "agree to disagree" rather than end up in discussions that will result in a deadlock. We don't think there is much to be gained from getting openly angry with each other. In fact, a lot of talking about disagreements seems to make matters worse. We feel that if you just relax about problems, they will have a way of working themselves out.

1 = Never
2 = Rarely
3 = Sometimes

4 = Often
5 = Very Often

C. In our relationship, when we are having conflict, we let each other know the other's opinions are valued and their emotions valid, even if we disagree with each other. Even when discussing a hot topic, we display a lot of self-control and are calm. When fighting we spend a lot of time validating each other as well as trying to persuade our partner or trying to find a compromise.

1 = Never
2 = Rarely
3 = Sometimes
4 = Often
5 = Very Often

D. We argue often and hotly. There are a lot of insults back and forth, name-calling, put-downs, and sarcasm. We don't really listen to what the other is saying, nor do we look at each other very much. One or the other of us can be quite detached and emotionally uninvolved, even though there may be brief episodes of attack and defensiveness. There are clearly more negatives than positives in our relationship.

1 = Never
2 = Rarely
3 = Sometimes
4 = Often
5 = Very Often

Source: Holman & Jarvis, 2000. Reprinted with permission. In terms of Gottman's couple types, scenario A reflects a volatile approach, B an avoiding approach, C a validating approach, and D a hostile approach.

but they balance the scales with even more affection and humor. Avoiders aren't particularly effusive or amiable, but they don't have a lot of negative vibes to overcome. As long as the positive, accepting components of their interactions substantially outnumber the negative, quarrelsome ones—you may recall from chapter 6 that an acceptable ratio is a minimum of 5 positive exchanges for every one negative—couples can fight loudly or not at all and do little damage to their relationship.

In some couples, however, arguments are harmful, caustic events. For Gottman, **hostiles** are couples that fail to maintain a 5-to-1 ratio of nice behavior to nasty conduct. Their discussions are sprinkled with too much criticism, contempt, defensiveness, and withdrawal, and the longer they last, the more oppressive they become. Some hostile couples actively address their disagreements but do so badly, whereas others remain more detached and uninvolved but snipe at each other in brief salvos of distaste. Still, whether or not they are actively arguing, hostiles are simply meaner to each other than other couples are, and that's why their conflicts are dangerous for their relationships.

It's also important for partners to be well-matched. A volatile person would be poorly wed to an avoider, and each would likely be frustrated by the other's approach to conflict. But heated arguments do not necessarily do harm to intimate relationships. As long as both partners prefer the same approach, they can fight passionately as long as they continue to obviously hold each other in high regard (Driver & Gottman, 2004).

THE OUTCOMES OF CONFLICT

Ending Conflict

Eventually, all conflicts end. Peterson (2002) described five ways in which conflicts can end, and we'll consider them in an order that ranges roughly from the most destructive and damaging to the most constructive and beneficial.

Separation occurs when one or both partners withdraw without resolving the conflict. Separation that ends a heated encounter may prevent irreparable harm to the relationship, and time apart may give combatants time to cool off and to think about their situation more constructively. It offers no solutions to a couple's problem, however, and may simply delay further discord.

Other conflicts end in conquest. In **domination,** one partner gets his or her way when the other capitulates. This happens routinely when one person is more powerful than the other, and the more powerful partner will typically be pleased with the outcome. Domination is aversive for the loser, however, and it may breed ill-will and resentment.

Compromise occurs when both parties reduce their aspirations so that a mutually acceptable alternative can be found. As Peterson suggested (2002, p. 380), the partners' "interests are diluted rather than reconciled"; neither partner gets everything he or she wants, but neither goes empty-handed. This may be the best outcome available when one person's gain can come only at the expense of the other, but in other situations, better solutions are usually available.

Integrative agreements satisfy both partners' original goals and aspirations, usually through creativity and flexibility. They're not easy to reach and they typically take some work; partners may need to refine and prioritize their wishes, make selective concessions, and invent new ways of attaining their goals that do not impose upon their partners. Nevertheless, through determination, ingenuity, imagination, and generous cooperation, partners can often get the things they really want.

Finally, on occasion, the partners not only get what they want, they also learn and grow and make desirable changes to their relationship. This pleasant outcome, **structural improvement,** isn't frequent, and when it occurs, it is usually the result of significant turmoil and upheaval. Partners may have encountered perilous stress and serious conflict to reach a point that leads them to rethink their habits and to muster both the courage and the will to change them. Still, structural improvement leaves a couple better off. As Peterson (2002, p. 382) wrote

> Some change will take place in one or more of the causal conditions governing the relationship. Each person will know more about the other than before. Each person may attribute more highly valued qualities to the other than before. Having weathered the storm of previous conflict, each person may trust the other and their relationship more than before, and thus be willing to approach other previously avoided issues in a more hopeful and productive way. With these changes, the quality of the relationship will be improved over many situations and beyond the time of the immediate conflict with which the process began.

Can Fighting Be Good for a Relationship?

Is Peterson right? Can fighting sometimes yield beneficial results? Perhaps. Consider this recommendation from John Gottman (1994b, p. 159): "The most important advice I can give to men who want their marriages to work is to try not to avoid conflict."

Even if we acknowledge that conflict is inevitable in intimate relationships, you may still feel that it would be better not to have quarrels, disagreements, and arguments. Some people certainly feel that way, believing that "disagreement is destructive" and that an argument is a sure sign that one's love is flawed (Eidelson & Epstein, 1982). But (as we noted in chapter 4) that's a dysfunctional belief, and relationship scientists generally take a different view. They recognize that the more unexpressed nuisances and irritants partners have, the less satisfied with their relationships they tend to be (Roloff & Cloven, 1990). Studies also find that newlyweds who withdraw from conflict without resolving their disagreements tend to be less happy years later (Noller et al., 1994).

Indeed, the prevailing view among conflict researchers is that, for all the problems it can bring, conflict is an essential tool with which to promote intimacy. Conflict brings problematic issues and incompatibilities into the open, allowing solutions to be sought. And handled well, conflict can defuse situations that would only fester and cause bigger problems later on. Confronting conflict head-on provides no guarantee that difficulties will be resolved and that contentment will follow (Fincham & Beach, 1999). Nevertheless, it is usually the deft and skillful management of conflict—and not its absence—that allows relationships to grow and prosper (Peterson, 2002).

In their book, *The Intimate Enemy: How to Fight Fair in Love and Marriage*, George Bach and Peter Wyden (1983) consider this proposition in great detail, contending that fighting increases intimacy when it is reasonably and adroitly done. Many of their suggestions for how to "fight fair," such as saying what we mean, active listening, and staying cool, have already been described (back in chapter 5), but Bach and Wyden go beyond providing rules for how to fight. They also provide guidelines for the results that should occur. Their scorecard, a "fight effects profile," is shown in Table 12.2. A "good fight" should have the positive effects listed in the table and should contribute to the growth of a good relationship.

Bach and Wyden do not underestimate how hard it is to fight fair and have a "good" fight. It requires self-discipline and genuine caring about one's partner. But the positive outcomes are usually worth the effort. From this perspective, instead of being a dreadful problem, conflict is a challenging opportunity—a chance to learn about one's partner and oneself and a possibility for one's relationship to grow in strength and intimacy. Consider using the Fight Effects Profile to grade your efforts the next time conflict puts your communication skills to the test.

VIOLENCE AND ABUSE IN RELATIONSHIPS

Many fights between intimate partners are entirely verbal, but some fights result in **violence** that involves "an act carried out with the intention of, or an act perceived as having the intention of, physically hurting another person" (Steinmetz, 1987, p. 729). Violence may be relatively minor or more severe (Newton, Connelly, & Landsverk, 2001), a point that a leading research tool, the **Conflict Tactics Scale** (or CTS), takes into consideration (Straus et al., 1996). With the CTS, people describe their use of psychological and physical aggression against their romantic partners, responding to such items as "I insulted or swore at my partner," "I threw something at my partner, "and "I pushed or shoved my partner." Violent actions range from those that do little harm, such as grabbing or pushing, to others that inflict atrocious injury, such as beatings and burnings (see Figure 12.3). And sadly, intimate violence of all types is more common than most people think. In this section of the chapter, we'll examine violence between romantic partners.

The Prevalence of Violence

In the middle 1990s, the Centers for Disease Control and Prevention teamed up with the National Institute of Justice to conduct detailed phone interviews with 16,000 men and women in a National Violence Against Women Survey in the U.S. (Tjaden & Thoennes, 1999). The survey found that violence is as American as apple pie. Most of the women (52 percent) and even more men (66 percent)

TABLE 12.2. The Fight Effects Profile

Each fight is scored by each person from his or her point of view. In a good fight, both partners win. That is, both partners have considerably more positive outcomes than negative ones.

Category	Positive Outcome	Negative Outcome
Hurt	Person feels less hurt, weak, or offended.	Person feels more hurt, weak, or offended.
Information	Person gains more information about relationship or partner's feelings.	Person learns nothing new.
Resolution	Open conflict has made it more likely the issue will be resolved.	Possibility of a solution is now less likely.
Control	Person has gained more mutually acceptable influence over the partner's behavior.	Person now has less mutually acceptable influence over the partner.
Fear	Fear of fighting and/or the partner is reduced.	Fear has increased.
Trust	Person has more confidence that the partner will deal with him or her "in good faith, with good will, and with positive regard."	Person has less confidence in partner's goodwill.
Revenge	Intentions to take revenge are not stimulated by the fight.	Intentions to take revenge are stimulated by the fight.
Reconciliation	Person makes active efforts to undo any harm he or she has caused and welcomes similar efforts by the partner.	Person does not attempt or encourage reconciliation.
Relational Evaluation	Person feels he or she is more central to the other's concern and interest.	Person feels he or she "counts less" with partner.
Self-Evaluation	Person feels better about himself or herself: more confidence, more self-esteem.	Person feels worse about himself or herself.
Cohesion-Affection	Closeness with and attraction to the partner have increased.	Closeness with and attraction to the partner have decreased.

Source: Adapted from Bach & Wyden, 1983.

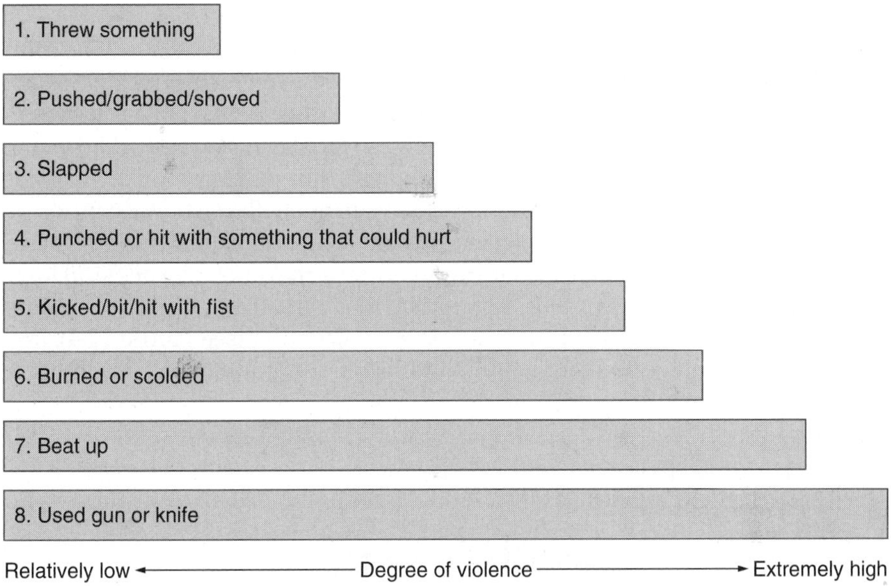

| 1. Threw something |
| 2. Pushed/grabbed/shoved |
| 3. Slapped |
| 4. Punched or hit with something that could hurt |
| 5. Kicked/bit/hit with fist |
| 6. Burned or scolded |
| 7. Beat up |
| 8. Used gun or knife |

Relatively low ◄——————————— Degree of violence ———————————► Extremely high

FIGURE 12.3. The Conflict Tactics Scale: Comparative ratings of physical violence.
Source: Straus, Hamby, Boney-McCoy, and Sugarman, 1996.

reported that they had been physically assaulted at some point in their lives, and 22 percent of the women and 7 percent of the men had experienced a violent assault by an intimate partner. The most common forms of violence were slapping or hitting, but on rare occasion guns and knives were used.

Interpersonal violence is nothing new. If anything, severe violence by husbands against their wives is actually less frequent today than it was 30 years ago (Straus, Gelles, & Steinmetz, 1980). Nevertheless, current estimates from the National Violence Against Women Survey are that approximately 1.3 million women and 835,000 men will be physically assaulted by their intimate partners this year.

The survey also found that one's ethnicity predicted one's risk of being victimized by one's partner. Assault rates were higher for American Indians and African Americans than for whites and Hispanics, with Asian/Pacific Islanders being less likely to encounter intimate violence than any other group. In addition, violence was more common in the same-sex relationships of men than women; lesbian women encountered only about half as much violence as heterosexual women did, but gay men experienced twice as much violence as heterosexual men (Tjaden & Thoennes, 1999). This may not be true among adolescents, however; in another sample, gay teens were less likely than lesbian teens to report any violence in their romantic partnerships (Halpern et al., 2004).

Types of Couple Violence

It's one thing to describe the specific acts of violence that occur in close relationships, and another to explain why they occur. Michael Johnson (1995, 2001;

Johnson & Ferraro, 2000) has suggested that there are four distinct types of violence in romantic couples, and they spring from different sources. The most familiar type is **situational couple violence** (or SCV), which typically erupts from heated conflicts that get out of hand. It occurs when both partners are angry and is tied to specific arguments, so it is only occasional and is usually mild, being unlikely to escalate into serious, life-threatening forms of aggression. Often, it is also mutual, with both partners angrily and impulsively flying out of control.

A notably different kind of violence is **intimate terrorism** (or IT) in which one partner uses violence as a tool to control and oppress the other. The physical force and coercion that occurs in intimate terrorism may be just one tactic in a general pattern of threats, isolation, and economic subordination (see Figure 12.4), and when it is present, it occurs more often than situational couple violence. Indeed,

FIGURE 12.4. The many facets of intimate terrorism.
Source: Johnson, 1995.

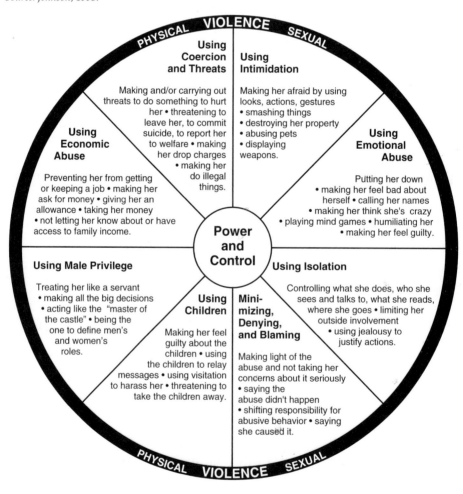

compared to SCV, intimate terrorism is more likely to be one-sided, to escalate over time, and to involve serious injury to its target (Johnson & Leone, 2005). Moreover, victims of intimate terrorism are less likely to fight back but much more likely to have left their partners (and then returned) several times.

A third type of couple violence is **mutual violent control,** in which both partners try to subjugate the other "in a situation that could be viewed as two intimate terrorists battling for control" (Johnson & Ferraro, 2000, p. 950). This is a rare situation, and **violent resistance,** in which a partner forcibly fights back against intimate terrorism, is more common. Nevertheless, situational couple violence and intimate terrorism occur much more frequently than either of these two, so researchers now consider SCV and IT to be the two major forms of couple violence (Graham-Kevan & Archer, 2003).

The distinctions among these different types are important because they occur at different rates in different demographic groups. In particular, Johnson (2001) found that men and women were equally likely to engage in situational couple violence but that a huge majority of those who employed intimate terrorism were men. As a result of this asymmetry, violent resistance was much more common in women than in men. Does this mean that men are more violent towards their intimate partners than women are? That's actually a thorny question. Let's consider it next.

Gender Differences in Partner Violence

Many people may find this surprising, but wives act violently toward their husbands just as often as husbands act violently toward their wives. For instance, in one national survey, 12.1 percent of the women and 11.3 percent of the men reported having committed at least one violent act against their spouses in the preceding year (Hampton, Gelles, & Harrop, 1989). Stereotypes may suggest that women engage in less intimate violence than men do, but if anything, it's the other way around; women are actually slightly more likely to use physical aggression against their partners than men are (Archer, 2000).

That sounds like a straightforward (if surprising) conclusion, but it has been the subject of considerable controversy and discussion among relationship scientists (e.g., Frieze, 2000; O'Leary, 2000). For one thing, most studies of couple violence do not determine whether a person's actions were offensive or defensive in nature; if, in an episode of situational couple violence, a man initiates a physical assault and his female partner responds in kind, each would have recently done some violence but for different reasons. Some studies find that women are just as likely to initiate violence as are men (Straus, 1999), but ambiguities remain. In addition, when an episode of SCV occurs, men tend to engage in more acts of violence than women do (Johnson, 2001), and many surveys do not keep track of such subtleties.

Men and women also tend to exhibit violent behavior of different severity. Women are more likely to throw something, kick, bite, or punch their partners, whereas men are more likely to choke or strangle, or beat up theirs (Archer, 2002). Thus, there's no question that men are more likely to cause meaningful

---

BOX 12.4
Stalking
Unwanted Intrusion

Another undesirable behavior that occurs in some relationships is intrusive pursuit of someone—often an ex-partner—who does not wish to be pursued. Legal definitions of *stalking* in most of the United States involve repeated, malicious following and harassing of an unwilling target that may include (depending on the state) unwanted phone calls and letters, surveillance, and other invasions of privacy (Matthews, 2004).

None of the United States had laws against stalking before 1990, but all of them now do. Stalking was outlawed because it is remarkably prevalent and it can injure its targets. Using a definition of stalking that required a victim to feel a high level of fear, the National Violence Against Women survey found that 8 percent of American women and 2 percent of men had been targets of a frightening stalker. Other studies that focused more broadly on unwanted communications and other intrusions converged on the estimate that one quarter of all women, and one tenth of all men, have experienced unwelcome harassment from a persistent pursuer (Cupach & Spitzberg, 2004). Most of the victims of stalking (75 percent) are women, and their stalkers are usually male (Cupach & Spitzberg, 2004).

Why do people pursue others who want nothing to do with them? There are

several reasons because there are various kinds of stalkers; as Finch (2001) colorfully put it, stalkers may be bad, mad, or sad. They may be motivated by desires for revenge or jealous possessiveness and may wish either to intimidate or to exert control over their targets (Brewster, 2003). Indeed, about half of all stalkers are people who pursue an ex-partner after the end of a romantic relationship, and they generally tend to be insecure men with low self-esteem who are very sensitive to rejection and who are disagreeable and hostile (Kamphuis, Emmelkamp, & de Vries, 2004). Alternatively, stalkers may be a little crazy, being obsessed with someone who is a mere acquaintanace or who they don't even know; stalkers are complete strangers to their targets about one fifth of the time. Or, finally, they may be lonely and possessed of poor social skills and may be seeking to form a relationship in an inept and hopeless way. One quarter of all stalkers are neighbors, coworkers, or other acquaintances such as teachers, bank tellers, or car mechanics.

Stalking is no trivial matter. Victims often become anxious and fearful, and some form of physical violence occurs in about one third of all cases. The police are consulted half of the time (Cupach & Spitzberg, 2004). Another dark cost of some relationships is that they don't fully end when one partner tries to exit them.

---

injury; when couple violence occurs, 62 percent of those who are injured are women (Archer, 2000). Moreover, men are much more likely than women to rape or murder their partners (Tjaden & Thoennes, 1999). These brutal acts are usually not assessed by studies of couple violence, but if they are included, men are clearly more aggressive than women are (O'Leary, 2000; Straus, 1999).

Sampling is also an issue. Studies of young adults tend to detect more violence from women than men, but studies focusing on distressed couples, such as those in marital therapy, usually find the husbands to be much more violent than their wives (Archer, 2002). Add all this up, and it appears that women can be just as violent as men, but they are less likely to cause injuries and less likely to use violence as a tool in an ongoing pattern of domination and influence. And when they are victims of intimate terrorism, women typically face persistent violence that often does them harm (Johnson & Leone, 2005). Why do men sometimes resort to force to hold sway over their female partners?

Correlates of Violence

Intimate violence is not restricted to any one social class, race, or ethnic background; it occurs throughout society. But there are a number of specific factors that are correlated with increased rates of spouse abuse (Tjaden & Thoennes, 1999):

Cohabitation instead of marriage

Stressful events, such as unemployment and unplanned pregnancy

Low socioeconomic status involving such factors as low income and little education

Family background, including growing up in a violent family

In particular, a man's work has something to do with whether he will be violent at home. Men in occupations that involve violence, such as law enforcement or the military, engage in 43 percent more intimate violence than do men in white-collar professions (Melzer, 2002). A low income is also key; violence is much more common in homes with low annual incomes than in homes that are affluent (Cunradi, Caetano, & Schafer, 2002). In addition, men who are plagued by feelings of inadequacy, who have low self-esteem and who feel dissatisfied with their lives (perhaps because they don't make much money), are more likely to be hostile toward women than are men with more self-respect (Cowan & Mills, 2004). And all this is wrapped up in a mindset in aggressive men that associates women with sex and hostility; such men are more likely than others to think of women as adversaries to be used for one's satisfaction and pleasure (Liebold & McConnell, 2004).

Such views may result, in part, from the lessons that youngsters receive from their families. Adults who witnessed intimate violence between their parents during their childhood are more likely to engage in violence in their own relationships than are people who had nonviolent homes (Kennedy, Bolger, & Shrout, 2002). They are also more likely to abuse their own children. It's regrettable that intimate aggression can be transmitted from one generation to the next, but we should note that this cycle is not inevitable. The National Family Violence Survey found that the sons of the most violent parents were ten times more likely than the sons of nonviolent parents to beat their wives. Yet even in this extreme group, only 20 percent had committed severe acts of violence against their spouses in the past 12 months; the other 80 percent of the children of very violent parents had not recently engaged in any severe violence in their intimate relationships (Johnson & Ferraro, 2000). Thus, children from violent homes are more likely to misbehave than others, but many never do. Nonetheless, their increased risk for such behavior is still disturbing because it translates into enormous suffering for many people. In the cycle of family violence, the evil that people do may, in fact, outlive them.

The Rationales of Violence

Overall, then, men who engage in intimate terrorism seem to subscribe to masculine codes that promote a man's authority over women, but many of them feel inadequate to the task (Melzer, 2002); they "often feel, or fear, that they do not measure up to those codes. Attempting to shore up their masculine self-concept, they may try to control others, particularly those who are physically weaker than they are" (Wood, 2004, p. 558). Do such men even realize that they are being abusive, or do they consider their use of force to be customary treatment of women by men?

Julia Wood (2004) provided insight into the minds of such men when she interviewed 22 incarcerated men who had abused their female partners. All of the men felt that their behavior had been a legitimate response to the disrespect they had faced from their partners, and all mentioned their partners' provocation as the genesis of their abuse. They also felt that men were supposed to be dominant and superior to women, and so were entitled to use violence to control and discipline them. On the other hand, most believed that they were not "real" wife abusers because they did not enjoy hurting women and they had limited their level of abuse, doing less harm than they could have. One man had stabbed his wife but only once, and another had brutally beaten his wife but argued that he hadn't hit her as hard as he could. Perhaps as a result of these rationalizations, only about half of the men expressed regret and remorse about their actions. They understood that their actions were illegal, but they didn't necessarily believe that their actions were wrong.

What do women feel in response to such treatment? In a broad review of the intimate violence literature, Sally Lloyd and Beth Emery (2000) noted that women are ordinarily surprised when they encounter intimate aggression, and they often struggle to make sense of it. They are influenced by romantic norms that encourage them to "forgive and forget"and by sexual norms that portray men as more impulsive and impetuous than women. They also labor under cultural norms that blame victims for their difficulties, so they "consistently ask themselves why they went out with the wrong kind of man, why they made him angry when they knew he had a violent temper, or why they were in the wrong place at the wrong time" (Lloyd & Emery, 2000, p. 508). As a result of these influences, women feel betrayed, but they sometimes also blame themselves for their partners' aggression and, due to shame, naïveté, or ignorance, they often remain silent about their plight.

Overall, intimate terrorism exacts a fearsome toll on its victims. Physical injuries are bad enough, but victims may also suffer negative psychological consequences ranging from lowered self-esteem and mistrust of men to depression and posttraumatic stress disorder (Johnson & Ferraro, 2000). There are also substantial social costs; battered women are often absent from work, and some become homeless when violence forces them to flee from their homes. And at its most basic level, intimate violence substantially lowers the quality of one's outcomes in a relationship, making it much less desirable than it otherwise might be. The end of the relationship may follow (Bradbury & Lawrence, 1999).

Why Don't They All Leave?

Indeed, intimate violence causes many people to leave their partners. One study (Campbell et al., 1994) that followed battered women over two-and-a-half years found that at the end of that period,

> 43 percent of the participants had left their original partners, either remaining unattached (20 percent) or entering new nonabusive relationships (23 percent),
>
> 23 percent remained with their partners but had successfully ended the violence for at least a year, and
>
> 33 percent were still in an abusive relationship, either as victims (25 percent) or as both victims and perpetrators of violence (8 percent).

Thus, in this sample, only a third of the women stayed in an abusive partnership for an extended period. Perseverance and determination are often required to escape an abusive relationship, but most people do, one way or the other. But why don't all victims run from their persecutors?

There's a simple answer to that question. They don't leave because, despite the abuse, they don't think they'll be better off if they go (Choice & Lamke, 1999)[3]. A decision to leave is complex. Some violent partners are sweet and loving part of the time, and intermittent violence may be one's only complaint about the relationship (Marshall, Weston, & Honeycutt, 2000). The costs of leaving may also seem too high; whatever investments one has made in the relationship will be lost, and one's alternatives may seem bleak (Rusbult & Martz, 1995). One's economic status is crucial in this regard; the financial expense of departing one's home may be too momentous to overcome if one is unemployed.

As if their economic dependence on the relationship and their psychological commitment to it were not enough, the fear of even greater violence may also prevent the victims of intimate terrorism from exiting the relationship. Some aggressive, controlling partners may react with extreme anger against

---

[3]This is an excellent example of the influence of our perceptions of the outcomes awaiting us outside our current relationships, which we labeled as our *comparison level for alternatives* back in chapter 6. We invite you to look back at pages 184–186 for more discussion of these ideas.

their lovers if they try to leave. The possibility of such violent reactions "argues strongly for maximum protection of women who are attempting to leave abusive relationships" (Dutton, 1987, p. 247).

Violence in Premarital Relationships

Our discussion, like the literature on couple violence, has focused on married spouses, but violence is also regrettably common in premarital partnerships. Cohabiting couples are more violent than married couples (Johnson & Ferraro, 2000), and in a survey of over 4,700 U.S. college students at 32 different institutions, 37 percent of the men and 35 percent of the women reported having engaged in some form of intimate violence in the previous year (White & Koss, 1991). In that sample, more men (39 percent) than women (32 percent) indicated that their partners had used force against them.

When young adults are asked why they act violently, the most frequent reason given by both men and women is anger. The second most common reason for men is to get control over their partners, whereas for women, it's self-defense (O'Keefe, 1997). Familiar influences are also correlated with violence in premarital partnerships: the belief that dating violence is justifiable, being the recipient of dating violence, and greater conflict in the dating relationship (O'Keefe, 1997). The sources of violence in dating relationships appear to be similar to those in more committed relationships, and it's clear that, whenever people enter into interdependent intimacy, the potential for conflict, and even violence, exists.

FOR YOUR CONSIDERATION

Jonathon's wife, Tina, is a bit hot-headed. When something bothers her, she wants to drop everything else and work on the problem, but she tends to do so with high emotion. She has a volatile temper; she gets angry easily, but she cools off just as fast. Jonathon is more placid, and he dislikes conflict. When he gets angry, he does so slowly, and he simmers rather than erupts. When there's something bothering him, he prefers to just get off by himself and engage in distracting entertainments instead of beginning a discussion that could turn into a fight.

Lately, Tina has become very frustrated because Jonathon is close-lipped and unresponsive when she brings up a complaint. His reluctance to discuss her grievances is just making her annoyance and dissatisfaction worse. What do you think the future holds for Tina and Jonathon? Why?

CHAPTER SUMMARY

The Nature of Conflict

What Is Conflict? *Interpersonal conflict* occurs whenever one person's motives, goals, beliefs, opinions, or behavior interfere with, or are incompatible with, those of another. Conflict occurs when one's wishes or actions actually obstruct or impede those of someone else, when people have to give up something that they want because of their partners' influence. Conflict is inescapable for two reasons. First, any two people will occasionally differ in their moods and preferences. Second, there are certain tensions known as *dialectics* that are woven into the fabric of close relationships that will, sooner or later, always cause some strain. These are the opposing motivations of autonomy and connection, openness and closedness, stability and change, and integration and separation. The dilemmas posed by fluctuating, opposing motives in close relationships never end. Sooner or later, conflict occurs.

The Frequency of Conflict. Conflict occurs often. Dating couples report 2.3 conflicts per week, and spouses experience one or two unpleasant disagreements each month. The frequency of conflicts in relationships is associated with personality characteristics such as neuroticism and agreeableness, an anxious attachment style, one's stage of life, incompatibility between partners, and the use of alcohol.

The Course of Conflict

Instigating Events. The interdependency that characterizes an intimate relationship provides abundant opportunities for dispute. Four different categories of events cause most conflicts; these are *criticism, illegitimate demands, rebuffs,* and *cumulative annoyances,* which often take the form of social allergies. Heterosexual men and women often fight over access to sex. Homosexuality has some, but not a major, influence on the sources of conflict between partners.

Attributions. Actor-observer effects guarantee that partners will have slightly different explanations for their actions than anyone else does, and self-serving biases lead them to judge their own actions more favorably than others do. As a result, partners often engage in *attributional conflict,* fighting over whose explanation is right and whose account is wrong. Nevertheless, whatever the truth, the explanations with which intimate partners account for the frustrations they encounter have a huge influence on how distressed they feel and how angrily they respond.

Engagement and Escalation. Once an instigating event occurs, partners must decide either to engage in conflict or to avoid the issue and let it drop. Avoidance occurs only when both partners wish to evade the issue. In some other cases, escalation occurs and the conflict heats up. The nasty things that partners say to each other may be of two types; direct tactics explicitly challenge one's partner whereas indirect tactics are more veiled and implicit.

The Demand/Withdraw Pattern. Couples may get bogged down in a demand/withdraw cycle in which one person approaches the other about a problem, and the partner responds by avoiding the issue or the person. Women tend to be the demanders and men the withdrawers more often than not. This pattern may emerge from gender differences: When anything's wrong in a relationship, women want to fix it, and their desire for renewed closeness makes them demanding. Another possibility is a social structure hypothesis, which argues that the pattern results from pervasive differences in the power of men and women in society and marriage alike. Men tend to have more power than women do, and if you're getting your way, you're likely to resist change. Both gender differences and social structure seem to create the demand/withdraw pattern.

Negotiation and Accommodation. Negotiation finally occurs when a couple works toward a solution in a sensible manner. In addition to negotiation, researchers recognize voice, loyalty, exit, and neglect as responses to dissatisfaction in close relationships. Voice is more likely when a partnership has been satisfying in the past, and it is most likely to be used by people with secure attachment styles. *Accommodation* occurs when partners inhibit the impulse to fight fire with fire and strive to react instead with constructive voice or loyalty.

Dealing with Conflict: Four Types of Couples. There are three discrete approaches to conflict that can lead to stable and enduring marriages. *Volatile* couples have frequent and passionate arguments. *Validators* have calmer, more relaxed discussions in which they appear to be working together on the problem. *Avoiders* rarely argue; they avoid confrontation, and if they do discuss their conflicts, they do so mildly and gingerly. Although they are very different, all three types of couples can last because they all maintain a high ratio of rewards to costs in their approaches to conflict. In contrast, the conflicts of *hostiles* are marked by negativity. Hostiles engage in such behaviors as criticism, contempt, defensiveness, and withdrawal, and their marriages are more fragile than those of the other three groups.

The Outcomes of Conflict

Ending Conflict. There are five ways conflicts can end: *separation, domination, compromise, integrative agreement,* and *structural improvement*. In separation, the parties withdraw without resolving the conflict. In domination, one person gets his or her way and the other gives in. In compromise, the two parties find an alternative that is acceptable to both but optimal to neither. In integrative agreement, both partners' original goals and aspirations are met. In structural improvement, the partners not only get what they want, they also make desirable changes to their relationship.

Can Fighting Be Good for a Relationship? The prevailing view among conflict researchers is that, for all the problems it can bring, conflict is an essential tool with which to promote intimacy. Deft and skillful management of conflict allows relationships to grow and prosper. A "fight effects profile" lists the desirable results a "good fight" should have.

Violence and Abuse in Relationships

Some fights result in *violence*, actions that intended to hurt someone else. The *Conflict Tactics Scale* is a research tool that assesses violence in couples.

The Prevalence of Violence. According to national surveys, 22 percent of women and 7 percent of men in the United States have experienced a violent assault by an intimate partner. The prevalence of violence varies across ethnic groups and is more common in the same-sex relationships of men than women.

Types of Couple Violence. There are four distinct types of violence in romantic couples. *Situational couple violence* typically erupts from heated arguments that get out of hand. In *intimate terrorism*, one partner uses violence as a tool to control and oppress the other. *Mutual violent control* occurs when both partners engage in intimate terrorism, and *violent resistance* occurs when a partner forcibly fights back. Men and women are equally likely to engage in situational couple violence, but a huge majority of those who employ intimate terrorism are men.

Gender Differences in Partner Violence. Wives act violently toward their husbands just as often as husbands act violently toward their wives. However, men and women engage in violent behavior of different severity; men are more likely to inflict injury, and when couples seek marital therapy, the husbands are typically more violent than the wives.

Correlates of Violence. Spouse abuse is associated with cohabitation, stressful events, low socioeconomic status, and growing up in a violent home. Men who are plagued by feelings of inadequacy are more likely to be hostile toward women. Children who witness violence between their parents are more likely than others to engage in intimate violence as adults.

The Rationales of Violence. Wife-abusing men feel superior to women and believe that their aggression is a legitimate response to the disrespect they receive from their wives. They also feel that they are not "real" abusers because they did less harm than they were capable of doing. Women often struggle to make sense of the violence they encounter, being influenced by romantic and sexual norms that sometimes lead them to blame themselves for their abuse.

Why Don't They All Leave? Some victims of abuse leave their relationships, others achieve a reduction in violence, and others remain in their abusive partnerships. Victims stay when they don't believe they'll be better off if they go. They are unlikely to leave the relationship when they do not have adequate economic resources or if they fear that by leaving they will suffer even greater physical harm.

Violence in Premarital Relationships. Violence is also regrettably common in premarital partnerships. The sources of violence in dating relationships appear to be similar to those in more committed relationships, and it's clear that, whenever people enter into interdependent intimacy, the potential for conflict, and even violence, exists.

PART FIVE

Losing and Enhancing Relationships

CHAPTER 13

The Dissolution and Loss of Relationships

THE CHANGING RATE OF DIVORCE ◆ The Prevalence of Divorce ◆ U.S. Divorce Rates in Comparative Perspectives ◆ Why Has the Divorce Rate Increased? ◆ THE PREDICTORS OF DIVORCE ◆ Levinger's Barrier Model ◆ Karney and Bradbury's Vulnerability-Stress-Adaptation Model ◆ Results from the PAIR Project ◆ Results from the Early Years of Marriage Project ◆ People's Personal Perceptions of the Causes of Divorce ◆ Specific Factors Associated with Divorce ◆ THE ROAD TO DIVORCE ◆ Breaking Up with Premarital Partners ◆ Steps to Divorce ◆ THE AFTERMATH OF SEPARATION AND DIVORCE ◆ Individuals' Perspectives ◆ Relationships Between Former Partners ◆ Children Whose Parents Divorce ◆ FOR YOUR CONSIDERATION ◆ CHAPTER SUMMARY

Sometimes the stresses and strains two partners experience catch up with them. Perhaps their conflict is too constant and too intense. Perhaps their partnership is inequitable, with one of them exploiting the other. Perhaps their passion has waned, and new attractions are distracting them. Or perhaps they are merely contented, instead of delighted, with each other, so they are disappointed that the "magic" has died.

There are myriad reasons why relationships may fail, and the deterioration of any particular partnership may involve events and processes that are unique to that specific couple. On the other hand, there are also personal and cultural influences that may have generic, widespread effects on the stability of many intimate relationships, and relationship scientists have been identifying and studying them for years. In this chapter, we consider the correlates and consequences of the decline and fall of satisfaction and intimacy. We will focus on marital relationships because a decision to divorce is often more deliberate and weighty, and the consequences more complicated, than those that emerge from less formal partnerships. Nevertheless, the dissolution of any intimate relationship—such as a cohabiting partnership, dating relationship, or friendship—can be momentous, and much of what we discuss will apply to those partnerships, as well. Let's start with a reminder that the cultural landscape we face today is quite different than the one our grandparents knew.

THE CHANGING RATE OF DIVORCE

The Prevalence of Divorce

As you recall, current divorce rates are much higher than they were when your grandparents married. The *refined divorce rate* in the United States, the number of divorces per 1,000 married women over age fifteen that occur in any given year[1], has increased dramatically in the last 50 years. Take a look back at Figure 1.3 on p. 11; the divorce rate is actually a bit lower than it was at its peak back in 1980, but the chance that a recent marriage will ultimately end in separation or divorce is still close to 50 percent (Popenoe & Whitehead, 2004). This is remarkable, because it suggests that despite all the good intentions and warm feelings with which people marry, the chances that they will succeed in living out their lives together are about the same as the chance of getting "heads" when you flip a coin.

Most people who divorce eventually remarry, but the steep rise in the divorce rate has also led to a notable increase in the number of adults who are currently divorced and single. In 1960, only 1.8 percent of men and 2.6 percent of women, tiny fractions of the population, were divorced and single. But by 2003, these percentages had quadrupled to 8.3 percent and 10.9 percent, respectively (Popenoe & Whitehead, 2004). This means that in the United States, millions and millions of people, including one out of every nine adult women, are presently divorced.

One of the results of the high divorce rate is that 27 percent of American children—more than 1 out of every 4 people under the age of 18—now live in single-parent families, most of them headed by their mothers (Popenoe & Whitehead, 2004). (This rate is three times higher than it was in 1960.) And some children who do have two parents are living with a stepmother or stepfather, so that, overall, more than one third (34 percent) of U.S. children are living apart from their biological fathers (Popenoe & Whitehead, 2004). (This is twice as many as in 1960.) Anyway you look at it, divorce is a larger part of the American way of life than it used to be.

U.S. Divorce Rates in Comparative Perspectives

Divorce rates increased in most Western countries during the second half of the twentieth century, but the United States had the dubious distinction of leading the pack. In 1995, the United States had a crude divorce rate (that's the number of divorces per 1,000 population) of 4.5 (United Nations, 1999). Most other countries had substantially lower rates (e.g., Mexico, 0.4; Chile, 0.4; South Africa, 0.8; Japan, 1.8; Netherlands, 2.2, Sweden, 2.4; Canada, 2.6; the United Kingdom, 2.9). Only a few countries (such as Russia, 4.5) had divorce rates close to that of the United States.

Obviously, the current divorce rate is a significant change from the past. On the other hand, the end of large numbers of marriages after only a few years is not

---

[1]The refined divorce rate is a more precise measure than the total number of divorces per year—or even the number of divorces per capita—because it takes note of both the size of the U.S. population and the changing sex ratios of men to women.

new at all. In former times, many marriages were terminated by the early death of one of the partners. The hazards of childbirth made it especially likely that a married woman would die young, and that her husband would remarry. In addition, many marriages in the past simply ended when one spouse deserted the other without ever obtaining a legal divorce. Those young men encouraged to "Go West!" in America during the 1800s often left wives and children behind. All things considered, given our longer life spans, the average time that spouses spend together when they stay married has increased "from about fifteen to twenty years in preindustrial Europe to about thirty-five years in 1900, and then to almost fifty years" in the late 1980s (Phillips, 1988, p. S93). And when anything is expected to last a longer time, there is an increased possibility that it will break down. Taken in their broader historical context—or in comparison with the breakup of other forms of close relationships (see Box 13.1)—the current high rate of divorce in the United States seems less deviant and less shocking. Nevertheless, what has clearly changed is the way that marriages end.

Why Has the Divorce Rate Increased?

There are no certain reasons why the second half of the twentieth century saw such a huge increase in American rates of divorce. But there are several possibilities, and all of them may (or may not) be contributing influences.

One possibility is that we hold different, more demanding expectations for marriage than people used to. Our great-grandparents generally believed that if you wanted to live with a romantic partner, if you wanted to have children, and if you wanted to pay the bills and live well, you had to get married. Nowadays, however, cohabitation is widespread, there are lots of single parents, and most women have entered the workforce (Nock, 2000). As a result, marriage is no longer the practical necessity it used to be; instead, in the opinion of some observers, people are more likely than ever before to pursue marriage as a path to personal fulfillment. Marriage is supposed to be play, not work; it's supposed to be exciting, not routine, and passionate, not warm (Myers, 2000). Thus, our expectations for marriage (or our *comparison levels*, if we use the language of interdependency theory) may be too high. A happy, warm, rewarding partnership may seem insufficient if it is measured against unrealistic expectations (Shulman, 2004).

For instance, almost 40 years ago, Slater (1968) warned that

> *Spouses are now asked to be lovers, friends, and mutual therapists in a society which is forcing the marriage bond to become the closest, deepest, most important and most enduring relationship of one's life. Paradoxically, then, it is increasingly likely to fall short of the emotional demands placed upon it and be dissolved. (p. 99)*

Twenty years later, Phillips (1988) expressed a similar point of view:

> *The same stress on romantic love, emotional intensity, and sexual satisfaction that has long been associated with premarital and extramarital relationships has spilled over into marriage . . . The higher these emotional expectations rise, the less likely they are to be fulfilled. (pp. 623–624)*

BOX 13.1

Dissolution in Four Types of Relationships

Separation Rates in Four Types of Relationships

Study	Marital	Cohabiting	Gay	Lesbian
Blumstein & Schwartz, 1983	4%	17%	16%	22%
Kurdek, 1998	7%		14%	16%
Bumpass & Sweet, 1989	20%	45%		
Wu & Balakrishnan, 1995	< 5%	24%		
Leridon, 1990	8%	16%		

Note: Blumstein and Schwartz (1983) solicited volunteer participants via the media; their index of relationship termination is the percentage of participants (N = 2,082) who broke up within 18 months of originally completing a questionnaire. Kurdek (1998b) conducted a five-year longitudinal study of 353 married, gay, and lesbian couples, who had respectively been living together, on average, for 4.7, 10.9 and 7.1 years at the beginning of the study; he assessed the percentage in each group that separated over the study period. Using the 1987–1988 National Survey of Families and Households, Bumpass and Sweet (1989) examined dissolution rates over the first five years of their relationship among 4,184 people involved in "first unions." Wu and Balakrishnan (1995) used data from Statistics Canada's 1990 General Social Survey (Family and Friends section). They report the percentage of marriages and first cohabitations (N = 2,876) that end in separation within three years. Leridon (1990) analyzed data from a French Family History Survey involving participants who became involved in first unions during the period 1968–1985. Breakdown results are the outcomes over the first five years for unions formed in the period 1977–1979.

The table presents the dissolution rates among married, cohabiting, gay, and lesbian couples in five different studies. What they all show is that married couples are less likely to separate over a given period of time than are cohabiting or same-sex couples. In the only study that compared all four kinds of couples (Blumstein & Schwartz, 1983), all of the unmarried couples were more likely to break up than married spouses were, so marriage appears to be more strongly related to relationship stability than sexual orientation is.

But don't take that to mean that married spouses are generally happier and more in love with each other than cohabiting, gay, or lesbian partners are;

on average, those unmarried couples report just as much attraction to one another as spouses do (Peplau & Spalding, 2000). What's different is that marriages may be harder to get out of. In most areas, gay and lesbian couples still "cannot marry legally, are less likely to own property jointly, are less likely to have children in common, may lack support from their families of origins, and so on" (Peplau & Spalding, 2000, pp. 120–121). Cohabiting heterosexual partners are also less likely to break up if they have children (Wu & Balkrishnan, 1995). Apparently, an important factor in the lower dissolution rates of married couples are the barriers linked with marriage that make it harder to leave the relationship.

People may simply be expecting too much of marriage. The percentage of American spouses who report that their marriages are "very happy" is lower now than it was 25 years ago (Popenoe & Whitehead, 2004), and the number of conflicts and problems that spouses report are higher (Amato et al., 2003). On the whole, the average perceived quality of American marriages has declined since 1970.

But the broader culture has changed, too, and several societal influences may be affecting both the expectations with which we begin our marriages and the situations we encounter once we are wed. For instance, most women in the U.S. now work outside the home, and their entry into the workforce may have had several effects. First, spouses report more conflict between work and family than they used to (Rogers & Amato, 2000), and the more hours a wife works during the week, the lower the quality of her marriage tends to be (Amato et al., 2003). Car repairs, child care, and the scheduling and cooking of meals (to name just a few examples) are more problematic when both spouses are employed and the amount of time spouses spend together tends to decline. Both spouses are also undoubtedly affected by their problems at work, so that decreases in job satisfaction are associated with increases in marital discord (Rogers & May, 2003). Second, participation in the labor force increases spouses' access to interesting, desirable, alternative partners, and divorce is more frequent when women work in occupations that surround them with men (South, Trent, & Shen, 2001).

In addition, women earn more money than they used to, and, around the world, divorce rates are higher when women are financially independent of men (Barber, 2003). Being able to support oneself increases one's freedom to choose divorce when a marriage deteriorates, and in the U.S. there is a straightforward, positive correlation between a woman's income and her odds of divorce: The more money she makes, the more likely it is that she will someday be divorced (Rogers, 2004). However, women are also more likely to divorce when they make about as much money as their husbands do; when they contribute either much less or much more to the total family income than their husbands do, the risk of divorce is lower (Rogers, 2004). Combined, these patterns support an **independence hypothesis** that suggests that the economic freedom to divorce makes divorce more likely; when either a husband or wife earns a lot less money than his or her spouse does, their marriage is less likely to end in divorce.

So, financial freedom increases the risk of divorce. But don't think that your marriage will be better off if you just do without money; poverty has even bigger effects on marital quality. In general, couples with money troubles who are experiencing financial strain are less content with their marriages than are those who are better off (Cutrona et al., 2003); in particular, couples with rather low incomes (under $25,000 per year) are twice as likely to divorce as are couples with reasonably high incomes (over $50,000 per year) (Karney, 2004; Popenoe & Whitehead, 2004). Having money may make it easier to divorce, but being poor may cause stress that undermines a marriage, too.

Overall, then, women's increased participation in the labor force has plausibly increased conflict at home, made alluring, new romantic partners more available, and decreased wives' economic dependence on their husbands. Perhaps for all of these reasons, the trend is clear: As the proportion of American women employed outside the home increased during the twentieth century, so, too, did the divorce rate (Fitch & Ruggles, 2000).[2]

Our gender roles, the behaviors we expect from men and women, are changing, too. Women are gradually becoming more instrumental, being more assertive and self-reliant (Twenge, 1997), and the partners in many marriages are dividing household responsibilities more equitably (Canary & Stafford, 2001). Over the last 25 years, less traditional gender roles and increases in the equality of family decision-making have been associated with higher marital quality for both husbands and wives. However, the new division of labor has had two different effects; husbands are less happy now that they're doing more household chores, but their wives are more content (Amato et al., 2003; Rogers & Amato, 2000).

By some accounts, Western culture is also becoming more individualistic, with people being less connected to the others around them than they used to be (Myers, 2000). Indeed, most of us are less tied to our communities than our grandparents were (Putnam, 2000). We're less likely to live near our extended families and less likely to know our neighbors; we participate in fewer clubs and social organizations, entertain at home less frequently, and move more often. As a result, we probably receive less social support and companionship from friends and acquaintances than our grandparents did, and we rely on our spouses for more (Magdol & Bessel, 2003), and this may affect divorce rates in two different ways. First, we ask more of our spouses than ever before. We expect them to fulfill a wider variety of interpersonal needs, and that increases the probability that they will disappoint us in some manner. In addition, people who are less connected to their communities are less affected by community norms that might discourage them from divorcing. And as it turns out, people who move often from place to place really are more prone to divorce than are those who stay in one place and put down roots (White, 1990).

The sex ratio of the culture has also changed. As we mentioned in chapter 1, the sex ratio in the United States is much lower than it was in 1960, and around the world, divorce rates are higher when women outnumber men (and the sex ratio is low) and lower when men outnumber women (and the sex ratio is high) (Barber, 2000a, 2003). Men tend to have more affairs than women do, and their sociosexual orientations are more unrestricted[3] (Simpson & Gagestad, 1991), so marriages tend to be more at risk when women outnumber men and men have lots of women available to them. In addition, when there are too few men to go

---

[2]As we describe these various patterns, do remember, please, that all of these links between social changes and divorce rates are *correlations* that allow diverse possibilities to exist. A connection between women's working and divorce does not necessarily mean that employment undermines women's commitment to their marriages. To the contrary, women are more likely to seek employment when there is preexisting discord and strife in their marriages, so it is just as likely that marital dissatisfaction causes women to find work as it is that women's work causes marital dissatisfaction (Rogers, 1999). Keep an open mind as you consider the implications of societal change.

[3]Need a reminder about sociosexuality? Look back at p. 285 in chapter 9.

around, teenaged girls are more likely to have children before they marry and are less likely to marry at all (Barber, 2002a; Gaughan, 2002), and such behavior further reduces the social significance and stability of marriage (Heaton, 2002).

Our shared perceptions of divorce are also less negative than they used to be. In many circles, a divorce used to be considered a shameful failure, and the event itself was often a messy, lurid, embarrassing spectacle in which blame had to be assigned to someone. The advent of no-fault divorce laws in the U.S. during the 1970s made a divorce much easier to obtain; for the first time in most jurisdictions, once they had agreed on the division of property and child custody, spouses merely had to certify that they faced "irreconcilable differences," and their marriage was dissolved. No-fault laws probably helped make the procedure more socially acceptable (Rodgers, Nakonezny, & Shull, 1999). On average, we feel that a divorce is a more reasonable and more desirable response to a bad marriage than our parents did, and more favorable attitudes toward divorce appear to reduce the quality of our marriages as time goes by (Amato & Rogers, 1999). We may be less likely to work hard to rescue a faltering relationship when divorce seems an expedient alternative.

Most couples also cohabit before they marry these days, and as we saw in chapter 1, people who cohabit encounter an increased risk of divorce later on. Despite the widespread belief that cohabitation is a valuable trial run that allows people to avoid later problems, cohabitation is *positively* associated with

---

BOX 13.2
Divorce: Another Reason to Marry

Divorce is usually an unwelcome event, but it does serve valuable legal functions. In most jurisdictions, there are few laws that clearly govern what happens when a cohabitating couple splits up, and the division of their assets can be very messy indeed. In contrast, in a divorce that works well, a couple's property and debt are divided fairly, and formal rules for child custody, visitation, and support are arranged. The legal protection provided by a divorce is one of several reasons why many gays and lesbians are seeking the right to form formal matrimonial unions in the U.S. (Leff, 2004).

"Gay marriage" is a contentious topic, but critics of the idea usually overlook the difficulties homosexual partners may face when they are denied access to a clean divorce. What do you think is fair when one member of a couple stays home to parent a child while the other gets rich working her way up the corporate ladder, and they finally decide to separate? In a case in California involving two lesbians, the woman who had been the stay-at-home mother found herself at a huge disadvantage when her partner wanted to keep most of the money she had earned (Leff, 2004). Only a small handful of states have formal procedures that guide cases like this, and the pursuit of justice when relationships end is another reason why gays and lesbians want state legislatures to legitimize their intimate relationships.

the probability of divorce (Meckler, 2002). The good news is that couples who start living together after they become engaged to marry, and who cohabit for a shorter, rather than longer, period of time, do not divorce more frequently than do those who marry without living together (Kline et al., 2004; Stafford, Kline, & Rankin, 2004). Brief cohabitation that is limited to one's fiancé does not seem to put a subsequent marriage at risk. (But it doesn't reduce the risk of divorce, either.) On the other hand, people who ever cohabit with more than one partner, or who cohabit before they become engaged, are more likely to later divorce (Teachman, 2003), probably because cohabitation changes their beliefs and expectations about marriage (Moors, 2000). Casual cohabitation seems to lead to (a) less respect for the institution of marriage, (b) less favorable expectations about the outcomes of marriage, and (c) greater willingness to divorce (McGinnis, 2003), and all of these make divorce more likely.

Finally, as more parents divorce, more children witness family conflict and grow up in "broken" homes. Common sense may suggest that youngsters who suffer family disruption might be especially determined to avoid making the same mistakes, but, in reality, divorce is passed down from one generation to the next: Children who experience the divorce of their parents are more likely to be divorced themselves when they become adults (Amato & DeBoer, 2001; Tallman, Rotolo, & Gray, 2001). Various processes may underlie this pattern. For one thing, children from divorced homes have less favorable views of marriage, and they report less trust in their partners when they begin their own romantic relationships (Boyer-Pennington, England, & Pennington, 2003; Jacquet & Surra, 2001); thus, compared to children from intact homes, they have less faith that their marriages will last (Boyer-Pennington et al., 2001). Furthermore, to some degree, children learn how to behave in intimate relationships from the lessons provided by their parents (Conger et al., 2000), and those who remember a childhood home full of strife and discord tend to have more acrimonious marriages of poorer quality themselves (Amato & Booth, 2001; Doucet & Aseltine, 2003). Thus, as divorce becomes more commonplace, more children seem to become more susceptible to divorce in later years.

So, why has the divorce rate increased? There are reasons to believe that, compared to our grandparents' day

- we expect more out of marriage, holding it to higher standards;
- working women have more financial freedom and better access to attractive alternatives, and they experience corrosive conflict between work and family;
- creeping individualism and social mobility leave us less tied to, and less affected by, community norms that discourage divorce;
- lower sex ratios promote teen births and undermine men's commitment to any one partner;
- new laws have made divorce more socially acceptable and easier to obtain;
- casual cohabitation weakens commitment to marriage; and
- children of divorce are more likely to divorce when they become adults.

All of these possible influences are merely correlated with the increasing prevalence of divorce in the United States, so they all may be symptoms, rather than causes, of the societal changes that have promoted divorce. It's a rather long list of possibilities, however, and it provides another good example of the manner in which cultural influences shape intimate relationships. Arguably, the cultural climate supports lasting marriages less effectively than it did 40 or 50 years ago. But even with such changes, at least half of the marriages that begin this year will not end in divorce. (Not all of them will be happy [Glenn, 1998], but at least they won't encounter a divorce.) What individual and relational characteristics predict who will and who will not ultimately separate? Let's turn to that next.

THE PREDICTORS OF DIVORCE

Whatever the cultural context, some marriages succeed and others fail, and as you'd expect, the differences between marital winners and losers have long been of interest to relationship scientists. Diverse models that explicate some of the sources of divorce have been proposed, and impressive longitudinal studies have now tracked some marriages for over twenty years. In this section, we'll inspect both theories and research results that identify some of the predictors of divorce.

Levinger's Barrier Model

George Levinger, a proponent of interdependency theory, used concepts like those we described in chapter 6 in a model (1976) that identified three types of factors that influence the breakup of relationships. The first of these is *attraction.* For Levinger, attraction is enhanced by the rewards a relationship offers (such as enjoyable companionship, sexual fulfillment, security, and social status), and it is diminished by its costs (such as irritating incompatibility and the investment of time and energy). The second key influence on breakups is the *alternatives* one possesses. The most obvious of these are other partners, but any alternative to a current relationship, such as being single or achieving occupational success, may lure someone away from an existing partnership. Finally, there are the *barriers* around the relationship that make it hard to leave; these include the legal and social pressures to remain married, religious and moral constraints, and the financial costs of obtaining a divorce and maintaining two households.

A major contribution of Levinger's approach was to highlight the fact that unhappy partners who would like to break up often stay together because it would cost them too much to leave. He also persuasively argued that many barriers to divorce are psychological rather than material; distressed spouses may certainly stay married because they do not have enough money to divorce, but they may also stay together (even when they have sufficient resources to leave) because of the guilt or embarrassment they would feel—or cause others—if they divorced.

Indeed, spouses report that there are several meaningful costs that would deter them from seeking a divorce. A survey of people married for twelve years demonstrated that they worry that their children would suffer, the threat of losing their children, religious norms, dependence on their spouses, and the fear of financial ruin were all perceived to be influential barriers that discouraged divorce (Knoester & Booth, 2000). However, over that twelve-year span, once other risk factors such as low education and parental divorce were taken into account, only two of those perceived barriers, dependence on one's spouse and religious beliefs, actually distinguished couples who divorced from those who did not. And if people had grown genuinely dissatisfied with their marriages, even those two barriers seemed insignificant: Once they wanted out of their marriages, there was no stopping them (Knoester & Booth, 2000).

Thus, people are usually aware of several obstacles that they would have to overcome in order to divorce, but once a marriage is on the rocks, those barriers may seem less momentous. Levinger's model helpfully reminds us of deterrents to divorce that run through people's minds, but it may not fully recognize how ineffective those deterrents may become once marital misery sets in.

Karney and Bradbury's Vulnerability-Stress-Adaptation Model

Benjamin Karney and Thomas Bradbury (1995) developed a general model of marital instability (which is shown in Figure 13.1) that highlighted another three influences that could contribute to divorce. According to this view, some people enter marriage with *enduring vulnerabilities* that increase their risk of divorce. Such vulnerabilities might include adverse experiences in one's family of origin, poor education, maladaptive personality traits, bad social skills, or dysfunctional attitudes toward marriage. None of these characteristics makes divorce inevitable, but all of them can shape the circumstances a couple encounters, and all of them influence the *adaptive processes* with which people try to cope with stress. If a couple gets lucky and encounters only infrequent

FIGURE 13.1. A vulnerability-stress-adaptation model of marriage.
Source: Karney & Bradbury, 1995.

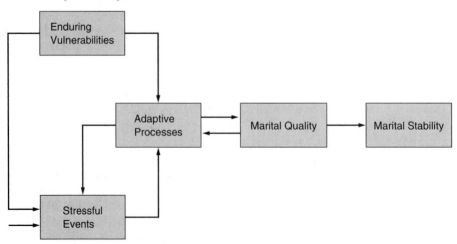

and mild difficulties, even those with poor coping and communication skills may live happily ever after.

However, almost every marriage must face occasional *stressful events* that require the partners to provide support to one another and to adjust to new circumstances. Some stressors (such as a period of unemployment or a major illness) befall some marriages and not others, whereas other stressors (such as pregnancy, childbirth, and parenting) are commonplace. When stressful events occur, a couple must cope and adapt, but, depending on their vulnerabilities, some people are better able to do that than are others. Failure to cope successfully can even make the stresses worse, and if poor coping causes marital quality to decline, a couple's coping may be further impaired (Neff & Karney, 2004). And ultimately, extended periods of dissatisfaction are presumed to lead to marital instability and divorce.

Overall, the vulnerability-stress-adaptation model makes the valuable point that the quality of our marriages emerges from the interplay of who we are, the circumstances we encounter, and the manner in which we respond to those circumstances, and, at least to some degree, these three important influences affect each other. It's possible for the roots of divorce to begin in childhood in an insecure attachment style or the lessons learned in a home filled with conflict, but if life treats us well or we work hard and well with our spouses to overcome life's difficulties (or perhaps just take a good college course on close relationships!), divorce need not occur.

Results from the PAIR Project

For decades, Ted Huston and his colleagues (Huston, Caughlin et al., 2001; Huston, Niehuis, & Smith, 2001) have been tracking 168 couples who married in 1981. The project has focused on the manner in which spouses adapt to their lives together (or fail to do so) and is known as the Processes of Adaptation in Intimate Relationships (or PAIR) Project. There's enormous value in longitudinal studies like this, but their results can be a little sobering. Indeed, in the PAIR project, after only 13 years, 35 percent of the couples had divorced and another 20 percent weren't happy; only 45 percent of the couples could be said to be happily married, and even they were less satisfied and less loving than they had been when they wed. And these, we should remind you, are typical results. Take a look back at Figure 6.7 on p. 199: Marital satisfaction routinely declines as time goes by.

Why? Huston and his colleagues examined three different explanations for why marriages go awry. One possibility, which is reminiscent of the enduring vulnerabilities noted by Karney and Bradbury (1995), is that spouses who are destined to be discontent begin their marriages being less in love and more at odds with each other than are those whose marriages ultimately succeed. This possibility, the *enduring dynamics* model, suggests that spouses bring to their marriages problems and incompatibilities that surface during their courtship; moreover, the partners are usually aware of these frustrations and shortcomings before they even wed. According to this model, then, marriages that are headed for divorce are weaker than others from the very beginning.

In contrast, a second possibility known as the *emergent distress* model suggests that the problematic behavior that ultimately destroys a couple begins after they marry. As time goes by, some couples fall into a rut of increasing conflict and negativity that did not exist when the marriage began. Thus, unlike the enduring dynamics model, the emergent distress approach suggests that, when they begin, there is no discernable difference between marriages that will succeed and those that will fail; the difficulties that ruin some marriages usually develop later.

Finally, a third possibility is the *disillusionment* model. This approach suggests that couples typically begin their marriages with rosy, romanticized views of their relationship that are unrealistically positive. Then, as time goes by, and as the spouses stop working as hard to be adorable and charming to each other, reality slowly erodes these pleasant fictions. Romance fades and disappointment gradually sets in as people realize that their spouses and their partnerships are less wonderful than they originally seemed.

The particulars of the three models are meaningful because each suggests a different way to improve marriages and to reduce the risk of divorce. According to the enduring dynamics model, rocky courtships lead to bad marriages, and premarital interventions that keep ambivalent couples from ever marrying should prevent many subsequent divorces. By comparison, the emergent distress model argues that couples need to guard against slow slides into disagreeableness and negativity, and interventions that encourage spouses to remain cheerful, generous, attentive, and kind should keep divorce from their door. And finally, the disillusionment model suggests that dispassionate and accurate perceptions of one's lover and one's relationship that preclude subsequent disappointment and disenchantment should also prevent divorce.

All of these are reasonable possibilities, but Huston and his colleagues found that only two of the three nicely fit the outcomes of the marriages they followed. (Let's pause a moment. Which two models do you think were the winners?) First, consistent with the enduring dynamics model, the researchers determined that, compared to spouses who were still happy after several years, couples who were unhappy had been less loving and affectionate and more ambivalent and negative toward each other when their marriages began. Couples who were destined to be distressed were less generous and less tender, and more uncertain and more temperamental, from the very start. Thus, any doubts or difficulties that people faced when they were engaged did not disappear once they were married. To the contrary, any indecision or incompatibilities were simply imported into their marital relationship, so that they remained less content over the years that followed.

So, the enduring dynamics model predicted how happy marriages would be. However, the best predictor of which couples would actually divorce was the disillusionment model. The drop in marital satisfaction during the first years of marriage was sharper and more pronounced in some couples than in others, and they were the spouses who were most at risk for divorce. These couples did not necessarily grow cantankerous or spiteful as the emergent distress model would expect; instead, they simply experienced the greatest change in their romantic feelings for each other. Their love faded more, and more rapidly, than did the romances of other couples.

In addition, a striking feature of the disillusionment that Huston and his colleagues observed was that many of the couples who were destined to divorce were more affectionate than most when their marriages began. Couples whose marriages were short-lived—who were divorced within six (or fewer) years—usually began their marriages with less love and more ambivalence than did couples whose marriages would succeed. (Thus, you can see why, when disillusionment set in, they were divorced relatively quickly.) However, couples who ultimately divorced after longer periods—after seven or more years of marriage—were especially affectionate and romantic when their marriages began. They were more adoring than other couples, on average, and thus had further to fall (and, perhaps, were more surprised than most) when the usual drop in affectionate behavior following the honeymoon began. They ended up no less sentimental toward each other than other couples, but they experienced the biggest changes—that is, the steepest declines—in romantic behavior, and those changes predicted a delayed divorce.

Overall, then, at this stage of the PAIR Project, two conclusions seem sound. First, the size and speed of changes in romance best predict which couples will divorce, and second, the problems couples bring to their marriage determine how quickly a divorce will occur. Similar results have been obtained from other studies (Arriaga, 2001; Kurdek, 2002; Surra & Gray, 2000), so we can safely assert that both the *level* of satisfaction a couple experiences and the *change* in that satisfaction over time are key players in relational outcomes. Importantly, couples that are doomed to divorce do not always turn surly and spiteful, but they do tend to lose the joy they once experienced (Gottman & Levenson, 2000).[4]

Results from the Early Years of Marriage Project

Another impressive longitudinal study, the Early Years of Marriage (EYM) project directed by Terri Orbuch and Joseph Veroff, has been following 174 white couples and 199 black couples in and around Detroit, Michigan, since they married in 1986 (Orbuch et al., 2002). The EYM researchers have been particularly interested in the manner in which the social conditions couples encounter may affect marital outcomes. And some sociological variables are important. In 2002, sixteen years after the project began, 46 percent of the couples had already divorced, but the couples' race seemed to make a big difference (Orbuch, Brown, & Veroff, 2004). Just over a third (36 percent) of the white couples had divorced, but more than half (55 percent) of the black couples had dissolved their marriages.

Why were black couples more prone to divorce? There could be several reasons. On average, the black couples had cohabitated for a longer period and

---

[4]We encourage you to take a moment to consider how this pattern maps onto people's appetitive and aversive motivations, which we introduced on p. 195 back in chapter 6. Apparently, some marriages fail not because they are aversive and unpleasant but because they are not pleasant and delightful enough.

were more likely to have had children before getting married. They also had lower incomes and were more likely to come from broken homes, and all of these influences are positively correlated with one's risk of divorce (Popenoe & Whitehead, 2004).

The number of years of education spouses had was also important. In general, the longer wives and white men had stayed in school, the less likely they were to divorce; curiously, however, education was not correlated with the risk of divorce for black men, a fact that may reflect the subtle interactions of social conditions and race (Tucker, 2000). Overall, though, the EYM project is demonstrating, as other studies have (Cutrona et al., 2003), that the social context in which couples conduct their relationships may have substantial effects on the outcomes they encounter. Being poor and poorly educated may put any couple at risk for divorce no matter how much they respect and value marriage (Karney, 2004).

People's Personal Perceptions of the Causes of Divorce

The various models and data we have examined to this point suggest that there are three general types of influences on our marital outcomes (Levinger & Levinger, 2003). At the broadest level are cultural norms and other variables that set the national stage for marriage. No-fault divorce laws, sex ratios, and discrimination that affects educational and economic opportunities are examples of the ways in which the *cultural context* may either support or undermine marital success.

More idiosyncratic are our *personal contexts*, the social networks of family and friends and the physical neighborhoods we inhabit. For instance, as we noted earlier, women who work with a wide variety of interesting male colleagues are more prone to divorce than are women who do not work outside their homes (South et al., 2001). Finally, there is a *relational context* that describes the intimate environment couples create through their own perceptions of, and interactions with, each other. The individual characteristics that lead us to react to our partners with either chronic good humor or pessimistic caution are some of the building blocks of the particular atmosphere that pervades a partnership.

We mention these three levels of analysis because people tend to focus on only one of them when they generate explanations for their marital problems. Yet another impressive longitudinal study, the Marital Instability Over the Life Course project conducted by Paul Amato and Alan Booth, has conducted phone interviews with a random sample of 1,078 Americans every few years since 1980 (Amato & Rogers, 1997). When those who have divorced were asked what caused their divorces, the most frequently reported reasons all involved some characteristic of their marital relationships, as Table 13.1 shows (Amato & Previti, 2003). Women complained of infidelity, substance use, or abuse more often than men, whereas men were more likely to complain of poor communication or to announce that they did not know what had gone wrong. Ex-wives also had more complaints than ex-husbands did, on average, but very few

---

BOX 13.3

The Rules of Relationships

Leslie Baxter (1986) once asked 64 male and 93 female college students in Oregon to write essays describing why they had ended a premarital romantic relationship. In all cases, the respondents had initiated the break-up, and their accounts (a term we explore further in Box 13.4 on page 417), provided an intriguing look at the implicit standards with which they judged their relationships. Eight themes appeared in at least 10 percent of the essays, and they appear to be specific prescriptions that take the form of *relationship rules:* They describe standards that are expected of us and our relationships, and our partners may leave us if we consistently break them. Here they are, listed in order of the frequency with which they were mentioned:

- *Autonomy:* Allow your partner to have friends and interests outside your relationship; don't be too possessive. (Problems with possessiveness were mentioned 37 percent of the time.)
- *Similarity:* You and your partner should share similar attitudes, values, and interests; don't be too different. (Mentioned 30 percent of the time.)
- *Supportiveness:* Enhance your partner's self-worth and self-esteem; don't be thoughtless or inconsiderate. (27 percent)
- *Openness:* Self-disclose, genuinely and authentically; don't be close-lipped. (22 percent)
- *Fidelity:* Be loyal and faithful to your partner; don't cheat. (17 percent)
- *Togetherness:* Share plenty of time together; don't take a night shift or move out of town. (16 percent)
- *Equity:* Be fair; don't exploit your partner. (12 percent)
- *Magic:* Be romantic; don't be ordinary. (10 percent)

Various other reasons were mentioned, but none as frequently as these. Men and women also differed some in the frequency of their complaints; women were troubled by problems with autonomy, openness, and equity more often than men, whereas men complained about missing magic more often than women. As we have seen before, women tend to be more pragmatic than men when they evaluate their relationships. But both sexes typically focus on their relationship and ignore their personal and cultural contexts when they explain the failure of their partnerships.

---

accounts from either sex acknowledged the possible influences of the cultural or personal contexts in which they conducted their relationships.

Nevertheless, those broader contexts may have been important. The higher a couple's income had been, the less often abuse was mentioned as a cause of divorce, and the more often personality clashes were mentioned. The more education the respondents had, the more often they complained of incompatibility with their ex-spouses. Thus, a couple's socioeconomic status, which derives in part from education and income, helped to predict the problems they would encounter. The age at which they married mattered, too; people who married at younger ages were more likely to report that they had grown apart or that alcohol and drug use had been a problem.

TABLE 13.1. "What Caused Your Divorce?"

Reason	% Total Cases	% Cases for Men	% Cases for Women
Infidelity	22	16	25
Incompatibility	19	19	19
Drinking or substance use	11	5	14
Grew apart	10	9	10
Personality problems	9	10	8
Communication difficulties	9	13	6
Physical or mental abuse	6	0	9
Love was lost	4	7	3
Don't know	3	9	0

The tabled values reflect the responses of 208 members of a random sample of spouses in the U.S. who were asked what had caused their divorces. Other causes such as financial problems or interference from family were mentioned on occasion, but the nine most frequent reasons are listed here.

Source: Amato & Previti, 2003.

Evidently, some problems were more likely to beset some couples than others, and there are clearly complexities here. Overall, however, the influences that may shape a couple's likelihood of divorce include not only the day-to-day interactions that may cause them pleasure or pain, but also the broader environments and culture that may promote or undermine their marriage, as well (Sprecher et al., 2002).

Specific Factors Associated with Divorce

We have touched on a variety of variables that may put people at risk for divorce, and we're about to list them and several more in the big table above. Before we do, however, we should note that divorce research faces particular challenges. First, many researchers treat separation and divorce as equivalent outcomes, although not all couples that separate get legally divorced. A marriage may be a failure in either case, but those who divorce may differ in important ways from those who merely separate.

Second, the samples of participants in studies of divorce are only rarely ethnically diverse. Seventy-five percent of the studies that were part of Karney and Bradbury's (1995) meta-analysis of 115 longitudinal research projects focused primarily on middle-class whites, and only 8 percent specifically recruited both blacks and whites. In addition, only 17 percent of the studies sought nationally representative samples. Obtaining diverse samples is expensive and difficult (Karney, Kreitz, & Sweeney, 2004), and as a result, for now, most of what we know about divorce is based on studies of white people.

Finally, statements of general trends sometimes gloss over important qualifications: No one generalization will apply to every marriage, predictors may hold for some groups or stages of marriage but not others, and the apparent influence of a particular variable may reflect the other factors to which it was compared in a given study. For instance, whereas having a child before marriage is generally associated with a higher risk of divorce, one study found this effect among blacks in the first years after marriage but *not* in a ten-year follow-up (Billy, Landale, & McLaughlin, 1986). Those couples that stayed together may have been able to gradually overcome the stresses of premarital childbirth, or—perhaps in wanting a child more—they may have been less susceptible to those stresses in the first place. Whatever the case, an important predictor of the risk of divorce lost its power as relationships matured. Similarly, some classic correlates of divorce (such as age at marriage and low income) may be more influential among young people in young marriages than in older marriages that have already lasted for some time (Booth et al., 1986). To some degree, marriages that survive the initial effects of certain stressors may be less susceptible to their influences many years later. Please keep these caveats in mind while inspecting Table 13.2, which presents a summary of key predictors of marital stability identified by modern research. The good news is that the effects of most of these influences probably haven't changed much for several decades (Teachman, 2002b). Most of them probably have similar effects on the satisfaction and stability gays and lesbians experience in their relationships, as well (Gottman et al., 2003).

TABLE 13.2. Predictors of Divorce: A Synthesis of the Literature

Predictor	Findings
Socioeconomic status	People with low-status occupations, less education, and lower incomes are more likely to divorce than are those with higher socioeconomic status. In particular, women with good educations are much less likely to divorce than women with poor educations are (Orbuch et al., 2002; Popenoe & Whitehead, 2004).
Race	Black Americans are more likely to divorce than white Americans are (Orbuch et al., 2002; Popenoe & Whitehead, 2004).
Sex ratios	Around the world, divorce rates are higher when women outnumber men and the sex ratio is low (Barber, 2003; Trent & South, 1989).
Social mobility	People who move often from place to place are more prone to divorce than are those who stay in one place and put down roots (Magdol & Bessel, 2003; White, 1990).
No-fault legislation	Laws that make a divorce easier to obtain seem to improve our attitudes toward divorce and thereby make divorce more likely (Amato & Rogers, 1999; Rodgers et al., 1999).
Working women	Divorce rates increase when higher proportions of women enter the work force (Fitch & Ruggles, 2000).
Age at marriage	People who marry as teenagers are more likely to divorce than are those who marry after age 25 (Heaton, 2002; Popenoe & Whitehead, 2004).
Prior marriage	Second marriages are more likely to end in divorce than first marriages are (White, 1990).

(continued)

TABLE 13.2. *(continued)*

Parental divorce	Parents who divorce increase the chances that their children will divorce (Amato & DeBoer, 2001; Tallman et al., 2001). However, as divorce becomes more commonplace, this effect is declining. Before 1975, adults whose parents had divorced were about 2.5 times as likely to divorce as those whose parents hadn't divorced. By 1996, this ratio had declined to 2.0 (Wolfinger, 1999).
Religion	Regular attendance at religious services is correlated with a lower risk of divorce, but the risk goes up when one spouse attends regularly but the other does not (Call & Heaton, 1997).
Premarital cohabitation	Premarital cohabitation is associated with higher divorce rates, but this effect generally disappears if the couple is engaged to be married when cohabitation begins (Kline et al., 2004; Stafford et al., 2004).
Premarital birth	Having a baby before marriage is associated with a higher risk of divorce for both the mother and the father (Nock, 1998; Heaton, 2002).
Children	Spouses who have no children are more likely to divorce (Wineberg, 1988), but the risk-reducing effect of children is most noticeable in the first few years of marriage (White, 1990). Thereafter, the presence of teenage children modestly elevates divorce rates. Parents who have sons are less likely to divorce than are those who have daughters (Katzev, Warner, & Acock, 1994; Waite & Lillard, 1991).
Attitude similarity	Spouses who have similar attitudes are less likely to divorce (Karney & Bradbury, 1995).
Personality attributes	The higher one's neuroticism, the more likely one is to divorce (Karney & Bradbury, 1995).
Attachment styles	People who are high in avoidance of intimacy are probably more likely to divorce (Jang, Smith, & Levine, 2002).
Genetics	A person who has an identical twin who gets divorced is about five times more likely to divorce than he or she would have been if the twin had not divorced, even if the two twins were separated at birth and have never met (Lykken, 2002).
Stress hormones	During their first year of marriage, couples who are destined to divorce have chronically higher amounts of the stress hormones epinephrine and norepinephrine in their blood than do couples who will not be divorced ten years later (Kiecolt-Glaser et al., 2003).
Stressful life events	The occurrence of stressful life events (other than parenthood) increases the likelihood of divorce (Karney & Bradbury, 1995).
Time together	Couples who share more time together are less likely to divorce (White, 1990).
Marital interaction	Positive interactions predict stability, and negative interactions predict divorce (Karney & Bradbury, 1995). Couples that fail to maintain a 5-to-1 ratio of positive to negative behaviors are more likely to divorce (Gottman et al., 1998).
Sexual satisfaction	Greater satisfaction with one's sex life is associated with a lower likelihood of divorce (Karney & Bradbury, 1995).
Marital satisfaction	"Marital satisfaction has larger effects on marital stability than do most other variables" (Karney & Bradbury, 1995, p. 20). Individuals who are more satisfied with their marriages are less likely to divorce. Even so, satisfaction is far from being a perfect predictor of divorce.

THE ROAD TO DIVORCE

We've spent some time describing who gets divorced, and now it's time to inspect *how*. How do partners proceed when they want to dissolve their relationship? The first thing to note is that they do not take such action lightly. Most divorce experiences are characterized by a long period of discontent, multiple complaints that are coupled with things that the partners like about each other, and ambivalence about separating. After intensive interviews with divorced spouses, Hopper (1993, p. 806) wrote

> *Prior to nearly every divorce, there was a long period of assessment, with both initiators and noninitiating partners describing similar experiences and feelings of indecision and ambivalence. They described pain, dissatisfaction, and feelings of being trapped; at the same time, they described good things that they did not want to forego. That is what made divorce such an agonizing decision and process, no matter what side of the divorce they were on.*

Recall, too, from our discussion of interdependency theory in chapter 6, that people do not usually depart their partnerships just because they are dissatisfied. Although a long period of unhappiness and distress precedes most divorces, people typically initiate divorce only when they come to believe that they will be better off without their spouses (that is, only when their CL_{alt}s promise better outcomes than they are experiencing now). The decision to divorce involves complex calculations of distress and delight and alternative, sometimes uncertain, possibilities.

Then, when that global decision is made, more choices await. Let's inspect what people do when they want to pull the plug on a failing partnership.

Breaking Up with Premarital Partners

The next time you want to end a romantic relationship, what do you think you'll do? Will you break the news to your partner straightforwardly, or will you simply block your partner's instant messages and start avoiding him or her? When she analyzed college students' accounts of their breakups, Leslie Baxter (1984) found that a major distinction between different trajectories of relationship dissolution involved the question of whether someone who wished to depart ever announced that intention to the partner who was to be left behind! In some instances, the effort to disengage was *direct,* or explicitly stated; however, in most cases, people used *indirect* strategies in which they tried to end the relationship without ever saying so.

A second key distinction, according to Baxter (1984), was whether one's effort to depart was *other-oriented,* trying to protect the partner's feelings, or *self-oriented,* being more selfish at the expense of the partner's feelings. On occasion, for instance, people announced their intention to end the relationship in a manner that allowed their partners a chance to respond and to save face; one direct, other-oriented strategy was to announce one's dissatisfaction but to talk things over and to negotiate, rather than demand, an end to the partnership. In contrast, when they were direct but more selfish, they sometimes simply announced that the relationship was over and ducked any further contact with their ex-partners.

A more indirect but rather selfish ploy was to behave badly, increasing the partner's costs so much that the partner decided to end the relationship. People were more considerate when they claimed that they wanted to be "just friends," but if they did so when they really wanted to end the relationship altogether, this, too, was an indirect approach, with them misrepresenting their desire to depart.

Obviously, people made various moves when they wanted to end their relationships, and the differences between direct and indirect, and other-oriented and self-oriented, strategies were just two of the distinctions that Baxter (1984) observed. Other distinctions included

- the gradual versus sudden onset of one's discontent. Only about a quarter of the time was there some critical incident that suddenly changed a partner's feelings about his or her relationship; more often, people gradually grew dissatisfied.
- an individual versus shared desire to end the partnership. Two thirds of the time only one partner wanted the relationship to end.
- the rapid versus protracted nature of one's exit. More often than not, people made several disguised efforts to end their relationships before they succeeded.
- the presence or absence of repair attempts. Most of the time, no formal effort to repair the relationship was made.

Add all this up, and the single most common manner in which premarital relationships ended involved gradual dissatisfaction that led one of the two partners to make repeated efforts to dissolve the relationship without ever announcing that intention and without engaging in any attempts to improve or repair the partnership. But even this most frequent pattern, which Baxter (1984) labeled as "persevering indirectness," occurred only one third of the time, so a variety of other specific trajectories were commonplace, too.

Nevertheless, people generally agree about the typical elements, if not the specific strategies, of partners' efforts to end their relationships (Battaglia et al., 1998). Surveys of young adults find that the end of a close relationship routinely involves several familiar elements that are listed in Table 13.3. The process usually begins when one partner grows bored with the relationship and begins noticing other people. Then one of them grows distant and less involved emotionally, but this often leads to an initial effort to restore the relationship and put things back the way they were. The partners spend less time together, however, and when a lack of interest resurfaces, thoughts of breaking up begin. Discussion of the relationship ensues, and the couple agrees to try again to work things out, but they continue to notice other people, and they become more withdrawn. They see others, but that engenders a short-lived desire to reunite that is followed by more contemplation of calling it quits. They prepare themselves psychologically and then break up.

TABLE 13.3. A Typical Script for the End of a Close Relationship

The next time one of your relationships ends, you may find it following this general sequence of events. The mixed feelings that partners often experience when they contemplate a break-up are apparent in this generic script:

Step 1	One of the partners begins to lose interest in the relationship
Step 2	The disinterested partner begins to notice other people
Step 3	The disinterested partner withdraws and acts more distant
Step 4	The partners try to work things out and resolve the problem
Step 5	The partners spend less time together
Step 6	Lack of interest resurfaces
Step 7	Someone considers breaking up
Step 8	They communicate their feelings in a "meeting of the minds"
Step 9	The partners again try to work things out
Step 10	One or both partners again notice other people
Step 11	They again spend less time together
Step 12	They go out with other potential partners
Step 13	They try to get back together
Step 14	One or both again consider breaking up
Step 15	They emotionally detach, with a sense of "moving on"
Step 16	They break up, and the relationship is dissolved

Actual break-ups are often very idiosyncratic, of course, but it's clear from this shared script that people generally expect the end of a close relationship to be characterized by ambivalence and twists and turns before the partnership finally ends.

Source: Battaglia et al., 1998.

Steps to Divorce

Obtaining a divorce is usually more complicated than breaking up with a premarital partner, but the ambivalence and vacillation that is evident in the typical sequence of events in Table 13.3 characterizes divorces, too. And marriages don't end overnight. Whereas someone's efforts to end a premarital romantic relationship may last several months (Lee, 1984), the process of ending a marriage may take several years. In one study of couples who stayed married for about a dozen years, the dissatisfied spouses typically spent the last five years of their marriages thinking about separating (Stewart et al., 1997)!

Over such a span of time, many idiosyncratic events may occur, but Steve Duck (1982) suggested that four general stages occur during the dissolution of most relationships. In an initial *personal phase,* a partner grows dissatisfied, often feeling frustration and disgruntlement. Then, in a subsequent *dyadic phase,* the unhappy partner reveals his or her discontent. Long periods of negotiation, confrontation, or attempts at accommodation may follow, and common feelings

Breaking up can be hard to do.

include shock, anger, hurt, and, sometimes, relief. But if the end of the relationship nears, a *social phase* begins. The partners publicize their distress, explaining their side of the story to family and friends and seeking support and understanding. Finally, as the relationship ends, a *grave-dressing phase* begins. Mourning decreases, and the partners begin to get over their loss by doing whatever cognitive work is required to put their past partnership behind them. Memories are revised and tidied up, and an acceptable story—an "account"—for the course of the relationship is created. Rationalization and reassessment is likely to occur.

Within this general framework, the manner in which people dissolve their partnerships is likely to affect their feelings about each other afterwards. In general, couples who do not identify and discuss the sources of their dissatisfaction have less positive feelings toward each other and are less likely to stay in touch than are those who do discuss their difficulties (Lee, 1984). In addition, couples who repeatedly swing back and forth between withdrawal and reconciliation before a divorce feel more hurt, angry, lonely, and confused after they

---

BOX 13.4

Accounts: What Are They? What Are Their Functions?

Before you read this box, we encourage you to try a short exercise proposed by Weber and Harvey (1994, p. 294):

1. Think of a difficult or troublesome experience you have had in a close relationship.
2. If you are recalling a past experience, what do you remember? What happened? What did you do? How did you feel?
3. Why did these events occur in your relationship?
4. Have you ever told anyone about this experience and your interpretation of what happened?

In answering these questions, you are giving an account, "a story-like narrative or explanation of one's experience, such as in a personal relationship, emphasizing the characters and events that have marked its course" (Weber, 1992, p. 178). Accounts are awash with descriptions, expectations, feelings, interpretations of people's actions, and explanations of how events occurred (Orbuch et al., 2004); they tend to bring order and a plot sequence to life's complex, messy events. Accounts of the ending of relationships may provide a history of the relationship's beginning, identification of factors that led to eventual breakup, identification of the relationship problems and partner's flaws that in retrospect had been present all along, reactions to separation, and ways

of coping. Accounts spring from the narrator's perceptions and aren't necessarily "true." Indeed, it is likely that many aspects of ex-partners' accounts of a past relationship will differ (Gray & Silver, 1990).

Accounts may serve several functions. We often paint ourselves in a favorable light to justify our behaviors and help maintain self-esteem (Gray & Silver, 1990). We can use accounts to influence the way others think of us, and in sharing our accounts with others, we get a chance to express and work through our emotions. Formulating narratives helps us find meaning in what has happened in our lives, and people who keep journals that express their feelings usually cope better, enjoying better mental and physical health, than do those who do not introspect as deeply (Lepore & Greenberg, 2002). And even if memories of past relationships persist indefinitely, account making may help bring some measure of closure to events. The more complete our narratives are—the more coherence and detail we bring to the characters, feelings, sequence of events, and causes that constructed our relationships—the better our adjustment is likely to be (Kellas & Manusov, 2003). Thoughtful accounts facilitate personal well-being, empathy for others, and a sense of growth (Tashiro & Frazier, 2003), and they may even be "essential to recovery from loss" (Weber & Harvey, 1994, p. 304).

---

finally separate than do those who decide to separate and then follow through on their decision.

Indeed, a variety of different outcomes are possible when intimate relationships end. Let's turn to those next.

THE AFTERMATH OF SEPARATION AND DIVORCE

When people are asked how much stress and change various events would cause in their lives, the death of a spouse and a divorce consistently show up at the top of the list (Miller & Rahe, 1997). What are the consequences of divorce? The spouses' lives change, of course, but so do their children's.

Individuals' Perspectives

Let's start with the good news. A few years afterwards, most people who divorce are again as happy as they were before their marriages began to dissolve (Lucas et al., 2003). After six years, most of them will have remarried, and over three fourths of them will look back and report that their divorce was a good thing (Hetherington, 2003). The bad news is that it can take years to adjust to the end of a marriage, and almost everyone who divorces encounters some rough bumps in the road. Worse, some people end up defeated by their divorces, suffering distress and difficulty in their lives and their relationships for many years thereafter (Hetherington, 2003; Lucas et al., 2003). As we describe general patterns and conclusions below, keep in mind that your outcomes, if you ever divorce, may be idiosyncratic; you may do better (or perhaps worse) than the norm.

Adjustment

Divorce is stressful. Negative emotions often run high in the few months before and after divorce proceedings. A study in the Boston area that followed 160 families with young children for eighteen months after they filed for divorce (Stewart et al., 1997) found that people routinely experienced confusion, anxiety, depression, and hostility as they approached the end of their marriages. Both men and women worried about "being alone." They probably were also driving poorly; people have more accidents and get more tickets than usual in the six months before and after they file for divorce (McMurray, 1970).

Some people fare better than others. The attachment dimension of anxiety over abandonment is associated with greater distress after a romance ends, with preoccupied and fearful people experiencing more rumination and anger and poorer coping, including the use of drugs and alcohol to blunt their pain. (Davis, Shaver, & Vernon, 2003). People with secure attachment styles respond more constructively, turning to friends and family for needed support, whereas avoidant people tend to keep their distance from others (Davis et al., 2003).

Nevertheless, overall, people who are divorced or separated are less content with their lives than are those who are still in a first marriage, and many of them remain disgruntled until they remarry (Forste & Heaton, 2004; Wang & Amato, 2000). One reason why is that the stresses people encounter do not end when the divorce is final; divorce changes one's social network and finances as well as one's intimate life (Johnson & Wu, 2002).

Social Networks

The amount of time people spend with friends increases after divorce, especially in the first year (Hanson, McLanahan, & Thompson, 1998). Friends and, to a lesser degree, various kin (such as parents, siblings, and children) are the most important sources of people's support during a separation (Duran-Aydintug, 1998). On the other hand, people usually lose about half of their friends and other members of their social networks (such as in-laws) after a divorce (Rands, 1988). Over time, some new network members are usually added, but two years later an ex-spouse's social network is typically 14 percent smaller on average than it was before the separation. The composition of the networks also changes, usually including fewer married people but more same-sex friends.

Moreover, not all of the remaining members of one's social network are likely to be supportive. About 50 percent of divorced people have interactions with their estranged spouses that are hostile or tense, and half of them also report that they have relatives who disapprove of their separation (Stewart et al., 1997). Not everyone who is close to a divorced person will offer desirable support.

Economic Resources

Women's finances usually deteriorate when they leave their marriages. In a National Survey of Families and Households in the U.S., over 10,000 people were interviewed in 1987 and again in 1993, and the household incomes of women who divorced between interviews dropped an average of 20 percent (Hanson et al., 1998). Part of the explanation for this pattern lies in the fact that only about 50 percent of fathers pay all the child support they are supposed to pay, and 25 percent ignore custody payments altogether (U.S. Bureau of the Census, 1995). Fathers are more likely to provide custody support if their own incomes are higher, but some ex-wives receive nothing unless such payments are automatically deducted from a father's paycheck (Meyer, 1999).

Men's economic well-being is less likely than women's to decline after divorce. The incomes of divorced men are about 10 percent lower than those of married men (Stroup & Pollock, 1994), but men are more likely to live by themselves after they divorce than are women, who are more likely to have children in their households. If one takes account of the number of mouths ex-spouses have to feed, the average income of a noncustodial father actually increases 28 percent in the year after he divorces, whereas custodial mothers' incomes drop 36 percent (Bianchi, Subaiya, & Kahn, 1999). On average, then, a woman's standard of living decreases after she divorces, whereas a man's improves.

Relationships between Former Partners

Of course, one of the key things that changes with separation is the partners' relationship. In some cases, partners will no longer have any contact with each other. In many cases, however, despite the acrimony that may have accompanied the divorce, it takes time for the bonds that connect the ex-partners to fade.

Based on his clinical work with divorced couples, Robert Weiss (1979) contended that the bonds ex-spouses feel for each other are often like the attachment bonds children have with their parents. In both childhood and adulthood, Weiss asserted, the loss of attachment can lead to separation distress, provoking such reactions as rage, protest over desertion, anxiety, restlessness, feelings of fear or panic, and hyperalertness to any possibility of the lost partner's return. Moments of euphoria and enhanced self-confidence can also occur. "Because they remain attached to each other and are simultaneously angry with each other," Weiss wrote, "the relationship of separated spouses is intensely ambivalent" (p. 209). There may be a paradoxical desire to rejoin the partner followed by outbursts of anger.

Still, certain patterns may underlie these conflicting feelings. Ahrons (1994) identified four types of postmarital relationships: **Fiery Foes, Angry Associates, Cooperative Colleagues,** and **Perfect Pals.** For both Fiery Foes and Angry Associates, the spouses' anger with each other is still part of their relationship. Angry Associates have some capacity to work together in coparenting their children; Fiery Foes have very little. Cooperative Colleagues aren't good friends, yet they are able to cooperate successfully in parenting tasks. Finally, Perfect Pals maintain "a strong friendship with mutual respect that did not get eroded by their decision to live separate lives" (p. 116). In a midwestern sample of divorced parents, Ahrons found that a year after their divorces, half the ex-spouses had amicable relationships (38 percent Cooperative Colleagues, 12 percent Perfect Pals) and half had distressed relationships (25 percent Angry Associates and 25 percent Fiery Foes).

Children Whose Parents Divorce

Relationship research has also focused on the outcomes encountered by children whose parents divorce. One meta-analysis combined 129 studies involving roughly 95,000 participants that compared youngsters whose parents divorced to those whose parents remained continuously married (Amato & Keith, 1991a, 1991b). Various outcomes were examined, and across the board, children of divorce exhibited lower levels of well-being when they reached adulthood than did those whose parents had stayed married. Children of divorced parents were more likely to be single parents, to have lower psychological adjustment (e.g., more depression and anxiety, and lower satisfaction with life), to engage in more problematic behavior (e.g., alcoholism, drug use, criminal behavior, suicide, or teen pregnancy), and to drop out of school. More recent studies have observed similar patterns (Amato, 2001); children of divorce get poorer grades in school, are less trusting toward others, and are more accepting of casual sex (Barber, 1998; King, 2002; Sun & Li, 2002). They are also more likely than other adults to be divorced themselves (Amato, 2003). However, these effects are usually not large. In other words, the global impact of having parents who divorced is consistently negative but relatively modest.

Why are children from broken homes less well off? Was their parent's divorce that influential or are other factors at work? A correlation between

---

BOX 13.5

Divorce Mediation

Since the late 1970s, divorce mediation has become a commonly used approach to assist divorcing couples Twaite, Keiser, & Luchow, 1998). It was created as an alternative to the adversarial model of the legal system—"You get your lawyer; I'll get mine; and we'll settle this in court." Although today there are various models of mediation, they generally emphasize open communication, negotiation, and mutual resolution of the emotional, financial, and child-related issues in divorce. Mediators are typically from legal or behavioral science backgrounds and need to be knowledgeable in both these fields. Agreements formulated during the course of mediation are put in written form, in order to serve as the basis for the divorce petition to the court. Mediators do not, however, serve as the lawyers in the divorce action itself, and most mediators require their clients to have separate legal counsel to inspect all agreements resulting from mediation.

A growing body of research testifies to the effectiveness of divorce mediation (see Benjamin & Irving, 1995; Kelly, 1996; Twaite et al., 1998). At least 40 per cent of couples that go through mediation can reach complete agreement and up to 80 percent reach at least partial agreement (see Benjamin & Irving, 1995). Emery (1999a) noted that: Compliance with agreements reached in mediation is somewhat better than with adversary settlements; parents, particularly fathers, are more satisfied with their experiences with mediation than with adversary procedures; and even many years later, mediation leads to less conflict and more cooperation in coparenting.

Concerns have been expressed that mediation does not afford the weaker spouse the benefits that litigation provides. But this does not seem to be the case: In both U.S. and Canadian studies women received higher child support and maintenance awards via mediation than litigation (see Twaite et al., 1998). Indeed, wives often find that in the mediation process they develop confidence in their ability to stand up for themselves (Twaite et al., 1998).

Participants believe that mediation helps them focus on the needs of their children, gives them an opportunity to express their feelings and grievances, and helps them deal with fundamental issues in greater depth than would occur in court procedures (Twaite et al., 1998). Although it does not always work, mediation does appear to usually offer a less acrimonious, more constructive approach to the divorce process. As such, it may help protect both adults and children from the sometimes disastrous consequences of an embittered, embattled divorce.

---

parental divorce and children's outcomes allows diverse possibilities, and there may be several reasons why such patterns exist. Spouses and families that go through a divorce may differ in several meaningful ways from those who live (more) happily ever after, and a number of influences may be at work (Leon, 2003). For instance, divorce often involves economic hardship, the loss of a parent, parental stress, and family conflict (Amato & Keith, 1991b; Hetherington & Kelly, 2002).

According to a **parental loss** view, children are presumed to benefit from having two parents who are devoted to their care (Barber, 2000b), and children who lose a parent for any reason, including divorce, are likely to be less well off (Teachman, 2002a). Indeed, if a divorce does occur, children fare better when they spend time with both parents (Fabricius, 2003), and they do worse if one of their parents moves some distance away (Braver, Ellman, & Fabricius, 2003).

In contrast, a **parental stress** model holds that the quality, not the quantity, of the parenting a child receives is key, and any stressor (including divorce) that distracts or debilitates one's parents can have detrimental effects. According to this view, children's outcomes depend on how well a custodial parent adjusts to a divorce, and, consistent with this perspective, children of divorce usually start doing more poorly in school before their parents actually break up, when marital disappointments begin (Sun, 2001). Of course, one major stressor is **economic hardship,** and it may be the impoverished circumstances that sometimes follow divorce, and not just the divorce per se, that adds to children's burdens. Any difficulties faced by the children are reduced if the custodial parent has sufficient resources to support them well (Sun & Li, 2002).

All of these factors may be influential, but there is even stronger and more consistent research support for a **parental conflict** model. Acrimonious interactions between parents appear to be hard on children, and whether or not a divorce occurs, conflict in the home is associated with greater anxiety (Riggio, 2004), less trust (King, 2002), poorer health (Luecken & Fabricius, 2003), and more problematic behavior (Krishnakumar, Buehler, & Barber, 2003) in children. Take a look at Figure 13.2: As you might expect, children are happiest when they live in an intact family in which little conflict or discord occurs, and their well-being is much lower when divorce occurs in a low-conflict home (Booth & Amato, 2001). But if they live amidst constant conflict, children are worse off when the parents *don't* divorce; when a divorce breaks up an angry, embattled household, there's almost no decrease in the children's well-being at all (Amato, 2003). Thus, the question of whether unhappy spouses should "stay together for the sake of the children" seems to depend on whether they can be civil toward each other; children suffer when a peaceable marriage is disrupted, but they are better off going through a divorce if their homes are full of conflict (Wagner & Ferreri, 2003).

There are two more points to make. First, there's no question that children are less affected by divorce if they are able to maintain high-quality relationships with their parents thereafter. Whatever their sources, the poorer outcomes often experienced by children of divorce largely disappear when the children continue to have meaningful, loving contact with their parents (Amato & Sobolewski, 2001; King, 2002). Second, many of the poorer outcomes experienced by children of divorce gradually fade with time (Amato & Keith, 1991b; Sun & Li, 2002). People are resilient, and children heal if they are provided sufficient love and support (Harvey & Fine, 2004). As Robert Emery (1999b, p. 18) observed

> *Divorce is a risk factor for a number of significant problems, but some*
> *problems were present prior to the marital separation, and in any case, the*

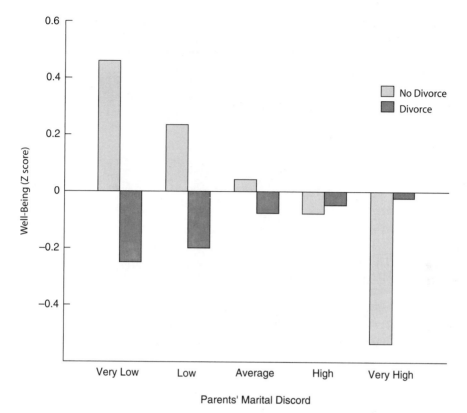

FIGURE 13.2. Associations of parents' marital discord and divorce with children's psychological well-being.

The figure compares the outcomes of children whose parents divorced to those of children who stayed in intact homes, and takes note of family discord and conflict. When divorce occurred in low-conflict families, children fared poorly, but they were even worse off when there was a lot of discord at home and the parents did not divorce. Spouses who ponder "staying together for the sake of the children" should consider whether they can provide their children a peaceable home. *Source: Amato, 2003.*

> *majority of children from divorced families successfully adjust to their new family and their new life circumstances. However, the successful adjustment does not mean that children have not struggled both directly with the stressors of divorce and less obviously with inner fears, worries, and regrets. To use a familiar metaphor, some children are irreparably wounded by divorce; the wounds of most children heal; but even healed wounds leave a scar.*

To Emery's reflections, we would add that it is one thing to analyze the effects of divorce on children and another to make sure that children receive what they need. Divorcing or remarrying parents may find it helpful to remember that with children the basics are what count: loving, effective parenting; peace between parents; and freedom from poverty.

Although many children's parents will divorce, low levels of postmarital conflict can contribute to children's well-being.

FOR YOUR CONSIDERATION

Connie and Bobby married during their senior year in high school when she became pregnant with their first child. They didn't have much money, and the baby demanded a lot of attention, so neither of them went to college, and after a few years and another child, it appeared that neither of them would. Bobby now works as a long-haul trucker, so he is gone for several days at a time. Connie is a cashier at a grocery store, and she is increasingly disgruntled. She has always felt that she deserved more than the modest life she leads, and she has started viewing Bobby with hidden disrespect. He is a cheerful, friendly man who is very warm to his children, but he lacks ambition, and Connie is beginning to think that he'll never "move up in the world." So, she feels very flattered by the flirtatious regional manager of the grocery store chain, who asks her out for drinks and dinner when Bobby is on the road. She fantasizes about how much more exciting her life would be if she were married to the manager, and she has decided to sleep with him to see what that's like.

In your opinion, what should Connie do? What does the future hold for Connie and Bobby? Why?

CHAPTER SUMMARY

There are many reasons why relationships may fail, and this chapter considered the correlates and consequences of the decline and fall of satisfaction and intimacy.

The Changing Rate of Divorce

The Prevalence of Divorce. The rate of divorce generally increased in the U.S. during the twentieth century, peaking around 1980 and then leveling off. The best guess is that about half of the American marriages that begin this year will end in divorce. As a result, about one quarter of the children in the U.S. live in single-parent homes.

U.S Divorce Rates in Comparative Perspectives. The U.S. divorce rate is high compared to other countries.

Why Has the Divorce Rate Increased? Several influences may underlie the sizable increase in American rates of divorce. People hold demanding expectations for marriage, and American women are more likely to work outside their homes, enjoying greater financial freedom and access to alternative partners, than ever before. Changing gender roles have reshaped marital interaction, Western cultures are more individualistic, and sex ratios are lower than they were a few decades back. Divorces are also easier to obtain, and the sharp rise in premarital cohabitation may have led young adults to have less respect for the institution of marriage. More people have also experienced the divorce of their parents, and people who come from broken homes are more likely to divorce as adults.

The Predictors of Divorce

The differences between marital winners and losers have long been of interest to relationship scientists.

Levinger's Barrier Model. George Levinger emphasized the attraction between partners, the barriers around their relationship, and their alternative attractions as determinants of divorce. When attraction and barriers are low but alternative attractions are high, divorce is likely. Levinger's approach highlights the fact that unhappy partners who would like to break up often stay together because it would cost them too much to leave, but barriers to divorce may not deter people who are certain they wish to divorce.

Karney and Bradbury's Vulnerability-Stress-Adaptation Model. This model describes the interplay of enduring personal vulnerabilities that put people at risk for divorce, the stressful events that trigger distress, and the adaptive processes with which people cope with their discontent. Difficult circumstances can put any marriage at risk, but some people cope with adversity less effectively than others do.

Results from the PAIR Project. Some research programs have tracked married couples for decades. The PAIR project has compared the roles of enduring dynamics, emergent distress, and disillusionment in producing marital difficulties. Enduring dynamics predict how happy marriages will be, but disillusionment best predicts which couples will actually divorce.

Results from the Early Years of Marriage Project. The EYM program has shown that the social context in which couples conduct their relationships is important; in the U.S., black couples are more likely to divorce than white couples are, but education generally reduces this difference.

People's Personal Perceptions of the Causes of Divorce. Divorced spouses identify infidelity, incompatibility, and drug use as the three most common reasons why they sought a divorce, but their focus on their past relationship overlooks a variety of societal influences.

Specific Factors Associated with Divorce. Along with various aspects of a couple's compatibility, socioeconomic status, social mobility, age at marriage, and cohabitation predict divorce.

The Road to Divorce

A long period of unhappiness and distress precedes most divorces, but people typically initiate divorce only when they finally come to believe that they will be better off without their spouses.

Breaking Up with Premarital Partners. There are patterns to the way people end intimate relationships. Most people never straightforwardly announce their intentions to break up with premarital partners; they choose instead to engage in repeated efforts to disengage without saying so. The usual sequence of events that follows is familiar; it involves ambivalence and vacillation that results in a lengthy process of relationship dissolution.

Steps to Divorce. When spouses divorce, they often go through a personal phase of dissatisfaction, a dyadic phase of negotiation and confrontation, a social phase of publicizing their problems and seeking support, and a grave-dressing phase of putting their loss behind them. The process of dissolving a relationship usually affects the feelings and interactions ex-partners experience after they separate.

The Aftermath of Separation and Divorce

Separation is a major life event that is very stressful.

Individuals' Perspectives. A few years later, most people who divorce are again as happy as they were before their marriages began to dissolve, but some people continue to suffer distress and difficulty for many years thereafter. Negative emotions are common during a divorce, and preoccupied and fearful people experience more pain than secure or dismissing people do. Social networks shrink, and depending on how many mouths they have to feed, the economic well-being of mothers declines while that of fathers improves.

Relationships between Former Partners. Many ex-spouses have tense, conflicted relationships, others can work together effectively in child rearing, and still others, a small subgroup, have positive friendships.

Children Whose Parents Divorce. The children of divorced parents typically exhibit lower well-being than the children of parents who remained married. The stress on parents, accompanied by less effective parenting, economic factors, and especially *parental conflict* probably all play a role in the adjustment of children of divorce. Many people experience wounds due to divorce, but injuries do heal. Members of divorced families often show remarkable resiliency in adjusting to their new family and their new life circumstances.

CHAPTER 14

Shyness and Loneliness

SHYNESS ◆ LONELINESS ◆ Measuring Loneliness ◆ How Does It Feel to Be Lonely? ◆ Does Loneliness Matter? ◆ Who's Lonely? ◆ Loneliness across the Lifespan ◆ POSSIBLE CAUSES AND MODERATORS OF LONELINESS ◆ Inadequacies in Our Relationships ◆ Changes in What We Want from Our Relationships ◆ Causal Attributions ◆ Interpersonal Behaviors ◆ COPING WITH LONELINESS ◆ What Helps People to Feel Less Lonely? ◆ Loneliness as a Growth Experience ◆ FOR YOUR CONSIDERATION ◆ CHAPTER SUMMARY

You're alone. You're without an intimate partner, and you want one. Perhaps you're lonely, having recently ended a close relationship, or having just moved away from home to go to school. Or perhaps you're shy; you've met someone you like a lot but you're nervous about making the first move. The problems we address in this chapter are very common difficulties, but their prevalence doesn't make them any easier to endure. As we'll see, people who are shy or lonely are often highly motivated to establish new intimate connections with others. But ironically, shyness and loneliness are states that engender styles of behavior that can actually make it harder for people to establish the new relationships they seek. Shyness and loneliness are born, in part, from a desire for intimacy, but they may prevent worthwhile relationships from ever beginning. Let's see how.

SHYNESS

Have you ever felt anxious and inhibited around other people, worrying about their evaluations of you and feeling ill-at-ease in your interactions with them? Most people have. Over 80 percent of us have experienced **shyness,** the syndrome that combines social reticence and inhibited interactive behavior with nervous discomfort in social settings (Bruch & Cheek, 1995; Leary & Kowalski, 1995). When people are shy, they fret about social disapproval and unhappily anticipate unfavorable judgments from others (Baldwin & Main, 2001). They also tend to be preoccupied with their own imagined inadequacies, so that they feel self-conscious and inept (van der Molen, 1990). They don't feel comfortable or effective at making small talk, and they are ill-at-ease when they meet new people (Capara et al., 2003). As a result, they interact with others in an impoverished manner. If they don't avoid an interaction altogether, they behave in an inhibited, guarded fashion; they look at others less, smile less, speak less

TABLE 14.1. The Shyness Scale

How shy are you? Rate how well each of the following statements describes you using this scale:

0 = Extremely uncharacteristic of me.
1 = Slightly characteristic of me.
2 = Moderately characteristic of me.
3 = Very characteristic of me.
4 = Extremely characteristic of me.

___1. I am socially somewhat awkward.
___2. I don't find it hard to talk to strangers.
___3. I feel tense when I'm with people I don't know well.
___4. When conversing, I worry about saying something dumb.
___5. I feel nervous when speaking to someone in authority.
___6. I am often uncomfortable at parties and other social functions.
___7. I feel inhibited in social situations.
___8. I have trouble looking someone right in the eye.
___9. I am more shy with members of the opposite sex.

The first thing you have to do to calculate your score is to reverse your answer to number 2. If you gave yourself a 0 on that item, change it to a 4; a 1 becomes a 3, a 3 becomes a 1, and a 4 should be changed to 0. (2 does not change.) Then add up your ratings. The average score for both men and women is about 14.5, with a standard deviation of close to six points. Thus, if your score is 8 or lower, you're less shy than most people, but if your score is 20 or higher, you're more shy.

Source: Cheek & Buss, 1981.

often, and converse less responsively, and they may even stand further away (Asendorpf, 1990; Bruch, 2001). Compared to people who are not shy, they manage "small talk" poorly.

Shyness may beset almost anyone now and then. It is especially common when people are in unfamiliar settings, meeting attractive, high-status strangers for the first time. It is unlikely when people are on familiar turf interacting with old friends (Leary & Kowalski, 1995). However, some people are *chronically* shy, experiencing shyness frequently, and there are three characteristics that distinguish them from people who are less shy. First, people who are routinely shy *fear negative evaluation* from others. The possibility that others might dislike them is rarely far from their minds, and the threat of derision or disdain from others is more frightening to them than it is to most people. They worry about social disapproval more than the rest of us do (Miller, 2001). Second, they tend to doubt themselves. *Poor self-regard* usually accompanies chronic shyness, and "shy people tend to have fairly extensive problems with low self-esteem" (Cheek & Melchior, 1990, p. 59). Finally, they feel less competent in their interactions with others, and overall, they have lower levels of *social skill* than do people who are not shy (Evans, 1993; Bruch, 2001; Jackson, Towson, & Narduzzi, 1997).

This unwelcome combination of perceptions and behavior puts shy people between a rock and a hard place. They worry about what people are thinking of them and dread disapproval from others but don't feel capable of making favorable impressions that would avoid such disapproval. As a result, they adopt a cautious, relatively withdrawn style of interaction that deflects interest and enthusiasm from others (Oakman, Gifford, & Chlebowsky, 2003). For instance, if they find an attractive woman looking at them, shy men won't look back, smile, and say hello; instead, they'll look away and say nothing (Garcia et al., 1991). Pleasant conversations that would have ensued had the men been less shy sometimes do not occur at all.

The irony here is that by behaving in such a timid manner, people who are either temporarily or chronically shy often make the negative impressions on others that they were hoping to avoid in the first place. Instead of eliciting sympathy, their aloof, unrewarding behavior often seems dull or disinterested to others. Let's think this through. Imagine that you're at a dance, and some acquaintances are out on the floor moving to the music in a small mob. They call to you—"C'mon!"—urging you to join them, but because you're not a confident dancer and you don't want to look silly, you stay on the sidelines. You'd like to join them, but your concern over the evaluations you might receive is too strong, so you hang back and watch. The problem with your reticence, of course, is that instead of being sociable and encouraging everyone's happy enthusiasm, you're just standing there. Inside you may feel friendly, but from your behavior it's hard to tell; you're certainly not being playful, and to all appearances you may seem awkward and a little dull. People who already know you may tolerate such timid detachment, but to anyone else, you might seem unsociable. Indeed, it's probably safe to say that you're making a poorer impression on others standing on the sidelines than you would by joining the mob and dancing clumsily; nobody much cares how well you dance as long as you're lively and light-hearted, but people do notice when you're simply no fun.

In fact, shy behavior does not make a good impression on others, as Figure 14.1 shows (Yost, 2002). The timid, reserved, and hesitant behavior that characterizes shyness can seem aloof and unfriendly, and it is likely to be met by reactions from others that are less sociable and engaging than those elicited by more gregarious behavior. Over time, shy people may be more likely to encounter neglect and rejection than understanding and empathy (Bruch & Cheek, 1995), and such outcomes may reinforce their shyness. For instance, in groups, the quiet reticence of shy people leads others to think they're not very smart (Paulhus & Morgan, 1997). Worse, shy people make new friends much more slowly and fall in love much less often than do those who are not shy (Asendorpf & Wilpers, 1998). They also tend to be more lonely (Dill & Anderson, 1999).

Thus, shy behavior may only make one's shyness worse, and obviously, it's usually better to feel confident than shy in social life. On occasion, shyness can be useful; when people really are confronted with novel situations and don't

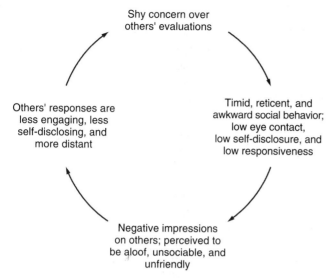

FIGURE 14.1. Interpersonal effects of shyness.
Shy behavior makes negative impressions on others, often
creating the unfavorable evaluations that shy people fear.
Source: Yost, 2002.

know how to behave, brief bouts of shy caution may keep them from doing
something inappropriate (Leary, 2001a). More often, however, shy people run
scared from the threat of social disapproval that hasn't occurred and never will,
so their shyness is an unnecessary and counterproductive burden (Miller, 2001).
Formal programs that help people overcome chronic shyness often teach them
a more positive frame of mind—helping them manage their anxiety and apprehension about social evaluation—and teach them social skills, focusing on how
to initiate conversations and how to be assertive; both positive thinking and effective behavior are then rehearsed in role-playing assignments and other practice settings until the clients feel comfortable enough to try them on their own
(Henderson & Zimbardo, 1998).

However, most shy people probably do not need formal training in interaction skills because they do just fine when they relax and quit worrying about
how they're being judged. If you're troubled by shyness now, you may make
better impressions on others if you actually care *less* about what they think.
Evidence for this possibility comes from an intriguing study by Mark Leary
(1986) who asked people to meet and greet a stranger in a noisy environment
that was said to simulate a crowded singles bar. Leary created a multi-track tape
of overlapping conversations, three different songs, radio static, and party noise
(such as laughing and yelling)—it was definitely "noise"—and played it at a
mildly obnoxious level as each couple conversed. Importantly, the tape was
always played at the same volume, but some people were told that the noise
was so loud that it would probably interfere with their conversation and make
it hard for them to have a nice chat, whereas others were told that the noise was

TABLE 14.2. Doing Better with an Excuse for Failure

In Leary's (1986) study, when noise that was said to be impossibly "loud" gave shy people an excuse for their interactions to go badly, they behaved no differently than did people who were not shy. In contrast, "soft" noise that was not supposed to interfere with their conversations left them tense and anxious, even though the noise was played at exactly the same volume in both the "loud" and "soft" conditions.

	Change in Heart Rate (in beats per minute)	
	Noise Volume	
Participants' Chronic Shyness	"Soft"	"Loud"
Low	5.3	4.7
High	15.8	4.5

soft enough that it wouldn't be a problem. Once these expectations were in place, people who were either shy or not shy were left alone with a stranger—a setting that is ordinarily threatening to shy people. Leary monitored the heart rates of his participants to track their anxiety and arousal, and Table 14.2 shows what he found. When the noise was "soft" and there wasn't a good excuse for their interactions to go poorly, shy people exhibited considerably more arousal and apprehension than normal people did; their heart rates increased three times as much. Even worse, they looked obviously shy and uncomfortable to people who later watched videotapes of their conversations. On the other hand, when they had an excuse—the impossibly "loud" noise—that lowered every-one's expectations, they behaved as if they weren't shy at all. They exhibited a normal, moderate increase in heart rate as their interactions began, and gave observers no clue that they were usually shy.

Interestingly, if they couldn't be blamed if their interactions went badly, the shy people in Leary's (1986) study stayed relatively relaxed and conducted their conversations without difficulty. In a sense, when they were given a non-threatening way to think about an upcoming interaction, their shyness disappeared. Such people—and that probably includes most people who feel shy— probably don't need additional training in basic social skills. What they do need is greater calm and self-confidence (Capara et al, 2003; Glass & Shea, 1986), and although that may not be easy to come by, shy people should consider the alternative: They're not winning friends and influencing people by acting shy, so what do they have to lose by trusting themselves and expecting interactions to go well?

LONELINESS

Whether or not we're shy, we may sometimes feel lonely. Loneliness sometimes involves, but is not the same as, physical isolation; people can feel very content in complete solitude (Leary, Herbst, & McCrary, 2003) but lonely in a crowd.

Instead, loneliness seems to emerge from a *discrepancy* between the kind of social relations we want and the kind of social relations we have. Unhappy feelings of deprivation and dissatisfaction result when we desire richer, more intimate connections with others than we presently enjoy (Perlman & Peplau, 1981). So, we can feel lonely when we are alone if we would rather be with someone. We can also feel lonely when we are surrounded by others if we feel unloved or if we would rather be with someone else.

Loneliness may also be of two different types. When people suffer **social isolation,** they are dissatisfied because they lack a social network of friends and acquaintances. In contrast, when they suffer **emotional isolation,** people are lonely because they lack a single intense relationship. According to Robert Weiss (1973), who first made this distinction, we can't ease one type of loneliness by substituting the other type of relationship. As a result, if a couple has just moved to a new town where they do not know anyone, they may experience the loneliness of social isolation even though their relationship with each other is close and fulfilling. Alternatively, a person can have an extensive social network and a very active social life but still feel lonely if he or she does not have a romantic partner. There has been some debate over whether these two types of isolation are just different routes to the same generic form of distress (Russell, Peplau, & Cutrona, 1980), but most researchers now accept a distinction between social and emotional lonesomeness (Green et al., 2001; DiTommaso & Spinner, 1995). If we lack the kind of relationship we desire, we can be lonely despite having other, quite rewarding social interactions.

Thus, loneliness depends on both our perceptions and our desires, and on a mismatch between the amount of intimacy we want and the amount we have. And as Figure 14.2 illustrates, a variety of influences may contribute to such a mismatch. The **discrepancy model** of loneliness developed by Dan Perlman and Letitia Peplau (1981, 1998) holds that both personal predispositions and adverse situations can contribute to temporary deficiencies in the quality of one's contact with others. Then, when such deficiencies occur, various cognitive processes such as causal attributions, social comparisons, and judgments of control moderate how intensely people react.

We'll soon say more about the predispositions and processes that shape lonely experiences. But before we do, let's characterize loneliness more thoroughly. How does it feel? How can we measure it?

Measuring Loneliness

Things would be simple if researchers could simply ask people, "How lonely are you?", and get valid answers. However, many people, particularly men, are reluctant to admit that they are lonely (Cramer & Neyedley, 1998)[1], so the most widely used measure of loneliness in adults never uses the word! This scale,

---

[1]Being reluctant to admit that there's anything wrong with one's social life is an example of a social desirability bias. Remember this problem with self-report data? It's back on page 61 in chapter 2.

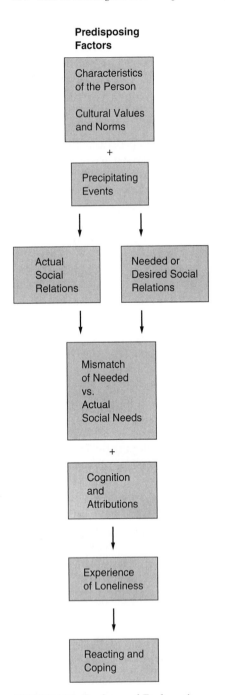

FIGURE 14.2. Peplau and Perlman's discrepancy view of loneliness.

TABLE 14.3. The UCLA Loneliness Scale (Version 3)

Instructions: The following statements describe how people sometimes feel. For each statement, please indicate how often you feel the way described by writing a number in the space provided. Here is an example:

How often do you feel happy?

If you never felt happy, you would respond "never"; if you always feel happy, you would respond "always."

NEVER	RARELY	SOMETIMES	ALWAYS
1	2	3	4

*1. How often do you feel that you are "in tune" with the people around you? ____

2. How often do you feel that you lack companionship? ____

3. How often do you feel that there is no one you can turn to? ____

4. How often do you feel alone? ____

*5. How often do you feel part of a group of friends? ____

*6. How often do you feel that you have a lot in common with the people around you? ____

7. How often do you feel that you are no longer close to anyone? ____

8. How often do you feel that your interests and ideas are not shared by those around you? ____

*9. How often do you feel outgoing and friendly? ____

*10. How often do you feel close to people? ____

11. How often do you feel left out? ____

12. How often do you feel that your relationships with others are not meaningful? ____

13. How often do you feel that no one really knows you well? ____

14. How often do you feel isolated from others? ____

*15. How often do you feel you can find companionship when you want it? ____

*16. How often do you feel that there are people who really understand you? ____

17. How often do you feel shy? ____

18. How often do you feel that people are around you but not with you? ____

*19. How often do you feel that there are people you can talk to? ____

*20. How often do you feel that there are people you can turn to? ____

*Reverse score item (i.e., 1 = 4, 2 = 3, 3 = 2, 4 =1).
Mean score among 489 college students in Russell's (1996) validation sample = 40.1.
Note: Copyright by Daniel W. Russell. Reprinted with permission.

the UCLA Loneliness Scale, was originally developed by Dan Russell, Letitia Peplau, and Carolyn Cutrona (1980) and is shown in Table 14.3.

As you can see, the items on the scale assess whether respondents feel connected and close to others, and there appear to be three different themes that produce high loneliness scores (Hawkley et al., 2004). The first is *isolation* from others. Lonely people feel alone and less in contact with others than they want to be. They also feel less *close connection* to others than they wish to have. They perceive their relationships with others to be less meaningful, supportive, and close than they want them to be. Finally, loneliness also results from experiencing too little *social connection* to people in general. Lonely people feel that they have insufficient ties to a network of friends and playmates, and altogether, they suffer from a sense of painful disconnection from others that is combined with a lack of pleasure and social support in their interactions with others (Joiner, Lewinsohn, & Seeley, 2002).

How Does It Feel to Be Lonely?

Add all this up, and lonely people feel dissatisfied, deprived, and distressed. Those feelings cover a lot of ground, and indeed, different people in different situations may have different kinds of feelings when they are lonely. A study on the loneliness of widows illustrated how many kinds of emotions and desires may be bound up with the experience of being lonely (Lopata, 1969). For these women, loneliness was associated with one or more of the following:

Desiring to be with the husband

Wanting to be loved by someone

Wanting to love and take care of someone

Wanting to share daily experiences with someone

Wanting to have someone around the house

Needing someone to share the work

Longing for the previous form of life

Experiencing loss of status

Experiencing loss of other people as a consequence of having lost the husband

Fearing the inability to make new friends

Thus, loneliness included longing for the past, frustration with the present, and fears about the future.

Even for individuals who have not experienced the devastating blow of losing a spouse, loneliness can involve many different kinds of feelings. A broad survey of loneliness found that people report four different sets of feelings when they are lonely: *desperation, impatient boredom, self-deprecation*, and *depression* (Rubenstein, Shaver, & Peplau, 1979). The specific feelings reported in each of these clusters are listed in Table 14.4. There are big differences among these feelings (for instance, desperation is quite different from boredom), but loneliness is complex enough to encompass all of them.

Does Loneliness Matter?

Loneliness is often a temporary state, but that doesn't mean it is inconsequential. Substantial evidence suggests that loneliness is associated with a variety of

TABLE 14.4. Feelings When Lonely

Desperation	Impatient Boredom	Self-Deprecation	Depression
Desperate	Impatient	Feeling unattractive	Sad
Helpless	Bored	Down on self	Depressed
Afraid	Desire to be elsewhere	Stupid	Empty
Without hope	Uneasy	Ashamed	Isolated
Abandoned	Angry	Insecure	Sorry for self
Vulnerable	Unable to concentrate		Melancholy
			Alienated
			Longing to be with one special person

Source: Rubenstein, Shaver, & Peplau, 1979.

serious conditions. Consider some examples:

Lonely adolescents in the U.S. are more likely than other teens to run away from home and to commit delinquent acts such as gambling, theft, and vandalism (Brennan & Auslander, 1979).

Compared to their non-lonely peers, lonely college students get poorer grades and are more likely to drop out of school (Burleson & Samter, 1992; Rotenberg & Morrison, 1993).

Among older adults, loneliness is associated with memory problems (Bazargan & Barbre, 1992).

Worse, loneliness is associated with a variety of clinical disorders. Lonely people are more likely than others to experience general maladjustment, personality disorders, bulimia nervosa, alcohol abuse, and schizophrenia (Ernst & Cacioppo, 1999; Jones & Carver, 1991). (These data are correlational, so it's not at all clear that loneliness helps cause such problems; it's just as likely that psychological difficulties interfere with rewarding interaction and help make people lonely. Still, because loneliness is a burdensome stressor, it may make existing problems worse.)

Lonely people sleep more poorly than others do (Cacioppo et al., 2002). They take longer to get to sleep, awaken more often during the night, and suffer more drowsiness during the day.

People who are chronically lonely have high levels of cortisol, a stress hormone that is a physiological indicator of anxiety (Cacioppo et al., 2000).

Perhaps most importantly, loneliness is also associated with poorer physical health. One study by Cutrona and her colleagues (1997) followed 3,000 elderly Iowans over a four-year period. When the study began, none of them were living in nursing homes; however, when the study ended, over 40 percent of the seniors who were high in loneliness had been admitted to nursing facilities,

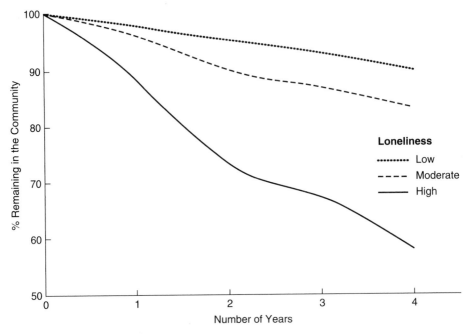

FIGURE 14.3. Loneliness and survival in the community.
Source: Cutrona et al., 1997.

whereas fewer than 10 percent of those who were not lonely had been institu-tionalized (see Figure 14.3). Even after control variables such as age, health at the beginning of the study, initial morale, and social ties were taken into consideration, those who were lonely at the beginning of the study were more likely to have subsequently been admitted to a nursing home.

Loneliness and health may be correlated because both are influenced by other factors such as income, and it's also plausible that, in limiting one's activity, poor health may make people more lonely. Nonetheless, it's likely that loneliness directly contributes to poor health. How might this occur? For one thing, loneli-ness is demoralizing, and it may lead people to neglect their self-care. Lonely peo-ple may also lack relationships with others that could promote improved health through the provision of social support and the encouragement of healthy behav-ior. But it's also likely that loneliness has physiological effects that have direct impact on health. Lonely people have higher blood pressure (Hawkley et al., 2003) and weaker immune systems that leave them more vulnerable to infection and illness (Dixon et al., 2001). In essence, there may be both psychological and physiological truth to the view that loneliness means having a broken heart.

Who's Lonely?

Most of us have experienced loneliness, and about one quarter of us (26 percent) have felt "very lonely or remote from other people" in just the past few weeks

TABLE 14.5.   Mean Level of Loneliness, 18 Nations, World Values Surveys, 1981–1983

Country	Males	Females	Country	Males	Females
Italy	1.30	1.67	Britain	.70	1.16
Japan	1.32	1.41	N. Ireland	.72	1.12
Spain	1.12	1.33	Australia	.76	1.05
U.S.	1.04	1.33	Iceland	.70	1.11
Canada	.92	1.22	Belgium	.70	1.09
France	.85	1.20	Norway	.71	1.03
USSR	.81	1.11	Sweden	.68	1.02
Ireland	.81	1.08	Netherlands	.70	.87
W. Germany	.74	1.14	Denmark	.57	.65

Note: Higher scores reflect greater loneliness.
Source: S. Stack, 1995.

(Weiss, 1973). Loneliness is evidently quite widespread. But are there some people who are more vulnerable (or predisposed) to loneliness than others? The answer, consistent with the discrepancy model of loneliness, is yes (Larose, Guay, & Boivin, 2002), with the major differences involving nationality, socioeconomic status, marital status, attachment style, genetics, and gender.

Nationality

Cross-cultural studies demonstrate that loneliness is more common in some countries than in others. In one comparison of eighteen countries, Italians and Japanese reported the most frequent feelings of loneliness, and Danes the least (Stack, 1995, 1998). And as you can see in Table 14.5, respondents from the U.S. were more lonely than most. One of the influences underlying these differences may be the amount of *social integration,* or connection to one's neighbors and community, a culture promotes (Green et al., 2001). People are less lonely in the Netherlands than in Italy, for instance, and a specific comparison of the two countries found that, even though many of the Dutch live alone, they enjoy more social integration; they have larger social networks of supportive friends, and they are more involved in civic organizations (van Tilburg et al., 1998). Importantly, some observers have argued that social integration in the U.S. has steadily declined in recent decades (Putnam, 2000).

Other factors may be influential, as well. People in Eastern cultures such as China and Japan are less prone to self-serving biases in attribution than are Westerners[2] (Mezulis et al., 2004); the Chinese, for instance, blame themselves more for failure and take less credit for success than Americans do. But, because attributions influence loneliness (as we will see shortly), they may be more prone to loneliness as a result of this comparatively dour outlook (Anderson, 1999).

---

[2]Need a reminder about the self-serving bias? Look back at page 119 in chapter 4.

Socioeconomic Factors

Social class is correlated with loneliness, too. Homeless people are often lonely (Rokach, 2004), and education and income are negatively correlated with loneliness (Pinquart & Sörensen, 2001). One survey of more than 8,000 households in the southwestern U.S. found that members of families with incomes of under $10,000 were four-and-a-half times more likely to be lonely than were members of families with incomes of $75,000 or more (Page & Cole, 1991) .

Marital Status

In general, married people are less lonely than those who are unmarried, but those who are divorced or widowed tend to be lonelier than people who have never married at all (Pinquart, 2003). Losing one's spouse appears to put one at risk for being lonely, and this seems to be true around the world (Stack, 1998). Cohabitation is associated with intermediate loneliness; cohabiting partners tend to be more lonely, on average, than spouses are, but they tend to be less lonely than single people (Page & Cole, 1991).

Thus, the more committed people are to a romantic relationship, the less lonely they tend to be. However, not all marriages are created equal, and loneliness is also associated with dissatisfaction with one's close relationships (Segrin et al., 2003); among those who are married, people in unhappy unions are lonelier than those who are more content with their marriages (Demir & Fisiloglu, 1999). We should also note that being single certainly doesn't doom people to being lonely. A study of older Dutch adults without partners found that they were unlikely to be lonely if they had plenty of supportive friends, were not distressed by being single, and believed that they could marry if they wished (Dykstra, 1995).

Attachment Style

People with secure attachment styles are less prone to both social and emotional loneliness than are those who are insecure, and one reason why is because they possess better social skills (Ireland & Power, 2004; DiTommaso et al., 2003). Skilled, pleasurable interaction with others helps stave off loneliness (a point to which we will return), and people who are anxious over abandonment or uncomfortable with closeness do not appear to enjoy interactions that are as close and rewarding, on average, as secure people do.

Genetics

Researchers aren't yet sure why—there may be a variety of personal characteristics at work—but if you have an identical twin who is lonely, you're likely to be lonely, too. There is also a correlation between the loneliness scores of ordinary brothers and sisters—if your sibling is lonely, you're a little more likely to be lonely, as well—but it's a much weaker pattern (McGuire & Clifford, 2000). To some degree, then, people inherit predispositions that result in loneliness later in life.

Gender

Unmarried men are lonelier than women (Pinquart, 2003), but they're less willing to admit it. When men and women are asked to rate how "lonely" they are, as they were in Stack's (1995) comparison of loneliness in eighteen different countries, women consistently report more loneliness than men do (take another look at Table 14.5). However, when social distress is assessed with the UCLA Loneliness Scale (which doesn't use the word "lonely"), unmarried men routinely get higher loneliness scores than women do (Borys & Perlman, 1985).

Men are apparently less willing than women to explicitly acknowledge that they are lonely (Cramer & Neyedley, 1998), and with good reason. Read this passage and see what you think:

> Jim, aged eighteen, is a first year student in University. He is very quiet and reserved, and he spends a lot of his time thinking about himself and his situation. Jim feels that he is alienated from other students on campus and that he is excluded from events that are happening around him. There is no one he feels he can turn to or depend upon. He has no close friends, although he often wishes he did. However, he feels that he doesn't know how to make friends, so he tends to avoid any social contacts. He never initiates any social activities, and whenever he is with a group of people, he feels like an outsider and doesn't have a good time. Therefore, Jim isolates himself from others, spending long hours concentrating on his course work. Often Jim feels that he is inferior and rejected and wonders if something is wrong with himself. He feels other people don't like him, and this makes him unhappy. Sometimes he becomes angry and can see only the worst in everything.

When Shelley Borys and Dan Perlman (1985, pp. 69–70) asked young adults to evaluate the person described by this passage, they judged the person more negatively when he was identified as a man ("Jim") than they did when she was said to be a woman (named "Sue"). Men appear to pay a larger price for seeming lonely than women do, and they may learn to avoid the "L-word."

The good news is that there's a handy cure for men's greater loneliness: an intimate relationship with a woman. Men who have a close partnership with a woman are much less lonely, on average, than are men who are between partners, as Table 14.6 shows. The reason why probably hearkens back to a point we made in chapter 5; women enjoy more meaningful and more fulfilling interactions with each other than men do. Women self-disclose more and talk about more personal topics, so they enjoy plenty of intimacy in their lives even when they're not dating anyone. Men, on the other hand, share relatively superficial interactions with other men, and they tend to really open up only when they're interacting with a woman. Thus, men seem to be dependent on women to avoid being lonely in a way that women are not dependent on them in return (Wheeler et al., 1983).

On the other hand, men don't all come in the same uniform package, and it's actually more correct to say that *macho* men need women to keep from being lonely. One of the psychological ingredients that allows people to have

TABLE 14.6. Loneliness in Men and Women with and without Romantic Partners

	With a Romantic Partner	Without a Romantic Partner
Men	16.9	31.2
Women	20.2	24.3

The table lists loneliness scores of young adults who do have romantic partners alongside the scores of those who do not. Women's loneliness does not depend much on whether or not they currently have a romantic partner, but men's loneliness does; men are much more lonely, on average, when they do not have an intimate relationship with a female partner.

Source: Wheeler, Reis, & Nezlek, 1983.

meaningful, fulfilling interactions with others is expressivity,[3] and the qualities that make someone warm, sensitive, and kind are negatively correlated with loneliness. That's probably a primary reason why women, who tend to be high in expressivity, are less lonely than men. But there are a lot of men who, in being androgynous, are also high in expressivity, and they tend not to be as lonely as more traditional, macho men are (Wheeler et al., 1983). So, the global difference between men and women in loneliness appears to be a gender difference rather than a sex difference. People who are low in expressivity (and that includes most men) tend towards loneliness when they are not paired with an expressive partner who brings intimacy into their lives, but many men (about one third of them) are just as expressive as most women (Bem, 1993), and they do not rely on women to keep from being lonely.

Loneliness across the Lifespan

Loneliness is also more likely at some ages than at others. You may hold the stereotype that elderly people tend to be lonely, but if you do, you're wrong.

Family Antecedents of Loneliness

As you might expect from the positive correlation between insecure attachment and loneliness, lonely people remember childhoods that were not particularly warm and fuzzy. They recall their parents as being remote, disagreeable, and untrustworthy and feel that their parents didn't spend enough time with them (Rubenstein & Shaver, 1982). These are just the sorts of memories that people with insecure attachment styles often have, and they again demonstrate that some people are more predisposed than others to become lonely.

Children of divorce are also prone to loneliness (Rubenstein and Shaver, 1982). Moreover, the younger children are when their parents divorce, the more loneliness they tend to experience as adults (see Figure 14.4). Curiously,

[3]Need a reminder about expressivity? Take a look back at page 24 in chapter 1.

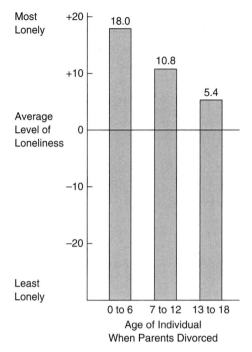

FIGURE 14.4. Loneliness scores by age at parents' divorce.
Source: Rubenstein, Shaver, & Peplau, 1979.

losing a parent to death does not have a similar effect: People who were bereaved during childhood report no more loneliness as adults than do people whose families remained intact during their youth. There seems to be something specific to divorce that increases the potential for feelings of loneliness as an adult.

Age Changes in Loneliness

Even young children get lonely. Eight-year-olds can define and describe loneliness (Hymel et al., 1999), and even kindergartners seem to understand its nature (Perlman & Landolt, 1999). But the folks that we assume are really lonely are the elderly; stereotypes portray elderly people as spending large amounts of time alone and gradually suffering the loss of most of their friends. There is some truth to this view (Cacioppo & Hawkley, 2003), and loneliness does tend to increase very late in life (Pinquart & Sörensen, 2001). On the whole, however, the elderly are less lonely than young adults are.

Dan Perlman (1991) combined the results of six surveys of more than 18,000 people in North America and found that loneliness has a "backward" check-shaped curve over the life span, with slightly different results for men and women. (See Figure 14.5.) People are lonelier, on average, when they are adolescents and young adults than when they are middle-aged. Loneliness actually declines with age until people enter their forties, when it levels off; thereafter, divorce, the death

Loneliness Across the Life Cycle

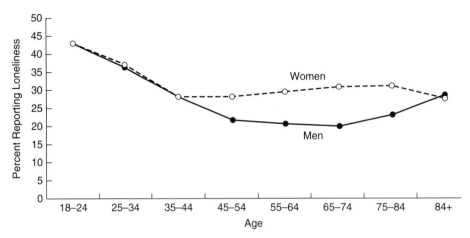

FIGURE 14.5. Loneliness across the life cycle.
Source: Perlman, 1991.

of a spouse, or ill health may all have a huge effect on the loneliness we encounter, but most of us will be less likely to be lonely than we were in college. Fewer than 15 percent of older adults report frequent loneliness, and that's a smaller proportion than is found in younger groups (Pinquart & Sörensen, 2001).

The exact reasons why are as yet unknown, but it's likely that years of experience have taught older adults to have more realistic expectations about the ups and downs of social life (Pinquart & Sörensen, 2001). Many younger folks probably have more romantic expectations of how wonderful their relationships will be when they meet the right friends and lovers, so they feel distressed and deprived when their interactions are merely pleasant instead of sublime.

POSSIBLE CAUSES AND MODERATORS OF LONELINESS

As you can see, there are a variety of personal and situational characteristics that are associated with loneliness, and some of us, in some situations, are more likely to become lonely than are others. But the correlates we have identified thus far may all be, to one degree or another, symptoms of the underlying processes from which loneliness springs. What are the actual primary causes of loneliness? There are several possibilities.

Inadequacies in Our Relationships

There are a number of reasons why we may be unfulfilled by our existing relationships, and a national survey of loneliness in the U.S. found that people gave five major reasons for being lonely (Rubenstein & Shaver, 1982):

1. Being unattached: Having no spouse; having no sexual partner; breaking up with spouse or lover

2. Alienation: Feeling different; being misunderstood; not being needed; having no close friends
3. Being alone: Coming home to an empty house
4. Forced isolation: Being housebound; being hospitalized; having no transportation
5. Dislocation: Being far from home; starting in a new job or school; moving too often; traveling often

Evidently, some people felt lonely due to emotional isolation (in being unattached and having no close, romantic partner) whereas others complained mostly of social isolation (being alienated from others or being dislocated from friends). Importantly, people also identified deficits that were produced by adverse situations (such as forced isolation and dislocation) and other problems that probably emerged more from their own characteristics and styles (such as being unattached and alienation). Indeed, both the situations we encounter and our own characteristics jointly determine how lonely we will be (Larose et al., 2002).

Changes in What We Want from Our Relationships

Discrepancies in what we want from our partnerships and what we've got may also develop as our relational goals and desires gradually change over time. Relationships that were once fulfilling may become less so as those changes occur.

Developmental changes are often involved (Peplau, Russell, & Heim, 1979; Perlman & Peplau, 1981). Playmates who were satisfying companions when we were fifteen may fail to be fulfilling partners when we are 25. Our circumstances may change, as well. We may not want to invest too much time and attention in any one partnership when we are starting our careers, spreading our wings, and heading out into the world. Later on, however, when our careers are established, and we have dated around, we may feel a great need for a more lasting, emotionally committed relationship. Whatever the reason, if we change our minds about what we want from our relationships and our relationships do not change accordingly, we may become lonely.

Causal Attributions

Once people become lonely, their attributions for their distress may help determine how long they stay lonely. Loneliness can be especially intense and long-lasting when people believe that their own enduring characteristics are to blame for their difficulties. Take a look at Table 14.7: Perceiving that any stable cause is responsible for one's loneliness robs one of hope that things will get better, and it's particularly disheartening to blame one's own personal and lasting deficiencies for one's current distress (Anderson et al., 1994). On the other hand, attributions to unstable causes—that is, perceiving that one's loneliness has resulted from temporary or changeable influences—offers optimistic possibilities that things will improve. In fact, a study of loneliness in college freshmen

TABLE 14.7. Explanations of Loneliness

	Locus of Causality	
Stability	Internal	External
Stable	I'm lonely because I'm unlovable, I'll never be worth loving.	The people here are cold and impersonal; none of them share my interests.
Unstable	I'm lonely now, but I won't be for long. I'll stop working so much and go out and meet some new people.	The first semester in college is always the worst, I'm sure things will get better.

Source: Based on Shaver & Rubenstein, 1980. From Brehm & Kassin, 1990.

found that those who made internal, stable attributions for their loneliness in the fall semester (for instance, thinking that they were lonely because of their personalities, their fears of being rejected, or their not knowing what to do to start a relationship) were more likely to still be lonely in the spring than were students who had attributed their loneliness to unstable causes (Cutrona, 1982). Hopeful outlooks are evidently more likely to cure loneliness than dour pessimism is (Anderson, 1999).

Interpersonal Behaviors

It's no fun being lonely, and the distress lonely people feel is evident in their behavior toward others. The interpersonal styles of lonely people differ from those of people who are not lonely in three important respects. First, lonely people have *low self-esteem* (McWhirter, 1997). Consistent with the sociometer model of self-esteem,[4] lonely people tend to take their unfulfilling social lives to heart and to feel badly about themselves. They regard themselves as relatively unlovable and unworthy, and therefore doubt that others will find them interesting and attractive. And as we saw in chapter 1, people with low self-esteem are likely to perceive disregard from others where it does not exist, and that's an outlook that may make loneliness worse.

Lonely people also have gloomy views of other people. Loneliness is associated with a variety of *negative attitudes toward others* (Check, Perlman, & Malamuth, 1985), with lonely people mistrusting others (Vaux, 1988b), judging their actions with suspicion (Hanley-Dunn, Maxwell, & Santos, 1985), and generally evaluating them negatively (Jones, Sansome, & Helm, 1983; Wittenberg & Reis, 1986). Thus, lonely individuals tend to dislike the very people from whom they seek acceptance and regard. This is a little ironic, but it does delineate the difficulties lonely people face and the pain they're in.

Finally, lonely people *lack social skills* (DiTommaso et al., 2003) and interact with others in a drab, dull way (Solano & Koester, 1989). They're passive and unresponsive. They are slow to respond to things said by their conversational partners, they don't ask many questions, and they change topics without warning,

[4]Need a reminder? Page 28 in chapter 1.

For Better or For Worse®   **by Lynn Johnston**

Lonely people tend to hold negative attitudes toward others, and that makes it harder for them to overcome their loneliness.

FOR BETTER OR FOR WORSE © 1989 Lynn Johnston Productions. Dist. by Universal Press Syndicate. Reprinted with permission. All rights reserved.

so they're not much fun to chat with (Hansson & Jones, 1981; Jones, Hobbs, & Hackenbury, 1982). In addition, they don't self-disclose much; their conversation is usually shallow and inconsequential, so it's hard for them to develop intimacy with others (Davis & Franzoi, 1986; Schwab et al., 1998).

Unfortunately, none of this escapes notice. The negative attitudes and dull, inept interpersonal behavior of lonely people often elicit negative reactions from others (Jones, 1990; Rook, 1988). Those who interact with lonely people usually feel that they don't know them very well (Solano, Batten, & Parish, 1982), and others often come to regard lonely people as socially incompetent (Spitzberg & Canery, 1985). Thus, lonely people are often caught in an unhappy loop in which their cynical outlook and off-putting, halfhearted style of interaction make it even harder for them to establish the intimacy and to gain the acceptance they long for.

This makes loneliness somewhat similar to shyness in its effects on social life, as Figure 14.6 suggests. However, loneliness may have more potent effects. Whereas shy behavior is essentially innocuous and aloof, lonely behavior is more corrosive and obnoxious. Shy people just keep their distance, but lonely people irritate and annoy us. Lonely college students do not differ from those who are not lonely in the number and diversity of social interactions they have each day, but they experience fewer positive outcomes such as support and affection and more negative outcomes such as conflict and distrust (Hawkley & Cacioppo, 2003). Thus, on college campuses, where they are frequently surrounded by other people, lonely people often behave in off-putting ways that can elicit rejection from others and that just makes their loneliness worse.

To add insult to injury, loneliness is also correlated with depression (Anderson & Harvey, 1988), which has its own deleterious effects on social life (Davila, 2001). Depression is characterized by negative mood (such as feelings of sadness and despair), pessimism, lack of initiative, and slowed thought processes (Holmes, 1991), and, like loneliness, it can both result from social rejection (Nolan, Flynn, & Garber, 2003) and make one's social difficulties worse

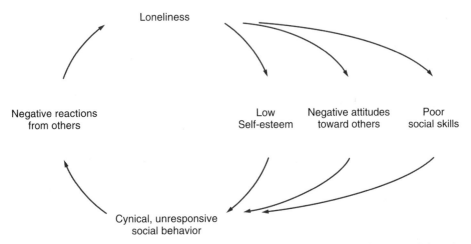

FIGURE 14.6.   Interpersonal effects of loneliness. Lonely behavior is dull, distrustful, and dreary, and it is likely to elicit rejection from others that will make one's loneliness worse.

(Beach et al., 2003). Depression is a broader, more global state of dissatisfaction and distress than loneliness is—loneliness emerges from interpersonal troubles, whereas depression stems from losses and setbacks of all sorts (Weeks et al., 1980)—but it can be depressing to stay lonely, and being depressed can make it even harder to behave in effective ways that will improve our relationships.

Finally, we should note that Figure 14.6 charts a cycle in which loneliness leads to poor social outcomes, but the converse can also be true. Loneliness can befall skilled, perfectly pleasant people who lose friends or lovers through no fault of their own, so adverse social outcomes can cause loneliness, too. However, once people become lonely, they often behave in ways that make their loneliness worse (Hawkley & Cacioppo, 2003), and that's the point we wish to emphasize with Figure 14.6. Regrettable, temporary situations can cause us to be lonely, but if we don't cope effectively, loneliness may become a sadly persistent burden.

COPING WITH LONELINESS

People do various things when they are lonely. Four major types of responses were reported by participants in a national survey on loneliness (Rubenstein & Shaver, 1982), and they are summarized in Table 14.8. As you can see, two types of responses seemed to involve positive, constructive behaviors; with *active solitude*, people sought ways to be at peace when they were alone, and with *social contact*, they sought to be with others. However, other responses to loneliness seemed less profitable. When they engaged in *sad passivity*, people tried to blunt their distress with intoxicants or, perhaps, did nothing at all. *Distractions* were more innocuous if people could afford them. A shopping spree could be a reasonable way to get your mind off things, but reckless spending of money you don't have is unlikely to be an effective cure for social dissatisfaction.

TABLE 14.8. What People Do When They Feel Lonely

Active Solitude	Social Contact	Distractions	Sad Passivity
Study or work	Call a friend	Spend money	Cry
Write	Visit someone	Go shopping	Sleep
Listen to music			Sit and think
Exercise, walk			Do nothing
Work on a hobby			Overeat
Go to a movie			Take tranquilizers
Read			Watch TV
Play music			Get drunk or stoned

Source: Rubenstein & Shaver, 1982.

Another distinction among responses to loneliness was made by Rook and Peplau (1982), who distinguished between cognitive and behavioral coping strategies. Various examples of these two types are listed in Tables 14.9 and 14.10, which also indicate the extent to which they were used by young adults. Most of these strategies are positive and constructive: for example, reminding yourself that you have some good relationships with other people, or trying to find new ways to meet people. But some negative, self-destructive reactions, such as taking your mind off feeling lonely by using drugs or alcohol were also reported fairly frequently.

What Helps People Feel Less Lonely?

Mindlessly watching TV, drinking to excess, or eating when you are not even hungry are undoubtedly all poor ways to cope with loneliness. None of these activities produce a more satisfying social life and, indeed, all of them could actually make it more difficult to establish good relationships. Obviously, it's better to cope with loneliness in positive and constructive ways (Rook, 1984). But how? There are some good suggestions among the strategies listed in Tables 14.9 and 14.10, and relationship research also offers some useful ideas.

Recall that there are at least three self-defeating characteristics of lonely people:

1. Making internal, stable attributions that blame oneself for unpleasant social outcomes
2. Having negative and cynical attitudes toward others
3. Behaving in passive and unresponsive ways with others

All of these characteristics make it more difficult to establish the rewarding social relationships that will vanquish loneliness, so there may be value in counteracting all three. If you feel lonely, here are some suggestions for how to do so.

1. First, address your pessimism. If a fear of possible social failure is keeping you from getting involved in some potentially interesting social interactions, try some rational cost analysis. If you go to that party, for example,

TABLE 14.9. Cognitive Strategies College Students Used to Cope with Loneliness

Strategy	Never	Sometimes	Often
Thought about things you could do to overcome your loneliness	4%	52%	44%
Reminded yourself that you actually do have good relationships with other people	7	33	60
Tried to figure out why you were lonely	7	54	39
Thought about good qualities that you possess (such as being warm, intelligent, sensitive, self-sufficient, etc.)	7	68	25
Told yourself that your loneliness would not last forever, that things would get better	10	38	52
Thought about things you can do extremely well (excelling at schoolwork, athletics, artwork, gourmet cooking, etc.)	10	47	23
Told yourself that most other people are lonely at one time or another	11	56	33
Took your mind off feeling lonely by deliberately thinking about other things (anything other than your loneliness)	13	61	26
Told yourself that you were overreacting, that you shouldn't be so upset	14	62	24
Thought about possible benefits of your experience of loneliness (such as telling yourself that you were learning to be self-reliant, that you would grow from the experience, etc.)	21	42	37
Changed your goals for social relationships (such as telling yourself that it is not that important to be popular, that at this point in you life it's all right not to have a boyfriend or girlfriend, etc.)	22	55	23

Source: Rook & Peplau, 1982.

and don't meet anyone, are you any worse off than you were? But if you go and have some enjoyable interactions, aren't you much better off than you were? Isn't the potential benefit worth the risk?

2. If you find yourself blaming your own inadequacies for feeling lonely, look around. Are you the only lonely person in your current situation? Usually, if you look carefully, you will discover that the answer is no; others are lonely, too, which suggests that situational factors are involved. For instance, college freshman are often lonely for a time after they leave home to come to school. In one study of more than 300 freshmen, two weeks after classes started in the fall, 75 percent of the participants were lonely occasionally, and

TABLE 14.10. **Behavioral Strategies College Students Used to Cope with Loneliness**

Strategy	Never	Sometimes	Often
Tried harder to be friendly to other people (such as making an effort to talk to people in your classes, etc.)	2%	62%	36%
Took your mind off feeling lonely through some mental activity (such as reading a novel, watching TV, going to a movie, etc.)	6	60	34
Worked particularly hard to succeed at some activity (such as studying extra hard for an exam, putting extra effort into practicing an instrument, pushing yourself on an athletic skill, etc.)	7	53	40
Did something helpful for someone else (such as helping a classmate with homework, doing volunteer work, etc.)	7	64	29
Did something you are very good at (schoolwork, athletics, artwork, etc.)	7	66	27
Took your mind off feeling lonely through some physical activity (such as jogging, playing basketball, shopping, washing the car, etc.)	12	51	37
Tried to find new ways to meet people (such as joining a club, moving into a dorm, going to dances, etc.)	18	64	18
Did something to make yourself more physically attractive to others (going on a diet, buying new clothes, changing your hairstyle, etc.)	20	61	19
Did something to improve your social skills (such as learning to dance, learning to be more assertive, improving conversational skills, etc.)	25	66	9
Talked to a friend or relative about ways to overcome your loneliness	40	45	15
Took your mind off feeling lonely by using drugs or alcohol	74	25	1
Talked to a counselor or therapist about ways to overcome your loneliness	91	6	3

Source: Rook & Peplau, 1982.

43 percent said they were moderately or severely lonely (Bragg, 1979; Weeks et al., 1980). Five weeks later, their loneliness had decreased, but it was still prevalent: 66 percent reported occasional loneliness, and 30 percent were moderately or severely lonely. Many of these students blamed their own inadequacies for being lonely, and yet, obviously, the situation—leaving home and being in a new environment—was very influential. The next time you are tempted to blame yourself for being lonely, think about this research and consider the situational influences that might be involved.

3. Identifying situational influences does not, however, mean that you should just sit back and wait for things to get better. Taking the initiative to meet some new people may pay off, but watch out for any sour, self-defeating attitudes. Do you find yourself getting more critical of others? Are you beginning to think that people are selfish, shallow, and uncaring? Such negative attitudes can have the force of a self-fulfilling prophecy: What you expect may be what you get. Armed with negative, even hostile, attitudes about others, your behavior is unlikely to be very charming, and their reactions are unlikely to provide the warm acceptance you desire. Taking a more positive approach—actively looking for others' good qualities—has a much better chance of success.

4. But what if you dutifully do all of the above and you are still lonely? Could this mean that, despite your good intentions, you are being tripped up by inadequate social skills? Possibly. Some people can benefit from social skills training provided by therapists or counseling centers. But there is another possible factor involved: What sort of relationship are you looking for? In another study of college freshmen across their entire first year in college (Cutrona, 1982), those who believed that only a successful romance could reduce their loneliness tended to stay lonely all year. In contrast, the students who became less lonely as the school year progressed placed greater emphasis on just forming new friendships. This pattern has also been obtained in other studies (Rook & Peplau, 1982; Schmidt & Sermat, 1983), so simply seeking new friends may be a better way of coping with loneliness than desperately seeking Mr. or Ms. Right.

Loneliness as a Growth Experience

Improving our social relations is one straightforward way to reduce or avoid loneliness. Another valuable approach is to turn the negative, unpleasant state of loneliness into the positive, enjoyable state of solitude. Too often, our reaction to even mild feelings of loneliness is to immediately seek others' company. As an alternative, consider the opportunities available in active solitude, particularly those that are pleasure-oriented rather than work-related. We all have things we really like to do but never seem to have the time for. Feelings of boredom, restlessness, and loneliness can be signals that now we do have the time. Perhaps you like long, leisurely bubble baths, or a walk in the woods, or good novels that you never have time to read. To turn loneliness into solitude, it's not the specific activity you choose that matters; what counts is your attitude toward the activity. If you seek distraction or oblivion, you have not found solitude (Leary et al., 2003). But if you immerse yourself in an activity that you enjoy for its own sake, you can appreciate your moment of solitude without fretting over being lonely.

One of the great benefits of being able to enjoy solitude is that we learn that we can take good care of ourselves and need not depend on other people to make us happy. Such an awareness is not a barrier to having intimate ties with others. Indeed, the ability to be comfortably alone with oneself may enhance our capacity to love others (Branden, 1980; Safilios-Rothschild, 1981). If we

Solitary activities can help widows and others avoid loneliness.

always need rewarding interactions with other people in order to be happy, this places a terrible burden on them—one they may not be willing or able to bear. Furthermore, being alone (physically or psychologically) can be used to develop an understanding of our own needs, feelings, and perspective on life. And the more self-knowledge we have, the better equipped we may be to have realistic, accepting, and loving relationships with others. It is by no means easy to face ourselves and our aloneness in the world; it can, however, be an enormously enriching experience. As the British historian Edward Gibbon once remarked, "I was never less alone than when by myself."

These two strategies of transformation—turning loneliness into solitude and using aloneness to gain self-knowledge—provide a balance to reducing loneliness through improving or extending our social relations. Much of healthy personal growth consists of promoting such a balance—of trying to develop satisfying relationships with other people and of trying to create a secure, internal base of satisfaction within ourselves.

FOR YOUR CONSIDERATION

Cary suffered a couple of unhappy blows during his senior year in high school when his parents divorced and his girlfriend moved to another state. He had always been a little shy, and it had taken him some time to get up the nerve to ask her out in the first place, and he was distraught when she left. So when he went off to college, he was eager to replace her. He looked forward to all the women he would meet, and he daydreamed about how assertive he would be when he talked to them. But every time he chatted with an attractive girl, he still felt shy and awkward, and when Fall Weekend arrived, he didn't have a date. His desire to have a girlfriend increased, and he started feeling lonely. He thought that all he needed to be happy was a girlfriend, but he began to think that most of the women he met were only interested in better-looking rich guys. He started blaming them for being shallow and selfish.

What do you think the future holds for Cary? Why?

CHAPTER SUMMARY

Shyness and loneliness are common problems that have interpersonal effects that may make it harder for people to establish the new relationships they seek.

Shyness

Most people have experienced shyness, the syndrome that combines inhibited social behavior with nervous discomfort in social settings. Shy people fret about social disapproval and manage small talk poorly. Those who are chronically shy display high fear of negative evaluation, low self-esteem, and poor social skills; thus, they worry about what other people are thinking of them but feel incapable of making favorable impressions that would avoid any disapproval. The irony in this is that by behaving in such a timid manner, shy people often make the negative impressions that they were hoping to avoid.

Programs designed to reduce shyness usually focus on positive thinking and social skills. Many shy people do not need skills training, however, because they stay relaxed and interact comfortably with others when they are given an excuse for the interaction to go poorly. Greater calm and self-confidence, however obtained, will help most of those who are shy.

Loneliness

Loneliness is a feeling of deprivation and dissatisfaction produced by a *discrepancy* between the kind of social relations one has and the kind one desires. Two different types of loneliness have been identified: *social isolation* created by lack of a social network of friends and acquaintances, and *emotional isolation* based on the lack of a single intense relationship.

Measuring Loneliness. The UCLA Loneliness Scale is the most widely used measure of adult loneliness. Its items have three themes: they assess isolation, deficiencies in close connections with others, and deficiencies in social connection to people in general.

How Does It Feel to Be Lonely? A variety of emotions and desires can accompany loneliness, but desperation, impatient boredom, self-deprecation, and depression are recurring feelings.

Does Loneliness Matter? Although some forms of loneliness are fleeting, minor experiences, loneliness is associated with several serious problems.

These include running away from home, crime and delinquency, academic problems, sleep disturbances, poor mental health, and poor physical health.

Who's Lonely? Loneliness is widespread, but Americans are more lonely, on average, than the citizens of many other countries. Wealthier people are less prone to loneliness, and married people are less lonely than are those who have experienced the loss of a relationship through separation, divorce, or death of the partner. People with insecure attachment styles and an identical twin who is lonely tend to be lonely, too.

Men are lonelier than women, but they're less willing to admit it, and with good reason: Lonely men are evaluated more negatively by others than are lonely women. An intimate relationship with a woman tends to make a macho man much less lonely, but androgynous men, who are high in expressivity, are less dependent on women to keep from being lonely.

Loneliness across the Lifespan. Lonely people recall having had cold, remote parents. Children of divorce are also prone to loneliness. In general, adolescents and young adults are lonelier than older people are; loneliness decreases with age from adolescence to middle-age. Loneliness may increase some in old age, especially among those who are incapacitated or widowed, but young adults are usually more lonely than the elderly are.

Possible Causes and Moderators of Loneliness

There are several possible primary causes of loneliness.

Inadequacies in Our Relationships. The reasons people give for being lonely involve five major categories: being unattached, alienation, being alone, forced isolation, and dislocation. These reasons cover a broad range, with some being situational in nature and others possibly involving personal characteristics of the lonely person.

Changes in What We Want from Our Relationships. As people change with age, what they want from their relationships may also change. If their relationships do not change accordingly, they may experience loneliness.

Causal Attributions. Explanations for loneliness may also increase its duration. College freshmen who make internal, stable attributions for their loneliness in the fall are more likely to still be lonely in the spring than are those who identify unstable reasons for their distress.

Interpersonal Behaviors. Lonely people tend to have low self-esteem, and they hold negative attitudes toward others and lack social skills. Their passive and unresponsive interpersonal behavior can irritate and annoy others, eliciting social rejection that can make their loneliness worse. Loneliness is also correlated with depression. Regrettable, temporary situations can cause us to be lonely, but if we don't cope effectively, loneliness may become a sadly persistent burden.

Coping with Loneliness

People appear to engage in a wide variety of behaviors when they are lonely. Some of these behaviors involve active, constructive coping, but others are potentially self-defeating.

What Helps People Feel Less Lonely? Adaptive ways to reduce loneliness may include (1) doing a rational cost analysis of risky social situations to decide whether the potential gain warrants taking the risk, (2) looking for situational causes of loneliness rather than blaming your own personal characteristics, (3) maintaining a positive attitude toward others, and (4) concentrating on enriching friendships rather than searching for a romantic partner.

Loneliness as a Growth Experience. Sometimes, loneliness can be transformed into a constructive experience. Using time alone to engage in pleasurable behaviors can turn loneliness into solitude. Using time alone effectively can also contribute to self-knowledge, which may strengthen our capacity for establishing intimate relationships with others.

CHAPTER 15

Maintaining and Repairing Relationships

MAINTAINING AND ENHANCING RELATIONSHIPS ◆ Staying Committed ◆
Staying Content ◆ REPAIRING RELATIONSHIPS ◆ Do It Yourself ◆
Preventive Maintenance ◆ Marital Therapy ◆ IN CONCLUSION ◆
FOR YOUR CONSIDERATION ◆ CHAPTER SUMMARY

This is our last chapter, and we're getting near the end of this book. So, it's time to take stock. What do you know now that you didn't know before we started? Only you know for sure, but here are some possibilities:

- The styles of behavior that are often expected of men—the styles that encourage them to be assertive and self-reliant but that do not encourage them to be warm and tender—do not train them to be very desirable partners in long-term intimate relationships.
- People with low self-esteem sometimes sabotage their own relationships by making mountains out of molehills and perceiving rejection where none exists.
- Proximity, familiarity, and convenience are influential in determining whether or not rewarding relationships ever begin. There may be lots of people with whom we could have wonderful relationships that we'll simply never meet.
- Looks matter, and if you're not physically attractive, a lot of people will pass you by instead of wanting to get to know you.
- We don't know or understand our romantic partners as well as we think we do; a lot of misperception persists even in successful relationships.
- People try hard to make good impressions on us when we're getting to know them, but they put less effort into being polite, decorous, and delightful once we like or love them.
- Men generally do not do as well at nonverbal communication as women do, and deficiencies in nonverbal communication are correlated with dissatisfaction in close relationships.
- More often than we realize, our partners do not receive the messages we intend to send when we talk with them.
- Bad is stronger than good, and the occasional sour or critical interactions we have with our partners are more influential than the nice things we do for them.

457

- Over the long haul, intimate relationships are much more costly than we usually expect them to be.
- Romantic, passionate love is one of the primary reasons we choose to marry, but it tends to decline over time.
- About one third of us are not comfortable and relaxed with interdependent intimacy; we either worry that our partners don't love us enough, or we are ill at ease when they get too close.
- Men tend to want more sex than women do, and frustration often results.
- Sooner or later, it's likely that our partners will betray us in some manner that causes us hurt and pain.
- Conflict is unavoidable.
- Marriages are less happy, on average, than they used to be, and divorce is more common.

Yikes. That's quite a list. And it's just a sampling of the various topics we have considered; several other influences, such as the personality traits of neuroticism and narcissism, or the states of jealousy or loneliness, create difficulties in close relationships, too.

Altogether, these patterns may paint a gloomy picture, and, indeed, the surprisingly low success rates of modern marriages suggest that many partnerships are not as wonderful as we hope they will be. On the other hand, there are also a lot of optimistic facts among the topics we have considered. Here are a few:

- A lot of men, about one third of them, are just as warm and tender and sensitive and kind as women routinely are. And those that aren't can probably learn to be warmer and more expressive than they are now.
- Happy lovers perceive their partners and explain their behavior in generous ways that give the partners the benefit of any doubt and portray them as kind and caring even when they occasionally misbehave.

Relationships are complex, and they are usually more costly than we expect them to be. But now that you've read this book, you shouldn't be as pessimistic as this comic strip character is.

Reprinted by permission of TMS Reprints.

Jeff Macnelly's Shoe

- Most people seek and are comfortable in an interdependent and intimate relationship with a romantic partner.
- In happy relationships, when passion decreases, it is replaced by a deep, affectionate friendship that is rich and warm and satisfying to those who experience it.
- Authentic forgiveness benefits both the recipient and the giver, and it is easiest to attain in those close, satisfying relationships that are most worth saving.
- Perhaps most importantly, almost all of us can be more thoughtful, more charming, and more rewarding romantic partners if we try to be. Men do as well as women at nonverbal communication when they are equally motivated to get it right. We can reduce or eliminate verbal misunderstandings when we take the time to check the accuracy of our interpretations. And with attentive effort, we can be more polite, less selfish, more considerate, and less critical toward our partners than we would otherwise be.

There are lots of reasons to hope that, with wisdom and work, we can live happily ever after. Indeed, the authors of your book firmly assert that "knowledge is power": With better understanding of close relationships, people are better equipped to prevent some problems and to readily overcome others. And the best news of all may be that people who are committed to their partnerships engage in a variety of actions that help to protect and maintain the satisfaction they enjoy. Furthermore, if they occur, many problems can be repaired, and many wounds can be healed. Couples who encounter disappointments in their relationships are often able to fully surmount their difficulties, if they wish.

In this concluding chapter, then, we survey both the mechanisms with which partners perpetuate their satisfaction and the interventions with which faltering contentment can be restored. Despite the hurdles that must be overcome, many relationships not only survive, they thrive.

MAINTAINING AND ENHANCING RELATIONSHIPS

We introduced the idea that people often behave in various ways that protect and maintain desirable relationships back in chapter 6 (on pages 213–214). **Relationship maintenance mechanisms,** the strategic actions people take to sustain their partnerships, have been studied by researchers from two different scholarly camps. Social psychologists schooled in Caryl Rusbult's *investment model*[1] have identified several behaviors that seem to follow from commitment to a relationship, and communication scholars have noted other actions that distinguish happy partners from those who are less content. Let's examine both sets of findings.

---

[1]We suspect a look back at page 211 will come in handy.

Staying Committed

People who are committed to a partnership, who want and expect it to continue, think and behave differently than less committed partners do (Reesing & Cate, 2004). They perceive themselves, their partners, and their relationship in ways that help to sustain the partnership, and they act in ways that avoid or defuse conflict and that enrich the relationship.

Cognitive Maintenance Mechanisms

People's perspectives change in several important ways when they are committed to their relationships. First, they think of themselves not as separate individuals but as part of a greater whole that includes them *and* their partners. They perceive greater overlap between their partners' lives and their own, and they use more plural pronouns, with *we, us,* and *ours* replacing *I, me,* and *mine* (Agnew et al., 1998). This change in self-definition is referred to as **cognitive interdependence,** and it probably makes some of the other maintenance mechanisms we mention below more likely to occur (Rusbult et al., 2001).

Second, committed partners think of each other with **positive illusions,** idealizing each other and perceiving their relationship in the best possible light (Gagné & Lydon, 2003; Murray et al., 1996b). A partner's faults are judged to be relatively trivial, the relationship's deficiencies are considered to be relatively unimportant, and a partner's misbehavior is dismissed as an unintentional or temporary aberration (Neff & Karney, 2003). A characteristic that makes these positive illusions interesting is that people are often well aware of the specific obnoxious and thoughtless things their partners sometimes do, but by misremembering them and explaining them away, they are able to maintain global evaluations of their partners that are more positive than the sum of their parts (Karney, McNulty, & Frye, 2001). And as long as they are not too unrealistic, these rose-colored perceptions help protect people's happiness by taking the sting out of a partner's occasional missteps.

A specific type of positive illusion can be said to be a third cognitive maintenance mechanism. Committed partners tend to think that their relationships are better than most, and the happier they are, the more exceptional they consider their relationships to be (Buunk, 2001). This **perceived superiority** makes one's partnership seem even more special (Buunk & Ybema, 2003) and really does make a relationship more likely to last (Rusbult et al., 2000).

Satisfied partners are also less likely to be on the prowl, looking for other lovers. Attractive rivals can distract our partners and lure them away from us only when our partners know they exist, but contented partners display an **inattention to alternatives** that leaves them relatively uninterested and unaware of how well they could be doing in alternative relationships. People who are not very committed to their current partnerships monitor their other options with more inquisitiveness and eagerness than do those who are more content with what they've already got; given the chance in a lab procedure, for instance, they linger longer and inspect more carefully photos of attractive members of the other sex (Miller, 1997a). Uncommitted lovers continue to shop around for better partners, and that puts their current relationships at risk: Young adults who are alert to their other options at the beginning of a college semester are less likely to still be with the same romantic partner when the semester is done (Simeon & Miller, 2005). In contrast, committed lovers are relatively heedless of how well they could be doing in other relationships— they're not paying much attention to such possibilities—and that helps to protect and maintain their current partnerships.

Finally, when committed partners do notice attractive rivals to their relationships, they judge them to be less desirable alternatives than others think them to be. Commitment leads people to disparage those who could lure them away from their existing relationships (Lydon, Fitzsimons, & Naidoo, 2003), and this **derogation of tempting alternatives** allows people to feel that other potential partners are less attractive than the ones they already have. One of the things that makes this perceptual bias interesting is that committed partners happily appreciate gorgeous others who are no threat to their relationships, but they find ways to undervalue those who could realistically undermine their existing loves (Lima, Thomas, & Maio, 2004). Here's an example. In one study of the derogation effect, students at Texas A&M University were presented with images of attractive members of the other sex who were said to be professional models in New York City (Simpson, Gangestad, & Lerma, 1990). Similar, very positive evaluations of the models were provided both by those who were and those who were not committed to a dating relationship, so there was no derogation effect when the models were supposedly somewhere far away. But other people were led to believe that the attractive images were of fellow students on campus, and in that condition, when the models could be potential threats to their relationships, committed partners considered them to be less attractive than uncommitted people did. In order to protect their relationships, then, happy lovers tend to underestimate how well they could be doing with other potential partners.

Behavioral Maintenance Mechanisms

As you can see, the cognitive things people do to maintain their relationships generally involve subtle changes in perception or judgment of others, their relationships, and themselves. Other maintenance mechanisms involve changes in the things people do.

For one thing, committed people are often willing to make various personal sacrifices, such as doing things they would prefer not to do, or not doing things that they would like to do, in order to promote the well-being of their partners or their relationships (Van Lange et al., 1997; Whitton, Stanley, & Markman, 2002). This **willingness to sacrifice** often involves trivial costs such as seeing a movie that doesn't interest you because your partner wants to go, but it can also involve substantial costs in which people endure rather long periods of deprivation in order to preserve or enrich their partnerships. If you're already married, for instance, your spouse may be having to go to a lot of trouble to help you go to school; but, if he or she is committed to your future together, that's a price that many spouses will be willing to pay.

Relationships are also likely to prosper when our partners behave toward us in ways that encourage us to gradually become the people that we want to be. When our partners encourage us to be all that we can be—supporting the development of skills we want to learn, endorsing our acceptance of promising new roles and responsibilities, and promoting the self-growth we seek—both our relationships and our personal well-being are enhanced (Drigotas, 2002). This is the **Michelangelo phenomenon,** named for the famous sculptor who created uplifting works of art from ordinary blocks of stone (Drigotas, Rusbult, Wieselquist, & Whitton, 1999). People are rarely done growing and changing when their partnerships begin, and they remain more committed to a relationship when their partners help them become who they wish to be.

Committed lovers also tend to swallow minor mistreatment from their partners without biting back. This is **accommodation,** the willingness to control the impulse to respond in kind to a partner's provocation and to instead respond constructively (Rusbult et al., 1998; Rusbult et al., 1991). Accommodation occurs when people tolerate a partner's bad mood, pointless criticism, thoughtlessness, and other nuisances with placidity and poise. It does not involve martyrdom; to the contrary, as long as a partner's offenses are only occasional or temporary, accommodation provides an effective means of avoiding useless conflict that might merely perpetuate an aversive interaction. And when both partners are inclined to "stay cool" instead of "fighting fire with fire," they tend to have a happy relationship (Rusbult et al., 2001).

We should note, however, that accommodation takes work. It involves active self-control—biting one's tongue and holding one's temper—and people are less able to be accommodating when they are stressed, distracted, or tired (Finkel & Campbell, 2001). This and other mechanisms of relationship maintenance, such as being inattentive to attractive alternatives (Vohs, 2004), require conscious effort, so lazy people are less likely than others to have satisfying, lasting relationships.

At least one behavioral maintenance mechanism, though, may be easier to enact: **play.** Couples are usually content when they find ways to engage in novel, challenging, exciting, and pleasant activities together (Aron et al., 2002). In short, those that play together tend to stay together. In formal studies of this simple truth, couples have been tied together on one side at the wrists and ankles and invited to crawl through an obstacle course while pushing a foam cylinder with their heads (Aron et al., 2000). Prizes could be won if they completed the course quickly enough, so the task was exciting, goofy fun. Compared to couples who engaged in a more mundane activity, those that played like this felt that their relationships were of higher quality when the day was done. And sure enough, out in the real world, spouses who get up and go out to hike, bike, dance, or to attend concerts, lectures, and shows feel that their marriages are of higher quality than do those who just stay home and watch television (Aron, Norman, & Aron, 2001). Finding time to play in inventive and creative ways is beneficial in close relationships.

Finally, those who are committed to a partnership are more likely to offer **forgiveness** after a partner's betrayal (Finkel et al., 2002). Forgiveness quickens the healing of both the relationship and the partner who was wronged—it is less stressful to forgive an intimate partner than to nurse a grudge—so forgiveness promotes good health both in relationships and in those who give it (Lewis & Adler, 2004).

Staying Content

A second collection of maintenance activities has been identified by communication scholars Dan Canary and Laura Stafford (2001), who distilled hundreds of reports (including 500 term papers from college students) describing what people did to maintain their relationships into the manageable number of categories that appear in Table 15.1. As you can see, contented partners try to foster *positivity*, being polite, staying cheerful, and remaining upbeat; they encourage *openness* and self-disclosure, sharing their own thoughts and feelings and inviting their partners to do the same; they provide *assurances* that announce their love, commitment, and regard for each other; they share a *social network*, having friends in common and spending time with their partner's family; and they *share tasks* around the home in an equitable fashion, handling their fair share of

TABLE 15.1. Canary and Stafford's Relational Maintenance Strategies

Strategy	Examples
Positivity	Try to be cheerful and to act nice Attempt to make our interactions enjoyable
Openness	Encourage him or her to disclose thoughts and feelings to me Seek to discuss the quality of our relationship
Assurances	Stress my commitment to him or her Imply that our relationship has a future
Sharing a Social Network	Focus on common friends and affiliations Show that I am willing to do things with his or her friends and family
Sharing Tasks	Help equally with tasks that need to be done Do my fair share of the work we have to do
Sharing Activities	Share time with him or her Share specific routine activities with him or her
Support	Seek advice Comfort him or her in time of need
Conflict Management	Apologize when I am wrong Be patient and forgiving with my partner
Avoidance	Avoid discussing certain topics Respect each other's privacy and his or her need to be alone
Humor	Call him or her by a funny nickname Tease him or her

Source: Stafford, 2003.

household responsibilities. There are some topics that contented partners choose to avoid, but they also seek to provide *support* to one another, to maintain good *humor,* and to spend sufficient time together, and they apologize when they are wrong.

Similar activities are used to maintain close friendships (Oswald, Clark, & Kelly, 2004), and that should be no surprise. If you take a look back at the components of intimacy (way back on p. 4 in chapter 1), you'll see that most of the maintenance mechanisms identified by Canary and Stafford promote and encourage intimacy between friends and lovers. Knowledge, caring, interdependence, mutuality, trust, and commitment are all likely to be enhanced by maintenance strategies that involve openness, assurances of one's love and commitment, reliable support, and plenty of shared friends and activities. The actions people take to stay happy in close relationships seem to involve the creation and preservation of rewarding intimacy with their partners.

Furthermore, these various actions seem to work. Partners who routinely do the things listed in Table 15.1 enjoy greater fondness for each other and greater commitment to their relationships than do those who work less hard to maintain their partnerships (Canary, Stafford, & Semic, 2002; Stafford, 2003). And don't fret if you find the long list of activities in Table 15.1 a little daunting because three of them may be more important than the others and they're easy to remember. Of the bunch, the best predictors of how happy a marriage will be are positivity, assurances, and sharing tasks (Canary et al., 2002; Dainton, 2000). Spouses who do their fair share of housework, who are typically in good spirits, and who regularly express their love and regard for their partners are especially likely to be happily wed.

We do have a cautionary note, however: Kindnesses done a partner on Valentine's Day are unlikely to still be keeping him or her satisfied on the Fourth of July. Canary and his colleagues (2002) found that the beneficial effects of these maintenance mechanisms were short-lived: If these desirable activities stopped, contentment soon began to decline. The clear implication is that in order to maintain happy relationships, we have to *keep at it.* We need to be routinely cheerful, loving, and fair, and those of us who take occasional breaks from being generous, jovial, and affectionate toward our partners do so at our peril.

REPAIRING RELATIONSHIPS

The maintenance mechanisms that protect and preserve relationships have something in common with taking good care of your car. If you shopped wisely and made a good buy, you're likely to be a happy driver if you conscientiously engage in a consistent program of thoughtful maintenance, regularly changing the oil, adding antifreeze, and generally taking care of business. Still, sooner or later, despite your efforts, things may break, and a repair rather than a tune-up will be in order. If the repair is simple, you may want to do it yourself, but there may also be occasions in which you'll need professional help. Happily, when relationships break, as with cars, help is available.

Do It Yourself

One way to solve the problems we encounter in our relationships is to fix them ourselves. No one knows our feelings better than we do, and motivated, attentive laypeople are often every bit as good at distinguishing happy from unhappy couples as trained professionals are (Ebling & Levenson, 2003). On the other hand, our perceptions of our own behavior tend to be contaminated by self-serving biases, and it's sometimes hard for people to recognize how they are contributing to the relational difficulties they face.

Nevertheless, if you want to do it yourself, there's plenty of advice available. Television shows, magazines, and self-help books are full of suggestions that may help you improve your relationships. And consumers of this material often feel that the advice has been helpful; people who read self-help books, for instance, usually feel that the books were beneficial to them (Ellis, 1993).

There are often problems, however, with the popular advice the media provide. For one thing, the backgrounds of people who freely give advice are sometimes as bogus as the advice itself; there are well-known authors who boast of their "Ph.D." degrees who either did not graduate from an accredited university or did not study a helping profession in graduate school. In addition, some advisors do not base their counsel on sound research; instead, they give voice to their personal opinions, which are sometimes at odds with the facts (Halliday, 1991).

On other occasions, advisors imply that change is simple and easy to achieve, thus encouraging people to be overly optimistic about their abilities to resolve their difficulties on their own. And because such advice is given to general audiences, it isn't tailored to the specific situations individuals face. Relevant, explicit directions on what to do are often lacking, and even if the guidelines provided are fairly clear, there may be no objective observer who can monitor the partners' compliance with the instructions or provide corrective feedback on implementing them.

The biggest problem of all, though, is that lay advice may be simply wrong, and its popularity often has nothing to do with its accuracy. Back in chapter 1, we mentioned that relationship scientists disagree strongly with the simple-minded notion that "men are from Mars and women are from Venus"; now that you've read this book, what do you think?

Here's another example. A book entitled, *The Rules: Time-Tested Secrets for Capturing the Heart of Mr. Right,* was a #1 "nonfiction" bestseller a few years ago. According to its authors (Fein & Schneider, 1995), *The Rules* described "a simple way of acting around men that can help any woman win the heart of the man of her dreams" (p. 5). If readers followed the advice provided, "he will not just marry you, but feel crazy about you forever! What we're promising you is 'happily ever after'" (p. 6). Sounds great, doesn't it? Unfortunately, the rules were wrong. In order to enhance their desirability, readers were advised to stay aloof and mysterious and to avoid seeming too eager to develop a new relationship. As the authors admitted, "in plain language, we're talking about playing hard to get" (p. 6). But playing hard-to-get doesn't work, and relationship science has known that for more than 30 years. Men are not particularly attracted to women who artificially delay the progress of a developing relationship; what's attractive to a man is a desirable woman who plays hard-to-get for everyone *but him* (Walster, Walster, & Piliavin, 1973). Specifically, *The Rules* instructed women to avoid seeing a man more than twice a week, to avoid much self-disclosure early on, and to avoid telling him what they did when they were apart, and these and other rules are *negatively* correlated with men's commitment to a new partner (Agnew & Gephart, 2000). On the whole, women who followed *The Rules* probably had more trouble attracting and keeping men than did other women. That's not very useful advice.

Of course, not all popular advice is flawed, and some of it is very credible. Some self-help books, for instance, are written by reputable, well-respected scientists (e.g., Doherty, 2001; Gottman & Silver, 1999). And on the positive side, such help is inexpensive. Readers of self-help books can refer to them many times, going back to absorb material at their own pace. Credible books may also be acceptable to people who are ashamed or who, for other reasons, can't or won't seek formal therapy. They may also provide readers a positive attitude and general encouragement that facilitates their efforts to address their problems.

Along those lines, let us acknowledge that we're glad you read *this* book. We did not design this text as a self-help book, but we hope that the information we gathered here has been useful to you. We believe that there is enormous value in the scientific study of close relationships, and we hope that we have provided you material that will help you understand your own relationships with more sophistication. We suspect that there's a lot here that you can apply to your own situation to enjoy even richer, more rewarding partnerships.

Preventive Maintenance

There are also occasions, when you're taking care of your car, when the smart thing to do is to invest in major maintenance *before* anything goes wrong. After a few years, for instance, you should replace your timing belt; it's a part inside a gasoline engine that, at best, will leave you stranded, or, at worse, will destroy your engine if it breaks. It's an expensive change to make, and when your engine is running fine, it's easy to put off. But there's no question that it's a wise choice.

Similarly, couples who are engaged to be married usually feel that they're sailing along just fine, and there's no need to prepare for the new phase of their relationship that wedlock will bring. However, some preventive maintenance may be valuable then, too. Before problems begin, fine-tuning a couple's expectations and communication skills may pay big dividends.

Premarital counseling is available in various forms ranging from informal visits with a pastor, priest, or rabbi to structured training under the guidance of psychologists or marriage and family therapists. (Monarch et al., 2002, provide a broad review of these programs.) To keep things simple here, we'll inspect the PREP program, which is perhaps the best known relationship skills course.

The Prevention and Relationship Enhancement Program, or PREP, typically involves about ten hours of training spread across five sessions (Markman et al.,

1994). Meetings focus on several topics that may be familiar by now to readers of this book:

- The power of commitment to change partners' outlooks and behavior. Couples are encouraged to take a long-range view of the future they are striving to create together.
- The importance of having fun together. Couples are urged to make a point of playing together on a regular basis.
- The value of open communication about sex. Couples are advised to express their desires clearly and openly and to try something new every now and then.
- The consequences of inappropriate expectations. Couples are encouraged to be aware of their expectations, to be reasonable in what they expect, and to communicate their expectations clearly.

Participants are also taught to manage conflict constructively and to solve problems collaboratively with a procedure that is the centerpiece of the PREP program, the **speaker-listener technique.** The technique provides a structure for calm, clear communication about contentious issues that promotes the use of active listening skills and increases the chances that partners will understand and validate each other despite their disagreement.[2] In particular, the speaker-listener technique is designed to interrupt the cycle of misperception that too often occurs when partners respond quickly to one another without checking their understanding of the other's intent.

To use the technique, the partners designate a small object as the *floor.* (See Table 15.2.) Whoever has the floor is the speaker. That partner's job is to concisely describe his or her feelings using "I-statements"; the listener's job is to listen without interrupting and then to paraphrase the speaker's message. When the speaker is satisfied that his or her feelings have been understood, the floor changes hands and the partners switch roles. This patient pattern of careful communication allows the partners to demonstrate their concern and respect for the other's feelings without falling into a noxious cycle of self-justification, mindreading, interruption, and defensiveness.

Does the PREP program work? In general, the answer seems to be yes. The average person who participates in a premarital prevention program like PREP is better off afterwards than 79 percent of those who do not participate (Carroll & Doherty, 2003). Some critics have argued that people are unlikely to use the speaker-listener technique when they most need it—that is, when they become frustrated or angry at what (they think) their partner is saying (Gottman et al., 2000)—but, regardless, the package of skills and insights provided by the PREP program are associated with increased satisfaction once a couple is married. For the first three or four years of their marriages, newlyweds who receive PREP training are more content than are those who do not receive such training (Freedman et al., 2002). Most of the participants in studies of the PREP approach

---

[2]If the terms "active listening" and "validation" don't ring any bells, we invite you to look back at pages 174–177 in chapter 5.

TABLE 15.2. The Speaker-Listener Technique

Want to stay cool when a discussion gets heated? Consider following these rules:

Rules for Both of You

1. *The Speaker has the floor.* Use a real object, such as a book or TV remote control, as the floor. Whoever holds the floor is the only person who gets to say anything until he or she is done.

2. *Share the floor.* When you're Speaker, don't go on and on. Keep each turn brief, and switch roles often as the floor changes hands.

3. *No problem solving.* The point of the technique is to delineate a disagreement, not to solve it. Collaborative brainstorming to solve the problem comes later.

Rules for the Speaker

4. *Speak for yourself. Don't try to be a mind reader.* Use "I" statements to describe your own thoughts, feelings, and concerns. Do not talk about your perceptions of your partner's motives or point of view.

5. *Stop and let the Listener paraphrase.* After a short time, stop and allow the Listener to paraphrase what you've just said. If he or she is not quite accurate, politely restate any points of confusion. The goal is to help the Listener really understand you.

Rules for the Listener

6. *Paraphrase what you hear.* Show the Speaker that you are listening by repeating back in your own words what you heard him or her say. The point is to make sure that you understood what was said.

7. *Focus on the Speaker's message. Don't rebut.* You should not offer your thoughts and opinions on the issue until you have the floor. Your job as Listener is to speak only in the service of understanding your partner.

Does this sound awkward? Perhaps, but it has its uses. As its creators suggest, the Speaker-Listener technique "isn't a normal way to communicate, but it is a relatively safe way to communicate on a difficult issue. Each person will get to talk, each will be heard, and both will show their commitment to discussing the problems constructively" (Markman et al., 1994, p. 67).

Note: Adapted from Markman, Stanley, & Blumberg, 1994.

---

have been middle-class whites, and the long-term effects of the training are uncertain; we still don't know, for instance, whether couples who received PREP training are less likely than other couples to ultimately divorce. Nevertheless, in this case, some premarital preventive maintenance appears to facilitate a few years of smooth sailing when marriages begin.

Marital Therapy

Once real problems emerge, more intensive interventions may be needed. Marital therapy takes several different forms, and there are several ways in which professionals can intervene. Consider these possibilities:

Individual therapy. One of the partners discusses the client's relationship with his or her own therapist.

Collaborative therapy. Both partners have their own therapists, and the two therapists consult each other about their clients.

Concurrent therapy. One therapist sees each of the two partners in separate, individual sessions.

Conjoint therapy. One therapist sees both partners together in the same session. Sometimes there are cotherapists (often one man and one woman) involved in the conjoint sessions.

Conjoint group therapy. One or more therapists works with several couples in group sessions.

Of these options, conjoint therapy is the most common, but people in troubled relationships often profit from individual therapy even when their partners refuse to seek help with them.

There are also a variety of therapeutic approaches that professional helpers may use. Three different broad types of therapies appear to be helpful for most people most of the time, and we'll survey them next. As we'll see, they differ with regard to (a) their focus on problematic behavior, thoughts, or feelings; (b) their focus on individual vulnerabilities or the couple and their interaction as the source of dysfunction; and (c) their emphasis on past events or present difficulties as the source of distress (Baucom, Epstein, & Stanton, in press).

Behavioral Approaches

Most of the time, unhappy spouses aren't very nice to each other, and a classic intervention, **behavioral couple therapy** (or BCT), encourages them to be more pleasant and rewarding partners. BCT focuses on the couple's present interactions and seeks to replace any negative and punishing behavior with more gracious and generous actions. Couples are taught communication skills that help them express affection and manage conflict coolly, and they are specifically encouraged to do things that benefit and please their partners. (See Box 15.1.)

Desirable behavior is elicited in several ways. Therapists may schedule "love days" (Weiss, Hops, & Patterson, 1973) in which one partner deliberately sets out to do favors and kindnesses that are requested by the other. Alternatively, the couple may enter into agreements to reward positive behavior from their partners with desirable behavior of their own. In one such agreement, a *quid pro quo contract*[3], behavior change from one partner is directly linked to behavior change by the other (Jacobson & Margolin, 1979). For instance, she may agree to do the laundry every Sunday if he cleans the bathroom on Saturday, and he'll clean the bathroom if she did the laundry on the previous Sunday. This sort of contract fails to increase positive exchanges if either partner falters, so *good faith contracts*, parallel agreements in which behavior change is rewarded

---

[3]*Quid pro quo* is Latin that means "something for something."

BOX 15.1

An Example of Behavioral Couple Therapy

Here is an example of BCT in action. (The names have been changed.) Sharon O'Sullivan was an attractive 32-year-old woman who said that her marriage was suffering from lack of communication, lack of mutual interests, sexual naiveté, and decreasing affection. She felt that she had a low tolerance for frustration and that she was depressed. She was a homemaker with three children, aged eight, five, and three. Sharon was very dissatisfied, she reported feeling like a prisoner, and she resented her husband's "over-involvement" in Alcoholics Anonymous. Paul O'Sullivan was a neat, reserved 35-year-old salesman who reported only one major marital problem, lack of communication. However, he reported that his wife displayed misdirected anger and had a minimal tolerance for the shortcomings of others. Paul had been a heavy drinker for the first nine years of their marriage but had been abstinent for the past three years after becoming an active member of A.A.

The O'Sullivans were initially interviewed separately for one hour and then seen for a total of ten conjoint sessions. The major treatment procedures included

1. Teaching communication skills; particular emphasis was placed on listening without interrupting and on avoiding punitive statements.

2. Encouraging Sharon to engage in more activities outside the home (for example, a women's group and Al Anon) to increase the positive feedback she might obtain from people other than her husband.

3. Encouraging both Sharon and Paul to volunteer to do things that satisfied each other's needs. They were asked to sign a weekly therapy plan sheet to indicate that they understood the nature of their behavior change agreements and that they were committed to making these changes. The necessity of mutual compromise as a vehicle for alleviating their marital distress was emphasized.

4. Prompting Paul to display some form of affectionate behavior once per day as improvements were made in the relationship.

5. Helping Sharon learn to ask Paul directly to meet more of her needs, especially her needs for his affection. In brief, she was encouraged to express her needs more straightforwardly.

6. Asking Sharon and Paul to consider the possibility that her criticism of A.A. and Paul's involvement in it (for example, "Most of the members are sick," and "You spend too much time there") resulted from his failure to be affectionate and to tell her at least several hours in advance that he would be going to a particular A.A. meeting.

7. Having Sharon contemplate the possibility that when Paul went to bed before she did and politely said "Good night," he was not putting her down and she need not feel unloved.

In summary, the treatment procedures included

1. Communication training.

2. Negotiation and compromise.

3. Behavior contracts to increase affectionate behavior.

4. The reinterpretation or relabeling of certain behaviors.

The therapy was deemed successful by the therapist and both clients.

Source: O'Leary & Turkewitz, 1978.

with special privileges, are also used (Weiss, Birchler, & Vincent, 1974). In a good faith contract, he may agree to clean the bathroom every Saturday, and when he does, he gets to choose the activity for that evening; she may agree to do the laundry every Sunday, and when she does, he assumes all the responsibility for bathing the children and putting them to bed that night.

Getting partners to behave more generously is important, but it doesn't always change the grudging disregard that distressed couples often feel for each other by the time they seek therapy. For that reason, a descendant of BCT focuses on partners' cognitions and judgments of their relationship as well as their conduct (Epstein & Baucom, 2002). In addition to encouraging desirable behavior, **cognitive-behavioral couple therapy** (or CBCT) seeks to change various aspects of the ways partners think about and appraise their partnership. The therapy addresses spouses' *selective attention*, their tendency to notice some things and to ignore others, and tries to instill more reasonable *expectancies*, more forgiving *attributions*, and more adaptive *relationship beliefs* in each partner. Participants are taught to track and test their thoughts, actively considering various attributions for any negative behavior, recognizing and challenging unrealistic beliefs, and generating lists of the pros and cons of the expectations they hold. CBCT acknowledges that people often import into their marriages problematic habits of thinking that they have learned in past relationships, but it still focuses mainly on current patterns in a couple's interaction; the idea is that, no matter where maladaptive cognition came from, a couple will be more content when they are able to perceive and judge each other fairly, kindly, and reasonably.

An even more recent descendant of BCT is **integrative behavioral couple therapy** (IBCT), an approach that seeks both to encourage more desirable behavior and to teach the partners to tolerantly accept the incompatibilities that they cannot change (Dimidjian, Martell, & Christensen, 2002). IBCT teaches the communication skills and employs the behavior modification techniques of BCT, but it also assumes that even when two partners behave desirably and well, some frustrating incompatibilities will always remain; for that reason, an important goal of therapy is to teach spouses adaptive emotional reactions to the nuisances they will inevitably face. Acceptance of one's own and one's partner's imperfections is promoted through three techniques (Wheeler & Christensen, 2002). With *empathic joining*, spouses are taught to express their pain and vulnerabilities without any blame or resentment that will make their partners defensive; the point is to engender empathy by helping each spouse understand the other's feelings. Spouses are also taught to view their problems with *unified detachment*, an intellectual perspective that defuses emotion and helps the couple understand their problematic patterns of interaction with cool dispassion. The couple is invited to describe the events that cause frustration and to identify the triggers that set them in motion while avoiding the negative emotion that usually results from such events. Finally, in *tolerance building*, spouses are taught to become less sensitive and to react less intensely when problematic behavior occurs; negative patterns of interaction are rehearsed and analyzed in therapy sessions, and the partners are actually encouraged to give

TABLE 15.3. Core Features of Marital Therapies

Therapeutic Approach	Behavior, Cognitions, or Emotions	Individual or Couple	Present or Past
	Primary Focus on		
Behavioral Couple Therapy	Behavior	Couple	Present
Cognitive-Behavioral Couple Therapy	Cognitions	Both	Present
Integrative Behavioral Couple Therapy	Emotions	Both	Present
Emotionally Focused Therapy	Emotions	Both	Present
Insight-Oriented Couple Therapy	Emotions & Cognitions	Individual	Past

Source: Adapted from Baucom, Epstein, & Stanton, in press.

up their efforts to change everything they dislike in each other. The focus of IBCT is on the couple's present patterns of interaction, whatever their origins, and it seeks collaborative change in both their interactive behavior and their individual emotional reactions to it.

Thus, the three behavioral approaches to marital therapy share a focus on the partners' actions with and toward each other, but they differ in their additional elements. BCT seeks to change spouses' behavior, whereas CBCT seeks to change their behavior and their cognitions, and IBCT seeks to change their behavior and their emotions. (See Table 15.4.) Each approach may appeal to some couples more than others, but, importantly, they all work (Baucom et al., in press). Between 60 and 70 percent of the couples who seriously undertake any of these therapies achieve notable reductions in their dissatisfaction and distress (Christensen et al., 2004).

Emotionally Focused Therapy

Another relatively recent innovation, emotionally focused couple therapy (or EFCT), is derived from attachment theory (Johnson, 2004). Like the behavioral approaches, EFCT seeks to reestablish desirable patterns of interaction between spouses, but its primary focus is on the emotions the partners experience as they seek to fulfill their attachment needs (Johnson & Denton, 2002). People are thought to need emotional security, and they seek it from their spouses, but frustration and distress can result when one spouse seeks reassurance and acceptance ineffectively and the other spouse responds in a negative manner. In one common pattern, a partner who wants more attention and affection will pursue it in a way that seems critical and blaming to the other, who then responds by retreating to an even greater distance. No one is soothed and no one is happy, and the cycle of obnoxious pursuit and withdrawal may intensify.

EFCT tries to identify such maladaptive cycles of emotional communication and to replace them with restructured interactions that allow the partners to feel

TABLE 15.4. Specific Steps in Emotionally Focused Couple Therapy

With the help of a therapist, couples who complete EFCT will encounter each of the following phases of treatment:

Stage One: Assessment of the Problem

    Step 1: Partners describe their problems, often describing a recent fight in detail.

    Step 2: Partners identify the emotional fears and needs that underlie their arguments.

    Step 3: Partners put their emotions into words, so that the other understands.

    Step 4: Partners realize that they're both hurting and neither of them is individually to blame.

Stage Two: Promoting New Styles of Interaction that Foster Bonding

    Step 5: Partners identify and admit their deepest feelings, including the need for reassurance, acceptance, and comfort.

    Step 6: Partners acknowledge and begin to accept the other's feelings; they also explore their own new responses to what they have learned.

    Step 7: Partners begin new patterns of interaction based in openness and understanding; they once again become allies rather than adversaries.

Stage Three: Rehearsal and Maintenance of Desirable New Styles of Interaction

    Step 8: Partners collaboratively invent new solutions to old problems.

    Step 9: Partners thoughtfully rehearse and consolidate their new, more accepting behavior toward one another.

Source: Adapted from Johnson & Denton, 2002, and Johnson, 2004.

safe, loved, and securely connected to one another. Three stages are involved (Johnson & Best, 2003). In the first, problematic patterns of communication of conflict are identified, and the couple is encouraged to think of themselves as collaborators united in a fight against a common foe; the therapist also helps the spouses explore the unmet needs for acceptance and security that fuel their conflict. In the second stage, the partners begin to establish constructive new patterns of interaction that acknowledge the other's needs and that provide more reassurance and comfort. Finally, in the third stage, the partners rehearse and reinforce their responsiveness to each other, and they rely on their newfound security to fearlessly seek new solutions to old problems. The entire process covers nine steps, which are listed in Table 15.4, during ten to twenty sessions of treatment.

    The focus of therapy is a couple's present interaction, but the partners are encouraged to consider how their individual needs contribute to their joint outcomes, so both individual and interactive sources of dysfunction are examined.

And EFCT is quite effective with couples who are moderately distressed, with about 70 percent of them overcoming their dissatisfaction by the time treatment is complete (Johnson, 2002).

Insight-Oriented Therapy

A final family of therapies has descended from the psychodynamic traditions of Sigmund Freud, who assumed that people often carried unconscious injuries and scars from their experiences in prior relationships that could, without their knowledge, complicate and contaminate their present partnerships. (See Box 15.2.) A variety of interventions seek to promote partners' insights into such problematic "baggage" (e.g., Gurman, 2002; Scharff & Bagnini, 2002), but a prototypical example of this approach is Douglas Snyder's (2002) insight-oriented couple therapy (IOCT). IOCT emphasizes individual vulnerabilities to a greater extent than the other therapies we have mentioned (see Table 15.3); it strives to help people comprehend how the personal habits and assumptions they developed in other relationships may be creating difficulty with their present partners. Thus, it also examines past events to a fuller extent than other therapies do; IOCT assumes that the origins of marital dissatisfaction often lie in difficulties the spouses encountered in prior relationships.

A primary tool of IOCT is *affective reconstruction*, the process through which a spouse re-imagines and revisits past relationships in an effort to identify the themes and coping styles that characterized conflicts with past partners (Snyder & Schneider, 2002). A person is guided through close inspection of his or her relational history, and careful attention is given to the patterns of any interpersonal injuries. The therapist then helps the client understand the connections that may exist between the themes of the person's past relationships and his or her present problems.

The insight that emerges from affective reconstruction helps the partners adopt more benign judgments of the other's behavior. Each spouse becomes more aware of his or her vulnerabilities, and the joint expression of fears and needs builds empathy between the partners. The therapist is also likely to portray both spouses as doing the best that they can, given their personal histories, so that blaming and acrimony are reduced. Then, because (as we've suggested before) knowledge is power, the spouses slowly construct new, more rewarding patterns of interaction that avoid the pitfalls of the past.

All of this typically takes fifteen to twenty sessions with a therapist. Like the emotionally focused and behavioral approaches to therapy, IOCT appears to help most couples, and in at least one study (Snyder, Wills, & Grady-Fletcher, 1991), it had substantial staying power, leaving spouses better adjusted four years later than BCT did.

Common Features of Marital Therapy

There are several other varieties of marital therapy available in the marketplace (see Gurman & Jacobson, 2002), but we focused on just the behavioral approaches, EFCT, and IOCT because careful studies suggest that they work for

---

BOX 15.2
Central Tenets of Insight-Oriented Therapy

Most marital therapists who use a psychodynamic orientation stress three fundamental propositions:

1. In the ways they choose a mate and behave toward their partners, people are frequently influenced by hidden tensions and unresolved needs of which they are unaware.

2. Many of these unconscious conflicts stem from events that took place either in one's family of origin or in prior romantic relationships.

3. The major therapeutic goal is for the clients to gain insight into their unconscious conflicts—to understand why they feel and act the way they do—so that they may have the freedom to choose to feel and act differently.

---

most couples (Baucom et al., in press). Most people who seriously participate in any of these therapies are likely to be better off afterwards, and (as a very rough average) about half of them will no longer be dissatisfied with their marriages (Christensen & Heavy, 1999). Other approaches, particularly those that combine elements of the behavioral, emotional, and insight-oriented approaches (e.g., Gurman, 2002), may also be generally effective, but less is known at this point about how well they do. Thus, there are no guarantees, and success in therapy is likely to depend on the sincerity of one's investment in, and the amount of effort one devotes to, the process. But *marital therapy helps* most couples. If you ever wish to repair a faltering intimate relationship, help is available.

So, which of these therapies is for you? Over the years, this question has aroused a lot of competition and occasional argument among professional helpers, but we have a very simple answer: Pick the therapy—and the therapist—that appeal to you the most. This is not an idle suggestion. The best therapy for you is very likely to be the one that sounded most interesting as you read these last few pages, and there are three reasons why.

First, despite their different labels and different emphases, the therapies we have introduced all share some common features, and that may be why they all work (Wampold, 2001). Each provides a reasonable explanation of why a couple has been experiencing difficulty, and each provides a hopeful new perspective on how such difficulties can be overcome. Towards that end, each provides a means of changing patterns of interaction that have been causing distress, and each increases a couple's repertoire of more effective, more desirable behavior. They pursue these ends with different rationales, but all of these therapies equip couples with more constructive and more satisfying ways of relating to each other. So, these various approaches all share some core elements that make them more similar than they may superficially seem (Messer & Wampold, 2002).

Second, given this, the *therapist* you select may be just as important as the therapy you choose. Marital therapy is much more likely to be successful when both members of the couple respect and trust their therapist (Summers & Barber, 2003), so you should seek an accomplished therapist who seems credible and persuasive to you. A professional helper who espouses a therapeutic approach you find plausible is likely to seem more skilled and knowledgeable than is one who uses an approach you find less compelling.

Finally, a therapeutic approach that interests you may be more likely to offer hope that real change is possible, and such optimism can be very influential (Baucom et al., in press). Positive expectations make therapy more effective. Compared to those who are pessimistic about the outcome of therapy, spouses who believe that benefits will result from their efforts are likely to work harder and to maintain higher spirits, and both increase the chances that the therapy will succeed.

Along those lines, let us remind you of the dangers in believing, as some people do, that "great relationships just happen" and "partners cannot change." We discussed these and other dysfunctional relationship beliefs back in chapter 4, and we hope that the disadvantages of such beliefs now seem (even more) clear. People who hold such views are less likely to seek therapy when problems arise in their marriages, and if they do enter therapy, they tend to do so halfheartedly. As a result, their situations are less likely to improve. You can lead a horse to water, but you can't make him drink.

Indeed, that old cliché suggests one last thing that all the marital therapies we have discussed have in common: They are all underutilized. Most people who divorce do so without ever consulting a marital therapist, and the minority who do usually wait to seek help until their problems are severe (Wolcott, 1986). Given the effectiveness of marital therapy, this is regrettable, but there is both good news and bad news here for readers of this book. The good news is that people with better educations are more likely than those with less schooling to seek therapy when they need it (Vessey & Howard, 1993). And, having read this book, you are almost certainly now better educated about close relationships than you used to be. We hope that, now that you know that you'll probably get your money's worth, you'll not delay in contacting a therapist if the need arises. The bad news is that men are less likely to seek therapy than women are; they're slower to recognize that problems exist, less likely to believe that therapy will help, and slower to seek therapy when it's warranted (Doss, Atkins, & Christensen, 2003). If help is to be obtained in a timely fashion, it will more often be a woman than a man who initially pursues it.

And time usually counts. The sooner marital problems are addressed, the easier they are to solve. The greater a couple's distress, the harder it is to reverse (Snyder, Mangrum, & Wills, 1993). Why wait? Consider the possibilities: Therapy doesn't always work, and there is always the chance, once a couple's problems are understood, that a therapist will recommend dissolving the marriage. But if that's the case, a great deal of distressing uncertainty and pain may be avoided. Alternatively, if a relationship is salvageable and therapy can be helpful, a couple can reduce their discomfort and return to profitable partnership the sooner therapy is sought. Either way, there's little point in waiting to address the inevitable difficulties intimate partners will face.

IN CONCLUSION

Overall, then, just like cars, relationships can get preventive maintenance that can keep them from breaking down, and they can often be fixed when they do falter. We think that this is a clever analogy (which is why we used it), but we need to point out that there's one way in which it is quite misleading: Sooner or later, no matter how you take care of them, cars wear out and must be replaced, and that's not necessarily true of intimate relationships at all. Sure, there are some people who regularly trade in their lovers, like their cars, for newer, flashier models (Campbell & Foster, 2002), but most readers of this book hope that they will ultimately construct an intimate relationship with a particular partner that they will find fulfilling for the rest of their lives.

And they may. We hope that, having now studied the modern science of close relationships, you are better equipped to create, understand, and manage successful, happy, rewarding relationships that last. We hope that, by shopping wisely and then making attentive and thoughtful investments in the care and feeding of your partnerships, you are able to develop and maintain relationships that remain gratifying to you forever. After all, some people do. When 100 couples who had been contentedly married for 45 years were asked to explain their success (Lauer, Lauer, & Kerr, 1990), they replied that

- they valued marriage and considered it a long-term commitment,
- a sense of humor was a big help,
- they were similar enough that they agreed about most things, and
- they genuinely liked their spouses and enjoyed spending time with them.

We hope that you're able to do the same.

FOR YOUR CONSIDERATION

When she reached the end of this book, Carolyn decided to talk with her husband about her increasing discontent with him and their marriage. He had been considerate and charming when they were engaged, but she had come to feel that he had stopped trying to please her, and she felt lonely and hurt. She felt that she was constantly changing to accommodate his wishes but that he was doing little to satisfy her in return. He never asked her how her day had been. It was a little thing, but it nettled her, and it was just one example of his self-absorption and apparent lack of care. However, when she suggested that they seek therapy, he resolutely refused. So, she decided to go by herself; she went to the website of the American Association for Marriage and Family Therapy at www.aamft.org, found a therapist, and made an individual appointment.

What do you think the future holds for Carolyn and her husband? Why?

CHAPTER SUMMARY

Relationships are complex, and there are many different ways they can go wrong. But with better understanding of close relationships, people are better equipped to prevent some problems and to overcome others. Moreover, committed partners work to protect and maintain the satisfaction they enjoy, and many problems can be repaired if they occur.

Maintaining and Enhancing Existing Relationships

Relationship maintenance mechanisms are strategic actions people take to sustain their partnerships.

Staying Committed. People who want a relationship to continue think and behave differently than less committed partners do. Cognitive maintenance mechanisms include *cognitive interdependence,* with people thinking of themselves as part of a couple instead of separate individuals; *positive illusions,* with partners idealizing each other and minimizing each other's faults; *perceived superiority,* with people considering their relationships to be better than most; *inattention to alternatives,* with people being relatively uninterested and unaware of how well they could be doing in alternative partnerships; and *derogation of alternatives,* with people underestimating how well they could be doing with other potential partners.

Behavioral maintenance mechanisms include *willingness to sacrifice,* with people doing things they would prefer not to do, and not doing things they would like to do, in order to promote and protect their relationships; the *Michelangelo phenomenon,* with partners encouraging each other's growth and development of new skills; *accommodation,* with people working to tolerate occasional provocation from their partners without fighting back; *play,* with partners seeking out novel, exciting, and pleasant activities together; and *forgiveness,* which occurs more easily among committed partners than among those with less commitment.

Staying Content. Communication scholars have identified several more activities that seem to help partners stay content. These include *positivity,* with people striving to be polite and cheerful; *openness,* with partners sharing their thoughts and feelings with each other; the provision of *assurances* of their love, commitment, and regard for each other; having friends in common with a shared *social network;* the *sharing* of *tasks;* good *humor;* and the provision of *support* to one another.

These various actions seem to work: Partners who routinely engage in these activities are happier than are those who work less hard to maintain their partnerships. However, the effects of these actions are short-lived, and people apparently need to *keep doing them* in order for them to be beneficial.

Repairing Relationships

Regular maintenance helps keep relationships in good condition, but they may still break down and need repair.

Do It Yourself. There's plenty of advice available to those who wish to fix their relationships themselves, but some of it is faulty. On occasion, even bestselling advice may be simply wrong, and people who try to follow it may find their problems getting worse instead of better. On the other hand, some self-help information is provided by reputable scientists, and when it is conveniently accessible, it may be very beneficial to its consumers.

Preventive Maintenance. Premarital counseling comes in various forms. One well-known program, the Prevention and Relationship Enhancement Program, or PREP, tries to instill realistic expectations, to open lines of communication, and to encourage play among partners. The centerpiece of PREP is the *speaker-listener technique,* a strategy that combines "I" statements and active listening skills to provide a safe way for partners to talk about contentious issues. PREP training seems to result in increased satisfaction during the first years of marriage.

Marital Therapy. Conjoint therapy, in which a therapist sees both partners together in the same sessions, is the most common form of marital therapy, but various other formats are common. There are also several different therapeutic approaches that professional helpers may use. They differ in their focus on behavior, thoughts, or feelings, their focus on partners' individual difficulties or those of the couple, and their emphasis on past events or present difficulties as the source of distress.

A classic intervention, *behavioral couple therapy,* or BCT, seeks to establish less punishing and more pleasant patterns of interaction between partners. Couples may enter into agreements to reward positive behavior from their partners with desirable behavior of their own. A descendant of BCT, *cognitive-behavioral couple therapy,* focuses on maladaptive cognitions and seeks to instill reasonable expectations and sensible beliefs in its participants, who are taught to track and test their thoughts by recognizing and challenging unrealistic beliefs and generating lists of the pros and cons of the expectations they hold. Another descendant of BCT, *integrative behavioral couple therapy,* tries to teach troubled spouses to accept the incompatibilities that they cannot change. One of its goals is to help partners understand their problems tolerantly and nondefensively. In general, all three of these therapies usually help those who undertake them, with 60 to 70 percent of clients becoming less dissatisfied with their marriages.

Another therapeutic approach, *emotionally focused couple therapy,* seeks to train spouses to treat each other in ways that allow them to feel safe, loved, and securely connected to one another. Partners are taught to provide reassurance and comfort that acknowledges and fulfills the other's needs. It, too, is usually effective, with most of its participants becoming less distressed.

A last approach, *insight-oriented couple therapy,* seeks to free spouses of some of the painful emotional baggage they carry from prior relationships that is causing them grief now. In particular, it strives to help people comprehend how the personal habits and assumptions they developed in other relationships may be creating difficulty with their present partners. Participants typically re-imagine their relationship histories in an effort to identify problematic patterns in their pasts.

All of these therapeutic approaches share certain core features. Each provides a reasonable explanation of why a couple has been experiencing difficulty, and each provides a hopeful new perspective on how such difficulties can be overcome. Towards that end, each provides a means of changing patterns of interaction that have been causing distress, and each increases a couple's repertoire of more effective, more desirable behavior. If one works with a therapist who engenders respect and trust, and if one enters any of these therapies with positive expectations, any of them is likely to provide real benefits to troubled spouses.

Thus, it is regrettable that all of these therapies tend to be underutilized. Most people who divorce do so without ever consulting a marital therapist, and the minority who do usually wait to seek help until their problems are severe. Time counts; the sooner marital problems are addressed, the easier they are to solve.

In Conclusion

Despite all the bumps in the road that may lie ahead, most readers of this book hope that they will ultimately construct an intimate relationship with a particular partner that they will find fulfilling for the rest of their lives. Our hope is that, having now studied the modern science of close relationships, you are better equipped to create, understand, and manage successful, happy, rewarding relationships that last. We wish you the very best in the interpersonal journey that awaits you.

References

Abbey, A. (1982). Sex differences in attributions for friendly behavior: Do males misperceive females' friendliness? *Journal of Personality and Social Psychology, 42,* 830–838.

Abrahams, M. F. (1994). Perceiving flirtatious communication: An exploration of the perceptual dimensions underlying judgments of flirtatiousness. *Journal of Sex Research, 31,* 283–292.

Acitelli, L. K. (1997). Sampling couples to understand them: Mixing the theoretical with the practical. *Journal of Social and Personal Relationships, 14,* 243–261.

Acitelli, L. K. (2001). Maintaining and enhancing a relationship by attending to it. In J. H. Harvey & A. E. Wenzel (Eds.), *Close romantic relationships: Maintenance and enhancement* (pp. 153–167). Mahwah, NJ: Erlbaum.

Acitelli, L. K., Douvan, E., & Veroff, J. (1993). Perceptions of conflict in the first year of marriage: How important are similarity and understanding? *Journal of Social and Personal Relationships, 10,* 5–19.

Acitelli, L. K., Kenny, D. A., & Weiner, D. (2001). The importance of similarity and understanding of partners' marital ideals to relationship satisfaction. *Personal Relationships, 8,* 167–185.

Acitelli, L. K., & Young, A. M. (1996). Gender and thought in relationships. In G. J. O. Fletcher & J. Fitness (Eds.), *Knowledge structures in close relationships: A social psychological approach* (pp. 147–168). Mahwah, NJ: Erlbaum.

Acker, M., & Davis, M. H. (1992). Intimacy, passion and commitment in adult romantic relationships: A test of the Triangular Theory of Love. *Journal of Social and Personal Relationships, 9,* 21–50.

Ackerman, D. (1994). *A natural history of love.* New York: Random House.

Adams, J. M., & Jones, W. H. (1997). The conceptualization of marital commitment: An integrative analysis. *Journal of Personality and Social Psychology, 72,* 1177–1196.

Adams, J. M., & Jones, W. H. (1999). Interpersonal commitment in historical perspective. In J. M. Adams & W. H. Jones (Eds.), *Handbook on interpersonal commitment and relationship stability* (pp. 3–33). New York: Kluwer Academic/Plenum.

Adams, R. G., & Blieszner, R. (1995). Aging well with friends and family. *American Behavioral Scientist, 39,* 209–224.

Afifi, W. S., Falato, W. L., & Weiner, J. L. (2001). Identity concerns following a severe relational transgression: The role of discovery method for the relational outcomes of infidelity. *Journal of Social and Personal Relationships, 18,* 291–308.

Afifi, W. A., & Faulkner, S. L. (2000). On being "just friends": The frequency and impact of sexual activity in cross-sex friendships. *Journal of Social and Personal Relationships, 17,* 205–222.

Afifi, W. A., & Metts, S. (1998). Characteristics and consequences of expectation violations in close relationships. *Journal of Social and Personal Relationships, 15,* 365–392.

Agnew, C. R. (2003, February). *The declaration of interdependence.* Paper presented at the meeting of the Society for Personality and Social Psychology, Los Angeles.

Agnew, C. R., & Gephart, J. M. (2000). Testing *The Rules* of commitment enhancement: Separating fact from fiction. *Representative Research in Social Psychology, 24,* 41–47.

Agnew, C. R., Loving, T. J., & Drigotas, S. M. (2001). Substituting the forest for the trees: Social networks and the prediction of romantic relationship state and fate. *Journal of Personality and Social Psychology, 81,* 1042–1057.

Agnew, C. R., Loving, T. J., Le, B., & Goodfriend, W. (2004). Thinking close: Measuring relational closeness as perceived self-other inclusion. In D. J. Mashek & A. Aron (Eds.), *Handbook of closeness and intimacy* (pp. 103–115). Mahwah, NJ: Erlbaum.

Agnew, C. R., Van Lange, P. A. M., Rusbult, C. E., & Langston, C. A. (1998). Cognitive interdependence: Commitment and the mental representation of close relationships. *Journal of Personality and Social Psychology, 74,* 939–954.

Aguinis, H., Simonsen, M. M., & Pierce, C. A. (1998). Effects of nonverbal behavior on perceptions of power bases. *Journal of Social Psychology, 138,* 455–470.

Ahrons, C. (1994). *The good divorce.* New York: HarperCollins.

Ainsworth, M. D. S., Blehar, M. C., Waters, E., & Wall, S. (1978). *Patterns of attachment: A psychological study of the strange situation.* Hillsdale, NJ: Erlbaum.

Akerlind, I., & Hornquist, J. O. (1992). Loneliness and alcohol abuse: A review of evidences of an interplay. *Social Science and Medicine, 34,* 405–414.

Albrecht, C. M., & Albrecht, D. E. (2001). Sex ratio and family structure in the nonmetropolitan United States. *Sociological Inquiry, 71,* 67–84.

Albrecht, S. L., & Kunz, P. R. (1980). The decision to divorce: A social exchange perspective. *Journal of Divorce, 3,* 319–337.

Albright, L., Cohen, A. I., Malloy, T. E., Christ, T., & Bromgard, G. (2004). Judgments of communicative intent in conversation. *Journal of Experimental Social Psychology, 40,* 290–302.

Ali, L., & Miller, L. (2004, July 12). The secret lives of wives. *Newsweek,* 46–54.

Allen, J. B., Kenrick, D. T., Linder, D. E., & McCall, M. A. (1989). Arousal and attribution: A response facilitation alternative to misattribution and negative-reinforcement models. *Journal of Personality and Social Psychology, 57,* 261–270.

Allen, K., & Ferrari, A. (1997). *101 of the world's most effective pickup lines.* New York: Ace Company Publishing.

Allen, K. (2003). Are pets a healthy pleasure? The influence of pets on blood pressure. *Current Directions in Psychological Science, 12,* 236–239.

Allen, K., Blascovich, J., & Mendes, W. B. (2002). Cardiovascular reactivity in the presence of pets, friends, and spouses: The truth about cats and dogs. *Psychosomatic Medicine, 64,* 727–739.

Allen, K., Shykoff, B. E., & Izzo, J. L., Jr. (2001). Pet ownership, but not ACE inhibitor therapy, blunts home blood pressure responses to mental stress. *Hypertension, 38,* 815–820.

Altman, I. (1973). Reciprocity of interpersonal exchange. *Journal for the Theory of Social Behaviour, 3,* 249–261.

Altman, I., & Taylor, D. A. (1973). *Social penetration: The development of interpersonal relationships.* New York: Holt, Rinehart & Winston.

Altman, I., Vinsel, A., & Brown, B. A. (1981). Dialectic conceptions in social psychology: An application to social penetration and privacy regulation. In L. Berkowitz (Ed.), *Advances in experimental social psychology* (Vol. 14, pp. 107–160). New York: Academic Press.

Amato, P. R. (2001). Children of divorce in the 1990s: An update of the Amato and Keith (1991) meta-analysis. *Journal of Family Psychology, 15,* 355–370.

Amato, P. R. (2003). Reconciling divergent perspectives: Judith Wallerstein, quantitative family research, and children of divorce. *Family Relations, 52,* 332–339.

Amato, P. R., & Booth, A. (2001). The legacy of parents' marital discord: Consequences for children's marital quality. *Journal of Personality and Social Psychology, 81,* 627–638.

Amato, P. R., & DeBoer, D. D. (2001). The transmission of marital instability across generations: Relationship skills or commitment to marriage? *Journal of Marriage and the Family, 63,* 1038–1051.

Amato, P. R., & Gilbreth, J. G. (1999). Nonresident fathers and children's well-being: A meta-analysis. *Journal of Marriage and the Family, 61,* 557–573.

Amato, P. R., Johnson, D. R., Booth, A., & Rogers, S. J. (2003). Continuity and change in marital quality between 1980 and 2000. *Journal of Marriage and the Family, 65,* 1–22.

Amato, P. R., & Keith, B. (1991a). Parental divorce and adult well-being: A meta-analysis. *Journal of Marriage and the Family, 53,* 43–58.

Amato, P. R., & Keith, B. (1991b). Parental divorce and the well-being of children: A meta-analysis. *Psychological Bulletin, 110,* 26–46.

Amato, P. R., & Previti, D. (2003). People's reasons for divorcing: Gender, social class, the life course, and adjustment. *Journal of Family Issues, 24,* 602–626.

Amato, P. R., & Rogers, S. J. (1997). A longitudinal study of marital problems and subsequent divorce. *Journal of Marriage and the Family , 59,* 612–624.

Amato, P. R., & Rogers, S. J. (1999). Do attitudes toward divorce affect marital quality? *Journal of Family Issues, 20,* 69–86.

Amato, P. R., & Sobolewski, J. M. (2001). The effects of divorce and marital discord on adult children's psychological well-being. *American Sociological Review, 66,* 900–921.

Ambady, N., Hallahan, M., & Conner, B. (1999). Accuracy of judgments of sexual orientation from thin slices of behavior. *Journal of Personality and Social Psychology, 77,* 538–547.

Ambady, N., Hallahan, M., & Rosenthal, R. (1995). On judging and being judged accurately in zero-acquaintance situations. *Journal of Personality and Social Psychology, 69,* 518–529.

Ambady, N., & Rosenthal, R. (1993). Half a minute: Predicting teacher evaluations from thin slices of nonverbal behavior and physical attractiveness. *Journal of Personality and Social Psychology, 64,* 431–441.

Andersen, P. (2001, June). *Warmth and immediacy in nonverbal communication.* Paper presented at the International Conference on Personal Relationships, Prescott, AZ.

Andersen, P. A., & Guerrero, L. K. (1998). Principles of communication and emotion in social interaction. In P. A. Andersen & L. K. Guerrero (Eds.), *Handbook of communication and emotion* (pp. 49–96). San Diego: Academic Press.

Andersen, S. M., & Chen, S. (2002). The relational self: An interpersonal social-cognitive theory. *Psychological Review, 109,* 619–645.

Anderson, C., Keltner, D., & John, O. P. (2003). Emotional convergence between people over time. *Journal of Personality and Social Psychology, 84,* 1054–1068.

Anderson, C. A. (1999). Attributional style, depression, and loneliness: A cross-cultural comparison of American and Chinese students. *Personality and Social Psychology Bulletin, 25,* 482–499.

Anderson, C. A., & Harvey, R. J. (1988). Discriminating between problems in living: An examination of depression, loneliness, shyness, and social anxiety. *Journal of Social and Clinical Psychology, 6,* 482–491.

Anderson, C. A., Miller, R. S., Riger, A. L., Dill, J. C., & Sedikides, C. (1994). Behavioral and characterological attributional styles as predictors of depression and loneliness: Review, refinement, and test. *Journal of Personality and Social Psychology, 66,* 549–558.

Anderson, D. E., DePaulo, B. M., & Ansfield, M. E. (2002). The development of deception detection skill: A longitudinal study of same-sex friends. *Personality and Social Psychology Bulletin, 28,* 536–545.

Anderson, D. E., DePaulo, B. M., Sternglanz, W., & Walker, M. (1999, June). *Eagle-eyed or starry-eyed? Deception detection in close relationships.* Paper presented at the meeting of the International Network on Personal Relationships, Louisville, KY.

Anderson, J. L., Crawford, C. B., Nadeau, J., & Lindberg, T. (1992). Was the Duchess of Windsor right? A cross-cultural review of the socioecology of ideals of female body shape. *Ethology and Sociobiology, 13,* 197–227.

Anderson, K. J., & Leaper, C. (1998). Meta-analyses of gender effects on conversational interruption: Who, what, when, where, and how. *Sex Roles, 39,* 225–252.

Antill, J. K. (1983). Sex role complementarity versus similarity in married couples. *Journal of Personality and Social Psychology, 45,* 145–155.

Archer, D. (1997). Unspoken diversity: Cultural differences in gestures. *Qualitative Sociology, 20,* 79–105.

Archer, J. (2000). Sex differences in aggression between heterosexual partners: A meta-analytic review. *Psychological Bulletin, 126,* 651–680.

Archer, J. (2002). Sex differences in physically aggressive acts between heterosexual partners: A meta-analytic review. *Aggression and Violent Behavior, 7,* 313–351.

Argyle, M., & Henderson, M. (1984). The rules of friendship. *Journal of Social and Personal Relationships, 1,* 211–237.

Argyle, M., & Henderson, M. (1985). *The anatomy of friendships.* London: Penguin Books.

Armas, G. C. (2003, March 13). Unmarried partners are more diverse. *Houston Chronicle,* p. 13A.

Aron, A., & Aron, E. N. (2000). Self-expansion motivation and including other in the self. In W. Ickes & S. Duck (Eds.), *The social psychology of personal relationships* (pp. 109–128). Chichester, England: Wiley.

Aron, A., Aron, E. N., & Allen, J. (1998). Motivations for unreciprocated love. *Personality and Social Psychology Bulletin, 24,* 787–796.

Aron, A., Dutton, D. G., Aron, E. N., & Iverson, A. (1989). Experiences of falling in love. *Journal of Social and Personal Relationships, 6,* 243–257.

Aron, A., Fisher, H., Mashek, D., Strong, G., Li, H., & Brown, L. L. (2004, July). *Passionate love as a reward-oriented behavioral and neural system: An fMRI study.* Paper presented at the meeting of the International Association for Relationship Research, Madison, WI.

Aron, A., Mashek, D. J., & Aron, E. N. (2004). Closeness as including the other in the self. In D. J. Mashek & A. Aron (Eds.), *Handbook of closeness and intimacy* (pp. 27–41). Mahwah, NJ: Erlbaum.

Aron, A., Melinat, E., Aron, E. N., Vallone, R. D., & Bator, R. J. (1997). The experimental generation of interpersonal closeness: A procedure and some preliminary findings. *Personality and Social Psychology Bulletin, 23,* 363–377.

Aron, A., Norman, C. C., & Aron, E. N. (2001). Shared self-expanding activities as a means of maintaining and enhancing close romantic relationships. In J. H. Harvey & A. E. Wenzel (Eds.), *Close romantic relationships: Maintenance and enhancement* (pp. 47–66). Mahwah, NJ: Erlbaum.

Aron, A., Norman, C. C., Aron, E. N., & Lewandowski, G. (2002). Shared participation in self-expanding activities: Positive effects on experienced marital quality. In P. Noller & J. A. Feeney (Eds.), *Understanding marriage: Developments in the study of couple interaction* (pp. 177–194). New York: Cambridge University Press.

Aron, A., Norman, C. C., Aron, E. N., McKenna, C., & Heyman, R. E. (2000). Couples' shared participation in novel and arousing activities and experienced relationship quality. *Journal of Personality and Social Psychology, 78,* 273–284.

Aron, A., Paris, M., & Aron, E. N. (1995). Falling in love: Prospective studies of self-concept change. *Journal of Personality and Social Psychology, 69,* 1102–1112.

Aron, A., & Westbay, L. (1996). Dimensions of the prototype of love. *Journal of Personality and Social Psychology, 70,* 535–551.

Aronson, E., & Cope, V. (1968). My enemy's enemy is my friend. *Journal of Personality and Social Psychology, 8,* 8–12.

Aronson, E., Wilson, T. D., & Akert, R. M. (2005). *Social psychology* (5th ed.). Upper Saddle River, NJ: Prentice Hall.

Arriaga, X. B. (2001). The ups and downs of dating: Fluctuations in satisfaction in newly formed romantic relationships. *Journal of Personality and Social Psychology, 80,* 754–765.

Arriaga, X. B., & Agnew, C. R. (2001). Being committed: Affective, cognitive, and conative components of relationship commitment. *Personality and Social Psychology Bulletin, 27,* 1190–1203.

Arriaga, X. B., & Rusbult, C. E. (1998). Standing in my partner's shoes: Partner perspective taking and reactions to accommodative dilemmas. *Personality and Social Psychology Bulletin, 24,* 927–948.

Asch, S. E. (1946). Forming impressions of personality. *Journal of Abnormal and Social Psychology, 41,* 258–290.

Asendorpf, J. (1990). The expression of shyness and embarrassment. In W. R. Crozier (Ed.), *Shyness and embarrassment: Perspectives from social psychology* (pp. 87–118). Cambridge: Cambridge University Press.

Asendorpf, J. B. (2002). Personality effects on personal relationships over the life span. In A. L. Vangelisti, H. T. Reis, & M. A. Fitzpatrick (Eds.), *Stability and change in relationships* (pp. 35–56). New York: Cambridge University Press.

Asendorpf, J. B., & Wilpers, S. (1998). Personality effects on social relationships. *Journal of Personality and Social Psychology, 74,* 1531–1544.

Assh, S. D., & Byers, E. S. (1996). Understanding the co-occurrence of marital distress and depression in women. *Journal of Social and Personal Relationships, 13,* 537–552.

Attridge, M., & Berscheid, E. (1994). Entitlement in romantic relationships in the United States: A social-exchange perspective. In M. J. Lerner & G. Mikula (Eds.), *Entitlement and the affectional bond: Justice in close relationships* (pp. 117–147). New York: Plenum.

Aubé, J., Norcliffe, H., Craig, J., & Koestner, R. (1995). Gender characteristics and adjustment-related outcomes: Questioning the masculinity model. *Personality and Social Psychology Bulletin, 21,* 284–295.

Ault, L. K., Cunningham, M. R., & Bettler, R. F., Jr. (1999, June). *The role of others in individuals' embarrassing predicaments: Preventative face-saving as a social support behavior.* Paper presented at the meeting of the International Network for Personal Relationships, Louisville, KY.

Aune, K. S., & Wong, N. C. H. (2002). Antecedents and consequences of adult play in romantic relationships. *Personal Relationships, 9,* 279–286.

Averill, J. R. (1982). *Anger and aggression: An essay on emotion.* New York: Springer.

Axinn, W. G., & Barber, J. S. (1997). Living arrangements and family formation attitudes in early adulthood. *Journal of Marriage and the Family, 59,* 595–611.

Axtell, R. E. (1991). *Gestures: The do's and taboos of body language around the world.* New York: Wiley.

Ayduk, O., Downey, G., Testa, A., Yen, Y., & Shoda, Y. (1999). Does rejection elicit hostility in rejection sensitive women? *Social Cognition, 17,* 245–271.

Babad, E., Bernieri, F., & Rosenthal, R. (1989). Nonverbal communication and leakage in the behavior of biased and unbiased teachers. *Journal of Personality and Social Psychology, 56,* 89–94.

Bach, G. R., & Wyden, P. (1983). *The intimate enemy: How to fight fair in love and marriage.* New York: Avon Books.

Bachman, J. G., Johnston, L. D., & O'Malley, P. M. (2001). *Monitoring the future: Questionnaire responses from the nation's high school seniors, 2000.* Ann Arbor, MI: Institute for Social Research.

Baeccman, C., Folkesson, P., & Norlander, T. (1999). Expectations of romantic relationships: A comparison between homosexual and heterosexual men with regard to Baxter's criteria. *Social Behavior and Personality, 27,* 363–374.

Bailenson, J. N., Blascovich, J., Beall, A. C., & Loomis, J. M. (2003). Interpersonal distance in immersive virtual environments. *Personality and Social Psychology Bulletin, 29,* 819–833.

Bailey, J. M., Kirk, K. M., Zhu, G., Dunne, M. P., & Martin, N. G. (2000). Do individual differences in sociosexuality represent different genetic or environmentally contingent strategies? Evidence from the Australian Twin Registry. *Journal of Personality and Social Psychology, 78,* 537–545.

Bakeman, R., & Gottman, J. M. (1997). *Observing interaction: An introduction to sequential analysis* (2nd ed.). New York: Cambridge University Press.

Baker, M., & Miller, R. S. (2004, January). *Mate preferences in parents and their young adult offspring.* Paper presented at the meeting of the Society for Personality and Social Psychology, Austin, TX.

Baldwin, M. W. (1995). Relational schemas and cognition in close relationships. *Journal of Social and Personal Relationships, 12,* 547–552.

Baldwin, M. W., & Fehr, B. (1995). On the instability of attachment style ratings. *Personal Relationships, 2,* 247–261.

Baldwin, M. W., & Keelan, J. P. R. (1999). Interpersonal expectations as a function of self-esteem and sex. *Journal of Social and Personal Relationships, 16,* 822–833.

Baldwin, M. W., & Main, K. J. (2001). Social anxiety and the cued activation of relational knowledge. *Personality and Social Psychology Bulletin, 27,* 1637–1647.

Bank, B. J., & Hansford, S. L. (2000). Gender and friendship: Why are men's best same-sex friendships less intimate and supportive? *Personal Relationships, 7,* 63–78.

Banse, R. (2004). Adult attachment and marital satisfaction: Evidence for dyadic configuration effects. *Journal of Social and Personal Relationships, 21,* 273–282.

Barber, N. (1998). Secular changes in standards in bodily attractiveness in women: Tests of a reproductive model. *International Journal of Eating Disorders, 23,* 449–453.

Barber, N. (1998). Sex differences in disposition towards kin, security of adult attachment, and sociosexuality as a function of parental divorce. *Evolution and Human Behavior, 19,* 125–132.

Barber, N. (1999). Reproductive and occupational stereotypes of bodily curvaceousness and weight. *Journal of Social Psychology, 139,* 247–249.

Barber, N. (1999). Women's dress fashions as a function of reproductive strategy. *Sex Roles, 40,* 459–471.

Barber, N. (2000a). On the relationship between country sex ratios and teen pregnancy rates: A replication. *Cross Cultural Research: The Journal of Comparative Social Science, 34,* 26–37.

Barber, N. (2000b). *Why parents matter: Parental investment and child outcomes.* Westport, CT: Bergin and Garvey.

Barber, N. (2001a). Mustache fashion covaries with a good marriage market for women. *Journal of Nonverbal Behavior, 25,* 261–272.

Barber, N. (2001b). On the relationship between marital opportunity and teen pregnancy: The sex ratio question. *Journal of Cross-Cultural Psychology, 32,* 259–267.

Barber, N. (2002a). Parental investment prospects and teen birth rates of Blacks and Whites in American metropolitan areas. *Cross Cultural Research: The Journal of Comparative Social Science, 36,* 183–199.

Barber, N. (2002b). *The science of romance: Secrets of the sexual brain.* Amherst, NY: Prometheus Books.

Barber, N. (2003). Divorce and reduced economic and emotional interdependence: A cross-national study. *Journal of Divorce and Remarriage, 39,* 113–124.

Bargh, J. A., & McKenna, K. Y. A. (2004). The Internet and social life. *Annual Review of Psychology, 55,* 573–590.

Barnes, S. B. (2001). *Online connections: Internet personal relationships.* Cresskill, NJ: Hampton Press.

Barrett, J. (2004, May 10). No time for wrinkles. *Newsweek, 143,* 82–85.

Barrett, L., Dunbar, R., & Lycett, J. (2002). *Human evolutionary psychology.* Princeton: Princeton University Press.

Bartels, A., & Zeki, S. (2000). The neural basis of romantic love. *NeuroReport, 11,* 3829–3834.

Bartholomew, K. (1990). Avoidance of intimacy: An attachment perspective. *Journal of Personal and Social Relationships, 7,* 147–178.

Bartholomew, K., & Horowitz, L. M. (1991). Attachment styles among young adults: A test of a four-category model. *Journal of Personality and Social Psychology, 61,* 226–244.

Bartholomew, K., & Shaver, P. R. (1998). Methods of assessing adult attachment: Do they converge? In J. A. Simpson & W. S. Rholes (Eds.), *Attachment theory and close relationships* (pp. 25–45). New York: Guilford Press.

Basow, S. A., & Rubenfeld, K. (2003). "Troubles talk": Effects of gender and gender-typing. *Sex Roles, 48,* 183–187.

Batson, C. D., Lishner, D. A., Carpenter, A., Dulin, L., Harjusola-Webb, S., Stocks, E. L., et al. (2003). ". . . As you would have them do unto you": Does imagining yourself in the other's place stimulate moral action? *Personality and Social Psychology Bulletin, 29,* 1190–1201.

Battaglia, D. M., Richard, F. D., Datteri, D. L., & Lord, C. G. (1998). Breaking up is (relatively) easy to do: A script for the dissolution of close relationships. *Journal of Social and Personal Relationships, 15,* 829–845.

Baucom, D. H., Epstein, N., & Stanton, S. (in press). The treatment of relationship distress: Theoretical perspectives and empirical findings. In A. Vangelisti & D. Perlman (Eds.) *The Cambridge handbook of personal relationships.* New York: Cambridge University Press.

Baumeister, R. F. (1998). The self. In D. T. Gilbert, S. T. Fiske, & G. Lindzey (Eds.), *The handbook of social psychology, Volume I* (2nd ed., pp. 680–740). Boston: McGraw-Hill.

Baumeister, R. F., & Bratslavsky, E. (1999). Passion, intimacy, and time: Passionate love as a function of change in intimacy. *Personality and Social Psychology Review, 3,* 49–67.

Baumeister, R. F., Bratslavsky, E., Finkenauer, C., & Vohs, K. D. (2001). Bad is stronger than good. *Review of General Psychology, 5,* 323–370.

Baumeister, R. F., & Campbell, W. K. (1999). The intrinsic appeal of evil: Sadism, sensational thrills, and threatened egotism. *Personality and Social Psychology Review, 3,* 210–221.

Baumeister, R. F., & Dhavale, D. (2001). Two sides of romantic rejection. In M. R. Leary (Ed.), *Interpersonal rejection* (pp. 55–71). New York: Oxford University Press.

Baumeister, R. F., & Leary, M. R. (1995). The need to belong: Desire for interpersonal attachments as a fundamental human motivation. *Psychological Bulletin, 117,* 497–529.

Baumeister, R. F., & Tice, D. M. (2001). *The social dimension of sex.* Boston: Allyn & Bacon.

Baumeister, R. F., Twenge, J. M., & Ciarocco, N. (2002). The inner world of rejection: Effects of social exclusion on emotion, cognition, and self-regulation. In J. P. Forgas & K. D. Williams (Eds.), *The social self: Cognitive, interpersonal, and intergroup perspectives* (pp. 161–174). New York: Psychology Press.

Baumeister, R. F., Twenge, J. M., & Nuss, C. K. (2002). Effects of social exclusion on cognitive processes: Anticipated aloneness reduces intelligent thought. *Journal of Personality and Social Psychology, 83,* 817–827.

Baumeister, R. F., & Vohs, K. D. (2004). Sexual economics: Sex as a female resource for social exchange in heterosexual interactions. *Personality and Social Psychology Review, 8,* 339–363.

Baumeister, R. F., & Wotman, S. R. (1992). *Breaking hearts: The two sides of unrequited love.* New York: Guilford Press.

Baumeister, R. F., Wotman, S. R., & Stillwell, A. M. (1993). Unrequited love: On heartbreak, anger, guilt, scriptlessness, and humiliation. *Journal of Personality and Social Psychology, 64,* 377–394.

Baxter, L. A. (1984). Trajectories of relationship disengagement. *Journal of Social and Personal Relationships, 1,* 29–48.

Baxter, L. A. (1985). Accomplishing relationship disengagement. In S. Duck & D. Perlman (Eds.), *Understanding personal relationships: An interdisciplinary approach* (pp. 243–265). London: Sage.

Baxter, L. A. (1986). Gender differences in the heterosexual relationship rules embedded in break-up accounts. *Journal of Social and Personal Relationships, 3,* 289–306.

Baxter, L. A. (1987). Self-disclosure and relationship disengagement. In V. Derlega & J. H. Berg (Eds.), *Self-disclosure: Theory, research, and therapy* (pp. 155–174). New York: Plenum.

Baxter, L. A. (2004). Relationships as dialogues. *Personal Relationships, 11,* 1–22.

Baxter, L. A., Mazanec, M., Nicholson, J., Pittman, G., Smith, K., & West, L. (1997). Everyday loyalties and betrayals in personal relationships. *Journal of Social and Personal Relationships, 14,* 655–678.

Baxter, L. A., & Montgomery, B. M. (1997). Rethinking communication in personal relationships from a dialectical perspective. In S. Duck (Ed.), *Handbook of personal relationships: Theory, research, and interventions* (2nd ed., pp. 325–349). Chichester, England: Wiley.

Baxter, L. A., & West, L. (2003). Couple perceptions of their similarities and differences: A dialectical perspective. *Journal of Social and Personal Relationships, 20,* 491–514.

Baxter, L. A., & Widenmann, S. (1993). Revealing and not revealing the status of romantic relationships to social networks. *Journal of Social and Personal Relationships, 10,* 321–337.

Baxter, L. A., & Wilmot, W. M. (1984). "Secret tests": Social strategies for acquiring information about the state of the relationship. *Human Communication Research. 11,* 171–201.

Baxter, L. A., & Wilmot, W. W. (1985). Taboo topics in close relationships. *Journal of Social and Personal Relationships, 2,* 253–269.

Bazargan, M., & Barbre, A. R. (1992). Self-reported memory problems among the Black elderly. *Educational Gerontology, 18,* 71–82.

Beach, S. R. H., Katz, J., Kim, S., & Brody, G. H. (2003). Prospective effects of marital satisfaction on depressive symptoms in established marriages: A dyadic model. *Journal of Social and Personal Relationships, 20,* 355–371.

Beach, S. R. H., Whitaker, D. J., Jones, D. J., & Tesser, A. (2001). When does performance feedback prompt complementarity in romantic relationships? *Personal Relationships, 8,* 231–248.

Bell, R. A., Buerkel-Rothfuss, N. L., & Gore, K. E. (1987). "Did you bring the yarmulke for the cabbage patch kid?" The idiomatic communication of young lovers. *Human Communication Research, 14,* 47–67.

Bellavia, G., & Murray, S. (2003). Did I do that? Self-esteem-related differences in reactions to romantic partners' moods. *Personal Relationships, 10,* 77–95.

Belsky, J. (1990). Children and marriage. In F. D. Fincham & T. N. Bradbury (Eds.), *The psychology of marriage: Basic issues and applications* (pp. 172–200). New York: Guilford.

Bem, S. L. (1993). *The lenses of gender: Transforming the debate on sexual inequality.* New Haven: Yale University Press.

Benin, M. H., & Agostinelli, J. (1988). Husbands' and wives' satisfaction with the division of labor. *Journal of Marriage and the Family, 50,* 349–361.

Benjamin, M., & Irving, H. H. (1995). Research in family mediation: Review and implications. *Mediation Quarterly, 13,* 53–82.

Bente, G., Donaghy, W. C., & Suwelack, D. (1998). Sex differences in body movement and visual attention: An integrated analysis of movement and gaze in mixed-sex dyads. *Journal of Nonverbal Behavior, 22,* 31–58.

Benz, J. J., Miller, R. L., & Anderson, M. K. (2004, June). *Attributions of deception in dating situations.* Paper presented at the meeting of the Society for Personality and Social Psychology, Austin, TX.

Berg, J. H. (1984). Development of friendship between roommates. *Journal of Personality and Social Psychology, 46,* 346–356.

Berg, J. H., & Clark, M. S. (1986). Differences in social exchange between intimate and other relationships: Gradually evolving or quickly apparent? In V. J. Derlega & B. A. Winstead (Eds.), *Friendship and social interaction* (pp. 101–128). New York: Springer-Verlag.

Berg, J. H., & McQuinn, R. D. (1986). Attraction and exchange in continuing and noncontinuing dating relationships. *Journal of Personality and Social Psychology, 50,* 942–952.

Berger, C. R. (1994). Power, dominance, and social interaction. In M. L. Knapp & G. R. Miller (Eds.), *Handbook of interpersonal communication* (2nd ed., pp. 450–507). Thousand Oaks, CA: Sage.

Berger, C. R., Gardner, R. R., Parks, M. R., Shulman, L., & Miller, G. R. (1976). Interpersonal epistemology and interpersonal communication. In G. R. Miller (Ed.), *Explorations in interpersonal communication* (pp. 149–172). Beverly Hills, CA: Sage.

Berger, D. G., & Wenger, M. G. (1973). The ideology of virginity. *Journal of Marriage and the Family, 35,* 666–676.

Berk, M. S., & Andersen, S. M. (2000). The impact of past relationships on interpersonal behavior: Behavioral confirmation in the social-cognitive process of transference. *Journal of Personality and Social Psychology, 79,* 546–562.

Berkman, L. F., & Glass, T. A. (2000). Social integration, social networks, social support and health. In L. F. Berkman & I. Kawachi (Eds.), *Social epidemiology* (pp. 137–174). New York: Oxford University Press.

Berkman, L., & Syme, S. (1979). Social networks, host resistance, and mortality: A nine year follow-up study of Alameda County residents. *American Journal of Epidemiology, 109,* 186–204.

Berman, J. S., & Bennett, J. B. (1982, August). *Love and power: Testing Waller's principle of least interest.* Paper presented at the meeting of the American Psychological Association, Washington, DC.

Berman, M. I., & Frazier, P. A. (2004, July). *Cheaters and victims after infidelity: Links between perceived control, forgiveness, relationship quality and psychological distress.* Paper presented at the meeting of the International Association for Relationship Research, Madison, WI.

Berndt, T. J. (1996). Friendships in adolescence. In N. Vanzetti & S. Duck (Eds.), *A lifetime of relationships* (pp. 181–212). Pacific Grove, CA: Brooks/Cole.

Bernieri, F. J., Zuckerman, M., Koestner, R., & Rosenthal, R. (1994). Measuring person perception accuracy: Another look at self-other agreement. *Personality and Social Psychology Bulletin, 20,* 367–378.

Bernstein, W. M., Stephenson, B. O., Snyder, M. L., & Wicklund, R. A. (1983). Causal ambiguity and heterosexual affiliation. *Journal of Experimental Social Psychology, 19,* 78–92.

Berscheid, E. (1999). The greening of relationship science. *American Psychologist, 54,* 260–266.

Berscheid, E., & Ammazzalorso, H. (2001). Emotional experience in close relationships. In G. J. O. Fletcher & M. S. Clark (Eds.), *Blackwell handbook of social psychology: Interpersonal processes* (pp. 308–330). Malden, MA: Blackwell.

Berscheid, E., & Lopes, J. (1997). A temporal model of relationship satisfaction and stability. In R. J. Sternberg & M. Hojjat (Eds.), *Satisfaction in close relationships* (pp. 129–159). New York: Guilford Press.

Berscheid, E., & Reis, H. T. (1998). Attraction and close relationships. In D. T. Gilbert, S. T. Fiske, & G. Lindzey (Eds.), *The handbook of social psychology* (Vol. 2, 4th ed., pp. 193–281). New York: McGraw-Hill.

Berscheid, E., Snyder, M., & Omoto, A. M. (1989). Issues in studying close relationships: Conceptualizing and measuring closeness. In C. Hendrick (Ed.), *Review of personality and social psychology: Vol. 10. Close relationships* (pp. 63–91). Newbury Park, CA: Sage.

Berscheid, E., Snyder, M., & Omoto, A. M. (2004). Measuring closeness: The Relationship Closeness Inventory (RCI) revisited. In D. J. Mashek & A. Aron (Eds.), *Handbook of closeness and intimacy* (pp. 81–101). Mahwah, NJ: Erlbaum.

Berscheid, E., & Walster, E. (1974). A little bit about love. In T. Huston (Ed.), *Foundations of interpersonal attraction* (pp. 355–381). New York: Academic Press.

Bettor, L., Hendrick, S. S., & Hendrick, C. (1995). Gender and sexual standards in dating relationships. *Personal Relationships, 2,* 359–369.

Bianchi, S. M., Subaiya, L., & Kahn, J. R. (1999). The gender gap in the economic well-being of nonresident fathers and custodial mothers. *Demography, 36,* 195–203.

Biddle, J. E., & Hamermesh, D. S. (1998). Beauty, productivity, and discrimination: Lawyers' looks and lucre. *Journal of Labor Economics, 16,* 172–181.

Biesanz, J. C., Neuberg, S. L., Smith, D. M., Asher, T., & Judice, T. N. (2001). When accuracy-motivated perceivers fail: Limited attentional resources and the reemerging self-fulfilling prophecy. *Personality and Social Psychology Bulletin, 27,* 621–629.

Billy, J. O., & Udry, J. R. (1985). The influence of male and female best friends on adolescent sexual behavior. *Adolescence, 20,* 21–32.

Billy, J. O. G., Landale, N. S., & McLaughlin, S. D. (1986). The effect of marital status at first birth on marital dissolution among adolescent mothers. *Demography, 23,* 329–349.

Birchler, G. R., & Webb, L. J. (1977). Discriminating interaction behavior in happy and unhappy marriages. *Journal of Consulting and Clinical Psychology, 45,* 494–495.

Birnbaum, M. H. (2004). Methodological and ethical issues in conducting social psychology research via the Internet. In C. Sansone, C. C. Morf, & A. T. Panter (Eds.), *The Sage handbook of methods in social psychology* (pp. 359–382). Thousand Oaks, CA: Sage.

Bissonnette, V. L., & Lipkus, I. M. (2002, June). *Subjective ambivalence in intimate relationships.* Paper presented at the meeting of the American Psychological Society, New Orleans.

Blascovich, J., Loomis, J., Beall, A., Swinth, K., Hoyt, C., & Bailenson, J. N. (2002). Immersive virtual environment technology as a methodological tool for social psychology. *Psychological Inquiry, 13,* 103–124.

Blau, P. M. (1964). *Exchange and power in social life.* New York: Wiley.

Bleske, A. L., & Shackelford, T. K. (2001). Poaching, promiscuity, and deceit: Combating mating rivalry in same-sex friendships. *Personal Relationships, 8,* 407–424.

Bleske-Rechek, A. L., & Buss, D. M. (2001). Opposite-sex friendship: Sex differences and similarities in initiation, selection, and dissolution. *Personality and Social Psychology Bulletin, 27,* 1310–1323.

Blieszner, R., & Roberto, K. A. (2004). Friendship across the life span: Reciprocity in individual and relationship development. In F. R. Lang & K. L. Fingerman (Eds.), *Growing together: Personal relationships across the life span* (pp. 159–182). Cambridge, UK: Cambridge University Press.

Blumstein, P., & Schwartz, P. (1983). *American couples: Money, work, sex.* New York: William Morrow.

Bolger, N., Zuckerman, A., & Kessler, R. C. (2000). Invisible support and adjustment to stress. *Journal of Personality and Social Psychology, 79,* 953–961.

Bollmer, J. M., Harris, M. J., Milich, R., & Georgesen, J. C. (2003). Taking offense: Effects of personality and teasing history on behavioral and emotional reactions to teasing. *Journal of Personality, 71,* 557–603.

Bombar, M. L., & Littig, L. W., Jr. (1996). Babytalk as a communication of intimate attachment: An initial study in adult romances and friendships. *Personal Relationships, 3,* 137–158.

Boneva, B., Kraut, R., & Frohlich, D. (2001). Using email for personal relationships: The difference gender makes. *American Behavioral Scientist, 45,* 530–549.

Bonner, B., Franiuk, R., & Logli, M. (2004, January). *Multi-dimensional romantic love.* Paper presented at the meeting of the Society for Personality and Social Psychology, Austin, TX.

Boon, S. D., & McLeod, B. A. (2001). Deception in romantic relationships: Subjective estimates of success at deceiving and attitudes toward deception. *Journal of Social and Personal Relationships, 18,* 463–476.

Booth, A., & Amato, P. R. (2001). Parental predivorce relations and offspring postdivorce well-being. *Journal of Marriage and the Family, 63,* 197–212.

Booth, A., & Crouter, A. C. (Eds.). (2002). *Just living together: Implications of cohabitation on families, children, and social policy.* Mahwah, NJ: Erlbaum.

Booth, A., Johnson, D. R., White, L. K., & Edwards, J. N. (1986). Divorce and marital instability over the life course. *Journal of Family Issues, 7,* 421–442.

Bornstein, R. F. (1989). Exposure and affect: Overview and meta-analysis of research, 1968–1987. *Psychological Bulletin, 106,* 265–289.

Borys, S., & Perlman, D. (1985). Gender differences in loneliness. *Personality and Social Psychology Bulletin, 11,* 63–76.

Bosson, J. K., & Swann, W. B., Jr. (2001). The paradox of the sincere chameleon: Strategic self-verification in close relationships. In J. H. Harvey & A. Wenzel (Eds.), *Close romantic relationships: Maintenance and enhancement* (pp. 67–86). Mahwah, NJ: Erlbaum.

Botwin, M. D., Buss, D. M., & Schackelford, T. K. (1997). Personality and mate preferences: Five factors in mate selection and marital satisfaction. *Journal of Personality, 65,* 107–136.

Bouchard, G., Lussier, Y., & Sabourin, S. (1999). Personality and marital adjustment: Utility of the five-factor model of personality. *Journal of Marriage and the Family, 61,* 651–660.

Bourgeois, K. S., & Leary, M. R. (2001). Coping with rejection: Derogating those who choose us last. *Motivation and Emotion, 25,* 101–111.

Bowlby, J. (1969). *Attachment and loss: Vol. 1. Attachment.* New York: Basic Books.

Boyer-Pennington, M. E., England, L. G., & Pennington, J. T. (2003, May). *College students' relationships as a function of parental marital stability and conflict.* Paper presented at the meeting of the American Psychological Society, Atlanta, GA.

Boyer-Pennington, M. E., Pennington, J., Spink, C., & Perkey, A. (2001, February). *The effect of parental marital status on single and married students' expectations for marriage and divorce.* Paper presented at the meeting of the Society for Personality and Social Psychology, San Antonio, TX.

Bradbury, T. N. (1994). Unintended effects of marital research on marital relationships. *Journal of Family Psychology, 8,* 187–201.

Bradbury, T. N. (Ed.). (1998). *The developmental course of marital dysfunction.* Cambridge, England: Cambridge University Press.

Bradbury, T. N. (2002). Invited program overview: Research on relationships as a prelude to action. *Journal of Social and Personal Relationships, 19,* 571–599.

Bradbury, T. N., Campbell, S. M., & Fincham, F. D. (1995). Longitudinal and behavioral analysis of masculinity and femininity in marriage. *Journal of Personality and Social Psychology, 68,* 328–341.

Bradbury, T. N., & Fincham, F. D. (1992). Attributions and behavior in marital interaction. *Journal of Personality and Social Psychology, 63,* 613–628.

Bradbury, T. N., & Lawrence, E. (1999). Physical aggression and the longitudinal course of newlywed marriage. In X. B. Arriaga & S. Oskamp (Eds.), *Violence in intimate relationships* (pp. 181–202). Thousand Oaks, CA: Sage.

Bradford, S. A., Feeney, J. A., & Campbell, L. (2002). Links between attachment orientations and dispositional and diary-based measures of disclosure in dating couples: A study of actor and partner effects. *Personal Relationships, 9,* 491–506.

Bramlett, M. D., & Mosher, W. D. (2002). Cohabitation, marriage, divorce and remarriage in the United States. *Vital Health Statistics, 23,* 1–103.

Branden, N. (1980). *The psychology of romantic love.* Los Angeles: Tarcher.

Brase, G. L., & Guy, E. C. (2004). The demographics of mate value and self-esteem. *Personality and Individual Differences, 36,* 471–484.

Braver, S. L., Ellman, I. M., & Fabricius, W. V. (2003). Relocation of children after divorce and children's best interests: New evidence and legal considerations. *Journal of Family Psychology, 17,* 206–219.

Brehm, S. S., & Brehm, J. W. (1981). *Psychological reactance: A theory of freedom and control.* New York: Academic Press.

Brehm, S. S., & Kassin, S. M. (1990). *Social psychology.* Boston: Houghton Mifflin.

Brennan, K. A., Clark, C. L., & Shaver, P. R. (1998). Self-report measurement of adult attachment: An integrative overview. In J. A. Simpson & W. S. Rholes (Eds.), *Attachment theory and close relationships* (pp. 46–76). New York: Guilford Press.

Brennan, K. A., & Morris, K. A. (1997). Attachment styles, self-esteem, and patterns of seeking feedback from romantic partners. *Personality and Social Psychology Bulletin, 23,* 23–31.

Brennan, T., & Auslander, N. (1979). *Adolescent loneliness: An exploratory study of social and psychological pre-dispositions and theory.* Boulder, CO: Behavioral Research Institute. (ERIC Document Reproduction Service No. ED 194822).

Brewer, M. B. (2004). Taking the social origins of human nature seriously: Toward a more imperialist social psychology. *Personality and Social Psychology Review, 8,* 107–113.

Brewster, M. P. (2003). Power and control dynamics in prestalking and stalking situations. *Journal of Family Violence, 18,* 207–217.

Bringle, R. G. (1995). Sexual jealousy in the relationships of homosexual and heterosexual men: 1980 and 1992. *Personal Relationships, 2,* 313–325.

Bringle, R. G., & Buunk, B. P. (1991). Extradyadic relationships and sexual jealousy. In K. McKinney & S. Sprecher (Eds.), *Sexuality in close relationships* (pp. 135–153). Hillsdale, NJ: Erlbaum.

Broderick, B. B. (1988). To arrive where we started: The field of family studies in the 1930s. *Journal of Marriage and the Family* , *50* , 569–584.

Brody, L. R., & Hall, J. A. (1993). Gender and emotion. In M. Lewis & J. M. Haviland (Eds.), *Handbook of emotion* (pp. 447–460). New York: Guilford Press.

Broemer, P., & Diehl, M. (2003). What you think is what you get: Comparative evaluations of close relationships. *Personality and Social Psychology Bulletin, 29,* 1560–1569.

Brown, C., Dovidio, J. F., & Ellyson, S. L. (1990). Reducing sex differences in visual displays of dominance. *Personality and Social Psychology Bulletin, 16,* 358–368.

Brown, J. L., Sheffield, D., Leary, M. R., & Robinson, M. E. (2003). Social support and experimental pain. *Psychosomatic Medicine, 65,* 276–283.

Brown, M., & Auerback, A. (1981). Communication patterns in initiation of marital sex. *Medical Aspects of Human Sexuality, 15,* 105–117.

Brown, N. R., & Sinclair, R. C. (1999). Estimating number of lifetime sexual partners: Men and women do it differently. *Journal of Sex Research, 36,* 292–297.

Browning, J. R., Hatfield, E., Kessler, D., & Levine, T. (2000). Sexual motives, gender, and sexual behavior. *Archives of Sexual Behavior, 29,* 135–153.

Bruch, M. A. (2001). Shyness and social interaction. In W. R. Crozier & L. E. Alden (Eds.), *International handbook of social anxiety: Concepts, research and interventions relating to the self and shyness* (pp. 195–215). Chichester, UK: Wiley.

Bruch, M. A., & Cheek, J. M. (1995). Developmental factors in childhood and adolescent shyness. In R. G. Heimberg, M. R. Liebowitz, D. A. Hope, & F. R. Schneier (Eds.), *Social phobia: Diagnosis, assessment, and treatment* (pp. 163–182). New York: Guilford Press.

Bruess, C. J. S., & Pearson, J. C. (1993). "Sweet pea" and "pussy cat": An examination of idiom use and marital satisfaction over the life cycle. *Journal of Social and Personal Relationships, 10,* 609–615.

Brunell, A. B., Campbell, W. K., Smith, L., & Krusemark, E. A. (2004, January). *Why do people date narcissists? A narrative study.* Paper presented at the meeting of the Society for Personality and Social Psychology, Austin, TX.

Bryant, A. N. (2003). Changes in attitudes toward women's roles: Predicting gender-role traditionalism among college students. *Sex Roles, 48,* 131–142.

Buckley, K. E., Winkel, R. E., & Leary, M. R. (2004). Reactions to acceptance and rejection: Effects of level and sequence of relational evaluation. *Journal of Experimental Social Psychology, 40,* 14–28.

Buehlman, K. T., Gottman, J. M., & Katz, L. F. (1992). How a couple views their past predicts their future: Predicting divorce from an oral history interview. *Journal of Family Psychology, 5,* 295–318.

Buhrmester, D., & Furman, W. (1986). The changing functions of friends in childhood: A neo-Sullivanian perspective. In V. J. Derlega & B. A. Winstead (Eds.), *Friendship and social interaction* (pp. 41–62). New York: Springer-Verlag.

Bui, K. T., Peplau, L. A., & Hill, C. T. (1996). Testing the Rusbult model of relationship commitment and stability in a 15-year study of heterosexual couples. *Personality and Social Psychology Bulletin, 22,* 1244–1257.

Bukowski, W. M., & Cillessen, A. H. (Eds.). (1998). *Sociometry then and now: Building on six decades of measuring children's experiences with the peer group.* San Francisco: Jossey-Bass.

Bulcroft, R. A., & White, J. M. (1997). Family research methods and levels of analysis. *Family Science Review, 10,* 136–153.

Buller, D. B., & Burgoon, J. K. (1994). Deception: Strategic and nonstrategic communication. In J. A. Daly & J. M. Wiemann (Eds.), *Strategic interpersonal communication* (pp. 191–223). Hillsdale, NJ: Erlbaum.

Bumpass, L. L., & Sweet, J. A. (1989). National estimates of cohabitation. *Demography, 26,* 615–625.

Burger, J. M., & Burns, L. (1988). The illusion of unique invulnerability and use of effective contraception. *Personality and Social Psychology Bulletin, 14,* 264–270.

Burgoon, J. K. (1994). Nonverbal signals. In M. L. Knapp & G. R. Miller (Eds.), *Handbook of interpersonal communication* (2nd ed., pp. 229–285). Thousand Oaks, CA: Sage.

Burgoon, J. K., & Bacue, A. E. (2003). Nonverbal communication skills. In J. O. Greene & B. R. Burleson (Eds.), *Handbook of communication and social interaction skills* (pp. 179–219). Mahwah, NJ: Erlbaum.

Burgoon, J. K., Buller, D. B., Grandpre, J. R., & Kalbfleisch, P. (1998). Sex differences in presenting and detecting deceptive messages. In D. J. Canary & K. Dindia (Eds.), *Sex differences and similarities in communication: Critical essays and empirical investigations of sex and gender in inter-action* (pp. 321–350). Mahwah, NJ: Erlbaum.

Burgoon, J. K., Buller, D. B., & Guerrero, L. K. (1995). Interpersonal deception: IX. Effects of social skill and nonverbal communication on deception success and detection accuracy. *Journal of Language and Social Psychology, 14,* 289–311.

Burgoon, J. K., Buller, D. B., White, C. H., Afifi, W., & Buslig, A. L. S. (1999). The role of conversational involvement in deceptive interpersonal interactions. *Personality and Social Psychology Bulletin, 25,* 669–685.

Burgoon, J., Buller, D. B., & Woodall, W. G. (1989). *Nonverbal communication: The unspoken dialogue.* New York: Harper & Row.

Burleson, B. R., Kunkel, A. W., Samter, W., & Werking, K. J. (1996). Men's and women's evaluations of communication skills in personal relationships: When sex differences make a difference—and when they don't. *Journal of Social and Personal Relationships, 13,* 201–224.

Burleson, B. R., & Samter, W. (1992). Are there gender differences in the relationship between academic performance and social behavior? *Human Communication Research, 19,* 155–175.

Burman, B., Margolin, G., & John, R. S. (1993). America's angriest home videos: Behavioral contingencies observed in home reenactments of marital conflict. *Journal of Consulting and Clinical Psychology, 61,* 28–39.

Burn, S. M. (1996). *The social psychology of gender.* New York: McGraw-Hill.

Burns, G. L., & Farina, A. (1992). The role of physical attractiveness in adjustment. *Genetic, Social, and General Psychology Monographs, 118,* 157–194.

Burton, K., Lydon, J., Bartz, J., & Bell, C. (2002, February). *Priming relationship commitment leads to increased relationship maintenance behavior.* Paper presented at the meeting of the Society for Personality and Social Psychology, Savannah, GA.

Bushman, B. J., Bonacci, A. M., van Dijk, M., & Baumeister, R. F. (2003). Narcissism, sexual refusal, and aggression: Testing a narcissistic reactance model of sexual coercion. *Journal of Personality and Social Psychology, 84,* 1027–1040.

Buss, D. M. (1985). Human mate selection. *American Scientist, 73,* 47–51.

Buss, D. M. (1989a). Conflict between the sexes: Strategic interference and the evocation of anger and upset. *Journal of Personality and Social Psychology, 56,* 735–747.

Buss, D. M. (1989b). Sex differences in human mate preferences: Evolutionary hypotheses tested in 37 cultures. *Behavioral and Brain Sciences, 12,* 1–14.

Buss, D. M. (1994). *The evolution of desire: Strategies of human mating.* New York: Basic Books.

Buss, D. M. (1995). Psychological sex differences: Origins through sexual selection. *American Psychologist, 50,* 164–168.

Buss, D. M. (2000). *The dangerous passion: Why jealousy is as necessary as love and sex.* New York: The Free Press.

Buss, D. M. (2004). *Evolutionary psychology: The new science of the mind* (2nd ed.). Boston: Allyn & Bacon.

Buss, D. M., & Barnes, M. (1986). Preferences in human mate selection. *Journal of Personality and Social Psychology, 50,* 559–570.

Buss, D. M., & Kenrick, D. T. (1998). Evolutionary social psychology. In D. T. Gilbert, S. T. Fiske, & G. Lindzey (Eds.), *The handbook of social psychology* (Vol. 2, 4th ed., pp. 982–1026). New York: McGraw-Hill.

Buss, D. M., Larsen, R. J., Westen, D., & Semmelroth, J. (1992). Sex differences in jealousy: Evolution, physiology, and psychology. *Psychological Science, 3,* 251–255.

Buss, D. M., & Schmitt, D. P. (1993). Sexual strategies theory: An evolutionary perspective on human mating. *Psychological Review, 100,* 204–232.

Buss, D. M., Shackelford, T. K., Choe, J., Buunk, B. P., & Dijkstra, P. (2000). Distress about mating rivals. *Personal Relationships, 7,* 235–243.

Buss, D. M., Shackelford, T. K., Kirkpatrick, L. A., Choe, J. C., Lim, H. K., Hasegawa, M., Hasegawa, T., & Bennett, K. (1999). Jealousy and the nature of beliefs about infidelity: Tests of competing hypotheses about sex differences in the United States, Korea, and Japan. *Personal Relationships, 6,* 125–150.

Buss, D. M., Shackelford, T. K., Kirkpatrick, L. A., & Larsen, R. J. (2001). A half century of mate preferences: The cultural evolution of values. *Journal of Marriage and the Family, 63,* 491–503.

Buunk, B. (1982). Anticipated sexual jealousy: Its relationship to self-esteem, dependency, and reciprocity. *Personality and Social Psychology Bulletin, 8,* 310–316.

Buunk, B. (1987). Conditions that promote breakups as a consequence of extra-dyadic involvements. *Journal of Social and Clinical Psychology, 5,* 271–284.

Buunk, B. P. (1995). Sex, self-esteem, dependency and extradyadic sexual experience as related to jealousy responses. *Journal of Social and Personal Relationships, 12,* 147–153.

Buunk, B. P. (1997). Personality, birth order and attachment styles as related to various types of jealousy. *Personality and Individual Differences, 23,* 997–1006.

Buunk, B. P. (2001). Perceived superiority of one's own relationship and perceived prevalence of happy and unhappy relationships. *British Journal of Social Psychology, 40,* 565–574.

Buunk, B. P., Angleitner, A., Oubaid, V., & Buss, D. M. (1996). Sex differences in jealousy in evolutionary and cultural perspective: Tests from the Netherlands, Germany, and the United States. *Psychological Science, 7,* 359–363.

Buunk, B. P., & Dijkstra, P. (2004). Men, women, and infidelity: Sex differences in extradyadic sex and jealousy. In J. Duncombe, K. Harrison, G. Allen, & D. Marsden (Eds.), *The state of affairs: Explorations in infidelity and commitment* (pp. 103–120). Mahwah, NJ: Erlbaum.

Buunk, B. P., Dijkstra, P., Fetchenhauer, D., & Kenrick, D. T. (2002). Age and gender differences in mate selection criteria for various involvement levels. *Personal Relationships, 9,* 271–278.

Buunk, B. P., Dijkstra, P., Kenrick, D. T., & Warntjes, A. (2001). Age preferences for mates as related to gender, own age, and involvement level. *Evolution and Human Behavior, 22,* 241–250.

Buunk, B., & Hupka, R. B. (1987). Cross-cultural differences in the elicitation of sexual jealousy. *Journal of Sex Research, 23,* 12–22.

Buunk, B. P., & Mutsaers, W. (1999). Equity perceptions and marital satisfaction in former and current marriage: A study among the remarried. *Journal of Social and Personal Relationships, 16,* 123–132.

Buunk, B. P., & van der Eijnden, R. J. J. M. (1997). Perceived prevalence, perceived superiority, and relationship satisfaction: Most relationships are good, but ours is the best. *Personality and Social Psychology Bulletin, 23,* 219–228.

Buunk, B. P., & VanYperen, N. W. (1991). Referential comparisons, relational comparisons, and exchange orientation: Their relation to marital satisfaction. *Personality and Social Psychology Bulletin, 17,* 709–717.

Buunk, B. P., & Ybema, J. F. (2003). Feeling bad, but satisfied: The effects of upward and downward comparison upon mood and marital satisfaction. *British Journal of Social Psychology, 42,* 613–628.

Byers, E. S., & Demmons, S. (1999). Sexual satisfaction and sexual self-disclosure within dating relationships. *Journal of Sex Research, 36,* 180–189.

Byers, E. S., Demmons, S., & Lawrance, K. (1998). Sexual satisfaction within dating relationships: A test of the interpersonal exchange model of sexual satisfaction. *Journal of Social and Personal Relationships, 15,* 257–267.

Byrne, D., & Blaylock, B. (1963). Similarity and assumed similarity of attitudes between husbands and wives. *Journal of Abnormal and Social Psychology, 67,* 636–640.

Byrne, D., & Clore, G. L. (1970). A reinforcement model of evaluative processes. *Personality: An International Journal, 1,* 103–128.

Byrne, D., Clore, G. L., & Smeaton, G. (1986). The attraction hypothesis: Do similar attitudes affect anything? *Journal of Personality and Social Psychology, 51,* 1167–1170.

Byrne, D., Ervin, C. E., & Lamberth, J. (1970). Continuity between the experimental study of attraction and real-life computer dating. *Journal of Personality and Social Psychology, 16,* 157–165.

Byrne, D., & Fisher, W. A. (1983). *Adolescents, sex, and contraception.* Hillsdale, NJ: Erlbaum.

Byrne, D., & Murnen, S. K. (1988). Maintaining loving relationships. In R. J. Sternberg & M. L. Barnes (Eds.), *The psychology of love* (pp. 293–310). New Haven, CT: Yale University Press.

Byrne, D., & Nelson, D. (1965a). Attraction as a linear function of proportion of positive reinforcements. *Journal of Personality and Social Psychology, 1,* 659–663.

Byrne, D., & Nelson, D. (1965b). The effect of topic importance and attitude similarity-dissimilarity on attraction in a multistranger design. *Psychonomic Science, 3,* 449–450.

Cacioppo, J. T., Ernst, J. M., Burleson, M. H., McClintock, M. K., Malarkey, W. B., Hawkley, L. C., Kowalewski, R. B., Paulsen, A., Hobson, J. A., Hugdahl, K., Spiegel, D., & Berntson, G. G. (2000). Lonely traits and concomitant physiological processes: The MacArthur social neuroscience studies. *International Journal of Psychophysiology, 35,* 143–154.

Cacioppo, J. T., & Gardner, W. L. (1999). Emotions. *Annual Review of Psychology, 50,* 191–214.

Cacioppo, J. T., & Hawkley, L. C. (2003, February). *Social isolation and health in older adults.* Paper presented at the meeting of the Society for Personality and Social Psychology, Los Angeles.

Cacioppo, J. T., Hawkley, L. C., Berntson, G. G., Ernst, J. M., Gibbs, A. C., Stickgold, R., & Hobson, J. A. (2002). Do lonely days invade the nights? Potential social modulation of sleep efficiency. *Psychological Science, 13,* 384–387.

Caldwell, M. A., & Peplau, L. A. (1984). The balance of power in lesbian relationships. *Sex Roles, 10,* 587–599.

Call, V. R. A., & Heaton, T. B. (1997). Religious influence on marital stability. *Journal for the Scientific Study of Religion, 36,* 382–392.

Call, V., Sprecher, S., & Schwartz, P. (1995). The incidence and frequency of marital sex in a national sample. *Journal of Marriage and the Family, 57,* 639–652.

Cameron, J. J., Ross, M., & Holmes, J. G. (2002). Loving the one you hurt: Positive effects of recounting a transgression against an intimate partner. *Journal of Experimental Social Psychology, 38,* 307–314.

Cameron, P., & Cameron, K. (1998). "Definitive" University of Chicago sex survey overestimated prevalence of homosexual identity. *Psychological Reports, 82,* 861–862.

Campbell, J., Miller, P., Cardwell, M., & Belknap, R. A. (1994). Relationship status of battered women over time. *Journal of Family Violence, 9,* 99–111.

Campbell, L., & Kashy, D. A. (2002). Estimating actor, partner, and interaction effects for dyadic data using PROC MIXED and HLM: A user-friendly guide. *Personal Relationships, 9,* 327–342.

Campbell, L., Simpson, J. A., Boldry, J., & Kashy, D. A. (2005). Perceptions of conflict and support in romantic relationships: The role of attachment anxiety. *Journal of Personality and Social Psychology, 88,* 510–531.

Campbell, L., Simpson, J. A., Kashy, D. A., & Rholes, W. S. (2001). Attachment orientations, dependence, and behavior in a stressful situation: An application of the actor-partner interdependence model. *Journal of Social and Personal Relationships, 18,* 821–843.

Campbell, S. M., Peplau, L. A., & DeBro, S. C. (1992). Women, men and condoms: Attitudes and experiences of heterosexual college students. *Psychology of Women Quarterly, 16,* 273–288.

Campbell, W. K., & Foster, C. A. (2002). Narcissism and commitment in romantic relationships: An investment model analysis. *Personality and Social Psychology Bulletin, 28,* 484–495.

Campbell, W. K., Foster, C. A., & Finkel, E. J. (2002). Does self-love lead to love for others? A story of narcissistic game playing. *Journal of Personality and Social Psychology, 83,* 340–354.

Canary, D. J. (2003). Managing interpersonal conflict: A model of events related to strategic choices. In J. O. Greene & B. R. Burleson (Eds.), *Handbook of commmunication and social interaction skills* (pp. 515–549). Mahwah, NJ: Erlbaum.

Canary, D. J., & Emmers-Sommer, T. M. (1997). *Sex and gender differences in personal relationships.* New York: Guilford Press.

Canary, D. J., & Stafford, L. (2001). Equity in the preservation of personal relationships. In J. H. Harvey & A. E. Wenzel (Eds.), *Close romantic relationships: Maintenance and enhancement,* (pp. 133–151). Mahwah, NJ: Erlbaum.

Canary, D. J., Stafford, L., & Semic, B. A. (2002). A panel study of the associations between maintenance strategies and relational characteristics. *Journal of Marriage and the Family, 64,* 395–406.

Cann, A., & Baucom, T. R. (2004). Former partners and new rivals as threats to a relationship: Infidelity type, gender, and commitment as factors related to distress and forgiveness. *Personal Relationships, 11,* 305–318.

Cantor, J. R., Zillmann, D., & Bryant, J. (1975). Enhancement of experienced sexual arousal in response to erotic stimuli through misattribution of unrelated residual arousal. *Journal of Personality and Social Psychology, 32,* 69–75.

Caporael, L. R., Lukaszewski, M. P., & Culbertson, G. H. (1983). Secondary baby talk: Judgments by institutionalized elderly and their caregivers. *Journal of Personality and Social Psychology, 44,* 746–754.

Caprara, G. V., Steca, P., Cervone, D., & Artistico, D. (2003). The contribution of self-efficacy beliefs to dispositional shyness: On social–cognitive systems and the development of personality dispositions. *Journal of Personality, 71,* 943–970.

Carducci, B. J. (1999). *Shyness: A bold new approach.* New York: HarperCollins.

Carli, L. L. (1990). Gender, language, and influence. *Journal of Personality and Social Psychology, 59,* 941–951.

Carli, L. L. (1999). Gender, interpersonal power, and social influence. *Journal of Social Issues, 55,* 81–98.

Carli, L. L. (2001). Gender and social influence. *Journal of Social Issues, 57,* 725–741.

Carli, L. L., Ganley, R., & Pierce-Otay, A. (1991). Similarity and satisfaction in roommate relationships. *Personality and Social Psychology Bulletin, 17,* 419–426.

Carli, L. L., LaFleur, S. J., & Loeber, C. C. (1995). Nonverbal behavior, gender, and influence. *Journal of Personality and Social Psychology, 68,* 1030–1041.

Carmichael, C. L., Gable, S. L., & Reis, H. T. (2003, February). *Who sees what in close relationships? Attachment and sensitivity to daily relationship behaviors using a quasi-signal detection paradigm.* Paper presented at the meeting of the Society for Personality and Social Psychology, Los Angeles.

Carmichael, C. L., & Reis, H. T. (2004, January). *The role of attachment insecurity in reduced sleep quality.* Paper presented at the meeting of the Society for Personality and Social Psychology, Austin, TX.

Carnegie, D. (1936). *How to win friends and influence people.* New York: Pocket Books.

Carney, D. R., Colvin, C. R., & Hall, J. A. (2004, January). *What? When? And for how long? A look at judgmental accuracy from "thin slices" of the behavioral stream.* Paper presented at the meeting of the Society for Personality and Social Psychology, Austin.

Carothers, B. J., & Allen, J. B. (1999). Relationships of employment status, gender roles, insult, and gender with use of influence tactics. *Sex Roles, 41,* 375–386.

Carothers, B. J., & Reis, H. T. (2004, January). *Men and women are from Earth: Examining the dimensional versus categorical structure of gender with taxometric procedures.* Paper presented at the meeting of the Society for Personality and Social Psychology, Austin, TX.

Carrère, S., & Gottman, J. M. (1999). Predicting divorce among newlyweds from the first three minutes of a marital conflict discussion. *Family Process, 38,* 293–301.

Carroll, J. S., & Doherty, W. J. (2003). Evaluating the effectiveness of premarital prevention programs: A meta-analytic review of outcome research. *Family Relations, 52,* 105–118.

Carroll, L. (1988). Concern with AIDS and the sexual behavior of college students. *Journal of Marriage and the Family, 50,* 405–411.

Carstensen, L. L., Isaacowitz, D. M., & Charles, S. T. (1999). Taking time seriously: A theory of socioemotional selectivity. *American Psychologist, 54,* 165–181.

Carter, S., & Snow, C. (2004, May). *Helping singles enter better marriages using predictive models of marital success.* Paper presented at the meeting of the American Psychological Society, Chicago.

Carton, J. S., Kessler, E. A., & Pape, C. L. (1999). Nonverbal decoding skills and relationship well-being in adults. *Journal of Nonverbal Behavior, 23,* 91–100.

Carver, C. S. (1997). Adult attachment and personality: Converging evidence and a new measure. *Personality and Social Psychology Bulletin, 23,* 865–883.

Cary, M. S. (1978). The role of gaze in the initiation of conversation. *Social Psychology, 41,* 269–271.

Cash, T. F., Thériault, J., & Annis, N. M. (2004). Body image in an interpersonal context: Adult attachment, fear of intimacy, and social anxiety. *Journal of Social and Clinical Psychology, 23,* 89–103.

Cashdan, E. (1998). Smiles, speech, and body posture: How women and men display sociometric status and power. *Journal of Nonverbal Behavior, 22,* 209–228.

Caspi, A., Harrington, H., Milne, B., Arnell, J. W., Theodore, R. F., & Moffitt, T. E. (2003). Children's behavioral styles at age 3 are linked to their adult personality traits at age 26. *Journal of Personality, 71,* 495–514.

Caspi, A., & Herbener, E. S. (1990). Continuity and change: Assortative marriage and the consistency of personality in adulthood. *Journal of Personality and Social Psychology, 58,* 250–258.

Cassidy, J., & Shaver, P. R. (Eds.). (1999). *Handbook of attachment: Theory, research and clinical applications.* New York: Guilford Press.

Catanese, K. R., Vohs, K. D., & Baumeister, R. F. (2004, February). *Bedtime stories: Examples of the social exchange model of sex.* Paper presented at the meeting of the Society for Personality and Social Psychology, Austin, TX.

Catania, J. A., Coates, T., Peterson, J., Dolcini, M., Kegeles, S., Siegel, D., Golden, E., & Fullilove, M. T. (1993). Changes in condom use among black, Hispanic, and white heterosexuals in San Francisco: The AMEN cohort survey. *Journal of Sex Research, 30,* 121–128.

Catania, J. A., Gibson, D. R., Chitwood, D. D., & Coates, T. J. (1990). Methodological problems in AIDS behavioral research: Influences on measurement error and participation bias in studies of sexual behavior. *Psychological Bulletin, 108,* 339–362.

Cate, R. M., Levin, L. A., & Richmond, L. S. (2002). Premarital relationship stability: A review of recent research. *Journal of Social and Personal Relationships, 19,* 261–284.

Cate, R. M., & Lloyd, S. A. (1992). *Courtship.* Thousand Oaks, CA: Sage.

Cate, R. M., Lloyd, S. A., & Henton, J. M. (1985). The effect of equity, equality, and reward level on the stability of students' premarital relationships. *Journal of Social Psychology, 125,* 715–721.

Cate, R. M., Lloyd, S. A., Henton, J. M., & Larson, J. (1982). Fairness and reward level as predictors of relationship satisfaction. *Social Psychology Quarterly, 45,* 177–181.

Cate, R. M., Lloyd, S. A., & Long, E. (1988). The role of rewards and fairness in developing premarital relationships. *Journal of Marriage and the Family, 50,* 443–452.

Caughlin, J. P., & Huston, T. L. (2002). A contextual analysis of the association between demand/withdraw and marital satisfaction. *Personal Relationships, 9,* 95–119.

Caughlin, J. P., Huston, T. L., & Houts, R. M. (2000). How does personality matter in marriage? An examination of trait anxiety, interpersonal negativity, and marital satisfaction. *Journal of Personality and Social Psychology, 78,* 326–336.

Caughlin, J. P., & Vangelisti, A. L. (2000). An individual difference explanation of why married couples engage in the demand/withdraw pattern of conflict. *Journal of Social and Personal Relationships, 17,* 523–551.

Cerda-Flores, R. M., Barton, S. A., Marty-Gonzalez, L. F., Rivas, F., & Chakraborty, R. (1999). Estimation of nonpaternity in the Mexican population of Nuevo Leon: A validation study of blood group markers. *American Journal of Physical Anthropology, 109,* 281–293.

Champion, C. D., & Kelly, A. E. (2004, May). *Clinton was right: Better to be technically truthful than to blatantly lie.* Paper presented at the meeting of the American Psychological Society, Chicago, IL.

Chan, C., & Margolin, G. (1994). The relationship between dual-earner couples' daily work mood and home affect. *Journal of Social and Personal Relationships, 11,* 573–586.

Chan, D. K.-S., & Cheng, G. H.-L. (2004). A comparison of offline and online friendship qualities at different stages of relationship development. *Journal of Social and Personal Relationships, 21,* 305–320.

Chaplin, W. F., Phillips, J. B., Brown, J. D., Clanton, N. R., & Stein, J. L. (2000). Handshaking, gender, personality, and first impressions. *Journal of Personality and Social Psychology, 79,* 110–117.

Check, J. V. P., Perlman, D., & Malamuth, N. M. (1985). Loneliness and aggressive behavior. *Journal of Social and Personal Relationships, 2,* 243–252.

Cheek, J. M., & Buss, A. H. (1981). Shyness and sociability. *Journal of Personality and Social Psychology, 41,* 330–339.

Cheek, J. M., & Melchior, L. A. (1990). Shyness, self–esteem, and self-consciousness. In H. Leitenberg (Ed.), *Handbook of social and evaluation anxiety* (pp. 47–82). New York: Plenum.

Chen, S., & Andersen, S. M. (2003, February). *Transference and the relational self.* Paper presented at the meeting of the Society for Personality and Social Psychology, Los Angeles.

Chen, S., Lee-Chai, A. Y., & Bargh, J. A. (2001). Relationship orientation as a moderator of the effects of social power. *Journal of Personality and Social Psychology, 80,* 173–187.

Cheng, C. M., Ferguson, M. J., & Chartrand, T. L. (2003, May). *Automatic evaluation of physical attractiveness: What is beautiful is automatically good.* Paper presented at the meeting of the American Psychological Society, Atlanta.

Choice, P., & Lamke, L. K. (1999). Stay/leave decision-making processes in abusive dating relationships. *Personal Relationships, 6,* 351–367.

Christensen, A. (1979). Naturalistic observation of families: A system for random audio recordings. *Behavior Therapy, 10,* 418–427.

Christensen, A., Atkins, D. C., Berns, S., Wheeler, J., Baucom, D. H., & Simpson, L. E. (2004). Traditional versus integrative behavioral couple therapy for significantly and chronically distressed married couples. *Journal of Consulting & Clinical Psychology, 72,* 176–191.

Christensen, A., & Heavey, C. L. (1993). Gender differences in marital conflict: The demand/withdraw interaction pattern. In S. Oskamp & M. Costanzo (Eds.), *Gender issues in contemporary society* (pp. 113–141). Newbury Park, CA: Sage.

Christensen, A., & Heavey, C. L. (1999). Intervention for couples. *Annual Review of Psychology, 50,* 165–190.

Christensen, A., Sullaway, M., & King, C. (1983). Systematic error in behavioral reports of dyadic interaction: Egocentric bias and content analysis. *Behavioral Therapy, 5,* 129–140.

Cialdini, R. B., Borden, R. J., Thorne, A., Walker, M. R., Freeman, S., & Sloan, L. R. (1976). Basking in reflected glory: Three (football) field studies. *Journal of Personality and Social Psychology, 34,* 366–375.

Ciarrochi, J., Hynes, K., & Crittenden, N. (2005). Can men do better if they try harder: Sex and motivational effects on emotional awareness. *Cognition and Emotion, 19,* 133–141.

Clanton, G. (1989). Jealousy in American culture 1945–1985: Reflections from popular literature. In D. D. Franks & E. D. McCarthy (Eds.), *The sociology of emotions: Original essays and research papers* (pp. 179–193). Greenwich, CT: JAI Press.

Clark, A. P. (2004). Self-perceived attractiveness and masculinization predict women's sociosexuality. *Evolution and Human Behavior, 25,* 113–124.

Clark, C. L., Shaver, P. R., & Abrahams, M.F. (1999). Strategic behaviors in romantic relationship initiation. *Personality and Social Psychology Bulletin, 25,* 707–720.

Clark, M. S. (1981). Noncomparability of benefits given and received: A cue to the existence of friendship. *Social Psychology Quarterly, 44,* 375–381.

Clark, M. S. (1984). Record keeping in two types of relationships. *Journal of Personality and Social Psychology, 47,* 549–577.

Clark, M. S. (1986). Evidence of the effectiveness of manipulations of communal and exchange relationships. *Personality and Social Psychology Bulletin, 12,* 414–425.

Clark, M. S. (2002, January). *Experiencing and expressing emotion: Relationship context matters.* Paper presented at the meeting of the Society for Personality and Social Psychology, Savannah, GA.

Clark, M. S., & Chrisman, K. (1994). Resource allocation in intimate relationships. In A. L. Weber & J. H. Harvey (Eds.), *Perspectives on close relationships* (pp. 176–192). Boston: Allyn & Bacon.

Clark, M. S., Finkel, E. J., Graham, S. M., & Pataki, S. P. (2004, January). *The thought counts: Giving and receiving benefits for communal reasons.* Paper presented at the meeting of the Society for Personality and Social Psychology, Austin, TX.

Clark, M. S., Graham, S., & Grote, N. (2002). Bases for giving benefits in marriage: What is ideal? What is realistic? What really happens? In P. Noller & J. A. Feeney (Eds.), *Understanding marriage: Developments in the study of couple interaction* (pp. 150–176). New York: Cambridge University Press.

Clark, M. S., & Grote, N. K. (1998). Why aren't indices of relationship costs always negatively related to indices of relationship quality? *Personality and Social Psychology Review, 2,* 2–17.

Clark, M. S., & Mills, J. (1979). Interpersonal attraction in exchange and communal relationships. *Journal of Personality and Social Psychology, 37,* 12–24.

Clark, M. S., & Mills, J. (1993). The difference between communal and exchange relationships: What it is and is not. *Personality and Social Psychology Bulletin, 15,* 684–691.

Clark, M. S., Mills, J. R., & Corcoran, D. M. (1989). Keeping track of needs and inputs of friends and strangers. *Personality and Social Psychology Bulletin, 15,* 533–542.

Clark, M. S., Mills, J., & Powell, M. C. (1986). Keeping track of needs in communal and exchange relationships. *Journal of Personality and Social Psychology, 51,* 333–338.

Clark, M. S., Pataki, S. P., & Carver, V. H. (1996). Some thoughts and findings on self-presentation of emotions in relationships. In G. J. O. Fletcher & J. Fitness (Eds.), *Knowledge structures in close relationships: A social psychological approach* (pp. 247–274). Mahwah, NJ: Erlbaum.

Clark, M. S., & Waddell, B. (1985). Perceptions of exploitations in communal and exchange relationships. *Journal of Social and Personal Relationships, 2,* 403–418.

Clark, R. A. (1998). A comparison of topics and objectives in a cross section of young men's and women's everyday conversations. In D. J. Canary & K. Dindia (Eds.), *Sex differences and similarities in communication: Critical essays and empirical investigations of sex and gender in interaction* (pp. 303–319). Mahwah, NJ: Erlbaum.

Clark, R. D., III, & Hatfield, E. (1989). Gender differences in receptivity to sexual offers. *Journal of Psychology and Human Sexuality, 2,* 39–55.

Clark, R. D., III, & Hatfield, E. (2003). Love in the afternoon. *Psychological Inquiry, 14,* 227–231.

Cleveland, H. H., Udry, J. R., & Chantala, K. (2001). Environmental and genetic influences on sex-typed behaviors and attitudes of male and female adolescents. *Personality and Social Psychology Bulletin, 27,* 1587–1598.

Clore, G. L., & Byrne, D. (1974). A reinforcement-affect model of attraction. In T. L. Huston (Ed.), *Foundations of interpersonal attraction* (pp. 143–170). New York: Academic Press.

Cohan, C. L., & Kleinbaum, S. (2002). Toward a greater understanding of the cohabitation effect: Premarital cohabitation and marital communication. *Journal of Marriage and the Family, 64,* 180–192.

Cohen, K. M. (2002). Relationships among childhood sex-atypical behavior, spatial ability, handedness, and sexual orientation in men. *Archives of Sexual Behavior, 31,* 129–143.

Coie, J. D., & Koeppl, G. K. (1990). Adapting interventions to the problems of aggressive and disruptive rejected children. In S. R. Asher & J. D. Coie (Eds.), *Peer rejection in childhood* (pp. 309–337). New York: Cambridge University Press.

Coker, D. A., & Burgoon, J. K. (1987). The nature of conversational involvement and nonverbal encoding patterns. *Human Communication Research, 13,* 463–494.

Cole, T. (2001). Lying to the one you love: The use of deception in romantic relationships. *Journal of Social and Personal Relationships, 18,* 107–129.

Collins, B. E. (2004, May). *What is beautiful is exciting and socially attractive.* Paper presented at the meeting of the American Psychological Society, Chicago.

Collins, N. L. (1996). Working models of attachment: Implications for explanation, emotion, and behavior. *Journal of Personality and Social Psychology, 71,* 810–832.

Collins, N. L., & Allard, L. M. (2001). Cognitive representations of attachment: The content and function of working models. In G. J. O. Fletcher & M. S. Clark (Eds.), *Blackwell handbook of social psychology: Interpersonal processes* (pp. 60–85). Malden, MA: Blackwell.

Collins, N. L., Cooper, M. L., Albino, A., & Allard, L. (2002). Psychosocial vulnerability from adolescence to adulthood: A prospective study of attachment style differences in relationship functioning and partner choice. *Journal of Personality, 70,* 965–1008.

Collins, N. L., & Feeney, B. C. (2000). A safe haven: An attachment theory perspective on support seeking and caregiving in intimate relationships. *Journal of Personality and Social Psychology, 78,* 1053–1073.

Collins, N. L., & Feeney, B. C. (2004). Working models of attachment shape perceptions of social support: Evidence from experimental and observational studies. *Journal of Personality and Social Psychology, 87,* 363–383.

Collins, N. L., & Miller, L. C. (1994). Self-disclosure and liking: A meta-analytic review. *Psychological Bulletin, 116,* 457–475.

Colvin, C. R., Vogt, D., & Ickes, W. (1997). Why do friends understand each other better than strangers do? In W. Ickes (Ed.), *Empathic accuracy* (pp. 169–193). New York: Guilford Press.

Condon, J. W., & Crano, W. D. (1988). Inferred evaluation and the relation between attitude similarity and interpersonal attraction. *Journal of Personality and Social Psychology, 54,* 789–797.

Conger, R. D., Cui, M., Bryant, C. M., & Elder, G. H., Jr. (2000). Competence in early adult romantic relationships: A developmental perspective on family influences. *Journal of Personality and Social Psychology, 79,* 224–237.

Conley, T. D., & Rabinowitz, J. L. (2004). Scripts, close relationships, and symbolic meanings of contraceptives. *Personal Relationships, 11,* 539–558.

Connolly, J., Craig, W., Goldberg, A., & Pepler, D. (1999). Conceptions of cross-sex friendships and romantic relationships in early adolescence. *Journal of Youth and Adolescence, 28,* 481–494.

Coogler, O. J. (1978). *Structured mediation in divorce settlement.* Lexington, MA: Lexington Books.

Cook, W. L. (2000). Understanding attachment security in family context. *Journal of Personality and Social Psychology, 78,* 285–294.

Cornetto, K. M. (2001, June). *Identity and illusion on the Internet: Interpersonal deception and detection in synchronous Internet environments.* Paper presented at the International Conference on Personal Relationships, Prescott, AZ.

Corrales, C. G. (1975). Power and satisfaction in early marriage. In R. E. Cromwell & D. H. Olson (Eds.), *Power in families* (pp. 197–216). New York: Wiley.

Couch, L. L., & Jones, W. H. (1997). Conceptualizing levels of trust. *Journal of Research in Personality, 31*, 319–336.

Couch, L. L., Jones, W. H., & Moore, D. S. (1999). Buffering the effects of betrayal: The role of apology, forgiveness, and commitment. In J. M. Adams & W. H. Jones (Eds.), *Handbook of interpersonal commitment and relationship stability* (pp. 451–469). New York: Kluwer Academic/Plenum.

Couch, L. L., & Olson, D. R. (2004, January). *Attachment as a predictor of psychological resolution after romantic betrayal.* Paper presented at the meeting of the Society for Personality and Social Psychology, Austin, TX.

Couch, L. L., Rogers, J., & Howard, A. (2000, February). *The impact of event characteristics on coping with interpersonal betrayal.* Paper presented at the meeting of the Society for Personality and Social Psychology, Nashville.

Cowan, G., Drinkard, J., & MacGavin, L. (1984). The effects of target, age, and gender on use of power strategies. *Journal of Personality and Social Psychology, 47*, 1391–1398.

Cowan, G., & Mills, R. D. (2004). Personal inadequacy and intimacy predictors of men's hostility toward women. *Sex Roles, 51*, 67–78.

Cox, C. L., Wexler, M. O., Rusbult, C. E., & Gaines, S. O., Jr. (1997). Prescriptive support and commitment processes in close relationships. *Social Psychology Quarterly, 60*, 79–90.

Cramer, D. (2004). Effect of the destructive disagreement belief on relationship satisfaction with a romantic partner or closest friend. *Psychology and Psychotherapy: Theory, Research, and Practice, 77*, 121–133.

Cramer, K. M., & Neyedley, K. A. (1998). Sex differences in loneliness: The role of masculinity and femininity. *Sex Roles, 38*, 645–653.

Crane, R. D., Dollahite, D. C., Griffin, W., & Taylor, V. L. (1987). Diagnosing relationships with spatial distance: An empirical test of a clinical principle. *Journal of Marital and Family Therapy, 13*, 307–310.

Crawford, C. (1998). Environments and adaptations: Then and now. In C. Crawford & D. L. Krebs (Eds.), *Handbook of evolutionary psychology: Ideas, issues, and applications* (pp. 275–302). Mahwah, NJ: Erlbaum.

Critelli, J. W., Myers, E. J., & Loos, V. E. (1986). The components of love: Romantic attraction and sex role orientation. *Journal of Personality, 54*, 354–370.

Crocker, J., & Luhtanen, R. K. (2003). Level of self-esteem and contingencies of self-worth: Unique effects on academic, social, and financial problems in college students. *Personality and Social Psychology Bulletin, 29*, 701–712.

Crohan, S. E. (1992). Marital happiness and spousal consensus on beliefs about marital conflict: A longitudinal investigation. *Journal of Social and Personal Relationships, 9*, 89–102.

Cromwell, R. E., & Olson, D. G. (1975). Multidisciplinary perspectives of power. In R. E. Cromwell & D. H. Olson (Eds.), *Power in families* (pp. 15–37). New York: Wiley.

Cui, M., Conger, R. D., Bryant, C. M., & Elder, G. H. (2002). Parental behavior and the quality of adolescent friendships: A social contextual perspective. *Journal of Marriage and the Family, 64*, 676–689.

Cumming, E., & Henry, W. E. (1961). *Growing old: The process of disengagement.* New York: Basic Books.

Cunningham, M. R. (1986). Measuring the physical in physical attractiveness: Quasi-experiments on the sociobiology of female facial beauty. *Journal of Personality and Social Psychology, 50*, 925–935.

Cunningham, M. R. (1989). Reactions to heterosexual opening gambits: Female selectivity and male responsiveness. *Personality and Social Psychology Bulletin, 15*, 27–41.

Cunningham, M. R. (2004, July). *Social allergies in love and work.* Paper presented at the meeting of the International Association for Relationship Research, Madison, WI.

Cunningham, M. R., Barbee, A. P., & Druen, P. B. (1997). Social allergens and the reactions they produce: Escalation of annoyance and disgust in love and work. In R. Kowalski (Ed.), *Aversive interpersonal interactions* (pp. 189–214). New York: Plenum.

Cunningham, M. R., Barbee, A. P., & Philhower, C. L. (2002). Dimensions of facial physical attractiveness: The intersection of biology and culture. In G. Rhodes & L. A. Zebrowitz (Eds.), *Facial attractiveness: Evolutionary, cognitive and social perspectives* (pp. 193–238). Westport, CT: Ablex.

Cunningham, M. R., Barbee, A. P., & Pike, C. L. (1990). What do women want? Facialmetric assessment of multiple motives in the perception of male facial physical attractiveness. *Journal of Personality and Social Psychology, 59*, 61–72.

Cunningham, M. R., Druen, P. B., & Barbee, A. P. (1997). Angels, mentors, and friends: Trade-offs among evolutionary, social, and individual variables in physical appearance. In J. A. Simpson & D. T. Kenrick (Eds.), *Evolutionary social psychology* (pp. 109–140). Mahwah, NJ: Erlbaum.

Cunningham, M. R., Roberts, A. R., Barbee, A. P., Druen, P. B., & Wu, C. (1995). "Their ideas of beauty are, on the whole, the same as ours": Consistency and variability in the cross-cultural perception of female physical attractiveness. *Journal of Personality and Social Psychology, 68,* 261–279.

Cunningham, M. R., Shamblen, S. R., Barbee, A. P., & Ault, L. K. (2005). Social allergies in romantic relationships: Behavioral repetition, emotional sensitization, and dissatisfaction in dating couples. *Personal Relationships, 12,* 273–295.

Cunradi, C. B., Caetano, R., & Schafer, J. (2002). Socioeconomic predictors of intimate partner violence among White, Black, and Hispanic couples in the United States. *Journal of Family Violence, 17,* 377–389.

Cupach, W. R., & Spitzberg, B. H. (2004). *The dark side of relationship pursuit: From attraction to obsession and stalking.* Mahwah, NJ: Erlbaum.

Curtin, S. C., & Martin, J. A. (2000). Births: Preliminary data for 1999. *National Vital Statistics Reports, 48 (14),* 1–21.

Curtis, R. C., & Miller, K. (1986). Believing another likes or dislikes you: Behaviors making the beliefs come true. *Journal of Personality and Social Psychology, 51,* 284–290.

Cutrona, C. E. (1982). Transition to college: Loneliness and the process of social adjustment. In L. A. Peplau & D. Perlman (Eds.), *Loneliness: A sourcebook of current theory, research, and therapy* (pp. 291–309). New York: Wiley Interscience.

Cutrona, C. E., Russell, D. W., Abraham, W. T., Gardner, K. A., Melby, J. N., Bryant, C., & Conger, R. D. (2003). Neighborhood context and financial strain as predictors of marital interaction and marital quality in African American couples. *Personal Relationships, 10,* 389–409.

Cutrona, C. E., Russell, D. W., de la Mora, A., & Wallace, R. B. (1997). Loneliness and nursing home admissions among rural older adults. *Psychology and Aging, 12,* 574–589.

Daigen, V., & Holmes, J. G. (2000). Don't interrupt! A good rule for marriage? *Personal Relationships, 7,* 185–201.

Dainton, M. (2000). Maintenance behaviors, expectations for maintenance, and satisfaction: Linking comparison levels to relational maintenance strategies. *Journal of Social and Personal Relationships, 17,* 827–842.

Dal Cin, S., Holmes, J. G., & Young, S. B. (2005, January). *Goal compatibility and relationship outcomes: It's the little things that matter.* Paper presented at the meeting of the Society for Personality and Social Psychology, New Orleans.

Daly, J. A., Hogg, E., Sacks, D., Smith, M., & Zimring, L. (1983). Sex and relationship affect social self-grooming. *Journal of Nonverbal Behavior, 7,* 183–189.

Darley, J. M., & Gross, P. H. (1983). A hypothesis-confirming bias in labeling effects. *Journal of Personality and Social Psychology, 44,* 20–33.

Davidson, B. (1984). A test of equity theory for marital adjustment. *Social Psychology Quarterly, 47,* 36–42.

Davidson, L. R., & Duberman, L. (1982). Friendship: Communication and interactional patterns in same-sex dyads. *Sex Roles, 8,* 809–822.

Davila, J. (2001). Paths to unhappiness: The overlapping courses of depression and romantic dysfunction. In S. R. H. Beach (Ed.), *Marital and family processes in depression: A scientific foundation for clinical practice* (pp. 71–87). Washington, DC: American Psychological Association.

Davila, J., Burge, D., & Hammen, C. (1997). Why does attachment style change? *Journal of Personality and Social Psychology, 73,* 826–838.

Davila, J., & Cobb, R. J. (2003). Predicting change in self-reported and interviewer-assessed adult attachment: Tests of the individual difference and life stress models of attachment change. *Personality and Social Psychology Bulletin, 29,* 859–870.

Davila, J., & Sargent, E. (2003). The meaning of life (events) predicts changes in attachment security. *Personality and Social Psychology Bulletin, 29,* 1383–1395.

Davis, D. (1981). Implications for interaction versus effectance as mediators of the similarity-attraction relationship. *Journal of Experimental Social Psychology, 17,* 96–117.

Davis, D., Shaver, P. R., & Vernon, M. L. (2003). Physical, emotional, and behavioral reactions to breaking up: The roles of gender, age, emotional involvement, and attachment style. *Personality and Social Psychology Bulletin, 29,* 871–884.

Davis, D., Shaver, P. R., & Vernon, M. L. (2004). Attachment style and subjective motivations for sex. *Personality and Social Psychology Bulletin, 30,* 1076–1090.

Davis, J. A., Smith, T. W., & Marsden, P. V. (2002). *The General Social Survey: 1972–2000 cumulative codebook.* Chicago: National Opinion Research Center.

Davis, J. L., & Rusbult, C. E. (2001). Attitude alignment in close relationships. *Journal of Personality and Social Psychology, 81,* 65–84.

Davis, K. E., & Latty-Mann, H. (1987). Love styles and relationship quality: A contribution to validation. *Journal of Social and Personal Relationships, 4,* 409–428.

Davis, K. E., & Todd, M. L. (1985). Assessing friendship: Prototypes, paradigm cases, and relationship description. In S. Duck & D. Perlman (Eds.), *Understanding personal relationships: An interdisciplinary approach* (pp. 17–38). London: Sage.

Davis, M. H., & Franzoi, S. L. (1986). Adolescent loneliness, self-disclosure, and private self-consciousness: A longitudinal investigation. *Journal of Personality and Social Psychology, 51,* 595–608.

Davis, M. H., & Kraus, L. A. (1997). Personality and empathic accuracy. In W. Ickes (Ed.), *Empathic accuracy* (pp. 144–168). New York: Guilford Press.

Davis, P. J. (1999). Gender differences in autobiographical memory for childhood emotional experiences. *Journal of Personality and Social Psychology, 76,* 498–510.

De Bro, S. C., Campbell, S. M., & Peplau, L. A. (1994). Influencing a partner to use a condom: A college student perspective. *Psychology of Women Quarterly, 18,* 165–182.

de Graaf, H., & Sandfort, T. G. M. (2004). Gender differences in affective responses to sexual rejection. *Archives of Sexual Behavior, 33,* 395–403.

de Jong Gierveld, J. (1995). Research into relationship research designs: Personal relationships under the microscope. *Journal of Social and Personal Relationships, 12,* 583–588.

De La Ronde, C., & Swann, W. B., Jr. (1998). Partner verification: Restoring shattered images of our intimates. *Journal of Personality and Social Psychology, 75,* 374–382.

de Rougemont, D. (1956). *Love in the Western world.* New York: Harper & Row.

de Vries, B. (1991). Friendship and kinship patterns over the life course: A family stage perspective. In L. Stones (Ed.), *Caring communities: Proceedings of the symposium on social support* (pp. 99–107). Ottawa: Industry, Science and Technology.

de Vries, B. (1996). The understanding of friendship: An adult life course perspective. In C. Magai & S. McFadden (Eds.), *Handbook of emotion, aging, and the life course* (pp. 249–268). New York: Academic Press.

Dean, K., K., & Gardner, W. L. (2003, February). *Satisfying the need to belong: Affective, motivational, and behavioral implications.* Paper presented at the meeting of the Society for Personality and Social Psychology, Los Angeles.

Demir, A., & Fisiloglu, H. (1999). Loneliness and marital adjustment of Turkish couples. *Journal of Psychology, 133,* 230–240.

DeNeve, K. M., & Cooper, H. (1998). The happy personality: A meta–analysis of 137 personality traits and subjective well-being. *Psychological Bulletin, 124,* 197–229.

DePaulo, B. M. (1992). Nonverbal behavior and self-presentation. *Psychological Bulletin, 111,* 203–243.

DePaulo, B. M. (1994). Spotting lies: Can humans learn to do better? *Current Directions in Psychological Science, 3,* 83–86.

DePaulo, B. M. (2004). The many faces of lies. In A. G. Miller (Ed.), *The social psychology of good and evil* (pp. 303–326). New York: Guilford Press.

DePaulo, B. M., Ansfield, M. E., Kirkendol, S. E., & Boden, J. M. (2000). Serious lies. *Basic & Applied Social Psychology, 26,* 147–167.

DePaulo, B. M., & Bell, K. L. (1996). Truth and investment: Lies are told to those who care. *Journal of Personality and Social Psychology, 71,* 703–716.

DePaulo, B. M., Charlton, K., Cooper, H., Lindsay, J. J., & Muhlenbruck, L. (1997). The accuracy-confidence correlation in the detection of deception. *Personality and Social Psychology Review, 1,* 346–357.

DePaulo, B. M., & Friedman, H. S. (1998). Nonverbal communication. In D. T. Gilbert, S. T. Fiske, & G. Lindzey (Eds.), *The handbook of social psychology: Vol. 2* (4th ed., pp. 3–40). New York: McGraw-Hill.

DePaulo, B. M., & Kashy, D. A. (1998). Everyday lies in close and casual relationships. *Journal of Personality and Social Psychology, 74,* 63–79.

DePaulo, B. M., Kashy, D. A., Kirkendol, S. E., Wyer, M. M., & Epstein, J. A. (1996). Lying in everyday life. *Journal of Personality and Social Psychology, 70*, 979–995.

DePaulo, B. M., Lanier, K., & Davis, T. (1983). Detecting the deceit of the motivated liar. *Journal of Personality and Social Psychology, 45*, 1096–1103.

DePaulo, B. M., Lindsay, J. J., Malone, B. E., Muhlenbruck, L., Charlton, K., & Cooper, H. (2003). Cues to deception. *Psychological Bulletin, 129*, 74–112.

DePaulo, B. M., & Pfeifer, R. L. (1986). On-the-job experience and skill at detecting deception. *Journal of Applied Social Psychology, 16*, 249–267.

DePaulo, B. M., Stone, J. I., & Lassiter, G. D. (1985). Telling ingratiating lies: Effects of target sex and target attractiveness on verbal and nonverbal deceptive success. *Journal of Personality and Social Psychology, 48*, 1191–1203.

Derlega, V. J., & Chaiken, A. L. (1977). Privacy and self-disclosure in social relationships. *Journal of Social Issues, 33*(3), 102–115.

Derlega, V. J., Wilson, M., & Chaikin, A. L. (1976). Friendship and disclosure reciprocity. *Journal of Personality and Social Psychology, 34*, 578–587.

Derlega, V. J., Winstead, B. A., Wong, P. T. P., & Hunter, S. (1985). Gender effects in an initial encounter: A case where men exceed women in disclosure. *Journal of Social and Personal Relationships, 2*, 25–44.

Dermer, M., & Pyszczynski, T. A. (1978). Effects of erotica upon men's loving and liking responses for women they love. *Journal of Personality and Social Psychology, 36*, 1302–1309.

Dermer, M., & Thiel, D. L. (1975). When beauty may fail. *Journal of Personality and Social Psychology, 31*, 1168–1176.

DeSteno, D., Bartlett, M. Y., Braverman, J., & Salovey, P. (2002). Sex differences in jealousy: Evolutionary mechanism or artifact of measurement? *Journal of Personality and Social Psychology, 83*, 1103–1116.

DeSteno, D. A., & Salovey, P. (1994). Jealousy in close relationships: Multiple perspectives on the green-eyed monster. In A. L. Weber & J. H. Harvey (Eds.), *Perspectives on close relationships* (pp. 217–242). Boston: Allyn & Bacon.

DeSteno, D. A., & Salovey, P. (1996a). Evolutionary origins of sex differences in jealousy? Questioning the "fitness" of the model. *Psychological Science, 7*, 367–372.

DeSteno, D. A., & Salovey, P. (1996b). Jealousy and the characteristics of one's rival: A self-evaluation maintenance perspective. *Personality and Social Psychology Bulletin, 22*, 920–932.

Devine, P. G., & Monteith, M. J. (1999). Automaticity and control in stereotyping. In S. Chaiken & Y. Trope (Eds.), *Dual-process theories in social psychology* (pp. 339–360). New York: Guilford Press.

Dewsbury, D. A. (1981). Effects of novelty on copulatory behavior: The Coolidge effect and related phenomena. *Psychological Bulletin, 89*, 464–482.

Diamond, L. M. (2004). Emerging perspectives on distinctions between romantic love and sexual desire. *Current Directions in Psychological Science, 13*, 116–119.

Diehl, M., Elnick, A. B., Bourbeau, L. S., & Labouvie-Vief, G. (1998). Adult attachment styles: Their relations to family context and personality. *Journal of Personality and Social Psychology, 74*, 1656–1669.

Diener, E. (2000). Subjective well-being: The science of happiness and a proposal for a national index. *American Psychologist, 55*, 34–43.

Diener, E., Gohm, C. L., Suh, E., & Oishi, S. (2000). Similarity of the relations between marital status and subjective well-being across cultures. *Journal of Cross-Cultural Psychology, 31*, 419–436.

Diener, E., Wolsic, B., & Fujita, F. (1995). Physical attractiveness and subjective well-being. *Journal of Personality and Social Psychology, 69*, 120–129.

Dijkstra, P., & Buunk, B. P. (1998). Jealousy as a function of rival characteristics: An evolutionary perspective. *Personality and Social Psychology Bulletin, 24*, 1158–1166.

Dijkstra, P., & Buunk, B. P. (2002). Sex differences in the jealousy-evoking effect of rival characteristics. *European Journal of Social Psychology, 32*, 829–852.

Dill, J. C., & Anderson, C. A. (1999). Loneliness, shyness, and depression: The etiology and interrelationships of everyday problems in living. In T. Joiner & J. C. Coyne (Eds.), *The interactional nature of depression* (pp. 93–125). Washington, DC: American Psychological Association.

Dimidjian, S., Martell, C. R., & Christensen, A. (2002). Integrative behavioral couple therapy. In A. S. Gurman & N. S. Jacobson (Eds.), *Clinical handbook of couple therapy* (3rd ed., pp. 251–277). New York: Guilford Press.

Dindia, K. (2000). Self-disclosure, identity, and relationship development: A dialectical perspective. In K. Dindia & S. Duck (Eds.), *Communication and personal relationships* (pp. 147–162). New York: John Wiley & Sons.

Dindia, K. (2000a). Relational maintenance. In C. Hendrick & S. S. Hendrick (Eds.), *Close relationships: A sourcebook.* (pp. 287–299). Thousand Oaks, CA: Sage.

Dindia, K. (2000b). Sex differences in self-disclosure, reciprocity of self-disclosure, and self-disclosure and liking: Three meta-analyses reviewed. In S. Petronio (Ed.), *Balancing the secrets of private disclosures* (pp. 21–35). Mahwah, NJ: Erlbaum.

Dindia, K. (2002). Self-disclosure research: Knowledge through meta-analysis. In M. Allen, R. W. Preiss et al. (Eds.), *Interpersonal communication research: Advances through meta-analysis* (pp. 169–185). Mahwah, NJ: Lawrence Erlbaum.

Dindia, K., & Allen, M. (1992). Sex differences in self-disclosure: A meta-analysis. *Psychological Bulletin, 112,* 106–124.

Dindia, K., & Fitzpatrick, M. A. (1985). Marital communication: Three approaches compared. In S. Duck & D. Perlman (Eds.), *Understanding personal relationships: An interdisciplinary approach* (pp. 137–157). London: Sage.

Dindia, K., Fitzpatrick, M. A., & Kenny, D. A. (1997). Self-disclosure in spouse and stranger interaction: A social relations analysis. *Human Communication Research, 23,* 388–412.

Dindia, K., & Timmerman, L. (2003). Accomplishing romantic relationships. In J. O. Greene & B. R. Burleson (Eds.), *Handbook of communication and social interaction skills* (pp. 685–721). Mahwah, NJ: Erlbaum.

Dion, K. K., & Dion, K. L. (1996). Cultural perspectives on romantic love. *Personal Relationships, 3,* 5–17.

Dion, K. K., Berscheid, E., & Walster, E. (1972). What is beautiful is good. *Journal of Personality and Social Psychology, 24,* 285–290.

DiTommaso, E., Brannen-McNulty, C., Ross, L., & Burgess, M. (2003). Attachment styles, social skills and loneliness in young adults. *Personality and Individual Differences, 35,* 303–312.

DiTommaso, E., & Spinner, B. (1995). Social and emotional loneliness: A re-examination of Weiss' typology of loneliness. *Personality and Individual Differences, 22,* 417–427.

Dixon, D., Cruess, S., Kilbourn, K., Klimas, N., & Fletcher, M. A. (2001). Social support mediates loneliness ad human herpes virus Type 6 (HHV-6) antibody titers. *Journal of Applied Social Psychology, 31,* 1111–1132.

Doherty, W. J. (2001). *Take back your marriage: Sticking together in a world that pulls us apart.* New York: Guilford Press.

Dolgin, K. G., & Minowa, N. (1997). Gender differences in self-presentation: A comparison of the roles of flatteringness and intimacy in self-disclosure to friends. *Sex Roles, 36,* 371–380.

Donaghue, N., & Fallon, B. J. (2003). Gender-role self-stereotyping and the relationship between equity and satisfaction in close relationships. *Sex Roles, 48,* 217–230.

Doss, B. D., Atkins, D. C., & Christensen, A. (2003). Who's dragging their feet? Husbands and wives seeking marital therapy. *Journal of Marital & Family Therapy, 29,* 165–177.

Doucet, J., & Aseltine, R. H., Jr. (2003). Childhood family adversity and the quality of marital relationships in young adulthood. *Journal of Social and Personal Relationships, 20,* 818–842.

Dovidio, J. F., Ellyson, S. L., Keating, C. F., Heltman, K., & Brown, C. E. (1988). The relationship of social power to visual displays of dominance between men and women. *Journal of Personality and Social Psychology, 54,* 233–242.

Downey, G., & Feldman, S. I. (1996). Implications of rejection sensitivity for intimate relationships. *Journal of Personality and Social Psychology, 70,* 1327–1343.

Downey, G., Feldman, S. I., & Ayduk, O. (2000). Rejection sensitivity and male violence in romantic relationships. *Personal Relationships, 7,* 45–61.

Downey, G., Freitas, A. L., Michaelis, B., & Khouri, H. (1998). The self-fulfilling prophecy in close relationships: Rejection sensitivity and rejection by romantic partners. *Journal of Personality and Social Psychology, 75,* 545–560.

Downs, A. C., & Lyons, P. M. (1991). Natural observations of the links between attractiveness and initial legal judgments. *Personality and Social Psychology Bulletin, 17,* 541–547.

Drach-Zahavy, A. (2004). Toward a multidimensional construct of social support: Implications of provider's self-reliance and support characteristics. *Journal of Applied Social Psychology, 34,* 1395–1420.

Drigotas, S. M. (2002). The Michelangelo phenomenon and personal well-being. *Journal of Personality, 70,* 59–70.

Drigotas, S. M., & Rusbult, C. E. (1992). Should I stay or should I go?: A dependence model of breakups. *Journal of Personality and Social Psychology, 62,* 62–87.

Drigotas, S. M., Rusbult, C. E., & Verette, J. (1999). Level of commitment, mutuality of commitment, and couple well-being. *Personal Relationships, 6,* 389–409.

Drigotas, S. M., Rusbult, C. E., Wieselquist, J., & Whitton, S. W. (1999). Close partner as sculptor of the ideal self: Behavioral affirmation and the Michelangelo phenomenon. *Journal of Personality and Social Psychology, 77,* 293–323.

Drigotas, S. M., Safstrom, C. A., & Gentila, T. (1999). An investment model prediction of dating infidelity. *Journal of Personality and Social Psychology, 77,* 509–524.

Driscoll, R., Davis, K. W., & Lipetz, M. E. (1972). Parental interference and romantic love. *Journal of Personality and Social Psychology, 24,* 1–10.

Driver, J. L., & Gottman, J. M. (2004). Daily marital interactions and positive affect during marital conflict among newlywed couples. *Family Process, 43,* 301–314.

Dryer, D. C., & Horowitz, L. M. (1997). When do opposites attract? Interpersonal complementarity versus similarity. *Journal of Personality and Social Psychology, 72,* 592–603.

Duck, S. (1982). A typography of relationship disengagement and dissolution. In S. Duck (Ed.), *Personal relationships. 4: Dissolving personal relationships* (1–30). London: Academic Press.

Duck, S. (Ed.). (1997). *Handbook of personal relationships: Theory, research and interventions* (2nd ed.). Chichester, England: Wiley.

Dunphy, D. C. (1963). The social structures of urban adolescent peer groups. *Sociometry, 26,* 230–246.

Duran-Aydintug, C. (1998). Emotional support during separation: Its sources and determinants. *Journal of Divorce and Remarriage, 29,* 121–141.

Dush, C. M. K., & Amato, P. R. (in press). Consequences of relationship status and quality for subjective well-being. *Journal of Social and Personal Relationships.*

Dutton, D. G. (1987). Wife assault: Social psychological contributions to criminal justice policy. In S. Oskamp (Ed.), *Applied social psychology annual: Vol. 7. Family process and problems: Social psychological aspects* (pp. 238–261). Newbury Park, CA: Sage.

Dutton, D. G., & Aron, A. P. (1974). Some evidence for heightened sexual attraction under conditions of high anxiety. *Journal of Personality and Social Psychology, 30,* 510–517.

Dweck, S., & Ivey, M. (1998). *Baby, all those curves and me with no brakes: Over 500 new no-fail pickup lines for men and women.* New York: Hyperion.

Dykstra, P. A. (1995). Loneliness among the never and formerly married: The importance of supportive friendships and a desire for independence. *Journal of Gerontology: Social Sciences, 50B,* S321–S329.

Eagly, A. H. (1997). Sex differences in social behavior: Comparing social role theory and evolutionary psychology. *American Psychologist, 52,* 1380–1383.

Eagly, A. H., Ashmore, R. D., Makhijani, M. G., & Longo, L. C. (1991). What is beautiful is good, but...: A meta-analytic review of research on the physical attractiveness stereotype. *Psychological Bulletin, 110,* 109–128.

Eagly, A. H., & Diekman, A. B. (2003). The malleability of sex differences in response to changing social roles. In L. G. Aspinwall & U. M. Staudinger (Eds.), *A psychology of human strengths: Fundamental questions and future directions for a positive psychology* (pp. 103–115). Washington, DC: American Psychological Association.

Eagly, A. H., & Wood, W. (1999). The origins of sex differences in human behavior: Evolved dispositions versus social roles. *American Psychologist, 54,* 408–423.

Ebbesen, E. B., Kjos, G. L., & Konecni, V. J. (1976). Spatial ecology: Its effects on the choice of friends and enemies. *Journal of Experimental Social Psychology, 12,* 505–518.

Ebling, R., & Levenson, R. W. (2003). Who are the marital experts? *Journal of Marriage and the Family, 65,* 130–142.

Egland, K. L., Spitzberg, B. H., & Zormeier, M. M. (1996). Flirtation and conversational competence in cross-sex platonic and romantic relationships. *Communication Reports, 9,* 105–117.

Eidelson, R. J. (1980). Interpersonal satisfaction and level of involvement: A curvilinear relationship. *Journal of Personality and Social Psychology, 39,* 460–470.

Eidelson, R. J. (1981). Affiliative rewards and restrictive costs in developing relationships. *British Journal of Social Psychology, 20,* 197–204.

Eidelson, R. J., & Epstein, N. (1982). Cognition and relationship maladjustment: Development of a measure of dysfunctional relationship beliefs. *Journal of Consulting and Clinical Psychology, 50,* 715–720.

Eisenberg, A. R. (1992). Conflicts between mothers and their young children. *Merrill-Palmer Quarterly, 38,* 21–43.

Eisenberger, N. I., Lieberman, M. D., & Williams, K. D. (2003, October). Does rejection hurt? An fMRI study of social exclusion. *Science, 302,* 290–292.

Eisenberger, R., Lynch, P., Aselage, J., & Rohdieck, S. (2004). Who takes the most revenge? Individual differences in negative reciprocity norm endorsement. *Personality and Social Psychology Bulletin, 30,* 787–799.

Ekman, P. (2003). *Emotions revealed: Recognizing faces and feelings to improve communication and emotional life.* New York: Times Books/Henry Holt.

Ekman, P., Friesen, W. V., & O'Sullivan, M. (1988). Smiles when lying. *Journal of Personality and Social Psychology, 54,* 414–420.

Ekman, P., Friesen, W. V., O'Sullivan, M., Chan, A., Diacoyanni-Tarlatzis, I., Heider, K., Krause, R., LeCompte, W. A., Pitcairn, T., Ricci-Bitti, P. E., Scherer, K., Tomita, M., & Tzavaras, A. (1987). Universals and cultural differences in the judgments of facial expressions of emotion. *Journal of Personality and Social Psychology, 53,* 712–717.

Ekman, P., & O'Sullivan, M. (1991). Who can catch a liar? *American Psychologist, 46,* 913–920.

Ekman, P., O'Sullivan, M., & Frank, M. G. (1999). A few can catch a liar. *Psychological Science, 10,* 263–266.

Elder, G. H., Jr. (1969). Appearance of education in marriage mobility. *American Sociological Review, 34,* 519–533.

Eldridge, K. A., & Christensen, A. (2002). Demand-withdraw communication during couple conflict: A review and analysis. In P. Noller & J. A. Feeney (Eds.), *Understanding marriage: Developments in the study of couple interaction* (pp. 289–322). Cambridge, UK: Cambridge University Press.

Elfenbein, H. A., & Ambady, N. (2003). Universals and cultural differences in recognizing emotions. *Current Directions in Psychological Science, 12,* 159–164.

Elizur, Y., & Mintzer, A. (2003). Gay males' intimate relationship quality: The roles of attachment security, gay identity, social support, and income. *Personal Relationships, 10,* 411–435.

Elliot, A. J., & Reis, H. T. (2003). Attachment and exploration in adulthood. *Journal of Personality and Social Psychology, 85,* 317–331.

Ellis, A. (1993). The advantages and disadvantages of self-help therapy materials. *Professional Psychology: Research & Practice, 24,* 335–339.

Ellis, B. J., Simpson, J. A., & Campbell, L. (2002). Trait-specific dependence in romantic relationships. *Journal of Personality, 70,* 611–659.

Ellyson, S. L., Dovidio, J. F., & Brown, C. E. (1992). The look of power: Gender differences and similarities in visual dominance behavior. In C. Ridgeway (Ed.), *Gender and interaction: The role of microstructures in inequality* (pp. 50–80). New York: Springer-Verlag.

Elwood, R. W., & Jacobson, N. S. (1982). Spouses' agreement in reporting their behavioral interactions: A clinical replication. *Journal of Consulting and Clinical Psychology, 50,* 783–784.

Emery, R. E. (1999a). *Marriage, divorce and children's adjustment* (2nd ed.). Thousand Oaks, CA: Sage.

Emery, R. E. (1999b). Postdivorce family life for children: An overview of research and some implications for policy. In R. A. Thompson & P. R. Amato (Eds.), *The postdivorce family: Children, parenting and society* (pp. 3–27). Thousand Oaks, CA: Sage.

Emmers, T. M., & Dindia, K. (1995). The effect of relational stage and intimacy on touch: An extension of Guerrero and Andersen. *Personal Relationships, 2,* 225–236.

Epley, S. W. (1974). Reduction of the behavioral effects of aversive stimulation by the presence of companions. *Psychological Bulletin, 81,* 271–283.

Epstein, N., & Baucom, D. H. (2002). *Enhanced cognitive-behavioral therapy for couples: A contextual approach.* Washington, DC: American Psychological Association.

Epstein, N., & Eidelson, R. J. (1981). Unrealistic beliefs of clinical couples: Their relationship to expectations, goals, and satisfaction. *American Journal of Family Therapy, 9,* 13–22.

Erbert, L. A. (2000). Conflict and dialectics: Perceptions of dialectical contradictions in marital conflict. *Journal of Social and Personal Relationships, 17,* 638–659.

Erikson, E. (1950). *Childhood and society.* New York: Norton.

Ernst, J. M., & Cacioppo, J. T. (1999). Lonely hearts: Psychological perspectives on loneliness. *Applied and Preventive Psychology, 8,* 1–22.

Etcheverry, P. E., & Le, B. (2004, January). *Thinking about commitment: Accessibility of commitment and the prediction of accommodation and willingness to sacrifice.* Paper presented at the meeting of the Society for Personality and Social Psychology, Austin, TX.

Etcoff, N. (1999). *Survival of the prettiest: The science of beauty.* New York: Doubleday.

Evans, M. A. (1993). Communicative competence as a dimension of shyness. In K. H. Rubin & J. B. Asendorpf (Eds.), *Social withdrawal, inhibition, and shyness in childhood* (pp. 189–212). Hillsdale, NJ: Erlbaum.

Fabricius, W. V. (2003). Listening to children of divorce: New findings that diverge from Wallerstein, Lewis, and Blakeslee. *Family Relations, 52,* 385–396.

Falbo, T. (1982). PAQ types and power strategies used in intimate relationships. *Psychology of Women Quarterly, 6,* 399–405.

Falbo, T., & Peplau, L. A. (1980). Power strategies in intimate relationships. *Journal of Personality and Social Psychology, 38,* 618–628.

Farber, B. (1987). The future of the American family: A dialectical account. *Journal of Family Issues, 8,* 431–433.

Fazzone, K. R., Kline, K. K., & Peeler, C. M. (2003, May). *Effects of women's hair length on ratings of perceived attractiveness by men.* Paper presented at the meeting of the American Psychological Society, Atlanta.

Feeney, B. C. (2004). A secure base: Responsive support of goal strivings and exploration in adult intimate relationships. *Journal of Personality and Social Psychology, 87,* 631–648.

Feeney, B. C., & Cassidy, J. (2003). Reconstructive memory related to adolescent-parent conflict interactions: The influence of attachment-related representations on immediate perceptions and changes in perceptions over time. *Journal of Personality and Social Psychology, 85,* 945–955.

Feeney, B. C., & Collins, N. L. (2001). Predictors of caregiving in adult intimate relationships: An attachment theoretical perspective. *Journal of Personality and Social Psychology, 80,* 972–994.

Feeney, B. C., & Collins, N. L. (2003). Motivations for caregiving in adult intimate relationships: Influences on caregiving behavior and relationship functioning. *Personality and Social Psychology Bulletin, 29,* 950–968.

Feeney, J. A. (1994). Attachment style, communication patterns, and satisfaction across the life cycle of marriage. *Personal Relationships, 1,* 333–348.

Feeney, J. A. (1998). Adult attachment and relationship-centered anxiety: Responses to physical and emotional distancing. In J. A. Simpson & W. S. Rholes (Eds.), *Attachment theory and close relationships* (pp. 189–218). New York: Guilford Press.

Feeney, J. A. (1999). Adult romantic attachment and couple relationships. In J. Cassidy & P. R. Shaver (Eds.), *Handbook of attachment: Theory, research and clinical applications* (pp. 355–377). New York: Guilford Press.

Feeney, J. A. (1999a). Adult attachment, emotional control, and marital satisfaction. *Personal Relationships, 6,* 169–185.

Feeney, J. A. (1999b). Romantic bonds in young adulthood: Links with family experiences. *Journal of Family Studies, 5,* 25–46.

Feeney, J. A. (2002). Attachment, marital interaction, and relationship satisfaction: A diary study. *Personal Relationships, 9,* 39–55.

Feeney, J. A. (2004). Hurt feelings in couple relationships: Towards integrative models of the negative effects of hurtful events. *Journal of Social and Personal Relationships, 21,* 487–508.

Feeney, J. A., Alexander, R., Noller, P., & Hohaus, L. (2003). Attachment insecurity, depression, and the transition to parenthood. *Personal Relationships, 10,* 475–493.

Feeney, J. A., & Noller, P. (1990). Attachment style as a predictor of adult romantic relationships. *Journal of Personality and Social Psychology, 58,* 281–291.

Feeney, J. A., & Noller, P. (2002). Allocation and performance of household tasks: A comparison of new parents and childless couples. In P. Noller & J. A. Feeney (Eds.), *Understanding marriage:*

Developments in the study of couple interaction (pp. 411–436). New York: Cambridge University Press.

Feeney, J. A., & Noller, P. (2004). Attachment and sexuality in close relationships. In J. H. Harvey, A. Wenzel, & S. Sprecher (Eds.), *The handbook of sexuality in close relationships* (pp. 183–201). Mahwah, NJ: Erlbaum.

Feeney, J. A., Noller, P., & Roberts, N. (2000). Attachment and close relationships. In C. Hendrick & S. S. Hendrick (Eds.), *Close relationships: A sourcebook* (pp. 185–201). Thousand Oaks, CA: Sage.

Feeney, J., Peterson, C., & Noller, P. (1994). Equity and marital satisfaction over the family life cycle. *Personal Relationships, 1,* 83–99.

Fehr, B. (1994). Prototype-based assessment of laypeople's views of love. *Personal Relationships, 1,* 309–331.

Fehr, B. (1996). *Friendship processes.* Thousand Oaks, CA: Sage.

Fehr, B. (1999a). Laypeople's conceptions of commitment. *Journal of Personality and Social Psychology, 76,* 90–103.

Fehr, B. (1999b). Stability and commitment in friendships. In J. M. Adams & W. H. Jones (Eds.), *Handbook of interpersonal commitment and stability* (pp. 259–280). New York: Kluwer Academic/ Plenum.

Fehr, B. (2001). The status of theory and research on love and commitment. In G. J. O. Fletcher & M. S. Clark (Eds.), *Blackwell handbook of social psychology: Interpersonal processes* (pp. 331–356). Malden, MA: Blackwell.

Fehr, B., & Broughton, R. (2001). Gender and personality differences in conceptions of love: An interpersonal theory analysis. *Personal Relationships, 8,* 115–136.

Fehr, B., & Russell, J. A. (1991). The concept of love viewed from a prototype perspective. *Journal of Personality and Social Psychology, 60,* 425–438.

Fehr, B., & Sprecher, S. (2004, July). *Compassionate love: Conceptual, relational, and behavioral issues.* Paper presented at the meeting of the International Association for Relationship Research, Madison, WI.

Fein, E., & Schneider, S. (1995). *The rules: Time-tested secrets for capturing the heart of Mr. Right.* New York: Warner Books.

Feingold, A. (1988). Matching for attractiveness in romantic partners and same-sex friends: A meta-analysis and theoretical critique. *Psychological Bulletin, 104,* 226–235.

Feingold, A. (1990). Gender differences in effects of physical attractiveness on romantic attraction: A comparison across five research paradigms. *Journal of Personality and Social Psychology, 59,* 981–993.

Feingold, A. (1992a). Gender differences in mate selection preferences: A test of the Parental Investment Model. *Psychological Bulletin, 112,* 125–139.

Feingold, A. (1992b). Good-looking people are not what we think. *Psychological Bulletin, 111,* 304–341.

Felmlee, D. H. (1995). Fatal attractions: Affection and disaffection in intimate relationships. *Journal of Social and Personal Relationships, 12,* 295–311.

Felmlee, D. H. (1998). "Be careful what you wish for. . . .": A quantitative and qualitative investigation of "fatal attractions." *Personal Relationships, 5,* 235–253.

Felmlee, D. H. (2001). From appealing to appalling: Disenchantment with a romantic partner. *Sociological Perspectives, 44,* 263–280.

Felmlee, D., & Flynn, H. K. (2004, July). *"Too much of a good thing:" Fatal attractions in adult intimate relationships.* Paper presented at the meeting of the International Association for Relationship Research, Madison, WI.

Felmlee, D. H., & Sprecher, S. (2000). Close relationships and social psychology: Intersections and future paths. *Social Psychology Quarterly, 63,* pp. 365–376.

Fenigstein, A., & Peltz, R. (2002). Distress over the infidelity of a child's spouse: A crucial test of evolutionary and socialization hypotheses. *Personal Relationships, 9,* 301–312.

Ferguson-Isaac, C., Ralston, T. K., & Couch, L. L. (1999, June). *Testing assumptions about coping with interpersonal betrayal.* Paper presented at the meeting of the International Network on Personal Relationships, Louisville, KY.

Festinger, L., Schachter, S., & Back, K. W. (1950). *Social pressures in informal groups: A study of human factors in housing.* New York: Harper & Brothers.

Filsinger, E. E., & Thoma, S. J. (1988). Behavioral antecedents of relationship stability and adjustment: A five-year longitudinal study. *Journal of Marriage and the Family, 50,* 785–795.

Finch, E. (2001). *The criminalization of stalking: Constructing the problem and evaluating the solution.* London: Cavendish.

Fincham, F. D. (2000). The kiss of porcupines: From attributing responsibility to forgiving. *Personal Relationships, 7,* 1–23.

Fincham, F. D. (2001). Attributions in close relationships: From Balkanization to integration. In G. J. O. Fletcher & M. S. Clark (Eds.), *Blackwell handbook of social psychology: Interpersonal processes* (pp. 3–31). Malden. MA: Blackwell.

Fincham, F. D., & Beach, S. R. H. (1999). Conflict in marriage: Implications for working with couples. *Annual Review of Psychology, 50,* 47–77.

Fincham, F. D., & Beach, S. R. H. (2002). Forgiveness in marriage: Implications for psychological aggression and constructive communication. *Personal Relationships, 9,* 239–251.

Fincham, F. D., & Bradbury, T. N. (1993). Marital satisfaction, depression, and attributions: A longitudinal analysis. *Journal of Personality and Social Psychology, 64,* 442–452.

Fincham, F. D., Harold, G. T., & Gano-Phillips, S. (2000). The longitudinal association between attributions and marital satisfaction: Direction of effects and role of efficacy expectations. *Journal of Family Psychology, 14,* 267–285.

Fincham, F. D., Paleari, F. G., & Regalia, C. (2002). Forgiveness in marriage: The role of relationship quality, attributions, and empathy. *Personal Relationships, 9,* 27–37.

Fink, B., Grammer, K., & Thornhill, R. (2001). Human (*Homo sapiens*) facial attractiveness in relation to skin texture and color. *Journal of Comparative Psychology, 115,* 92–99.

Finkel, E. J., & Campbell, W. K. (2001). Self-control and accommodation in close relationships: An interdependence analysis. *Journal of Personality and Social Psychology, 81,* 253–277.

Finkel, E. J., Rusbult, C. E., Kumashiro, M., & Hannon, P. A. (2002). Dealing with betrayal in close relationships: Does commitment promote forgiveness? *Journal of Personality and Social Psychology, 82,* 956–974.

Finkenauer, C., & Hazam, H. (2000). Disclosure and secrecy in marriage: Do both contribute to marital satisfaction? *Journal of Social and Personal Relationships, 17,* 245–263.

Firestone, R. W., & Catlett, J. (1999). *Fear of intimacy.* Washington, DC: American Psychological Association.

Fisher, H. (1995). The nature and evolution of romantic love. In W. Jankowiak (Ed.), *Romantic passion: A universal experience?* (pp. 23–41). New York: Columbia University Press.

Fisher, H. E., Aron, A., Mashek, D., Li, H., & Brown, L. L. (2002). Defining the brain systems of lust, romantic attraction, and attachment. *Archives of Sexual Behavior, 31,* 413–419.

Fisher, M. (2004, June 6). What happened to old-fashioned intimacy? *Houston Chronicle,* p. 1C.

Fisher, W. A. (1986). A psychological approach to human sexuality: The sexual behavior sequence. In D. Byrne & K. Kelley (Eds.), *Alternative approaches to the study of sexual behavior* (pp. 131–171). Hillsdale, NJ: Erlbaum.

Fisher, W. A., & Barak, A. (2001). Internet pornography: A social psychological perspective on Internet sexuality. *Journal of Sex Research, 38,* 312–323.

Fisher, W. A., Miller, C. T., Byrne, D., & White, L. A. (1980). Talking dirty: Responses to communicating a sexual message as a function of situational and personality factors. *Basic and Applied Psychology, 1,* 111–115.

Fiske, S. T. (2004). Developing a program of research. In C. Sansone, C. C. Morf, & A. T. Panter (Eds.), *The Sage handbook of methods in social psychology* (pp. 71–90). Thousand Oaks, CA: Sage.

Fitch, C. A., & Ruggles, S. (2000). Historical trends in marriage formation: The United States 1850–1990. In L. J. Waite (Ed.), *The ties that bind: Perspectives on marriage and cohabitation* (pp. 59–88). New York: Aldine de Gruyter.

Fitness, J. (2001). Betrayal, rejection, revenge, and forgiveness. In M. R. Leary (Ed.), *Interpersonal rejection* (pp. 73–103). New York: Oxford University Press.

Fitzpatrick, J., & Sollie, D. L. (1999a). Influence of individual and interpersonal factors on satisfaction and stability in romantic relationships. *Personal Relationships, 6,* 337–350.

Fitzpatrick, J., & Sollie, D. L. (1999b). Unrealistic gendered and relationship-specific beliefs: Contributions to investments and commitment in dating relationships. *Journal of Social and Personal Relationships, 16,* 852–867.

Fitzsimons, G. M., & Bargh, J. A. (2003). Thinking of you: Nonconscious pursuit of interpersonal goals associated with relationship partners. *Journal of Personality and Social Psychology, 84,* 148–164.

Fitzsimons, G. M., & Kay, A. C. (2004). Language and interpersonal cognition: Causal effects of variations in pronoun usage on perceptions of closeness. *Personality and Social Psychology Bulletin, 30,* 547–557.

Fleeson, W. (2004). The quality of American life at the end of the century. In O. G. Brim, C. D. Ryff, & R. C. Kessler (Eds.), *How healthy are we? A national study of well-being at midlife* (pp. 252–269). Chicago: University of Chicago Press.

Fletcher, G. (2002). *The new science of intimate relationships.* Malden, MA: Blackwell.

Fletcher, G. J. O., Simpson, J. A., & Thomas, G. (2000a). Ideals, perceptions, and evaluations in early relationship development. *Journal of Personality and Social Psychology, 80,* 933–940.

Fletcher, G. J. O., Simpson, J. A., & Thomas, G. (2000b). The measurement of perceived relationship quality components: A confirmatory factor analytic approach. *Personality and Social Psychology Bulletin, 26,* 340–354.

Fletcher, G. J. O., Simpson, J. A., Thomas, G., & Giles, L. (1999). Ideals in intimate relationships. *Journal of Personality and Social Psychology, 76,* 72–89.

Fletcher, G. J. O., Tither, J. M., O'Loughlin, C., Friesen, M., & Overall, N. (2004). Warm and homely or cold and beautiful? Sex differences in trading off traits in mate selection. *Personality and Social Psychology Bulletin, 30,* 659–672.

Foa, U. G., Converse, J., Törnblom, K. Y., & Foa, E. B. (Eds.). (1993). *Resource theory: Explorations and applications.* San Diego: Academic Press.

Folkes, V. S. (1982). Forming relationships and the matching hypothesis. *Personality and Social Psychology Bulletin, 8,* 631–636.

Fonagy, P., Steele, H., & Steele, M. (1991). Maternal representations of attachment during pregnancy predict the organization of infant–mother attachment at one year of age. *Child Development, 62,* 891–905.

Forestell, C. A., Humphrey, T. M., & Stewart, S. H. (2004). Involvement of body weight and shape factors in ratings of attractiveness by women: A replication and extension of Tassinary and Hansen (1998). *Personality and Individual Differences, 36,* 295–305.

Forgas, J. P., Levinger, G., & Moylan, S. J. (1994). Feeling good and feeling close: Affective influences on the perception of intimate relationships. *Personal Relationships, 1,* 165–184.

Forrest, J. A., & Feldman, R. S. (2000). Detecting deception and judge's involvement: Lower task involvement leads to better lie detection. *Personality and Social Psychology Bulletin, 26,* 118–125.

Forste, R., & Heaton, T. B. (2004). The divorce generation: Well-being, family attitudes, and socioeconomic consequences of marital disruption. *Journal of Divorce and Remarriage, 41,* 95–114.

Forste, R., & Tanfer, K. (1996). Sexual exclusivity among dating, cohabiting, and married women. *Journal of Marriage and the Family, 58,* 33–47.

Forsyth, D. R., & Schlenker, B. R. (1977). Attributional egocentrism following performance of a competitive task. *Journal of Social Psychology, 102,* 215–222.

Foster, C. A., Witcher, B. S., Campbell, W. K., & Green, J. D. (1998). Arousal and attraction: Evidence for automatic and controlled processes. *Journal of Personality and Social Psychology, 74,* 86–101.

Foster, J. D., Shrira, I., & Campbell, W. K. (2004, February). *Subsequent relationships of the mate poached.* Paper presented at the meeting of the Society for Personality and Social Psychology, Austin, TX.

Fraley, R. C. (2002). Attachment stability from infancy to adulthood: Meta-analysis and dynamic modeling of developmental mechanisms. *Personality and Social Psychology Review, 6,* 123–151.

Fraley, R. C., & Davis, K. E. (1997). Attachment formation and transfer in young adults' close friendships and romantic relationships. *Personal Relationships, 4,* 131–144.

Fraley, R. C., & Waller, N. G. (1998). Adult attachment patterns: A test of the typological model. In J. A. Simpson & W. S. Rholes (Eds.), *Attachment theory and close relationships* (pp. 77–114). New York: Guilford Press.

Fraley, R. C., Waller, N. G., & Brennan, K. A. (2000). An item response theory analysis of self-report measures of adult attachment. *Journal of Personality and Social Psychology, 78,* 350–365.

Franiuk, R., Cohen, D., & Pomerantz, E. M. (2002). Implicit theories of relationships: Implications for relationship satisfaction and longevity. *Personal Relationships, 9,* 345–367.

Frazier, P. A., Byer, A. L., Fischer, A. R., Wright, D. M., & DeBord, K. A. (1996). Adult attachment style and partner choice: Correlational and experimental findings. *Personal Relationships, 3,* 117–136.

Frederick, D. A., & Haselton, M. G. (2004, January). *Male muscularity as a good-genes indicator: Evidence from women's preferences for short-term and long-term mates.* Paper presented at the Evolutionary Psychology Pre-Conference at the meeting of the Society for Personality and Social Psychology, Austin, TX.

Frederick, S., & Lowenstein, G. (1999). Hedonic adaptation. In D. Kahneman, E. Diener, & N. Schwarz (Eds.), *Well-being: The foundations of hedonic psychology* (pp. 302–329). New York: Russell Sage Foundation.

Freedman, C. M., Low, S. M., Markman, H. J., & Stanley, S. M. (2002). Equipping couples with the tools to cope with predictable and unpredictable crisis events: The PREP program. *International Journal of Emergency Mental Health, 4,* 49–56.

Frei, J. R., & Shaver, P. R. (2002). Respect in close relationships: Prototype definition, self-report assessment, and initial correlates. *Personal Relationships, 9,* 121–139.

French, J. R. P., Jr., & Raven, B. H. (1959). The bases of social power. In D. Cartwright (Ed.), *Studies in social power* (pp. 150–167). Ann Arbor: University of Michigan Press.

Friedman, H. S., DiMatteo, M. R., & Mertz, T. J. (1980). Nonverbal communication on television news: The facial expressions of broadcasters during coverage of a presidential election campaign. *Personality and Social Psychology Bulletin, 6,* 427–435.

Frieze, I. H. (2000). Violence in close relationships—development of a research area: Comment on Archer (2000). *Psychological Bulletin, 126,* 681–684.

Frieze, I. H., & McHugh, M. C. (1992). Power and influence strategies in violent and nonviolent marriages. *Psychology of Women Quarterly, 16,* 449–465.

Frieze, I. H., Olson, J. E., & Russell, J. (1991). Attractiveness and income for men and women in management. *Journal of Applied Social Psychology, 21,* 1039–1057.

Frieze, I. H., Parsons, J. E., Johnson, P. B., Ruble, D. N., & Zellman, G. L. (1978). *Women and sex roles: A social psychological perspective.* New York: W. W. Norton.

Fritz, H. L., Nagurney, A. J., & Helgeson, V. S. (2003). Social interactions and cardiovascular reactivity during problem disclosure among friends. *Personality and Social Psychology Bulletin, 29,* 713–725.

Frye, N. E., & Karney, B. R. (2002). Being better or getting better? Social and temporal comparisons as coping mechanisms in close relationships. *Personality and Social Psychology Bulletin, 28,* 1287–1299.

Frye, N. E., & Karney, B. R. (2004). Revision in memories of relationship development: Do biases persist over time? *Personal Relationships, 11,* 79–97.

Fuendeling, J. M. (1998). Affect regulation as a stylistic process within adult attachment. *Journal of Social and Personal Relationships, 15,* 291–322.

Fuller T. L., & Fincham, F. D. (1995). Attachment style in married couples: Relation to current marital functioning, stability over time, and method of assessment. *Personal Relationships, 2,* 17–34.

Funder, D. C., Kolar, D. C., & Blackman, M. C. (1995). Agreement among judges of personality: Interpersonal relations, similarity, and acquaintanceship. *Journal of Personality and Social Psychology, 69,* 656–672.

Fung, H. H., & Carstensen, L. F. (2004). Motivational changes in response to blocked goals and foreshortened time: Testing alternatives to Socioemotional Selectivity Theory. *Psychology and Aging, 19,* 68–78.

Fung, H. H., Carstensen, L. F., & Lang, F. R. (2001). Age-related patterns in social networks among European Americans and African Americans: Implications for socioemotional selectivity across the life span. *International Journal of Aging and Human Development, 52,* 185–206.

Furnham, A., Dias, M., & McClelland, A. (1998). The role of body weight, waist-to-hip ratio, and breast size in judgments of female attractiveness. *Sex Roles, 39,* 311–326.

Furnham, A., McClelland, A., & Omer, L. (2003). A cross-cultural comparison of ratings of perceived fecundity and sexual attractiveness as a function of body weight and waist-to-hip ratio. *Health and Medicine, 8,* 219–230.

Furr, R. M., & Funder, D. C. (1998). A multimodal analysis of personal negativity. *Journal of Personality and Social Psychology, 74,* 1580–1591.

Gable, S. L. (2005, January). *Will you be there for me when things go right? Supportive responses to positive events.* Paper presented at the Relationships Preconference of the Society for Personality and Social Psychology, New Orleans.

Gable, S. L., & Reis, H. T. (2001). Appetitive and aversive social interaction. In J. H. Harvey & A. Wenzel (Eds.), *Close romantic relationships: Maintenance and enhancement* (pp. 169–194). Mahwah, NJ: Erlbaum.

Gable, S. L., Reis, H. T., & Downey, G. (2003). He said, she said: A quasi-signal detection analysis of daily interactions between close relationship partners. *Psychological Science, 14,* 100–105.

Gable, S. L., Reis, H. T., & Elliot, A. J. (2003). Evidence for bivariate systems: An empirical test of appetition and aversion across domains. *Journal of Research in Personality, 37,* 349–372.

Gable, S. L., Reis, H. T., Impett, E. A., & Asher, E. R. (2004). What do you do when things go right? The intrapersonal and interpersonal benefits of sharing positive events. *Journal of Personality and Social Psychology, 87,* 228–245.

Gaelick, L., Bodenhausen, G. V., & Wyer, R. S., Jr. (1985). Emotional communication in close relationships. *Journal of Personality and Social Psychology, 49,* 1246–1265.

Gagné, F. M., & Lydon, J. E. (2001a). Mind-set and close relationships: When bias leads to (in)accurate predictions. *Journal of Personality and Social Psychology, 81,* 85–96.

Gagné, F. M., & Lydon, J. E. (2001b). Mindset and relationship illusions: The moderating effects of domain specificity and relationship commitment. *Personality and Social Psychology Bulletin, 27,* 1144–1155.

Gagné, F. M., & Lydon, J. E. (2003). Identification and the commitment shift: Accounting for gender differences in relationship illusions. *Personality and Social Psychology Bulletin, 29,* 907–919.

Galati, D., Scherer, K. R., & Ricci-Bitti, P. E. (1997). Voluntary facial expression of emotion: Comparing congenitally blind with normally sighted encoders. *Journal of Personality and Social Psychology, 73,* 1363–1379.

Gambrill, E., Florian, V., & Thomas, K. (1999). *Rules people use in making and keeping friends.* Unpublished manuscript, University of California, Berkeley.

Gangestad, S. (2004, January). *A window into male-female conflicts of interests: When and with whom women have extra-pair sexual attraction.* Paper presented at the Evolutionary Psychology Pre-Conference at the meeting of the Society for Personality and Social Psychology, Austin, TX.

Gangestad, S. W., & Buss, D. M. (1993). Pathogen prevalence and human mate preference. *Ethology and Sociobiology, 14,* 89–96.

Gangestad, S. W., & Cousins, A. J. (2001). Adaptive design, female mate preferences, and shifts across the menstrual cycle. *Annual Review of Sex Research, 12,* 145–185.

Gangestad, S. W., & Simpson, J. A. (1993). Toward an evolutionary history of female sociosexual variation. *Journal of Personality, 58,* 69–96.

Gangestad, S. W., & Simpson, J. A. (2000). The evolution of human mating: Trade-offs and strategic pluralism. *Behavioral and Brain Sciences, 23,* 573–644.

Gangestad, S. W., Simpson, J. A., Cousins, A. J., Garver-Apgar, C. E., & Christensen, P. N. (2004). Women's preferences for male behavioral displays change across the menstrual cycle. *Psychological Science, 15,* 203–207.

Gangestad, S. W., & Snyder, M. (2000). Self-monitoring: Appraisal and reappraisal. *Psychological Bulletin, 126,* 530–555.

Garcia, S., Stinson, L., Ickes, W., Bissonnette, V., & Briggs, S. R. (1991). Shyness and physical attractiveness in mixed-sex dyads. *Journal of Personality and Social Psychology, 61,* 35–49.

Gardner, W. L., & Seeley, E. A. (2001). Confucius, 'jen,' and the benevolent use of power: The interdependent self as a psychological contract preventing exploitation. In A. Y. Lee-Chai & J. A. Bargh (Eds.), *The use and abuse of power: Multiple perspectives on the causes of corruption* (pp. 263–280). Philadelphia: Psychology Press.

Gaughan, M. (2002). The substitution hypothesis: The impact of premarital liaisons and human capital on marital timing. *Journal of Marriage and the Family, 64,* 407–419.

Gaulin, S. J. C., & McBurney, D. H. (2001). *Psychology: An evolutionary approach.* Upper Saddle River, NJ: Prentice-Hall.

Gayle, B. M., Preiss, R. W., & Allen, M. (2002). A meta-analytic interpretation of intimate and nonintimate interpersonal conflict. In M. Allen, R. W. Preiss, B. M. Gayle, & N. A. Burrell (Eds.), *Interpersonal communication research: Advances through meta-analysis* (pp. 345–368). Mahwah, NJ: Erlbaum.

Geary, D. C. (1998). *Male, female: The evolution of human sex differences.* Washington, DC: American Psychological Association.

Geary, D. C. (2000). Evolution and proximate expression of human paternal investment. *Psychological Bulletin, 126,* 55–77.

Gehl, B. K., & Watson, D. (2003, February). *Defining the structure of jealousy through factor analysis.* Poster presented at the annual meeting of the Society for Personality and Social Psychology, Los Angeles, CA.

Geis, B. D., & Gerrard, M. (1984). Predicting male and female contraceptive behavior: A discriminant analysis of groups high, moderate, and low in contraceptive effectiveness. *Journal of Personality and Social Psychology, 46,* 669–680.

Geiss, S. K., & O'Leary, K. D. (1981). Therapist ratings of frequency and severity of marital problems: Implications for research. *Journal of Marital and Family Therapy, 7,* 515–520.

Gentry, M. (1998). The sexual double standard: The influence of number of relationships and level of sexual activity on judgments of women and men. *Psychology of Women Quarterly, 22,* 505–511.

Gentzler, A. L., & Kerns, K. A. (2004). Associations between insecure attachment and sexual experiences. *Personal Relationships, 11,* 249–265.

Gephart, J. M., & Agnew, C. R. (1997, August). *Power strategies in romantic relationships.* Paper presented at the meeting of the American Psychological Association, Chicago, IL.

Gerrard, M., & Warner, T. D. (1994). Comparison of Marine and college women's HIV/AIDS-relevant sexual behaviors. *Journal of Applied Social Psychology, 24,* 959–980.

Gifford, R., & Gallagher, T. M. B. (1985). Sociability: Personality, social context, and physical setting. *Journal of Personality and Social Psychology, 48,* 1015–1023.

Gilbert, D. T., Krull, D. S., & Pelham, B. W. (1988). Of thoughts unspoken: Social inference and the self-regulation of behavior. *Journal of Personality and Social Psychology, 55,* 685–694.

Gilbert, D. T., & Osborne, R. E. (1989). Thinking backward: Some curable and incurable consequences of cognitive busyness. *Journal of Personality and Social Psychology, 57,* 940–949.

Gilbertson, J., Dindia, K., & Allen, M. (1998). Relational continuity constructional units and the maintenance of relationships. *Journal of Social and Personal Relationships, 15,* 774–790.

Gill, M. J., & Swann, W. B., Jr. (2004). On what it means to know someone: A matter of pragmatics. *Journal of Personality and Social Psychology, 86,* 405–418.

Gilovich, T., Savitsky, K., & Medvec, V. H. (1998). The illusion of transparency: Biased assessments of others' ability to read one's emotional states. *Journal of Personality and Social Psychology, 75,* 332–346.

Gladue, B. A., & Delaney, H. J. (1990). Gender differences in perception of attractiveness of men and women in bars. *Personality and Social Psychology Bulletin, 16,* 378–391.

Glass, C. R., & Shea, C. A. (1986). Cognitive therapy for shyness and social anxiety. In W. H. Jones, J. M. Cheek, & S. R. Briggs (Eds.), *Shyness: Perspectives on research and treatment* (pp. 315–327). New York: Plenum.

Glass, S. P., & Wright, T. L. (1992). Justifications for extramarital relationships: The association between attitudes, behaviors, and gender. *Journal of Sex Research, 29,* 361–387.

Gleason, M. E. J., Bolger, N., & Shrout, P. E. (2005, January). *Do we like those who give us advice and support? An experimental test of the effects of support receipt and provision on closeness and liking.* Paper presented at the meeting of the Society for Personality and Social Psychology, New Orleans.

Glenn, N. D. (1996). Values, attitudes, and the state of the American marriage. In D. Popenoe, J. B. Elshtain, & D. Blankenhorn (Eds.), *Promises to keep: Decline and renewal of marriage in America* (pp. 15–33). Lanham, MD: Rowman & Littlefield.

Glenn, N. D. (1998). The course of marital success and failure in five American 10-year marriage cohorts. *Journal of Marriage & the Family, 60,* 569–576.

Glenn, N. D., & Weaver, C. N. (1988). The changing relationship of marital status to reported happiness. *Journal of Marriage and the Family, 50,* 317–324.

Glynn, L. M., Christenfeld, N., & Gerin, W. (1999). Gender, social support, and cardiovascular responses to stress. *Psychosomatic Medicine, 61,* 234–242.

Gold, J. A., Ryckman, R. M., & Mosley, N. R. (1984). Romantic mood induction and attraction to a dissimilar other: Is love blind? *Personality and Social Psychology Bulletin, 10,* 358–368.

Goldfarb, L., Gerrard, M., Gibbons, F. X., & Plante, T. (1988). Attitudes toward sex, arousal, and the retention of contraceptive information. *Journal of Personality and Social Psychology, 55,* 634–641.

Gonzalez, R., & Griffin, D. (2000). On the statistics of interdependence. Treating dyadic data with respect. In W. Ickes & S. Duck (Eds.), *The social psychology of personal relationships* (pp. 181–213). Chichester, England: Wiley.

Gonzalez, R., & Griffin, D. (2004). Measuring individuals in a social environment: Conceptualizing dyadic and group interaction. In C. Sansone, C. C. Morf, & A. T. Panter (Eds.), *The Sage handbook of methods in social psychology* (pp. 313–334). Thousand Oaks, CA: Sage.

Goodfriend, W. (2004, January). *Partner-esteem: Romantic partners' biased perceptions of each other's faculties and flaws.* Paper presented at the meeting of the Society for Personality and Social Psychology, Austin, TX.

Goodfriend, W., & Agnew, C. R. (2002, February). *Tangible and intangible investments: A longitudinal study of their association with relationship longevity.* Paper presented at the meeting of the Society for Personality and Social Psychology, Savannah, GA.

Goodfriend, W., & Agnew, C. R. (2004, July). *A factor analytic investigation of the investment construct in romantic relationships.* Paper presented at the meeting of the International Association for Relationship Research, Madison, WI.

Goodwin, R., & Cramer, D. (2002). Inappropriate relationships in a time of social change. Some reflections on culture, history, and relational dimensions. In R. Goodwin & D. Cramer (Eds.), *Inappropriate relationships: The unconventional, the disapproved, & the forbidden* (pp. 247–263). Mahwah, NJ: Erlbaum.

Goodwin, S. A., Fiske, S. T., Rosen, L. D., & Rosenthal, A. M. (2002). The eye of the beholder: Romantic goals and impression biases. *Journal of Experimental Social Psychology, 38,* 232–241.

Goodwin, R., & Gaines, S., O., Jr. (2004). Relationship beliefs and relationship quality across cultures: Country as a moderator of dysfunctional beliefs and relationship quality in three former Communist societies. *Personal Relationships, 11,* 267–279.

Gordon, A. K., & Miller, A. G. (2000). Perspective differences in the construal of lies: Is deception in the eye of the beholder? *Personality and Social Psychology Bulletin, 26,* 46–55.

Gordon, R. A. (1996). Impact of ingratiation on judgments and evaluations: A meta-analytic investigation. *Journal of Personality and Social Psychology, 71,* 54–70.

Gosling, S. D., Vazire, S., Srivastava, S., & John, O. P. (2004). Should we trust web-based studies? A comparative analysis of six preconceptions about Internet questionnaires. *American Psychologist, 59,* 93–104.

Gotlib, I. H., & Whiffen, V. E. (1991). The interpersonal context of depression: Implications for theory and research. In W. H. Jones & D. Perlman (Eds.), *Advances in personal relationships: A research annual* (Vol. 3, pp. 177–206). London: Jessica Kingsley.

Gottman, J. M. (1993). The roles of conflict engagement, escalation, and avoidance in marital interaction: A longitudinal view of five types of couples. *Journal of Consulting and Clinical Psychology, 61,* 6–15.

Gottman, J. M. (1994a). *What predicts divorce? The relationship between marital processes and marital outcomes.* Hillsdale, NJ: Erlbaum.

Gottman, J. M. (1994b). *Why marriages succeed or fail.* New York: Simon & Schuster.

Gottman, J. M. (1999). *The marriage clinic: A scientifically-based marital therapy.* New York: W. W. Norton.

Gottman, J. M., & Carrère, S. (1994). Why can't men and women get along? Developmental roots and marital inequities. In D. J. Canary & L. Stafford (Eds.), *Communication and relational maintenance* (pp. 203–229). San Diego: Academic Press.

Gottman, J. M., Carrère, S., Swanson, C., & Coan, J. (2000). Reply to "From Basic Research to Interventions." *Journal of Marriage and the Family, 62,* 265–273.

Gottman, J. M., Coan, J., Carrère, S., & Swanson, C. (1998). Predicting marital happiness and stability from newlywed interactions. *Journal of Marriage and the Family, 60,* 5–22.

Gottman, J. M., & Levenson, R. W. (1992). Marital processes predictive of later dissolution: Behavior, physiology, and health. *Journal of Personality and Social Psychology, 63,* 221–233.

Gottman, J. M., & Levenson, R. W. (2000). The timing of divorce: Predicting when a couple will divorce over a 14–year period. *Journal of Marriage and the Family, 62,* 737–745.

Gottman, J. M., Levenson, R. W., Gross, J., Frederickson, B. L., McCoy, K., Rosenthal, L., et al. (2003). Correlates of gay and lesbian couples' relationship satisfaction and relationship dissolution. *Journal of Homosexuality, 45,* 23–43.

Gottman, J. M., & Notarius, C. I. (2000). Decade review: Observing marital interaction. *Journal of Marriage and the Family, 62,* 927–947.

Gottman, J. M., & Notarius, C. I. (2002). Marital research in the 20th century and a research agenda for the 21st century. *Family Process, 41,* 159–197.

Gottman, J. M., Notarius, C., Gonso, J., & Markman, H. (1976). *A couple's guide to communication.* Champaign, IL: Research Press.

Gottman, J. M., Notarius, C., Markman, H., Bank, S., Yoppi, B., & Rubin, M. E. (1976). Behavior exchange theory and marital decision making. *Journal of Personality and Social Psychology, 34,* 14–23.

Gottman, J. M., & Porterfield, A. L. (1981). Communication dysfunction in the non-verbal behavior of marital couples. *Journal of Marriage and the Family, 43,* 817–827.

Gottman, J. M., & Silver, N. (1999). *The seven principles for making marriage work.* New York: Crown.

Gracia, E., & Herrero, J. (2004). Personal and situational determinants of relationship-specific perceptions of social support. *Social Behavior and Personality, 32,* 459–476.

Graham, T., & Ickes, W. (1997). When women's intuition isn't greater than men's. In W. Ickes (Ed.), *Empathic accuracy* (pp. 117–143). New York: Guilford Press.

Graham-Kevan, N., & Archer, J. (2003). Intimate terrorism and common couple violence: A test of Johnson's predictions in four British samples. *Journal of Interpersonal Violence, 18,* 1247–1270.

Grammer, K., & Thornhill, R. (1994). Human (Homo sapiens) facial attractiveness and sexual selection: The role of symmetry and averageness. *Journal of Comparative Psychology, 108,* 233–242.

Gray, J. (1992). *Men are from Mars, women are from Venus.* New York: HarperCollins.

Gray, J. D., & Silver, R. C. (1990). Opposite sides of the same coin: Former spouses' divergent perspectives in coping with their divorce. *Journal of Personality and Social Psychology, 59,* 1180–1191.

Gray-Little, B., & Burks, N. (1983). Power and satisfaction in marriage: A review and critique. *Psychological Bulletin, 93,* 513–538.

Green, B. L., & Kenrick, D. T. (1994). The attractiveness of gender-typed traits at different relationship levels: Androgynous characteristics may be desirable after all. *Personality and Social Psychology Bulletin, 20,* 244–253.

Green, L. R., Richardson, D. S., Lago, T., & Schatten-Jones, E. C. (2001). Network correlates of social and emotional loneliness in young and older adults. *Personality and Social Psychology Bulletin, 27,* 281–288.

Green, S. K., Buchanan, D. R., & Heuer, S. K. (1984). Winners, losers, and choosers: A field investigation of dating initiation. *Personality and Social Psychology Bulletin, 10,* 501–511.

Greenfield, S., & Thelen, M. (1997). Validation of the Fear of Intimacy Scale with a lesbian and gay male population. *Journal of Social and Personal Relationships, 14,* 707–716.

Green-Hennessy, S., & Reis, H. T. (1998). Openness in processing social information among attachment types. *Personal Relationships, 5,* 449–466.

Greer, A. E., & Buss, D. M. (1994). Tactics for promoting sexual encounters. *Journal of Sex Research, 31,* 185–201.

Greiling, H., & Buss, D. M. (2000). Women's sexual strategies: The hidden dimension of extra-pair mating. *Personality and Individual Differences, 28,* 929–963.

Grice, J. W., & Seely, E. (2000). The evolution of sex differences in jealousy: Failure to replicate previous results. *Journal of Research in Personality, 34,* 348–356.

Griffiths, M. (2001). Sex on the Internet: Observations and implications for Internet sex addiction. *Journal of Sex Research, 38,* 333–342.

Griffitt, W., & Veitch, R. (1974). Preacquaintance attitude similarity and attraction revisited: Ten days in a fall-out shelter. *Sociometry, 37,* 163–173.

Griggs, L. (1990, July 2). A losing battle with AIDS. *Time,* pp. 41–43.

Grimm, L. G., & Yarnold, P. R. (Eds.). (1995). *Reading and understanding multivariate statistics.* Washington, DC: American Psychological Association.

Gronlund, N. E., & Holmlund, W. S. (1958). The value of elementary school sociometric status scores for predicting pupils' adjustment in high school. *Education Administration and Supervision, 44,* 255–260.

Grote, N. K., & Clark, M. S. (2001). Perceiving unfairness in the family: Cause or consequence of marital distress? *Journal of Personality and Social Psychology, 80,* 281–293.

Grote, N. K., & Frieze, I. H. (1994). The measurement of friendship-based love in intimate relationships. *Personal Relationships, 1,* 275–300.

Grote, N. K., & Frieze, I. H. (1998). "Remembrance of things past": Perceptions of marital love from its beginnings to the present. *Journal of Social and Personal Relationships, 15,* 91–109.

Grote, N. K., Frieze, I. H., & Stone, C. A. (1996). Children, traditionalism in the division of family work, and marital satisfaction: "What's love got to do with it?" *Personal Relationships, 3,* 211–228.

Guerrero, L. K. (1997). Nonverbal involvement across interactions with same-sex friends, opposite-sex friends and romantic partners: Consistency or change? *Journal of Social and Personal Relationships, 14,* 31–58.

Guerrero, L. K. (1998). Attachment-style differences in the experience and expression of romantic jealousy. *Personal Relationships, 5,* 273–291.

Guerrero, L. (2004, July). *Communicative responses to jealousy.* Paper presented at the meeting of the International Association for Relationship Research, Madison, WI.

Guerrero, L. K., & Andersen, P. A. (1998a). The dark side of jealousy and envy: Desire, delusion, desperation, and destructive communication. In B. H. Spitzberg & W. R. Cupach (Eds.), *The dark side of close relationships* (pp. 33–70). Mahwah, NJ: Erlbaum.

Guerrero, L. K., & Andersen, P. A. (1998b). Jealousy experience and expression in romantic relationships. In P. A. Andersen & L. K. Guerrero (Eds.), *Handbook of communication and emotion* (pp. 155–188). San Diego: Academic Press.

Guerrero, L. K., Andersen, P. A., Jorgensen, P. F., Spitzberg, B. H., & Eloy, S. V. (1995). Coping with the green-eyed monster: Conceptualizing and measuring communicative responses to romantic jealousy. *Western Journal of Communication, 59,* 270–304.

Guerrero, L. K., & Reiter, R. L. (1998). Expressing emotion: Sex differences in social skills and communicative responses to anger, sadness, and jealousy. In D. J. Canary & K. Dindia (Eds.), *Sex differences and similarities in communication: Critical essays and empirical investigations of sex and gender in interaction* (pp. 321–350). Mahwah, NJ: Erlbaum.

Gulliford, R. A., Murray, S. L., Bellavia, G. M., & Rose, P. (2002, February). *Positive illusions and perceptions of positive and negative events in marriage.* Paper presented at the meeting of the Society for Personality and Social Psychology, Savannah, GA.

Gunn, D. O., Guillory, C., & Gunn, C. W. (2002, June). *The development of intimacy in electronic chat rooms.* Paper presented at the meeting of the American Psychological Society, New Orleans.

Gupta, U., & Singh, P. (1982). Exploratory study of love and liking and type of marriages. *Indian Journal of Applied Psychology, 19,* 92–97.

Gurman, A. S. (2002). Brief integrative marital therapy: A depth-behavioral approach. In A. S. Gurman & N. S. Jacobson (Eds.), *Clinical handbook of couple therapy* (3rd ed., pp. 180–220). New York: Guilford Press.

Gurman, A. S., & Jacobson, N. S. (2002). *Clinical handbook of couple therapy* (3rd ed.). New York: Guilford Press.

Guttentag, M., & Secord, P. F. (1983). *Too many women? The sex ratio question.* Beverly Hills, CA: Sage.

Haas, A. (1979). Male and female spoken language differences: Stereotypes and evidence. *Psychological Bulletin, 86,* 616–626.

Haden, S. C., Hojjat, M., Ouimet, C., & Yock, S. (2004, July). *Young adults' hypothesized responses to betrayal in romantic relationships and close friendships.* Paper presented at the meeting of the International Association for Relationship Research, Madison, WI.

Hall, E. T. (1966). *The hidden dimension.* Garden City, NY: Doubleday.

Hall, J. A. (1998). How big are nonverbal sex differences? The case of smiling and sensitivity to nonverbal cues. In D. J. Canary & K. Dindia (Eds.), *Sex differences and similarities in communication: Critical essays and empirical investigations of sex and gender in interaction* (pp. 155–177). Mahwah, NJ: Erlbaum.

Hall, J. A., & Matsumoto, D. (2004). Gender differences in judgments of multiple emotions from facial expressions. *Emotion, 4,* 201–206.

Hall, J. A., & Veccia, E. M. (1990). More "touching" observations: New insights in men, women, and interpersonal touch. *Journal of Personality and Social Psychology, 59,* 1155–1162.

Halliday, G. (1991). Psychological self-help books: How dangerous are they? *Psychotherapy, 28,* 678–680.

Halpern, C. T., Young, M. L., Waller, M. W., Martin, S. L., & Kupper, L. L. (2004). Prevalence of partner violence in same-sex romantic and sexual relationships in a national sample of adolescents. *Journal of Adolescent Health, 35,* 124–131.

Hamermesh, D. S., & Biddle, J. E. (1994). Beauty and the labor market. *American Economic Review, 84,* 1174–1195.

Hamermesh, D. S., & Parker, A. M. (2005). Beauty in the classroom: Instructors' pulchritude and putative pedagogical productivity. *Economics of Education Review, 24,* 369–376.

Hammes, S. K., & Swann, W. B., Jr. (2004, January). *Alone we stand strong, together we fall apart: Precarious couples in dating relationships.* Paper presented at the meeting of the Society for Personality and Social Psychology, Austin, TX.

Hammock, G., Rosen, S., Richardson, D., & Bernstein, S. (1989). Aggression as equity restoration. *Journal of Research in Personality, 23,* 398–409.

Hamon, R. R., & Ingoldsby, B. B. (Eds.). (2003). *Mate selection across cultures.* Thousand Oaks, CA: Sage.

Hampton, R. L., Gelles, R. J., & Harrop, J. W. (1989). Is violence in black families increasing? A comparison of 1975 and 1985 national survey rates. *Journal of Marriage and the Family, 51,* 969–980.

Hancock, J. T., Thom-Santelli, J., & Ritchie, T. (2004). Deception and design: The impact of communication technology on lying behavior. *Proceedings of the Conference on Computer Human Interaction, 6,* 130–136.

Hancock, M., & Ickes, W. (1996). Empathic accuracy: When does the perceiver-target relationship make a difference? *Journal of Social and Personal Relationships, 13,* 179–199.

Hanley-Dunn, P., Maxwell, S. E., & Santos, J. P. (1985). Interpretation of interpersonal interactions: The influence of loneliness. *Personality and Social Psychology Bulletin, 11,* 445–456.

Hansen, G. L. (1985a). Dating jealousy among college students. *Sex Roles, 12,* 713–721.

Hansen, G. L. (1985b). Perceived threats and marital jealousy. *Social Psychology Quarterly, 48,* 262–268.

Hansson, R. O., & Jones, W. H. (1981). Loneliness, cooperation, and conformity among American undergraduates. *Journal of Social Psychology, 115,* 103–108.

Harris, C. R. (2000). Psychophysiological responses to imagined infidelity: The specific innate modular view of jealousy reconsidered. *Journal of Personality and Social Psychology, 78,* 1082–1091.

Harris, C. R. (2002). Sexual and romantic jealousy in the heterosexual and homosexual adults. *Psychological Science, 13,* 7–12.

Harris, C. R. (2003). A review of sex differences in sexual jealousy, including self-report data, psychophysiological responses, interpersonal violence, and morbid jealousy. *Personality and Social Psychology Review, 7,* 102–128.

Harris, C. R., & Christenfeld, N. (1996). Gender, jealousy, and reason. *Psychological Science, 7,* 364–366.

Harris, M. J., & Rosenthal, R. (1985). Mediation of interpersonal expectancy effects: 31 meta-analyses. *Psychological Bulletin, 97,* 363–386.

Hartup, W. W. (1993). Adolescents and their friends. In B. Laursen (Ed.), *Close friendships in adolescence: No. 60. New directions for child development* (pp. 3–22). San Francisco: Jossey-Bass.

Harvey, J. H., & Fine, M. A. (2004). *Children of divorce: Stories of loss and growth.* Mahwah, NJ: Lawrence Erlbaum.

Harvey, J. H., Hendrick, S. S., & Tucker, K. (1988). Self-report methods in studying personal relationships. In S. Duck (Ed.), *Handbook of personal relationships: Theory, research, and interventions* (pp. 99–113). New York: Wiley.

Harvey, J. H., Wells, G. L., & Alvarez, M. D. (1978). Attribution in the context of conflict and separation in close relationships. In J. H. Harvey, W. J. Ickes, & R. F. Kidd (Eds.), *New directions in attributional research* (Vol. 2, pp. 235–260). Hillsdale, NJ: Erlbaum.

Harvey, S. M., Beckman, L. J., Browner, C. H., & Sherman, C. A. (2002). Relationship power, decision making, and sexual relations: An exploratory study couple of Mexican origin. *Journal of Sex Research, 39,* 284–291.

Haselton, M. G. (2002). The sexual overperception bias: Evidence of a systematic bias in men from a survey of naturally occurring events. *Journal of Research in Personality, 37,* 34–47.

Haselton, M. G., & Buss, D. M. (2000). Error Management Theory: A new perspective on biases in cross-sex mind reading. *Journal of Personality and Social Psychology, 78,* 81–91.

Haslam, N., & Fiske, A. P. (1999). Relational models theory: A confirmatory factor analysis. *Personal Relationships, 6,* 241–250.

Haslam, S. A., & McGarty, C. (2004). Experimental design and causality in social psychological research. In C. Sansone, C. C. Morf, & A. T. Panter (Eds.), *The Sage handbook of methods in social psychology* (pp. 237–264). Thousand Oaks, CA: Sage.

Hatala, M. N., Baack, D. W., & Parmenter, R. (1998). Dating with HIV: A content analysis of gay male HIV-positive and HIV-negative personal advertisements. *Journal of Social and Personal Relationships, 15,* 268–276.

Hatfield, E. (1983). Equity theory and research: An overview. In H. H. Blumberg, A. P. Hare, V. Kent, & M. Davies (Eds.), *Small groups and social interaction* (Vol. 2, pp. 401–412). Chichester, England: Wiley.

Hatfield, E. (1984). The dangers of intimacy. In V. J. Derlega (Ed.), *Communication, intimacy, and close relationships* (pp. 207–220). Orlando: Academic Press.

Hatfield, E., Greenberger, D., Traupmann, J., & Lambert, P. (1982). Equity and sexual satisfaction in recently married couples. *Journal of Sex Research, 17,* 18–32.

Hatfield, E., & Rapson, R. L. (1987). Passionate love: New directions in research. In W. H. Jones & D. Perlman (Eds.), *Advances in personal relationships* (Vol. 1, pp. 109–139). Greenwich, CT: JAI Press.

Hatfield, E., & Rapson, R. L. (2002). Passionate love and sexual desire: Cultural and historical perspectives. In A. L. Vangelisti, H.T. Reis, & Fitzpatrick, M. A. (Eds.), *Stability and change in relationships* (pp. 306–324). New York: Cambridge University Press.

Hatfield, E., & Sprecher, S. (1986). Measuring passionate love in intimate relationships. *Journal of Adolescence, 9,* 383–410.

Havighurst, R. J. (1961). Successful aging. *Gerontologist, 1,* 8–13.

Hawkley, L. C., Browne, M. W., Ernst, J. M., Burleson, M. H., & Cacioppo, J. T. (2004, January). *The structure of loneliness: Replicable facets that matter.* Paper presented at the meeting of the Society for Personality and Social Psychology, Austin, TX.

Hawkley, L. C., Burleson, M. H., Berntson, G. G., & Cacioppo, J. T. (2003). Loneliness in everyday life: Cardiovascular activity, psychosocial context, and health behaviors. *Journal of Personality and Social Psychology, 85,* 105–120.

Hawkley, L. C., & Cacioppo, J. T. (2003, February). *Loneliness, social interactions, and affect in everyday life.* Paper presented at the meeting of the Society for Personality and Social Psychology, Los Angeles, CA.

Haynes, J. M. (1981). *Divorce mediation.* New York: Springer.

Hays, R. B. (1985). A longitudinal study of friendship development. *Journal of Personality and Social Psychology, 48,* 909–924.

Hazan, C., & Shaver, P. (1987). Romantic love conceptualized as an attachment process. *Journal of Personality and Social Psychology, 52,* 511–524.

Hazan, C., & Zeifman, D. (1994). Sex and the psychological tether. In K. Bartholomew & D. Perlman (Eds.), *Attachment processes in adulthood* (pp. 151–178). London: Jessica Kingsley.

Heaton, T. B. (2002). Factors contributing to increasing marital stability in the US. *Journal of Family Issues, 23,* 392–409.

Heaton, T. B., & Albrecht, S. L. (1991). Stable unhappy marriages. *Journal of Marriage and the Family, 53,* 747–758.

Heavy, C. L., Layne, C., & Christensen, A. (1993). Gender and conflict structure in marital interaction: A replication and extension. *Journal of Consulting and Clinical Psychology, 61,* 16–27.

Hebl, M. R., & Heatherton, T. F. (1998). The stigma of obesity in women: The difference is black and white. *Personality and Social Psychology Bulletin, 24,* 417–426.

Hebl, M. R., Bigazzi Foster, J., Mannix, L. M., & Dovidio, J. F. (2002). Formal and interpersonal discrimination: A field study of bias toward homosexual applicants. *Personality and Social Psychology Bulletin, 28,* 815–825.

Hecht, M. A., & LaFrance, M. (1998). License or obligation to smile: The effect of power and sex on amount and type of smiling. *Personality and Social Psychology Bulletin, 24,* 1332–1342.

Hecht, M. L., Marston, P. J., & Larkey, L. K. (1994). Love ways and relationship quality in heterosexual relationships. *Journal of Social and Personal Relationships, 11,* 25–43.

Heider, F. (1958). *The psychology of interpersonal relations.* New York: Wiley.

Helgeson, V. S., & Fritz, H. L. (1999). Unmitigated agency and unmitigated communion: Distinctions from agency and communion. *Journal of Research in Personality, 33,* 131–158.

Helms-Erickson, H., McHale, S. M., & Proulx, C. M. (2002, July). *Patterns of spouses' sex-typed personal qualities and their links with marriage in midlife.* Paper presented at the International Conference on Personal Relationships, Halifax, Nova Scotia.

Henderson, L., & Zimbardo, P. (1998). Shyness. In H. S. Friedman (Ed.), *Encyclopedia of mental health* (Vol. 3, pp. 497–509). San Diego, CA: Academic Press.

Henderson, M. (2004, May 5). Experts figure out why men prefer Marilyn. *The Times,* p. 13.

Henderson-King, D. H., & Veroff, J. (1994). Sexual satisfaction and marital well-being in the first years of marriages. *Journal of Social and Personal Relationships, 11,* 509–534.

Hendrick, C., & Hendrick, S. S. (2003). Romantic love: Measuring cupid's arrow. In S. J. Lopez & C. R. Snyder (Eds.), *Positive psychological assessment: A handbook of models and measures* (pp. 235–249). Washington, DC: American Psychological Association.

Hendrick, C., Hendrick, S. S., & Dicke, A. (1998). The Love Attitudes Scale: Short Form. *Journal of Social and Personal Relationships, 15,* 147–159.

Hendrick, S. S. (1981). Self-disclosure and marital satisfaction. *Journal of Personality and Social Psychology, 40,* 1150–1159.

Hendrick, S. S., & Hendrick, C. (1993). Lovers as friends. *Journal of Social and Personal Relationships, 10,* 459–466.

Hendrick, S. S., & Hendrick, C. (1995). Gender differences and similarities in sex and love. *Personal Relationships, 2,* 55–65.

Hendrick, S. S., & Hendrick, C. (2004, January). *Respect in close romantic relationships.* Paper presented at the meeting of the Society for Personality and Social Psychology, Austin, TX.

Hendrick, S. S., Dicke, A., & Hendrick, C. (1998). The Relationship Assessment Scale. *Journal of Social and Personal Relationships, 15,* 137–142.

Henley, N. M. (1977). *Body politics: Power, sex, and nonverbal communication.* Englewood Cliffs, NJ: Prentice-Hall.

Henningsen, D. D. (2004). Flirting with meaning: An examination of miscommunication in flirting interactions. *Sex Roles, 50,* 481–489.

Hensley, W. E. (1994). Height as a basis for interpersonal attraction. *Adolescence, 29,* 469–474.

Herbst, K. C., Gaertner, L., & Insko, C. A. (2003). My head says yes but my heart says no: Cognitive and affective attraction as a function of similarity to the ideal self. *Journal of Personality and Social Psychology, 84,* 1206–1219.

Herek, G. M., & Capitanio, J. P. (1996). "Some of my best friends": Intergroup contact, concealable stigma, and heterosexuals' attitudes toward gay men and lesbians. *Personality and Social Psychology Bulletin, 22,* 412–424.

Herek, G. M., & Glunt, E. K. (1993). Interpersonal contact and heterosexuals' attitudes toward gay men: Results from a national survey. *Journal of Sex Research, 30,* 239–244.

Herz, R. S., & Inzlicht, M. (2002). Sex differences in response to physical and social factors involved in human mate selection. *Evolution and Human Behavior, 23,* 359–364.

Hetherington, E. M. (2003). Intimate pathways: Changing patterns in close personal relationships across time. *Family Relations, 52,* 318–331.

Hetherington, E. M., & Kelly, J. (2002). *For better or for worse: Divorce reconsidered.* New York: W. W. Norton.

Hickman, S. E., & Muehlenhard, C. L. (1999). "By the semi-mystical appearance of a condom": How young women and men communicate sexual consent in heterosexual situations. *Journal of Sex Research, 36,* 258–272.

Hill, C. A., Blakemore, J. E. O., & Drumm, P. (1997). Mutual and unrequited love in adolescence and young adulthood. *Personal Relationships, 4,* 15–23.

Hill, C. A., & Preston, L. K. (1996). Individual differences in the experience of sexual motivation: Theory and measurement of dispositional sexual motives. *Journal of Sex Research, 33,* 27–45.

Hill, C. T., Rubin, Z., Peplau, L. A., & Willard, S. G. (1979). The volunteer couple: Sex differences, couple commitment, and participation in research on interpersonal relationships. *Social Psychology Quarterly, 41,* 415–420.

Hill, M. E. (2002). Skin color and the perception of attractiveness among African Americans: Does gender make a difference? *Social Psychology Quarterly, 65,* 77–91.

Hinchliff, S., & Gott, M. (2004). Intimacy, commitment, and adaptation: Sexual relationships within long-term marriages. *Journal of Social and Personal Relationships, 21,* 595–609.

Hines, D., Saris, R. N., & Throckmorton-Belzer, L. (2002). Pluralistic ignorance and health risk behaviors: Do college students misperceive social approval for risky behavior on campus and in media? *Journal of Applied Social Psychology, 32,* 2621–2640.

Hinsz, V. B., Matz, D. C., & Patience, R. A. (2001). Does women's hair signal reproductive potential? *Journal of Experimental Social Psychology, 37,* 166–172.

Holland, R. W., Roeder, U. R., van Baaren, R. B., Brandt, A. C., & Hannover, B. (2004). Don't stand so close to me: The effects of self-construal on interpersonal closeness. *Psychological Science, 15,* 237–242.

Holman, T. B., & Jarvis, M. O. (2003). Hostile, volatile, avoiding, and validating couple-conflict types: An investigation of Gottman's couple-conflict types. *Personal Relationships, 10,* 267–282.

Holmes, D. S. (1991). *Abnormal psychology.* New York: Harper & Row.

Holmes, J. G. (1991). Trust and the appraisal process in close relationships. In W. H. Jones & D. Perlman (Eds.), *Advances in personal relationships* (Vol. 2, pp. 57–106). London: Jessica Kingsley.

Holmes, J. G. (2002). Interpersonal expectations as the building blocks of social cognition: An interdependence theory perspective. *Personal Relationships, 9,* 1–26.

Holmes, J. G. (2004). The benefits of abstract functional analysis in theory construction: The case of interdependence theory. *Personality and Social Psychology Review, 8,* 146–155.

Holmes, J. G., & Levinger, G. (1994). Paradoxical effects of closeness in relationships on perceptions of justice: An interdependence-theory perspective. In M. J. Lerner & G. Mikula (Eds.), *Entitlement and the affectional bond: Justice in close relationships* (pp. 149–173). New York: Plenum.

Holtzworth-Munroe, A., & Jacobson, N. S. (1985). Causal attributions of marital couples: When do they search for causes? What do they conclude when they do? *Journal of Personality and Social Psychology, 48,* 1398–1412.

Homans, G. C. (1961). *Social behavior.* New York: Hartcourt, Brace & World.

Honeycutt, J. M. (1996). How "helpful" are self–help relational books? Common sense or counter-intuitive information. *Personal Relationship Issues, 3,* 1–3.

Honeycutt, J. M., Cantrill, J. G., Kelly, P., & Lambkin, D. (1998). How do I love thee? Let me consider my options: Cognition, verbal strategies, and the escalation of intimacy. *Human Communication Research, 25,* 39–63.

Hoobler, G. D. (1999, June). *Ten years of personal relationships research: Where have we been and where are we going?* Paper presented at the meeting of the International Network on Personal Relationships, Louisville, KY.

Hopper, J. (1993). The rhetoric of motives in divorce. *Journal of Marriage and the Family, 55,* 801–813.

Horneffer, K. J., & Fincham, F. D. (1996). Attributional models of depression and marital distress. *Personality and Social Psychology Bulletin, 22,* 678–689.

Hornstein, G. A., & Truesdell, S. E. (1988). Development of intimate conversation in close relationships. *Journal of Social and Clinical Psychology, 7,* 49–64.

Horstmann, G. (2003). What do facial expressions convey: Feeling states, behavioral intentions, or action requests? *Emotion, 3,* 150–166.

Hotchkiss, S. (2003). *Why is it always about you? The seven deadly sins of narcissism.* New York: Free Press.

Houston, J. P. (1981). *The pursuit of happiness.* Glenview, IL: Scott, Foresman.

Houts, A. C., Cook, T. D., & Shadish, W. R., Jr. (1986). The person-situation debate: A critical multiplist perspective. *Journal of Personality, 54,* 52–105.

Howard, J. W., & Dawes, R. M. (1976). Linear prediction of marital happiness. *Personality and Social Psychology Bulletin, 2,* 478–480.

Howard, M. (2003, October 18). Honeymoon never lasts forever. *The Bryan-College Station Eagle,* p. B6.

Howes, C. (1996). The earliest friendships. In W. M. Bukowski, A. F. Newcomb, & W. W. Hartup (Eds.), *The company they keep: Friendship in childhood and adolescence* (pp. 66–86). New York: Cambridge University Press.

Hughes, D. K., & Surra, C. A. (2000). The reported influence of research participation on premarital relationships. *Journal of Marriage and the Family, 62,* 822–832.

Hume, D. K., & Montgomerie, R. (2001). Facial attractiveness signals different aspects of "quality" in women and men. *Evolution and Human Behavior, 22,* 93–112.

Hunt, M. (1974). *Sexual behavior in the 1970s.* Chicago: Playboy Press.

Hunt, M. M. (1959). *The natural history of love.* New York: Knopf.

Hupka, R. B., & Bank, A. L. (1996). Sex differences in jealousy: Evolution or social construction? *Cross-Cultural Research, 30,* 24–59.

Hupka, R. B., Buunk, B., Falus, G., Fulgosi, A., Ortega, E., Swain, R., & Tarabrina, N. V. (1985). Romantic jealousy and romantic envy: A seven-nation study. *Journal of Cross-Cultural Psychology, 16,* 423–446.

Huppe, M., & Cyr, M. (1997). Division of household labor and marital satisfaction of dual income couples according to family life cycle. *Canadian Journal of Counseling, 31,* 145–162.

Huston, T. L. (1973). Ambiguity of acceptance, social desirability, and dating choice. *Journal of Experimental Social Psychology, 9,* 32–42.

Huston, T. L. (1999). *The connubial crucible: Newlywed years as predictors of marital delight, distress, and divorce.* Paper presented at the meeting of the American Psychological Association, Boston.

Huston, T. L. (2000). The social ecology of marriage and other intimate unions. *Journal of Marriage and the Family, 62,* 298–320.

Huston, T. L. (2002). Power. In H. H. Kelley, E. Berscheid, A. Christensen et al. (Eds.), *Close relationships* (pp. 265–314). Clinton Corners, NY: Percheron Press.

Huston, T. L., Caughlin, J. P., Houts, R. M., Smith, S. E., & George, L. J. (2001). The connubial crucible: Newlywed years as predictors of marital delight, distress, and divorce. *Journal of Personality and Social Psychology, 80,* 237–252.

Huston, T. L., & Chorost, A. F. (1994). Behavioral buffers on the effect of negativity on marital satisfaction: A longitudinal study. *Personal Relationships, 1,* 223–239.

Huston, T. L., & Houts, R. M. (1998). The psychological infrastructure of courtship and marriage: The role of personality and compatibility in romantic relationships. In T. N. Bradbury (Ed.), *The developmental course of marital dysfunction* (pp. 114–151). New York: Cambridge University Press.

Huston, T. L., Niehuis, S., & Smith, S. E. (2001). The early marital roots of conjugal distress and divorce. *Current Directions in Psychological Science, 10,* 116–119.

Hwang, J., & Dabbs, J. M., Jr. (2002, February). *Testosterone and adult attachment style.* Paper presented at the meeting of the Society for Personality and Social Psychology, Savannah, GA.

Hyde, J. S., & DeLamater, J. (2000). *Understanding human sexuality* (7th ed.) New York: McGraw-Hill.

Hymel, S., Tarulli, D., Hayden Thompson, L., & Terrell-Deutsch, B. (1999). Loneliness through the eyes of children. In K. J. Rotenberg & S. Hymel (Eds.), *Loneliness in childhood and adolescence* (pp. 80–106). New York: Cambridge University Press.

Ickes, W. (1985). Sex-role influences on compatibility in relationships. In W. Ickes (Ed.), *Compatible and incompatible relationships* (pp. 187–208). New York: Springer-Verlag.

Ickes, W. J. (Ed.). (1997). *Empathic accuracy.* New York: Guilford Press.

Ickes, W. (2000). Methods of studying close relationships. In W. Ickes & S. Duck (Eds.), *The social psychology of personal relationships* (pp. 159–180). Chichester, England: Wiley.

Ickes, W. (2003). *Everyday mind reading: Understanding what other people think and feel.* Amherst, NY: Prometheus Books.

Ickes, W., & Barnes, R. D. (1978). Boys and girls together—and alienated: On enacting stereotyped sex roles in mixed-sex dyads. *Journal of Personality and Social Psychology, 36,* 669–683.

Ickes, W., & Simpson, J. A. (1997). Managing empathic accuracy in close relationships. In W. J. Ickes (Ed.), *Empathic accuracy* (pp. 218–250). New York: Guilford Press.

Ickes, W., & Simpson, J. A. (2001). Motivational aspects of empathic accuracy. In G. J. O. Fletcher & M. S. Clark (Eds.), *Blackwell handbook of social psychology: Interpersonal processes* (pp. 229–249). Malden. MA: Blackwell.

Iida, M., Bolger, N., & Shrout, P. E. (2004, January). *Restoring equity in close relationships: Do people reciprocate support to restore equity?* Paper presented at the meeting of the Society for Personality and Social Psychology, Austin, TX.

Ijsendoorn, M. H., & Sagi, A. (1999). Cross–cultural patterns of attachment: Universal and contextual dimensions. In J. Cassidy & P. R. Shaver (Eds.), *Handbook of attachment: Theory, research and clinical applications* (pp. 713–734). New York: Guilford Press.

Impett, E., & Peplau, L. A. (2003). Sexual compliance: Gender, motivational, and relationship perspectives. *Journal of Sex Research, 40*, 87–100.

Ireland, J. L., & Power, C. L. (2004). Attachment, emotional loneliness, and bullying behaviour: A study of adult and young offenders. *Aggressive Behavior, 30*, 298–312.

Isabella, R. A. (1998). Origins of attachment: The role of context, duration, frequency of observation, and infant age in measuring maternal behavior. *Journal of Social and Personal Relationships, 15*, 538–554.

Jackson, T., Towson, S., & Narduzzi, K. (1997). Predictors of shyness: A test of variables associated with self-presentational models. *Social Behavior and Personality, 25*, 149–154.

Jacobson, N. S., Follette, W. C., & McDonald, D. W. (1982). Reactivity to positive and negative behavior in distressed and nondistressed married couples. *Journal of Consulting and Clinical Psychology, 50*, 706–714.

Jacobson, N. S., & Margolin, G. (1979). *Marital therapy: Strategies based on social learning and behavior exchange principles.* New York: Brunner/Mazel.

Jacques, A. J., Parkhill, M. R., Zawacki, T., Buck, P. O., & Abbey, A. (2004, May). *Behavioral and attitudinal predictors of misperception of sexual intent.* Paper presented at the meeting of the American Psychological Society, Chicago.

Jacquet, S. E., & Surra, C. A. (2001). Parental divorce and premarital couples: Commitment and other relationship characteristics. *Journal of Marriage and the Family, 63*, 627–638.

Jang, S., Smith, S. W., & Levine, T. R. (2002). To stay or to leave? The role of attachment styles in communication patterns and potential termination of romantic relationships following discovery of deception. *Communication Monographs, 69*, 236–252.

Jankowiak, W., & Fischer, E. (1992). A cross-cultural perspective on romantic love. *Ethnology, 31*, 149–155.

Jensen-Campbell, L. A., & Graziano, W. G. (2001). Agreeableness as a moderator of interpersonal conflict. *Journal of Personality, 69*, 323–362.

Jensen-Campbell, L. A., Graziano, W. G., & West, S. G. (1995). Dominance, prosocial orientation, and female preferences: Do nice guys really finish last? *Journal of Personality and Social Psychology, 68*, 427–440.

Jessor, R., Costa, F., Jessor, L., & Donovan, J. E. (1983). Time of first intercourse: A prospective study. *Journal of Personality and Social Psychology, 44*, 608–626.

Jöchle, W. (1973). Coitus-induced ovulation. *Contraception, 7*, 523–564.

Johannesen-Schmidt, M. C., & Eagly, A. H. (2002). Another look at sex differences in preferred mate characteristics: The effects of endorsing the traditional female gender role. *Psychology of Women Quarterly, 26*, 322–328.

Johnson, C. L. (1975). Authority and power in Japanese-American marriage. In R. E. Cromwell & D. H. Olson (Eds.), *Power in families* (pp. 182–196). New York: Wiley.

Johnson, D. R., & Wu, J. (2002). An empirical test of crisis, social selection, and role explanations of the relationship between marital disruption and psychological distress: A pooled time-series analysis of four-wave panel data. *Journal of Marriage and the Family, 64*, 211–224.

Johnson, M. P. (1995). Patriarchal terrorism and common couple violence: Two forms of violence against women. *Journal of Marriage and the Family, 57*, 283–294.

Johnson, M. P. (1999). Personal, moral, and structural commitment to relationships: Experiences of choice and constraint. In J. M. Adams & W. H. Jones (Eds.), *Handbook on interpersonal commitment and relationship stability* (pp. 73–87). New York: Kluwer Academic/Plenum.

Johnson, M. P. (2001). Conflict and control: Symmetry and asymmetry in domestic violence. In A. Booth, A. C. Crouter, & M. Clements (Eds.), *Couples in conflict* (pp. 95–104). Mahwah, NJ: Erlbaum.

Johnson, M. P., Caughlin, J. P., & Huston, T. L. (1999). The tripartite nature of marital commitment: Personal, moral, and structural reasons to stay married. *Journal of Marriage and the Family, 61*, 160–177.

Johnson, M. P., & Ferraro, K. J. (2000). Research on domestic violence in the 1990s: Making distinctions. *Journal of Marriage and the Family, 62*, 948–963.

Johnson, M. P., & Leone, J. M. (2005). The differential effects of intimate terrorism and situational couple violence: Findings from the National Violence Against Women Survey. *Journal of Family Issues, 26,* 322–349.

Johnson, S. M. (2002). Marital problems. In D. H. Sprenkle (Ed.), *Effectiveness research in marriage and family therapy* (pp. 163–190). Alexandria, VA: American Association for Marriage and Family Therapy.

Johnson, S. M. (2004). Attachment theory: A guide for healing couple relationships. In W. S. Rholes & J. A. Simpson (Eds.), *Adult attachment: Theory, research, and clinical implications* (pp. 367–387). New York: Guilford Press.

Johnson, S. M., & Best, M. (2003). A systemic approach to restructuring adult attachment: The EFT model of couples therapy. In P. Erdman & T. Caffery (Eds.), *Attachment and family systems: Conceptual, empirical, and therapeutic relatedness* (pp. 165–189). New York: Brunner-Routledge.

Johnson, S. M., & Denton, W. (2002). Emotionally Focused Couple Therapy: Creating secure connections. In A. S. Gurman & N. S. Jacobson (Eds.), *Clinical handbook of couple therapy* (3rd ed., pp. 221–250). New York: Guilford Press.

Johnson, W., McGue, M., Krueger, R. F., & Bouchard, T. J., Jr. (2004). Marriage and personality: A genetic analysis. *Journal of Personality and Social Psychology, 86,* 285–294.

Johnston, L. D., Fabrigar, L. R., & Wilson, A. (2005, January). *Adult attachment styles and responses to partner dissatisfaction in romantic relationships.* Paper presented at the meeting of the Society for Personality and Social Psychology, New Orleans.

Joiner, T. E., Jr., Lewisohn, P. M., & Seeley, J. R. (2002). The core of loneliness: Lack of pleasurable engagement—more so than painful disconnection—predicts social impairment, depression onset, recovery from depressive disorders among adolescents. *Journal of Personality Assessment, 79,* 472–491.

Joiner, T. E., Jr., & Metalsky, G. I. (2001). Excessive reassurance seeking: Delineating a risk factor in the development of depressive symptoms. *Psychological Science, 12,* 371–378.

Joiner, T. E., Jr., Metalsky, G. I., Katz, J., & Beach, S. R. H. (1999). Depression and excessive reassurance-seeking. *Psychological Inquiry, 10,* 269–278.

Jones, D. (1995). Sexual selection, physical attractiveness, and facial neotony: Cross-cultural evidence and implications. *Current Anthropology, 36,* 723–748.

Jones, E. E., & Pittman, T. (1982). Toward a general theory of strategic self-presentation. In J. Suls (Ed.), *Psychological perspectives on the self* (pp. 231–262). Hillsdale, NJ: Erlbaum.

Jones, J. T., & Cunningham, J. D. (1996). Attachment styles and other predictors of relationship satisfaction in dating couples. *Personal Relationships, 3,* 387–399.

Jones, J. T., Carvallo, M. R., Pelham, B. W., & Mirenberg, M. C. (2003, February). *Implicit egotism: Implications for interpersonal attraction.* Paper presented at the meeting of the Society for Personality and Social Psychology, Los Angeles.

Jones, W. H. (1990). Loneliness and social exclusion. *Journal of Social and Clinical Psychology, 9,* 214–220.

Jones, W. H. (2000, June). *Loneliness and relationship dynamics: Betrayal, apology, and forgiveness.* Paper presented at the meeting of the International Society for the Study of Personal Relationships, Brisbane.

Jones, W. H., & Burdette, M. P. (1994). Betrayal in relationships. In A. L. Weber & J. H. Harvey (Eds.), *Perspectives on close relationships* (pp. 243–262). Boston: Allyn & Bacon.

Jones, W. H., & Carver, M. D. (1991). Adjustment and coping implications of loneliness. In C. R. Snyder & D. R. Forsyth (Eds.), *Handbook of social and clinical psychology: The health perspective* (pp. 395–415). New York: Pergamon Press.

Jones, W. H., Crouch, L. L., & Scott, S. (1997). Trust and betrayal: The psychology of trust violations. In R. Hogan, J. Johnson, & S. R. Briggs (Eds.), *Handbook of personality psychology* (pp. 466–482). New York: Academic Press.

Jones, W. H., Freemon, J. E., & Goswick, R. A. (1981). The persistence of loneliness: Self and other determinants. *Journal of Personality, 49,* 27–48.

Jones, W. H., Hobbs, S. A., & Hackenbury, D. (1982). Loneliness and social skills deficits. *Journal of Personality and Social Psychology, 42,* 682–689.

Jones, W. H., Moore, D. S., Schratter, A., & Negel, L. A. (2001). Interpersonal transgressions and betrayals. In R. M. Kowalski (Ed.), *Behaving badly: Aversive behaviors in interpersonal relationships* (pp. 233–256). Washington DC: American Psychological Association.

Jones, W. H., Sansome, C., & Helm, B. (1983). Loneliness and interpersonal judgments. *Personality and Social Psychology Bulletin, 9,* 437–442.

Judge, T. A., & Cable, D. M. (2004). The effect of physical height on workplace success and income: Preliminary test of a theoretical model. *Journal of Applied Psychology, 89,* 428–441.

Kachadourian, L. K., Fincham, F., & Davila, J. (2004). The tendency to forgive in dating and married couples: The role of attachment and relationship satisfaction. *Personal Relationships, 11,* 373–393.

Kafetsios, K. (2004). Attachment and emotional intelligence abilities across the life course. *Personality and Individual Differences, 37,* 129–145.

Kafetsios, K., & Nezlek, J. B. (2002). Attachment styles in everyday social interaction. *European Journal of Social Psychology, 32,* 719–735.

Kahneman, D., & Tversky, A. (1982). The psychology of preferences. *Scientific American, 246,* 160–173.

Kalick, S. M., & Hamilton, T. E. (1986). The matching hypothesis reexamined. *Journal of Personality and Social Psychology, 51,* 673–682.

Kalick, S. M., Zebrowitz, L. A., Langlois, J. H., & Johnson, R. M. (1998). Does human facial physical attractiveness honestly advertise health? Longitudinal data on an evolutionary question. *Psychological Science, 9,* 8–13.

Kamphuis, J. H., Emmelkamp, P. M. G., & de Vries, V. (2004). Informant personality descriptions of postintimate stalkers using the Five Factor Profile. *Journal of Personality Assessment, 82,* 169–178.

Kandel, D. B. (1978). Similarity in real-life adolescent friendship pairs. *Journal of Personality and Social Psychology, 36,* 306–312.

Kane, H., Ford, M., Guichard, A., & Collins, N. L. (2005, January). *Attachment style differences in the desire for support and perceptions of support during a stressful task.* Paper presented at the meeting of the Society for Personality and Social Psychology, New Orleans.

Kanouse, D. E., Duan, N., Lever, J., Carson, S., Perlman, J. F., & Levitan, B. (1999). Drawing a probability sample of female street prostitutes in Los Angeles County. *Journal of Sex Research, 36,* 45–51.

Karakurt, G., Sheese, B., & Graziano, W. G. (2004, May). *The interplay among personality traits, attachment dimensions, and jealousy.* Paper presented at the meeting of the American Psychological Society, Chicago, IL.

Karney, B. (2004, January). *The potential impact of federal marriage initiatives on theory and research in close relationships.* Paper presented at the meeting of the Society for Personality and Social Psychology, Austin, TX.

Karney, B. R., & Bradbury, T. N. (1995). The longitudinal course of marital quality and stability: A review of theory, methods, and research. *Psychological Bulletin, 118,* 3–34.

Karney, B. R., & Bradbury, T. N. (1997). Neuroticism, marital interaction, and the trajectory of marital satisfaction. *Journal of Personality and Social Psychology, 72,* 1075–1092.

Karney, B. R., & Bradbury, T. N. (2000). Attributions in marriage: State or trait? A growth curve analysis. *Journal of Personality and Social Psychology, 78,* 295–309.

Karney, B. R., & Coombs, R. H. (2000). Memory bias in long-term close relationships: Consistency or improvement? *Personality and Social Psychology Bulletin, 26,* 959–970.

Karney, B. R., Davila, J., Cohan, C. L., Sullivan, K. T., Johnson, M. D., & Bradbury, T. N. (1995). An empirical investigation of sampling strategies in marital research. *Journal of Marriage and the Family, 57 ,* 909–920.

Karney, B. R., & Frye, N. E. (2002). "But we've been getting better lately": Comparing prospective and retrospective views of relationship development. *Journal of Personality and Social Psychology, 82,* 222–238.

Karney, B. R., Kreitz, M. A., & Sweeney, K. E. (2004). Obstacles to ethnic diversity in marital research: On the failure of good intentions. *Journal of Social and Personal Relationships, 21,* 509–526.

Karney, B. R., McNulty, J. K., & Fry, N. E. (2001). A social-cognitive perspective on the maintenance and deterioration of relationship satisfaction. In J. H. Harvey & A. E. Wenzel (Eds.), *Close romantic relationships: Maintenance and enhancement* (pp. 195–214). Mahwah, NJ: Erlbaum.

Karremans, J. C., Van Lange, P. A. M., Ouwerkerk, J. W., & Kluwer, E. S. (2003). When forgiving enhances psychological well-being: The role of interpersonal commitment. *Journal of Personality and Social Psychology, 84,* 1011–1026.

Kashy, D. A., & DePaulo, B. M. (1996). Who lies? *Journal of Personality and Social Psychology, 70,* 1037–1051.

Katvez, A. R., Warner, R. L., & Acock, A. C. (1994). Girls or boys? The relationship of child gender to marital instability. *Journal of Marriage and the Family, 56,* 89–100.

Katz, J., & Beach, S. R. H. (2000). Looking for love? Self-verification and self-enhancement effects on initial romantic attraction. *Personality and Social Psychology Bulletin, 26,* 1526–1539.

Katz, J., Joiner, T. E., Jr. (2002). Being known, intimate, and valued: Global self-verification and dyadic adjustment in couples and roommates. *Journal of Personality, 70,* 33–58.

Kaul, M., & Lakey, B. (2003). Where is the support in perceived support? The role of generic relationship satisfaction and enacted support in perceived support's relation to low distress. *Journal of Social and Clinical Psychology, 22,* 59–78.

Kearns, J. N., & Fincham, F. D. (2004). A prototype analysis of forgiveness. *Personality and Social Psychology Bulletin, 30,* 838–855.

Keelan, J. P. R., Dion, K. K., & Dion, K. L. (1998). Attachment style and relationship satisfaction: Test of a self-disclosure explanation. *Canadian Journal of Behavioural Science, 30,* 24–35.

Kellas, J. K., & Manusov, V. (2003). What's in a story? The relationship between narrative completeness and adjustment to relationship dissolution. *Journal of Social and Personal Relationships, 20,* 285–307.

Kellerman, J., Lewis, J., & Laird, J. D. (1989). Looking and loving: The effects of mutual gaze on feelings of love. *Journal of Research in Personality, 23,* 145–161.

Kelley, H. H. (1979). *Personal relationships: Their structures and processes.* Hillsdale, NJ: Erlbaum.

Kelley, H. H. (2002). Love and commitment. In H. H. Kelley, E. Berscheid, A. Christensen et al. (Eds.), *Close relationships* (pp. 265–314). Clinton Corners, NY: Percheron Press.

Kelley, H. H., & Thibaut, J. W. (1978). *Interpersonal relations: A theory of interdependence.* New York: Wiley.

Kelln, B. R. C., & Ellard, J. H. (1999). An equity theory analysis of the impact of forgiveness and retribution on transgressor compliance. *Personality and Social Psychology Bulletin, 25,* 864–872.

Kelly, E. L., & Conley, J. J. (1987). Personality and compatibility: A prospective analysis of marital stability and marital satisfaction. *Journal of Personality and Social Psychology, 52,* 27–40.

Kelly, J. B. (1996). A decade of divorce mediation research: Some answers and questions. *Family and Conciliation Courts Review, 34,* 373–385.

Keltner, D. (1995). Signs of appeasement: Evidence for the distinct displays of embarrassment, amusement, and shame. *Journal of Personality and Social Psychology, 68,* 441–454.

Keltner, D., & Shiota, M. N. (2003). New displays and new emotions: A commentary on Rozin and Cohen (2003). *Emotion, 3,* 86–91.

Kennedy, J. K., Bolger, N., & Shrout, P. E. (2002). Witnessing interpersonal aggression in childhood: Implications for daily conflict in adult intimate relationships. *Journal of Personality, 70,* 1051–1077.

Kenny, D. A. (1994). *Interpersonal perception: A social relations analysis.* New York: Guilford Press.

Kenny, D. A, & Acitelli, L. K. (2001). Accuracy and bias in the perception of the partner in a close relationship. *Journal of Personality and Social Psychology, 80,* 439–448.

Kenny, D. A., Bolger, N., & Kashy, D. A. (2002). Traditional methods for estimating multilevel models. In D. S. Moskowitz & S. L. Hershberger (Eds.), *Modeling intraindividual variability with repeated measures data: Methods and applications* (pp. 1–24). Mahwah, NJ: Erlbaum.

Kenrick, D. T., & Gutierres, S. E. (1989). Influence of popular erotica on judgments of strangers and mates. *Journal of Experimental Social Psychology, 25,* 159–167.

Kenrick, D. T., & Keefe, R. C. (1992). Age preferences in mates reflect sex differences in reproductive strategies. *Behavioral and Brain Sciences, 15,* 75–133.

Kenrick, D. T., Keefe, R. C., Bryan, A., Barr, A., & Brown, S. (1995). Age preferences and mate choice among homosexuals and heterosexuals: A case for modular psychological mechanisms. *Journal of Personality and Social Psychology, 69,* 1166–1172.

Kenrick, D. T., Montello, D. R., Gutierres, S. E., & Trost, M. R. (1993). Effects of physical attractiveness on affect and perceptual judgments: When social comparison overrides social reinforcement. *Personality and Social Psychology Bulletin, 19,* 195–199.

Kenrick, D. T., Sadalla, E. K., Groth, G., & Trost, M. R. (1990). Evolution, traits, and the stages of human courtship: Qualifying the parental investment model. *Journal of Personality, 58,* 97–116.

Kenrick, D. T., Sundie, J. M., Nicastle, L. D., & Stone, G. O. (2001). Can one ever be too wealthy or too chaste? Searching for nonlinearities in mate judgment. *Journal of Personality and Social Psychology, 80,* 462–471.

Kenrick, D. T., & Trost, M. R. (2000). An evolutionary perspective on human relationships. In W. Ickes & S. Duck (Eds.), *The social psychology of personal relationships* (pp. 9–35). Chichester, England: Wiley.

Kephart, W. (1967). Some correlates of romantic love. *Journal of Marriage and the Family, 29,* 470–479.

Keysar, B., & Henly, A. S. (2002). Speakers' overestimation of their effectiveness. *Psychological Science, 13,* 207–212.

Kiecolt-Glaser, J. K. (1999). Stress, personal relationships, and immune function: Health implications. *Brain, Behavior and Immunity, 13,* 61–72.

Kiecolt-Glaser, J. K., Bane, C., Glaser, R., & Malarkey, W. B. (2003). Love, marriage, and divorce: Newlyweds' stress hormones foreshadow relationship changes. *Journal of Consulting and Clinical Psychology, 71,* 176–188.

Kiecolt-Glaser, J. K., Fisher, L. D., Ogrocki, P., Stout, J. C., Speicher, C. E., & Glaser, R. (1987). Marital quality, marital disruption, and immune function. *Psychosomatic Medicine, 49,* 13–34.

Kiecolt-Glaser, J. K., Malarkey, W. B., Chee, M., Newton, T., Cacioppo, J. T., Hsiao-Yin, M., & Glaser, R. (1993). Negative behavior during marital conflict is associated with immunological down–regulation. *Psychosomatic Medicine, 55,* 395–409.

Kiecolt-Glaser, J. K., McGuire, L., Robles, T. F., & Glaser, R. (2002). Emotions, morbidity, and mortality: New perspectives from psychoneuroimmunology. *Annual Review of Psychology, 53,* 83–107.

Kiecolt-Glaser, J. K., & Newton, T. L. (2001). Marriage and health: His and hers. *Psychological Bulletin, 127,* 472–503.

Kiesler, S. B., & Baral, R. L. (1970). The search for a romantic partner: The effects of self-esteem and physical attractiveness on romantic behavior. In K. J. Gergen & D. Marlowe (Eds.), *Personality and social behavior* (pp. 155–166). Reading, MA: Addison-Wesley.

Kilpatrick, S. D., Bissonnette, V. L., & Rusbult, C. E. (2002). Empathic accuracy and accommodative behavior among newly married couples. *Personal Relationships, 9,* 369–393.

Kim, H. K., & McKenry, P. C. (2002). The relationship between marriage and psychological well-being: A longitudinal analysis. *Journal of Family Issues, 23,* 885–911.

Kimmel, A. J. (2004). Ethical issues in social psychology research. In C. Sansone, C. C. Morf, & A. T. Panter (Eds.), *The Sage handbook of methods in social psychology* (pp. 45–70). Thousand Oaks, CA: Sage.

King, V. (2002). Parental divorce and interpersonal trust in adult offspring. *Journal of Marriage and the Family, 64,* 642–656.

Kirkpatrick, L. A., & Davis, K. E. (1994). Attachment style, gender, and relationship stability: A longitudinal analysis. *Journal of Personality and Social Psychology, 66,* 502–512.

Kirkpatrick, L. A., & Hazan, C. (1994). Attachment styles and close relationships: A four-year prospective study. *Personal Relationships, 1,* 123–142.

Kitson, G. C., & Morgan, L. A. (1990). The multiple consequences of divorce: A decade review. *Journal of Marriage and the Family, 44,* 924–973.

Klein, K. J. K., & Hodges, S. D. (2001). Gender differences, motivation, and empathic accuracy: When it pays to understand. *Personality and Social Psychology Bulletin, 27,* 720–730.

Kleinke, C. L. (1986). Gaze and eye contact: A research review. *Psychological Bulletin, 100,* 78–100.

Kleinke, C. L., & Dean, G. O. (1990). Evaluation of men and women receiving positive and negative responses with various acquaintance strategies. *Journal of Social Behavior and Personality, 5,* 369–377.

Kline, G. H., Stanley, S. M., Markman, H. J., Olmos-Gallo, P. A., St. Peters, M., Whitton, S. W., & Prado, L. M. (2004). Timing is everything: Pre-engagement cohabitation and increased risk for poor marital outcomes. *Journal of Family Psychology, 18,* 311–318.

Klinetob, N. A., & Smith, D. A. (1996). Demand-withdraw communication in marital interaction: Tests of interpersonal contingency and gender role hypotheses. *Journal of Marriage and the Family, 58,* 945–957.

Klohnen, E. C., & Bera, S. (1998). Behavioral and experiential patterns of avoidantly and securely attached women across adulthood: A 31-year longitudinal perspective. *Journal of Personality and Social Psychology, 74*, 211–223.

Klohnen, E. C., & Luo, S. (2003). Interpersonal attraction and personality: What is attractive—Self similarity, ideal similarity, complementarity, or attachment security? *Journal of Personality and Social Psychology, 85*, 709–722.

Klusmann, D. (2002). Sexual motivation and the duration of partnership. *Archives of Sexual Behavior, 31*, 275–287.

Knee, C. R. (1998). Implicit theories of relationships: Assessment and prediction of romantic relationship initiation, coping, and longevity. *Journal of Personality and Social Psychology, 74*, 360–370.

Knee, C. R., Nanayakkara, A., Vietor, N. A., Neighbors, C., & Patrick, H. (2001). Implicit theories of relationships: Who cares if romantic partners are less than ideal? *Personality and Social Psychology Bulletin, 27*, 808–819.

Knee, C. R., Patrick, H., & Lonsbary, C. (2003). Implicit theories of relationships: Orientations toward evaluation and cultivation. *Personality and Social Psychology Review, 7*, 41–55.

Knee, C. R., Patrick, H., Vietor, N. A., & Neighbors, C. (2004). Implicit theories of relationships: Moderators of the link between conflict and commitment. *Personality and Social Psychology Bulletin, 30*, 617–628.

Knobloch, L. K., & Solomon, D. H. (2004). Interference and facilitation from partners in the development of interdependence within romantic relationships. *Personal Relationships, 11*, 115–130.

Knobloch, L. K., Solomon, D. H., & Cruz, M. G. (2001). The role of relationship development and attachment in the experience of romantic jealousy. *Personal Relationships, 8*, 205–224.

Knoester, C., & Booth, A. (2000). Barriers to divorce: When are they effective? When are they not? *Journal of Family Issues, 21*, 78–99.

Kobak, R. R., & Sceery, A. (1988). Attachment in late adolescence: Working models, affect regulation, and representations of self and others. *Child Development, 59*, 135–146.

Koeppel, L. B., Montagne-Miller, Y., O'Hair, D., & Cody, M. J. (1993). Friendly? Flirting? Wrong? In P. J. Kalbfleisch (Ed.), *Interpersonal communication: Evolving interpersonal relationships* (pp. 13–32). Hillsdale, NJ: Erlbaum.

Koestner, R., & Wheeler, L. (1988). Self-presentation in personal advertisements: The influence of implicit notions of attraction and role expectations. *Journal of Social and Personal Relationships, 5*, 149–160.

Kollock, P., Blumstein, P., & Schwartz, P. (1985). Sex and power in interaction: Conversational privileges and duties. *American Sociological Review, 50*, 34–46.

Konrad, R. (2004, May 28). Love is blind, but not data. *Houston Chronicle*, p. 10C.

Koski, L. R., & Shaver, P. R. (1997). Attachment and relationship satisfaction across the lifespan. In R. J. Sternberg & M. Hojjat (Eds.), *Satisfaction in close relationships* (pp. 26–55). New York: Guilford Press.

Kouri, K. M., & Lasswell, M. (1993). Black-White marriages: Social change and intergenerational mobility. *Marriage and Family Review, 19*, 241–255.

Kowalski, R. M. (Ed.). (1997). *Aversive interpersonal behaviors.* New York: Plenum.

Kowalski, R. M. (2000). "I was only kidding!": Victims' and perpetrators' perceptions of teasing. *Personality and Social Psychology Bulletin, 26*, 231–241.

Kowalski, R. M. (Ed.). (2000). *Behaving badly: Aversive behaviors in interpersonal relationships.* Washington, DC: American Psychological Association.

Kowalski, R. M. (2003). *Complaining, teasing, and other annoying behaviors.* New Haven: Yale University Press.

Kowalski, R. M., Walker, S., Wilkinson, R., Queen, A., & Sharpe, B. (2003). Lying, cheating, complaining, and other aversive interpersonal behaviors: A narrative examination of the darker side of relationships. *Journal of Social and Personal Relationships, 20*, 471–490.

Koziel, S., & Pawlowski, B. (2003). Comparison between primary and secondary mate markets: An analysis of data from lonely hearts columns. *Personality and Individual Differences, 35*, 1849–1857.

Krause, N., & Shaw, B. A. (2002). Negative interaction and changes in functional disability during late life. *Journal of Social and Personal Relationships, 19*, 339–359.

Kraut, R. E., & Poe, D. B. (1980). Behavioral roots of person perception: The deception judgments of customs inspectors and laymen. *Journal of Personality and Social Psychology, 39*, 784–798.

Kreider, R. M., & Fields, J. M. (2002). *Number, timing, and duration of marriages and divorces: 1996.* (Current Population Reports, P70–80). Washington, D.C.: U.S. Census Bureau.

Kreider, R. M., & Simmons, T. (2003). *Marital status: 2000, a census 2000 brief.* Washington, D.C.: U.S. Census Bureau.

Krishnakumar, A., Buehler, C., & Barber, B. K. (2003). Youth perceptions of interparental conflict, ineffective parenting, and youth problem behaviors in European-American and African-American families. *Journal of Social and Personal Relationships, 20,* 239–260.

Krishnan, V. (1998). Premarital cohabitation and marital disruption. *Journal of Divorce and Remarriage, 28,* 157–170.

Kropp, J. P., & Haynes, O. M. (1987). Abusive and nonabusive mothers' ability to identify general and specific emotion signals of infants. *Child Development, 58,* 187–190.

Krueger, J., Ham, J. J., & Linford, K. M. (1996). Perceptions of behavioral consistency: Are people aware of the actor-observer effect? *Psychological Science, 7,* 259–264.

Kruger, J., & Gilovich, T. (1999). "Naïve cynicism" in everyday theories of responsibility assessment: On biased assumption of bias. *Journal of Personality and Social Psychology, 76,* 743–753.

Kruger, J., & Gilovich, T. (2004). Actions, intentions, and self-assessment: The road to self-enhancement is paved with good intentions. *Personality and Social Psychology Bulletin, 30,* 328–339.

Kruglanski, A. W. (1996). Motivated social cognition: Principles of the interface. In E. T. Higgins & A. W. Kruglanski (Eds.), *Social psychology: Handbook of basic principles* (pp. 493–520). New York: Guilford Press.

Kubitschek, W. N., & Hallinan, M. T. (1998). Tracking and students' friendships. *Social Psychology Quarterly, 61,* 1–15.

Kuczmarski, R. J., Flegal, K. M., Campbell, S. M., & Johnson, C. L. (1994). Increasing prevalence of overweight among US adults: The national health and nutrition examination surveys, 1960 to 1991. *Journal of the American Medical Association, 272,* 205–211.

Kuijer, R. G., Buunk, B. P., Ybema, J. F., & Wobbes, T. (2002). The relation between perceived inequity, marital satisfaction and emotions among couples facing cancer. *British Journal of Social Psychology, 41,* 39–56.

Kunda, Z. (1999). *Social cognition: Making sense of people.* Cambridge, MA: MIT Press.

Kupersmidt, J. B., Coie, J. D., & Dodge, K. A. (1990). The role of poor peer relationships in the development of disorder. In S. R. Asher & J. D. Coie (Eds.), *Peer rejection in childhood* (pp. 274–305). New York: Cambridge University Press.

Kurdek, L. A. (1991). Sexuality in homosexual and heterosexual couples. In K. McKinney & S. Sprecher, *Sexuality in close relationships* (pp. 177–191). Hillsdale, NJ: Erlbaum.

Kurdek, L. A. (1992). Relationship stability and relationship satisfaction in cohabiting gay and lesbian couples: A prospective longitudinal test of the contextual and interdependence models. *Journal of Social and Personal Relationships, 9,* 125–142.

Kurdek, L. A. (1993). Nature and prediction of changes in marital quality for first-time parent and nonparent husbands and wives. *Journal of Family Psychology, 6,* 255–265.

Kurdek, L. A. (1994a). Areas of conflict for gay, lesbian, and heterosexual couples: What couples argue about influences relationship satisfaction. *Journal of Marriage and the Family, 56,* 923–934.

Kurdek, L. A. (1994b). The nature and correlates of relationship quality in gay, lesbian, and heterosexual cohabiting couples: A test of the individual difference, interdependence, and discrepancy models. In B. Greene & G. M. Herek (Eds.), *Lesbian and gay psychology: Theory, research, and clinical applications* (pp. 133–155). Thousand Oaks, CA: Sage.

Kurdek, L. A. (1998a). Developmental changes in marital satisfaction: A 6-year prospective longitudinal study of newlywed couples. In T. N. Bradbury (Ed.), *The developmental course of marital dysfunction* (pp. 180–204). Cambridge: Cambridge University Press.

Kurdek, L. A. (1998b). Relationship outcomes and their predictors: Longitudinal evidence from heterosexual married, gay cohabiting, and lesbian cohabiting couples. *Journal of Marriage and the Family, 60,* 553–568.

Kurdek, L. A. (1999). The nature and predictors of the trajectory of change in marital quality for husbands and wives over the first 10 years of marriage. *Developmental Psychology, 35,* 1283–1296.

Kurdek, L. A. (2000). Attractions and constraints as determinants of relationship commitment: Longitudinal evidence from gay, lesbian, and heterosexual couples. *Personal Relationships, 7,* 245–262.

Kurdek, L. A. (2002). Predicting the timing of separation and marital satisfaction: An eight-year prospective longitudinal study. *Journal of Marriage and the Family, 64,* 163–179.

Kurdek, L. A. (2003). Negative representations of the self/spouse and marital distress. *Personal Relationships, 10,* 511–534.

Kurdek, L. A., & Schmitt, J. P. (1986a). Interaction of sex role self-concept with relationship quality and relationship beliefs in married, heterosexual cohabiting, gay, and lesbian couples. *Journal of Personality and Social Psychology, 51,* 365–370.

Kurdek, L. A., & Schmitt, J. P. (1986b). Relationship quality in heterosexual married, heterosexual cohabitating, and gay and lesbian relationships. *Journal of Personality and Social Psychology, 51,* 711–720.

Kurtz, J. E., & Sherker, J. L. (2003). Relationship quality, trait similarity, and self-other agreement on personality ratings in college roommates. *Journal of Personality, 71,* 21–48.

Kyes, K. B., Brown, I. S., & Pollack, R. H. (1991). The effect of exposure to a condom script on attitudes toward condoms. *Journal of Psychology and Human Sexuality, 4,* 21–36.

LaFrance, M. (1992). Gender and interruptions: Individual infraction or violation of the social order? *Psychology of Women Quarterly, 16,* 497–512.

LaFrance, M., Hecht, M. A., & Levy Paluck, E. (2003). The contingent smile: A meta-analysis of sex differences in smiling. *Psychological Bulletin, 129,* 305–334.

Lakey, B., Adams, K., Neely, L., Rhodes, G., Lutz, C. J., & Sielky, K. (2002). Perceived support and low emotional distress: The role of enacted support, dyad similarity and provider personality. *Personality and Social Psychology Bulletin, 28,* 1546–1555.

Lakey, B., Drew, J. B., Anan, R. M., Sirl, K., & Butler, C. (2004). Negative interpretations of interpersonal situations and the relation between low perceived support and psychological distress among divorced adults. *Journal of Applied Social Psychology, 34,* 1030–1047.

Lakey, B., & Scoboria, A. (2005). The relative contribution of trait and social influences to the links among perceived social support, affect, and self-esteem. *Journal of Personality, 73,* 361–388.

Lakoff, R. (1975). *Language and woman's place.* New York: Harper & Row.

Lam, A. G., Mak, A., & Lindsay, P. D. (2004). What really works? An exploratory study of condom negotiation strategies. *AIDS Education & Prevention, 16,* 160–171.

Lambert, T. A., Kahn, A. S., & Apple, K. J. (2003). Pluralistic ignorance and hooking up. *Journal of Sex Research, 40,* 129–133.

Lamm, H., & Wiesmann, U. (1997). Subjective attributes of attraction: How people characterize their liking, their love, and their being in love. *Personal Relationships, 4,* 271–284.

Landers, A. (1982). *Love or sex . . . and how to tell the difference.* Chicago: Field Enterprises.

Landers, A. (1997, March 22). Nurse offers article to help families, friends of bereaved parents. *The Bryan-College Station Eagle,* p. C7.

Lane, J. D., & Wegner, D. M. (1994). Secret relationships: The back alley to love. In R. Erber & R. Gilmour (Eds.), *Theoretical frameworks for personal relationships* (pp. 67–85). Hillsdale, NJ: Erlbaum.

Lane, J. D., & Wegner, D. M. (1995). The cognitive consequences of secrecy. *Journal of Personality and Social Psychology, 69,* 237–253.

Lang, F. R. (2004). Social motivation across the life span. In F. R. Lang & K. L. Fingerman (Eds.), *Growing together: Personal relationships across the life span* (pp. 341–367). Cambridge, UK: Cambridge University Press.

Lang, F. R., & Carstensen, L. L. (1994). Close emotional relationships in late life: Further support for proactive aging in the social domain. *Psychology and Aging, 9,* 315–324.

Langlois, J. (2004, January). *Facial attractiveness and cognitive averaging: An evolutionary approach.* Paper presented at the Evolutionary Psychology Pre-Conference at the meeting of the Society for Personality and Social Psychology, Austin, TX.

Langlois, J. H., Kalakanis, L., Rubenstein, A. J., Larson, A., Hallam, M., & Smoot, M. (2000). Maxims or myths of beauty? A meta-analytic and theoretical review. *Psychological Bulletin, 126,* 390–423.

Langlois, J. H., Ritter, J. M., Roggman, L. A., & Vaughn, L. S. (1991). Facial diversity and infant preferences for attractive faces. *Developmental Psychology, 27,* 79–84.

Langlois, J. H., & Roggman, L. A. (1990). Attractive faces are only average. *Psychological Science, 1,* 115–121.

Lansford, J. E., Sherman, A. M., & Antonucci, T. C. (1998). Satisfaction with social networks: An examination of socioemotional selectivity theory across cohorts. *Psychology and Aging, 13,* 544–552.

Larose, S., Guay, F., & Boivin M. (2002). Attachment, social support, and loneliness in young adulthood: A test of two models. *Personality and Social Psychology Bulletin, 28,* 684–693.

Larson, R. W., & Bradney, N. (1988). Precious moments with family members and friends. In R. M. Milardo (Ed.), *Families and social networks* (pp. 107–126). Thousand Oaks, CA: Sage.

Larson, R., & Richards, M. H. (1991). Daily companionship in late childhood and early adolescence: Changing developmental contexts. *Child Development, 62,* 284–300.

Larson, R., Richards, M. H., Moneta, G., Holmbeck, G., & Duckett, E. (1996). Changes in adolescents' daily interactions with their families from ages 10 to 18: Disengagement and transformation. *Developmental Psychology, 32,* 744–754.

Lauer, J., & Lauer, R. (1985, June). Marriages made to last. *Psychology Today,* pp. 22–26.

Lauer, R. H., Lauer, J. C., & Kerr, S. T. (1990). The long-term marriage: Perceptions of stability and satisfaction. *International Journal of Aging and Human Development, 31,* 189–195.

Laumann, E. O., Gagnon, J. H., Michael, R. T., & Michaels, S. (1994). *The social organization of sexuality: Sexual practices in the United States.* Chicago: University of Chicago Press.

Laurenceau, J., Barrett, L. F., & Pietromonaco, P. R. (1998). Intimacy as an interpersonal process: The importance of self-disclosure, partner disclosure, and perceived partner responsiveness in interpersonal exchanges. *Journal of Personality and Social Psychology, 74,* 1238–1251.

Laurenceau, J., Rivera, L. M., Schaffer, A. R., & Pietromonaco, P. R. (2004). Intimacy as an interpersonal process: Current status and future directions. In D. J. Mashek & A. Aron (Eds.), *Handbook of closeness and intimacy* (pp. 81–101). Mahwah, NJ: Erlbaum.

Laursen, B., & Collins, W. A. (1994). Interpersonal conflict during adolescence. *Psychological Bulletin, 115,* 197–209.

Laursen, B., Coy, K. C., & Collins, W. A. (1998). Reconsidering changes in parent-child conflict across adolescence: A meta-analysis. *Child Development, 69,* 817–832.

Lavee, Y., & Katz, R. (2002). Division of labor, perceived fairness, and marital quality: The effect of gender ideology. *Journal of Marriage and the Family, 64,* 27–39.

Lawrance, K., & Byers, E. S. (1995). Sexual satisfaction in long-term heterosexual relationships: The interpersonal exchange model of sexual satisfaction. *Personal Relationships, 2,* 267–285.

Le, B., & Agnew, C. R. (2001). Need fulfillment and emotional experience in interdependent romantic relationships. *Journal of Social and Personal Relationships, 18,* 423–440.

Le, B., & Agnew, C. R. (2003). Commitment and its theorized determinants: A meta-analysis of the investment model. *Personal Relationships, 10,* 37–57.

Leaper, C., & Holliday, H. (1995). Gossip in same-gender and cross-gender friends' conversations. *Personal Relationships, 2,* 237–246.

Leary, M. R. (1986). The impact of interactional impediments on social anxiety and self-presentation. *Journal of Experimental Social Psychology, 22,* 122–135.

Leary, M. R. (1990). Responses to social exclusion: Social anxiety, jealousy, loneliness, depression, and low self-esteem. *Journal of Social and Clinical Psychology, 9,* 221–229.

Leary, M. R. (1995). *Self-presentation: Impression management and interpersonal behavior.* Madison, WI: Brown & Benchmark.

Leary, M. R. (2001a). Social anxiety as an early warning system: A refinement and extension of the self-presentational theory of social anxiety. In S. G. Hofmann & P. M. DiBartolo (Eds.), *Social phobia and social anxiety: An integration* (pp. 321–334). New York: Allyn & Bacon.

Leary, M. R. (2001b). Toward a conceptualization of interpersonal rejection. In M. R. Leary (Ed.), *Interpersonal rejection* (pp. 3–20). New York: Oxford University Press.

Leary, M. R. (2002, June). *The potent and pervasive effects of interpersonal rejection.* Paper presented at the meeting of the American Psychological Society, New Orleans, LA.

Leary, M. R. (2003). Commentary on Self-Esteem as an Interpersonal Monitor: The Sociometer Hypothesis (1995). *Psychological Inquiry, 14,* 270–274.

Leary, M. R. (2004). The sociometer, self-esteem, and the regulation of interpersonal behavior. In K. D. Vohs & R. F. Baumeister (Eds.), *Handbook of self-regulation: Research, theory, and applications* (pp. 373–391). New York: Guilford Press.

Leary, M. R., & Baumeister, R. F. (2000). The nature and function of self-esteem: Sociometer theory. In M. Zanna (Ed.), *Advances in experimental social psychology* (Vol. 32, pp. 1–62). San Diego: Academic Press.

Leary, M. R., Gallagher, B., Fors, E., Buttermore, N., Baldwin, E., Kennedy, K., & Mills, A. (2003). The invalidity of disclaimers about the effects of social feedback on self-esteem. *Personality and Social Psychology Bulletin, 29,* 623–636.

Leary, M. R., Haupt, A. L., Strausser, K. S., & Chokel, J. T. (1998). Calibrating the sociometer: The relationship between interpersonal appraisals and state self-esteem. *Journal of Personality and Social Psychology, 74,* 1290–1299.

Leary, M. R., Herbst, K. C., & McCrary, F. (2003). Finding pleasure in solitary activities: Desire for aloneness or disinterest in social contact? *Personality and Individual Differences, 35,* 59–68.

Leary, M. R., & Kowalski, R. M. (1995). *Social anxiety.* New York: Guilford Press.

Leary, M. R., Kowalski, R. M., Smith, L., & Phillips, S. (2003). Teasing, rejection, and violence: Case studies of the school shootings. *Aggressive Behavior, 29,* 202–214.

Leary, M. R., & MacDonald, G. (2003, February). *Emotional reactions to interpersonal rejection: Why do hurt feelings hurt?* Paper presented at the meeting of the Society for Personality and Social Psychology, Los Angeles, CA.

Leary, M. R., & Miller, R. S. (1986). *Social psychology and dysfunctional behavior: Origins, diagnosis, and treatment.* New York: Guilford Press.

Leary, M. R., & Miller, R. S. (2000). Self-presentational perspectives on personal relationships. In W. Ickes & S. Duck (Eds.), *The social psychology of personal relationships* (pp. 129–155). Chichester, England: Wiley.

Leary, M. R., Nezlek, J. B., Downs, D. L., Radford-Davenport, J., Martin, J., & McMullen, A. (1994). Self-presentation in everyday interactions. *Journal of Personality and Social Psychology, 67,* 664–673.

Leary, M. R., & Rice, S. C. (2004, July). *When rejection isn't rejecting: Separating the effects of social exclusion and relational evaluation.* Paper presented at the meeting of the International Association for Relationship Research, Madison, WI.

Leary, M. R., & Springer, C. A. (2001). Hurt feelings: The neglected emotion. In R. M. Kowalski (Ed.), *Behaving badly: Aversive behaviors in interpersonal relationships* (pp. 151–175). Washington DC: American Psychological Association.

Leary, M. R., Springer, C., Negel, L., Ansell, E., & Evans, K. (1998). The causes, phenomenology, and consequences of hurt feelings. *Journal of Personality and Social Psychology, 74,* 1225–1237.

Lebow, J. L, & Gurman, A. S. (1995). Research assessing couple and family therapy. *Annual Review of Psychology, 46,* 27–57.

Leck, K., & Simpson, J. A. (1999). Feigning romantic interest: The role of self-monitoring. *Journal of Research in Personality, 33,* 69–91.

Lee, E. (2002, July). *Relationship quality and emotional responses as predictors of truth-telling behavior after deception in intimate relationships.* Paper presented at the International Conference on Personal Relationships, Halifax.

Lee, J. A. (1977). A typology of styles of loving. *Personality and Social Psychology Bulletin, 3,* 173–182.

Lee, J. A. (1988). Love-styles. In R. J. Sternberg & M. L. Barnes (Eds.), *The psychology of love* (pp. 38–67). New Haven, CT: Yale University Press.

Lee, L. (1984). Sequences in separation: A framework for investigating endings of the personal (romantic) relationship. *Journal of Social and Personal Relationships, 1,* 49–73.

Lee-Chai, A. Y., Chen, S., & Chartrand, T. L. (2001). From Moses to Marco: Individual differences in the use and abuse of power. In A. Y. Lee-Chai & J. A. Bargh (Eds.), *The use and abuse of power: Multiple perspectives on the causes of corruption* (pp. 57–74). Philadelphia: Psychology Press.

Leff, L. (2004, May 23). Divorce "most important" benefit of gay marriage. *The Bryan College Station Eagle,* p. B6.

Leffler, A., Gillespie, D. L., & Conaty, J. C. (1982). The effects of status differentiation on nonverbal behavior. *Social Psychology Quarterly, 45,* 153–161.

Lehman, D. R., Ellard, J. H., & Wortman, C. B. (1986). Social support for the bereaved: Recipients' and providers' perspectives on what is helpful. *Journal of Consulting and Clinical Psychology, 54,* 438–446.

Lehmiller, J. L., Agnew, C. R., Etcheverry, P. E. (2004, May). *Commitment in romantic relationships: Linking own and perceived partner levels to relationships.* Paper presented at the meeting of the American Psychological Society, Chicago.

Lehrer, E. L., & Chiswick, C. U. (1993). Religion as a determinant of marital stability. *Demography, 30,* 385–404.

Leitenberg, H., & Henning, K. (1995). Sexual fantasy. *Psychological Bulletin, 117,* 469–496.

Lemp, G., Hirozawa, A., et al. (1994). Seroprevalence of HIV and risk behaviors among young homosexual and bisexual men. *Journal of the American Medical Association, 272,* 449–454.

Leon, K. (2003). Risk and protective factors in young children's adjustment to parental divorce: A review of the research. *Family Relations, 52,* 258–270.

Leonard, K. E., & Roberts, L. J. (1997). Marital aggression, quality, and stability in the first year of marriage: Findings from the Buffalo Newlywed Study. In T. N. Bradbury (Ed.), *The developmental course of marital dysfunction* (pp. 44–73). Cambridge: Cambridge University Press.

Leone, P., Robins, S., & Connell, J. (2003, May). *Beauty is in the job status and gender of the beholder: Evolutionary psychology vs. social role theory.* Paper presented at the meeting of the American Psychological Society, Atlanta.

Lepore, S. J., & Greenberg, M. A. (2002). Mending broken hearts: Effects of expressive writing on mood, cognitive processing, social adjustment and health following a relationship breakup. *Psychology and Health, 17,* 547–560.

Leridon, H. (1990). Cohabitation, marriage, separation: An analysis of life histories of French cohorts from 1968 to 1985. *Populations Studies, 44,* 127–144.

Leslie, L. A., Huston, T. L., & Johnson, M. P. (1986). Parental reactions to dating relationships: Do they make a difference? *Journal of Marriage and the Family, 48,* 57–66.

Levenson, R. W., Carstensen, L. L., & Gottman, J. M. (1993). Long-term marriage: Age, gender, and satisfaction. *Psychology and Aging, 8,* 301–313.

Levenson, R. W., Carstensen, L. L., & Gottman, R. M. (1994). Influence of age and gender on affect, physiology, and their interrelations: A study of long-term marriages. *Journal of Personality and Social Psychology, 67,* 56–68.

Levin, J. (2000). A prolegomenon to an epidemiology of love: Theory, measurement, and health outcomes. *Journal of Social and Clinical Psychology, 19,* 117–136.

Levine, T. R., & McCornack, S. A. (1992). Linking love and lies: A formal test of the McCornack and Parks model of deception detection. *Journal of Social and Personal Relationships, 9,* 143–154.

Levinger, G. (1976). A social psychological perspective on marital dissolution. *Journal of Social Issues, 32,* 21–47.

Levinger, G. (1979). A social exchange view on the dissolution of pair relationships. In R. L. Burgess & T. L. Huston (Eds.), *Social exchange in developing relationships* (pp. 169–193). New York: Academic Press.

Levinger, G. (1999). Duty toward whom? Reconsidering attractions and barriers as determinants of commitment in a relationship. In J. M. Adams & W. H. Jones (Eds.), *Handbook on interpersonal commitment and relationship stability* (pp. 37–52). New York: Kluwer Academic/Plenum.

Levinger, G., & Breedlove, J. (1966). Interpersonal attraction and agreement: A study of marriage partners. *Journal of Personality and Social Psychology, 3,* 367–372.

Levinger, G., & Levinger, A. C. (2003). Winds of time and place: How context has affected a 50-year marriage. *Personal Relationships, 10,* 285–306.

Levinger, G., & Snoek, J. D. (1972). *Attraction in relationships: A new look at interpersonal attraction.* Morristown, NJ: General Learning Press.

Levitt, M. J., Silver, M. E., & Franco, N. (1996). Troublesome relationships: A part of human experience. *Journal of Social and Personal Relationships, 13,* 523–536.

Levy, M. B., & Davis, K. E. (1988). Love styles and attachment styles compared: Their relations to each other and to various relationship characteristics. *Journal of Social and Personal Relationships, 5,* 439–471.

Levy, S. R., Ayduk, O., & Downey, G. (2001). The role of rejection sensitivity in people's relationships with significant others and valued social groups. In M. R. Leary (Ed.), *Interpersonal rejection* (pp. 251–289). London: Oxford University Press.

Lewis, J., & Adler, J. (2004, September 27). Forgive and let live. *Newsweek*, p. 52.

Lewis, R., Jr., Yancey, G., & Bletzer, S. S. (1997). Racial and nonracial factors that influence spouse choice in Black/White marriages. *Journal of Black Studies, 28,* 60–78.

Li, N. P., Bailey, J. M., Kenrick, D. T., & Linsenmeier, J. A. W. (2002). The necessities and luxuries of mate preferences: Testing the tradeoffs. *Journal of Personality and Social Psychology, 82,* 947–955.

Liebold, J. M., & McConnell, A. R. (2004). Women, sex, hostility, power, and suspicion: Sexually aggressive men's cognitive associations. *Journal of Experimental Social Psychology, 40,* 256–263.

Liebowitz, M. R. (1983). *The chemistry of love.* Boston: Little, Brown.

Lima, M. V., Thomas, G., & Maio, G. (2004, July). *Resisting temptation in non-relationship and relationship contexts: The role of self-persuasion.* Paper presented at the meeting of the International Association for Relationship Research, Madison, WI.

Lin, Y. W., & Rusbult, C. E. (1995). Commitment to dating relationships and cross-sex friendships in America and China. *Journal of Social and Personal Relationships, 12,* 7–26.

Lippa, R., & Hershberger, S. (1999). Genetic and environmental influences on individual differences in masculinity, femininity, and gender diagnosticity: Analyzing data from a classic twin study. *Journal of Personality, 67,* 127–155.

Lippert, T., & Prager, K. J. (2001). Daily experiences of intimacy: A study of couples. *Personal Relationships, 8,* 283–298.

Lipton, D., McDonel, E. C., & McFall, R. M. (1987). Heterosocial perception in rapists. *Journal of Consulting and Clinical Psychology, 55,* 17–21.

Little, A. C., Penton-Voak, I. S., Burt, M., & Perrett, D. I. (2002). Evolution and individual differences in the perception of attractiveness: How cyclic hormonal changes and self-perceived attractiveness influence female preferences for male faces. In G. Rhodes & L. A. Zebrowitz (Eds.), *Facial attractiveness: Evolutionary, cognitive and social perspectives* (pp. 59–90). Westport, CT: Ablex.

Livingston, R. W. (2001). What you see is what you get: Systematic variability in perceptual-based social judgment. *Personality and Social Psychology Bulletin, 27,* 1086–1096.

Lloyd, S. A. (1987). Conflict in premarital relationships: Differential perceptions of males and females. *Family Relations, 36,* 290–294.

Lloyd, S. A., & Emery, B. C. (2000). The context and dynamics of intimate aggression against women. *Journal of Social and Personal Relationships, 17,* 503–521.

Locke, K. D., & Horowitz, L. M. (1990). Satisfaction in interpersonal interactions as a function of similarity in level of dysphoria. *Journal of Personality and Social Psychology, 58,* 823–831.

Löckenhoff, C. E., & Carstensen, L. F. (2004). Socioemotional Selectivity Theory, aging, and health: The increasingly delicate balance between regulating emotions and making tough choices. *Journal of Personality, 72,* 1395–1424.

Loftus, J. (2001). America's liberalization in attitudes toward homosexuality, 1973 to 1998. *American Sociological Review, 66,* 762–782.

Lokey, W. D., & Schmidt, G. W. (2000, February). *Association between adult attachment style and extramarital affairs in men.* Paper presented at the meeting of the Society for Personality and Social Psychology, Nashville, TN.

Lomore, C., & Cohen, D. (2002, February). *Soulmate and work-it-out theorists: Defensive and practical strategies for coping with relationship transgressions.* Paper presented at the meeting of the Society for Personality and Social Psychology, Savannah, GA.

Long, E. C. J., Angera, J. J., Carter, S. J., Nakamoto, M., & Kalso, M. (1999). Understanding the one you love: A longitudinal assessment of an empathy training program for couples in romantic relationships. *Family Relations, 48,* 235–242.

Lopata, H. Z. (1969). Loneliness, forms and components. *Social Problems, 17,* 248–261.

Lott, A. J., & Lott, B. E. (1974). The role of reward in the formation of positive interpersonal attitudes. In T. Huston (Ed.), *Foundations of interpersonal attraction* (pp. 171–189). New York: Academic Press.

Loving, T. J. (2004, January). *Undergraduate disclosure to friends about dating relationships: What they say and why they say it.* Paper presented at the meeting of the Social Psychologists in Texas, Corpus Christi, TX.

Loving, T. J., & Agnew, C. R. (2001). Socially desirable responding in close relationships: A dual-component approach and measure. *Journal of Social and Personal Relationships, 18,* 551–574.

Lucas, R. E., Clark, A. E., Georgellis, Y., & Diener, E. (2003). Reexamining adaptation and the set point model of happiness: Reactions to changes in marital status. *Journal of Personality and Social Psychology, 84,* 527–539.

Luecken, L. J., & Fabricius, W. V. (2003). Physical health vulnerability in adult children from divorced and intact families. *Journal of Psychosomatic Research, 55,* 221–228.

Luo, S., & Klohnen, E. C. (2003, February). *Unraveling perceptual processes of romantic attraction: Perceived similarity to actual self, perceived similarity to ideal self, and perceived partner security.* Paper presented at the meeting of the Society for Personality and Social Psychology, Los Angeles.

Lydon, J. E., Fitzsimons, G. M., & Naidoo, L. (2003). Devaluation versus enhancement of attractive alternatives: A critical test using the calibration paradigm. *Personality and Social Psychology Bulletin, 29,* 349–359.

Lydon, J., Pierce, T., & O'Regan, S. (1997). Coping with moral commitment to long-distance dating relationships. *Journal of Personality and Social Psychology, 73,* 104–113.

Lykken, D. T. (2002). How relationships begin and end: A genetic perspective. In A. L. Vangelisti, H. T. Reis, & M. A. Fitzpatrick (Eds.), *Stability and change in relationships* (pp. 83–102). Cambridge, UK: Cambridge University Press.

Lykken, D. T., & Tellegen, A. (1993). Is human mating adventitious or the result of lawful choice? A twin study of mate selection. *Journal of Personality and Social Psychology, 65,* 56–68.

Lynn, M., & Shurgot, B. A. (1984). Responses to lonely hearts advertisements: Effects of reported physical attractiveness, physique, and coloration. *Personality and Social Psychology Bulletin, 10,* 349–357.

MacDonald, G., Zanna, M. P., & Holmes, J. G. (2000). An experimental test of the role of alcohol in relationship conflict. *Journal of Experimental Social Psychology, 36,* 182–193.

MacDonald, T. K., MacDonald, G., Zanna, M. P., & Fong, G. (2000). Alcohol, sexual arousal, and intentions to use condoms in young men: Applying alcohol myopia theory to risky sexual behavior. *Health Psychology, 19,* 290–298.

MacDonald, T. K., & Ross, M. (1999). Assessing the accuracy of predictions about dating relationships: How and why do lovers' predictions differ from those made by observers? *Personality and Social Psychology Bulletin, 25,* 1417–1429.

Mackey, R. A., Diemer, M. A, & O'Brien, B. A. (2000). Psychological intimacy in the lasting relationships of heterosexual and same-gender couples. *Sex Roles, 43,* 201–227.

Macrae, C. N., Alnwick, K. A., Milne, A. B., & Schloerscheidt, A. M. (2002). Person perception across the menstrual cycle: Hormonal influences on social-cognitive functioning. *Psychological Science, 13,* 532–536.

Madey, S. F., Simo, M., Dillworth, D., Kemper, D., Toczynski, A., & Perella, A. (1996). They do get more attractive at closing time, but only when you are not in a relationship. *Basic and Applied Social Psychology, 18,* 387–393.

Madon, S., Guyll, M., Spoth, R. L., Cross, S. E., & Hilbert, S. J. (2003). The self-fulfilling influence of mother expectations on children's underage drinking. *Journal of Personality and Social Psychology, 84,* 1188–1205.

Magdol, L., & Bessel, D. R. (2003). Social capital, social currency, and portable assets: The impact of residential mobility on exchanges of social support. *Personal Relationships, 10,* 149–169.

Mahoney, A., Pargament, K. I., Tarakeshwar, N., & Swank, A. B. (in press). Religion in the home in the 1980s and 90s: Meta-analyses and conceptual analyses of links between religion, marriage and parenting. *Journal of Family Psychology.*

Major, B., Carrington, P. I., & Carnevale, P. J. D. (1984). Physical attractiveness and self-esteem: Attributions for praise from an other-sex evaluator. *Personality and Social Psychology Bulletin, 10,* 43–50.

Major, B., & Heslin, R. (1982). Perceptions of same-sex and cross-sex nonreciprocal touch: It's better to give than to receive. *Journal of Nonverbal Behavior, 6,* 148–162.

Major, B., Schmidlin, A. M., & Williams, L. (1990). Gender patterns in social touch: The impact of setting and age. *Journal of Personality and Social Psychology, 58,* 634–643.

Malle, B. F., & Pearce, G. E. (2001). Attention to behavioral events during interaction: Two actor-observer gaps and three attempts to close them. *Journal of Personality and Social Psychology, 81,* 278–294.

Marchand, M. A. G., & Vonk, R. (2004, January). I bet you say that to all the girls (boys): When flattery does not work. Paper presented at the meeting of the Society for Personality and Social Psychology, Austin, TX.

Marcus, D. K., & Miller, R. S. (2003). Sex differences in judgments of physical attractiveness: A social relations analysis. *Personality and Social Psychology Bulletin, 29,* 325–335.

Marecek, J. (1987). Counseling adolescents with problem pregnancies. *American Psychologist, 42,* 89–93.

Margolin, L., & White, L. (1987). The continuing role of physical attractiveness in marriage. *Journal of Marriage and the Family, 49,* 21–28.

Mark, M. M., & Reichardt, C. S. (2004). Quasi-experimental and correlational designs: Methods for the real world when random assignment isn't feasible. In C. Sansone, C. C. Morf, & A. T. Panter (Eds.), *The Sage handbook of methods in social psychology* (pp. 265–286). Thousand Oaks, CA: Sage.

Markey, P. M., Funder, D. C., & Ozer, D. J. (2003). Complementarity of interpersonal behaviors in dyadic interactions. *Personality and Social Psychology Bulletin, 29,* 1082–1090.

Markman, H. J. (1981). Prediction of marital distress: A 5-year follow-up. *Journal of Consulting and Clinical Psychology, 49,* 760–762.

Markman, H., Stanley, S., & Blumberg, S. L. (1994). *Fighting for your marriage: Positive steps for preventing divorce and preserving a lasting love.* San Francisco: Jossey-Bass.

Marks, G., & Miller, N. (1982). Target attractiveness as a mediator of assumed attitude similarity. *Personality and Social Psychology Bulletin, 8,* 728–735.

Marshall, G. D., & Zimbardo, P. G. (1979). Affective consequences of inadequately explained physiological arousal. *Journal of Personality and Social Psychology, 37,* 970–988.

Marshall, L. L., Weston, R., & Honeycutt, T. C. (2000). Does men's positivity moderate or mediate the effect of their abuse on women's relationship quality? *Journal of Social and Personal Relationships, 17,* 660–675.

Marston, P. J., Hecht, M. L., Manke, M. L., McDaniel, S., & Reeder, H. (1998). The subjective experience of intimacy, passion, and commitment in heterosexual loving relationships. *Personal Relationships, 5,* 15–30.

Martin, J. (1997, October 21). Bereaved may face insensitivity. *Houston Chronicle,* p. 10F.

Martin, R. (1997). "Girls don't talk about garages!": Perceptions of conversation in same- and cross-sex friendships. *Personal Relationships, 4,* 115–130.

Martin, T. C., & Bumpass, L. (1989). Recent trends in marital disruption. *Demography, 26,* 37–51.

Masciuch, S., & Kienapple, K. (1993). The emergence of jealousy in children 4 months to 7 years of age. *Journal of Social and Personal Relationships, 10,* 421–435.

Mason, A., & Blankenship, V. (1987). Power and affiliation motivation, stress, and abuse in intimate relationships. *Journal of Personality and Social Psychology, 52,* 203–210.

Masters, W. H., & Johnson, V. F. (1970). *Human sexual inadequacy.* Boston: Little, Brown.

Mathes, E. W., Adams, H. E., & Davies, R. M. (1985). Jealousy: Loss of relationship rewards, loss of self-esteem, depression, anxiety, and anger. *Journal of Personality and Social Psychology, 48,* 1552–1561.

Mathews, A., Derlega, V. J., Morrow, J. A., & Winstead, B. A. (2004, July). *Development of a taxonomy of reasons for and against self-disclosure in close relationships.* Paper presented at the meeting of the International Association for Relationship Research, Madison, WI.

Matthews, D. D. (Ed.). (2004). *Domestic violence sourcebook* (2nd ed.). Detroit: Omnigraphics.

Matthews, L. S., Wickrama, K. A. S., & Conger, R. D. (1996). Predicting marital instability from spouse and observer reports of marital interaction. *Journal of Marriage and the Family, 58,* 641–655.

Mayseless, O., Sharabany, R., & Sagi, A. (1997). Attachment concerns of mothers as manifested in parental, spousal, and friendship relationships. *Personal Relationships, 4,* 255–269.

McAdams, D. P. (1985). Motivation and friendship. In S. Duck & D. Perlman (Eds.), *Understanding personal relationships: An interdisciplinary approach* (pp. 85–105). London: Sage.

McAdams, D. P., & Bryant, F. B. (1987). Intimacy motivation and subjective mental health in a nationwide sample. *Journal of Personality, 55,* 395–414.

McAdams, D. P., Healy, S., & Krause, S. (1984). Social motives and friendship patterns. *Journal of Personality and Social Psychology, 47,* 828–838.

McAdams, D. P., & Vaillant, G. E. (1982). Intimacy motivation and psychosocial adjustment: A longitudinal study. *Journal of Personality Assessment, 46,* 586–593.

McCornack, S. A. (1997). The generation of deceptive messages: Laying the groundwork for a viable theory of interpersonal deception. In J. O. Greene (Ed.), *Message production: Advances in communication theory* (pp. 91–126). Mahwah, NJ: Erlbaum.

McCornack, S. A, & Levine, T. R. (1990a). When lies are uncovered: Emotional and relational outcomes of discovered deception. *Communication Monographs, 57,* 119–138.

McCornack, S. A, & Levine, T. R. (1990b). When lovers become leery: The relationship between suspicion and accuracy in detecting deception. *Communication Monographs, 57,* 219–230.

McCornack, S. A, & Parks, M. R. (1990). What women know that men don't: Sex differences in determining the truth behind deceptive messages. *Journal of Social and Personal Relationships, 7,* 107–118.

McCown, J. A. (2000, August). *Internet relationships: People who meet people.* Paper presented at the meeting of the American Psychological Association, Washington, DC.

McCrae, R. R., & Costa, P. T., Jr. (1997). Personality trait structure as a human universal. *American Psychologist, 52,* 509–516.

McCreary, J., & Branscum, E. (2004, January). *Stability and change in attachment models.* Paper presented at the meeting of the Society for Personality and Social Psychology, Austin, TX.

McCullough, M. E. (2000). Forgiveness as human strength: Theory, measurement, and links to well-being. *Journal of Social and Clinical Psychology, 19,* 43–55.

McCullough, M. E., Bellah, C. G., Kilpatrick, S. D., & Johnson, J. L. (2001). Vengefulness: Relationships with forgiveness, rumination, well-being, and the Big Five. *Personality and Social Psychology Bulletin, 27,* 601–610.

McCullough, M. E., Emmons, R. A., Kilpatrick, S. D., & Mooney, C. N. (2003). Narcissists as "victims": The role of narcissism in the perception of transgressions. *Personality and Social Psychology Bulletin, 29,* 885–893.

McCullough, M. E., Rachal, K. C., Sandage, S. J., Worthington, E. L., Jr., Brown, S. W., & Hight, T. L. (1998). Interpersonal forgiving in close relationships: II. Theoretical elaboration and measurement. *Journal of Personality and Social Psychology, 75,* 1586–1603.

McDonald, G. W. (1981). Structural exchange and marital interaction. *Journal of Marriage and the Family, 43,* 825–839.

McFarland, C., & Ross, M. (1987). The relation between current impression and memories of self and dating partners. *Personality and Social Psychology Bulletin, 13,* 228–238.

McGinn, D. (2004, October 4). Mating behavior 101. *Newsweek,* 44–45.

McGinnis, S. L. (2003). Cohabiting, dating, and perceived costs of marriage: A model of marriage entry. *Journal of Marriage and the Family, 65,* 105–116.

McGonagle, K. A., Kessler, R. C., & Schilling, E. A. (1992). The frequency and determinants of marital disagreements in a community sample. *Journal of Social and Personal Relationships, 9,* 507–524.

McGowan, S. (2002). Mental representations in stressful situations: The calming and distressing of significant others. *Journal of Experimental Social Psychology, 38,* 152–161.

McGregor, I., & Holmes, J. G. (1999). How storytelling shapes memory and impressions of relationship events over time. *Journal of Personality and Social Psychology, 76,* 403–419.

McGuire, S., & Clifford, J. (2000). Genetic and environmental contributions to loneliness in children. *Psychological Science, 11,* 487–491.

McKenna, K. Y. A., & Bargh, J. A. (2000). Plan 9 from cyberspace: The implications of the Internet for personality and social psychology. *Personality and Social Psychology Review, 4,* 57–75.

McKenna, K. Y. A., Green, A. S., & Gleason, M. E. J. (2002). Relationship formation on the Internet: What's the big attraction? *Journal of Social Issues, 58,* 9–31.

McMurray, L. (1970). Emotional stress and driving performance: The effect of divorce. *Behavioral Research in Highway Safety, 1,* 100–114.

McNulty, J. K., & Karney, B. R. (2002). Expectancy confirmation in appraisals of marital interactions. *Personality and Social Psychology Bulletin, 28,* 764–775.

McNulty, J. K., & Karney, B. R. (2004). Positive expectations in the early years of marriage: Should couples expect the best or brace for the worst? *Journal of Personality and Social Psychology, 86,* 729–743.

McPherson, M., Smith-Lovin, L., & Cook, J. M. (2001). Birds of a feather: Homophily in social networks. *Annual Review of Sociology, 27,* 415–444.

McWhirter, B. T. (1997). Loneliness, learned resourcefulness, and self-esteem in college students. *Journal of Counseling and Development, 75,* 460–469.

Mealey, L., Bridgstock, R., & Townsend, G. C. (1999). Symmetry and perceived facial attractiveness: A monozygotic co-twin comparison. *Journal of Personality and Social Psychology, 76,* 151–158.

Meckler, L. (2002, July 25). Keeping the knot tied. *Houston Chronicle,* p. 10A.

Meeks, B. S., Hendrick, S. S., & Hendrick, C. (1998). Communication, love and relationship satisfaction. *Journal of Social and Personal Relationships, 15,* 755–773.

Mehl, M. R., & Pennebaker, J. W. (2003). The sounds of social life: A psychometric analysis of students' daily social environments and natural conversations. *Journal of Personality and Social Psychology, 84,* 857–870.

Meier, B. P., & Robinson, M. D. (2004). Does quick to blame mean quick to anger? The role of agreeableness in dissociating blame and anger. *Personality and Social Psychology Bulletin, 30,* 856–867.

Melzer, S. A. (2002). Gender, work, and intimate violence: Men's occupational violence spillover and compensatory violence. *Journal of Marriage and the Family, 64,* 820–832.

Mendes de Leon, C. F., Glass, T. A., Beckett, L. A., Seeman, T. E., Evans, D. A., & Berkman, L. F. (1999). Social networks and disability transitions across eight intervals of yearly data in the New Haven EPESE. *Journals of Gerontology: Series B: Psychological Sciences and Social Sciences, 54B(3),* S162–S172.

Messer, S. B., & Wampold, B. E. (2002). Let's face facts: Common factors are more potent than specific therapy ingredients. *Clinical Psychology: Science & Practice, 9,* 21–25.

Messman, S. J., Canary, D. J., & Hause, K. S. (2000). Motives to remain platonic, equity, and the use of maintenance strategies in opposite-sex friendships. *Journal of Social and Personal Relationships, 17,* 67–94.

Metts, S. (1989). An exploratory investigation of deception in close relationships. *Journal of Social and Personal Relationships, 6,* 159–179.

Metts, S. (1994). Relational transgressions. In W. R. Cupach & B. H. Spitzberg (Eds.), *The dark side of interpersonal communication* (pp. 217–239). Hillsdale, NJ: Erlbaum.

Metts, S. (2004). First sexual involvement in romantic relationships: An empirical investigation of communicative framing, romantic beliefs and attachment orientation in the passion turning point. In J. H. Harvey, A. Wenzel, & S. Sprecher (Eds.), *The handbook of sexuality in close relationships* (pp. 135–158). Mahwah, NJ: Erlbaum.

Metts, S., & Cupach, W. R. (1990). The influence of romantic beliefs and problem-solving responses on satisfaction in romantic relationships. *Human Communication Research, 17,* 170–185.

Metts, S., Sprecher, S., & Regan, P. C. (1998). Communication and sexual desire. In P. A. Andersen and L. K. Guerrero (Eds.), Handbook of communication and emotion: Research, theory, applications, and contexts (pp. 353–377). San Diego: Academic Press.

Meyer, D. R. (1999). Compliance with child support orders in paternity and divorce cases. In R. A. Thompson & P. R. Amato (Eds.), *The postdivorce family: Children, parenting and society* (pp. 127–157). Thousand Oaks, CA: Sage.

Meyers, S. A., & Landsberger, S. A. (2002). Direct and indirect pathways between adult attachment style and marital satisfaction. *Personal Relationships, 9,* 159–172.

Mezulis, A. H., Abramson, L. Y., Hyde, J. S., & Hankin, B. J. (2004). Is there a universal positivity bias in attributions? A meta-analytic review of individual, developmental, and cultural differences in the self-serving attributional bias. *Psychological Bulletin, 130,* 711–747.

Michael, R. T., Gagnon, J. H., Laumann, E. O., & Kolata, G. (1994). *Sex in America: A definitive survey.* Boston: Little, Brown.

Michaels, S. (1996). The prevalence of homosexuality in the United States. In R. P. Cabaj & T. S. Stein (Eds.), *Textbook of homosexuality and mental health* (pp. 43–63). Washington, DC: American Psychiatric Press.

Mickelson, K. D., Kessler, R. C., & Shaver, P. R. (1997). Adult attachment in a nationally representative sample. *Journal of Personality and Social Psychology, 73,* 1092–1106.

Mikula, G., Athenstaedt, U., Heschgl, S., & Heimgartner, A. (1998). Does it only depend on the point of view? Perspective-related differences in justice evaluations of negative incidents in personal relationships. *European Journal of Social Psychology, 28,* 931–962.

Mikulincer, M. (1997). Adult attachment style and information processing: Individual differences in curiosity and cognitive closure. *Journal of Personality and Social Psychology, 72,* 1217–1230.

Mikulincer, M. (1998). Attachment working models and the sense of trust: An exploration of interaction goals and affect regulation. *Journal of Personality and Social Psychology, 74,* 1209–1224.

Mikulincer, M., Orbach, I., & Iavnieli, D. (1998). Adult attachment style and affect regulation: Strategic variations in subjective self-other similarity. *Journal of Personality and Social Psychology, 75,* 436–448.

Mikulincer, M., & Shaver, P. R. (2005). Attachment, security, compassion, and altruism. *Current Directions in Psychological Science, 14,* 34–38.

Milardo, R. M., Johnson, M. P., & Huston, T. L. (1983). Developing close relationships: Changing patterns of interaction between pair members and social networks. *Journal of Personality and Social Psychology, 44,* 964–976.

Miles, L. (2003, February). *Not all smiles are created equal: An investigation of the implicit impact of posed and genuine smiles on the social perceiver.* Paper presented at the meeting of the Society for Personality and Social Psychology, Los Angeles.

Milhausen, R. R., & Herold, E. S. (1999). Does the sexual double standard still exist? Perceptions of university women. *Journal of Sex Research, 36,* 361–368.

Miller, J. B. (1976). *Toward a new psychology of women.* Boston: Beacon Press.

Miller, J. B., & Noirot, M. (1999). Attachment memories, models and information processing. *Journal of Social and Personal Relationships, 16,* 147–173.

Miller, J. G. (2004). Culturally sensitive research questions and methods in social psychology. In C. Sansone, C. C. Morf, & A. T. Panter (Eds.), *The Sage handbook of methods in social psychology* (pp. 93–116). Thousand Oaks, CA: Sage.

Miller, L. C. (1990). Intimacy and liking: Mutual influence and the role of unique relationships. *Journal of Personality and Social Psychology, 59,* 50–60.

Miller, L. C., Berg, J. H., & Archer, R. L. (1983). Openers: Individuals who elicit intimate self-disclosure. *Journal of Personality and Social Psychology, 44,* 1234–1244.

Miller, M. A., & Rahe, R. H. (1997). Life changes scaling for the 1990s. *Journal of Psychomatic Research, 43,* 279–292.

Miller, P. J. E., Huston, T. L., & Caughlin, J. P. (2003). Trait expressiveness and marital satisfaction: The role of idealization processes. *Journal of Marriage and the Family, 65,* 978–995.

Miller, P. J. E., & Rempel, J. K. (2004). Trust and partner-enhancing attributions in close relationships. *Personality and Social Psychology Bulletin, 30,* 695–705.

Miller, R. S. (1996). *Embarrassment: Poise and peril in everyday life.* New York: Guilford Press.

Miller, R. S. (1997a). Inattentive and contented: Relationship commitment and attention to alternatives. *Journal of Personality and Social Psychology, 73,* 758–766.

Miller, R. S. (1997b). We always hurt the ones we love: Aversive interactions in close relationships. In R. Kowalski (Ed.), *Aversive interpersonal interactions* (pp. 11–29). New York: Plenum.

Miller, R. S. (2001). Breaches of propriety. In R. M. Kowalski (Ed.), *Behaving badly: Aversive behaviors in interpersonal relationships* (pp. 29–58). Washington, DC: American Psychological Association.

Miller, R. S. (2001). Shyness and embarrassment compared: Siblings in the service of social evaluation. In W. R. Crozier & L. E. Alden (Eds.), *International handbook of social anxiety: Concepts, research and interventions relating to the self and shyness* (pp. 281–300). Chichester, UK: Wiley.

Miller, R. S. (2003). On being admired but overlooked: Reflections on "attention to alternatives" in close relationships. *Psychological Inquiry, 14,* 284–288.

Miller, R. S., & Schlenker, B. R. (1985). Egotism in group members: Public and private attributions of responsibility for group performance. *Social Psychology Quarterly, 48,* 85–89.

Mills, J., & Clark, M. S. (2001). Viewing close romantic relationships as communal relationships: Implications for maintenance and enhancement. In J. H. Harvey & A. Wenzel (Eds.), *Close romantic relationships: Maintenance and enhancement* (pp. 13–25). Mahwah, NJ: Erlbaum.

Mills, J., Clark, M. S., Ford, T. E., & Johnson, M. (2004). Measurement of communal strength. *Personal Relationships, 11,* 213–230.

Mitchell, K., & Sugar, M. (2003, September 30). Trust is often hard to recover. *The Bryan-College Station Eagle,* p. B4.

Mitchell, S. A. (2002). *Can love last? The fate of romance over time.* New York: Norton.

Monarch, N. D., Hartman, S. G., Whitton, S. W., & Markman, H. J. (2002). The role of clinicians in the prevention of marital distress and divorce. In J. H. Harvey & A. Wenzel (Eds.), *A clinician's guide to maintaining and enhancing close relationships* (pp. 233–258). Mahwah, NJ: Erlbaum.

Mondloch, C. J., Lewis, T. L., Budreau, D. R., Maurer, D., Dannemiller, J. L., Stephens, B. R., & Kleiner-Gathercoal, K. A. (1999). Face perception during early infancy. *Psychological Science, 10*, 419–422.

Monroe, W. S. (1898). Discussion and reports. Social consciousness in children. *Psychological Review, 5*, 68–70.

Monsour, M. (1992). Meanings of intimacy in cross- and same-sex friendships. *Journal of Social and Personal Relationships, 9*, 277–295.

Montano, D., Kasprzyk, D., von Haeften, I., & Fishbein, M. (2001). Toward an understanding of condom use behaviours: A theoretical and methodological overview of Project SAFER. *Psychology, Health & Medicine, 6*, 139–150.

Montepare, J. M., & Vega, C. (1988). Women's vocal reactions to intimate and casual male friends. *Personality and Social Psychology Bulletin, 14*, 103–113.

Montoya, R. M., & Horton, R. S. (2004). On the importance of cognitive evaluation as a determinant of interpersonal attraction. *Journal of Personality & Social Psychology, 86*, 696–712.

Moors, G. (2000). Values and living arrangements: A recursive relationship. In L. J. Waite (Ed.), *The ties that bind: Perspectives on marriage and cohabitation* (pp. 212–226). New York: Aldine de Gruyter.

Moreland, R. L., & Beach, S. R. (1992). Exposure effects in the classroom: The development of affinity among students. *Journal of Experimental Social Psychology, 28*, 255–276.

Moreno, J. L. (1934). *Who shall survive? A new approach to the problem of human interrelationships.* Washington, DC: Nervous and Mental Disease Publishing.

Morgentaler, A. (2003). *The Viagra myth: The surprising impact on love and relationships.* San Francisco: Jossey-Bass.

Morier, D., & Seroy, C. (1994). The effect of interpersonal expectancies on men's self-presentation of gender role attitudes to women. *Sex Roles, 31*, 493–504.

Morris, A. B. (2001). Alcohol consumption and HIV risk behaviours: Integrating the theories of alcohol myopia and outcome expectancies. *Addiction Research & Theory, 9*, 73–86.

Morrow, G. D., Clark, E. M., & Brock, K. F. (1995). Individual and partner love styles: Implications for the quality of romantic involvements. *Journal of Social and Personal Relationships, 12*, 363–387.

Morrow, J., & Cikara, M. (2004, May). *Effects of gender and dominance on overt sexuality, attractiveness, warmth, and competence.* Paper presented at the meeting of the American Psychological Society, Chicago.

Muehlenhard, C. L., Andrews, S. L., & Beal, G. K. (1995). Beyond "just saying no": Dealing with men's unwanted sexual advances in heterosexual dating contexts. *Journal of Psychology & Human Sexuality, 8*, 141–168.

Muehlenhard, C. L., & Hollabaugh, L. C. (1988). Do women sometimes say no when they mean yes? The prevalence and correlates of women's token resistance to sex. *Journal of Personality and Social Psychology, 54*, 872–879.

Muehlenhard, C. L., & Miller, E. N. (1988). Traditional and nontraditional men's responses to women's dating initiation. *Behavior Modification, 12*, 385–403.

Muehlenhard, C. L., & Rodgers, C. S. (1998). Token resistance to sex: New perspectives on an old stereotype. *Psychology of Women Quarterly, 22*, 443–463.

Mulac, A. (1998). The gender-linked language effect: Do language differences really make a difference? In D. J. Canary & K. Dindia (Eds.), *Sex differences and similarities in communication: Critical essays and empirical investigations of sex and gender in interaction* (pp. 127–153). Mahwah, NJ: Erlbaum.

Mullen, B., Futrell, D., Stairs, D., Tice, D. M., Baumeister, R. F., Dawson, K. E., Riordan, C. A., Radloff, C. E., Goethals, G. R., Kennedy, J. G., & Rosenfeld, P. (1986). Newscasters' facial expressions and voting behavior of viewers: Can a smile elect a president? *Journal of Personality and Social Psychology, 51*, 291–295.

Mullen, P. E., & Martin, J. L. (1994). Jealousy: A community study. *British Journal of Psychiatry, 164*, 35–43.

Munger, K., & Harris, S. J. (1989). Effects of an observer on handwashing in a public restroom. *Perceptual and Motor Skills, 69,* 733–734.

Murray, S. L. (1999). The quest for conviction: Motivated cognition in romantic relationships. *Psychological Inquiry, 10,* 23–34.

Murray, S. L., & Holmes, J. G. (1997). A leap of faith? Positive illusions in romantic relationships. *Personality and Social Psychology Bulletin, 23,* 586–604.

Murray, S. L., Bellavia, G. M., Rose, P., & Griffin, D. W. (2003). Once hurt, twice hurtful: How perceived regard regulates daily marital interactions. *Journal of Personality and Social Psychology, 84,* 126–147.

Murray, S. L., Griffin, D. W., Rose, P., & Bellavia, G. M. (2003). Calibrating the sociometer: The relational contingencies of self-esteem. *Journal of Personality and Social Psychology, 85,* 63–84.

Murray, S. L., & Holmes, J. G. (1999). The (mental) ties that bind: Cognitive structures that predict relationship resilience. *Journal of Personality and Social Psychology, 77,* 1228–1244.

Murray, S. L., Holmes, J. G., & Griffin, D. W. (1996a). The benefits of positive illusions: Idealization and the construction of satisfaction in close relationships. *Journal of Personality and Social Psychology, 70,* 79–98.

Murray, S. L., Holmes, J. G., & Griffin, D. W. (1996b). The self-fulfilling nature of positive illusions in romantic relationships: Love is not blind, but prescient. *Journal of Personality and Social Psychology, 71,* 1155–1180.

Murray, S. L., Holmes, J. G., & Griffin, D. W. (2000). Self-esteem and the quest for felt security: How perceived regard regulates attachment processes. *Journal of Personality and Social Psychology, 78,* 478–498.

Murray, S. L., Holmes, J. G., Griffin, D. W., Bellavia, G., & Rose, P. (2001). The mismeasure of love: How self-doubt contaminates relationship beliefs. *Personality and Social Psychology Bulletin, 27,* 423–436.

Murray, S. L., Holmes, J. G., MacDonald, G., & Ellsworth, P. C. (1998). Through the looking glass darkly? When self-doubts turn into relationship insecurities. *Journal of Personality and Social Psychology, 75,* 1459–1480.

Murray, S. L., Rose, P., Bellavia, G. M., Holmes, J. G., & Kusche, A. G. (2002). When rejection stings: How self-esteem constrains relationship-enhancement processes. *Journal of Personality and Social Psychology, 83,* 556–573.

Murstein, B. I. (1987). A clarification and extension of the SVR theory of dyadic pairing. *Journal of Marriage and the Family, 49,* 929–933.

Myers, D. G. (2000). *The American paradox: Spiritual hunger in an age of plenty.* New Haven: Yale University Press.

Myers, D. G., & Diener, E. (1995). Who is happy? *Psychological Science, 6,* 10–19.

Myers, S. A., & Berscheid, E. (1997). The language of love: The difference a preposition makes. *Personality and Social Psychology Bulletin, 23,* 347–362.

Nathan, C. P., Logan, A., & Andersen, P. A. (2002, July). *Testing the triangle: The effects of intimacy, passion, and commitment on relational satisfaction in dating relationships.* Paper presented at the International Conference on Personal Relationships, Halifax, Nova Scotia.

National Center for Health Statistics. (2005). Births, marriages, divorces, and deaths: Provisional data for 2004. *National Vital Statistics Report, 53* (21), 1–7.

Neff, L. A., & Karney, B. R. (2002). Judgments of a relationship partner: Specific accuracy but global enhancement. *Journal of Personality, 70,* 1079–1112.

Neff, L. A., & Karney, B. R. (2003). The dynamic structure of relationship perceptions: Differential importance as a strategy of relationship maintenance. *Personality and Social Psychology Bulletin, 29,* 1433–1446.

Neff, L. A., & Karney, B. R. (2004). How does context affect intimate relationships? Linking external stress and cognitive processes within marriage. *Personality and Social Psychology Bulletin, 30,* 134–148.

Neimeyer, G. J. (1984). Cognitive complexity and marital satisfaction. *Journal of Social and Clinical Psychology, 2,* 258–263.

Neria, Y., Guttmann-Steinmetz, S., Koenen, K., Levinovsky, L., Zakin, G., & Dekel, R. (2001). Do attachment and hardiness relate to each other and to mental health in real-life stress? *Journal of Social and Personal Relationships, 18,* 844–858.

Newby-Clark, I. R., & Ross, M. (2003). Conceiving the past and future. *Personality and Social Psychology Bulletin, 29,* 807–818.

Newcomb, M. D., Huba, G. J., & Bentler, P. M. (1986). Determinants of sexual and dating behaviors among adolescents. *Journal of Personality and Social Psychology, 50,* 428–438.

Newcomb, T. M. (1961). *The acquaintance process.* New York: Holt, Rinehart & Winston.

Newman, M. L., Pennebaker, J. W., Berry, D. S., & Richards, J. M. (2003). Lying words: Predicting deception from linguistic styles. *Personality and Social Psychology Bulletin, 29,* 665–675.

Newton, R. R., Connelly, C. D., & Landsverk, J. A. (2001). An examination of measurement characteristics and factorial validity of the Revised Conflict Tactics Scale. *Educational and Psychological Measurement, 61,* 317–335.

Neyer, F. J. (1997). Free recall or recognition in collecting egocentered networks: The role of survey techniques. *Journal of Social and Personal Relationships, 14,* 305–316.

Nezlek, J. B. (2001). Causal relationships between perceived social skills and day-to-day social interaction: Extending the sociometer hypothesis. *Journal of Social and Personal Relationships, 18,* 386–403.

Nezlek, J. B., & Leary, M. R. (2002). Individual differences in self-presentational motives in daily social interaction. *Personality and Social Psychology Bulletin, 28,* 211–223.

Nezlek, J. B., Kowalski, R. M., Leary, M. R., Blevins, T., & Holgate, S. (1997). Personality moderators of reactions to interpersonal rejection: Depression and trait self-esteem. *Personality and Social Psychology Bulletin, 23,* 1235–1244.

Nezlek, J. B., Richardson, D. S., Green, L. R., & Schatten-Jones, E. C. (2002). Psychological well-being and day-to-day social interaction among older adults. *Personal Relationships, 9,* 57–71.

Nock, S. L. (1998). The consequences of premarital fatherhood. *American Sociological Review, 63,* 250–263.

Nock, S. L. (2000). The divorce of marriage and parenthood. *Journal of Family Therapy, 22,* 245–263.

Nolan, S. A., Flynn, C., & Garber, J. (2003). Prospective relations between rejection and depression in young adolescents. *Journal of Personality and Social Psychology, 85,* 745–755.

Noller, P. (1980). Misunderstandings in marital communication: A study of couples' nonverbal communications. *Journal of Personality and Social Psychology, 39,* 1135–1148.

Noller, P. (1981). Gender and marital adjustment level differences in decoding messages from spouses and strangers. *Journal of Personality and Social Psychology, 41,* 272–278.

Noller, P. (1987). Nonverbal communication in marriage. In D. Perlman & S. Duck (Eds.), *Intimate relationships: Development, dynamics, and deterioration* (pp. 149–175). Newbury Park, CA: Sage.

Noller, P. (1996). What is this thing called love? Defining the love that supports marriage and family. *Personal Relationships, 3,* 97–115.

Noller, P., & Feeney, J. A. (1994). Relationship satisfaction, attachment, and nonverbal accuracy in early marriage. *Journal of Nonverbal Behavior, 18,* 199–221.

Noller, P., Feeney, J. A., Bonnell, D., & Callan, V. J. (1994). A longitudinal study of conflict in early marriage. *Journal of Social and Personal Relationships, 11,* 233–252.

Noller, P., & Vernardos, C. (1986). Communication awareness in married couples. *Journal of Social and Personal Relationships, 3,* 31–42.

Notarius, C. I., Lashley, S. L., & Sullivan, D. J. (1997). Angry at your partner?: Think again. In R. J. Sternberg & M. Hojjat (Eds.), *Satisfaction in close relationships* (pp. 219–248). New York: Guilford Press.

O'Keefe, M. (1997). Predictors of dating violence among high school students. *Journal of Interpersonal Violence, 12,* 546–568.

O'Leary, K. D. (2000). Are women really more aggressive than men in intimate relationships?: Comment on Archer (2000). *Psychological Bulletin, 126,* 685–689.

O'Leary, K. D., & Turkewitz, H. (1978). Marital therapy from a behavioral perspective. In T. J. Paolino & B. McCrady (Eds.), *Marriage and marital therapy: Psychoanalytic, behavioral and systems theory perspectives* (pp. 240–297). New York: Brunner/Mazel.

O'Meara, J. D. (1989). Cross-sex friendship: Four basic challenges of an ignored relationship. *Sex Roles, 21,* 525–543.

O'Rourke, J. F. (1963). Field and laboratory: The decision making behavior of family groups in two experimental conditions. *Sociometry, 26,* 422–435.

O'Sullivan, L. F., & Gaines, M. E. (1998). Decision-making in college students' heterosexual dating relationships: Ambivalence about engaging in sexual activity. *Journal of Social and Personal Relationships, 15*, 347–363.

O'Sullivan, M. (2003). The fundamental attribution error in detecting deception: The boy-who-cried-wolf effect. *Personality and Social Psychology Bulletin, 29*, 1316–1327.

Oakman, J., Gifford, S., & Chlebowsky, N. (2003). A multilevel analysis of the interpersonal behavior of socially anxious people. *Journal of Personality, 71*, 397–434.

Okdie, B., Mclarney-Vesotski, A., Bernieri, F., & Oberleitner, D. (2004, June). *Reported truthfulness across mediums.* Paper presented at the meeting of the Society for Personality and Social Psychology, Austin, TX.

Okonski, B. (1996, May 6). Just say something. *Newsweek, 131*, 14.

Oliver, M. B., & Hyde, J. S. (1993). Gender differences in sexuality: A meta-analysis. *Psychological Bulletin, 114*, 29–51.

Oliver, M. B., & Sedikides, C. (1992). Effects of sexual permissiveness on desirability of partner as a function of low and high commitment to relationship. *Social Psychology Quarterly, 55*, 321–333.

Olson, D. H., & Cromwell, R. E. (1975). Methodological issues in family power. In R. E. Cromwell & D. H. Olson (Eds.), *Power in families* (pp. 131–150). New York: Wiley.

Olson, M. H., Colburn, J., Dessouki, A., & Heinbaugh, M. (2004, May). *Attractiveness increases at "closing time."* Paper presented at the meeting of the American Psychological Society, Chicago.

Orbuch, T. L., Brown, E., & Veroff, J. (2004, July). *The early development of marriage and accounts of divorce 16 years later.* Paper presented at the meeting of the International Association for Relationship Research, Madison, WI.

Orbuch, T. L., & Veroff, J. (2002). A programmatic review: Building a two-way bridge between social psychology and the study of the early years of marriage. *Journal of Social and Personal Relationships, 19*, 549–568.

Orbuch, T. L., Veroff, J., Hassan, H., & Horrocks, J. (2002). Who will divorce: A 14-year longitudinal study of black couples and white couples. *Journal of Social and Personal Relationships, 19*, 179–202.

Orr, A. (2004). *Meeting, mating, and cheating: Sex, love, and the new world of online dating.* Upper Saddle River, NJ: Reuters.

Orvis, B. R., Kelley, H. H., & Butler, D. (1976). Attributional conflict in young couples. In J. H. Harvey, W. J. Ickes, & R. E. Kidd (Eds.), *New directions in attribution research* (Vol. 1, pp. 353–386). Hillsdale, NJ: Erlbaum.

Osborne, R. E., & Gilbert, D. T. (1992). The preoccupational hazards of social life. *Journal of Personality and Social Psychology, 62*, 219–228.

Ostovich, J. M., & Sabini, J. (2004). How are sociosexuality, sex drive, and lifetime number of sexual partners related? *Personality and Social Psychology Bulletin, 30*, 1255–1266.

Oswald, D. L., Clark, E. M., & Kelly, C. M. (2004). Friendship maintenance: An analysis of individual and dyad behaviors. *Journal of Social and Clinical Psychology, 23*, 413–441.

Overall, N. C., Fletcher, G. J. O., & Friesen, M. D. (2003). Mapping the intimate relationship mind: Comparisons between three models of attachment representations. *Personality and Social Psychology Bulletin, 29*, 1479–1493.

Owen, P. R., & Laurel-Seller, E. (2000). Weight and shape ideals: Thin is dangerously in. *Journal of Applied Social Psychology, 30*, 979–990.

Page, R. M., & Cole, G. E. (1991). Demographic predictors of self-reported loneliness in adults. *Psychological Reports, 68*, 939–945.

Pakaluk, M. (Ed.). (1991). *Other selves: Philosophers on friendship.* Indianapolis, IN: Hackett.

Papero, D. V. (1995). Bowen family systems and marriage. In N. S. Jacobson & A. S. Gurman (Eds.), *Clinical handbook of couple therapy* (pp. 11–30). New York: Guilford.

Park, B., Kraus, S., & Ryan, C. S. (1997). Longitudinal changes in consensus as a function of acquaintance and agreement in liking. *Journal of Personality and Social Psychology, 72*, 604–616.

Parks, M. R., & Floyd, K. (1996). Meanings for closeness and intimacy in friendship. *Journal of Social and Personal Relationships, 13*, 85–107.

Parrott, W. G. (1991). The emotional experiences of envy and jealousy. In P. Salovey (Ed.), *The psychology of jealousy and envy* (pp. 3–30). New York: Guilford Press.

Parrott, W. G., & Smith, R. H. (1993). Distinguishing the experiences of envy and jealousy. *Journal of Personality and Social Psychology, 64*, 906–920.

Pasch, L. A., & Bradbury, T. N. (1998). Social support, conflict, and the development of marital dysfunction. *Journal of Consulting and Clinical Psychology, 66*, 219–230.

Pataki, S. P., & Clark, M. S. (2004). Self-presentations of happiness: Sincere, polite, or cautious? *Personality and Social Psychology Bulletin, 30*, 905–914.

Patterson, M. L. (1988). Functions of nonverbal behavior in close relationships. In S. Duck (Ed.), *Handbook of personal relationships: Theory, research, and interventions* (pp. 41–56). New York: Wiley.

Patterson, M. L. (1990). Functions of non-verbal behavior in social interaction. In H. Giles & W. P. Robinson (Eds.), *Handbook of language and social psychology* (pp. 101–120). Chichester, England: Wiley.

Paul, E. L., & Hayes, K. A. (2002). The casualties of "casual" sex: A qualitative exploration of the phenomenology of college students' hookups. *Journal of Social and Personal Relationships, 19*, 639–661.

Paul, E. L., McManus, B., & Hayes, A. (2000). "Hookups": Characteristics and correlates of college students' spontaneous and anonymous sexual experiences. *Journal of Sex Research, 37*, 76–88.

Paul, L., Foss, M. A., & Galloway, J. (1993). Sexual jealousy in young men and women: Aggressive responsiveness to partner and rival. *Aggressive Behavior, 19*, 401–420.

Paulhus, D. L., & Morgan, K. L. (1997). Perceptions of intelligence in leaderless groups: The dynamic effects of shyness and acquaintance. *Journal of Personality and Social Psychology, 72*, 581–591.

Pedersen, F. A. (1991). Secular trends in human sex ratios: Their influence on individual and family behavior. *Human Nature, 2*, 271–291.

Pedersen, W. C., Miller, L. C., Putcha-Bhagavatula, A. D., & Yang, Y. (2002). Evolved sex differences in the number of partners desired? The long and the short of it. *Psychological Science, 13*, 157–161.

Pegalis, L. J., Shaffer, D. R., Bazzini, D. G., & Greenier, K. (1994). On the ability to elicit self-disclosure: Are there gender-based and contextual limitations on the opener effect? *Personality and Social Psychology Bulletin, 20*, 412–420.

Pelham, B. W., Mirenberg, M. C., & Jones, J. T. (2002). Why Susie sells seashells by the seashore: Implicit egotism and major life decisions. *Journal of Personality & Social Psychology, 82*, 469–487.

Pennebaker, J. W. (1997). Writing about emotional experiences as a therapeutic process. *Psychological Science, 8*, 162–166.

Pennebaker, J. W., Dyer, M. A., Caulkins, R. J., Litowitz, D. L., Ackerman, P. L., Anderson, D. B., & McGraw, K. M. (1979). Don't the girls get prettier at closing time: A country and western application to psychology. *Personality and Social Psychology Bulletin, 5*, 122–125.

Penton-Voak, I. S., & Perrett, D. I. (2000). Female preference for male faces changes cyclically—further evidence. *Evolution and Human Behavior, 21*, 39–48.

Penton-Voak, I. S., Perrett, D. I., Castles, D. L., Kobayashi, T., Burt, D. M., Murray, L. K., & Minamisawa, R. (1999). Menstrual cycle alters face preference. *Nature, 399*, 741–742.

Peplau, L. A. (2003). Human sexuality: How do men and women differ? *Current Directions in Psychological Science, 12*, 37–40.

Peplau, L. A., Fingerhut, A., & Beals, K. P. (2004). Sexuality in the relationships of lesbians and gay men. In J. H. Harvey, A. Wenzel, & S. Sprecher (Eds.), *The handbook of sexuality in close relationships* (pp. 349–369). Mahwah, NJ: Erlbaum.

Peplau, L. A., Russell, D., & Heim, M. (1979). The experience of loneliness. In I. Frieze, D. Bar-Tal, & J. Carroll (Eds.), *New approaches to social problems: Applications of attribution theory* (pp. 53–78). San Francisco: Jossey-Bass.

Peplau, L. A., & Spalding, L. R. (2000). The close relationships of lesbians, gay men and bisexuals. In C. Hendrick & S. S. Hendrick (Eds.), *Close relationships: A sourcebook* (pp. 111–123). Thousand Oaks, CA: Sage.

Perlman, D. (1989, August). *You bug me: A preliminary report on hassles in relationships.* Paper presented at the meeting of the American Psychological Association, New Orleans.

Perlman, D. (1991). *Age differences in loneliness: A meta analysis.* Vancouver, Canada: University of British Columbia. (ERIC Document Reproduction Service No. ED 326767).

Perlman, D., & Landolt, M. A. (1999). Examination of loneliness in children/adolescents and in adults: Two solitudes or unified enterprise? In K. J. Rotenberg & S. Hymel (Eds.), *Loneliness in childhood and adolescence* (pp. 325–347). New York: Cambridge University Press.

Perlman, D., & Peplau, L. A. (1981). Toward a social psychology of loneliness. In S. Duck & R. Gilmour (Eds.), *Personal relationships. 3: Personal relationships in disorder* (pp. 31–56). New York: Academic Press.

Perlman, D., & Peplau, L. A. (1998). Loneliness. In H. Friedman (Ed.), *Encyclopedia of mental health* (Vol. 2, pp. 571–581). San Diego, CA: Academic Press.

Perrett, D. I., Burt, D. M., Penton-Voak, I. S., Lee, K. J., Rowland, D. A., & Edwards, R. (1999). Symmetry and human facial attractiveness. *Evolution and Human Behavior, 20,* 295–307.

Perrett, D. I., Lee, K. J., Penton-Voak, I., Rowland, D., Yoshikawa, S., Burt, D. M., Henzi, S. P., Castles, D. L., & Akamatsu, S. (1998). Effects of sexual dimorphism on facial attractiveness. *Nature, 394,* 884–887.

Perrett, D. I., May, K. A., & Yoshikawa, S. (1994). Facial shape and judgments of female attractiveness. *Nature, 368,* 239–242.

Peterson, D. R. (2002). Conflict. In H. H. Kelley, E. Berscheid, A. Christensen et al. (Eds.), *Close relationships* (pp. 265–314). Clinton Corners, NY: Percheron Press.

Petronio, S. (2002). *Boundaries of privacy: Dialectics of disclosure.* Albany, NY: State University of New York Press.

Petronio, S., Olson, C., & Dollar, N. (1989). Privacy issues in relational embarrassment: Impact on relational quality and communication satisfaction. *Communication Research Reports, 6,* 21–27.

Pettijohn, T. F., II, & Jungeberg, B. J. (2004). *Playboy* playmate curves: Changes in facial and body feature preferences across social and economic conditions. *Personality and Social Psychology Bulletin, 30,* 1186–1197.

Phillips, R. (1988). *Putting asunder: A history of divorce in Western society.* Cambridge: Cambridge University Press.

Pierce, C. A. (1996). Body height and romantic attraction: A meta-analytic test of the male-taller norm. *Social Behavior and Personality, 24,* 143–149.

Pines, A. M. (1998). *Romantic jealousy: Causes, symptoms, cures.* New York: Routledge.

Pines, A., & Aronson, E. (1983). Antecedents, correlates, and consequences of sexual jealousy. *Journal of Personality, 51,* 108–136.

Pinquart, M. (2003). Loneliness in married, widowed, divorced, and never-married older adults. *Journal of Social and Personal Relationships, 20,* 31–53.

Pinquart, M., & Sörensen, S. (2001). Influences on loneliness in older adults: A meta-analysis. *Basic and Applied Social Psychology, 23,* 245–266.

Pitts, M. K., Smith, A. M. A., Grierson, J., O'Brien, M., & Misson, S. (2004). Who pays for sex and why? An analysis of social and motivational factors associated with male clients of sex workers. *Archives of Sexual Behavior, 33,* 353–358.

Planalp, S., & Benson, A. (1992). Friends' and acquaintances' conversations I: Perceived differences. *Journal of Social and Personal Relationships, 9,* 483–506.

Pliner, P., & Chaiken, S. (1990). Eating, social motives, and self-presentation in men and women. *Journal of Experimental Social Psychology, 26,* 240–254.

Pollard, J. S. (1995). Attractiveness of composite faces: A comparative study. *International Journal of Comparative Psychology, 8,* 77–83.

Pomerantz, E. M., Ruble, D. N., & Bolger, N. (2004). Supplementing the snapshots with video footage: Taking a developmental approach to understanding social psychological phenomena. In C. Sansone, C. C. Morf, & A. T. Panter (Eds.), *The Sage handbook of methods in social psychology* (pp. 405–425). Thousand Oaks, CA: Sage.

Pontari, B. A., & Dockery, K. (2004, January). *Strategic social help for friends: Providing beneficial impression management through videotaped descriptions.* Paper presented at the meeting of the Society for Personality and Social Psychology, Austin, TX.

Pontari, B. A., & Schlenker, B. R. (2000). The influence of cognitive load on self-presentation: Can cognitive busyness help as well as harm social performance? *Journal of Personality and Social Psychology, 78,* 1092–1108.

Pontari, B. A., & Schlenker, B. R. (2004). Providing and withholding impression management support for romantic partners: Gender of the audience matters. *Journal of Experimental Social Psychology, 40,* 41–51.

Popenoe, D., & Whitehead, B. D. (2002). *Should we live together? What young adults need to know about cohabitation before marriage* (2nd ed.). Piscataway, NJ: The National Marriage Project.

Popenoe, D., & Whitehead, B. D. (2004). *The state of our unions, 2004.* Piscataway, NJ: The National Marriage Project.

Porter, S., & Yuille, J. C. (1996). The language of deceit: An investigation of the verbal clues to deception in the interrogation context. *Law and Human Behavior, 20,* 443–458.

Porterfield, E. (1982). Black-American intermarriage in the United States. *Marriage and Family Review, 5,* 17–34.

Prager, K. J., & Roberts, L. J. (2004). Deep intimate connection: Self and intimacy in couple relationships. In D. J. Mashek & A. Aron (Eds.), *Handbook of closeness and intimacy* (pp. 43–60). Mahwah, NJ: Erlbaum.

Pratto, F., & Walker, A. (2001). Dominance in disguise: Power, beneficence, and exploitation in personal relationships. In A. Y. Lee-Chai & J. A. Bargh (Eds.), *The use and abuse of power: Multiple perspectives on the causes of corruption* (pp. 93–114). Philadelphia: Psychology Press.

Prentice, D. A., & Carranza, E. (2002). What women should be, shouldn't be, are allowed to be, and don't have to be: The contents of prescriptive gender stereotypes. *Psychology of Women Quarterly, 26,* 269–281.

Price, R. A., & Vandenberg, S. S. (1979). Matching for physical attractiveness. *Personality and Social Psychology Bulletin, 5,* 398–400.

Prins, K. S., Buunk, B. P., & VanYperen, N. W. (1993). Equity, normative disapproval and extramarital relationships. *Journal of Social and Personal Relationships, 10,* 39–53.

Pronin, E., Gilovich, T., & Ross, L. (2004). Objectivity in the eye of the beholder: Divergent perceptions of bias in self versus others. *Psychological Review, 111,* 781–799.

Pronin, E., Lin, D. Y., & Ross, L. (2002). The bias blind spot: Perceptions of bias in self versus others. *Personality and Social Psychology Bulletin, 28,* 369–381.

Puente, S., & Cohen, D. (2003). Jealousy and the meaning (or nonmeaning) of violence. *Personality and Social Psychology Bulletin, 29,* 449–460.

Purvis, J. A., Dabbs, J. M., Jr., & Hopper, C. H. (1984). The "opener": Skilled user of facial expression and speech pattern. *Personality and Social Psychology Bulletin, 10,* 61–66.

Putnam, R. D. (2000). *Bowling alone: The collapse and revival of American community.* New York: Simon & Schuster.

Pyke, K. D. (1994). Women's employment as a gift or burden? Marital power across marriage, divorce, and remarriage. *Gender and Society, 8,* 73–91.

Rands, M. (1988). Changes in social networks following marital separation and divorce. In R. M. Milardo (Ed.), *Families and social networks* (pp. 127–146). Newbury Park, CA: Sage.

Rashotte, L. S. (2002). What does that smile mean? The meaning of nonverbal behaviors in social interaction. *Social Psychology Quarterly, 65,* 92–102.

Rauscher, F. H., Krauss, R. M., & Chen, Y. (1996). Gesture, speech, and lexical access: The role of lexical movements in speech production. *Psychological Science, 7,* 226–231.

Raven, B. H. (2001). Power/interaction and interpersonal influence: Experimental investigations and case studies. In A. Y. Lee-Chai & J. A. Bargh (Eds.), *The use and abuse of power: Multiple perspectives on the causes of corruption* (pp. 217–240). Philadelphia: Psychology Press.

Realo, A., Allik, J. Nõlvak, A., Valk, R., Ruus, T., Schmidt, M., & Eilola, T. (2003). Mind-reading ability: Beliefs and performance. *Journal of Research in Personality, 37,* 420–445.

Reeder, H. M. (2000). "I like you . . . as a friend": The role of attraction in cross-sex friendship. *Journal of Social and Personal Relationships, 17,* 329–348.

Reesing, A. L., & Cate, R. M. (2004, July). *Relationship commitment and its association with relationship maintenance: An application of the commitment framework.* Paper presented at the meeting of the International Association for Relationship Research, Madison, WI.

Regan, P. C. (1998). Of lust and love: Beliefs about the role of sexual desire in romantic relationships. *Personal Relationships, 5,* 139–157.

Regan, P. (2003). *The mating game: A primer on love, sex, and marriage.* Thousand Oaks, CA: Sage.

Regan, P. C. (2004). Sex and the attraction process: Lessons from science (and Shakespeare) on lust, love, chastity, and fidelity. In J. H. Harvey, A. Wenzel, & S. Sprecher (Eds.), *The handbook of sexuality in close relationships* (pp. 115–133). Mahwah, NJ: Erlbaum.

Regan, P. C., Kocan, E. R., & Whitlock, T. (1998). Ain't love grand! A prototype analysis of the concept of romantic love. *Journal of Social and Personal Relationships, 15,* 411–420.

Regan, P. C., & Sprecher, S. (1995). Gender differences in the value of contributions to intimate relationships: Egalitarian relationships are not always perceived to be equitable. *Sex Roles, 33,* 221–238.

Reich, D. (2004). What you expect is not always what you get: The roles of extremity, optimism, and pessimism in the behavioral confirmation process. *Journal of Experimental Social Psychology, 40,* 199–215.

Reis, H. T. (1986). Gender effects in social participation: Intimacy, loneliness, and the conduct of social interaction. In R. Gilmour & S. Duck (Eds.), *The emerging field of personal relationships* (pp. 91–105). London: Academic Press.

Reis, H. T. (1998). Gender differences in intimacy and related behaviors: Context and process. In D. J. Canary & K. Dindia (Eds.), *Sex differences and similarities in communication: Critical essays and empirical investigations of sex and gender in interaction* (pp. 203–234). Mahwah, NJ: Erlbaum.

Reis, H. T. (2002a). Action matters, but relationship science is basic. *Journal of Social and Personal Relationships, 19,* 601–611.

Reis, H. T. (2002b, July). *How do you see the me that I see? Understanding and validation in marital relationships.* Paper presented at the International Conference on Personal Relationships, Halifax, Nova Scotia.

Reis, H. T. (2004, July). *The R word: Perceived partner responsiveness and the ripening of relationship science.* Paper presented at the meeting of the International Association for Relationship Research, Madison, WI.

Reis, H. T., Capobianco, A., & Tsai, F. (2002). Finding the person in personal relationships. *Journal of Personality, 70,* 813–850.

Reis, H. T., Clark, M. S., & Holmes, J. G. (2004). Perceived partner responsiveness as an organizing construct in the study of intimacy and closeness. In D. J. Mashek & A. Aron (Eds.), *Handbook of closeness and intimacy* (pp. 201–225). Mahwah, NJ: Erlbaum.

Reis, H. T., & Gable, S. L. (2003). Toward a positive psychology of relationships. In C. L. M. Keyes & J. Haidt (Eds.), *Flourishing: Positive psychology and the life well-lived* (pp. 129–159). Washington, D.C.: American Psychological Association.

Reis, H. T., Lin, Y., Bennett, M. E., & Nezlek, J. B. (1993). Change and consistency in social participation during early adulthood. *Developmental Psychology, 29,* 633–645.

Reis, H. T., Nezlek, J., & Wheeler, L. (1980). Physical attractiveness in social interaction. *Journal of Personality and Social Psychology, 38,* 604–617.

Reis, H. T., & Patrick, B. C. (1996). Attachment and intimacy: Component processes. In E. T. Higgins & A. W. Kruglanski (Eds.), *Social psychology: Handbook of basic principles* (pp. 523–563). New York: Guilford Press.

Reis, H. T., Senchak, M., & Solomon, B. (1985). Sex differences in the intimacy of social interaction: Further examination of potential explanations. *Journal of Personality and Social Psychology, 48,* 1204–1217.

Reis, H. T., Sheldon, R. M., Gable, S. L., Roscoe, J., & Ryan, R. M. (2000). Daily well-being: The role of autonomy, competence, and relatedness. *Personality and Social Psychology Bulletin, 26,* 419–435.

Reis, H. T., Wheeler, L., Spiegel, N., Kernis, M. H., Nezlek, J., & Perri, M. (1982). Physical attractiveness in social interaction: II. Why does appearance affect social experience? *Journal of Personality and Social Psychology, 43,* 979–996.

Reisenzein, R. (1983). The Schachter theory of emotion: Two decades later. *Psychological Bulletin, 94,* 239–264.

Reiss, I. (1967). *The social context of premarital sex permissiveness.* New York: Holt.

Rempel, J. K., Ross, M., & Holmes, J. G. (2001). Trust and communicated attributions in close relationships. *Journal of Personality and Social Psychology, 81,* 57–64.

Rhodes, G., Harwood, K., Yoshikawa, S., Nishitani, M., & MacLean, I. (2002). The attractiveness of average faces: Cross-cultural evidence and possible biological basis. In G. Rhodes & L. A.

Zebrowitz (Eds.), *Facial attractiveness: Evolutionary, cognitive and social perspectives* (pp. 35–58). Westport, CT: Ablex.

Rhodes, G., Sumich, A., & Byatt, G. (1999). Are average facial configurations attractive only because of their symmetry? *Psychological Science, 10,* 52–58.

Rhodes, G., & Tremewan, T. (1996). Averageness, exaggeration, and facial attractiveness. *Psychological Science, 7,* 105–110.

Rhodewalt, F., & Eddings, S. K. (2002). Narcissus reflects: Memory distortion in response to ego-relevant feedback among high- and low-narcissistic men. *Journal of Research in Personality, 36,* 97–116.

Rhodewalt, F., & Sorrow, D. L. (2003). Interpersonal self-regulation: Lessons from the study of narcissism. In M. R. Leary & J. P. Tangney (Eds.), *Handbook of self and identity* (pp. 519–535). New York: Guilford.

Rholes, W. S., Simpson, J. A., Campbell, L., & Grich, J. (2001). Adult attachment and the transition to parenthood. *Journal of Personality and Social Psychology, 81,* 421–435.

Rholes, W. S., Simpson, J. A., & Oriña, M. M. (1999). Attachment and anger in an anxiety-provoking situation. *Journal of Personality and Social Psychology, 76,* 940–957.

Richard, L. S., Wakefield, J. A., & Lewak, R. (1990). Similarity of personality variables as predictors of marital satisfaction: A Minnesota Multiphasic Personality Inventory (MMPI) item analysis. *Personality and Individual Differences, 11,* 39–43.

Ridge, R. D, & Reber, J. S. (2002). "I think she's attracted to me": The effect of men's beliefs on women's behavior in a job interview scenario. *Basic and Applied Social Psychology, 24,* 1–14.

Ridge, S. R., & Feeney, J. A. (1998). Relationship history and relationship attitudes in gay males and lesbians: Attachment style and gender differences. *Australian and New Zealand Journal of Psychiatry, 32,* 848–859.

Ridley, C., Busboom, A., Collins, D., Gilson, M., Almeida, D., Feldman, C., & Cate, R. (2000, June). *Lusting after one's partner: Changing patterns within the relational context.* Presented at the meeting of the International Society for the Study of Personal Relationships, Brisbane.

Riesch, S. K., Bush, L., Nelson, C. J., Ohm, B. J., Portz, P. A., Abell, B., Wightman, M. R., & Jenkins, P. (2000). Topics of conflict between parents and young adolescents. *Journal of the Society of Pediatric Nurses, 5,* 27–40.

Riggio, H. R. (2004). Parental marital conflict and divorce, parent–child relationships, social support, and relationship anxiety in young adulthood. *Personal Relationships, 11,* 99–114.

Rindfuss, R. R., & Stephen, E. H. (1990). Marital noncohabitation: Separation does not make the heart grow fonder. *Journal of Marriage and the Family, 52,* 259–270.

Robbins, C., Kaplan, H. B., & Martin, S. S. (1985). Antecedents of pregnancy among unmarried adolescents. *Journal of Marriage and the Family, 47,* 567–583.

Robins, R. W., Caspi, A., & Moffitt, T. E. (2000). Two personalities, one relationship: Both partners' personality traits shape the quality of their relationship. *Journal of Personality and Social Psychology, 79,* 251–259.

Robins, R. W., Caspi, A., & Moffitt, T. E. (2002). It's not just who you're with, it's who you are: Personality and relationship experiences across multiple relationships. *Journal of Personality, 70,* 925–964.

Robins, R. W., Mendelsohn, G. A., Connell, J. B., & Kwan, V. S. Y. (2004). Do people agree about the causes of behavior? A social relations analysis of behavior ratings and causal attributions. *Journal of Personality and Social Psychology, 86,* 334–344.

Robles, T. F., & Kiecolt-Glaser, J. K. (2003). The physiology of marriage: Pathways to health. *Physiology and Behavior, 79,* 409–416.

Rodgers, J. L., Nakonezny, P. A., & Shull, R. D. (1999). Did no-fault divorce legislation matter? Definitely yes and sometimes no. *Journal of Marriage and the Family, 61,* 803–809.

Rogers, S. J. (1999). Wives' income and marital quality: Are there reciprocal effects? *Journal of Marriage and the Family, 61,* 123–132.

Rogers, S. J. (2004). Dollars, dependency, and divorce: Four perspectives on the role of wives' income. *Journal of Marriage and the Family, 66,* 59–74.

Rogers, S. J., & Amato, P. R. (2000). Have changes in gender relations affected marital quality? *Social Forces, 79,* 731–753.

Rogers, S. J., & May, D. C. (2003). Spillover between marital quality and job satisfaction: Long-term patterns and gender differences. *Journal of Marriage and the Family, 65,* 482–495.

Rokach, A. (2004). The lonely and homeless: Causes and consequences. *Social Indicators Research, 69,* 37–50.

Roloff, M., & Cloven, D. H. (1990). The chilling effect in interpersonal relationships: The reluctance to speak one's mind. In D. D. Cahn (Ed.), *Intimates in conflict: A communication perspective* (pp. 49–76). Hillsdale, NJ: Erlbaum.

Roloff, M. E., & Ifert, D. (1998). Antecedents and consequences of explicit agreements to declare a taboo topic in dating relationships. *Personal Relationships, 5,* 191–205.

Roloff, M. E., & Ifert, D. E. (2000). Conflict management through avoidance: Withholding arguments, suppressing arguments, and declaring topics taboo. In S. Petronio (Ed.), *Balancing the secrets of private disclosures* (pp. 151–163). Mahwah, NJ: Erlbaum.

Romance on the Web. (2003, May 12). *Newsweek, 142,* E20.

Rook, K. S. (1984). Promoting social bonding: Strategies for helping the lonely and socially isolated. *American Psychologist, 39,* 1389–1407.

Rook, K. S. (1988). Toward a more differentiated view of loneliness. In S. Duck (Ed.), *Handbook of personal relationships: Theory, research, and interventions* (pp. 571–589). New York: Wiley.

Rook, K. S. (1998). Investigating the positive and negative sides of personal relationships: Through a lens darkly? In B. H. Spitzberg & W. R. Cupach (Eds.), *The dark side of close relationships* (pp. 369–393). Mahwah, NJ: Erlbaum.

Rook, K. S., & Peplau, L. A. (1982). Perspectives on helping the lonely. In L. A. Peplau & D. Perlman (Eds.), *Loneliness: A sourcebook of current theory, research, and therapy* (pp. 351–378). New York: Wiley Interscience.

Rose, S. M. (1985). Same- and cross-sex friendships and the psychology of homosociality. *Sex Roles, 12,* 63–74.

Rosenbaum, M. E. (1986). The repulsion hypothesis: On the nondevelopment of relationships. *Journal of Personality and Social Psychology, 51,* 1156–1166.

Rosenthal, D. A., Smith, A. M. A., & de Visser, R. (1999). Personal and social factors influencing age at first sexual intercourse. *Archives of Sexual Behavior, 28,* 319–333.

Rosenthal, R. (1994). Interpersonal expectancy effects: A 30-year perspective. *Current Directions in Psychological Science, 3,* 176–179.

Rosenthal, R. (2003). Covert communication in laboratories, classrooms, and the truly real world. *Current Directions in Psychological Science, 12,* 151–154.

Rosenthal, R., & DePaulo, B. M. (1979). Sex differences in eavesdropping on nonverbal cues. *Journal of Personality and Social Psychology, 37,* 273–285.

Ross, L. R., & Spinner, B. (2001). General and specific attachment representations in adulthood: Is there a relationship? *Journal of Social and Personal Relationships, 18,* 747–766.

Ross, M., & Sicoly, F. (1979). Egocentric biases in availability and attribution. *Journal of Personality and Social Psychology, 37,* 322–336.

Ross, S. R., Kendall, A. C., Maters, K. G., Rye, M. S., & Wrobel, T. A. (2004). A personological examination of self- and other-forgiveness in the five factor model. *Journal of Personality Assessment, 82,* 207–214.

Rotenberg, K. J., & Morrison, J. (1993). Loneliness and college achievement: Do Loneliness Scale scores predict college drop-out? *Psychological Reports, 73,* 1283–1288.

Rothblum, E. D., & Factor, R. (2001). Lesbians and their sisters as a control group: Demographic and mental health factors. *Psychological Science, 12,* 63–69.

Rowatt, W. C., Cunningham, M. R., & Druen, P. B. (1999). Lying to get a date: The effect of facial physical attractiveness on the willingness to deceive prospective dating partners. *Journal of Social and Personal Relationships, 16,* 209–223.

Rowe, A., & Carnelley, K. B. (2003). Attachment style differences in the processing of attachment-relevant information: Primed-style effects on recall, interpersonal expectations, and affect. *Personal Relationships, 10,* 59–75.

Ruane, M. E. (1999, December 26). FWIW, Internet slang is running wild on ur kids' e-mail, etc. etc. *Houston Chronicle,* p. 2A.

Rubenstein, A. J., Langlois, J. H., & Roggman, L. A. (2002). What makes a face attractive and why: The role of averageness in defining facial beauty. In G. Rhodes & L. A. Zebrowitz (Eds.), *Facial attractiveness: Evolutionary, cognitive and social perspectives* (pp. 1–33). Westport, CT: Ablex.

Rubenstein, C. M., & Shaver, P. (1980). Loneliness in two northeastern cities. In J. Hartog, J. R. Audy, & Y. A. Cohen (Eds.), *The anatomy of loneliness* (pp. 319–337). New York: International Universities Press.

Rubenstein, C. M., & Shaver, P. (1982). *In search of intimacy.* New York: Delacorte Press.

Rubenstein, C. M., Shaver, P., & Peplau, L. A. (1979). Loneliness. *Human Nature, 2,* 58–65.

Rubin, L. B. (1986). On men and friendship. *Psychoanalytic Review, 73,* 165–181.

Rubin, Z. (1973). *Liking and loving.* New York: Holt, Rinehart & Winston.

Rubin, Z. (1980). *Children's friendships.* Cambridge, MA: Harvard University Press.

Rubin, Z., & Mitchell, C. (1976). Couples research as couples counseling: Some unintended effects of studying close relationships. *American Psychologist, 31,* 17–25.

Rudman, L. A. (1998). Self–promotion as a risk factor for women: The costs and benefits of counter-stereotypical impression management. *Journal of Personality and Social Psychology, 74,* 629–645.

Rudman, L. A., & Glick, P. (1999). Feminized management and backlash toward agentic women: The hidden costs to women of a kinder, gentler image of middle managers. *Journal of Personality and Social Psychology, 77,* 1004–1010.

Rusbult, C. E. (1987). Responses to dissatisfaction in close relationships: The exit-voice-loyalty-neglect model. In D. Perlman & S. Duck (Eds.), *Intimate relationships: Development, dynamics, and deterioration* (pp. 209–237). Thousand Oaks, CA: Sage.

Rusbult, C. E., Arriaga, X. B., & Agnew, C. R. (2001). Interdependence in close relationships. In G. J. O. Fletcher & M. S. Clark (Eds.), *Blackwell handbook of social psychology: Interpersonal processes* (pp. 359–387). Malden, MA: Blackwell.

Rusbult, C. E., Bissonnette, V. L., Arriaga, X. B., & Cox, C. L. (1998). Accommodation processes during the early years of marriage. In T. N. Bradbury (Ed.), *The developmental course of marital dysfunction* (pp. 74–113). New York: Cambridge University Press.

Rusbult, C. E., Drigotas, S. M., & Verette, J. (1994). The investment model: An interdependence analysis of commitment processes and relationship maintenance phenomena. In D. J. Canary & L. Stafford (Eds.), *Communication and relational maintenance* (pp. 115–139). San Diego: Academic Press.

Rusbult, C. E., Johnson, D. J., & Morrow, G. D. (1986). Impact of couple patterns of problem solving on distress and nondistress in dating relationships. *Journal of Personality and Social Psychology, 50,* 744–753.

Rusbult, C. E., & Martz, J. M. (1995). Remaining in abusive relationships: An investment model analysis of nonvoluntary dependence. *Personality and Social Psychology Bulletin, 21,* 558–571.

Rusbult, C. E., Olsen, N., Davis, J. L., & Hannon, M. A. (2001). Commitment and relationship maintenance mechanisms. In J. H. Harvey & A. E. Wenzel (Eds.), *Close romantic relationships: Maintenance and enhancement* (pp. 87–113). Mahwah, NJ: Erlbaum.

Rusbult, C. E., Van Lange, P. A. M., Wildschut, T., Yovetich, N. A., & Verette, J. (2000). Perceived superiority in close relationships: Why it exists and persists. *Journal of Personality and Social Psychology, 79,* 521–545.

Rusbult, C. E., Verette, J., Whitney, G. A., Slovik, L. F., & Lipkus, I. (1991). Accommodation processes in close relationships: Theory and preliminary empirical evidence. *Journal of Personality and Social Psychology, 60,* 53–78.

Rusbult, C. E., Wieselquist, J., Foster, C. A., & Witcher, B. S. (1999). Commitment and trust in close relationships: An interdependence analysis. In J. M. Adams & W. H. Jones (Eds.), *Handbook on interpersonal commitment and relationship stability* (pp. 427–449). New York: Kluwer Academic/Plenum.

Rusbult, C. E., Zembrodt, I. M., & Gunn, L. K. (1982). Exit, voice, loyalty, and neglect: Responses to dissatisfaction in romantic involvements. *Journal of Personality and Social Psychology, 43,* 1230–1242.

Rusbult, C. E., Zembrodt, I. M., & Iwaniszek, J. (1986). The impact of gender and sex-role orientation on responses to dissatisfaction in close relationships. *Sex Roles, 15,* 1–20.

Russell, D. W. (1996). The UCLA Loneliness Scale (Version 3): Reliability, validity and factorial structure. *Journal of Personality Assessment, 66,* 20–40.

Russell, D., Peplau, L. A., & Cutrona, C. E. (1980). The revised UCLA Loneliness Scale: Concurrent and discriminant validity evidence. *Journal of Personality and Social Psychology, 39,* 472–480.

Ruvolo, A. P. (1998). Marital well-being and general happiness of newlywed couples: Relationships across time. *Journal of Social and Personal Relationships, 15,* 470–489.

Ruvolo, A. P., Fabin, L. A., & Ruvolo, C. M. (2001). Relationship experiences and change in attachment characteristics of young adults: The role of relationship breakups and conflict avoidance. *Personal Relationships, 8,* 265–281.

Ruvolo, A. P., & Ruvolo, C. M. (2000). Creating Mr. Right and Ms. Right: Interpersonal ideals and personal change in newlyweds. *Personal Relationships, 7,* 341–362.

Ruvolo, A. P., & Veroff, J. (1997). For better or for worse: Real-ideal discrepancies and the marital well-being of newlyweds. *Journal of Social and Personal Relationships, 14,* 223–242.

Ryff, C. D., & Singer, B. (2000). Interpersonal flourishing: A positive health agenda for the new millenium. *Personality and Social Psychology Review, 4,* 30–44.

Saal, F. E., Johnson, C. B., & Weber, N. (1989). Friendly or sexy? It may depend on whom you ask. *Psychology of Women Quarterly, 13,* 263–276.

Sabatelli, R. M., Buck, R., & Dreyer, A. (1980). Communication via facial cues in intimate dyads. *Personality and Social Psychology Bulletin, 6,* 242–247.

Sabatelli, R. M., Buck, R., & Dreyer, A. (1982). Nonverbal communication accuracy in married couples: Relationship with marital complaints. *Journal of Personality and Social Psychology, 43,* 1088–1097.

Sabin, E. P. (1993). Social relationships and mortality among the elderly. *Journal of Applied Gerontology, 12,* 44–60.

Safilios-Rothschild, C. (1981). Toward a social psychology of relationships. *Psychology of Women Quarterly, 5,* 377–384.

Sagarin, B. J., Becker, D. V., Guadagno, R. E., Nicastle, L. D., & Millevoi, A. (2003). Sex differences (and similarities) in jealousy. The moderating influence of infidelity experience and sexual orientation of the infidelity. *Evolution and Human Behavior, 24,* 17–23.

Sagarin, B. J., Rhoads, K. V. L., & Cialdini, R. B. (1998). Deceiver's distrust: Denigration as a consequence of undiscovered deception. *Personality and Social Psychology Bulletin, 24,* 1167–1176.

Sagrestano, L. M. (1992a). Power strategies in interpersonal relationships: The effects of expertise and gender. *Psychology of Women Quarterly, 16,* 481–495.

Sagrestano, L. M. (1992b). The use of power and influence in a gendered world. *Psychology of Women Quarterly, 16,* 439–447.

Sahlstein, E. M., & Baxter, L. A. (2001). Improvising commitment in close relationships: A relational dialectics perspective. In J. Harvey & A. Wenzel (Eds.), *Close romantic relationships: Maintenance and enhancement* (pp. 115–132). Mahwah, NJ: Erlbaum.

Sallee, R. (2003, October 25). Fewer mothers of infants hold jobs. *Houston Chronicle,* p. 31A.

Salovey, P. (Ed.). (1991). *The psychology of jealousy and envy.* New York: Guilford Press.

Salovey, P., & Rodin, J. (1988). Coping with envy and jealousy. *Journal of Social and Clinical Psychology, 7,* 15–33.

Saluter, A. F. (1996, February). Marital status and living arrangements: March, 1994. *Current population reports: Population characteristics (P20-484).* Washington, DC: U.S. Bureau of the Census.

Sanders, S. A., & Reinisch, J. M. (1999). Would you say you "had sex" if . . .? *Journal of the American Medical Association, 281,* 275–277.

Sandnabba, N. K., & Ahlberg, C. (1999). Parents' attitudes and expectations about children's cross-gender behavior. *Sex Roles, 40,* 249–263.

Sanford, K. (1997). Two dimensions of adult attachment: Further validation. *Journal of Social and Personal Relationships, 14,* 133–143.

Sanitioso, R. B., & Wlodarski, R. (2004). In search of information that confirms a desired self-perception: Motivated processing of social feedback and choice of social interactions. *Personality and Social Psychology Bulletin, 30,* 412–422.

Sansone, C., Morf, C. C., & Panter, A. T. (Eds.). (2004). *The Sage handbook of methods in social psychology.* Thousand Oaks, CA: Sage.

Sapadin, L. A. (1988). Friendship and gender: Perspectives of professional men and women. *Journal of Social and Personal Relationships, 5,* 387–403.

Saragovi, C., Aubé, J., Koestner, R., & Zuroff, D. (2002). Traits, motives, and depressive styles as reflections of agency and communion. *Personality and Social Psychology Bulletin, 28,* 563–577.

Satterfield, A. T., & Muehlenhard, C. L. (1997). Shaken confidence: The effects of an authority figure's flirtatiousness on women's and men's self-rated creativity. *Psychology of Women Quarterly, 21,* 395–416.

Schachner, D. A., & Shaver, P. R. (2002, June). *Attachment style and personality variables predict human mate poaching behaviors.* Paper presented at the meeting of the American Psychological Society, New Orleans, LA.

Schachner, D. A., & Shaver, P. R. (2004). Attachment dimensions and sexual motives. *Personal Relationships, 11,* 179–195.

Schachter, S. (1959). *The psychology of affiliation: Experimental studies of the sources of gregariousness.* Stanford, CA: Stanford University Press.

Schachter, S. (1964). The interaction of cognitive and physiological determinants of emotional state. In L. Berkowitz (Ed.), *Advances in experimental social psychology* (Vol. 1, pp. 49–80). New York: Academic Press.

Schacter, D. L. (1996). *Searching for memory: The brain, the mind, and the past.* New York: Basic Books.

Schafer, R. B., & Keith, P. M. (1990). Matching by weight in married couples: A life cycle perspective. *Journal of Social Psychology, 130,* 657–664.

Scharfe, E., & Bartholomew, K. (1994). Reliability and stability of adult attachment patterns. *Personal Relationships, 1,* 23–43.

Scharfe, E., & Bartholomew, K. (1998). Do you remember?: Recollections of adult attachment patterns. *Personal Relationships, 5,* 219–234.

Scharff, J. S., & Bagnini, C. (2002). Object relations couple therapy. In A. S. Gurman & N. S. Jacobson (Eds.), *Clinical handbook of couple therapy* (3rd ed., pp. 59–85). New York: Guilford Press.

Scheib, J. E. (2001). Context-specific mate choice criteria: Women's trade-offs in the contexts of long-term and extra-pair mateships. *Personal Relationships, 8,* 371–389.

Schlenker, B. R. (2003). Self-presentation. In M. R. Leary & J. P. Tangney (Eds.), *Handbook of self and identity* (pp. 492–518). New York: Guilford Press.

Schlenker, B. R., & Britt, T. W. (1999). Beneficial impression management: Strategically controlling information to help friends. *Journal of Personality and Social Psychology, 76,* 559–573.

Schlenker, B. R., & Pontari, B. A. (2000). The strategic control of information: Impression management and self-presentation in daily life. In A. Tesser, R. B. Felson, & J. M. Suls (Eds.), *Psychological perspectives on self and identity* (pp. 199–232). Washington, DC: American Psychological Association.

Schmidt, N., & Sermat, V. (1983). Measuring loneliness in different relationships. *Journal of Personality and Social Psychology, 44,* 1038–1047.

Schmitt, D. P., Alcalay, L., Allensworth, M., Allik, J., Ault, L., Austers, I., et al. (2003). Are men universally more dismissing than women? Gender differences in romantic attachment across 62 cultural regions. *Personal Relationships, 10,* 307–331.

Schmitt, D. P., & Buss, D. M. (2001). Human mate poaching: Tactics and temptations for infiltrating existing mateships. *Journal of Personality and Social Psychology, 80,* 894–917.

Schmitt, D. P., Couden, A., & Baker, M. (2001). The effects of sex and temporal context on feelings of romantic desire: An experimental evaluation of sexual strategies theory. *Personality and Social Psychology Bulletin, 27,* 833–847.

Schmitt, D. P., & Shackelford, T. K. (2003). Nifty ways to leave your lover: The tactics people use to entice and disguise the process of human mate poaching. *Personality and Social Psychology Bulletin, 29,* 1018–1035.

Schmitt, D. P., Shackelford, T. K., & Buss, D. M. (2001). Are men really more 'oriented' toward short-term mating than women? A critical review of theory and research. *Psychology, Evolution and Gender, 3,* 211–239.

Schmitt, D. P., Shackelford, T. K., Duntley, J., Tooke, W., & Buss, D. M. (2001). The desire for sexual variety as a key to understanding basic human mating strategies. *Personal Relationships, 8,* 425–455.

Schmitt, D. P., & the International Sexuality Description Project. (2003). Universal sex differences in the desire for sexual variety: Tests from 52 nations, 6 continents, and 13 islands. *Journal of Personality and Social Psychology, 85,* 85–104.

Schmitt, D. P., & the International Sexuality Description Project. (2004). Patterns and universals of mate poaching across 53 nations: The effects of sex, culture, and personality on romantically attracting another person's partner. *Journal of Personality and Social Psychology, 86,* 560–584.

Schratter, A. K. (2001). Accounts of betrayal in interpersonal relationships. *Dissertation Abstracts International, 61*(11), 6189B.

Schutz, A. (1999). It was your fault! Self-serving biases in autobiographical accounts of conflicts in married couples. *Journal of Social and Personal Relationships, 16,* 193–208.

Schwab, S. H., Scalise, J. J., Ginter, E. J., & Whipple, G. (1998). Self-disclosure, loneliness and four interpersonal targets: Friend, group of friends, stranger, and group of strangers. *Psychological Reports, 82,* 1264–1266.

Schwartz, P. (2000). *Everything you know about love and sex is wrong.* New York: Putnam.

Schwartz, P., & Rutter, V. (1998). *The gender of sexuality.* Thousand Oaks, CA: Pine Forge Press.

Schweinle, W. E., & Ickes, W. (2002). On empathic accuracy and husbands' abusiveness: The "overattribution bias." In P. Noller & J. A. Feeney (Eds.), *Understanding marriage: Developments in the study of couple interaction* (pp. 228–250). Cambridge, UK: Cambridge University Press.

Schweinle, W. E., Ickes, W., & Bernstein, I. H. (2002). Empathic accuracy in husband to wife aggression: The overattribution bias. *Personal Relationships, 9,* 141–158.

Seal, S. W., Agostinelli, G., & Hannett, C. A. (1994). Extradyadic romantic involvement: Moderating effects of sociosexuality and gender. *Sex Roles, 3,* 1–22.

Sears, D. O. (1986). College sophomores in the laboratory: Influences of a narrow data base on social psychology's view of human nature. *Journal of Personality and Social Psychology, 51,* 515–530.

Secord, P. F. (1983). Imbalanced sex ratios: The social consequences. *Personality and Social Psychology Bulletin, 9,* 525–543.

Sedikides, C., Campbell, W. K., Reeder, G. D., & Elliot, A. J. (1998). The self-serving bias in relational context. *Journal of Personality and Social Psychology, 74,* 378–386.

Sedikides, C., Oliver, M. B., & Campbell, W. K. (1994). Perceived benefits and costs of romantic relationships for women and men: Implications for exchange theory. *Personal Relationships, 1,* 5–21.

Sedikides, C., & Strube, M. J. (1997). Self-evaluation: To thine own self be good, to thine own self be true, and to thine own self be better. In M. Zanna (Ed.), *Advances in experimental social psychology* (Vol. 29, pp. 209–269). San Diego: Academic Press.

Seeman, T. E., Singer, B. H., Ryff, C. D., Love, G. D., & Levy-Storms, L. (2002). Social relationships, gender, and allostatic load across two age cohorts. *Psychosomatic Medicine, 64,* 395–406.

Segal, M. W. (1974). Alphabet and attraction: An unobtrusive measure of the effect of propinquity in a field setting. *Journal of Personality and Social Psychology, 30,* 654–657.

Segrin, C. (1998). Disrupted interpersonal relationships and mental health problems. In B. H. Spitzberg & W. R. Cupach (Eds.), *The dark side of close relationships* (pp. 327–365). Mahwah, NJ: Erlbaum.

Segrin, C., Powell, H. L., Givertz, M., & Brackin, A. (2003). Symptoms of depression, relational quality, and loneliness in dating relationships, *Personal Relationships, 10,* 25–36.

Selman, R. L. (1981). The child as a friendship philosopher. In S. R. Asher & J. M. Gottman (Eds.), *The development of children's friendships* (pp. 242–272). New York: Cambridge University Press.

Sermat, V. (1980). Some situational and personality correlates of loneliness. In J. Hartog, J. R. Audy, & Y. A. Cohen (Eds.), *The anatomy of loneliness* (pp. 305–318). New York: International Universities Press.

Shackelford, T. K., & Buss, D. M. (1997a). Cues to infidelity. *Personality and Social Psychology Bulletin, 23,* 1034–1045.

Shackelford, T. K., & Buss, D. M. (1997b). Marital satisfaction in evolutionary psychological perspective. In R. J. Sternberg & M. Hojjat (Eds.), *Satisfaction in close relationships* (pp. 7–25). New York: Guilford.

Shackelford, T. K., & Larsen, R. J. (1997). Facial asymmetry as an indicator of psychological, emotional, and physiological distress. *Journal of Personality and Social Psychology, 72,* 456–466.

Shaffer, D. R., & Bazzini, D. G. (1997). What do you look for in a prospective date? Reexamining the preferences of men and women who differ in self-monitoring propensities. *Personality and Social Psychology Bulletin, 23,* 605–616.

Shaffer, D. R., Pegalis, L. J., & Bazzini, D. G. (1996). When boy meets girl (revisited): Gender, gender-role orientation, and prospect of future interaction as determinants of self-disclosure among same- and opposite-sex acquaintances. *Personality and Social Psychology Bulletin, 22,* 495–506.

Shaffer, D. R., Ruammake, C., & Pegalis, L. J. (1990). The "opener": Highly skilled as interviewer or interviewee. *Personality and Social Psychology Bulletin, 16,* 511–520.

Shah, J. (2003). Automatic for the people: How representations of significant others implicitly affect goal pursuit. *Journal of Personality and Social Psychology, 84,* 661–681.

Shanteau, J., & Nagy, G. F. (1979). Probability of acceptance in dating choice. *Journal of Personality and Social Psychology, 37,* 522–533.

Sharp, E. A., & Ganong, L. H. (2000). Raising awareness about marital expectations: Are unrealistic beliefs changed by integrative teaching? *Family Relations, 49,* 71–76.

Sharpsteen, D. J. (1993). Romantic jealousy as an emotion concept: A prototype analysis. *Journal of Social and Personal Relationships, 10,* 69–82.

Sharpsteen, D. J., & Kirkpatrick, L. A. (1997). Romantic jealousy and adult romantic attachment. *Journal of Personality and Social Psychology, 72,* 627–640.

Shaver, P., Furman, W., & Buhrmester, D. (1985). Transition to college: Network changes, social skills, and loneliness. In S. Duck & D. Perlman (Eds.), *Understanding personal relationships: An interdisciplinary approach* (pp. 193–219). London: Sage.

Shaver, P. R., & Hazan, C. (1988). A biased overview of the study of love. *Journal of Social and Personal Relationships, 5,* 473–501.

Shaver, P. R., Hazan, C., & Bradshaw, D. (1988). Love as attachment: The integration of three behavioral systems. In R. J. Sternberg & M. L. Barnes (Eds.), *The psychology of love* (pp. 68–99). New Haven, CT: Yale University Press.

Shaver, P. R., Morgan, H. J., & Wu, S. (1996). Is love a "basic" emotion? *Personal Relationships, 3,* 81–96.

Shaver, P., & Rubenstein, C. (1980). Childhood attachment experience and adult loneliness. In L. Wheeler (Ed.), *Review of personality and social psychology* (Vol. 1, pp. 42–73). Beverly Hills, CA: Sage.

Shaver, P. R., Schachner, D. A., & Mikulincer, M. (2005). Attachment style, excessive reassurance seeking, relationship processes, and depression. *Personality and Social Psychology Bulletin, 31,* 343–359.

Shettel-Neuber, J., Bryson, J. B., & Young, L. E. (1978). Physical attractiveness of the "other person" and jealousy. *Personality and Social Psychology Bulletin, 4,* 612–615.

Shibazaki, K., & Brennan, K. A. (1998). When birds of different feathers flock together: A preliminary comparison of intra-ethnic and inter-ethnic dating relationships. *Journal of Social and Personal Relationships, 15,* 248–256.

Shiner, R. L., Masten, A. S., & Roberts, J. M. (2003). Childhood personality foreshadows adult personality and life outcomes two decades later. *Journal of Personality, 71,* 1145–1170.

Shoda, Y. (2004). Individual differences in social psychology: Understanding situations to understand people, understanding people to understand situations. In C. Sansone, C. C. Morf, & A. T. Panter (Eds.), *The Sage handbook of methods in social psychology* (pp. 117–141). Thousand Oaks, CA: Sage.

Shulman, P. (2004). Great expectations. *Psychology Today, March/April,* 33–42.

Siciliani, J., & Pride, R. E. (2003, May). *Sex and ethnicity differences in perceptions of body image and desirable physique.* Paper presented at the meeting of the American Psychological Society, Atlanta.

Sillars, A. L. (1985). Interpersonal perception in relationships. In W. Ickes (Ed.), *Compatible and incompatible relationships* (pp. 277–305). New York: Springer-Verlag.

Sillars, A. L. (1998). (Mis)understanding. In B. H. Spitzberg & W. R. Cupach (Eds.), *The dark side of close relationships* (pp. 73–102). Mahwah, NJ: Erlbaum.

Sillars, A. L., Folwell, A. L., Hill, K. C., Maki, B. K., Hurst, A. P., & Casano, R. A. (1994). Marital communication and the persistence of understanding. *Journal of Social and Personal Relationships, 11,* 611–617.

Simeon, J. R., & Miller, R. S. (2005, January). *Relationship functioning, personalities, and attention to attractive alternatives over time.* Paper presented at the meeting of the Society for Personality and Social Psychology, New Orleans.

Simpson, J. A. (1990). Influence of attachment styles on romantic relationships. *Journal of Personality and Social Psychology, 59,* 971–980.

Simpson, J. A. (2004, January). *28 days (plus or minus a few)*. Paper presented at the Personal Relationships Pre-Conference at the meeting of the Society for Personality and Social Psychology, Austin, TX.

Simpson, J. A., Campbell, B., & Berscheid, E. (1986). The association between romantic love and marriage: Kephart (1967) twice revisited. *Personality and Social Psychology Bulletin, 12,* 363–372.

Simpson, J. A., Fletcher, G. J. O., & Campbell, L. (2001). The structure and function of ideal standards in close relationships. In G. J. O. Fletcher & M. S. Clark (Eds.), *Blackwell handbook of social psychology: Interpersonal processes* (pp. 86–106). Malden. MA: Blackwell.

Simpson, J. A., & Gangestad, S. W. (1991). Individual differences in sociosexuality: Evidence for convergent and discriminant validity. *Journal of Personality and Social Psychology, 60,* 870–883.

Simpson, J. A., & Gangestad, S. W. (2001). Evolution and relationships: A call for integration. *Personal Relationships, 8,* 341–355.

Simpson, J. A., Gangestad, S. W., & Biek, M. (1993). Personality and nonverbal social behavior: An ethological perspective of relationship initiation. *Journal of Experimental Social Psychology, 29,* 434–461.

Simpson, J. A., Gangestad, S. W., & Lerma, M. (1990). Perception of physical attractiveness: Mechanisms involved in the maintenance of romantic relationships. *Journal of Personality & Social Psychology, 59,* 1192–1201.

Simpson, J. A., Ickes, W., & Blackstone, T. (1995). When the head protects the heart: Empathic accuracy in dating relationships. *Journal of Personality and Social Psychology, 69,* 629–641.

Simpson, J. A., Ickes, W., & Grich, J. (1999). When accuracy hurts: Reactions of anxious-ambivalent dating partners to a relationship-threatening situation. *Journal of Personality and Social Psychology, 76,* 754–769.

Simpson, J. A., Ickes, W., & Oriña, M. (2001). Empathic accuracy and preemptive relationship maintenance. In J. H. Harvey & A. E. Wenzel (Eds.), *Close romantic relationships: Maintenance and enhancement,* (pp. 27–46). Mahwah, NJ: Erlbaum.

Simpson, J. A., Oriña, M. M., & Ickes, W. (2003). When accuracy hurts, and when it helps: A test of the empathic accuracy model in marital interactions. *Journal of Personality and Social Psychology, 85,* 881–893.

Simpson, J. A., & Rholes, W. S. (2002). Attachment orientations, marriage, and the transition to parenthood. *Journal of Research in Personality, 36,* 622–628.

Simpson, J. A., Rholes, W. S., Campbell, L., & Wilson, C. L. (2003). Changes in attachment orientations across the transitions to parenthood. *Journal of Experimental Social Psychology, 39,* 317–331.

Simpson, J. A., Rholes, W. S., & Nelligan, J. S. (1992). Support seeking and support giving within couples in an anxiety-provoking situation: The role of attachment styles. *Journal of Personality and Social Psychology, 62,* 434–446.

Simpson, J. A., Rholes, W. S., Oriña, M. M., & Grich, J. (2002). Working models of attachment, support giving, and support seeking in a stressful situation. *Personality and Social Psychology Bulletin, 28,* 598–608.

Simpson, J. A., Wilson, C. L., & Winterheld, H. A. (2004). Sociosexuality and romantic relationships. In J. H. Harvey, A. Wenzel, & S. Sprecher (Eds.), *The handbook of sexuality in close relationships* (pp. 87–112). Mahwah, NJ: Erlbaum.

Singh, D. (1993). Adaptive significance of waist-to-hip ratio and female physical attractiveness. *Journal of Personality and Social Psychology, 65,* 293–307.

Singh, D. (1994). Is thin really beautiful and good? Relationship between waist-to-hip ratio (WHR) and female attractiveness. *Personality and Individual Differences, 16,* 123–132.

Singh, D. (1995). Female judgment of male attractiveness and desirability for relationships: Role of waist-to-hip ratio and financial status. *Journal of Personality and Social Psychology, 69,* 1089–1101.

Singh, D. & Luis, S. (1995). Ethnic and gender consensus for the effect of waist-to-hip ratio on judgments of women's attractiveness. *Human Nature, 6,* 51–65.

Singh, R., & Teoh, J. B. P. (1999). Attitudes and attraction: A test of two hypotheses for the similarity-dissimilarity asymmetry. *British Journal of Social Psychology, 39,* 537–554.

Slater, A., Von der Schulennurg, C., Brown, E., Badenoch, M., Butterworth, G., Parsons, S., & Samuels, C. (1998). Newborn infants prefer attractive faces. *Infant Behavior and Development, 21,* 345–354.

Slater, P. E. (1968). Some social consequences of temporary systems. In W. G. Bennes & P. E. Slater (Eds.), *The temporary society* (pp. 77–96). New York: Harper & Row.

Smith, A. E., Jussim, L., & Eccles, J. (1999). Do self-fulfilling prophecies accumulate, dissipate, or remain stable over time? *Journal of Personality and Social Psychology, 77,* 548–565.

Smith, T. W., Ruiz, J. M., & Uchino, B. N. (2004). Mental activation of supportive ties, hostility, and cardiovascular reactivity to laboratory stress in young men and women. *Health Psychology, 23,* 476–785.

Smock, P. J. (2000). Cohabitation in the United States: An appraisal of research themes, findings, and implications. *Annual Review of Sociology, 26,* 1–20.

Snodgrass, S. E. (1985). Women's intuition: The effect of subordinate role on interpersonal sensitivity. *Journal of Personality and Social Psychology, 49,* 146–155.

Snodgrass, S. E. (1992). Further effects of role versus gender on interpersonal sensitivity. *Journal of Personality and Social Psychology, 62,* 154–158.

Snyder, D. K. (2002). Integrating insight-oriented techniques into couple therapy. In J. H. Harvey & A. Wenzel (Eds.), *A clinician's guide to maintaining and enhancing close relationships* (pp. 259–275). Mahwah, NJ: Erlbaum.

Snyder, D. K., Mangrum, L. F., & Wills, R. M. (1993). Predicting couples' response to marital therapy: A comparison of short- and long-term predictors. *Journal of Consulting & Clinical Psychology, 61,* 61–69.

Snyder, D. K., & Schneider, W. J. (2002). Affective reconstruction: A pluralistic, developmental approach. In A. S. Gurman & N. S. Jacobson (Eds.), *Clinical handbook of couple therapy* (3rd ed., pp. 151–179). New York: Guilford Press.

Snyder, D. K., Wills, R. M., & Grady-Fletcher, A. (1991). Long-term effectiveness of behavioral versus insight-oriented therapy: A four-year follow-up study. *Journal of Consulting and Clinical Psychology, 59,* 138–141.

Snyder, M. (1974). The self-monitoring of expressive behavior. *Journal of Personality and Social Psychology, 30,* 526–537.

Snyder, M. (1981). Seek, and ye shall find: Testing hypotheses about other people. In E. T. Higgins, C. P. Herman, & M. P. Zanna (Eds.), *Social cognition: The Ontario symposium* (Vol. 1, pp. 277–303). Hillsdale, NJ: Erlbaum.

Snyder, M. (1987). *Public appearances, private realities: The psychology of self-monitoring.* New York: W. H. Freeman.

Snyder, M., Berscheid, E., & Glick, P. (1985). Focusing on the exterior and the interior: Two investigations of the initiation of personal relationships. *Journal of Personality and Social Psychology, 48,* 1427–1439.

Snyder, M., Berscheid, E., & Matwychuk, A. (1988). Orientations toward personnel selection: Differential reliance on appearance and personality. *Journal of Personality and Social Psychology, 54,* 972–979.

Snyder, M., & DeBono, K. G. (1985). Appeals to image and claims about quality: Understanding the psychology of advertising. *Journal of Personality and Social Psychology, 49,* 586–597.

Snyder, M., & Gangestad, S. (1986). On the nature of self-monitoring: Matters of assessment, matters of validity. *Journal of Personality and Social Psychology, 51,* 125–139.

Snyder, M., Gangestad, S., & Simpson, J. A. (1983). Choosing friends as activity partners: The role of self-monitoring. *Journal of Personality and Social Psychology, 45,* 1061–1072.

Snyder, M., & Simpson, J. A. (1984). Self-monitoring and dating relationships. *Journal of Personality and Social Psychology, 47,* 1281–1291.

Snyder, M., & Simpson, J. A. (1987). Orientations toward romantic relationships. In D. Perlman & S. Duck (Eds.), *Intimate relationships: Development, dynamics, and deterioration* (pp. 45–62). Newbury Park, CA: Sage.

Snyder, M., Simpson, J. A., & Gangestad, S. (1986). Personality and sexual relations. *Journal of Personality and Social Psychology, 51,* 181–190.

Snyder, M., & Swann, W. B., Jr. (1978a). Behavioral confirmation in social interaction: From social perception to social reality. *Journal of Experimental Social Psychology, 14,* 148–163.

Snyder, M., & Swann, W. B., Jr. (1978b). Hypothesis-testing processes in social interaction. *Journal of Personality and Social Psychology, 36,* 1202–1212.

Snyder, M., Tanke, E. D., & Berscheid, E. (1977). Social perception and interpersonal behavior: On the self-fulfilling nature of social stereotypes. *Journal of Personality and Social Psychology, 35,* 656–666.

Solano, C. H., Batten, P. G., & Parish, E. A. (1982). Loneliness and patterns of self-disclosure. *Journal of Personality and Social Psychology, 43,* 524–531.

Solano, C. H., & Koester, N. H. (1989). Loneliness and communication problems: Subjective anxiety or objective skills? *Personality and Social Psychology Bulletin, 15,* 126–133.

Soldz, S., & Vaillant, G. E. (1999). The Big Five personality traits and the life course: A 45-year longitudinal study. *Journal of Research in Personality, 33,* 208–232.

Solomon, D. H., & Knobloch, L. K. (2001). Relationship uncertainty, partner interference, and intimacy within dating relationships. *Journal of Social and Personal Relationships, 18,* 804–820.

Somers, C. L., & Paulson, C. E. (2000). Students' perceptions of parent-adolescent closeness and communication about sexuality: Relations with sexual knowledge, attitudes, and behaviors. *Journal of Adolescence, 23,* 629–644.

Sommer, K. L. (2001). Coping with rejection: Ego-defensive strategies, self-esteem, and interpersonal relationships. In M. R. Leary (Ed.), *Interpersonal rejection* (pp. 167–188). New York: Oxford University Press.

Sommer, K. L., Williams, K. D., Ciarocco, N. J., & Baumeister, R. F. (2001). When silence speaks louder than words: Explorations into the intrapsychic and interpersonal consequences of social ostracism. *Basic and Applied Social Psychology, 23,* 225–243.

South, S. J., & Lloyd, K. M. (1995). Spousal alternatives and marital dissolution. *American Sociological Review, 60,* 21–35.

South, S. J., Trent, K., & Shen, Y. (2001). Changing partners: Toward a macrostructural-opportunity theory of marital dissolution. *Journal of Marriage and the Family, 63,* 743–754.

Spence, J. T., & Helmreich, R. (1981). Androgyny vs. gender schema: A comment on Bem's gender schema theory. *Psychological Review, 88,* 365–368.

Spitzberg, B. H. (1999). An analysis of empirical estimates of sexual aggression, victimization, and perpetration. *Violence and Victims, 14,* 241–260.

Spitzberg, B. H., & Canary, D. J. (1985). Loneliness and relationally competent communication. *Journal of Social and Personal Relationships, 2,* 387–402.

Spitzberg, B. H., & Cupach, W. R. (Eds.). (1998). *The dark side of close relationships.* Mahwah, NJ: Erlbaum.

Spitzer, B. L., Henderson, K. A., & Zivian, M. T. (1999). Gender differences in population versus media body sizes: A comparison over four decades. *Sex Roles, 40,* 545–565.

Sprecher, S. (1986). The relation between inequity and emotions in close relationships. *Social Psychology Quarterly, 49,* 309–321.

Sprecher, S. (1987). The effects of self-disclosure given and received on affection for an intimate partner and stability of the relationship. *Journal of Social and Personal Relationships, 4,* 115–127.

Sprecher, S. (1989). The importance to males and females of physical attractiveness, earning potential, and expressiveness in initial attraction. *Sex Roles, 21,* 591–607.

Sprecher, S. (1992). How men and women expect to feel and behave in response to inequity in close relationships. *Social Psychology Quarterly, 55,* 57–69.

Sprecher, S. (1998a). The effect of exchange orientation on close relationships. *Social Psychology Quarterly, 61,* 220–231.

Sprecher, S. (1998b). Insiders' perspectives on reasons for attraction to a close other. *Social Psychology Quarterly, 61,* 287–300.

Sprecher, S. (1998c). Social exchange theories and sexuality. *Journal of Sex Research, 35,* 32–44.

Sprecher, S. (1999, June). *Equity and other social exchange variables in close, heterosexual relationships: Associations with satisfaction, commitment, and stability.* Paper presented at the meeting of the American Sociological Association, Chicago.

Sprecher, S. (2001). A comparison of emotional consequences of and changes in equity over time using global and domain-specific measures of equity. *Journal of Social and Personal Relationships, 18,* 477–501.

Sprecher, S. (2002). Sexual satisfaction in premarital relationships: Associations with satisfaction, love, commitment, and stability. *Journal of Sex Research, 39,* 190–196.

Sprecher, S., Aron, A., Hatfield, E., Cortese, A., Potapova, E., & Levitskaya, A. (1994). Love: American style, Russian style, and Japanese style. *Personal Relationships, 1,* 349–369.

Sprecher, S., Barbee, A., & Schwartz, P. (1995). "Was it good for you, too?": Gender differences in first sexual intercourse experiences. *Journal of Sex Research, 32,* 3–15.

Sprecher, S., & Cate, R. M. (2004). Sexual satisfaction and sexual expression as predictors of relationship satisfaction and stability. In J. H. Harvey, A. Wenzel, & S. Sprecher (Eds.), *The handbook of sexuality in close relationships* (pp. 235–256). Mahwah, NJ: Erlbaum.

Sprecher, S., & Duck, S. (1994). Sweet talk: The importance of perceived communication for romantic and friendship attraction experienced during a get-acquainted date. *Personality and Social Psychology Bulletin, 20,* 391–400.

Sprecher, S., & Fehr, B. (2005). Compassionate love for close others and humanity. *Journal of Social and Personal Relationships.*

Sprecher, S., & Felmlee, D. (1997). The balance of power in romantic heterosexual couples over time from "his" and "her" perspectives. *Sex Roles, 37,* 361–380.

Sprecher, S., & Felmlee, D. (2000). Romantic partners' perceptions of social network attributes with the passage of time and relationship transitions. *Personal Relationships, 7,* 325–340.

Sprecher, S., Felmlee, D., Orbuch, T. L., & Willetts, M. C. (2002). Social networks and change in personal relationships. In A. L. Vangelisti, H. T. Reis, & M. A. Fitzpatrick (Eds.), *Stability and change in relationships* (pp. 257–284). Cambridge, UK: Cambridge University Press.

Sprecher, S., McKinney, K., & Orbuch, T. L. (1987). Has the double standard disappeared? An experimental test. *Social Psychology Quarterly, 50,* 24–31.

Sprecher, S., & Metts, S. (1989). Development of the "Romantic Beliefs Scale" and examination of the effects of gender and gender-role orientation. *Journal of Social and Personal Relationships, 6,* 387–411.

Sprecher, S., & Metts, S. (1999). Romantic beliefs: Their influence on relationships and patterns of change over time. *Journal of Social and Personal Relationships, 16,* 834–851.

Sprecher, S., Metts, S., Burleson, B., Hatfield, E., & Thompson, A. (1995). Domains of expressive interaction in intimate relationships: Associations with satisfaction and commitment. *Family Relations, 44,* 203–210.

Sprecher, S., & Regan, P. C. (1998). Passionate and companionate love in courting and young married couples. *Sociological Inquiry, 68,* 163–185.

Sprecher, S., & Regan, P. C. (2002). Liking some things (in some people) more than others: Partner preferences in romantic relationships and friendships. *Journal of Social and Personal Relationships, 19,* 463–481.

Sprecher, S., Regan, P. C., & McKinney, K. (1998). Beliefs about the outcomes of extramarital sexual relationships as a function of the gender of the "cheating spouse." *Sex Roles, 38,* 301–311.

Sprecher, S., Regan, P. C., McKinney, K., Maxwell, K., & Wazienski, R. (1997). Preferred level of sexual experience in a date or mate: The merger of two methodologies. *Journal of Sex Research, 34,* 327–337.

Sprecher, S., & Schwartz, P. (1994). Equity and balance in the exchange of contributions in close relationships. In M. J. Lerner & G. Mikula (Eds.), *Entitlement and the affectional bond: Justice in close relationships* (pp. 11–41). New York: Plenum.

Stack, S. (1995). *Gender, marriage and loneliness: A cross—national study.* Unpublished manuscript, Wayne State University.

Stack, S. (1998). Marriage, family and loneliness: A cross—national study. *Sociological Perspectives, 41,* 415–432.

Stackert, R. A., & Bursik, K. (2003). Why am I unsatisfied? Adult attachment style, gendered irrational relationship beliefs, and young adult romantic relationship satisfaction. *Personality and Individual Differences, 34,* 1419–1429.

Stafford, L. (2003). Maintaining romantic relationships: A summary and analysis of one research program. In D. J. Canary & M. Dainton (Eds.), *Maintaining relationships through communication: Relational, contextual, and cultural variations* (pp. 58–59). Mahwah, NJ: Erlbaum.

Stafford, L., & Dainton, M. (1994). The dark side of "normal" family interaction. In W. R. Cupach & B. H. Spitzberg (Eds.), *The dark side of interpersonal communication* (pp. 259–280). Hillsdale, NJ: Erlbaum.

Stafford, L., Kline, S. L., & Rankin, C. T. (2004). Married individuals, cohabiters, and cohabiters who marry: A longitudinal study of relational and individual well-being. *Journal of Social and Personal Relationships, 21,* 231–248.

Stall, R. D., Coates, T. J., & Hoff, C. (1988). Behavioral risk reduction for HIV infection among gay and bisexual men. *American Psychologist, 43,* 878–885.

Stanfield, J. R., & Stanfield, J. B. (1997). Where has love gone? Reciprocity, redistribution, and the Nurturance Gap. *Journal of Socio-Economics, 26,* 111–126.

Stanley, S. M., Bradbury, T. N., & Markman, H. J. (2000). Structural flaws in the bridge from basic research on marriage to interventions. *Journal of Marriage and the Family, 62,* 256–264.

Stanovich, K. (2004). *How to think straight about psychology* (7th ed.). New York: Longman.

Steele, C. M., & Josephs, R. A. (1990). Alcohol myopia: Its prized and dangerous effects. *American Psychologist, 45,* 921–933.

Steiner-Pappalardo, N. L., & Gurung, R. A. R. (2002). The femininity effect: Relationship quality, sex, gender, attachment, and significant-other concepts. *Personal Relationships, 9,* 313–325.

Steinmetz, S. K. (1987). Family violence: Past, present, and future. In M. B. Sussman & S. K. Steinmetz (Eds.), *Handbook of marriage and the family* (pp. 725–765). New York: Plenum.

Stephan, W., Berscheid, E., & Walster, E. (1971). Sexual arousal and heterosexual perception. *Journal of Personality and Social Psychology, 20,* 93–101.

Sternberg, R. J. (1986). A triangular theory of love. *Psychological Review, 93,* 119–135.

Sternberg, R. J. (1987). *The triangle of love: Intimacy, passion, commitment.* New York: Basic Books.

Sternberg, R. J. (1998). *Cupid's arrow: The course of love through time.* New York: Cambridge University Press.

Sternglanz, R. W. (2004, June). *Exoneration of serious wrongdoing via confession to a lesser offense.* Paper presented at the meeting of the Society for Personality and Social Psychology, Austin, TX.

Stevens, C. K., & Kristof, A. L. (1995). Making the right impression: A field study of applicant impression management during job interviews. *Journal of Applied Psychology, 80,* 587–606.

Stevens, J., Kumanyika, S. K., & Keil, J. E. (1994). Attitudes towards body size and dieting: Differences between elderly Black and White women. *American Journal of Public Health, 84,* 1322–1325.

Stewart, A. J., Copeland, A. P., Chester, N. L., Malley, J. E., & Barenbaum, N. B. (1997). *Separating together: How divorce transforms families.* New York: Guilford Press.

Stewart, S., Stinnett, H., & Rosenfeld, L. B. (2000). Sex differences in desired characteristics of short-term and long-term relationship partners. *Journal of Social and Personal Relationships, 17,* 843–853.

Stiles, W. B., Walz, N. C., Schroeder, M. A. B., Williams, L. L., & Ickes, W. (1996). Attractiveness and disclosure in initial encounters of mixed-sex dyads. *Journal of Social and Personal Relationships, 13,* 303–312.

Stillwell, A. M., & Baumeister, R. F. (1997). The construction of victim and perpetrator memories: Accuracy and distortion in role-based accounts. *Personality and Social Psychology Bulletin, 23,* 1157–1172.

Stinson, L., & Ickes, W. (1992). Empathic accuracy in the interactions of male friends versus male strangers. *Journal of Personality and Social Psychology, 62,* 787–797.

Storms, M. D. (1980). Theories of sexual orientation. *Journal of Personality and Social Psychology, 38,* 783–792.

Storrs, D., & Kleinke, C. L. (1990). Evaluation of high and equal status male and female touchers. *Journal of Nonverbal Behavior, 14,* 87–95.

Strachman, A., & Gable, S. L. (2005, January). *Responses to positive event sharing in romantic couples.* Paper presented at the meeting of the Society for Personality and Social Psychology, New Orleans.

Straus, M. A. (1999). The controversy over domestic violence by women: A methological, theoretical, and sociology of science analysis. In X. B. Arriaga & S. Oskamp (Eds.), *Violence in intimate relationships* (pp. 17–44). Thousand Oaks, CA: Sage.

Straus, M. A., Gelles, R. J., & Steinmetz, S. K. (1980). *Behind closed doors.* Garden City, NY: Anchor Books.

Straus, M. A., Hamby, S. L., Boney-McCoy, S., & Sugarman, D. B. (1996). The revised Conflict Tactics Scales (CTS2): Development and preliminary psychometric data. *Journal of Family Issues, 17,* 283–316.

Strodl, E., & Noller, P. (2003). The relationship of adult attachment dimensions to depression and agoraphobia. *Personal Relationships, 10,* 171–185.

Strong, G., & Aron, A. (2004, January). *Relation of high positive and low negative affective states with experienced romantic relationship quality.* Paper presented at the meeting of the Society for Personality and Social Psychology, Austin, TX.

Stroup, A. L., & Pollock, G. E. (1994). Economic consequences of marital dissolution. *Journal of Divorce and Remarriage, 22,* 37–54.

Strube, M. J. (1988). The decision to leave an abusive relationship: Empirical evidence and theoretical issues. *Psychological Bulletin, 104,* 236–250.

Stucke, T. S. (2003). Who's to blame? Narcissism and self-serving attributions following feedback. *European Journal of Personality, 17,* 465–478.

Stukas, A. A., Jr., & Snyder, M. (2002). Targets' awareness of expectations and behavioral confirmation in ongoing interactions. *Journal of Experimental Social Psychology, 38,* 31–40.

Sümer, N., & Cozzarelli, C. The impact of adult attachment on partner and self-attributions and relationship quality. *Personal Relationships, 11,* 355–371.

Summers, R. F., & Barber, J. P. (2003). Therapeutic alliance as a measurable psychotherapy skill. *Academic Psychiatry, 27,* 160–165.

Sun, Y. (2001). Family environment and adolescents' well-being before and after parents' marital disruption: A longitudinal analysis. *Journal of Marriage and the Family, 63,* 697–713.

Sun, Y., & Li, Y. (2002). Children's well-being during parents' marital disruption process: A pooled time-series analysis. *Journal of Marriage and the Family, 64,* 472–488.

Sunnafrank, M., & Ramirez, A., Jr. (2004). At first sight: Persistent relational effects of get-acquainted conversations. *Journal of Social and Personal Relationships, 21,* 361–379.

Surra, C. A., & Gray, C. R. (2000). A typology of processes of commitment to marriage: Why do partners commit to problematic relationships? In L. J. Waite (Ed.), *The ties that bind: Perspectives on marriage and cohabitation* (pp. 253–280). New York: Aldine de Gruyter.

Surra, C. A., & Longstreth, M. (1990). Similarity of outcomes, interdependence, and conflict in dating relationships. *Journal of Personality and Social Psychology, 59,* 501–516.

Swann, W. B., Jr. (1996). *Self-traps: The elusive quest for higher self-esteem.* New York: W. H. Freeman.

Swann, W. B., Jr. (1997). The trouble with change: Self-verification and allegiance to the self. *Psychological Science, 8,* 177–180.

Swann, W. B., Jr., Bosson, J. K., & Pelham, B. W. (2002). Different partners, different selves: Strategic verification of circumscribed identities. *Personality and Social Psychology Bulletin, 28,* 1215–1228.

Swann, W. B., Jr., De La Ronde, C., & Hixon, J. G. (1994). Authenticity and positivity strivings in marriage and courtship. *Journal of Personality and Social Psychology, 66,* 857–869.

Swann, W. B., Jr., & Ely, R. J. (1984). A battle of wills: Self-verification versus behavioral confirmation. *Journal of Personality and Social Psychology, 46,* 1287–1302.

Swann, W. B., Jr., & Gill, M. J. (1997). Confidence and accuracy in person perception: Do we know what we think we know about our relationship partners? *Journal of Personality and Social Psychology, 73,* 747–757.

Swann, W. B., Jr., Hixon, J. G., Stein-Seroussi, A., & Gilbert, D. T. (1990). The fleeting gleam of praise: Cognitive processes underlying behavioral reactions to self-relevant feedback. *Journal of Personality and Social Psychology, 59,* 17–26.

Swann, W. B., Jr., & Pelham, B. (2002). Who wants out when the going gets good? Psychological investment and preference for self-verifying roommates. *Self and Identity, 1,* 219–233.

Swann, W. B., Jr., Rentfrow, P. J., & Gosling, S. D. (2003). The precarious couple effect: Verbally inhibited men + critical, disinhibited women = bad chemistry. *Journal of Personality and Social Psychology, 85,* 1095–1106.

Swann, W. B., Jr., Silvera, D. H., & Proske, C. U. (1995). On "knowing your partner": Dangerous illusions in the age of AIDS? *Personal Relationships, 2,* 173–186.

Sweeney, P. D., Anderson, K., & Bailey, S. (1986). Attributional style in depression: A meta-analytic review. *Journal of Personality and Social Psychology, 50,* 974–991.

Tafoya, M., & Spitzberg, B. H. (in press). Communicative infidelity. In B. H. Spitzberg & W. R. Cupach (Eds.), *The dark side of interpersonal communication* (2nd ed.). Mahwah, NJ: LEA.

Tallman, I., Rotolo, T., & Gray, L. N. (2001). Continuity or change? The impact of parents' divorce on newly married couples. *Social Psychology Quarterly, 64,* 333–346.

Tan, D. T. Y., & Singh, R. (1995). Attitudes and attraction: A developmental study of the similarity-attraction and dissimilarity–repulsion hypotheses. *Personality and Social Psychology Bulletin, 21,* 975–986.

Tashiro, T., & Frazier, P. (2003). "I'll never be in a relationship like that again": Personal growth following romantic relationship breakups. *Personal Relationships, 10,* 113–128.

Tavris, C. (1982). *Anger: The misunderstood emotion.* New York: Simon and Schuster.

Taylor, M. (1999). *Imaginary companions and the children who create them.* New York: Oxford University Press.

Teachman, J. D. (2002a). Childhood living arrangements and the intergenerational transmission of divorce. *Journal of Marriage and the Family, 64,* 717–729.

Teachman, J. D. (2002b). Stability across cohorts in divorce risk factors. *Demography, 39,* 331–351.

Teachman, J. D. (2003). Premarital sex, premarital cohabitation and the risk of subsequent marital dissolution among women. *Journal of Marriage and the Family, 65,* 444–455.

Tellegen, A., Lykken, D. T., Bouchard, T. J., Wilcox, K. J., Segal, N. L., & Rich, S. (1988). Personality similarity in twins reared apart and together. *Journal of Personality and Social Psychology, 54,* 1031–1039.

Tesser, A., Beach, S. R. H., Mendolia, M., Crepaz, N., Davies, B., & Pennebaker, J. (1998). Similarity and uniqueness focus: A paper tiger and a surprise. *Personality and Social Psychology Bulletin, 24,* 1190–1204.

Tesser, A., & Paulus, D. L. (1976). Toward a causal model of love. *Journal of Personality and Social Psychology, 34,* 1095–1105.

Testa, R. J., Kinder, B. N., & Ironson, G. (1987). Heterosexual bias in the perception of loving relationships of gay males and lesbians. *Journal of Sex Research, 23,* 163–172.

Thibaut, J. W., & Kelley, H. H. (1959). *The social psychology of groups.* New York: Wiley.

Thomas, G. (2000, June). *Empathic accuracy in intimate relationships.* Paper presented at the meeting of the International Society for the Study of Personal Relationships, Brisbane.

Thomas, G., & Fletcher, G. J. O. (1997). Empathic accuracy in close relationships. In W. Ickes (Ed.), *Empathic accuracy* (pp. 194–217). New York: Guilford Press.

Thomas, G., Fletcher, G. J. O., & Lange, C. (1997). On-line empathic accuracy in marital interaction. *Journal of Personality and Social Psychology, 72,* 839–850.

Thompson, S. C., & Kelley, H. H. (1981). Judgments of responsibility for activities in close relationships. *Journal of Personality and Social Psychology, 41,* 469–477.

Thornhill, R., Gangestad, S. W., Miller, R., Scheyd, G., McCollough, J. K., & Franklin, M. (2003). Major histocompatibility complex genes, symmetry, and body scent attractiveness in men and women. *Behavioral Ecology, 14,* 668–678.

Thornhill, R., & Grammer, K. (1999). The body and face of woman: One ornament that signals quality? *Evolution and Human Behavior, 20,* 105–120.

Thornton, B., & Moore, S. (1993). Physical attractiveness contrast effect: Implications for self-esteem and evaluations of the social self. *Personality and Social Psychology Bulletin, 19,* 474–480.

Thorton, A., & Young-DeMarco, L. (2001). Four decades of trends in attitudes toward family issues in the United States: The 1960s through the 1990s. *Journal of Marriage and the Family, 63,* 1009–1037.

Tice, D. M., & Baumeister, R. F. (1993). Controlling anger: Self-induced emotion change. In D. M. Wegner & J. W. Pennebaker (Eds.), *Handbook of mental control* (pp. 393–409). Englewood Cliffs, NJ: Prentice Hall.

Tice, D. M., Butler, J. L., Muraven, M. B., & Stillwell, A. M. (1995). When modesty prevails: Differential favorability of self-presentation to friends and strangers. *Journal of Personality and Social Psychology, 69,* 1120–1138.

Tice, D. M., Twenge, J. M., & Schmeichel, B. J. (2002). Threatened selves: The effects of social exclusion on prosocial and antisocial behavior. In J. P. Forgas & K. D. Williams (Eds.), *The social self: Cognitive, interpersonal, and intergroup perspectives* (pp. 175–187). New York: Psychology Press.

Tjaden, P., & Thoennes, N. (1999). *Extent, nature, and consequences of intimate partner violence: Findings from the National Violence Against Women Survey.* Washington, DC: National Institute of Justice / Centers for Disease Control and Prevention.

Tolmacz, R. (2004). Attachment style and willingness to compromise when choosing a mate. *Journal of Social and Personal Relationships, 21,* 267–272.

Tolstedt, B. E., & Stokes, J. P. (1984). Self-disclosure, intimacy, and the de-penetration process. *Journal of Personality and Social Psychology, 46,* 84–90.

Tracy, J. L., & Robins, R. W. (2004, January). *The automaticity of emotion recognition.* Paper presented at the meeting of the Society for Personality and Social Psychology, Austin, TX.

Tracy, J. L., Shaver, P. R., Albino, A. W., & Cooper, M. L. (2003). Attachment styles and adolescent sexuality. In P. Florsheim (Ed.), *Adolescent romantic relations and sexual behavior: Theory, research, and practical implications* (pp. 137–159). Mahwah, NJ: Erlbaum.

Treas, J., & Giesen, D. (2000). Sexual infidelity among married and cohabiting Americans. *Journal of Marriage and the Family, 62,* 48–60.

Trent, K., & South, S. J. (1989). Structural determinants of the divorce rate: A cross-societal analysis. *Journal of Marriage and the Family, 51,* 391–404.

Triandis, H. C., McCusker, C., & Hui, C. H. (1990). Multimethod probe of individualism and collectivism. *Journal of Personality and Social Psychology, 59,* 1006–1020.

Trinke, S. J., & Bartholomew, K. (1997). Hierarchies of attachment relationships in young adulthood. *Journal of Social and Personal Relationships, 14,* 603–625.

Tucker, J. S., & Anders, S. L. (1998). Adult attachment style and nonverbal closeness in dating couples. *Journal of Nonverbal Behavior, 22,* 109–124.

Tucker, J. S., & Anders, S. L. (1999). Attachment style, interpersonal perception accuracy, and relationship satisfaction in dating couples. *Personality and Social Psychology Bulletin, 25,* 403–412.

Tucker, M. B. (2000). Marital values and expectations in context: Results from a 21-city survey. In L. J. Waite (Ed.), *The ties that bind: Perspectives on marriage and cohabitation* (pp. 166–187). New York: Aldine de Gruyter.

Tucker, P., & Aron, A. (1993). Passionate love and marital satisfaction at key transition points in the family life cycle. *Journal of Social and Clinical Psychology, 12,* 135–147.

Turk, J. L., & Bell, N. W. (1972). Measuring power in families. *Journal of Marriage and the Family, 34,* 215–227.

Turque, B. (1992, September 14). Gays under fire. *Newsweek,* 35–40.

Twaite, J. A., Keiser, S., & Luchow, A. K. (1998). Divorce mediation: Promises, criticisms, achievements and current challenges. *Journal of Psychiatry and Law, 26,* 353–381.

Twenge, J. M. (1997). Changes in masculine and feminine traits over time: A meta-analysis. *Sex Roles, 36,* 305–325.

Twenge, J. M., & Campbell, W. K. (2003). "Isn't it fun to get the respect that we're going to deserve?" Narcissism, social rejection, and aggression. *Personality and Social Psychology Bulletin, 29,* 261–272.

Twenge, J. M., Catanese, K. R., & Baumeister, R. F. (2002). Social exclusion causes self-defeating behavior. *Journal of Personality and Social Psychology, 83,* 606–615.

Twenge, J. M., Catanese, K. R., & Baumeister, R. F. (2003). Social exclusion and the deconstructed state: Time perception, meaninglessness, lethargy, lack of emotion, and self-awareness. *Journal of Personality and Social Psychology, 85,* 409–423.

Tyler, T. R. (2002). Is the Internet changing social life? It seems the more things change, the more they stay the same. *Journal of Social Issues, 58,* 195–205.

U.S. Bureau of the Census. (1995). Child support for custodial mothers and fathers: 1989. *Current Population Reports,* Series P-60, no. 187.

United Nations Department of Economic and Social Affairs. (1999). *Demographic yearbook: 1997* (49th ed.). New York: Author.

Urbaniak, G. C., & Kilmann, P. R. (2003). Physical attractiveness and the "nice guy paradox": Do nice guys really finish last? *Sex Roles, 49,* 413–426.

van den Boom (1994). The influence of temperament and mothering on attachment and exploration: An experimental manipulation of sensitive responsiveness among lower-class mothers with irritable infants. *Child Development, 65,* 1457–1477.

van den Boom (1995). Do first-year intervention effects endure? Follow-up during toddlerhood of a sample of Dutch irritable infants. *Child Development, 66,* 1798–1816.

van der Molen, H. T. (1990). A definition of shyness and its implications for clinical practice. In W. R. Crozier (Ed.), *Shyness and embarrassment: Perspectives from social psychology* (pp. 255–285). Cambridge: Cambridge University Press.

Van Horn, K. R., Arnone, A., Nesbitt, K., Desilets, L., Sears, T., Giffin, M., & Brudi, R. (1997). Physical distance and interpersonal characteristics in college students' romantic relationships. *Personal Relationships, 4,* 25–34.

Van Lange, P. A. M., & Rusbult, C. E. (1995). My relationship is better than—and not as bad as—yours is: The perception of superiority in close relationships. *Personality and Social Psychology Bulletin, 21,* 32–44.

Van Lange, P. A. M., Rusbult, C. E., Drigotas, S. M., Arriaga, X. B., Witcher, B. S., & Cox, C. L. (1997). Willingness to sacrifice in close relationships. *Journal of Personality and Social Psychology, 72,* 1373–1395.

Van Lange, P. A. M., Rusbult, C. E., Semin-Goossens, A., Görts, C. A., & Stalpers, M. (1999). Being better than others but otherwise perfectly normal: Perceptions of uniqueness and similarity in close relationships. *Personal Relationships, 6,* 269–289.

Van Leeuwen, M. (2003, May). *Insecurity in attachment: Is it related to addiction?* Paper presented at the meeting of the American Psychological Society, Atlanta.

van Tilburg, T., de Jong Gierveld, J., Lecchini, L., & Marsiglia, D. (1998). Social integration and loneliness: A comparative study among older adults in the Netherlands and Tuscany, Italy. *Journal of Social and Personal Relationships, 15,* 740–754.

Vangelisti, A. (2004, July). *The sticks and stones fallacy: Hurt feelings in close relationships.* Paper presented at the meeting of the International Association for Relationship Research, Madison, WI.

Vangelisti, A. L., & Young, S. L. (2000). When words hurt: The effects of perceived intentionality on interpersonal relationships. *Journal of Social and Personal Relationships, 17,* 393–424.

Vaughan, C. A., Stewart, V., Ceo, D., & Sacco, W. P. (2003, May). *Ethnicity moderates the relationship between body mass index and self-perceived physical attractiveness.* Paper presented at the meeting of the American Psychological Society, Atlanta.

Vaughn, B. E., & Bost, K. K. (1999). Attachment and temperament: Redundant, independent, or interacting influences on interpersonal adaptation and personality development? In J. Cassidy & P. R. Shaver (Eds.), *Handbook of attachment: Theory, research, and clinical applications* (pp. 198–225). New York: Guilford Press.

Vaux, A. (1988). Social and personal factors in loneliness. *Journal of Social and Clinical Psychology, 6,* 462–471.

Veniegas, R. C., & Peplau, L. A. (1997). Power and the quality of same-sex friendships. *Psychology of Women Quarterly, 21,* 279–297.

Veroff, J., Hatchett, S. & Douvan, E. (1992). Consequences of participating in a longitudinal study of marriage. *Public Opinion Quarterly, 56,* 315–327.

Vessey, J. T., & Howard, K. I. (1993). Who seeks psychotherapy? *Psychotherapy: Theory, Research, Practice, Training, 30,* 546–553.

Vincent, J. P., Weiss, R. L., & Birchler, G. R. (1975). Dyadic problem solving behavior as a function of marital distress and spousal vs. stranger interactions. *Behavior Therapy, 6,* 475–487.

Vittengl, J. R., & Holt, C. S. (1998). A time-series diary study of mood and social interaction. *Motivation and Emotion, 22,* 255–275.

Vittengl, J. R., & Holt, C. S. (2000). Getting acquainted: The relationship of self-disclosure and social attraction to positive affect. *Journal of Social and Personal Relationships, 17,* 53–66.

Vogel, D. L., & Karney, B. R. (2002). Demands and withdrawal in newlyweds: Elaborating on the social structure hypothesis. *Journal of Social and Personal Relationships, 19,* 685–701.

Vohs, K. D. (2004, January). *The health of romantic relationships relies on self-regulation.* Paper presented at the meeting of the Society for Personality and Social Psychology, Austin, TX.

Vohs, K. D., & Baumeister, R. F. (2004). Sexual passion, intimacy, and gender. In D. J. Mashek & A. Aron (Eds.), *Handbook of closeness and intimacy* (pp. 189–200). Mahwah, NJ: Erlbaum.

Vohs, K. D., Catanese, K. R., & Baumeister, R. F. (2004). Sex in "his" versus "her" relationship. In J. H. Harvey, A. Wenzel, & S. Sprecher (Eds.), *The handbook of sexuality in close relationships* (pp. 455–474). Mahwah, NJ: Erlbaum.

Vonk, R. (1998). The slime effect: Suspicion and dislike of likeable behavior toward superiors. *Journal of Personality and Social Psychology, 74,* 849–864.

Vorauer, J. D., & Ratner, R. K. (1996). Who's going to make the first move? Pluralistic ignorance as an impediment to relationship formation. *Journal of Social and Personal Relationships, 13,* 483–506.

vos Savant, M. (2004, March 14). Ask Marilyn. *Parade,* 12.

Vrij, A., Edward, K., & Bull, R. (2001). Stereotypical verbal and nonverbal responses while deceiving others. *Personality and Social Psychology Bulletin, 27,* 899–909.

Vrij, A., Paterson, B., Nunkoosing, K., Soukara, S., & Oosterwegel, A. (2003). Perceived advantages and disadvantages of secrets disclosure. *Personality and Individual Differences, 35,* 593–602.

Vuchinich, S. (1987). Starting and stopping spontaneous family conflicts. *Journal of Marriage and the Family, 49,* 591–601.

Waas, G. A., & Graczyk, P. A. (1998). Group interventions for the peer-rejected child. In K. C. Stoiber & T. R. Kratochwill (Eds.), *Handbook of group intervention for children and families* (pp. 141–158). Needham Heights, MA: Allyn & Bacon.

Wagner, M., & Ferreri, G. N. (2003, May). *Affects of family conflict on self-concept and attitudes toward romantic relationships.* Paper presented at the meeting of the American Psychological Society, Atlanta, GA.

Waite, L. J., & Gallagher, M. (2000). *The case for marriage: Why married people are happier, healthier, and better off financially.* New York: Broadway Books.

Waite, L. J., & Lillard, L. A. (1991). Children and marital disruption. *American Journal of Sociology, 96,* 930–953.

Waller, N. G., & Shaver, P. R. (1994). The importance of nongenetic influences on romantic love styles: A twin-family study. *Psychological Science, 5,* 268–274.

Waller, W. (1937). The rating and dating complex. *American Sociological Review, 2,* 727–734.

Waller, W. W., & Hill, R. (1951). *The family, a dynamic interpretation.* New York: Dryden Press.

Walster, E., Aronson, V., Abrahams, D., & Rottman, L. (1966). The importance of physical attractiveness in dating behavior. *Journal of Personality and Social Psychology, 4,* 508–516.

Walster, E., Traupmann, J., & Walster, G. W. (1978). Equity and extramarital sexuality. *Archives of Sexual Behavior, 7,* 127–141.

Walster, E., & Walster, G. W. (1978). *A new look at love.* Reading, MA: Addison-Wesley.

Walster, E., Walster, G. W., & Piliavin, J. (1973). "Playing hard to get": Understanding an elusive phenomenon. *Journal of Personality & Social Psychology, 26,* 113–121.

Walster, E., Walster, G. W., & Traupmann, J. (1978). Equity and premarital sex. *Journal of Personality, 36,* 82–92.

Wampold, B. E. (2001). *The great psychotherapy debate: Models, methods, and findings.* Mahwah, NJ: Erlbaum.

Wang, H., & Amato, P. R. (2000). Predictors of divorce adjustment: Stressors, resources, and definitions. *Journal of Marriage and the Family, 62,* 655–668.

Warren, B. L. (1966). A multiple variable approach to the assortive mating phenomenon. *Eugenics Quarterly, 13,* 285–298.

Watson, D. (2000, February). *Personality similarity and relationship satisfaction.* Paper presented at the meeting of the Society for Personality and Social Psychology, Nashville.

Watson, D., Hubbard, B., & Wiese, D. (2000a). General traits of personality and affectivity as predictors of satisfaction in intimate relationships: Evidence from self- and partner-ratings. *Journal of Personality, 68,* 413–449.

Watson, D., Hubbard, B., & Wiese, D. (2000b). Self-other agreement in personality and affectivity: The role of acquaintanceship, trait visibility, and assumed similarity. *Journal of Personality and Social Psychology, 78,* 546–558.

Way, N., Cowal, K., Gingold, R., Pahl, K., & Bissessar, N. (2001). Friendship patterns among African American, Asian American, and Latino adolescents from low-income families. *Journal of Social and Personal Relationships, 18,* 29–53.

Weaver, S. E., & Ganong, L. H. (2004). The factor structure of the Romantic Beliefs Scale for African Americans and European Americans. *Journal of Social and Personal Relationships, 21,* 171–185.

Webb, E. J., Campbell, D. T., Schwartz, R. D., Sechrest, L., & Grove, J. B. (1981). *Nonreactive measures in the social sciences* (2nd ed.). Boston: Houghton Mifflin.

Weber, A. L. (1992). The account-making process: A phenomenological approach. In T. L. Orbuch (Ed.), *Close relationship loss: Theoretical approaches* (pp. 174–191). New York: Springer-Verlag.

Weber, A. L., & Harvey, J. H. (1994). Accounts in coping with relationship loss. In A. L. Weber & J. H. Harvey (Eds.), *Perspectives on close relationships* (pp. 285–306). Boston: Allyn & Bacon.

Weeks, D. G., Michela, J. L., Peplau, L. A., & Bragg, M. E. (1980). The relation between loneliness and depression: A structural equation analysis. *Journal of Personality and Social Psychology 39,* 1238–1244.

Wegener, D. T., & Fabrigar, L. R. (2004). Constructing and evaluating quantitative measures for social psychological research. In C. Sansone, C. C. Morf, & A. T. Panter (Eds.), *The Sage handbook of methods in social psychology* (pp. 145–172). Thousand Oaks, CA: Sage.

Wegner, D. M., Erber, R., & Raymond, P. (1991). Transactive memory in close relationships. *Journal of Personality and Social Psychology, 61,* 923–929.

Wegner, D. M., & Gold, D. B. (1995). Fanning old flames: Emotional and cognitive effects of suppressing thoughts of a past relationship. *Journal of Personality and Social Psychology, 68*, 782–792.

Wegner, D. M., & Lane, J. D. (1995). From secrecy to psychopathology. In J. W. Pennebaker (Ed.), *Emotion, disclosure, & health* (pp. 25–46). Washington, DC: American Psychological Association.

Wegner, D. M., Lane, J. D., & Dimitri, S. (1994). The allure of secret relationships. *Journal of Personality and Social Psychology, 66*, 287–300.

Weigel, D. J., & Ballard-Reisch, D. S. (2002). Investigating the behavioral indicators of relational commitment. *Journal of Social and Personal Relationships, 19*, 403–423.

Weigel, D. J., Bennett, K. K., & Ballard-Reisch, D. S. (2003). Family influences on commitment: Explaining the family of origin correlates of relationship commitment attitudes. *Personal Relationships, 10*, 453–474.

Weiss, R. L., Birchler, G. R., & Vincent, J. P. (1974). Contractual models for negotiating training in marital dyads. *Journal of Marriage and the Family, 36*, 321–330.

Weiss, R. L., Hops, H., & Patterson, G. R. (1973). A framework for conceptualizing marital conflict, a technology for altering it, some data for evaluating it. In L. A. Hamerlynck, L. C. Handy, & E. J. Mash (Eds.), *Behavior change: Methodology, concepts and practice* (pp. 309–342). Champaign, IL: Research Press.

Weiss, R. S. (1973). *Loneliness.* Cambridge, MA: MIT Press.

Weiss, R. S. (1979). The emotional impact of marital separation. In G. Levinger & O. C. Moles (Eds.), *Divorce and separation: Context, causes, and consequences* (pp. 201–210). New York: Basic Books.

Werking, K. (1997). *We're just good friends: Women and men in nonromantic relationships.* New York: Guilford Press.

Werking, K. J. (2000). Cross-sex friendship research as ideological practice. In K. Dindia & S. Duck (Eds.), *Communication and personal relationships* (pp. 113–130). New York: Wiley.

West, C., & Zimmerman, D. H. (1983). Small insults: A study of interruptions in cross-sex conversations between unacquainted persons. In B. Thorne, C. Kramarge, & N. Henley (Eds.), *Language, gender and society* (pp. 102–117). Rowley, MA: Newbury House.

West, S. G., Biesanz, J. C., & Kwok, O. (2004). Within-subject and longitudinal experiments: Design and analysis issues. In C. Sansone, C. C. Morf, & A. T. Panter (Eds.), *The Sage handbook of methods in social psychology* (pp. 287–312). Thousand Oaks, CA: Sage.

Wheeler, J., & Christensen, A. (2002). Creating a context for change: Integrative Couple Therapy. In A. L. Vangelisti, H. T. Reis, & M. A. Fitzpatrick (Eds.), *Stability and change in relationships* (pp. 285–305). Cambridge, UK: Cambridge University Press.

Wheeler, L., & Kim, Y. (1997). What is beautiful is culturally good: The physical attractiveness stereotype has different content in collectivistic cultures. *Personality and Social Psychology Bulletin, 23*, 795–800.

Wheeler, L., Reis, H., & Nezlek, J. (1983). Loneliness, social interaction, and sex roles. *Journal of Personality and Social Psychology, 45*, 943–953.

Whisman, M. A., & Allan, L. E. (1996). Attachment and social cognition theories of romantic relationships: Convergent or complementary perspectives? *Journal of Social and Personal Relationships, 13*, 263–278.

Whitcher, S. J., & Fisher, J. D. (1979). Multidimensional reaction to therapeutic touch in a hospital setting. *Journal of Personality and Social Psychology, 37*, 87–96.

White, G. L. (1980a). Inducing jealousy: A power perspective. *Personality and Social Psychology Bullein, 6*, 222–227.

White, G. L. (1980b). Physical attractiveness and courtship progress. *Journal of Personality and Social Psychology, 39*, 660–668.

White, G. L. (1981a). A model of romantic jealousy. *Motivation and Emotion, 5*, 295–310.

White, G. L. (1981b). Some correlates of romantic jealousy. *Journal of Personality, 49*, 129–147.

White, G. L., Fishbein, S., & Rutstin, J. (1981). Passionate love: The misattribution of arousal. *Journal of Personality and Social Psychology, 41*, 56–62.

White, G. L., & Kight, T. D. (1984). Misattribution of arousal and attraction: Effects of salience of explanation of arousal. *Journal of Experimental Social Psychology, 20*, 55–64.

White, G. L., & Mullen, P. E. (1989). *Jealousy: Theory, research, and clinical strategies.* New York: Guilford Press.

White, J. W., & Koss, M. P. (1991). Courtship violence: Incidence in a national sample of higher education students. *Violence and Victims, 6,* 247–256.

White, L. K. (1990). Determinants of divorce: A review of research in the eighties. *Journal of Marriage and the Family, 52,* 904–912.

White, L. K., & Booth, A. (1991). Divorce over the life course: The role of marital happiness. *Journal of Family Issues, 12,* 5–21.

Whitley, B. E., Jr. (1993). Reliability and aspects of the construct validity of Sternberg's Triangular Love Scale. *Journal of Social and Personal Relationships, 10,* 475–480.

Whitton, S., Stanley, S., & Markman, H. (2002). Sacrifice in romantic relationships: An exploration of relevant research and theory. In A. L. Vangelisti, H. T. Reis, & M. A. Fitzpatrick (Eds.), *Stability and change in relationships* (pp. 156–181). Cambridge, UK: Cambridge University Press.

Whitty, M. T. (2002). Liar, liar! An examination of how open, supportive and honest people are in chat rooms. *Computers in Human Behavior, 18,* 343–352.

Whitty, M. T. (2004). Cyber-flirting: An examination of men's and women's flirting behaviour both offline and on the Internet. *Behaviour Change, 21,* 115–126.

Whitty, M., & Gavin, J. (2001). Age/sex/location: Uncovering the social cues in the development of online relationships. *Cyber Psychology and Behavior, 4,* 623–630.

Whyte, W. F. (1955). *Street corner society: The social structure of an Italian slum.* Chicago: University of Chicago Press.

Widmer, E. D. (1997). Influence of older siblings on initiation of sexual intercourse. *Journal of Marriage and the Family, 59,* 928–938.

Widmer, E. D., Treas, J., & Newcomb, R. (1998). Attitudes toward nonmarital sex in 24 countries. *Journal of Sex Research, 35,* 349–358.

Wiederman, M. W. (1999). Volunteer bias in sexuality research using college student participants. *Journal of Sex Research, 36,* 59–66.

Wiederman, M. W. (2004). Methodological issues in studying sexuality in close relationships. In J. H. Harvey, A. Wenzel, & S. Sprecher (Eds.), *The handbook of sexuality in close relationships* (pp. 31–56). Mahwah, NJ: Erlbaum.

Wiederman, M. W., & Hurd, C. (1999). Extradyadic involvement during dating. *Journal of Social and Personal Relationships, 16,* 265–274.

Wiederman, M. W., & Kendall, E. (1999). Evolution, sex, and jealousy: Investigation with a sample from Sweden. *Evolution and Human Behavior, 20,* 121–128.

Wieselquist, J., Rusbult, C. E., Foster, C. A., & Agnew, C. R. (1999). Commitment, pro-relationship behavior, and trust in close relationships. *Journal of Personality and Social Psychology, 77,* 942–966.

Wiggins, J. S. (Ed.). (1996). *The five-factor model of personality: Theoretical perspectives.* New York: Guilford Press.

Wile, D. B. (1995). *After the fight: Using your disagreements to build a stronger relationship.* New York: Guilford Press.

Wilkie, J. R., Ferree, M., & Ratcliff, K. S. (1998). Gender and fairness: Marital satisfaction in two-earner couples. *Journal of Marriage and the Family, 60,* 577–594.

Willetts, M. C., Sprecher, S., & Beck, F. D. (2004). Overview of sexual practices and attitudes within relational contexts. In J. H. Harvey, A. Wenzel, & S. Sprecher (Eds.), *The handbook of sexuality in close relationships* (pp. 57–85). Mahwah, NJ: Erlbaum.

Williams, J. C., & Solano, C. H. (1983). The social reality of feeling lonely: Friendship and reciprocation. *Personality and Social Psychology Bulletin, 9,* 237–242.

Williams, J. E., & Best, D. L. (1990). *Measuring sex stereotypes: A multination study* (Rev. ed.). Newbury Park, CA: Sage.

Williams, K. D. (2001). *Ostracism: The power of silence.* New York: Guilford Press.

Williams, K. D., Cheung, C. K. T., & Choi, W. (2000). Cyberostracism: Effects of being ignored over the Internet. *Journal of Personality and Social Psychology, 79,* 748–762.

Williams, K. D., & Zadro, L. (2001). Ostracism: On being ignored, excluded, and rejected. In M. R. Leary (Ed.), *Interpersonal rejection* (pp. 21–53). New York: Oxford University Press.

Williamson, G. M., & Clark, M. S. (1989). Providing help and desired relationship type as determinants of changes in moods and self-evaluations. *Journal of Personality and Social Psychology, 56,* 722–734.

Williamson, G. M., Clark, M. S., Pegalis, L. J., & Behan, A. (1996). Affective consequences of refusing to help in communal and exchange relationships. *Personality and Social Psychology Bulletin, 22,* 34–47.

Wills, T. A., Weiss, R. L., & Patterson, G. R. (1974). A behavioral analysis of the determinants of marital satisfaction. *Journal of Consulting and Clinical Psychology, 42,* 802–811.

Wilson, C., Simpson, J., Campbell, L., & Fletcher, G. (2002, February). *The influence of mindsets on perceptions of partners and relationships.* Paper presented at the meeting of the Society for Personality and Social Psychology, Savannah, GA.

Wineberg, H. (1988). Duration between marriage and first birth and marital instability. *Social Biology, 35,* 91–102.

Winstead, B. A., Derlega, V. J., & Rose, S. (1997). *Gender and close relationships.* Thousand Oaks, CA: Sage.

Winston, R. (2002). *Human instinct.* London: Bantam Press.

Winter, D. G. (1973). *The power motive.* New York: Free Press.

Winter, D. G. (1988). The power motive in women—and men. *Journal of Personality and Social Psychology, 54,* 510–519.

Wiseman, J., & Duck, S. (1995). Having and managing enemies: A very challenging relationship. In S. Duck & J. T. Wood (Eds.), *Confronting relationship challenges* (pp. 43–72). Thousand Oaks, CA: Sage.

Wittenberg, M. T., & Reis, H. T. (1986). Loneliness, social skills, and social perception. *Personality and Social Psychology Bulletin, 12,* 121–130.

Wolcott, I. H. (1986). Seeking help for marital problems before separation. *Australian Journal of Sex, Marriage & Family, 7,* 154–164.

Wolfinger, N. H. (1999). Trends in the intergenerational transmission of divorce. *Demography, 36,* 420–425.

Woll, S. B. (1989). Personality and relationship correlates of loving styles. *Journal of Research in Personality, 23,* 480–505.

Wood, J. T. (2004). Monsters and victims: Male felons' accounts of intimate partner violence. *Journal of Social and Personal Relationships, 21,* 555–576.

Wood, J. T., & Dindia, K. (1998). What's the difference? A dialogue about differences and similarities between men and women. In D. J. Canary & K. Dindia (Eds.), *Sex differences and similarities in communication: Critical essays and empirical investigations of sex and gender in interaction* (pp. 19–39). Mahwah, NJ: Erlbaum.

Wood, W., & Christensen, P. N. (2004). Quantitative research synthesis: Examining study outcomes over settings, samples, and time. In C. Sansone, C. C. Morf, & A. T. Panter (Eds.), *The Sage handbook of methods in social psychology* (pp. 335–356). Thousand Oaks, CA: Sage.

Wood, W., & Eagly, A. H. (2002). A cross-cultural analysis of the behavior of women and men: Implications for the origins of sex differences. *Psychological Bulletin, 128,* 699–727.

Wright, P. H. (1982). Men's friendships, women's friendships and the alleged inferiority of the latter. *Sex Roles, 8,* 1–20.

Wright, P. H. (1989). Gender differences in adults' same- and cross-gender friendships. In R. G. Adams & R. Blieszner (Eds.), *Older adult friendship: Structure and process* (pp. 197–221). Thousand Oaks, CA: Sage.

Wright, P. H. (1998). Toward an expanded orientation to the study of sex differences in friendship. In D. J. Canary and K. Dindia (Eds.), *Sex differences and similarities in communication: Critical essays and empirical investigations of sex and gender in interaction* (pp. 41–63). Mahwah, NJ: Erlbaum.

Wright, T. L., Ingraham, L. J., & Blackmer, D. R. (1985). Simultaneous study of individual differences and relationship effects in attraction. *Journal of Personality and Social Psychology, 47,* 1059–1062.

Wright, T. M., & Riese, S. P. (1997). Personality and unrestricted sexual behavior: Correlations of sociosexuality in Caucasian and Asian college students. *Journal of Research in Personality, 31,* 166–192.

Wu, Z., & Balakrishnan, T. R. (1995). Dissolution of premarital cohabitation in Canada. *Demography, 32,* 521–532.

Xiaohe, X., & Whyte, M. K. (1990). Love matches and arranged marriages: A Chinese replication. *Journal of Marriage and the Family, 52,* 709–722.

Yager, J. (1997). *Friendshifts: The power of friendship and how it shapes our lives.* Stamford, CT: Hannacroix Creek Books.

Yarab, P. E., Allgeier, E. R., & Sensibaugh, C. C. (1999). Looking deeper: Extradyadic behaviors, jealousy, and perceived unfaithfulness in hypothetical dating relationships. *Personal Relationships, 6,* 305–316.

Ybema, J. F., Kuijer, R. G., Hagedoorn, M., & Buunk, B. P. (2002). Caregiver burnout among intimate partners of patients with a severe illness: An equity perspective. *Personal Relationships, 9,* 73–88.

Yoshimura, S. (2004, July). *Fifteen types of revenge activities enacted against current and past romantic partners.* Paper presented at the meeting of the International Association for Relationship Research, Madison, WI.

Yost, J. H. (2002). *It's not me, it's my interaction style: The self-defeating nature of a protective self-presentation style in shyness.* Paper presented at the meeting of the Society for Personality and Social Psychology, Savannah, GA.

Yum, Y. (2004). Culture and self-construal as predictors of responses to accommodative dilemmas in dating relationships. *Journal of Social and Personal Relationships, 21,* 817–835.

Zaalberg, R., Manstead, A. S. R., & Fischer, A. H. (2004). Relations between emotions, display rules, social motives, and facial behaviour. *Cognition and Emotion, 18,* 183–207.

Zadro, L., & Williams, K. D. (2000, June). *The silent treatment: Ostracism in intimate relationships.* Paper presented at the meeting of the International Society for the Study of Personal Relationships, Brisbane.

Zadro, L., Williams, K. D., & Richardson, R. (2004). How low can you go? Ostracism by a computer is sufficient to lower self-reported levels of belonging, control, self-esteem, and meaningful existence. *Journal of Experimental Social Psychology, 40,* 560–567.

Zammichieli, M. E., Gilroy, F. D., & Sherman, M. F. (1988). Relation between sex-role orientation and marital satisfaction. *Personality and Social Psychology Bulletin, 14,* 747–754.

Zanna, M. P., & Pack, S. J. (1975). On the self–fulfilling nature of apparent sex differences in behavior. *Journal of Experimental Social Psychology, 11,* 583–591.

Zayas, V., Shoda, Y., & Ayduk, O. N. (2002). Personality in context: An interpersonal systems perspective. *Journal of Personality, 70,* 851–900.

Zechmeister, J. S., Garcia, S., Romero, C., & Vas, S. N. (2004). Don't apologize unless you mean it: A laboratory investigation of forgiveness and retaliation. *Journal of Social and Clinical Psychology, 23,* 532–564.

Zhang, F., & Hazan, C. (2002). Working models of attachment and person perception processes. *Personal Relationships, 9,* 225–235.

Zillman, D. (1978). Attribution and misattribution of excitatory reactions. In J. H. Harvey, W. Ickes, & R. F. Kidd (Eds.), *New directions in attribution research* (Vol. 2, pp. 335–368). Hillsdale, NJ: Erlbaum.

Zillman, D. (1984). *Connections between sex and aggression.* Hillsdale, NJ: Erlbaum.

Zillman, D. (1993). Mental control of angry aggression. In D. M. Wegner & J. W. Pennebaker (Eds.), *Handbook of mental control* (pp. 370–392). Englewood Cliffs, NJ: Prentice Hall.

Zimmer-Gembeck, M. J. (1999). Stability, change and individual differences in involvement with friends and romantic partners among adolescent females. *Journal of Youth and Adolescence, 28,* 419–438.

Zimmerman, D. H., & West, C. (1975). Sex roles, interruptions and silences in conversations. In B. Thorne & N. Henley (Eds.), *Language and sex: Difference and dominance* (pp. 105–129). Rowley, MA: Newbury House.

Zuckerman, M., DePaulo, B. M., & Rosenthal, R. (1981). Verbal and nonverbal communication of deception. In L. Berkowitz (Ed.), *Advances in experimental social psychology* (Vol. 14, pp. 1–59). New York: Academic Press.

Zuckerman, M., Driver, R., & Koestner, R. (1982). Discrepancy as a cue to actual and perceived deception. *Journal of Nonverbal Behavior, 7,* 95–100.

Zuckerman, M., Koestner, R., & Alton, A. O. (1984). Learning to detect deception. *Journal of Personality and Social Psychology, 46,* 519–528.

Credits

Nature of Self-Monitoring: Matters of Assessment, Matters of Validity," Journal of Personality and Social Psychology, 51, 125–139, 1986. Copyright © 1986 by the American Psychological Association. Reprinted with permission. **Figure 4.4:** Source: Leary & Miller, 1986.

Chapter 5: Figure 5.1: Adapted from Gottman, Notarius, Gonso & Markman, 1976. **Table 5.1:** From Patterson (1988). **Figure 5.3:** Adapted from Frieze et al., 1978, p. 330. **Cartoon 5.1:** CATHY © 1983 Cathy Guisewite. Reprinted with permission of UNIVERSAL PRESS SYNDICATE. All rights reserved.

Chapter 6: Figure 6.2: From J. M. Gottman and R. W. Levenson, "Marital Processes Predictive of Later Dissolution: Behavior, Physiology and Health," Journal of Personality and Social Psychology, 63, 221–233, 1992. Copyright © 1992 by the American Psychological Association. Reprinted with permission. **Figure 6.3:** From J. M. Gottman and R. W. Levenson, "Marital Processes Predictive of Later Dissolution: Behavior, Physiology and Health," Journal of Personality and Social Psychology, 63, 221–233, 1992. Copyright © 1992 by the American Psychological Association. Reprinted with permission. **Figure 6.4:** From "Toward a Positive psychology of relationships" by H. T. Reis and S. L. Gable in C. L. M. Keyes and J. Haidt, eds., FLOURISHING: Positive Psychology and the life well-lived, pp. 129–159. **Figure 6.5:** Figure from "Affilative Rewards and Restrictive Costs in Developing Relationships" by R. J. Eidelson in BRITISH JOURNAL OF SOCIAL PSYCHOLOGY, pp. 197–204. Copyright © 1981. Reprinted with permission from the British Journal of Social Psychology. **Figure 6.6:** Adapted from Eidelson, 1980. **Figure 6.7:** "The nature and predictors of the trajectory of change in marital quality for husbands and wives over the first 10 years of marriage" by L. A. Kurdek in DEVELOPMENTAL PSYCHOL-OGY, 35, 1283–1296, 1999. **Cartoon 6.1:** "If I Had Two Dead Rats" from book CAT by B. Kliban (1935–1990). Use by Permission Only. All Rights Reserved. © Judith K. Kliban. **Table 6.1:** Sources: Clark & Mills, 1979; Clark, Mills & Corcoran, 1989; Clark, Mills & Powell, 1986; Clark & Waddell, 1985; Wililamson & Clark, 1989; and Williamson et al., 1996. **Table 6.2:** "Measurement of communal strength" by J. Mills, M. S. Clark, T. E. Ford and M. Johnson in PERSONAL RELATIONSHIPS, 11, 2004, pp. 213–230. **Table 6.3:** Source: Arriaga & Agnew, 2001. **Figure 6.8:** "The Investment Model of Commitment" by C. E. Rusbult, S. M. Drigotas and J. Verette from "The Investment Model: An Interdependence Analysis of Commitment Processes and Relationship Maintenance Phenomena" in COMMUNICATION AND RELA-TIONAL MAINTENANCE ed. by D. J. Canary and L. Stafford, pp. 115–139. Copyright © 1994. Reprinted with permission from Elsevier.

Chapter 7: Table 7.1: Source: Argyle and Henderson, 1985.

Chapter 8: Table 8.1: Brehm, Sharon S., and Saul Kassin, Social Psychology. Copyright © 1990 by Houghton Mifflin Company. Used with permission. **Table 8.2:** Source: White, Fishbein & Rutstein (1981). **Table 8.3:** E. Hatfield and R. L. Rapson, "Passionate Love: New Directions in Research," in Advances in Personal Relationships, W. L. Jones and D. Perlman, eds. Vol. 1, pp. 109–139, 1987. Copyright © Jessica Kingsley Publishers. **Figure 8.1:** Source: Goodwin et al., 2002. Table 8.5: Source: Grote & Frieze (1994). **Table 8.6:** Brehm, Sharon S., and Saul Kassin, Social Psychology. Copyright © 1990 by Houghton Mifflin Company. Used with permission. **Table 8.7:** Source: Bartholomew, 1990. **Figure 8.2:** Adapted from Bartholomew, 1990. **Figure 8.3:** Adapted from Brennan, Clark & Shaver (1998). **Table 8.8:** Source: Brennan, Clark & Shaver (1998). **Figure 8.5:** Data from Call, Sprecher & Schwartz, 1992.

Chapter 9: Table 9.1: Adapted from Widmer, Treas & Newcomb (1998). **Table 9.2:** Source: Spitzberg, 1999. **Figure 9.1:** Source: Blumstein & Schwartz, 1993.

Chapter 10: Table 10.1: "Calibrating the sociometer: The relationship between interpersonal appraisals and the state self-estate" by M. R. Leary, A. L. Haupt, K. S. Strausser and J. T. Chokel from JOURNAL OF PERSONALITY AND SOCIAL PSYCHOLOGY, 74, 1998, pp. 1290–1299. **Table 10.3:** From Weber, A. & Harvey, J. H. PERSPECTIVES ON CLOSE RELATIONSHIP © 1994. Published by Allyn and Bacon, Boston, MA. Copyright © 1994 by Pearson Education. Reprinted by permission of the publisher. **Figure 10.1:** Source: Leary, Haupt, Strausser, & Chokel (1998). **Figure 10.2:** Courtesy Mark Leary.

Chapter 11: Table 11.1: Based on Raven, 2001. **Cartoon 11.1:** Reprinted by permission of United Media. **Table 11.2:** Data from Corrales, 1975. **Table 11.3:** Data from Johnson, 1975.

Chapter 12: Box 12.3: "Hostile, volatile, avoiding and validating couple conflict types: an investigation of Gottman's couple conflict types" by J. B. Holman and M. O. Jarvis from PERSONAL RELATIONSHIPS, 10, pp. 267–282, 2003. **Table 12.1:** Source: Christensen & Heavey, 1993. **Table 12.2:** Adapted from Bach & Wyden, 1968. **Figure 12.1:** From Close Relationships by H. H. Kelley, E. Bershceid, A. Christensen, J. H. Harvey, T. L. Huston, G. Levinger, E. McClintock, L. A. Peplau, and D. R. Peterson © 1983 by W. H. Freeman and Company. Used with permission. **Figure 12.2:** Adapted from Rusbult (1987). **Figure 12.3:** Source: Straus, Hamby, Boney-McCoy, and Sugarman, 1996. **Figure 12.4:** "Power and Control Wheel" from E. Pence and M. Paymar, EDUCATION GROUPS FOR MEN WHO BATTER: The Duluth Model, 1993. Reprinted by permission of Springer Publishing Company, Inc., New York 10036.

Chapter 13: Table 13.1: Source: Amato & Previti (2003). **Table 13.3:** From "Breaking up is (relatively) easy to do: A Script for the dissolution of close relationships" by D. M. Battaglia et al., in JOURNAL OF SOCIAL AND PERSONAL RELATIONSHIPS, Vol. 15, No. 6, pp. 829–845. Copyright © 1998. Reprinted by permission of Sage Publications, Ltd. **Figure 13.1:** Source: Karney & Bradbury, 1995. **Figure 13.2:** From "Reconciling Divergent Perspectives" by Paul Amato from FAMILY RELATIONS, 52(4), 2003, pp. 332–339. Copyright © 2003 by the National Council on Family Relations, 3989 Central Ave. NE, Suite 550, Minneapolis, MN 55421. Reprinted by permission.

Chapter 14: Table 14.1: Reprinted with permission of Daniel W. Russell. **Figure 14.1:** Source: Yost (2002). **Figure 14.2:** From D. W. Russell, C. E. Cutrona, A. de la Mora, and R. B. Wallace, "Loneliness and Nursing Home Admission Among Rural Older Adults," Psychology and Aging, 12, 574–589, 1997. Copyright © 1997 by the American Psychological Association. Reprinted with permission. **Table 14.6:** Source: Wheeler, Reis, & Nezlek (1983). **Cartoon 14.1:** FOR BETTER OR FOR WORSE © 1989 Lynn Johnston Productions. Dist. by Universal Press Syndicate. Reprinted with permission. All rights reserved. **Table 14.8:** From In Search of Intimacy by Carin Rubenstein and Phillip Shaver, copyright © 1982 by Carin Rubenstein and Phillip Shaver. Used by permission of Dell Publishing, a division of Random House, Inc. **Figure 14.3:** From D. W. Russell, C. E. Cutrona, A. de la Mora, and R. B. Wallace, "Loneliness and Nursing Home Admission Among Rural Older Adults," Psychology and Aging, 12, 574–589, 1997. Copyright © 1997 by the American Psychological Association. Reprinted with permission. **Table 14.4:** Source: Rubenstein, Shaver &

Peplau, 1979. **Table 14.5:** Source: S. Stack, 1995. **Figure 14.4:** Source: Rubenstein, Shaver & Peplau, 1979. **Figure 14.5:** Source: Perlman, 1991. **Table 14.7:** "Helping the Lonely" by K. S. Rook and L. A. Peplau in LONELINESS: A CURRENT THEORY, RESEARCH & THERAPY ed. by L. A. Peplau and D. Perlman. Reprinted by permission of John Wiley & Sons, Inc. **Table 14.10:** "Helping the Lonely" by K. S. Rook and L. A. Peplau in LONELINESS: A CURRENT THEORY, RESEARCH & THERAPY ed. by L. A. Peplau and D. Perlman. Reprinted by permission of John Wiley & Sons, Inc.

Chapter 15: Cartoon 15.1: Reprinted by permission of TMS Reprints. **Table 15.1:** From "Maintaining Romantic Relationships: A Summary and Analysis of One Research Program," by Laura Stafford. In D. J. Canary & M. Dainton (Eds.), (2003), MAINTAINING RELATIONSHIPS THROUGH COMMUNICATION: Relational, Contextual, and Cultural Variations (pp. 58–59). Mahwah, NJ: Erlbaum. Copyright 2003 by Lawrence Erlbaum Associates. Reprinted with permission. **Table 15.2:** Adapted from Markman, Stanley & Blumberg (1994). **Table 15.3:** Source: Adapted from Johnson & Denton (2002) and Johnson & Patz (2003). **Table 15.4:** Source: Adapted from Baucom, Epstein, & Stanton.

Name Index

Hill, M. E., 86
Hill, R., 188, 345
Hinchliff, S., 292
Hines, D., 290
Hinsz, V. B., 86
Hixon, J. G., 132
Hobbs, S. A., 447
Hodges, S., 139
Hodges, S. D., 159
Hoff, C., 290
Hollabaugh, L. C., 300
Holland, R. W., 154
Holliday, H., 168
Holman, T. B., 376
Holmes, D. S., 447
Holmes, J. G., 5, 30, 65, 117, 118,
  122, 130, 171, 209, 222, 334,
  362, 365
Holt, C. S., 26
Holtzworth-Munroe, A., 120
Homans, G. C., 182
Honeycutt, J. M., 40, 134
Honeycutt, T. C., 387
Hopper, C. H., 164
Hopper, J., 413
Hops, H., 469
Hornstein, G. A., 162
Horowitz, L. M., 97, 103, 262
Horstmann, G., 150
Horton, R. S., 102
Hotchkiss, S., 132
Houston, J. P., 190
Houts, A. C., 50
Houts, R. M., 27, 45, 192, 198, 365
Howard, A., 337
Howard, J. W., 194
Howard, K. I., 476
Howard, M., 201
Howes, C., 227
Huba, G. J., 281
Hubbard, B., 26
Hughes, D. K., 66
Hui, C. H., 12
Hume, D. K., 86
Humphrey, T. M., 85
Hunt, M., 277
Hunt, M. M., 245
Hupka, R. B., 315, 316
Huppe, M., 372
Huppe, M., 209
Hurd, C., 315
Huston, T., 201
Huston, T. L., 11, 25, 27, 45, 55,
  93, 104, 177, 192, 198, 199, 212,
  233, 271, 344, 365, 371,
  405–407
Hwang, J., 267
Hyde, J. S., 21, 277, 284
Hymel, S., 443
Hynes, K., 352

Iavnieli, D., 140
Ickes, W., 24, 44, 68, 138, 139,
  140, 141, 157, 160
Ifert, D., 165
Ifert, D. E., 369
Iida, M., 207

Ijsendoorn, M. H., 268
Impett, E., 297
Ingoldsby, B. B., 244, 246
Ingraham, L. J., 76
Insko, C. A., 102
Inzlicht, M., 86
Ireland, J. L., 440
Ironson, G., 279
Irving, H. H., 421
Isaacowitz, D. M., 233
Isabella, R. A., 17
Ivey, M., 95
Iwaniszek, J., 374
Izzo, J. L., Jr., 234

Jackson, T., 430
Jacobson, N. S., 65, 120, 205,
  469, 474
Jacques, A. J., 298
Jacquet, S. E., 402
Jang, S., 412
Jankowiak, W., 244
Jarvis, M. O., 376
Jensen-Campbell, L. A., 106, 365
Jessor, R., 281
Jöchle, W., 87
Johannesen-Schmidt, M. C., 34
John, O. P., 102
John, R. S., 175
Johnson, C. B., 157
Johnson, C. L., 357
Johnson, D. J., 374
Johnson, D. R., 418
Johnson, M., 212, 381
Johnson, M. P., 104, 212, 233,
  382, 383, 385, 386, 387, 388
Johnson, S. M., 28, 473
Johnson, V., 298
Johnston, L. D., 11, 374
Joiner, T. E., Jr., 131, 240, 436
Jones, D., 83, 86
Jones, E. E., 134
Jones, J. T., 19, 76, 96
Jones, W. H., 5, 212, 333, 334,
  335, 336, 437, 446, 447
Josephs, R. A., 291
Judge, T. A., 85
Jungeberg, B. J., 88
Jussim, L., 130

Kachadourian, L. K., 338
Kafetsios, K., 169, 267
Kahn, A. S., 290
Kahn, J. R., 419
Kahneman, D., 192
Kalick, S. M., 88, 93
Kamphuis, J. H., 384
Kandel, D. B., 96, 97
Kane, H., 225
Kanouse, D. E., 284
Kaplan, H. B., 281
Karakurt, G., 317
Karney, B., 201, 399, 404–405,
  405, 408, 412, 425
Karney, B. R., 27, 48, 56, 117, 120,
  122, 126, 131, 191, 192, 199,
  372, 460

Karremans, J. C., 338
Kashy, D. A., 67, 68, 328, 329
Kassin, S. M., 121, 260, 446
Katz, J., 131
Katz, L. F., 122
Katz, R., 208
Katzev, A. R., 412
Kaul, M., 225
Kay, A. C., 5
Kearns, J. N., 337
Keefe, R. C., 33, 98, 100
Keelan, J. P. R., 130, 266
Keil, J. E., 88
Keiser, S., 421
Keith, B., 420, 421, 422
Keith, P. M., 96
Kellas, J. K., 417
Kellerman, J., 152
Kelley, H., 183
Kelley, H. H., 119, 185, 202,
  345, 367
Kelln, B. R. C., 338
Kelly, A. E., 336
Kelly, C. M., 464
Kelly, E. L., 27
Kelly, J., 421
Kelly, J. B., 421
Keltner, D., 102, 150
Kendall, E., 323
Kennedy, J. K., 385
Kenny, D. A., 67, 102, 138, 163
Kenrick, D. T., 26, 31, 32, 33, 34,
  91, 92, 98, 100, 269
Kephart, W., 244
Kerns, K. A., 267
Kerr, S. T., 477
Kessler, E. A., 156
Kessler, R. C., 17, 192, 224,
  265, 364
Keysar, B., 148
Kiecolt-Glaser, J. K., 7, 36,
  64, 412
Kienapple, K., 315
Kiesler, S. B., 185
Kilmann, P. R., 105
Kilpatrick, S. D., 139
Kim, H. K., 7
Kim, Y., 81
Kimmel, A. J., 66
Kinder, B. N., 279
King, C., 65
King, V., 420, 422
Kirkpatrick, L. A., 18, 317, 365
Kjos, G. L., 80
Klein, K., 139
Klein, K. J. K., 159
Kleinbaum, S., 12
Kleinke, C. L., 95, 152, 154
Kline, G. H., 412
Kline, K. K., 86
Kline, S. L., 402
Klinetob, N. A., 372
Klohnen, E. C., 18, 97, 102
Klusmann, D., 272, 288
Knee, C. R., 124, 125
Knobloch, L. K., 198, 316
Knoester, C., 404

Subject Index

Note: Page numbers in *italic* type refer to boxes, tables, or figures.